Active Directory

Other Microsoft .NET resources from O'Reilly

Related titles   Active Directory Cookbook™   Windows Server 2003
                 Learning Windows 2003   Network Administration
                 Windows Server Hacks™   Windows Server 2008: The
                                              Definitive Guide

.NET Books   *dotnet.oreilly.com* is a complete catalog of O'Reilly's books on
Resource Center   .NET and related technologies, including sample chapters and
                 code examples.

ONDotnet.com provides independent coverage of fundamental, interoperable, and emerging Microsoft .NET programming and web services technologies.

Conferences   O'Reilly & Associates bring diverse innovators together to nurture the ideas that spark revolutionary industries. We specialize in documenting the latest tools and systems, translating the innovator's knowledge into useful skills for those in the trenches. Visit *conferences.oreilly.com* for our upcoming events.

Safari Bookshelf (*safari.oreilly.com*) is the premier online reference library for programmers and IT professionals. Conduct searches across more than 1,000 books. Subscribers can zero in on answers to time-critical questions in a matter of seconds. Read the books on your Bookshelf from cover to cover or simply flip to the page you need. Try it today with a free trial.

FOURTH EDITION

Active Directory

Brian Desmond, Joe Richards, Robbie Allen, and Alistair G. Lowe-Norris

O'REILLY®

Beijing · Cambridge · Farnham · Köln · Sebastopol · Taipei · Tokyo

Active Directory, Fourth Edition

by Brian Desmond, Joe Richards, Robbie Allen, and Alistair G. Lowe-Norris

Copyright © 2009 O'Reilly Media. All rights reserved.
Printed in the United States of America.

Published by O'Reilly Media, Inc., 1005 Gravenstein Highway North, Sebastopol, CA 95472.

O'Reilly books may be purchased for educational, business, or sales promotional use. Online editions are also available for most titles (*http://safari.oreilly.com*). For more information, contact our corporate/institutional sales department: (800) 998-9938 or *corporate@oreilly.com*.

Editors: John Osborn and Laurel Ruma

Production Editor: Loranah Dimant

Production Services: Appingo, Inc.

Indexer: Ellen Troutman Zaig

Cover Designer: Karen Montgomery

Interior Designer: David Futato

Illustrator: Jessamyn Read

Printing History:

January 2000:	First Edition.
April 2003:	Second Edition.
January 2006:	Third Edition.
November 2008:	Fourth Edition.

ISBN: 978-0-596-52059-5

[C]   [2/10]

1265418068

Table of Contents

Part II. Designing an Active Directory Infrastructure

Preface

Active Directory is a common repository for information about objects that reside on the network, such as users, groups, computers, printers, applications, and files. The default Active Directory schema supports numerous attributes for each object class that can be used to store a variety of information. Access Control Lists (ACLs) are also stored with each object, which allows you to maintain permissions for who can access and manage the object. Having a single source for this information makes it more accessible and easier to manage; however, to accomplish this requires a significant amount of knowledge on such topics as LDAP, Kerberos, DNS, multimaster replication, group policies, and data partitioning, to name a few. This book will be your guide through this maze of technologies, showing you how to deploy a scalable and reliable Active Directory infrastructure.

Windows 2000 Active Directory has proven itself to be very solid in terms of features and reliability, but after several years of real-world deployments, there was much room for improvement. When Microsoft released Windows Server 2003, they focused on security, manageability, and scalability enhancements. Windows Server 2003 R2 takes this evolution further and combines Windows Server 2003 Service Pack 1 with some feature packs, which makes Windows Server even more secure, manageable, and scalable and also adds considerable new functionality, such as a stand-alone LDAP server service and increased Unix system integration functions right in the box.

Windows Server 2008 introduces some highly sought-after features to Active Directory. At the top of the list for many administrators will be such features as read-only domain controllers, support for Server Core, and fine-grained password policies. The list of new features and major enhancements is lengthy, and we have taken the time to cover them all in this book.

This book is a major update to the very successful third edition. All of the existing chapters have been brought up to date with Windows Server 2008 changes, as well as updates in concepts and approaches to managing Active Directory and script updates. There are eight new chapters (Chapters 7, 9, 18, 19, 29, 30, 31, and 33) to explain features or concepts not covered in the third edition. These chapters include in-depth coverage of read-only domain controllers, fine-grained password policies, Windows PowerShell, and Exchange 2007. We also cover programming Active Directory with .NET. While we have made updates to every chapter in this book, it is worthwhile to highlight the major enhancements to Chapters 8, 13, and 15 that cover significant Windows Server 2008 Active Directory changes.

This book describes Active Directory in depth, but not in the traditional way of going through the graphical user interface screen by screen. Instead, the book sets out to tell administrators how to design, manage, and maintain a small, medium, or enterprise Active Directory infrastructure. To this end, the book is split up into three parts.

Part I introduces in general terms much of how Active Directory works, giving you a thorough grounding in its concepts. Some of the topics include Active Directory replication, the schema, application partitions, group policies, interaction with DNS, domain controllers, and password policies.

In Part II, we describe in copious detail the issues around properly designing the directory infrastructure. Topics include in-depth looks at designing the namespace, creating a site topology, designing group policies, auditing, permissions, backup and recovery, Active Directory Lightweight Directory Services, upgrading Active Directory, and Microsoft Exchange.

Part III is all about managing Active Directory via automation with Active Directory Service Interface (ADSI), ActiveX Data Objects (ADO), Windows Management Instrumentation (WMI), PowerShell, and .NET. This section covers how to create and manipulate users, groups, printers, and other objects that you may need in your everyday management of Active Directory. It also describes in depth how you can utilize the strengths of WMI, Windows PowerShell, and the .NET namespace `System.DirectoryServices` to manage Active Directory programmatically via those interfaces.

If you're looking for in-depth coverage of how to use the MMC snap-ins or Resource Kit tools, look elsewhere. However, if you want a book that lays bare the design and management of an enterprise or departmental Active Directory, you need not look any further.

Intended Audience

This book is intended for all Active Directory administrators, whether you manage a single server or a global multinational with thousands of servers. Even if you have a previous edition, you will find this fourth edition to be full of updates and corrections and a worthy addition to your "good" bookshelf: the bookshelf next to your PC with the books you really read that are all dog-eared with soda drink spills and pizza grease on them. To get the most out of the book, you will probably find it useful to have a server running Windows Server 2008 available so that you can check out various items as we point them out.

If you have no experience with VBScript, the scripting language we use in Part III, don't worry. The syntax is straightforward, and you should have no difficulty grasping the principles of scripting with ADSI, ADO, and WMI. Likewise, the syntax we use in Part III to cover .NET is straightforward, and for those looking to learn PowerShell, Chapter 30 provides a jumpstart to the PowerShell language.

Contents of the Book

This book is split into three parts.

Part 1, Active Directory Basics

Chapter 1, *A Brief Introduction*
Reviews the evolution of the Microsoft NOS and some of the major features and benefits of Active Directory.

Chapter 2, *Active Directory Fundamentals*
Provides a high-level look at how objects are stored in Active Directory and explains some of the internal structures and concepts that it relies on.

Chapter 3, *Naming Contexts and Application Partitions*
Reviews the predefined Naming Contexts within Active Directory, what is contained within each, and the purpose of Application Partitions.

Chapter 4, *Active Directory Schema*
Gives you information on how the blueprint for each object and each object's attributes are stored in Active Directory.

Chapter 5, *Site Topology and Replication*
Details how the actual replication process for data takes place between domain controllers.

Chapter 6, *Active Directory and DNS*
Describes the importance of the Domain Name System (DNS) and what it is used for within Active Directory.

Chapter 7, *Read-Only Domain Controllers*
Describes the deployment and operation of Read-Only Domain Controllers (RODCs).

Chapter 8, *Group Policy Primer*
Gives you a detailed introduction to the capabilities of Group Policy Objects and how to manage them.

Chapter 9, *Fine-Grained Password Policies*
Comprehensive coverage of how to design, implement, and manage fine-grained password policies.

Part 2, Designing an Active Directory Infrastructure

Chapter 10, *Designing the Namespace*
Introduces the steps and techniques involved in properly preparing a design that reduces the number of domains and increases administrative control through the use of Organizational Units.

Chapter 11, *Creating a Site Topology*
Shows you how to design a representation of your physical infrastructure within Active Directory to gain very fine-grained control over intrasite and intersite replication.

Chapter 12, *Designing Organization-Wide Group Policies*
Explains how Group Policy Objects function in Active Directory and how you can properly design an Active Directory structure to make the most effective use of these functions.

Chapter 13, *Active Directory Security: Permissions and Auditing*
Describes how you can design effective security for all areas of your Active Directory, in terms of both access to objects and their properties; includes information on how to design effective security access logging in any areas you choose.

Chapter 14, *Designing and Implementing Schema Extensions*
Covers procedures for extending the classes and attributes in the Active Directory schema.

Chapter 15, *Backup, Recovery, and Maintenance*
Describes how you can back up and restore Active Directory down to the object level or the entire directory.

Chapter 16, *Upgrading to Windows Server 2003*
Outlines how you can upgrade your existing Active Directory infrastructure to Windows Server 2003.

Chapter 17, *Upgrading to Windows Server 2003 R2*
Outlines the process to upgrade your existing Active Directory to Windows Server 2003 R2.

Chapter 18, *Upgrading to Windows Server 2008*
Outlines the process to upgrade your existing Active Directory to Windows Server 2008.

Chapter 19, *Integrating Microsoft Exchange*
Covers some of the important Active Directory-related issues when implementing Microsoft Exchange.

Chapter 20, *Active Directory Lightweight Directory Service (a.k.a. ADAM)*
Introduces Active Directory Lightweight Directory Service (AD LDS, formerly ADAM).

Part 3, Scripting Active Directory with ADSI, ADO, and WMI

Chapter 21, *Scripting with ADSI*

Introduces ADSI scripting by leading you through a series of step-by-step examples.

Chapter 22, *IADs and the Property Cache*

Delves into the concept of the property cache used extensively by ADSI and shows you how to properly manipulate any attribute of any object within it.

Chapter 23, *Using ADO for Searching*

Demonstrates how to make use of a technology normally reserved for databases and now extended to allow rapid searching for objects in Active Directory.

Chapter 24, *Users and Groups*

Gives you the lowdown on how to rapidly create users and groups, giving them whatever attributes you desire.

Chapter 25, *Permissions and Auditing*

Describes how each object contains its own list of permissions and auditing entries that governs how it can be accessed and how access is logged. The chapter then details how you can create and manipulate permission and auditing entries as you choose. It closes with a complete script to enumerate the entire security descriptor for any Active Directory object including proper constant names for all values, perfect for anyone looking to script Active Directory delegation and wanting to know what values should be set.

Chapter 26, *Extending the Schema and the Active Directory Snap-ins*

Covers creation of new classes and attributes programmatically in the schema, and modification of the existing Active Directory snap-ins to perform additional customized functions.

Chapter 27, *Scripting with WMI*

Gives a quick overview of WMI and goes through several examples for managing a system, including services, the registry, and the event log. Accessing AD with WMI is also covered, along with the TrustMon and Replication WMI Providers.

Chapter 28, *Scripting DNS*

Describes how to manipulate DNS server configuration, zones, and resource records with the WMI DNS Provider.

Chapter 29, *Programming the Directory with the .NET Framework*

Starts off by providing some background information on the .NET Framework and then dives into several examples using the System.DirectoryServices namespaces with VB.NET.

Chapter 30, *PowerShell Basics*

Provides a jumpstart to Windows PowerShell and a quick reference for PowerShell scripting concepts.

Chapter 31, *Scripting Active Directory with PowerShell*

> Describes how to manage and manipulate Active Directory using Windows PowerShell.

Chapter 32, *Scripting Basic Exchange 2003 Tasks*

> Tackles common Active Directory-related user and group management tasks for Microsoft Exchange 2000/2003.

Chapter 33, *Scripting Basic Exchange 2007 Tasks*

> Tackles common Active Directory-related tasks for Microsoft Exchange 2007 using Windows PowerShell.

Conventions Used in This Book

The following typographical conventions are used in this book:

Constant width

> Indicates command-line elements, computer output, and code examples.

Constant width italic

> Indicates variables in examples and registry keys.

Constant width bold

> Indicates user input.

Italic

> Introduces new terms and indicates URLs, commands, file extensions, filenames, directory or folder names, and UNC pathnames.

 Indicates a tip, suggestion, or general note. For example, we'll tell you if you need to use a particular version or if an operation requires certain privileges.

 Indicates a warning or caution. For example, we'll tell you if Active Directory does not behave as you'd expect or if a particular operation has a negative impact on performance.

Using Code Examples

This book is here to help you get your job done. In general, you may use the code in this book in your programs and documentation. You do not need to contact us for permission unless you're reproducing a significant portion of the code. For example, writing a program that uses several chunks of code from this book does not require permission. Selling or distributing a CD-ROM of examples from O'Reilly books *does* require permission. Answering a question by citing this book and quoting example code does not require permission. Incorporating a significant amount of example code from this book into your product's documentation *does* require permission.

We appreciate, but do not require, attribution. An attribution usually includes the title, author, publisher, and ISBN. For example: "*Active Directory*, Fourth Edition, by Brian Desmond, Robbie Allen, Joe Richards, and Alistair G. Lowe-Norris. Copyright 2009 O'Reilly Media, Inc., 9780596520595."

If you feel your use of code examples falls outside fair use or the permission given above, feel free to contact us at *permissions@oreilly.com*.

Safari® Books Online

When you see a Safari® Books Online icon on the cover of your favorite technology book, that means the book is available online through the O'Reilly Network Safari Bookshelf.

Safari offers a solution that's better than e-books. It's a virtual library that lets you easily search thousands of top tech books, cut and paste code samples, download chapters, and find quick answers when you need the most accurate, current information. Try it for free at *http://safari.oreilly.com*.

How to Contact Us

We have tested and verified the information in this book to the best of our ability, but you might find that features have changed (or even that we have made mistakes!). Please let us know about any errors you find, as well as your suggestions for future editions, by writing to:

> O'Reilly Media, Inc.
> 1005 Gravenstein Highway North
> Sebastopol, CA 95472
> 800-998-9938 (in the United States or Canada)
> 707-829-0515 (international/local)
> 707-829-0104 (fax)

To ask technical questions or comment on the book, send email to:

> *bookquestions@oreilly.com*

We have a web page for this book where we list examples and any plans for future editions. You can access this information at:

> *http://www.oreilly.com/catalog/9780596520595*

For more information about books, conferences, Resource Centers, and the O'Reilly Network, see the O'Reilly web site at:

> *http://www.oreilly.com*

Acknowledgments

For the Fourth Edition (Brian)

I wouldn't be here if it weren't for the fine folks at O'Reilly who decided to entrust this project to me. Special thanks to my editor Laurel Ruma who made this a very smooth running adventure. Joe, Robbie, and Alistair have of course provided an excellent foundation, which made this project so much easier. I would not have been able to get this done in the time I did without their hard work.

There are numerous individuals whose contributions to the depth and accuracy of the content in this edition are irreplaceable. Without their help, this book would not be what it is:

- PowerShell guru Brandon Shell and .NET expert Joe Kaplan contributed the fine content in this book on these important topics.
- Technical reviewers Joe Richards, Michael B. Smith, and Guido Grillenmeier, thank you for the comments, corrections, and invaluable feedback. Guido, thank you for voluntarily taking the time out of your day and vacation to provide your expertise.
- Special thanks to Eric Kotz, unofficial reviewer. Your feedback from the perspective of an Active Directory beginner brought clarity to the chapters you read.
- Thank you to Microsoft experts James McColl, Siddharth Bhai, Dmitri Gavrilov, Eric Fleischman, and Stephanie Cheung for your help with the details that made this book what it is!
- Darren Mar-Elia (C-GPO), your feedback on the Group Policy chapters was instrumental.
- Dean Wells, your crucial assistance in decrypting English phraseology is priceless, and of course thanks for your help in consistently transforming complex technical content to plain English.
- Susan Bradley, Small Business Server Diva, your contributions were critical.
- Jorge de Almeida Pinto (Princess), thank you for the last minute contributions to our list of new Active Directory features in Windows Server 2008.
- James Manning and Ted Kolvoord, thank you for the last minute reviews of the PowerShell chapters!

John Tanner, thanks for all your help behind the scenes making this project successful. Matt Wagner at Fresh Books, your assistance and expertise in handling the business end of this project was key.

Patrick Sheren and Scott Weyandt, thank you for the opportunity you gave me just four years ago. I would not be where I am today if it weren't for the three years we spent working together. And yes, you too, Kurt.

To the special people in my life who are always trying to get me to explain what I do all day, you have provided the impetus for this project.

To my readers, I had a lot of fun on this project, and I hope you have as much fun reading this book as I had writing it.

For the Third Edition (Joe)

I want to thank Robbie Allen for my introduction into the world of book writing and for putting up with my often-grumpy responses to silly issues we encountered on this project. Truly, I wouldn't have worked on this book had it not been for Robbie; if I did not say it before, I am happy I had the opportunity to have this experience—thank you.

Thanks to Alistair for the first edition. I recall being involved with the decision to migrate a company of 200k+ users to Windows 2000 and realizing that I knew nothing about Active Directory (AD) other than it was supposed to be "super-cool" and fixed everything that was broken in NT. "The Cat Book," the *only* book on AD around at the time, prepared me with the essential concepts and ideas to get started. After five years, I am happy to be able to give back some of what I have learned to that very same book.

Thanks to the folks who had the onerous task of finding the mistakes. I was lucky to have very knowledgeable reviewers who spent a lot of time reading every word (old and new) and bluntly telling me the issues. To Hunter Colman and Stuart Fuller: you guys were afraid you wouldn't add value. You were completely wrong; you added a lot of value. To Lee Flight: thanks for reviewing another edition of this book; your comments were invaluable. To Laura Hunter: I will never look at a comma the same way again; you helped the structure and flow immensely. To Ulf B. Simon-Weidner: your comments and ideas were a great help. Finally, thanks to Dean Wells, a great source of information, fear, and humorous English phrases. Dean couldn't review everything but he happily helped me out when I asked. He spent at least 90 minutes on the phone one night just discussing changes that needed to be made to a few pages of Chapter 5. All of these guys (and gal) are extremely knowledgeable, opinionated, and professional. It was an honor having them tell me what was screwed up. Thanks to my friend Vern Rottman for being an "unofficial" reviewer and running interference for me when I worked with him.

Thanks to the Microsoft Directory Service Developers: because of you, we have a "super-cool" DS. P.S. AD/AM rocks. Thanks to Dmitri Gavrilov for going above and beyond by responding to my unsolicited emails. Thanks to Stuart Kwan (of the Ottawa Kwan Clan) for being one of the most insanely energetic speakers and, at the same time, actually listening to what we thought was wrong and working to get corrections. I am thrilled that someday I will be able to run DCs without IE loaded. May your energizer battery never run out of juice. Thanks to Brett Shirley for telling me to correct stuff in Chapter 13 and writing the most brilliant parts of REPADMIN and being a killer JET Blue (ESE) dev. Thanks to Eric Fleischman for answering all the random AD questions from myself as well as everyone else at all hours of the day and night. Your answers, comments, thoughts, and insight into the actual questions themselves are all greatly appreciated.

Thanks to the *activedir.org* listserv crowd. Hands down, that list is the best Active Directory (and often Exchange) resource outside of Microsoft. It has helped me a lot.

Thanks to my family, great people I love without bound. Yes, Dawn, even you.

And last but not least, thanks to my guardian angel, Di. She put up with a lot of griping from me, as well as the loss of my companionship for most of the summer as I sat in the corner typing away. Through it all, she always had a smile on her face and was willing to burn a grilled cheese sandwich for me as needed. She never once reminded me that I said I would tile the kitchen floor this summer. I'll start tiling next week, only three months late....

For the Second Edition (Robbie)

I would like to thank the people at O'Reilly for giving me the opportunity to work on this book. Special thanks goes to Robert Denn, who was a great editor to work with.

I would like to thank Alistair Lowe-Norris for providing such a solid foundation in the first edition. While there was a lot of new material to include, much of the information in the first edition was still pertinent and useful. He deserves a lot of credit since the first edition was done before Windows 2000 had even been released to the public, and there was virtually no information on Active Directory available.

Thanks to Alistair, Mitch Tulloch, and Paul Turcotte for providing very insightful feedback during the review process. Their comments rounded out the rough edges in the book.

And no acknowledgments section would be complete without recognition to my significant other, Janet. She was supportive during the many late nights and weekends I spent writing. I appreciate everything she does for me.

For the First Edition (Alistair)

Many people have encouraged me in the writing of this book, principally Vicky Launders, my partner, friend, and fountain of useful information, who has been a pinnacle of understanding during all the late nights and early mornings. Without you my life would not be complete.

My parents, Pauline and Peter Norris, also have encouraged me at every step of the way; many thanks to you both.

For keeping me sane, my thanks go to my good friend Keith Cooper, a natural polymath, superb scientist, and original skeptic; to Steve Joint for keeping my enthusiasm for Microsoft in check; to Dave and Sue Peace for "Tuesdays," and the ability to look interested in what I was saying and how the book was going no matter how uninterested they must have felt; and to Mike Felmeri for his interest in this book and his eagerness to read an early draft.

I had a lot of help from my colleagues at Leicester University. To Lee Flight, a true networking guru without peer, many thanks for all the discussions, arguments, suggestions, and solutions. I'll remember forever how one morning very early you took the first draft of my 11-chapter book and spread it all over the floor to produce the 21 chapters that now constitute the book. It's so much better for it. Chris Heaton gave many years of dedicated and enjoyable teamwork; you have my thanks. Brian Kerr, who came onto the fast-moving train at high speed, managed to hold on tight through all the twists and turns along the way, and then finally took over the helm. Thanks to Paul Crow for his remarkable work on the Windows 2000 client rollout and GPOs at Leicester. And thanks to Phil Beesley, Carl Nelson, Paul Youngman, and Peter Burnham for all the discussions and arguments along the way. A special thank you goes to Wendy Ferguson for our chats over the past few years.

To the Cormyr crew: Paul Burke, for his in-depth knowledge across all aspects of technology and databases in particular, who really is without peer, and thanks for being so eager to read the book that you were daft enough to take it on your honeymoon; Simon Williams for discussions on enterprise infrastructure consulting and practices, how you can't get the staff these days, and everything else under the sun that came up; Richard Lang for acting as a sounding board for the most complex parts of replication internals, as I struggled to make sense of what was going on; Jason Norton for his constant ability to cheer me up; Mark Newell for his gadgets and Ian Harcombe for his wit, two of the best analyst programmers that I've ever met; and finally, Paul "Vaguely" Buxton for simply being himself. Many thanks to you all.

To Allan Kelly, another analyst programmer par excellence, for various discussions that he probably doesn't remember but that helped in a number of ways.

At Microsoft: Walter Dickson for his insightful ability to get right to the root of any problem, his constant accessibility via email and phone, and his desire to make sure that any job is done to the best of its ability; Bob Wells for his personal enthusiasm and interest in what I was doing; Daniel Turner for his help, enthusiasm, and key role in getting Leicester University involved in the Windows 2000 RDP; Oliver Bell for actually getting Leicester University accepted on the Windows 2000 RDP and taking a chance by allocating free consultancy time to the project; Brad Tipp, whose enthusiasm and ability galvanized me into action at the U.K. Professional Developers Conference in 1997; Julius Davies for various discussions and, among other things, telling me how the auditing and permissions aspects of Active Directory had all changed just after I finished the chapter; Karl Noakes, Steve Douglas, Jonathan Phillips, Stuart Hudman, Stuart Okin, Nick McGrath, and Alan Bennett for various discussions.

To Tony Lees, director of Avantek Computer Ltd., for being attentive, thoughtful, and the best all-round salesman I have ever met—many thanks for taking the time to get Leicester University onto the Windows 2000 RDP.

Thanks to Amit D. Chaudhary and Cricket Liu for reviewing parts of the book.

I also would like to thank everyone at O'Reilly, especially my editor Robert Denn for his encouragement, patience, and keen desire to get this book crafted properly.

## PART I

Active Directory Basics

## CHAPTER 1

A Brief Introduction

Active Directory (AD) is Microsoft's network operating system (NOS), built on top of Windows 2000, Windows Server 2003, and now Windows Server 2008. It enables administrators to manage enterprise-wide information efficiently from a central repository that can be globally distributed. Once information about users and groups, computers and printers, and applications and services has been added to Active Directory, it can be made available for use throughout the entire enterprise to as many or as few people as you like. The structure of the information can match the structure of your organization, and your users can query Active Directory to find the location of a printer or the email address of a colleague. With Organizational Units, you can delegate control and management of the data however you see fit. If you are like most organizations, you may have a significant amount of data (e.g., thousands of employees or computers). It may seem intimidating if you are faced with importing all of this data into Active Directory and managing it, but fortunately, Microsoft has some very robust yet easy-to-use Application Programming Interfaces (APIs) to help facilitate programmatic data management.

This book is a comprehensive introduction to Active Directory with a broad scope. In Part I, we cover many of the basic concepts of Active Directory to give you a good grounding in some of the fundamentals that every administrator should understand. In Part II, we focus on various design issues and methodologies, to enable you to map your organization's business requirements into your Active Directory infrastructure. Getting the design right the first time around is critical to a successful implementation, but it can be extremely difficult if you have no experience deploying Active Directory. In Part III, we cover in detailed management of Active Directory programmatically through scripts based on Active Directory Service Interface (ADSI), ActiveX Data Objects (ADO), Windows Management Instrumentation (WMI), the .NET Framework, and Windows PowerShell. No matter how good your design is, unless you can automate your environment, problems will creep in, causing decreased uniformity and reliability.

Before moving on to some of the basic components within Active Directory, we will take a moment to review how Microsoft came to the point of implementing a Lightweight Directory Access Protocol (LDAP)-based directory service to support their NOS environment.

Evolution of the Microsoft NOS

Network operating system, or "NOS," is the term used to describe a networked environment in which various types of resources, such as user, group, and computer accounts, are stored in a central repository that is controlled by administrators and accessible to end users. Typically, a NOS environment is comprised of one or more servers that provide NOS services, such as authentication, authorization, and account manipulation, and multiple end users that access those services.

Microsoft's first integrated NOS environment became available in 1990 with the release of Windows NT 3.0, which combined many features of the LAN Manager protocols and of the OS/2 operating system. The NT NOS slowly evolved over the next eight years until Active Directory was first released in beta form in 1997.

Under Windows NT, the "domain" concept was introduced, providing a way to group resources based on administrative and security boundaries. NT domains are flat structures limited to about 40,000 objects (users, groups, and computers). For large organizations, this limitation imposed superficial boundaries on the design of the domain structure. Often, domains were geographically limited as well because the replication of data between domain controllers (i.e., servers providing the NOS services to end users) performed poorly over high-latency or low-bandwidth links. Another significant problem with the NT NOS was delegation of administration, which typically tended to be an all-or-nothing matter at the domain level.

Microsoft was well aware of these limitations and needed to re-architect their NOS model into something that would be much more scalable and flexible. For that reason, they looked to LDAP-based directory services as a possible solution.

Brief History of Directories

In general terms, a *directory service* is a repository of network, application, or NOS information that is useful to multiple applications or users. Under this definition, the Windows NT NOS is a type of directory service. In fact, there are many different types of directories, including Internet white pages, email systems, and even the Domain Name System (DNS). Although each of these systems has characteristics of a directory service, X.500 and the Lightweight Directory Access Protocol (LDAP) define the standards for how a true directory service is implemented and accessed.

In 1988, the International Telecommunication Union (ITU) and International Organization of Standardization (ISO) teamed up to develop a series of standards around directory services, which has come to be known as X.500. While X.500 proved to be a good model for structuring a directory and provided a lot of functionality around advanced operations and security, it was difficult to implement clients that could utilize it. One reason is that X.500 is based on the OSI (Open System Interconnection) protocol stack instead of TCP/IP, which had become the standard for the Internet. The X.500 Directory Access Protocol (DAP) was very complex and implemented many features most clients never needed. This prevented large-scale adoption. It is for this reason that a group headed by the University of Michigan started work on a "lightweight" X.500 access protocol that would make X.500 easier to utilize.

The first version of the Lightweight Directory Access Protocol (LDAP) was released in 1993 as Request for Comments (RFC) 1487[*] but due to the absence of many features provided by X.500, it never really took off. It wasn't until LDAPv2 was released in 1995 as RFC 1777 that LDAP started to gain popularity. Prior to LDAPv2, the primary use of LDAP was as a gateway between X.500 servers. Simplified clients would interface with the LDAP gateway, which would translate the requests and submit them to the X.500 server. The University of Michigan team thought that if LDAP could provide most of the functionality necessary to most clients, they could remove the middleman (the gateway) and develop an LDAP-enabled directory server. This directory server could use many of the concepts from X.500, including the data model, but would leave out all the overhead resulting from the numerous features it implemented. Thus, the first LDAP directory server was released in late 1995 by the University of Michigan team, and it turned into the basis for many future directory servers.

In 1997, the last major update to the LDAP specification, LDAPv3, was described in RFC 2251. It provided several new features and made LDAP robust enough and extensible enough to be suitable for most vendors to implement. Since then, companies such as Netscape, Sun, Novell, IBM, OpenLDAP Foundation, and Microsoft have developed LDAP-based directory servers. Most recently, RFC 3377 was released, which lists all of the major LDAP RFCs. For a Microsoft whitepaper on their LDAPv3 implementation and conformance, see *http://www.microsoft.com/windowsserver2003/te chinfo/overview/ldapcomp.mspx.*

Windows NT Versus Active Directory

As we mentioned earlier, Windows NT and Active Directory both provide directory services to clients. Although both share some common concepts, such as Security Identifiers (SIDs) to identify security principals, they are very different from a feature, scalability, and functionality point of view. Table 1-1 contains a comparison of features between Windows NT and Active Directory.

---

[*] You can look up the text of this RFC at *http//www.ietf.org/rfc.html,*

Table 1-1. A comparison between Windows NT and Active Directory

Windows NT	Active Directory
Single-master replication is used, from the Primary Domain Controller (PDC) master to the Backup Domain Controller (BDC) subordinates.	Multimaster replication is used between all domain controllers.
Domain is the smallest unit of partitioning.	Naming Contexts are the smallest units of partitioning.
System policies can be used locally on machines or set at the domain level.	Group policies can be managed centrally and used by clients throughout the forest based on domain, site, or Organizational Unit (OU) criteria.
Data cannot be stored hierarchically within a domain.	Data can be stored in a hierarchical manner using OUs.
Domain is the smallest unit of security delegation and administration.	A property of an object is the smallest unit of security delegation/administration.
Domain is a policy, replication, and security boundary.	Domain is a policy and replication boundary. Forest is the security boundary.
NetBIOS and WINS are used for name resolution.	DNS is used for name resolution. WINS may be required for applications or legacy clients.
Object is the smallest unit of replication.	Attribute is the smallest unit of replication. In Windows Server 2003 Active Directory and above, some attributes replicate on a per-value basis (such as the member attribute of group objects).
Maximum recommended database size for the Security Accounts Manager (SAM) is 40 MB.	Recommended maximum database size for Active Directory is 16 TB.
Maximum effective number of users is 40,000 (if you accept the recommended 40 MB maximum).	The maximum number of objects per forest is in the tens of millions. Microsoft has tested to 1 billion users; for more information see *http://technet.microsoft.com/en-us/library/cc756101.aspx*.
Four domain models (single, single-master, multimaster, complete-trust) are required to solve per-domain admin-boundary and user-limit problems.	No domain models required as the complete-trust model is implemented. One-way trusts with external domains, forests, and UNIX Kerberos realms can be implemented manually.
Schema is not extensible.	Schema is fully extensible.
Data can only be accessed through a Microsoft API.	Data can be accessed through a Microsoft API or through LDAP, which is the standard protocol used by directories, applications, and clients that want to access directory data. Allows for cross-platform data access and management.

First, Windows NT Primary Domain Controllers and Backup Domain Controllers have been replaced by Active Directory Domain Controllers. It is possible under Active Directory to promote member servers to Domain Controllers (DCs) and demote DCs to ordinary member servers, all without needing a reinstallation of the operating system; this was not the case under Windows NT. If you want to make a member server a DC, you can promote it using the *dcpromo.exe* wizard. *Dcpromo* asks you a number of questions, such as whether you are creating the first domain in a domain tree or joining an existing tree, whether this new tree is part of an existing forest or a new forest to be created, and so on.

 UTOOLS provides a tool called UPromote through *http://utools.com/ UPromote.asp* that allows you to demote NT4 DCs to member servers. Although this functionality is *not* supported by Microsoft, many companies and universities have successfully used the product to demote NT4 BDCs from Active Directory domains. This is useful if for some reason you cannot upgrade or reinstall the operating system on the NT4 BDC.

Organizational Units are an important change with Active Directory. Under Windows NT, administration was delegated on a per-domain basis. Active Directory allows the administrators to define administration boundaries that encompass anything from the entire forest, domain, or Organizational Unit, all the way down to individual objects and attributes. This can significantly reduce the number of domains you require and offers far greater flexibility in your management choices.

Windows NT uses NetBIOS as its primary network communication mechanism, whereas Active Directory requires DNS and uses TCP/IP as its exclusive transport protocol. Under previous versions, administrators were required to maintain two computer lookup databases (DNS for name resolution and WINS for NetBIOS name resolution) but Active Directory does not require NetBIOS name resolution. Instead, it relies on DNS. You may still encounter a need to install and run a WINS server, and for many organizations, retiring an existing WINS infrastructure is a daunting prospect. Running WINS in conjunction with Active Directory is only be required for compatibility for applications or older legacy clients that still require NetBIOS name resolution.

The significant difference in replication is that Active Directory will replicate at the attribute and, in some cases, even the value level rather than object level. With Windows NT, if you changed the full name of a user object, the whole object had to be replicated out. In the same scenario with Active Directory, only the modified attribute will be replicated. This functionality was further improved in Windows Server 2003 Active Directory, where value-level replication was enabled for linked attributes. This allowed common attributes such as group membership to be replicated at a more granular value level. For example, instead of replicating all members of a group, you only replicate the members that were added or removed. Coupled with some very clever changes to the way replication works, this means that you replicate less data for shorter periods, thereby reducing the two most important factors in replication. See Chapters 5 and 10 for more on replication.

The suggested maximum Windows NT Security Accounts Manager (SAM) database size was 40 MB, which was roughly equivalent to about 40,000 objects, depending on the proportion of computer, user, and group accounts you had in your domain. Many companies have gone above 75 MB for the SAM for one domain due to the huge number of groups that they were using, so this rule was never hard and fast as long as you understood the problems you were likely to experience if you went past the recommended limit. Active Directory is based on the Extensible Storage Engine (ESE) database used by Exchange and was developed to hold millions of objects with a maximum database size of 16 TB. This should be enough for most people's needs, and the number of objects is only a recommended maximum limit. Remember, however, that this new database holds all classes of objects, not just the users, groups, and computers of the previous version's SAM. As more and more Active Directory-enabled applications are developed, more classes of objects will be added to the schema, and more objects will be added to the directory.

For administrators of Windows NT, the significant increase in scalability may be the most important change of all. It was extremely easy to hit the 40 MB SAM recommendation within an NT domain, forcing you to split the domain. You ended up managing multiple domains when you really didn't want to, which could be quite frustrating. None of the domains were organized into a domain tree or anything of the sort, so they had no automatic trusts between them. This meant that NT administrators had to set up manual trusts between domains, and these had to be initiated at both domains to set up a single one-way trust. As you added more domains, you ended up managing greater numbers of trusts. There are four domain models that you could use as templates for your Windows NT design: the single-domain model, the single-master domain model, the multimaster domain model, and the complete-trust domain model. All four are shown in Figure 1-1. The most common model after the single-domain model is probably the multimaster domain model.

The single-domain model had, as the name implied, only one domain with a SAM smaller than 40 MB and no trusts. Where multiple domains were needed for resource access but the SAM was still less than 40 MB, the single-master domain model was used. The single-master domain model was made up of one user (or account) domain and multiple resource domains. The important point was that the resource domains had one-way trusts with the user domain that held all the accounts. Due to the one-way trusts, the administrators of the resource domains could set permissions as they wished to their own resources for any accounts in the user domain. This meant that one central set of administrators could manage the accounts, while individual departments maintained autonomy over their own resources. The multimaster model came into play when the SAM limitations were approached, when you needed to separate out user management to different administrative groups, or when you wanted to better control replication traffic geographically. The administrators of the user domain split the user accounts into two or more domains, giving them two-way (i.e., complete) trust between each other, and then each resource domain had to have a one-way trust with each user domain. Scaling this up, for a multimaster domain with 10 user domains and 100 resource domains, that's 90 trusts to make up the intrauser trusts and 1,000 separate resource-to-user trusts that must be manually set. Finally, in some cases, the

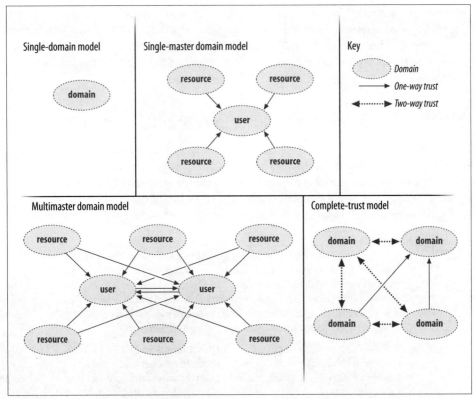

Figure 1-1. The four Windows NT domain models

complete-trust model was used where any domain could create accounts, and those accounts could be used to access shared resources to any other domain.

By contrast, all Active Directory domains within a forest trust each other via transitive trusts. This results in an automatic complete-trust model within the forest. In Windows Server 2003 Active Directory, transitive forest trusts are also available so that all of the domains in two different forests can completely trust each other via a single explicit trust between the forest root domains.

> Windows NT had simple trusts. This means that if DomA trusted DomB, and DomB trusted DomC, there was no automatic connection between DomA and DomC.
>
> Active Directory gave us transitive trusts; with transitive trusts, if DomA trusted DomB, and DomB trusted DomC, DomA could trust DomC through the trust transitivity.

Finally, the Windows NT schema was not extensible. No new object types could be added to it, which was a significant limitation for many enterprises. When Microsoft products that extended Windows NT—such as Terminal Server and File and Print for NetWare—were released, each had to store any attribute data that it wanted all together within one existing attribute. Under Active Directory, the schema is fully extensible, so any new applications can extend the schema and add in objects and attributes as required.

Windows 2000 Versus Windows Server 2003

Although the first version of Active Directory available with Windows 2000 was very stable and feature-rich, it still had room for improvement, primarily around manageability and performance. With Windows Server 2003, Microsoft has addressed many of these issues. To utilize these features, you have to upgrade your domain controllers to Windows Server 2003 and raise the domain and forest functional levels as necessary.

Windows 2000 Active Directory introduced us to the concept of mixed mode and native mode. This was a domain concept that indicated whether or not all domain controllers in a domain were Windows 2000 and could therefore use a new capability that wasn't available in Windows NT. Switching from mixed mode to native mode was a purposeful configuration change made by the domain administrators.

Windows Server 2003 Active Directory further refined this by adding functional levels. It introduced both domain functional levels and forest functional levels. Like mixed mode and native mode, domain functional mode depends on the types of domain controllers in the forest. If you have all Windows Server 2003 domain controllers, you can switch Windows Server 2003 domain functional mode and gain access to many new functions. Microsoft also added new functions that could be used only if all domain controllers in the forest were upgraded to Windows Server 2003, so they added forest functional mode. When all DCs in the forest are upgraded, the enterprise administrators can increase the forest functional mode.

The difference between Windows 2000 Active Directory and Windows Server 2003 Active Directory is more evolutionary than revolutionary. While the decision to upgrade from Windows 2000 is a subjective one, based on your needs, Windows 2000 is in the extended support phase so you should definitely be considering migration to Windows Server 2008 if you are still running Windows 2000. On the whole, Microsoft added or updated more than 100 features within Active Directory during the Windows Server 2003 release, and we will now discuss some of the more significant ones.

For information on upgrading to Windows Server 2003 from Windows 2000, check out Chapter 16.

Some of the new features are available as soon as you promote the first Windows Server 2003 domain controller into an existing Windows 2000 Active Directory domain. In Table 1-2, the features available when you do so are listed, along with a description. Note that, with the exception of Windows Management Instrumentation (WMI) Filtering for Group Policy Objects (GPOs), these features will apply only to the Windows Server 2003 domain controllers in the domain.

Table 1-2. Windows 2000 domain functional level feature list

Feature	Description
Application partitions	You can create your own partitions to store data separately from the default partitions, and you can configure which domain controllers (DC) in the forest replicate it.
Global Catalog (GC); not required for logon (i.e., universal group caching)	Under Windows 2000, a DC had to contact a GC to determine universal group membership and subsequently to allow users to log on. This feature allows DCs to cache universal group membership so that it may not be necessary to contact a GC for logins.
Microsoft Management Console (MMC) enhancements and new command-line tools	The new Active Directory Users and Computers console allows you to save queries, drag and drop, and edit multiple users at once, and it is much more efficient about scrolling through a large number of objects. In addition, several new command-line tools (dsadd, dsmod, dsrm, dsquery, dsget, and dsmove) come installed with the server, allowing for greater flexibility in managing Active Directory.
Install from Media	Administrators can create new DCs for an existing domain by installing from a backup of an existing DC that resides on media such as a CD or DVD.
WMI filtering for GPOs	You can apply a WMI filter, which is a query that can utilize any WMI information on a client, to a GPO, and that query will be run against each targeted client. If the query succeeds, the GPO will continue to process; otherwise, it will stop processing. The feature requires clients to be Windows XP or better.
GC replication tuning	After an attribute has been added to the GC, a sync of the contents of the GC for every GC server will no longer be performed as it was with Windows 2000. This occurs only with Windows Server 2003 to Windows Server 2003 replication.

In Table 1-3, the features available in domains running the Windows Server 2003 functional level are listed. A domain can be changed to the Windows Server 2003 functional level when all domain controllers in the domain are running Windows Server 2003.

Table 1-3. Windows Server 2003 domain functional level feature list

Feature	Description
Domain controller rename	With Windows 2000, you had to demote, rename, and repromote a DC if you wanted to rename it. With Windows Server 2003 domains, you can rename domain controllers, and it requires only a single reboot.
Logon timestamp replicated	Under Windows 2000, the lastLogon attribute contained a user's last logon timestamp, but that attribute was not replicated among the DCs. With Windows Server 2003, the lastLogon TimeStamp attribute is occasionally updated approximately every 10 days.
Quotas	Users and computers that have write access to AD can cause a Denial of Service (DOS) attack by creating objects until a DC's disk fills up. You can prevent this type of attack by using quotas.

Feature	Description
	With a quota, you can restrict the number of objects a security principal can create in a partition, container, or OU. Windows Server 2003 DCs can enforce quotas even when not at the Windows Server 2003 domain functional level, but for it to be enforced everywhere, all DCs must be running Windows Server 2003.

In Table 1-4, the features available to forests running the Windows Server 2003 functional level are listed. A forest can be raised to the Windows Server 2003 functional level when all domains contained within the forest are at the Windows Server 2003 domain functional level.

Table 1-4. Windows Server 2003 forest functional level feature list

Feature	Description
Reuse of critical schema identification properties	This feature allows certain critical identification properties to become available for reuse in the event a schema extension was originally misdefined and has since been defuncted.
Forest trust	A forest trust is a transitive trust between two forest root domains that allows all domains within the two forests to trust each other. To accomplish something similar with Windows 2000, you would have to implement trusts between each domain in the two forests.
Per-value replication	This feature allows certain linked-value attributes to replicate on a per-value basis instead of a per-attribute basis (i.e., all values). This is vital for group objects because under Windows 2000, a change in the member attribute caused the entire set of values for that attribute to unnecessarily be replicated.
Improved replication topology generation	The Intersite Topology Generator (ISTG) and Knowledge Consistency Checker (KCC) have been greatly improved and will create more efficient replication topologies.
Dynamic auxiliary classes	This feature allows for dynamically assigned per-object auxiliary classes. Under Windows 2000, an object could only utilize auxiliary classes that were statically defined in the schema for its object class.
Dynamic objects	Dynamic objects have a defined time to live (TTL) after which they will be removed from Active Directory unless the TTL is updated. This can help facilitate data management for short-lived objects.
inetOrgPerson class for users	The inetOrgPerson object class is a standard (RFC 2798) commonly used by directory vendors to represent users. With Windows Server 2003, you can use either the Microsoft-defined user object class or the inetOrgPerson object class for user accounts.
Domain rename	A domain can be renamed, which was not previously possible under Windows 2000. The impact to the environment is pretty significant (i.e., all member computers must be rebooted), and there are special considerations if Exchange is involved, so it should be done conservatively. Domain Renames are supported *only* under Exchange 2003.

Windows Server 2003 Versus Windows Server 2003 R2

The release time frame for Windows Server 2008 was extended repeatedly, so Microsoft decided to release an interim update to Windows Server 2003—Windows Server 2003 R2. R2 includes Windows Server 2003 SP1 as well as a number of optional Active Directory add-on components. Some of these new optional components, such as Active Directory Application Mode (ADAM), are available via Web downloads, but Microsoft chose to package them on the R2 CD to make them available to a wider audience. In addition, some users question Microsoft's commitment to software that is only available from its web site; making the components part of the Core OS dispels any doubts on Microsoft's support position.

Service Pack 1 offers a considerable number of improvements for Windows Server 2003. As with Windows XP Service Pack 2, many of the changes are security-related, correcting issues in Internet Explorer and offering new firewall functionality, Table 1-5 gives an overview of the Active Directory specific updates.

Table 1-5. Windows Server 2003 SP1 Active Directory enhancements

Feature	Description
Directory service backup reminders	Special messages logged to the Directory Service event log if directory partitions are not backed up.
Additional replication security and fewer replication errors	Replication metadata for domain controllers removed from the domain is now removed. This enhances directory security and eliminates replication error messages related to the deleted domain controllers.
Install from Media improvements for installing DNS Servers	New option to include application directory partitions in the backup media eliminates the requirement for network replication of DomainDNSZone and ForestDNSZones application directory partitions before the DNS Server is operational.
Updated tools	Newer versions of DcDiag, NTDSUtil, IADSTools.DLL, AdPrep, and other tools to aid in management, updates, and troubleshooting.
Virtual server support	Official support for running domain controllers within Microsoft Virtual Server 2005. Additional logic was added to guard against directory corruption due to improper backup and restoration procedures.
Extended storage of deleted objects	Tombstone lifetime on new forests increased from 60 to 180 days. Existing forests are not modified. Note that due to a regression bug, new Windows Server 2003 R2 forests have a tombstone lifetime of 60 days. This was subsequently corrected in Windows Server 2003 SP2 and Windows Server 2008.
Improved domain controller name resolution	To avoid replication failures due to DNS name-resolution issues, Windows Server 2003 with SP1 will request other variations of the server name that could be registered.
Confidential attributes	Ability to mark attributes as confidential so they cannot be read without additional permissions granted. By default, any attribute marked confidential can only be read by trustees with full control access to the object; however, this can be delegated in a granular manner.
SID History attribute retained on object deletion	The SID History attribute has been added to the default list of attributes retained on an object tombstone. When the object is undeleted, the attribute will be restored with the object.
Operations master health and status reporting	Operations that require a Flexible Single Master Operator (FSMO) domain controller that cannot be performed will generate Directory Service event log messages.
Drag and drop changes in Active Directory Users and Computers (ADUC) Console	Ability to disable drag and drop functionality in ADUC and display confirmation dialogs when initiating a move operation.

Although Service Pack 1 is certainly full of great updates that any domain administrator would want loaded on their domain controllers, the real meat in Windows Server 2003

R2 is in the optional components. If the optional components do not interest you, then R2 will probably not be an upgrade you will spend a lot of time on. Table 1-6 lists the various new components available in R2 specific to Active Directory.

Table 1-6. Windows Server 2003 R2 optional Active Directory-specific components

Feature	Description
Active Directory Application Mode (ADAM)	Standalone LDAP service that is Active Directory with the NOS-specific components and requirements stripped out.
Active Directory Federated Services (ADFS)	Standards-based technology that enables distributed identification, authentication, and authorization across organizational and platform boundaries.
Identity Management for UNIX (IMU)	Manage user accounts and passwords on Windows and Unix via Network Information Service (NIS). Automatically synchronize passwords between Windows and Unix.

Windows Server 2003 R2 Versus Windows Server 2008

Windows Server 2008 introduces substantial and, in some cases, complicated improvements to Active Directory. Perhaps the most important and well-known features are the introduction of *Server Core* and support for running Active Directory on Server Core along with the introduction of read-only domain controllers (RODCs). The differences between the fundamental Active Directory services in Windows Server 2003 R2 and Windows Server 2008 can again be considered evolutionary changes, as opposed to revolutionary. When evaluating your timeline to migrate to Windows Server 2008, consider the numerous new and improved features to aid your decision. Undoubtedly, one of the most compelling scenarios for upgrading to Windows Server 2008 Active Directory is for deployment into branch offices. A list of many of the key new features in Windows Server 2008 Active Directory are outlined in Table 1-7 and will be discussed in detail throughout the remainder of this book.

Table 1-7. Windows Server 2008 Active Directory enhancements

Feature	Description
Read-only domain controllers (RODCs)	RODCs do not allow local writes and do not store passwords and other secrets by default. This feature adds a great deal of security to domain controllers in locations with questionable physical security.
Server Core support	Domain controllers can now run on a version of the Windows Server 2008 operating system that is substantially lighter and thus more secure.
Fine-grained password policies	Password policies can now be defined on a per user or group basis.
Administrative role separation	Users who are not domain administrators can be securely delegated administrative control of RODCs without providing access to Active Directory.
Read-only DNS	RODCs can host dynamic DNS zones and refer the updates to writeable domain controllers.
GlobalNames DNS zone	A new type of DNS zone which can help pave the way to migrating away from WINS.

Feature	Description
New auditing and logging infrastructure	Auditing of Active Directory access and changes as well as various other actions have been completely overhauled.
Last logon statistics	Windows Vista and Windows Server 2008 clients can store and display detailed last logon success and failure information directly on user objects in the directory.
Active Directory database snapshots	Point-in-time snapshots of the Active Directory database can be taken and mounted as a basis for disaster recovery and other object restore operations.
Restartable Directory service	Active Directory can be stopped to allow for certain offline operations to be performed without restarting the domain controller in Directory Service Repair Mode.
Improved user interface and tools	The core Active Directory graphical user interface (GUI) tools have been improved so that they can connect to mounted snapshots as well as Active Directory Lightweight Directory Services (AD LDS) instances.
ADMX repository	Upgraded Group Policy template files can now be stored once per domain in the Sysvol, thus greatly reducing the size of the Sysvol for many organizations.
Group Policy Preferences	A product Microsoft purchased from Desktop Standard, Group Policy Preferences allows you to control numerous settings and Windows features which were previously only accessible via scripts.
Starter Group policies	Group Policy templates can be defined which administrators can base new policies on.
Group Policy user interface enhancements	Numerous improvements to the Group Policy Management Console (GPMC) and GPO Editor tools such as searching for settings and filtering displays.
DFS-R Sysvol replication	Sysvol can now be replicated with the new Distribution File System Replication (DFS-R) replication engine which is much more reliable and scalable than the NT File Replication Service (NTFRS).
ESE single bit error correction	The JET database engine that Active Directory uses is now capable of detecting single bit errors and correcting them and thus reducing incidences of database corruption.
Owner access restrictions	An additional well-known security principal representing the owner of an object is now available.
Delegated DCPromo	Domain controllers can now be promoted by users other than domain administrators.
Phonetic name indexing	The `displayName` attribute is phonetically sortable on Japanese locale domain controllers.
Kerberos AES256 support	Kerberos support for Advanced Encryption Standard (AES) has been improved to support a maximum key length of 256 bits.

Summary

This chapter is a brief introduction to the origins of Active Directory and some of the new features available in Windows Server 2003, Window Server 2003 R2, and Windows Server 2008. The rest of the chapters in Part I cover the conceptual introduction to Active Directory and equip you with the skills necessary to gain the most from Parts II and III.

## CHAPTER 2

Active Directory Fundamentals

This chapter aims to bring you up to speed on the basic concepts and terminology used with Active Directory. It is important to understand each component of Active Directory before embarking on a design, or your design may leave out a critical element.

How Objects Are Stored and Identified

Data stored within Active Directory is presented to the user in a hierarchical fashion similar to the way data is stored in a filesystem. Each entry is referred to as an object. At the structural level, there are two types of objects: containers and non-containers, which are also known as leaf nodes. One or more containers branch off in a hierarchical fashion from a root container. Each container may contain leaf nodes or other containers. As the name implies, however, a leaf node may not contain any other objects.

 Although the data in Active Directory is presented hierarchically, it is actually stored in flat database rows and columns. The Directory Information Tree (DIT) file is an Extensible Storage Engine (ESE) database file. This answers the question "Does Active Directory use JET or ESE Database technology?" ESE *is* a JET technology.

Consider the parent-child relationships of the containers and leaves in Figure 2-1. The root of this tree has two children, Finance and Sales. Both of these are containers of other objects. Sales has two children of its own, Pre-Sales and Post-Sales. Only the Pre-Sales container is shown as containing additional child objects. The Pre-Sales container holds user, group, and computer objects as an example.[*] Each of these child nodes is said to have the Pre-Sales container as its parent. Figure 2-1 represents what is known in Active Directory as a domain.

---

[*] User, group, and computer objects are actually containers, as they can contain other objects such as printers. However, they are not normally drawn as containers in domain diagrams such as this.

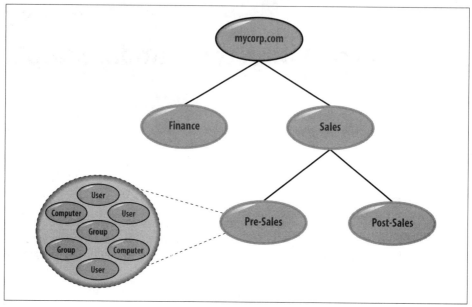

Figure 2-1. A hierarchy of objects

The most common type of container you will create in Active Directory is an organizational unit (OU), but there are others as well, such as the type called Container. Each of these has its place as we'll show later, but the one that we will be using most frequently is the organizational unit.

Uniquely Identifying Objects

When you are potentially storing millions of objects in Active Directory, each object has to be uniquely locatable and identifiable. To that end, objects have a Globally Unique Identifier (GUID) assigned to them by the system at creation. This 128-bit number is the Microsoft implementation of the UUID concept from Digital Equipment Corporation. UUIDs/GUIDs are commonly misunderstood to be guaranteed to be unique. This is not the case; the number is just statistically improbable to be duplicated before the year 3400 AD. In the documentation for the GUID creation API function, Microsoft says, "To a very high degree of certainty, this function returns a unique value." The object's GUID stays with the object until it is deleted, regardless of whether it is renamed or moved within the Directory Information Tree (DIT).

Although an object's GUID is resilient, it is not very easy to remember, nor is it based on the directory hierarchy. For that reason, another way to reference objects, called a *distinguished name* (DN), is more commonly used.

Distinguished names

Hierarchical paths in Active Directory are known as distinguished names and can be used to uniquely reference an object. Distinguished names are defined in the LDAP standard as a means of referring to any object in the directory.

Distinguished names for Active Directory objects are normally represented using the syntax and rules defined in the LDAP standards. Let's take a look at how a path to the root of Figure 2-1 looks:

```
dc=mycorp,dc=com
```

In the previous distinguished name, you represent the domain root, *mycorp.com* by separating each part with a comma and prefixing each part with the letters "dc." If the domain had been called *mydomain.mycorp.com*, the distinguished name of the root would have looked like this:

```
dc=mydomain,dc=mycorp,dc=com
```

> DC stands for domain component and is used to specify domain or application partition objects. Application partitions are covered in Chapter 3.

A relative distinguished name (RDN) is the name used to uniquely reference an object within its parent container in the directory. For example, this is the DN for the default Administrator account in the Users container in the *mycorp.com* domain:

```
cn=Administrator,cn=Users,dc=mycorp,dc=com
```

This is the RDN of the user:

```
cn=Administrator
```

RDNs must always be unique within the container they exist. It is permissible to have two objects with cn=Administrator in the directory; however, they must be located inside different parent containers. There could not be two objects with an RDN of cn=Administrator in the Users container.

DNs are made up of names and prefixes separated by the equal sign (=). Another prefix that will become very familiar to you is OU, which stands for Organizational Unit. Here is an example:

```
cn=Keith Cooper,ou=Northlight IT Ltd,dc=mycorp,dc=com
```

All RDNs use a prefix to indicate the class of the object that is being referred to. Any object class that does not have a specific letter code uses the default of cn, which stands for common name. Table 2-1 provides a complete list of the most common attribute types amongst directory server implementations. The list is from RFC 2253, Lightweight Directory Access Protocol (v3): UTF-8 String Representation of Distinguished Names, and the full text can be found at *http://www.ietf.org/rfc/rfc2253.txt*.

Table 2-1. Attribute Types from RFC2253

Key	Attribute
CN	Common Name
L	Locality Name
ST	State or Province Name
O	Organization Name
OU	Organizational Unit Name
C	Country Name
STREET	Street Address
DC	Domain Component
UID	Userid

Active Directory supports using CN, L, O, OU, C, and DC. CN is used in the majority of cases.

Examples

Let's take a look at Figure 2-1 again. If all the containers were Organizational Units, the distinguished names for Pre-Sales and Post-Sales would be as follows:

```
ou=Pre-Sales,ou=Sales,dc=mycorp,dc=com
ou=Post-Sales,ou=Sales,dc=mycorp,dc=com
```

And if you wanted to specify a user named Richard Lang, a group called My Group, and a computer called Moose in the Pre-Sales OU, you would use the following:

```
cn=Richard Lang,ou=Pre-Sales,ou=Sales,dc=mycorp,dc=com
cn=My Group,ou=Pre-Sales,ou=Sales,dc=mycorp,dc=com
cn=Moose,ou=Pre-Sales,ou=Sales,dc=mycorp,dc=com
```

Building Blocks

Now that we've shown how objects are structured and referenced, let's look at the core concepts behind Active Directory.

Domains and Domain Trees

Active Directory's logical structure is built around the concept of domains. Domains were introduced in Windows NT 3.x and 4.0. However, in Active Directory, domains have been updated significantly from the flat and inflexible structure imposed by Windows NT. An Active Directory domain is made up of the following components:

- An X.500-based hierarchical structure of containers and objects
- A DNS domain name as a unique identifier

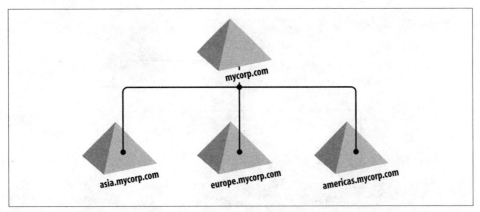

Figure 2-2. The mycorp.com domain tree

- A security service, which authenticates and authorizes any access to resources via accounts in the domain or trusts with other domains
- Policies that dictate how functionality is restricted for users or machines within that domain

A domain controller (DC) can be authoritative for one and only one domain. It is not possible to host multiple domains on a single DC. For example, Mycorp has already been allocated a DNS domain name for their company called *mycorp.com*, so they decide that the first Active Directory domain that they are going to build is to be named *mycorp.com*. However, this is only the first domain in a series that may need to be created, and *mycorp.com* is in fact the root of a domain tree.

The *mycorp.com* domain itself, ignoring its contents, is automatically created as the root node of a hierarchical structure called a domain tree. This is literally a series of domains connected together in a hierarchical fashion, all using a contiguous naming scheme. If Mycorp were to add domains called Europe, Asia, and Americas, then the names would be *europe.mycorp.com*, *asia.mycorp.com*, and *americas.mycorp.com*. Each domain tree is called by the name given to the root of the tree; hence, this domain tree is known as the *mycorp.com* tree, as illustrated in Figure 2-2. You can see that in Mycorp's setup we now have a contiguous set of domains that all fit into a neat tree. Even if we had only one domain, it would still be a domain tree, albeit with only one domain.

Trees ease management and access to resources, as all the domains in a domain tree trust one another implicitly with transitive trusts. In a transitive trust, if Domain A trusts Domain B and Domain B trusts Domain C, this implies that Domain A trusts Domain C as well. This is illustrated in Figure 2-3. Put much more simply, the administrator of *asia.mycorp.com* can allow any user in the tree access to any of the resources in the Asia domain that the administrator wishes. The user accessing the resource does not have to be in the same domain.

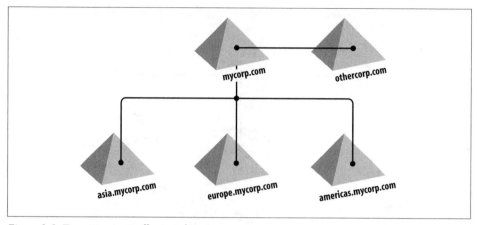

Figure 2-3. Transitive trusts illustrated

 Trust relationships do not compromise security; they are just setting up the potential to allow access to resources. Actual access permissions still have to be granted by administrators. This is why you should avoid granting access to Everyone or Authenticated Users on resources. Once a trust is established, everyone in the trusted domain could be able to access those resources as well.

Forests

Now that you understand what a domain tree is, we move on to the next piece of the Active Directory structure, the forest. Where a domain tree was a collection of domains, a forest is a collection of one or more domain trees. These domain trees share a common Configuration container and Schema, and the whole trees are connected together through transitive trusts. As soon as you create a single domain, you have a forest. If you add any domains to the initial domain tree or add new domain trees, you still have one forest.

Forests are named after the first domain that is created when creating a new forest, also known as the forest root domain. The forest root domain is important because it has special properties.

 In Active Directory, you can never remove the forest root domain. If you try to do so, the forest is irretrievably destroyed. Under Windows Server 2003 and newer Active Directories, you can rename the forest root domain, but you cannot change its status as the forest root domain or make a different domain the root. In order to rename the forest root domain, your forest must be at Windows Server 2003 forest functional level.

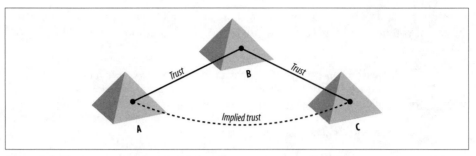

Figure 2-4. The mycorp.com forest with the othercorp.com tree added

As we continue with Mycorp, we find that it has a subsidiary business called Othercorp. The DNS domain name allocated and used by Othercorp is *othercorp.com*. In Othercorp's case, all you would need to do is create the root of the *othercorp.com* tree as a member of the existing forest; thus, *othercorp.com* and *mycorp.com* can exist together and share resources similar to Figure 2-4. The forest containing the *mycorp.com* and *othercorp.com* domain trees is known as the *mycorp.com* forest, in which *mycorp.com* is the forest root domain.

> While multiple domain trees in a forest can be configured, you should seriously consider all the implications of such a configuration before implementation. It can be confusing for troubleshooting efforts when you are working on an issue in the domain *othercorp.com*, but the configuration information for the forest is maintained in the partition `cn=configuration,dc=mycorp,dc=com`. This is especially true when bringing in outside resources not familiar with the implementation.
>
> While legitimate reasons exist to create multitree forests, we recommend that you endeavor to simplify your Active Directory design as much as possible and limit yourself to one domain tree and as few domains as possible.

Individual companies often implement their own forest. If Othercorp elected to deploy their Active Directory as a separate forest, you would need to employ a forest trust between Mycorp and Othercorp to provide seamless resource access between the two companies.

A forest trust is a new type of trust in Windows Server 2003 that allows an administrator to create a single transitive one-way or two-way trust between two forest root domains. This trust allows all the domains in one forest to trust all the domains in another forest, and vice versa.

If you have business units that are independent and, in fact, wish to be isolated from each other, then you must not combine them in a single forest. If you simply give each business unit its own domain, these business units are given the impression that they are autonomous and isolated from each other. However, in Active Directory, this level of autonomy and isolation can be achieved only through separate forests . This is also the case if you need to comply with regulatory or legal isolation requirements.

 Building environments with separate forests has become popular in larger organizations implementing Exchange to get true separation of responsibilities. See *http://www.microsoft.com/technet/prodtechnol/win dowsserver2003/technologies/directory/activedirectory/mtfstwp.mspx* for considerations for multiforest deployments.

Organizational Units

Having covered the large-scale (domains, trees, and forests) view of Active Directory, we'll now talk about the small scale. When you look inside an Active Directory domain, you will see a hierarchical structure of objects. This hierarchy is made up of objects that can act as containers and objects that cannot. The primary type of container that you will create to house objects is called an organizational unit (OU). Another type of container, which is actually called a *Container*, can also be used to store a hierarchy of objects and containers.

Although both can contain huge hierarchies of containers and objects, an Organizational Unit can have group policies applied to it. For more information on group policy, see Chapter 8. For this reason, OUs are often used almost exclusively for building object hierarchies within a domain.

Let's illustrate this with an example. Imagine that you are the administrator of the *asia .mycorp.com* domain from Figure 2-2. You have 500 users and 500 computer accounts in the domain. Most of the day-to-day account and machine management is very simple, but the manufacturing section is currently undergoing restructuring and an extensive recruitment program; people keep being transferred in or hired from the outside. You would like to be able to give this group autonomy by allowing one of the senior administrators to manage their own section of the tree. The manufacturing tree isn't large enough to justify creating another domain to manage along with the associated domain controllers. You can instead create an Organizational Unit in your hierarchy called Manufacturing. You then give the senior engineer authority over that Organizational Unit to create and delete accounts, change passwords, and create other Organizational Units within the Manufacturing OU. Obviously, the permissions that the senior engineer would be given would be properly tailored so that he had control over only that Organizational Unit and not the *asia.mycorp.com* domain tree as a whole. You could do this manually or delegate control using the Delegation of Control wizard, discussed in more depth in Chapter 13.

When you install an Active Directory domain, a number of default containers (and one Organizational Unit) are created automatically, including the Users and Computers containers and Domain Controllers OU. If you try to create a new Container, you will find that there is no option to do so from within the *Active Directory Users and*

Computers (ADUC) MMC snap-in. This also applies to Organization, Locality, and Country container objects. This is intentional; in almost all cases, you would want to create an Organizational Unit instead of a Container. It is possible to create the other types of containers from within scripts and other LDAP tools, but generally it is not necessary. So, throughout this book, whenever we advocate creating hierarchies within domains, we always recommend that you use Organizational Units. After all, an Organizational Unit is just a superset of a Container. There is nothing a Container can do that an Organizational Unit cannot.

> The Windows Support Tools can be installed from the support folder of any Windows CD or service pack CD. They are also available for download from *http://download.microsoft.com* by searching for "support tools." Windows Server 2008 includes the support tools natively.

Global Catalog

The Global Catalog (GC) is a very important part of Active Directory because it is used to perform forest-wide searches. As its name implies, the Global Catalog is a catalog of all objects in a forest which contains a subset of attributes for each object. The GC can be accessed via LDAP over port 3268. The global catalog is read-only and cannot be updated directly.

In multidomain forests, typically you first need to perform a query against the GC to locate the objects of interest. Then you can perform a more directed query against a domain controller for the domain the object is in if you want to access all the attributes available on the object.

The attributes that are available in the global catalog are members of the *partial attribute set* (PAS). You can add and remove attributes from the PAS using tools such as the Active Directory Schema snap-in or by modifying the `attributeSchema` object for the attribute directly in the schema.

> Under Windows 2000, adding an attribute to the PAS caused all global catalogs in a forest to resync the entire contents of the GC. This could have major replication and network traffic implications. Fortunately, this has been resolved with Windows Server 2003 (and later) so that a GC resync no longer happens after a PAS addition. This functionality becomes immediately available on Windows Server 2003 and newer domain controllers as soon as you add them to the forest.

Flexible Single Master Operator (FSMO)

Even though Active Directory is a multimaster directory, there are some situations in which there should only be a single *domain controller* (DC) that can perform certain functions. In these cases, Active Directory nominates one server to act as the master for those functions. There are five such functions that need to take place on one server only. The server that is the master for a particular function or role is known as the Flexible Single Master Operator (FSMO, pronounced "fizmo") role owner.

Of the five roles, three exist for every domain, and two apply to the entire forest. If there are four domains in your forest, there will be 14 FSMO roles:

4 lots of 3 domain-wide FSMOs
2 single forest-wide FSMOs

The number of different role owners can vary greatly depending on whether you have domain controllers serving multiple roles, as is often the case.

The different FSMO roles are the following:

Schema Master (forest-wide)
> The Schema Master role owner is the domain controller that is allowed to make updates to the schema. No other server can process changes to the schema. If you attempt to update the schema on a DC that doesn't hold the Schema FSMO, the DC will return a referral to the schema master role holder. The default schema master role owner is the first server to be promoted to a domain controller in the forest.

Domain Naming Master (forest-wide)
> The Domain Naming Master role owner is the server that controls changes to the forest-wide namespace. This server adds and removes domains and is required to rename or move domains within a forest, as well as to authorize creation of application partitions and the addition/removal of their replicas. Like the Schema Master, this role owner defaults to the first DC you promote in a forest.

 It is a common misunderstanding that the schema and domain naming masters cannot be hosted outside of the root domain. Any domain controller in the forest (from any domain) can host the schema and domain naming master FSMO roles. In general, we recommend that these FSMOs be kept on a domain controller in the forest root unless you have a reason to place them elsewhere.

PDC Emulator (domain-wide)
> For backward-compatibility purposes, one Active Directory DC has to act as the Windows NT Primary Domain Controller (PDC). This server acts as the Windows NT master browser, and it also acts as the PDC for down-level clients and Backup Domain Controllers (BDCs). While doing this, it replicates the Windows NT SAM database to Windows NT 4.0 and Windows 3.51 BDCs. Even though the PDC has very important legacy functions, don't be fooled into thinking that once you have removed all older DCs and clients, it is no longer important.

Windows Server 2008 no longer supports Windows NT4 BDC replication. Therefore you must remove all Windows NT BDCs from a domain before beginning to migrate that domain to Windows Server 2008.

However, the PDC emulator has other important functions: it attempts to maintain the latest password for any account. This is enforced by having the other DCs immediately forward any account password changes directly to the PDC. The significance of this feature is in helping to support PDC-chaining functions. PDC-chaining occurs when an account attempts to authenticate and the local DC doesn't think the password is correct. The local DC will then "chain" the authentication attempt to the PDC to see if the PDC thinks the password is okay.

The PDC is also the target server of most Group Policy management tools. This is done to lessen the possibility of the same policy being modified in different ways by different administrators on different DCs at the same time. One other function of the PDC is that the PDC in each domain is the primary time source for the domain and the PDC of the forest root domain is the primary time source for the entire forest.

The PDC-Chaining and the matching forwarding of the passwords to the PDC across Active Directory site boundaries can be disabled by setting the `AvoidPdcOnWan` registry value to 1. This is found in the registry key `HKLM\SYSTEM\CurrentControlSet\Services\Netlogon \Parameters`. If you suspect that PDC-Chaining isn't working, make sure this registry value isn't configured. You can find more information about this registry setting at *http://support.microsoft .com/kb/225511*.

RID Master (domain-wide)

A *Relative-Identifier* (RID) Master exists per domain. Every security principal in a domain has a *Security Identifier* (SID) that is comprised of several components including a RID. The system uses the SID to uniquely identify that object for security permissions. In a way, this is similar to the GUID that every object has, but the SID is given only to security-enabled objects and is used only for security verification purposes. For more information about SIDs, see the sidebar "What's in a Security Identifier (SID)?" While you may log on or authenticate using the SAM account name or Universal Principal Name (UPN) to reference an object, the system always references you for authorization functions by the SID.

In a domain, the SIDs must be unique across the entire domain. As each DC can create security-enabled objects, some mechanism has to exist so that two identical SIDs are never created. To keep conflicts from occurring, the RID Master maintains a large pool of unique RID values. When a DC is added to the network, it is allocated a subset of 500 values from the RID pool for its own use. Whenever a DC needs to create a SID, it takes the next available value from its own RID pool to create the SID with a unique value.

In this way, the RID Master makes sure that all SIDs in a domain use unique RID values. When a Windows 2000 Pre-SP4 DC's RID pool drops to 100 free values, the DC contacts the RID Master for another set of RID values. With Windows 2000 SP4, this was changed to 50% of the RID pool size, and the default RID pool size is 500 RIDs. The threshold is not set to 0 to ensure that the RID Master can be unavailable to other DCs for a brief time without immediately impacting object creations. The RID Master itself is in charge of generating and maintaining a pool of unique values across the entire domain.

 RID pool size can be configured by setting the RID Block Size value in the registry key HKLM\SYSTEM\CurrentControlSet\Services\NTDS \RID values on the RID Master FSMO role holder. If you decide to use this registry setting, it is a recommended practice to set this value on *any* domain controller that could become the RID Master so you do not have any inconsistencies in RID pool sizes after a RID Master FSMO transfer. A common scenario where you might use this registry setting is if you have a distributed environment where there can be prolonged connectivity issues between domain controllers and the RID master.

What's in a Security Identifier (SID)?

Many Windows administrators know what a SID is: a unique, variable-length identifier used to identify a trustee or security principal. However, few understand what components a SID is comprised of. A little bit of time spent understanding how SIDs are composed can possibly help an administrator understand the underpinnings of Windows security.

A Windows SID is generally composed of two fixed fields and up to 15 additional fields, all separated by dashes like so:

S-v-id-s1-s2-s3-s4-s5-s6-s7-s8-s9-s10-s11-s12-s13-s14-s15

The first fixed field (v) describes the version of the SID structure. Microsoft has never changed this, so it is always 1.

The second fixed field (id) is called the identifier authority. In Windows domains and Windows computers, it uniquely identifies the authority involved such as NULL (0), World (1), Local (2), NT Authority (5), etc.

The next 15 fields (s1–s15) are not required for every SID and, in fact, most SIDs only have a few of these fields populated. These additional fields are called sub-authorities and help uniquely identify the object being referenced. The last sub-authority on most SIDs is generally called the RID. This is the value that a domain or computer increments to create unique SIDs.

With that information, you can now look at a SID such as S-1-5-10 and determine that it is a version 1 SID issued by the NT Authority. This SID is special and is called a Well-Known SID, representing NTAUTHORITY\SELF. Another Well-Known SID is S-1-1-0, which is a version 1 World SID; it represents Everyone.

There are several other Well-Known SIDs with various values. They are easily identifiable because they don't fit the format of normal computer and domain SIDs. These normal SIDs usually look like this:

`S-1-21-xxx-yyy-zzz-r`

where the values for *xxx*, *yyy*, and *zzz* are randomly generated when the computer or domain is created. The RID value r could either be a consecutive number issued by the RID generation routine or a Well-Known RID assigned to certain security principals that exist in every domain. An example of a Well-Known RID is 500, which translates to the built-in administrator account.

Infrastructure Master (domain-wide)

The Infrastructure Master is used to maintain references to objects in other domains, known as phantoms. If three users from Domain B are members of a group in Domain A, the Infrastructure Manager on Domain A is used to maintain references to the phantom Domain B user members. These phantoms are not manageable or even visible through ordinary means; they are an implementation construct to maintain consistency.

The Infrastructure Master FSMO role owner is used to continually maintain the phantoms whenever the objects they refer to are changed or moved in the object's domain. When an object in one domain references an object in another domain, it represents that reference by the GUID, the SID (for references to security principals), and the DN of the object being referenced. The Infrastructure FSMO role holder is the DC responsible for updating an object's SID and distinguished name in a cross-domain object reference.

The Infrastructure Master is responsible for fixing up stale references from objects in its domain to objects in other domains ("stale" means references to objects that have been moved or renamed so that the local copy of the remote object's name is out of date). It does this by comparing its (potentially stale) naming data with that of a global catalog, which automatically receives regular replication updates for objects in all domains and hence has no stale data. The Infrastructure FSMO writes any updates it finds to its objects and then replicates the updated information around to other DCs in the domain. However, if a GC also holds the Infrastructure role, then by definition that server hosting the GC will always be up to date and will therefore have no stale references. If it never notices that anything needs changing, it will never update any non-GC servers with Infrastructure updates.

The Infrastructure Master is also responsible for performing updates to the domain when upgrading to Windows Server 2003 or 2008—the adprep /domainprep command must be run on the infrastructure master. We discuss **adprep** in Chapters 16 and 18.

The placement of the infrastructure master and whether or not it can be placed on a global catalog without causing issues is often a source of great confusion. Table 2-2 provides a matrix of permitted permutations.

Table 2-2. Infrastructure master placement rules

	Single domain forest	Multiple domain forest	
		All domain controllers are GCs	All domain controllers are *not* GCs
Infrastructure master relevant	No	No	Yes
Infrastructure master permitted on GC	Yes	Yes	No

 An Infrastructure Master technically exists for each application partition in the forest in addition to domains. Historically, the infrastructure master has not performed any functions for application partitions. However, Windows Server 2008 setup now enforces a consistency check to make sure that the specified infrastructure master for each application partition is valid. For more information on this, reference *http://support.microsoft.com/kb/949257*. Application partitions are covered in detail in Chapter 3.

FSMO roles can be transferred between domain controllers. You can transfer the Domain Naming FSMO with the Active Directory Domains and Trusts snap-in, the Schema FSMO with the Active Directory Schema snap-in, and the RID, Infrastructure, and PDC Emulator FSMOs using the Active Directory Users and Computers snap-in. Alternatively, you can use the *NTDSUTIL* utility available on Windows 2000 Server and newer to perform transfers from a command line. For more information on using *NTDSUTIL* to transfer FSMO roles, see Chapter 15.

Although the AD snap-ins and *NTDSUTIL* can trivially transfer a role from one server to another while both servers are available, there will be some cases in which a FSMO role owner becomes unavailable without previously transferring the role. In this case, you have to use *NTDSUTIL* to force an ungraceful transfer of the role to a server, known as seizing the role. When you seize a FSMO role, you should not bring the original role owner back online. Instead, you should perform a metadata cleanup and then rebuild the domain controller. For more information on using *NTDSUTIL* to seize FSMO roles, see Chapter 15.

To remove the metadata from the directory after a failed DCPROMO, or if a domain controller cannot be brought back online for any reason, see *http://support.microsoft.com/kb/216498*.

If you are using the Windows Server 2008 version of Active Directory Users and Computers, you can delete a domain controller from the Domain Controllers OU and metadata cleanup will be performed. This mitigates the need to use NTDSUTIL as outlined in the previously mentioned article.

If a server with a role becomes unavailable, another server is not automatically promoted to assume the role. The administrator must move the role to a new owner manually.

If you lose one of the FSMO masters for a domain, you should always make sure that you are in control of the situation and are promoting a new DC to be the relevant master, forcibly moving the role to an existing DC, or swiftly bringing back the DC that is the relevant master. Many Active Directory administrators spend a great deal of time worrying about the well-being of their FSMO role owners and the "what-if" scenario of scrambling to bring them back into service if one of the role holders goes offline. It is worthwhile to consider just how important the immediate availability of each FSMO role owner is to your environment:

Schema master
> The schema master is only necessary when you are making changes to the schema. These are generally planned well in advance, so if your schema master goes offline you can afford to wait before bringing it back online.

Domain naming master
> The domain naming master is only necessary when adding domains and application partitions. This is another change that is planned well in advance, so, again, if your domain naming master goes offline, you can probably wait to bring it back online.

Infrastructure master
> If the infrastructure master is offline, you can't run `adprep /domainprep`, and cross-domain phantom updates will stop. The first task is, of course, planned well in advance. The second seems important at first glance, but the infrastructure master updates phantoms over the period of a couple days, so if you wait a bit to bring it back online, chances are you'll be fine.

RID master
> If the RID master is offline, then you can't issue RID pools to DCs when they're requested. Recall from the earlier section on the RID master that Windows 2000 SP4 and newer domain controllers request RID pools in blocks of 500 when they get down to 250 RIDs remaining. So, unless you expect to exhaust the RID pools on your domain controllers very rapidly (where "rapidly" is faster than you restore

the RID master), you're probably not going to have any issues if the RID master is offline for a period of time. One scenario where RID master availability could be more important is if you are provisioning large numbers of new security principals (users or groups) and the provisioning system targets a single domain controller or set of domain controllers for this task.

PDC emulator

The importance of the availability of the PDC emulator varies from environment to environment. The PDC emulator is the domain controller that applications that use legacy APIs will often contact; it is also how trust paths are resolved, how passwords are chained, where the time sync hierarchy is rooted, and so forth. Whether or not you should rush to bring the PDC emulator back online is really quite subjective to your environment, but, generally speaking, out of the five FSMO roles, the PDC emulator is probably the most important role-holder in your environment.

The fSMORoleOwner Attribute

The FSMO role owners are stored in Active Directory in different locations depending on the role. The DN of the server holding the role is actually stored as the fSMORoleOwner attribute of various objects. For the *mycorp.com* domain, here are the containers that hold that attribute for their respective FSMO roles:

```
PDC Emulator - dc=mycorp,dc=com
Infrastructure Master - cn=Infrastructure,dc=mycorp,dc=com
RID Master - cn=RID Manager$,cn=System,dc=mycorp,dc=com
Schema Master - cn=Schema,cn=Configuration,dc=mycorp,dc=com
Domain Naming Master -
cn=Partitions,cn=Configuration,dc=mycorp,dc=com
```

The information in the attribute is stored as a DN, representing the NTDS Settings object of the domain controller that is the role owner. So, example contents for this attribute might be:

```
CN=NTDS Settings, CN=MYSERVER1, CN=Servers, CN=My Site,
CN=Sites, CN=Configuration, DC=mycorp, DC=com
```

FSMO role placement has been a subject of some debate over the years. Some administrators advocate placing each role on a different DC, while others advocate keeping all roles together. For the sake of simplicity, keep the roles together on a single DC in each domain unless the load on the FSMO role holder DC demands splitting them up onto different servers. However, if you want to split them up, see *http://support.micro soft.com/kb/223346* for the latest guidance on how to best place these roles.

If you are concerned about being able to restore FSMO role holders from backup, you should split the roles accordingly. It is specifically a bad idea to restore the RID master from backup, so you should keep the RID master on a separate domain controller if you want to be able to restore the other FSMO role holders from backup.

Time Synchronization in Active Directory

Active Directory is highly dependent on all of the domain controllers and domain members having synchronized clocks. Kerberos (which is the underlying authentication protocol for Active Directory clients) uses system clocks to verify authenticity of Kerberos packets. By default, Active Directory supports a tolerance of plus or minus five minutes for clocks. If the time variance exceeds this setting, clients will be unable to authenticate and, in the case of domain controllers, replication will not occur.

Fortunately, Active Directory and Windows collectively implement a time synchronization system based on *Network Time* (NTP) ensures that every machine in the forest has a synchronized clock. The *w32time* service implements time synchronization on every Windows 2000 or newer machine in the forest. The time synchronization hierarchy is outlined in the list below and in Figure 2-5:

1. The forest root domain PDC emulator synchronizes its clock with a reliable outside time source (such as a hardware clock, a government source, or another reliable NTP server).

2. Each child domain PDC emulator synchronizes its clock with the PDC emulator of its parent domain.

3. Each domain controller synchronizes its clock with the PDC emulator of its domain.

4. Each domain member synchronizes its clock with the domain controller it authenticates to.

 Network Time Protocol was defined in RFC 1305, which is available at *http://www.faqs.org/rfcs/rfc1305.html*

You should not need to configure the *w32time* service on any machine other than your root domain PDC emulator. While it is permissible to do so, our experience has been that many organizations who elect to use a different time sync hierarchy (such as using local routers or dedicated NTP servers) end up suffering from Kerberos issues later on. For information on how to configure the *w32time* service on the PDC emulator, see the upcoming sidebar "Configuring W32Time on the PDC Emulator."

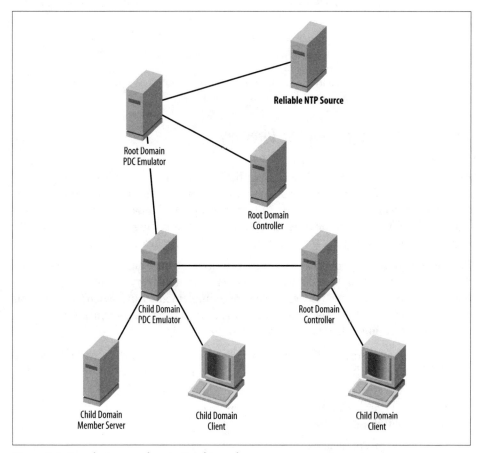

Figure 2-5. Sample time synchronization hierarchy

 It is crucial that you remember to reconfigure the w32time service on any domain controller that you transfer the PDC emulator FSMO role to or from in your root domain. Many organizations proactively configure all of the possible candidates for holding the PDC emulator FSMO to synchronize with an external reliable time source ahead of time.

Configuring W32Time on the PDC Emulator

In order to configure the PDC emulator, you will need to identify one or more authoritative external time sources. For this example we will use the NTP Pool Project's (*http://www.pool.ntp.org*) NTP servers.

```
w32tm/config/manualpeerlist:"0.pool.ntp.org,1.pool.ntp.org,2.pool.ntp.org"
/syncfromflags:manual
w32tm /config /update
w32tm /resync
```

For more information on configuring the w32time service in this scenario, reference *http://support.microsoft.com/?id=816042*. You may also wish to subscribe to the blog located at *http://blogs.msdn.com/w32time/*.

For troubleshooting time sync issues, the w32time service will log events to the System event log. The **w32tm /monitor** and **w32tm /stripchart /computer:*TargetMachineName*** commands are often useful for troubleshooting as well.

Domain and Forest Functional Levels

For the Windows Server 2003 release of Active Directory, Microsoft expanded on the domain mode concept by introducing functional levels. Whereas the domain modes applied only to domains, functional levels apply to both forests and domains. Like the domain mode, functional levels dictate what type of operating systems can assume the role of a domain controller in a domain or forest. Each functional level also has an associated list of features that become available when the domain or forest reaches that particular functional level. We covered many of the features that are available for each functional level in Chapter 1.

Functional levels are introduced into a domain and forest when the first domain controller running Windows Server 2003 is added to a domain. By default, the domain functional level is set to "Windows 2000 Mixed," and the forest functional level is set to "Windows 2000." As with domain modes under Windows 2000, functional levels can be set via the Active Directory Domains and Trusts snap-in and, once "elevated" to a higher status, cannot be changed back.

Tables 2-3 and 2-4 show the operating systems that are supported by the various domain and forest functional levels.

Table 2-3. Domain functional levels

Functional level	Supported domain controller OS
Windows 2000 Mixed	Windows NT 4.0
	Windows 2000
	Windows Server 2003

Functional level	Supported domain controller OS
Windows 2000 Native	Windows 2000
	Windows Server 2003
	Windows Server 2008
Windows Server 2003 Interim	Windows NT 4.0
	Windows Server 2003
Windows Server 2003	Windows Server 2003
	Windows Server 2008
Windows Server 2008	Windows Server 2008

Table 2-4. Forest functional levels

Functional level	Supported domain controller OS
Windows 2000	Windows NT 4.0
	Windows 2000
	Windows Server 2003
	Windows Server 2008
Windows Server 2003 Interim	Windows NT 4.0
	Windows Server 2003
	Windows Server 2008
Windows Server 2003	Windows Server 2003
	Windows Server 2008
Windows Server 2008	Windows Server 2008

> For more information on upgrading to Windows Server 2008, check out Chapter 18.

Windows 2000 Domain Mode

Each Windows 2000 Active Directory domain runs in one of two modes: mixed mode (the default) or native mode. A mixed-mode domain allows servers running previous versions of Windows NT to exist as domain controllers in the domain. A native-mode domain supports only Windows 2000 or later domain controllers. Supporting a mixed-mode domain is necessary to allow administrators to update Windows NT domains to Active Directory. A mixed-mode Active Directory domain emulates some of the behaviors of a Windows NT domain. Remember that with previous versions of Windows NT, networks used to have a Primary Domain Controller (PDC) for a domain that held a writeable copy of the accounts database, and zero or more Backup Domain

Controllers (BDCs) that held a read-only accounts database copied from the PDC. For an Active Directory network to support older Windows NT domain controllers, one (and only one) of the Active Directory servers has to act as a PDC. The Windows NT PDC notifies the BDCs when a change occurs, and the BDCs then request a copy of the accounts database from the PDC to get the relevant user, group, and computer accounts from Active Directory. While all accounts are replicated out, the total attributes for each object are a much smaller subset of the total attributes that Active Directory now holds for these types of objects.

Going from mixed mode to native mode is a simple, but one-way, change. Since this is a one-way change, you should test it in your lab and plan accordingly. Once you have decided to move forward with the procedure, you simply connect to a DC with the Active Directory Domains and Trusts snap-in and change the mode under the General tab to native mode. After you have done this, the only way to go back is to reinstall all domain controllers of the domain and restore from a backup made prior to the upgrade.

Never upgrade to Windows 2000 native mode unless you are certain that you will not require any BDCs to exist anywhere in that domain.

Moving any domain from mixed mode to native mode has no bearing in any way on any other domain. It doesn't matter if it is the root domain or a subdomain you are converting, because you are only removing the ability of that domain to replicate data to older Windows NT BDCs within the domain, not affecting its ability to replicate and interact with Windows 2000 domain controllers in other domains.

The specific differences between mixed mode and native mode are shown in Table 2-5.

Table 2-5. The differences between mixed mode and native mode

Action	Windows 2000 mixed mode	Windows 2000 native mode
Replication	PDC FSMO master sends updates to Windows NT BDCs; same DC acts like ordinary Active Directory DC when communicating with other Active Directory DCs. All Active Directory DCs use multimaster replication between themselves.	Only Active Directory DCs allowed, so all DCs use multimaster replication.
NetBIOS	Can't disable.	Can disable.
Group functions	Windows NT Group Nesting rules; same scope group nesting disallowed for global and domain local groups. Domain local groups limited to DCs. Universal groups cannot be security enabled, but can be nested in other universal groups. No conversion between group types or scopes.	Windows AD Group Nesting rules; same scope group nesting allowed. Domain local groups available on all domain members. Universal groups can be security enabled. Conversion between group types and scopes allowed.
Account migration	sIDHistory is not available; cannot use Movetree or ADMT to move objects into the domain.	sIDHistory is available. Movetree and ADMT can be used.

One important difference between Windows 2000 native-mode and Windows 2000 mixed-mode domains has to do with groups. We'll go in more detail about those differences later in the chapter.

Groups

Active Directory supports three group scopes: domain local, domain global, and universal. Each of these groups behaves slightly differently based on the domain and forest functional levels. To complicate matters further, each group scope can have two types: distribution and security.

The type is the easiest piece to define. If the type is distribution, the group's SID is not added to a user's security token during logon, so it cannot be used for Windows security purposes. Distribution groups are generally used as a messaging list (a set of users that you can mail or send instant messages to all at once), though it is possible to use them for security groups for LDAP-based applications or for other applications that don't use the standard Windows security model. Microsoft Exchange represents distribution lists with Active Directory distribution groups. Security groups, by contrast, are enumerated during logon, and the SIDs of any groups of which the user is a member are added to the user's security token. Security groups can also be leveraged by Exchange as distribution lists.

 In the move from Exchange 5.5 to Exchange 2000, Exchange security was changed to use the standard Windows security. Any Distribution Lists used to secure any Exchange resources, such as mailboxes, mailbox folders, or calendars will automatically be made into a security-enabled group by Exchange. This is often very confusing to administrators because it doesn't require an administrator to initiate the conversion; any mailbox-enabled user can do it.

All Windows editions that support *Kerberos* will encounter problems if security principals are members of too many groups. The issue is that the token of the security principal becomes too large for Windows to handle, and users may experience authentication or other Kerberos issues. This phenomenon is often referred to as *token bloat*. For more information on token size issues, reference *http://support.microsoft.com/kb/327825*. The three different scopes of mailing lists and security groups result from the legacy of Windows NT and the introduction of the GC. Global groups and domain local groups are the direct descendants of Windows NT groups; the membership of these groups is only available from domain controllers of the domains they are created in. Universal groups are a new type of group in Active Directory, and their membership is available from domain controllers of the domains they are created in, as well as all Global Catalogs in the forest. Universal and global groups can be used in access control lists (ACLs) on any resource in the forest or in trusting domains. Domain local groups can only be used in ACLs in the domain they are created in.

In order to fully understand how groups work in Active Directory, we will explain the following items in this section:

- How Windows NT groups have a bearing on Active Directory
- Which groups are available in mixed, native, and Windows Server 2003/2008 functional levels
- Which security principals each group may contain in mixed, native, and Windows Server 2003/2008 functional levels
- How you can nest groups across domain boundaries
- What options are available to you for converting between different group scopes in mixed, native, and Windows Server 2003/2008 functional levels

To start with, let's take a look at how Windows NT handles groups.

Groups in Windows NT

Back in Windows NT, domains could have two scopes of groups: domain local and global. Both were security groups. The domain local group could contain users and global groups. The global group could contain only users. Both could have permissions assigned to them. Member servers and workstations had local groups that were similar to domain local groups in that they were security groups and could contain users or global groups. Administrators typically took advantage of the fact that global groups could nest into domain local or local groups. Users went into global groups, and local groups were given access to resources on local machines, such as file servers, and domain local groups were given access to resources on domain controllers. Then you simply put the global groups in the appropriate local or domain local groups to assign the permissions.

Windows NT groups are still important in Windows 2000 mixed domains, since downlevel Windows NT BDCs will need to replicate these groups from the Active Directory PDC emulator FSMO role owner. During an upgrade of a PDC from Windows NT to Active Directory, Windows NT domain local and global groups are migrated to Active Directory domain local security groups and global security groups, although they still appear as domain local and global groups to any Windows NT BDCs.

If you are running in Windows 2000 mixed mode, the key limitation you should be aware of is that universal security groups are not permitted. Table 2-6 shows which group options are only available beginning with Windows 2000 native mode.

Group nesting in different functional levels

When you convert a domain to Windows 2000 Native or Windows Server 2003/2008 functional level, certain groups become available, but you do not lose any group nesting options that you had in mixed mode. The new options can be summarized quite easily as follows:

- Domain local security groups can contain domain local security and domain local distribution groups. Local security groups on member servers can contain domain local security groups.
- Domain global security groups can contain domain global security and domain global distribution groups.
- Universal security groups become available.

Let's look at this summary using a table. Consider Table 2-6, with the extra options available only in Windows 2000 Native mode and newer emphasized in bold.

Table 2-6. Windows 2000 Native and newer restrictions on group membership based on group scope

Scope	Type	Can contain domain local		Can contain domain global		Can contain universal	
		Distribution groups	Security groups	Distribution groups	Security groups	Distribution groups	Security groups
Domain local	Distribution groups	Yes	Yes	Yes	Yes	Yes	Yes
	Security groups	**Yes**	Yes	Yes	Yes	Yes	Yes
Domain global	Distribution groups	No	No	Yes	Yes	No	No
	Security groups	No	No	Yes	Yes	No	No
Universal	Distribution groups	No	No	Yes	Yes	Yes	Yes
	Security groups	No	No	Yes	Yes	Yes	Yes

Although these tables are fine, there is one other complicating factor that needs to be taken into account: cross-domain group membership.

Group membership across domain boundaries

Restrictions for all groups are shown in Tables 2-7 and 2-8. Two items are listed as "Special," which signifies distribution groups in Windows 2000 Mixed, and distribution and security groups in Windows 2000 Native and Windows Server 2003/2008 modes.

Table 2-7. Restrictions on group membership based on group scope

Group scope	Can contain users and computers from		Can contain domain local groups from	
	Same domain	Different domain	Same domain	Different domain
Domain local groups	Yes	Yes	Special	No
Domain global groups	Yes	No	No	No
Universal groups	Yes	Yes	No	No

Table 2-8. Restrictions on group membership based on domain

Group scope	Can contain domain global groups from		Can contain universal groups from	
	Same domain	Different domain	Same domain	Different domain
Domain local groups	Yes	Yes	Yes	Yes
Domain global groups	Special	No	No	No
Universal groups	Yes	Yes	Yes	Yes

Tables 2-7 and 2-8 work in conjunction with Table 2-6. You would normally check which groups may be members from Table 2-6 (if any) and then cross reference with Tables 2-7 and 2-8 to identify what options you have across domain boundaries.

Converting groups

Converting groups from one scope to another is available only in Windows 2000 Native and newer modes. There are limits on what groups can be converted based on the existing members of the group and the current type and scope of the group. The former should be fairly obvious based on the existing restrictions shown in Table 2-6. The conversion process cannot work if the existing group members would not be valid members of the new group type once the conversion had taken place. However, when you upgrade to Windows 2000 Native or newer, you gain the ability to convert between groups based on these restrictions:

- Security groups can be converted to distribution groups.
- Distribution groups can be converted to security groups.
- A domain local group can be converted to a universal group provided that the domain local group is not already a member of another domain local group.
- A domain global group can be converted to a universal group provided that the domain global group does not contain any other domain global groups.
- A universal group can be converted to a domain global group provided all members in the group are users from the domain the group existed in.
- A universal group can be converted to a domain local group.

The benefit of converting a distribution group to a security group is probably obvious: you get to use the group for Windows security purposes. The benefit of converting a security group to a distribution group is usually not so obvious. The most useful aspect of this conversion is that you can safely disable a security group to verify whether or not it is being used for Windows security. Previously, if you didn't know whether a group was being used for Windows security, you would have to delete it and hope that nothing broke. If anything did break, you found yourself figuring out how to restore the group or how to use a new group. Now you can simply convert the group to a distribution group, and if anything breaks, you simply change the group back into a security group, thereby restoring the old functionality.

Wrap-up

Although this all looks complicated, using the tables helps to simplify the relationships between the group types. Ultimately, you need to decide how long you will be staying in Windows 2000 mixed mode before going to Windows 2000 Native mode or newer so that you can decide what sort of groups are best for your needs. You also have to consider that in Windows 2000 Native and Windows Server 2003 and 2008, the more universal groups you add, the larger the global catalog and the longer members of those groups will take to log on. Chapters 10 and 12 explain more about when and how to use groups in your designs.

Summary

In this chapter, we've gone over the groundwork for some of the main internals of Active Directory. We covered such concepts as domains, trees, forests, Organizational Units, the Global Catalog, FSMOs, Windows 2000 domain modes, and forest and domain functional levels. We then delved into how groups work in Active Directory and what features are available under the various domain modes and functional levels.

With this information under our belts, let's now take a look at how data is organized in Active Directory with Naming Contexts and Application Partitions.

## CHAPTER 3

Naming Contexts and Application Partitions

Due to the distributed nature of Active Directory, it is necessary to segregate data into partitions. If data partitions were not used, every domain controller would have to replicate all the data within a forest. Often it is advantageous to group data based on geographical or political requirements. Think of a domain as a big data partition, which is also referred to as a *naming context* (NC). Only domain controllers that are authoritative for a domain need replicate all of the information within that domain. Information about other domains is not needed on those domain controllers. On the other hand, there is some Active Directory data that must be replicated to all domain controllers within a forest. There are three predefined naming contexts within Active Directory:

- A *Domain Naming Context* for each domain
- The *Configuration Naming Context* for the forest
- The *Schema Naming Context* for the forest

Each of these naming contexts represents a different type of Active Directory data. The Configuration NC holds data pertaining to the configuration of the forest (or of forest-wide applications), such as the objects representing naming contexts, LDAP policies, sites, subnets, Microsoft Exchange, and so forth. The Schema NC contains the set of object class and attribute definitions for the types of data that can be stored in Active Directory. Each domain in a forest also has a Domain NC, which contains data specific to the domain—for example, users, groups, computers, etc.

In Windows Server 2003 Active Directory, Microsoft extended the naming context concept by allowing user-defined partitions called *application partitions*. Application partitions can contain any type of object except for security principals. A major benefit of application partitions is that administrators can define which domain controllers replicate the data contained within these partitions. Application partitions are not restricted by domain boundaries, as is the case with Domain NCs; they can exist on any domain controller running Windows Server 2003 or later in a forest, regardless of the domain the DC hosts.

You can retrieve a list of the naming contexts and application partitions a specific domain controller maintains by querying its *RootDSE* entry. You can view the RootDSE attributes by opening the Ldp utility, which is available as a part of Windows Support Tools and is included in Windows Server 2008. To see how to view the RootDSE information, see the sidebar "Querying RootDSE with Ldp," next.

Querying RootDSE with Ldp

Ldp is a tool that is included with Windows Server 2008 and in the support tools for Windows 2000, XP, and 2003. You can use Ldp to view raw data from any LDAP server. We will leverage Ldp throughout this book when appropriate. Unless otherwise noted, you should assume that the version of Ldp we are using is the version that ships with Windows Server 2008.

RootDSE is viewable by anonymously binding to any domain controller in the forest. The steps to use Ldp to view this information are:

1. Launch Ldp by running **ldp.exe.**
2. Click Connection→Connect, enter the name of a domain controller, and click OK. Figure 3-1 shows connecting to the domain controller **k8devdc01** on port 389 (the LDAP port).
3. Ldp will connect to the domain controller and immediately display all of the anonymously viewable RootDSE output as shown in Figure 3-2.

There is a great deal of data displayed in this screen and we will not cover it all at this time. A good deal of the information will be covered throughout this book when it is relevant. The information of particular interest to us right now is the data corresponding to the attributes in Table 3-1.

We can see the distinguished name of the root domain in this forest (DC=k8dev01,DC=brianlab,DC=local), the DNs of the application partitions hosted on this domain controller (such as DC=DomainDnsZones,DC=k8dev01,DC=brianlab,DC=local), and so forth.

This output is particularly useful when writing scripts and programs that query Active Directory. By utilizing the RootDSE attributes, you can avoid hardcoding paths into your code. We will cover scripting beginning in Part III.

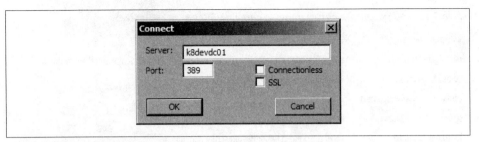

Figure 3-1. Ldp connection dialog

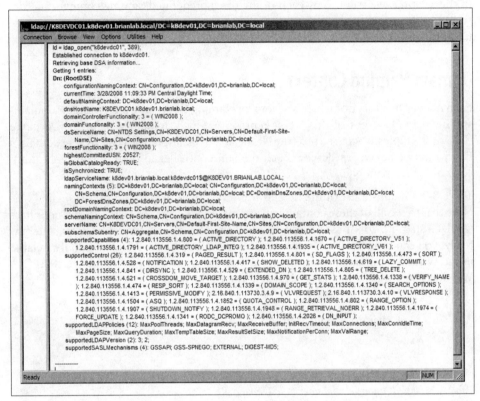

Figure 3-2. Ldp RootDSE output on a Windows 2008 domain controller

Table 3-1. RootDSE attributes pertaining to naming contexts

Attribute Name	Description
namingContexts	List of DNs of all the naming contexts and application partitions maintained by the DC
defaultNamingContext	DN of the Domain NC the DC is authoritative for
configurationNamingContext	DN of the Configuration NC
schemaNamingContext	DN of the Schema NC
rootNamingContext	DN of the Domain NC for the forest root domain

In this chapter, we will review each of the three predefined naming contexts and describe the data contained within each, and then cover application partitions and sample uses of them.

Domain Naming Context

Each Active Directory domain has a Domain Naming Context, which contains domain-specific data. The root of this NC is represented by a domain's distinguished name (DN) and is typically referred to as the NC head. For example, the *mycorp.com* domain's DN would be dc=mycorp,dc=com. Each domain controller in the domain replicates a copy of the Domain NC.

Table 3-2 contains a list of the default top-level containers found in a Domain NC. Note that to see all of these containers with the Active Directory Users and Computers (ADUC) snap-in, you must select View→Advanced Features from the menu. Alternatively, you can browse all of these containers with Ldp or the ADSI Edit tool available in the Windows Support Tools on any Windows Server 2003 or Windows 2000 CD. Windows Server 2008 includes ADSI Edit out of the box.

> To start ADSI Edit, go to Start→Run→**adsiedit.msc.**

Table 3-2. Default top-level containers of a Domain NC

Relative distinguished name	Description
cn=Builtin	Container for predefined built-in local security groups. Examples include Administrators, Domain Users, and Account Operators.
cn=Computers	Default container for computer objects representing member servers and workstations. You can change the default container used in Windows Server 2003 and newer with the *redircmp.exe* utility.
ou=Domain Controllers	Default organizational unit for computer objects representing domain controllers.

Relative distinguished name	Description
cn=ForeignSecurityPrincipals	Container for placeholder objects representing members of groups in the domain that are from a domain external to the forest.
cn=LostandFound	Container for orphaned objects. Orphaned objects are objects that were created in a container that was deleted from another domain controller within the same replication period.
cn=NTDS Quotas	Container to store quota objects, which are used to restrict the number of objects a security principal can create in a partition or container. This container is new in Windows Server 2003.
cn=Program Data	Container for applications to store data instead of using a custom top-level container. This container is new in Windows Server 2003.
cn=System	Container for miscellaneous domain configuration objects. Examples include trust objects, DNS objects, and group policy objects.
cn=Users	Default container for user and group objects. You can change the default container used in Windows Server 2003 and newer with the *redirusr.exe* utility.

Configuration Naming Context

The Configuration NC is the primary repository for configuration information for a forest and is replicated to every domain controller in the forest. Additionally, every writeable domain controller in the forest holds a *writeable* copy of the configuration NC. The root of the Configuration NC is found in the Configuration container, which is a sub-container of the forest root domain. For example, the *mycorp.com* forest would have a Configuration NC located at cn=configuration,dc=mycorp,dc=com.

Table 3-3 contains a list of the default top-level containers found in the Configuration NC.

Table 3-3. Default top-level containers of the Configuration NC

Relative distinguished name	Description
cn=DisplaySpecifiers	Container that holds display specifier objects, which define various display formats for the Active Directory MMC Snap-ins.
cn=Extended-Rights	Container for extended rights (controlAccessRight) objects.
cn=ForestUpdates	Contains objects that are used to represent the state of forest and domain functional level changes. This container is new in Windows Server 2003.
cn=LostandFoundConfig	Container for orphaned objects.
cn=NTDS Quotas	Container to store quota objects, which are used to restrict the number of objects that security principals can create in a partition or container. This container is new in Windows Server 2003.
cn=Partitions	Contains objects for each naming context, application partition, and external LDAP directory reference.

Relative distinguished name	Description
cn=Physical Locations	Contains location objects (physicalLocation), which can be associated with other objects to denote location of the object.
cn=Services	Store of configuration information about services such as FRS, Exchange, and Active Directory itself.
cn=Sites	Contains all of the site topology and replication objects. This includes site, subnet, siteLink, server, and nTDSConnection objects, to name a few.
cn=WellKnown Security Principals	Holds objects representing commonly used foreign security principals, such as Everyone, Interactive, and Authenticated Users.

Schema Naming Context

The Schema NC contains objects representing the classes and attributes that Active Directory supports. The schema is defined on a forest-wide basis, so the Schema NC is replicated to every domain controller in the forest. Recall that the Schema NC is writeable *only* on the domain controller holding the schema master FSMO role. The root of the Schema NC can be found in the Schema container, which is a sub-container of the Configuration container. For example, in the *mycorp.com* forest, the Schema NC would be located at cn=schema,cn=configuration,dc=mycorp,dc=com.

Although the Schema container appears to be a child of the Configuration container, it is actually a separate naming context in its own right. Figure 3-3 shows how the Schema and Configuration NCs are segregated in the ADSI Edit tool.

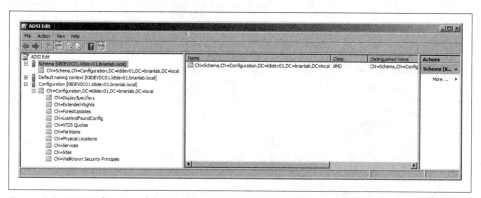

Figure 3-3. ADSI Edit view of the Configuration and Schema naming contexts

You may be wondering why the schema isn't just contained within the Configuration NC. As we discussed in Chapter 2, there is a Schema FSMO role that is the single master for updates to schema objects. The Schema FSMO role is necessary due to the highly sensitive nature of the schema. Schema modifications need to be processed prior to any updates that utilize the schema. The mechanism to most easily guarantee this with the replication model AD uses is to put the schema into its own partition so it can replicate separately prior to other changes.

Unlike the Domain and Configuration NCs, the Schema NC does not maintain a hierarchy of containers or organizational units. Instead, it is a single container that has `classSchema`, `attributeSchema`, and `subSchema` objects. The `classSchema` objects define the different types of classes and their associated attributes. The `attributeSchema` objects define all the attributes that are used as part of `classSchema` definitions. There is also a single `subSchema` instance that represents the abstract schema as defined in the LDAPv3 RFC (*http://www.ietf.org/rfc/rfc2254.txt*).

Chapters 4 and 14 deal with the schema in more depth.

Application Partitions

Application partitions are a feature introduced to Active Directory in Windows Server 2003. They enable administrators to create areas in Active Directory to store data on specific domain controllers they choose, rather than on every DC in a domain or forest. You can define which domain controllers hold a copy of each application partition, which is known as a replica. There is no limitation based on domain or site membership, which means that you can configure any domain controller running Windows Server 2003 or later within a forest to hold any application partition replica. The existing site topology will be used to automatically create the necessary connection objects to replicate among the servers that hold replicas of an application partition. Domain controllers will also register the necessary Service Location (SRV) records (explained in more detail in Chapter 6), so that clients can use the DC locator process to find the optimal domain controller for an application partition, just as they would for a domain.

There are a few limitations to be aware of regarding application partitions:

- Application partitions cannot contain security principals, which most notably includes `user`, `inetOrgPerson`, `group`, and `computer` objects. Any other type of object can be created in an application partition.

- None of the objects contained in an application partition are replicated to the global catalog. Even if a domain controller that holds a replica of an application partition is also a global catalog server, the domain controller will not return any objects from the application partition during a global catalog search.

- Objects in an application partition cannot be moved outside the partition. This is different from objects contained in domains, which can be moved between domains.

- The Domain Naming FSMO must be on a Windows Server 2003 (or newer) domain controller to create an application partition. After the application partition has been created, you can move the Domain Naming FSMO back to a Windows 2000 domain controller (if necessary).

Application partitions are named similarly to domains. For example, if you created an application partition called "apps" directly under the *mycorp.com* domain, the DNS name would be *apps.mycorp.com* and the distinguished name would be `dc=apps,dc=mycorp,dc=com`. Application partitions can be rooted under domains, as shown in the previous example; nested under other application partitions (for example, `dc=sales,dc=apps,dc=mycorp,dc=com`); or as part of a new domain tree (for example, `dc=apps,dc=local`). For more information on creating and managing application partitions, refer to the sidebar "Creating Application Partitions," next.

Creating Application Partitions

Application partitions are commonly managed with the *ntdsutil* utility. With *ntdsutil*, you can manage application partitions in Active Directory and AD LDS. The types of operations you can perform include creating and deleting new application partitions, and adding and removing domain controllers and AD LDS instances to the list of replicas for an application partition.

In this example, we will create an application partition under the `k8dev01.brian lab.local` domain called `BigAppPart`. This domain is at the Windows Server 2008 functional level. We will enable the application partition to replicate to domain controllers `K8DEVDC01` and `K8DEVDC02`.

Creating the application partition

1. From a command prompt, launch **ntdsutil**.
2. Enter partition management mode by entering **partition management**.
3. Enter the distinguished name of the application partition and a server to create the partition on:

   ```
   create nc "dc=BigAppPart,dc=k8dev01,dc=brianlab,dc=local"
   k8devdc01.k8dev01.brianlab.local
   ```

4. Enter **quit** to exit the partition management menu, and then enter **quit** again to exit ntdsutil.

Adding the k8devdc02 replica

1. From a command prompt, launch **ntdsutil**.
2. Enter partition management mode by entering **partition management**.
3. Enter **connections** to move to the connections submenu.
4. Enter **connect to server k8devdc02**. You must always connect to the server to which you will be adding the replica.

---

5. Enter **quit** to return to the `partition management` menu.

6. Enter the following nc replica to add the replica to k8devdc02:

    ```
    "dc=BigAppPart,dc=k8dev01,dc=brianlab,dc=local" k8devdc02.k8dev01.brianlab.local
    ```

7. Enter **quit** to exit the `partition management` menu, and then enter **quit** again to exit `ntdsutil`.

    On Windows Server 2003, you should replace the **partition management** command with the **domain management** command. The rest of the syntax is identical.

Application partitions tend to store dynamic data—that is, data which has a limited lifespan. See the section on "Storing Dynamic Data" for more on this. Dynamic data from network services such as DNS and Dynamic Host Configuration Protocol (DHCP) can both reside in an application partition in AD. This allows uniformity of access from applications via a single methodology. This enables developers to write to a special area only available on specific servers rather than into a domain partition that is replicated to every DC. In fact, application partitions could allow multiple versions of COM+ applications to be installed and configured on the same computer, resulting in more cost-effective management of server applications.

The availability of *Active Directory Lightweight Directory Service* (AD LDS), formerly known as *Active Directory Application Mode (ADAM)*, has given administrators another option for storing directory data outside of the normal domain-naming contexts while still using Windows security and authentication. Instead of putting application data in an application partition, you can instead place that data in a dedicated AD LDS instance. This allows you to offload administrative control of that information to application owners or other administrators, as well as lessening the chance of an application negatively impacting a domain controller's primary NOS function. We discuss AD LDS specifics in Chapter 20.

Storing Dynamic Data

Although application partitions give administrators more control over how to replicate application data, the problem of data cleanup still exists. That is, applications that add data to Active Directory are not always good about cleaning it up after it is no longer needed. That's why the ability to create dynamic data was also added as a feature in Windows Server 2003 Active Directory. Dynamic objects are objects that have a time-to-live (TTL) value that determines how long the object will exist before being automatically deleted by Active Directory. Dynamic objects typically have a fairly short life span (i.e., days or less). An example use of dynamic objects is an e-commerce web site that needs to store user session information temporarily. Because a directory is likely going to be where the user profile information resides, it can be advantageous to use the same store for session-based information, which is generally short-lived. The default TTL that is set for dynamic objects is 1 day, but can be configured to be as short as 15 minutes.

The default TTL and minimum TTL can be modified by changing the `DynamicObjectDefaultTTLSeconds` and `DynamicObjectMinTTLSeconds` values in the `ms-DS-Other-Settings` attribute of the `CN=Directory Service,CN=Windows NT,CN=Services,CN=Configuration,DC=…`object.

To create a dynamic object, you simply have to add `dynamicObject` to the `objectClass` attribute when creating the object. Microsoft has specifically disabled the ability to add this objectClass to existing objects for safety reasons. This is why you cannot convert existing static objects into dynamic objects. The `entryTTL` attribute can also be set at creation time to set the TTL to something other than the one-day default. To prevent a dynamic object from being automatically deleted, you can "refresh" the object by resetting the `entryTTL` attribute for the object to a new TTL value (time specified in seconds).

 Dynamic objects do not get tombstoned like normal objects when they are deleted; they are just removed from the directory. A tombstone is not needed since the TTL mechanism allows them to be immediately removed from all domain controllers simultaneously. For more information on tombstones, see the section "Preserve attribute in tombstone" in Chapter 4.

Summary

In this chapter, we covered how objects are grouped at a high level into naming contexts and application partitions, which are used as replication boundaries. The Domain NC contains domain-specific data such as users, groups, and computers. The Configuration NC contains forest-wide configuration data such as the site topology objects and objects that represent naming contexts and application partitions. The Schema NC contains all the schema objects that define how data is structured and represented in Active Directory.

Application partitions were introduced in Windows Server 2003 Active Directory as a way for administrators to define their own groupings of objects and, subsequently, replication boundaries. Storage of DNS data for AD-integrated DNS zones is the classic example of when it makes sense to use application partitions, due to the increased control they give you over which domain controllers replicate the data. Dynamic objects are also new to Windows Server 2003 Active Directory. This feature allows you to create objects that have a TTL value; after the TTL expires, Active Directory automatically deletes the object.

## CHAPTER 4

Active Directory Schema

The schema is the blueprint for data storage in Active Directory. Each object in Active Directory is an instance of a class in the schema. A user object, for example, exists as an instance of the user class. Attributes define the pieces of information that a class, and thus an instance of that class, can hold. Syntaxes define the type of data that can be placed into an attribute. As an example, if an attribute is defined with a syntax of Boolean, it can store True or False as its value, or it can be null. A null value has an implementation-specific meaning; it could mean True or False depending on the application using the value.

Active Directory contains many attributes and classes in the default schema, some of which are based on standards and some of which Microsoft needed for its own use. Each release of Active Directory since Windows 2000 has included updates to the default schema. For background information on schema versions, see the sidebar "Schema Versions," next. However, the Active Directory schema was designed to be extensible, so that administrators could add classes or attributes they deemed necessary. In fact, extending the schema is not a difficult task; it is often more difficult to design the changes that you would like to incorporate. Schema design issues are covered in Chapter 14, and in Chapter 26, we cover how to extend the schema programmatically. In this chapter, we're concerned only with the fundamentals of the schema.

COMMAND-LINE REFERENCE

Schema Versions

Each time Microsoft releases an update to the default Active Directory schema, they update the `schemaVersion` attribute in Active Directory. To date, there have been four versions of the default Active Directory schema released that are outlined in Table 4-1.

You can easily query the schema version with the adfind command-line tool. Use this command to do so:

```
adfind -schema -s base objectVersion
```

Table 4-1. Active Directory default schema versions

Schema version	Release
13	Windows 2000
30	Windows Server 2003
31	Windows Server 2003 R2
44	Windows Server 2008

Structure of the Schema

The Schema Container is located in Active Directory under the Configuration Container. For example, the distinguished name of the Schema Container in the *mycorp .com* forest would be cn=schema,cn=Configuration,dc=mycorp,dc=com. You can view the contents of the container directly by pointing an Active Directory viewer such as *ADSIEdit* or *LDP* at it. You can also use the Active Directory Schema MMC snap-in, which splits the classes and attributes in separate containers for easy viewing, even though in reality all the schema objects are stored directly in the Schema Container.

 The Active Directory Schema MMC snap-in is not fully enabled by default. In order to enable the schema management snap-in on a domain controller, you must first register the DLL which it depends on. To do that, run this command: regsvr32 schmmgmt.dll.

The schema itself is made up of two types of Active Directory objects: classes and attributes. In Active Directory, these are known respectively as classSchema (Class-Schema) and attributeSchema (Attribute-Schema) objects. The two distinct forms of the same names result from the fact that the cn (Common-Name) attribute of a class contains the hyphenated easy-to-read name of the class, and the lDAPDisplayName (LDAP-Display-Name) attribute of a class contains the concatenated string format that is used when querying Active Directory with LDAP or ADSI. In the schema, the lDAPDisplayName attribute of each object is normally made by capitalizing the first letter of each word of the Common-Name, and then removing the hyphens and concatenating all the words together. Finally, the first letter is made lowercase.* This creates simple names like user, as well as the more unusual sAMAccountName and lDAPDisplayName. We'll specify the more commonly used LDAP display name format from now on.

Whenever you need to create new types of objects in Active Directory, you must first create a classSchema object, defining the class of the object and the attributes it contains. Once the class is properly designed and added to the schema, you can then create objects in Active Directory that use the class. If the class you are adding will have custom

---

* Names defined by the X.500 standard don't tend to follow this method. For example, the Common-Name attribute has an LDAP-Display-Name of cn, and the Surname attribute has an LDAP-Display-Name of sn.

attributes that are required to be populated when new instances of that class are created, you must define the `attributeSchema` objects first. If you just want to add a new attribute to an existing class, you must create the `attributeSchema` object and associate the attribute with whatever classes you want to use it with.

Before we delve into what makes up an Active Directory class or attribute, we need to explain how each class that you create is unique not just within your Active Directory but also throughout the world.

X.500 and the OID Namespace

Active Directory is based on LDAP, which was originally based on the X.500 standard created by the ISO (International Organization for Standardization) and ITU (International Telecommunications Union) organizations in 1988. To properly understand how the Active Directory schema works, you really need to understand some of the basics of X.500; we'll run through them next.

The X.500 standard specifies that individual object classes in an organization can be uniquely defined using a special identifying process. The process has to be able to take into account the fact that classes can inherit from one another, as well as the potential need for any organization in the world to define and export a class of their own design.

To that end, the X.500 standard defined an Object Identifier (OID) to uniquely identify every schema object. This OID is composed of two parts:

- The first part indicates the unique path to the branch holding the object in the X.500 tree-like structure.
- The second part uniquely indicates the object in that branch.

OID notation uses integers for each branch and object, as in the following example OID for an object:

```
1.3.6.1.4.1.3385.12.497
```

This uniquely references object 497 in branch 1.3.6.1.4.1.3385.12. The 1.3.6.1.4.1.3385.12 branch is contained in a branch whose OID is 1.3.6.1.4.1.3385, and so on.

> Each branch within an OID number also corresponds to a name. This means that the dotted notation 1.3.6.1.4.1, for example, is equivalent to *iso.org.dod.internet.private.enterprise*. As the names are of no relevance to us with Active Directory, we don't cover them in this book.

This notation continues today and is used in the Active Directory schema. If you wish to create a schema object, you need to obtain a unique OID branch for your organization. Using this as your root, you can then create further branches and leaf nodes within the root, as your organization requires.

The Internet Assigned Numbers Authority (IANA) maintains the main set of root branches and defines itself as "the central coordinator for the assignment of unique parameter values for Internet protocols." The IANA says of its mission:

> The IANA is chartered by the Internet Society (ISOC) and the Federal Network Council (FNC) to act as the clearinghouse to assign and coordinate the use of numerous Internet protocol parameters. The Internet protocol suite, as defined by the Internet Engineering Task Force (IETF) and its steering group (the IESG), contains numerous parameters, such as Internet addresses, domain names, autonomous system numbers (used in some routing protocols), protocol numbers, port numbers, management information base object identifiers, including private enterprise numbers, and many others. The common use of the Internet protocols by the Internet community requires that the particular values used in these parameter fields be assigned uniquely. It is the task of the IANA to make those unique assignments as requested and to maintain a registry of the currently assigned values. The IANA is located at and operated by the Information Sciences Institute (ISI) of the University of Southern California (USC).

You can find the IANA web page at *http://www.iana.org*.

You can request an OID namespace—i.e., a root OID number from which you can create your own branches—directly from the IANA if you like. These numbers are known as Enterprise Numbers. The entire list of Enterprise Numbers assigned by the IANA can be found at *http://www.iana.org/assignments/enterprise-numbers*. This list of numbers is updated every time a new one is added.

At the top of the file, you can see that the root that the IANA uses is 1.3.6.1.4.1. If you look down the list, you will see that Microsoft has been allocated branch 311 of that part of the tree, so Microsoft's OID namespace is 1.3.6.1.4.1.311. Leicester University's OID namespace is 1.3.6.1.4.1.3385. As each number also has a contact email address alongside it in the list, you can search through the file for any member of your organization that has already been allocated a number. It is likely that large organizations that already have an X.500 directory or that have developed SNMP MIBs will have obtained an OID.

In addition to Enterprise Numbers, country-specific OIDs can be purchased as well. An organization's Enterprise Number registration has no bearing on whether it has obtained a country-based OID namespace to use. If you don't see the company listed in the Enterprise Numbers list, don't be fooled; the organization could still have a number.

For example, Microsoft has been issued the Enterprise Number 1.3.6.1.4.1.311, yet all of its new schema classes use a U.S.-issued OID namespace of 1.2.840.113556 as their root. The 1.2.840 part is uniquely allotted to the United States. In other words, Microsoft has obtained two OID namespaces that it can use but is choosing to use only the U.S.-issued namespace.

If you want to obtain an Enterprise Number, fill in the online form at at *http://pen.iana .org/pen/PenApplication*.page. If this URL changes, you can navigate to it from the main IANA web page.

Microsoft used to issue unique OID namespaces to customers on request; however, they no longer do this. Instead, Microsoft provides a script that will generate a statistically unique OID branch each time it is run. This script is available from *http://go .microsoft.com/fwlink/?LinkId=100725*.

Using a unique prefix for schema extensions may not seem important at first glance. The benefit of unique prefixes comes into play if a company finds out another company is also using the same prefix. This can become extremely problematic if the other company is an application vendor.

For example, say that MyCorp Financial Services is prefixing their schema extensions with the "mycorp" prefix. MyCorp Financial has extended their schema with two new attributes: `mycorpAttrib1` and `mycorpAttrib2`. MyCorp Financial purchases a software package from another company, MyCorp Software Solutions, who also chose to use attribute names of `mycorpAttrib1` and `mycorpAttrib2`.

In this scenario, MyCorp Financial Services would be in a very bad position. MyCorp Financial's only option would be changing all previous uses of their attributes so that the names could be reused by the application. If MyCorp Financial did not rename their attributes, they would not be able to use the application that they purchased.

Once an organization has an OID namespace, it can add unique branches and leaves in any manner desired under the root. For example, Leicester University could decide to have no branches underneath and just give any new object an incrementing integer starting from 1 underneath the 1.3.6.1.4.1.3385 root. Alternatively, they could decide to make a series of numbered branches starting from 1, each corresponding to a certain set of classes or attributes that they wish to create. Thus, the fifth object under the third branch would have an OID of 1.3.6.1.4.1. 3385.3.5.

The range of values in any part of an OID namespace for the Active Directory schema goes from 1 to 268,435,455, i.e., from 2^0 through $2^{28} - 1$.

This limitation has caused issues with schema extensions for some companies in Australia. Australia has the OID 1.2.36, and according to the Australia Standards document MP-75, companies may use their Australian Company Number (excluding leading zeros) to formulate their OID without needing to request an OID. Unfortunately the ACN is nine digits, so it could easily exceed the limitation listed above. This has been filed as a bug and Microsoft is aware of the issue.

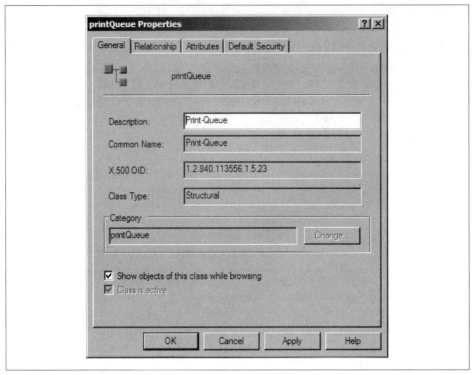

Figure 4-1. printQueue Schema class properties

To reinforce this point, let's look at a couple of examples directly from the Active Directory schema. If you open the Active Directory Schema snap-in, you can look at the schema class OIDs very easily. Navigating through the classes when we open the property page for the `printQueue` class, we get Figure 4-1. You can see that the unique OID is 1.2.840.113556.1.5.23. This tells us that the number is a defined part of Microsoft's object class hierarchy.

Figure 4-2 shows the property page for the `organizationalPerson` class. Here, you can see that the unique OID 2.5.6.7 is very different, because within the original X.500 standard, a set of original classes was defined. One was `organizationalPerson`, and this is a copy of that class. Microsoft included the entire set of base X.500 classes within Active Directory.

 The OID numbering notation has nothing to do with inheritance. Numbering a set of objects a certain way does nothing other than create a structure for you to reference the objects; it does not indicate how objects inherit from one another.

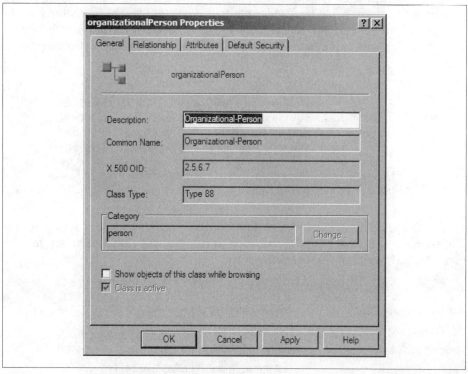

Figure 4-2. organizationalPerson Schema class properties

Let's dissect an example attribute and class to see what they contain. With that information, you will be able to see what is required when you create a new schema object.

Attributes (attributeSchema Objects)

Just as class information is stored in Active Directory as instances of the class called classSchema, attributes are represented by instances of the class called attributeSchema. As with all objects, the attributeSchema class has a number of attributes that can be set when specifying a new instance. The attributeSchema class inherits attributes from the class called top. However, most of the top attributes are not relevant here. All of the attributes of the attributeSchema class are documented in the Platforms SDK at *http://msdn2.microsoft.com/en-us/library/ms680969(VS.85).aspx*.

Dissecting an Example Active Directory Attribute

The userPrincipalName (UPN) attribute is used on user objects to provide a unique method of identifying each user across a forest. Users can log on to a workstation in any domain in the forest using the UPN if they so desire. The UPN attribute, in fact, accepts valid RFC 2822 (email) addresses, so the UPN for user *tpood* in the *europe .mycorp.com* domain could be *tpood@mycorp.com* or *tpood@europe.mycorp.com*, or even *tpood@logon.local*. In fact, any UPN suffix, such as *@mycorp.com*, can be used in a forest. The only requirement is that the UPN value for a user is unique across all users in a forest.

 Active Directory does not enforce uniqueness of a UPN when it is set. If two different users in the same forest are assigned the same UPN, neither will be able to log on using the UPN. When duplicate UPNs are detected, domain controllers will log an event from source Key Distribution Center (KDC) with event ID 11. Many large organizations implement scripts or other tools to scan their directories on a regular basis to check for duplicate UPNs.

To dissect the attribute, we need to find out what values had been set for it. Table 4-2 shows a subset of the values of attributes that have been set for the userPrincipalName attributeSchema instance.

Table 4-2. userPrincipalName's attributes

Attribute lDAPDisplayName	Attribute syntax	Attribute value
adminDescription	CASE_IGNORE_STRING	User-Principal-Name
adminDisplayName	CASE_IGNORE_STRING	User-Principal-Name
attributeID	CASE_IGNORE_STRING	1.2.840.113556.1.4.656
attributeSyntax	CASE_IGNORE_STRING	2.5.5.12
cn	CASE_IGNORE_STRING	User-Principal-Name
isMemberOfPartialAttributeSet	BOOLEAN	True
isSingleValued	BOOLEAN	True
lDAPDisplayName	CASE_IGNORE_STRING	userPrincipalName
name	CASE_IGNORE_STRING	User-Principal-Name
objectCategory	DN_STRING	cn=Attribute-Schema, cn=Schema, cn=Configuration, dc=mycorp,dc=com
objectClass	CASE_IGNORE_STRING	top; attributeSchema (two values of a multivalued attribute)
oMSyntax	INTEGER	64
searchFlags	INTEGER	1 (Indexed)
showInAdvancedViewOnly	BOOLEAN	True
systemFlags	INTEGER	18 (Category 1 attribute, replicated to GC)
systemOnly	BOOLEAN	False

We can see that the name of the attribute is `User-Principal-Name` (`adminDescription`, `adminDisplayName`, `cn`, `name`), that it is an instance of the `attributeSchema` class (`objectCategory` and `objectClass`), that it inherits attributes from both `top` and `attributeSchema` (`objectClass`), and that the UPN attribute is not visible to casual browsing (`showInAdvancedViewOnly`).

The `userPrincipalName` attributes show the following:

- It is to be stored in the GC (`isMemberOfPartialAttributeSet` and `systemFlags`).
- It is to be indexed (`searchFlags`).
- It has an OID of 1.2.840.113556.1.4.656 (`attributeID`).
- We should use `userPrincipalName` (`lDAPDisplayName`) when binding to it with ADSI.
- Instances can be created by anyone (`systemOnly`).
- It stores single (`isSingleValued`) Unicode strings (`attributeSyntax` and `oMSyntax`).

In Figure 4-3, you can see many of the values for the UPN attribute. We have indicated which attributes are changed by checking or unchecking each checkbox.

Attribute Properties

There are several properties on attributes that have significant and varied impact on attribute use and functionality. Here we give a little more detailed information on a few of these attributes that you need to understand when modifying the schema.

Attribute Syntax

The syntax of an attribute represents the kind of data it can hold; people with a programming background are probably more familiar with the term "data type." Unlike attributes and classes, the supported syntaxes are not represented as objects in Active Directory. Instead, Microsoft has coded these syntaxes internally into Active Directory itself. Consequently, any new attributes you create in the schema must use one of the predefined syntaxes.

Whenever you create a new attribute, you must specify its syntax. To uniquely identify the syntax among the total set of 21 syntaxes, you must specify two pieces of information: the OID of the syntax and a so-called OM syntax. This pair of values must be set together and correctly correlate with Table 4-3. More than one syntax has the same OID, which may seem strange; and to uniquely distinguish between different syntaxes, you thus need a second identifier. This is the result of Microsoft requiring some syntaxes that X.500 did not provide. Table 4-3 shows the 21 expanded syntaxes, including the name of the syntax with alternate names followed in parentheses.

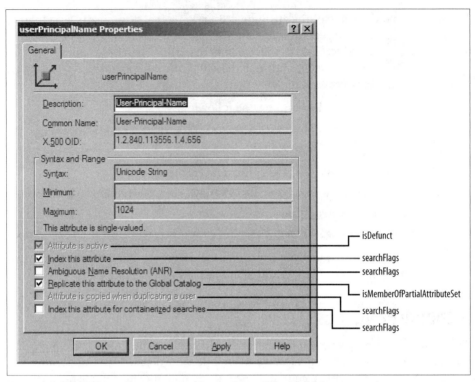

Figure 4-3. The UPN attribute as viewed by the Active Directory Schema snap-in

Table 4-3. Syntax definitions

Syntax	OID	OM syntax	Description
Address	2.5.5.13	127	Used internally by the system.
Boolean	2.5.5.8	1	True or false.
Case-insensitive string	2.5.5.4	20	A string that does not differentiate between uppercase and lowercase.
Case-sensitive string	2.5.5.3	27	A string that differentiates between uppercase and lowercase.
Distinguished name	2.5.5.1	127	The Fully Qualified Domain Name (FQDN) of an object in Active Directory.
DN-Binary	2.5.5.7	127	Octet string with binary value and DN. Format: B:<char count>:<binary value>:<object DN>.
DN-String	2.5.5.14	127	Octet string with string value and DN. Format: S:<char count>:<string value>:<object DN>.
Generalized-Time	2.5.5.11	24	ASN1.1 time format, e.g., 20040625234417.0Z.
Integer (enumeration)	2.5.5.9	10	A 32-bit number.
Integer (integer)	2.5.5.9	2	A 32-bit number.
Large integer	2.5.5.16	65	A 64-bit number.

Syntax	OID	OM syntax	Description
NT Security Descriptor	2.5.5.15	66	A Security Descriptor (SD).
Numeric string	2.5.5.6	18	A string of digits.
Object ID	2.5.5.2	6	OID.
Octet string (Octet-String)	2.5.5.10	4	A byte string.
Print case string (IA5-String)	2.5.5.5	22	A normal printable string.
Print case string (Printable-String)	2.5.5.5	19	A normal printable string.
Replica-Link	2.5.5.10	127	Replication information.
SID	2.5.5.17	4	A security identifier (SID).
Undefined	2.5.5.0	N/A	Not a valid syntax.
Unicode	2.5.5.12	64	A wide string.
UTC-Time	2.5.5.11	23	The number of seconds elapsed since 1 January 1970.

Most of these are standard programming types. If you're not sure which syntax to use, take a look at a preexisting attribute and see if you can find an appropriate syntax for the attribute you wish to create. For example, the userPrincipalName attribute has an attributeSyntax of 2.5.5.12 and an oMSyntax of 64, so it must contain Unicode strings.

System Flags

The systemFlags attribute is an often overlooked but important attribute. The attribute is a bitmask that represents how the attribute should be handled. For more information on bitmasks, see the upcoming sidebar "How to Work with Bitmasks." New bit values can be defined any time that Microsoft updates the directory service binaries. The systemFlags attribute is configured both on schema definitions of attributes and classes as well as on any instantiated object throughout the forest. This can be confusing, but the various bits in the attribute can mean various things depending on the object the attribute applies to. Table 4-4 lists only the values for systemFlags on attributeSchema and classSchema objects. A complete listing of valid systemFlags settings is available in the Platform SDK at *http://msdn2.microsoft.com/en-us/library/ms680022(VS.85).aspx*.

Table 4-4. System flag values for class and attributes objects

Value	Description
1 (0x0001)	Attribute is not replicated.
2 (0x0002)	Attribute will be replicated to the global catalog. This value should only be set by Microsoft; do not use. Instead, use isMemberOfPartialAttributeSet attribute for adding attributes to PAS.
4 (0x0004)	Attribute is constructed, not stored in the database. This should only be set by Microsoft; do not use.

Value	Description
16 (0x0010)	Category 1 attribute or class. Category 1 objects are classes and attributes that are included in the base schema with the system. Note that not all classes and attributes included in the base schema are marked as category 1.
134217728 (0x08000000)	The schema object cannot be renamed.

How to Work with Bitmasks

Masks are a fundamental concept in computer science, and perhaps the most common type of mask is the bitmask. A fair number of attributes in Active Directory are actually bitmasks. Bitmasks are a series of binary values that often represent a series of settings. Bitmasks can be confusing to administrators since they are sometimes displayed as a decimal number whereas the actual data is a series of bits (binary data).

Let's examine the bitmask below which describes a very limited set of animals:

Description	Alive	Mammal	Bird	Cat	Dog	Parrot	Tiger	Monkey
Bit Number	0	1	2	3	4	5	6	7
Bit	0	1	0	0	0	0	0	1
Decimal Representation	1	2	4	8	16	32	64	128

In this case I've set the necessary bits to describe a Monkey who is not currently living. The binary representation of this mask is 01000001, and in decimal, 130 (2 + 128). Each of the bits represents a distinct characteristic of an animal. In order to fully describe our monkey, it was necessary to set two bits.

Now, we probably wouldn't even have a mask representing the monkey in this state if the monkey wasn't in the production process, so once the monkey is born, we'll need to update the mask to reflect it's "Alive" state (a.k.a. bit one). In order to do this, you need to do a binary OR operation, which is equivalent to addition.

```
01000001 OR 10000000 = 11000001 (01000001 + 10000000)
```

You can use the scientific view in the Windows calculator to perform binary arithmetic operations. The new decimal representation is 131.

This may seem simple; however, it is a very common error for administrators to modify an attribute that is a bitmask by replacing the decimal value shown in the administrative tool with another decimal value. When you do this, data can be lost or added inadvertently. Consider, for example, if you were updating the monkey's mask to represent its alive status and you copied the decimal value from a live parrot, you would replace the live monkey's mask with 37, which then describes the monkey as a parrot.

The moral of the story here is that you should always treat bitmasks as binary data and alter them accordingly.

Constructed attributes

Most attributes are directly stored in the Active Directory database. Constructed attributes are the exception, and they are handled by the directory service in order to offer special functionality. This functionality can range from telling you approximately how many objects are contained directly under a container type object (msDS-Approx-Immed-Subordinates) to telling you the types of objects that can be instantiated under a given object (possibleInferiors) to telling you which attributes you have write access to on a given object (allowedAttributesEffective), and many other things. These attributes, because they are special, have some rules you should be aware of:

- Constructed attributes are not replicated. They are constructed by each directory instance separately.
- Constructed attributes cannot be used in server-side sorting.
- Constructed attributes generally cannot be used for queries. The attribute aNR is an exception here as it is used for constructing the special ANR queries. ANR is covered in the section "Ambiguous Name Resolution."
- In some cases, a BASE scope query may be required to retrieve certain constructed attributes; e.g., tokenGroups can only be returned with a BASE scope query.

Category 1 objects

Category 1 objects are a subset of the attributes and classes that come with AD LDS or Active Directory. They are marked with a special bit flag so that Microsoft can track and protect them from certain types of modifications.

Schema FlagsEx

The schemaFlagsEx attribute is an attribute that has existed since Windows 2000 but was not put into use until Windows Server 2008. The schemaFlagsEx attribute is designed to hold flags that further define the properties of an attribute. There is currently only one flag implemented in this bitmask as outlined in Table 4-5.

Table 4-5. schemaFlagsEx values

Bit Number	Value	Description
1	1 (0x1)	Marks an attribute as critical. Critical attributes cannot be added to the filtered attribute set regardless of the value of the tenth bit of the searchFlags attribute.

Search Flags

The searchFlags attribute is another bitmask that is best known as the attribute used to control indexing, but it is a little more involved than that. As indicated by the name, searchFlags is similar to systemFlags in that it is a series of bits representing how the attribute should be handled. Unlike `systemFlags`, `searchFlags` are only set on schema attribute definitions. See Table 4-6 for all of the values as of Windows Server 2008.

Table 4-6. Search flag bits

Bit Number	Value	Description
1	1 (0x0001)	Create an index for the attribute. All other index-based flags require this flag to be enabled as well. Marking linked attributes to be indexed has no effect.
2	2 (0x0002)	Create an index for the attribute in each container. This is only useful for one-level LDAP queries.
3	4 (0x0004)	Add attribute to Ambiguous Name Resolution (ANR) set. ANR queries are primarily used for Exchange and other address book tools. ANR attributes must be indexed and must be either UNICODE or Teletex string attribute syntax. Adding attributes to this set can have performance implications on Microsoft Exchange.
4	8 (0x0008)	Preserve this attribute in a tombstone object. This flag controls what attributes are kept when an object is deleted.
5	16 (0x0010)	Copy this value when the object is copied. This flag doesn't do anything in Active Directory; tools such as Active Directory Users and Computers that copy objects can look at this flag to determine what attributes should be copied.
6	32 (0x0020)	Create tuple index. Tuple indexing is useful for medial searches. A medial search has a wildcard at the beginning or in the middle of the search string. For example, the medial search (`drink=*coke`) would match Cherry Coke, Diet Coke, etc. This flag requires Windows Server 2003 or ADAM V1.0.
7	64 (0x0040)	Create subtree index. This index is only available in ADAM R2 or newer and is designed to increase performance of VLV queries. See the section "ADAM Schema" in Chapter 20.
8	128 (0x0080)	Mark attribute as confidential. Only users with both read property *and* Control Access right to the attribute so marked can view it when it is so marked. This is a new feature as of Windows Server 2003 SP1. SP1 domain controllers will not allow you to mark Category 1 attributes with this flag.
9	256 (0x0100)	Never audit changes to this attribute. This flag is new in Windows Server 2008. Windows Server 2008 auditing enhancements are covered in Chapter 13.
10	512 (0x0200)	Include this attribute in the RODC filtered attribute set. RODCs and the filtered attribute set are covered in Chapter 7.

Indexed attributes

Attribute indexing is available to boost performance of queries. When an attribute is indexed, the values are placed in a special table in a sorted order so that a query using the attribute can be completed by looking at a subset of all the information in the directory. The type of index created can be modified by additional bit flags configured in the `searchFlags` attribute. There are several points to know about indexes:

- A query that contains bitwise operations on an indexed attribute diminishes the usefulness of the index. A bitwise operation can't be directly looked up in the index table and the entire set of values in the index will have to be enumerated and tested.

Bitwise queries are queries that query a bitmask, for example, the `systemFlags` or `userAccountControl` attributes.

- A query that contains a NOT of an indexed attribute negates the use of the index for that portion of the query. A NOT of an attribute requires enumerating all objects in the search scope to determine which objects don't have the attribute or which objects have permissions applied that disallow the trustee to view the attribute value.

- Linked attributes are implicitly indexed, and beginning with Windows Server 2003, the necessary logic to use these indexes was implemented. If you modify the flag, it will have no effect due to the implicit indexing behavior.

- It is often assumed that indexes cannot be built or do not work well for attributes with multiple values or non-unique values. This is incorrect. In the early days of the original Active Directory beta, there was concern about multiple values and non-unique values, but the issues surrounding them were addressed. This topic is most often raised in regards to the `objectClass` attribute and is stated as the reason why Microsoft didn't index the attribute by default prior to Windows Server 2008.

  If you have installed the Exchange Server 2007 schema extensions in your forest, `objectClass` is indexed as part of this schema extension.

  Windows Server 2008 domain controllers implement a special behavior that indexes `objectClass` by default regardless of the `searchFlags` setting in Active Directory. Note that this is considered a special behavior because the attribute will not be indexed on Windows 2000 or Windows Server 2003 domain controllers once you import the Windows Server 2008 schema extensions; however, the attribute will be indexed on any Windows Server 2008 servers. This could cause performance deltas in applications that randomly select domain controllers for use. You may consider indexing `objectclass` when you apply the Windows Server 2008 schema updates so that you will have a consistent LDAP query experience across your enterprise once Windows Server 2008 domain controllers are introduced.

While indexing attributes can very frequently improve the performance of LDAP queries, it is important to realize that indexes also consume disk space. Adding an index to an attribute that is populated across a large percentage of directory objects may consume a substantial amount of disk space.

Domain controller performance will also be impacted while indexes are being generated. Index data is not replicated, so every domain controller in the forest must build its own copy of an index when it detects a new attribute index must be created. The speed at which an index is created is dependent on how much data must be indexed and also the hardware the domain controller is running on.

Ambiguous Name Resolution

Ambiguous Name Resolution (ANR) is used for address book look-ups. It allows a single small query to be expanded into searching as many fields as the administrator would like searched so that users can enter a single piece of information and hopefully find all possible "hits" on the value they are interested in. When an ANR query such as (anr=brian)is submitted, the Active Directory Query Processor expands the simple filter into a more complex OR wildcard filter that contains all attributes marked as part of the ANR set. The specified filter on a default Windows Server 2008 Active Directory would expand that simple query to:

```
(|
    (displayName=brian*)
    (givenName=brian*)
    (legacyExchangeDN=brian*)
    (msDS-AdditionalSamAccountName=brian*)
    (msDS-PhoneticCompanyName=brian*)
    (msDS-PhoneticDepartment=brian*)
    (msDS-PhoneticDisplayName=brian*)
    (msDS-PhoneticFirstName=brian*)
    (msDS-PhoneticLastName=brian*)
    (physicalDeliveryOfficeName=brian*)
    (proxyAddresses=brian*)
    (name=brian*)
    (sAMAccountName=brian*)
    (sn=brian*)
)
```

A Windows Server 2008 Active Directory domain with Exchange Server 2007 SP1 installed would expand the query to:

```
(|
    (displayName-brian*)
    (givenName=brian*)
    (legacyExchangeDN=brian*)
    (msDS-AdditionalSamAccountName=brian*)
    (msDS-PhoneticCompanyName=brian*)
    (msDS-PhoneticDepartment=brian*)
    (msDS-PhoneticDisplayName=brian*)
    (msDS-PhoneticFirstName=brian*)
    (msDS-PhoneticLastName=brian*)
    (physicalDeliveryOfficeName=brian*)
    (proxyAddresses=brian*)
    (name=brian*)
    (sAMAccountName=brian*)
    (sn=brian*)
    (mail=brian*)
    (mailNickname=brian*)
    (msExchResourceSearchProperties=brian*)
)
```

As you can see, a very simple query can quickly be expanded into a very large query. For this reason, you should avoid adding additional ANR attributes.

Preserve attribute in tombstone

When a delete request is processed for an object, the object is not immediately deleted. Instead, the object is stripped of most of its attributes and moved to the *Deleted*

Objects container of the partition the object exists in. Deleted objects that have been moved to the Deleted Objects containers are referred to as *tombstones*. Tombstones remain in the Deleted Objects container for the length of the tombstone period. The default tombstone periods or lifetimes for new forests are documented in Table 4-7. Tombstoning an object allows the delete operation to replicate to all domain controllers holding a copy of the object. The process of undeleting an object in Active Directory is known as *tombstone reanimation*.

 Administrators can modify the tombstone lifetime for a forest by changing the `tombstoneLifetime` attribute of the `CN=Directory Service,` `CN=Windows NT, CN=Services,CN=Configuration,DC=mycorp,DC=com` object.

The attributes that are retained when an object is tombstoned are configured through a combination of the `searchFlags` setting and some hard-coded internal functionality. The *preserve on tombstone* `searchFlags` setting is configurable by administrators so they can choose to add more attributes to what is kept on a tombstoned object. The purpose of keeping more attributes on tombstones is directly related to the new capability available in ADAM and Windows Server 2003 Active Directory to reanimate tombstoned objects. The more attributes you allow the directory to retain on the tombstoned object, the fewer attributes you have to recover through other means after the object is reanimated.

Unfortunately, not all attributes can successfully be added to the tombstone when the proper `searchFlags` bit is set. The most obvious examples are linked attributes such as group membership. Linked attributes are handled differently by the directory, and thus there is no way to force them to be retained. If you configure a linked attribute to be preserved, Active Directory will simply ignore the setting. This is unfortunate, as it means that critical information such as group membership must be either manually maintained in an additional attribute that can survive the tombstone process, or else the group membership must be maintained outside of AD.

While some attributes won't survive the tombstone regardless of what you set, some attributes will survive the tombstone but will not survive the *reanimation* process. The attribute `pwdLastSet` attribute, for example, falls into this category. When you reanimate an object with `pwdLastSet`, even though the attribute may be preserved in the tombstone, it will be overwritten when the object is reanimated.

Unfortunately, Microsoft has not documented what can and cannot survive a tombstone and subsequent reanimation. So make sure you test any attributes you have configured to be retained to make sure they can actually be reanimated. You don't want to find yourself in a situation where you discover that an attribute didn't survive reanimation when it comes time to reanimate an object.

Table 4-7. Tombstone lifetime values for new forests

Operating system	Tombstone lifetime
Windows 2000	60 days
Windows Server 2003	180 days
Windows Server 2003 R2	60 days (this was a regression bug in R2)
Windows Server 2003 SP2	180 days
Windows Server 2008	180 days

Tuple index

When you create an index, it is optimized for direct look-ups and, if the attribute syntax supports it, trailing wildcards—e.g., (name=joe*). If you use medial queries—that is, queries with wildcards anywhere but the end of the string, such as (name=*oe)—performance tends to be rather less than optimal. Generally, this is okay, but in the cases where an important application is being significantly impacted due to poor medial query performance, you may want to consider enabling a tuple index for the attribute. This is just like enabling a normal index; you simply enable another bit on the attribute's searchFlags mask to specify that a tuple index should be created.

A tuple index is considered an expensive index, and it will increase the Active Directory database (*ntds.dit*) size more than a "normal" index. In addition, new attribute insertion performance will be impacted slightly. This performance hit will not be noticeable for single attribute insertions, but if you are updating a large number of attributes at once, the performance hit may be more noticeable.

Confidential

A new bit for the `searchFlags` attribute was defined for Windows Server 2003 Service Pack 1: the *confidential attribute* flag. Any attribute that has this flag enabled requires two permissions in order to be viewed by a trustee (trustees are the security principals who are granted permissions). The trustee needs *read property* for the attribute and also needs *control access* for the attribute. This functionality was put into place primarily to protect sensitive user attributes such as Social Security numbers and other personal information. By default, only the administrators and account operators have full control on all user objects, which means they will be able to view any confidential attributes. Anyone else who has full control over a user object will also be able to view the confidential data, so this is yet another reason to not grant unnecessary rights in the directory. If you have domain controllers in the domain (or global catalogs in the forest if you are dealing with an attribute in the partial attribute set) that are not running Windows Server 2003 Service Pack 1 or newer, then any attributes marked as confidential will still be viewable without the special access rights on those domain controllers or global catalogs.

The confidential attribute capability was added as a workaround to issues that exist in the current security model in Active Directory. Unfortunately, there are a large number of explicit read property grant permissions on objects in Active Directory that are terribly difficult to override. This new flag allows you to step in despite all the default grant permissions and quickly deny access to an attribute.

This new function was welcomed with open arms in the Active Directory community until administrators started to realize that Microsoft purposely crippled the functionality by not allowing you to set Category 1 attributes as confidential. Category 1 attributes are many of the attributes defined in the default AD schema, and that list of attributes contains many of the attributes you probably want to make confidential such as telephone numbers, addresses, employee IDs, and so on. It seems the intent is simply to give AD administrators a way to better secure custom attributes they have added to the directory with schema extensions. This limitation drastically reduces the usefulness of this capability for companies that stick to the default schema.

 As mentioned, modification of `searchFlags` to enable confidential functions on Category 1 attributes is strictly disallowed by Windows Server 2003 SP1 domain controllers. If you try to change `searchFlags` on one of these DCs so that the confidential flag is set, you will get either an "Unwilling to perform" or a poorly worded "The search flags for the attribute are invalid. The ANR bit is valid only on attributes of Unicode or Teletex strings" error for your troubles.

This new capability is almost wholly underwhelming for AD LDS. The default security descriptors on all AD LDS base schema objects are configured with no explicit Access Control Entries (ACEs). The result is very few explicit read property grant permissions on objects when they are instantiated, which means you can more easily secure attributes with inherited deny permissions and will not need to depend on the confidential attribute functionality.

Next, we need to discuss the tools that Microsoft has made available starting with Windows Server 2003 Service Pack 1 to handle managing access to confidential attributes. The answer is easy: *none*. In order to grant a trustee the ability to view a specific confidential attribute on an attribute, a grant ACE with control access permission for the specific attribute needs to be added to the ACL of the object. For more information on modifying the ACL of an object, see Chapter 13.

The GUI tools available for assigning permissions not only do not have the ability to assign this type of permission, but they can't even display the permission if something else grants it. The command-line tool dsacls.exe is only marginally better; it can display the permission, but cannot grant the permission. The best that the GUI and dsacls.exe tool can do is assign either full control to the object or ALL control access rights to the object, but neither of these is optimal if you prefer to give minimum rights necessary to get the job done. In Windows Server 2003 SP1, the only way to set granular permissions to view a specific confidential attribute is to write a custom program or script to handle the delegation.

 Beginning with Windows Server 2003 R2, there is a GUI tool to handle this delegation. The new version of LDP that is loaded in the *%windir %\adam* directory when you install R2 ADAM has a new ACL editor. This version of updated version of LDP is also available in the free download of ADAM SP1. The version of LDP that is installed with Windows Server 2008 also includes this functionality. If you need to modify this delegation, we recommend you use one of the updated versions of the LDP tool.

Attribute change auditing

The Windows Server 2008 auditing infrastructure has been substantially updated compared to its predecessors. In Windows 2000 Server and Windows Server 2003, there was a single domain-wide directory service auditing setting called *Audit Directory Service Access*. When this setting was enabled, all directory services auditing events were enabled. In a busy environment, the consequence of this was a substantial amount of security audit traffic in the event logs, to the point that it could easily become unmanageable and thus impractical to have enabled.

Windows Server 2008 domain controllers separate directory services auditing into four subcategories:

- Directory Service Access
- Directory Service Changes
- Directory Service Replication
- Detailed Directory Service Replication

Of particular interest to us right now is the *Directory Service Changes subcategory*. We will discuss the new auditing infrastructure in much more detail in Chapter 13.

By default, all attribute changes will continue to be audited as required by the *System ACL* (SACL). In order to control noise, however, you can set bit 9 on an attribute's `searchFlags` mask to disable all change audits for that attribute. The Windows Server 2008 GUI tools do not expose an interactive method to easily set this bit. For directions on setting this bit, reference the sidebar "Controlling Attribute Change Auditing," next.

COMMAND-LINE REFERENCE

Controlling Attribute Change Auditing

The Windows Server 2008 GUI tools do not expose an easy mechanism for controlling bit 9 in an attribute's `searchFlags` mask without performing the binary arithmetic by hand. Fortunately, this change can easily be enacted by combining the adfind and admod tools.

In this example we will disable change auditing for the description attribute:

```
adfind -sc s:description searchFlags -adcsv | admod -safety 1 -expand
searchFlags::{{searchFlags:SET:0x0100}}
```

In this example we will enable change auditing for the description attribute:

```
adfind -sc s:description searchFlags -adcsv | admod -safety 1 -expand
searchFlags::{{searchFlags:CLR:0x0100}}
```

Note that you can apply this pattern to toggle any bitmask flag in Active Directory.

Filtered attribute set

The filtered attribute set is part of the overall new Read-Only Domain Controller (RODC) functionality in Windows Server 2008 Active Directory. RODCs can be configured to not replicate certain attributes in the Active Directory schema. There is an in depth discussion of the RODC in Chapter 7; however, we will discuss RODCs briefly in the context of the filtered attribute set here.

RODCs were designed with the mentality that the server that they are running on is compromised by default. Consequentially there are some attributes that we might not wish to have stored on an RODC as they could contain sensitive information. Examples might be schema extensions that contain application-specific secrets, confidential data such as Social Security numbers, and so forth.

You can apply the process illustrated in the sidebar "Controlling Attribute Change Auditing" to control whether or not attributes are included in the filtered attribute set. Instead of toggling bit 0x100, you should toggle bit 0x200.

 You cannot include attributes that are defined as critical in the schema FlagsEx attribute in the filtered attribute set.

Property Sets and attributeSecurityGUID

Property sets are described in our Chapter 13 discussion on Active Directory security. We mention them here because the creation, modification, and identification of property sets involve the schema partition. Part of the information for a property set is maintained in the configuration container in the cn=extended-rights sub-container, and the rest is maintained in the schema.

The property sets are defined in the cn=extended-rights sub-container as controlAccessRight objects. Two of the attributes of the controlAccessRight object link it to the schema. The first attribute is the appliesTo attribute; the second is the rightsGuid. The appliesTo attribute is the string representation of the schemaIDGUID attribute of the classSchema objects that the property set applies to. The rightsGuid is the string representation of the binary GUID stamped on the `attributeSecurityGUID` attribute of `attributeSchema` objects to identify them as members of the property set.

Linked Attributes

Microsoft allows distinguished name attributes with `attributeSyntax` values of 2.5.5.1, 2.5.5.7, and 2.5.5.14 to be linked to attributes with an `attributeSyntax` of 2.5.5.1. These are called linked attributes and consist of a forward link and a back link. An example of a pair of linked attributes is `member` and `memberOf`.

Attributes are linked by setting the `linkID` attributes of two `attributeSchema` objects to valid link values. The values must be unique for all `attributeSchema` objects. The value of the forward link is a positive even value and the back link is the forward `linkID` value plus one to make it a positive odd value. Attributes must be linked when they are first defined in the schema.

You can use any random `linkID` values as long as they result in a unique `linkID` pair; however, it is *highly* recommended that you auto-generate link IDs. You cannot use auto-generated link IDs in the case that you need your schema extension to support Windows 2000. If you need to support Windows 2000, you should email *schemreg@microsoft.com* to request unique link IDs.

In order to auto-generate link ID pairs, there are four steps you must follow:

1. Create the forward link attribute and populate the `linkID` attribute with the value `1.2.840.113556.1.2.50`.
2. Reload the schema cache.
3. Create the back link attribute and populate the `linkID` attribute with the `lDAPDisplayName` of the forward link attribute you created in step 1.
4. Reload the schema cache.

Classes (classSchema Objects)

Schema classes are defined as instances of the `classSchema` class. A complete listing of the attributes on the `classSchema` class is available from the Platform SDK at *http://msdn2.microsoft.com/en-us/library/ms680982(VS.85).aspx*.

Object Class Category and Inheritance

Classes are special in that they can inherit from one another. For example, let's say that we wanted to store two new types of objects in the schema, representing a marketing user and a finance user, respectively. These users both need all the attributes of the existing `user` class as a base. However, the finance user needs seven special attributes, while the marketing user needs three. The extra attributes required by both users do not match in any way. In this example, we can create a `Marketing-User` class, a

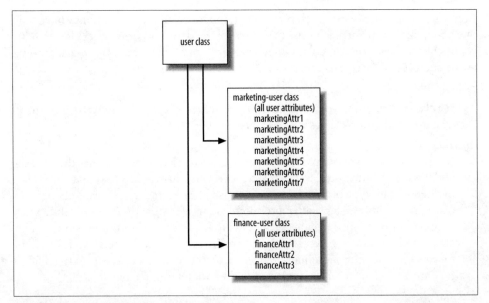

Figure 4-4. Marketing and Finance subclasses

Finance-User class, and 10 distinctly new attributes. However, rather than having to specify that the Marketing-User and Finance-User classes have each of the attributes of the original user class individually, all we need to do is specify that the new classes inherit from the user class by setting the subClassOf attribute to user. When we do this, both of the new classes inherit every single attribute that the user class had. We can then add the extra attributes to each class and we have two new classes. This example is outlined in Figure 4-4.

You have another option when using Windows Server 2003 Forest Functional Mode or ADAM to resolve this issue. First, define the additional attributes and then create two auxiliary classes and assign the attributes to the classes. Then you can dynamically assign the auxiliary classes to users on ad hoc basis. This is far more flexible in that you can easily reconfigure individual users as necessary. If a user moves from Marketing to Finance, using special inherited classes would require deleting the user and recreating the user with the finance-user class. With dynamic auxiliary classes, you would simply clear the marketing attributes, remove the Marketing auxiliary class, and add the Finance auxiliary class and attributes.

You can think of the Active Directory schema as a treelike structure, with multiple classes branching down or inheriting from one base class at the top that has the attributes all objects need to begin with. This class, unsurprisingly enough, is called top, which was originally defined in the X.500 specification. Some classes inherit directly from **top**, while others exist much lower down the tree. While each class may have only one parent in this layout, each class may also inherit attributes from other classes. This is possible because you can create three categories of **classSchema** object, also known as the **objectClassCategory**: *structural, abstract*, and *auxiliary*:

Structural
> If a class is structural, you can directly create objects of its type in Active Directory. The user and group classes are examples of structural classes.

Abstract
> It is possible that you would want to create a class that inherits from other classes and has certain attributes, but that is not one you will ever need to create instances of directly. This type of class is known as abstract. Abstract classes can inherit from other classes and can have attributes defined on them directly. The only difference between abstract and structural classes is that an object that is an instance of an abstract class cannot be created in Active Directory. If you are familiar with an object-oriented programming language, abstract schema classes in Active Directory are analogous to abstract classes in the programming language.

Auxiliary
> An auxiliary class is used to store sets of attributes that other classes can inherit. Auxiliary classes are a way for structural and abstract classes to inherit collections of attributes that do not have to be defined directly within the classes themselves. Auxiliary classes are primarily a grouping mechanism.

The X.500 specifications indicate that an auxiliary class cannot inherit from a structural class, and an abstract class can inherit only from another abstract class.

> To comply with the X.500 standards, there are actually four types of **objectClassCategory**. While objects are required to be classified as one of structural, abstract, or auxiliary by the 1993 X.500 specifications, objects defined before 1993 using the 1988 specifications are not required to comply with these categories. Such objects have no corresponding 1993 category and so are defined in the schema as having a special category known as the 88-Class.

Let's take a look at the **user** and **computer** classes that are used to create user and computer accounts within Active Directory. The **computer** class and **user** class are each structural, which means that you can instantiate objects of those classes directly in Active Directory. The **computer** class inherits from the **user** class, so the **computer** class is a special type of user in a way. The **user** class inherits from the **organizationalPerson** abstract class. This means that the total attributes available to objects of class **computer** include not only the attributes defined specifically on the **computer** and **user** classes themselves, but also all the attributes that are inherited from the **organizationalPerson** class. The **organizationalPerson** class is a subclass of the

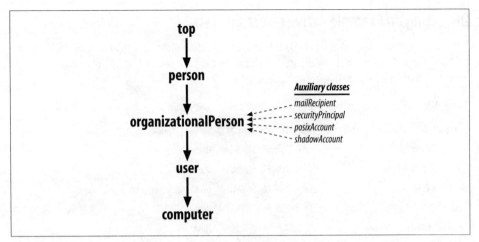

Figure 4-5. The computer class

person abstract class, which is a subclass of the abstract top class. Recall that there are no classes above top; it is the root class. This relationship is outlined in Figure 4-5.

The user class that Microsoft needed to define in Active Directory had to be more than just the sum of the X.500 standard parts. After all, Microsoft uses *Security Identifiers* (SIDs) to identify users, and these were not contained in the original X.500 standards. So, to extend the attributes that make up a user, Microsoft defined some auxiliary classes and included these in the user class makeup. The auxiliary classes are mailRecipient, securityPrincipal, posixAccount, and shadowAccount. mailRecipient is a collection of attributes that allow a user to hold information relating to the email address and mail account associated with that user. The securityPrincipal attribute is used to hold the SID and other user-related security attributes that Microsoft needed. The shadowAccount and posixAccount auxiliary classes were added in Windows Server 2003 R2 to support Microsoft *Services for UNIX*.

If you were to use a tool such as ADSI Edit, you could see the inheritance and class relationships quite clearly. For example, looking at the objectClass attribute of any user object, you would see that at a minimum, the values held in this attribute were top, person, organizationalPerson, and user. In other words, this attribute indicates that each user object inherits attributes from all these classes. Similarly, for any computer object, the objectClass attribute holds top, person, organizationalPerson, user, and computer. If you were to look at the subclassOf attribute on the computer class object itself in the schema, you would see the user class. The user class has a subClassOf attribute that indicates organizationalPerson, and so on. You can see this relationship in Figure 4-5.

Dissecting an Example Active Directory Class

Let's now look at the user class in a little more depth. Using a tool like ADSIEdit, we can see the values of each attribute for the user classSchema object. Table 4-8 contains a partial listing of the attributes and values.

Table 4-8. Partial listing of attributes and values for the user class

User attribute's LDAP-Display-Name	User attribute's syntax	Value contained in user's attribute
adminDescription	CASE_IGNORE_STRING	User
adminDisplayName	CASE_IGNORE_STRING	User
auxiliaryClass	CASE_IGNORE_STRING	posixAccount shadowAccount
cn	CASE_IGNORE_STRING	User
defaultHidingValue	BOOLEAN	False
defaultSecurityDescriptor	CASE_IGNORE_STRING	SDDL text-encoded representation of the default security descriptor
governsID	CASE_IGNORE_STRING	1.2.840.113556.1.5.9
lDAPDisplayName	CASE_IGNORE_STRING	user
name	CASE_IGNORE_STRING	User
nTSecurityDescriptor	SECURITY_DESCRIPTOR	Binary representation of the Security Descriptor for the class
objectCategory	DN_STRING	cn=Class-Schema, cn=Schema, cn=Configuration, dc=mycorp, dc=com
objectClass	CASE_IGNORE_STRING	top; classSchema (two values of a multivalued attribute)
objectClassCategory	INTEGER	1
rDNAttID	CASE_IGNORE_STRING	cn
schemaIDGUID	OCTET_STRING	<GUID> that uniquely identifies this class
showInAdvancedViewOnly	BOOLEAN	True
subClassOf	CASE_IGNORE_STRING	organizationalPerson
systemAuxiliaryClass	CASE_IGNORE_STRING	securityPrincipal mailRecipient
systemMayContain	CASE_IGNORE_STRING	Various attributes. See discussion.
systemPossSuperiors	CASE_IGNORE_STRING	builtinDomain organizationalUnit domainDNS

You can learn the following about the user class by inspecting these attribute values:

- The name of the class is User (adminDescription, adminDisplayName, cn, name).
- It is an instance of the classSchema class (objectCategory and objectClass).
- It inherits attributes from both top and classSchema (objectClass).

- This object class has a security descriptor governing who can access and manipulate it (`nTSecurityDescriptor`).
- A default Security Descriptor should be applied to new instances of the user class if one is not specified on creation (`defaultSecurityDescriptor`).
- The instances of the user class are visible in normal browsing (`defaultHidingValue`).
- The user class itself is not hidden from casual browsing (`showInAdvancedViewOnly`).
- The user class has an OID of 1.2.840.113556.1.5.9 (`governsID`).
- It inherits attributes not only from `top` and `classSchema` but also from `security-Principal` and `mailRecipient` (`objectClass` and `systemAuxiliaryClass`).
- The `shadowAccount` and `posixAccount` auxiliary classes can be associated with `user` objects.
- The user class is a direct subclass of the `organizationalPerson` class (`subClassOf`).
- When connecting to instances of the class via LDAP, the two-letter prefix used should be `cn` (`rDNAttID`).
- This class can be created directly under only three different parents in Active Directory (`systemPossSuperiors`).
- The class is structural (`objectClassCategory`).
- There are a large number of attributes that instances of the user class can have values for (`systemMayContain`).

How inheritance affects mustContain, mayContain, possSuperiors, and auxiliaryClass

Let's look at the `mustContain`, `mayContain`, `auxiliaryClass`, `possSuperiors`, and their system attribute pairs. You can see that the only values set are `systemPossSuperiors`, `systemMayContain`, and `systemAuxiliaryClass`. These were the values set on the initial creation of the user class and cannot be changed. Note that there were no mandatory attributes set at the creation of the original class because the attribute `systemMustContain` is not listed. If you later wished to add an extra set of attributes or a new optional attribute to the user class, you could use `auxiliaryClass` or `mayContain` and modify the base definition. This occurs if, for example, you install the Exchange schema updates in your forest. If you were to do this, the user class would be directly modified to include three of these Exchange-related auxiliary classes in the `auxiliaryClass` attribute:

- `msExchMailStorage`
- `msExchCustomAttributes`
- `msExchCertificateInformation`

Exchange is discussed in more detail in Chapter 19.

The attributes that are required when you create a new user are not listed in the `mustContain` attribute. That's because `objectSID`, `sAMAccountName`, and the other attributes are inherited from other classes that make up this one. The mustContain attributes can be defined directly in auxiliaryClass or systemAuxiliaryClass, or they can be defined on the classes inherited from further up the tree. Both sAMAccountName and objectSID, for example, are defined on the securityPrincipal class.

 Do not mistake attributes that a class must contain with the attributes that you must explicitly set on object instantiation. Unfortunately there is no effective way to programmatically determine what attributes you need to set on an object when you create an instance of the class. Some of the attributes that an object must contain are system-owned and can only be set by the system; other attributes are optional and will be populated automatically; and finally some attributes are actually required to be specified by the objects creator. To confuse the situation even more, various versions of the OS or AD LDS change the requirements.

The same principle applies to the mayContain attribute. The entire set of these attributes is available only when you recurse back up the tree and identify all the inherited mayContain attributes on all inherited classes.

The possSuperiors attribute, on the other hand, can be made up of only those items defined directly on the class, those defined on the class in the subClassOf attribute, or any inherited classes defined on any other subClassOf attributes up the subClassOf tree. If that was too confusing, try this: an instance of the user class can have possSuperiors from itself, from the organizationalPerson class defined in the subClassOf attribute, from the person class (the organizationalPerson class's subClassOf attribute), and from top (the person class's subClassOf attribute).

Viewing the user class with the Active Directory Schema snap-in

Take a look at Figure 4-6. This shows the user class viewed with the Active Directory Schema snap-in. You can see the relevant general user data.

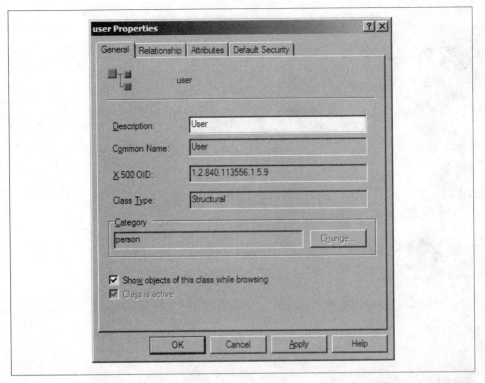

Figure 4-6. User class schema entry general settings

Notice that quite a bit of the user class is not configurable after the initial configuration, including:

- governsID
- subClassOf
- schemaIDGUID
- systemMustContain
- rDNAttID
- systemPossSuperiors
- objectClassCategory
- systemMayContain
- systemOnly
- systemAuxiliaryClass
- objectClass
- subClassOf

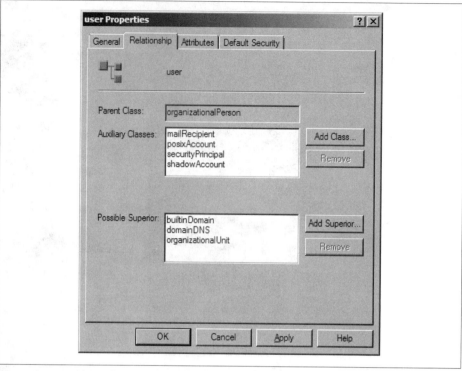

Figure 4-7. User class schema entry relationship settings

To see the so-called relationship settings (subClassOf, auxiliaryClass, possSuperiors, systemAuxiliaryClass, systemPossSuperiors), look at Figure 4-7. In this screen, you can see that the user class in this schema is inheriting attributes from the four auxiliary classes.

The third and final screen is the Attributes tab for the user class and is displayed in Figure 4-8. This shows the mustContain, systemMustContain, mayContain, and systemMayContain attributes of the user class.

Dynamically Linked Auxiliary Classes

With Windows 2000, auxiliary classes were statically linked to structural classes via the auxiliaryClass and systemAuxiliaryClass attributes. This went against how most directory services implemented auxiliary classes, which was typically allowing dynamically assigned auxiliary classes on instances of objects. A new feature in Windows Server 2003 is the ability to dynamically assign auxiliary classes to individual objects instead of to an entire class of objects in the schema. Having the dynamic auxiliary class mechanism provides much more flexibility for application developers who may want to utilize existing structural and auxiliary classes, but do not want to extend the schema to define such relationships.

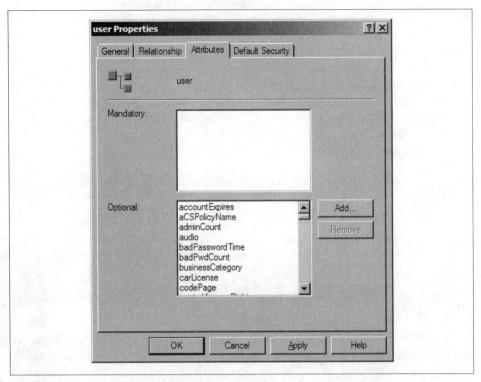

Figure 4-8. User class schema entry attribute settings

 Dynamic linking of auxiliary classes requires Windows Server 2003 Forest Functional Level, or higher.

To dynamically link an auxiliary class to an object, you only need to modify the `objectClass` attribute of the object to include the name of the auxiliary class. Any auxiliary class can be used, provided that all `mustContain` and `systemMustContain` attributes contained within the auxiliary class are set at the same time. You can also remove a dynamically linked auxiliary class by clearing any values that have been set for attributes defined by the auxiliary class and then removing the auxiliary class name from the object's `objectClass` attribute.

Now let's illustrate why dynamically linking auxiliary classes is a good idea. Assume we have a forest with several domains, each representing divisions within a company. Each division manages its own user objects. One of the divisions, named Toasters, wants to assign additional attributes to their user objects. These new attributes would only apply to employees within the Toasters division. Under Windows 2000, the only way to accomplish this would be to create the new attributes in the schema, create a new auxiliary class, and include the new attributes in the auxiliary class. At that point, the new auxiliary class could be added to the `auxiliaryClass` of the user `classSchema` object. That means every user object contained within the forest would then have the new attributes available. If each division wanted to do something similar, you can see how the number of attributes on all user objects within the forest could grow very quickly and unnecessarily. With Windows Server 2003, you would still create the new attributes and auxiliary classes in the schema, but you would not modify the `auxiliaryClass` of the user object. Instead, each division would dynamically link their auxiliary class to *their* user objects. This provides for a cleaner and much more efficient implementation than was possible under Windows 2000.

 When you dynamically link an auxiliary class to an object, the auxiliary class is listed in the `objectClass` attribute for the object. When an auxiliary class is statically linked, the auxiliary class is not listed in the `objectClass` listing. This can cause issues with applications that determine available attributes on an object and only look at the schema definitions of an object class or at the `objectClass` attribute of the object itself.

Summary

In this chapter, we've shown you how the internal blueprint for all objects in Active Directory, known as the schema, was derived from the X.500 directory service. We explained the purpose of the OID numbering system and how it can be used as well as the various elements that must be unique in an Active Directory schema extension such as prefix names and link IDs.

We then detailed how an attribute and its syntax are structured in the schema as `attributeSchema` objects, using the `userPrincipalName` attribute as an example. We showed how attributes are added to classes by detailing how classes are stored in the schema as instances of `classSchema` objects. To make this clearer we dug into the details of the user class to see how it was constructed. Finally, we covered how auxiliary classes can be dynamically linked starting in Windows Server 2003 and why it is significant.

Chapter 14 builds on what you've learned here to demonstrate how you can design and implement schema extensions.

## CHAPTER 5

Site Topology and Replication

This chapter introduces a major feature of Active Directory: multimaster replication. Active Directory was one of the first LDAP-based directories to offer multimaster replication. Most directories replicate data from a single master server to subordinate servers. This is how replication worked in Windows NT 4.0 for example. Obviously, there are several potential problems with a single-master replication scheme, including single point of failure for updates, geographic distance from master to clients performing the updates, and less efficient replication due to single originating location of updates. Active Directory replication addresses these issues, but with a price. To get the benefit of a multimaster replication, you must first create a site topology that describes the network and helps define how domain controllers should replicate with each other. In large environments, building and maintaining a site topology can be a significant amount of work.

This chapter looks at the basics of how sites and replication work in Active Directory. In Chapter 11, we'll describe the physical infrastructure of a network layout using sites. We'll also discuss in that chapter how the Knowledge Consistency Checker (KCC) sets up and manages the replication connections and details on how to effectively design and tailor sites, site links, and replication in Active Directory.

Site Topology

The Active Directory site topology is the map that describes the network connectivity, Active Directory Replication guidelines, and locations for resources as it relates to the Active Directory forest. The major components of this topology are sites, subnets, site links, site link bridges, and connection objects. These are all Active Directory objects that are maintained in the forest's configuration container to allow the information to be locally available on all domain controllers so the DCs can properly communicate.

Subnets

A *subnet* is a portion of the IP space of a network. Subnets are described by their IP network address combined with a subnet mask measured in bits. For instance, the subnet mask 255.255.255.0 is a 24-bit subnet mask. If you have a 24-bit mask for the 10.5.20.0 network, your subnet object would be described as 10.5.20.0/24. The subnet objects in Active Directory are a logical representation of the subnets in your environment; they may, but do not necessarily have to, reflect your actual physical subnet definitions. For example, you may have a building that has two 24-bit subnets of 10.5.20.0 and 10.5.21.0, which for the purposes of Active Directory could be included in a single AD subnet of 10.5.20.0/23, which specifies a 23-bit subnet mask. These examples all represent IP version 4 (IPv4) subnets. Windows Server 2008 introduces support for IP version 6 (IPv6) subnets and domain controllers in Active Directory. The same concepts for subnetting apply; however, the addresses and subnets are much larger. IPv4 uses 32-bit addressing whereas IPv6 uses 128-bit addressing.

You must define subnet information in the directory because the only key available for determining relative location on a network is the IP addresses of the machines. The subnets are, in turn, associated with sites. Without these definitions, there is no way for a machine to make an efficient determination of what distributed resources it should try to use. By default, no subnets are defined in Active Directory. For more information on defining subnets in Active Directory, see the sidebar "Adding Subnets to a Site," next.

Adding Subnets to a Site

When adding subnets to sites via the Active Directory Sites and Services snap-in, you must enter the name of the subnet in the form network address/bits masked; e.g., 10.186.149.0/24 is network address 10.186.149.0 with subnet mask 255.255.255.0. In Windows Server 2008, the dialog supports entry of both IPv4 and IPv6 subnets.

The bits masked in the subnet name are the number of bits set in the subnet mask for that subnet. It can be between 0 and 32. The subnet mask is made up of four octets or bytes (four sets of eight bits). To convert the subnet mask to bits, convert each octet from the subnet mask to binary. The subnet mask 255.255.255.0 is 11111111.11111111.11111111.00000000 in binary, which uses 8+8+8 bits (i.e., 24) to define the subnet mask. A subnet mask of 255.255.248.0 would be 11111111.11111111.11111000.00000000, which is 8+8+5, or 21.

If subnets and IP addresses mean very little to you, check out Chuck Semeria's whitepaper "Understanding IP Addressing: Everything You Ever Wanted to Know" at *http://www.3com.com/other/pdfs/infra/corpinfo/en_US/501302.pdf*. The whitepaper covers both IPv4 and IPv6.

It is very important to make sure that you have up-to-date subnet information stored in Active Directory any time you are working with a multisite environment. If subnet information is not accurate, unnecessary WAN traffic may be generated as domain members authenticate to domain controllers in other sites. Domain controllers will also log events warning you of missing subnet definitions.

A *supernet* is a term used to describe a single subnet that encompasses one or more smaller subnets into a single Active Directory subnet object. For example, you may define a subnet object of 10.0.0.0/8, as well as many subnets in the same space with larger subnet masks, such as 10.1.0.0/16, 10.1.2.0/24, or even 10.1.2.209/32. When Active Directory works out which subnet a machine is associated with, it chooses the most specific subnet defined. So if the IP address is 10.1.2.209, the subnet 10.1.2.209/32 would be used; but if the IP address were 10.2.56.3, the 10.0.0.0/8 subnet would be used.

You may be wondering why someone would do this. The supernet objects can be assigned to any site just like any other subnet object. This means you can assign these "catchall" subnets to hub-based sites for machines that are running from subnets that are not otherwise defined. This causes the machines to use the hub resources versus randomly finding and selecting resources to use.

Figure 5-1 shows a perfect example of an organization whose subnet design lends well to the deployment of supernets in Active Directory. There are three hub sites in this topology—Chicago, São Paulo, and London. If you look closely, all of the subnets under Chicago can be summarized as 10.1.0.0/16, all of the subnets under London can be summarized as 10.2.0.0/16, and all of the subnets under São Paulo can be summarized as 10.3.0.0/16. By creating each of these subnets in Active Directory and associating them with their respective hub sites, you will create a safety net for new subnets which might come up at each of the locations.

Sites

Active Directory *sites* are generally defined as a collection of well-connected AD subnets. You use sites to group subnets together into a logical collection to help define replication flow and resource location boundaries. Active Directory uses sites directly to generate its replication topology and also to help clients find the "nearest" distributed resources to use in the environment such as DFS shares or domain controllers. The client's IP address is used to determine which Active Directory subnet they belong to, and then that subnet information, in turn, is used to look up their AD site. The site information can then be used to perform DNS queries via the DC Locator service to determine the closest domain controller or global catalog. For a discussion of the DC Locator process, refer to the DC Locator section in Chapter 6.

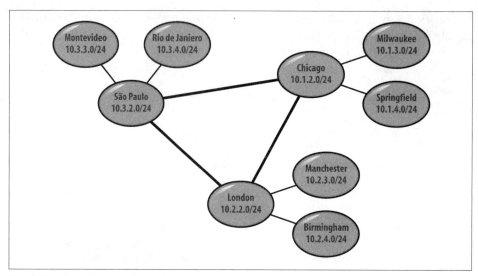

Figure 5-1. Sample site and subnet topology

Most members of a domain dynamically determine their site when they start up, and they continue to validate what site they are in the background. This allows administrators to make modifications to the site topology and have it properly take effect in relatively short order with the least amount of manual work. Domain controllers, on the other hand, select their site when they are promoted and will not automatically change unless an administrator wants a DC to become part of another site. Moving a domain controller to another site is an administrative task that is most easily performed via the Active Directory Sites and Services tool.

By default, there is one site defined in Active Directory, the *Default-First-Site-Name* site. If there are no subnets objects defined, all members of the domain are "magically" assumed to be part of this initial site, or any other single defined site if you have replaced the default site with another site. Once there are multiple site objects or after subnet objects are defined and assigned, the "magic" feature goes away and subnet objects must be defined for the subnets which domain members reside in. There is nothing special about this initial site other than it is the first one created; you can rename as you see fit. You can even delete it as long as you have created at least one other site and moved any domain controllers located within the Default-First-Site-Name to another site.

Multiple sites can be defined for a single physical location. This can allow you to better segregate what resources are used for what requestors. For instance, it is common practice in large companies to build a separate site just to harbor the Microsoft Exchange 2000 and 2003 servers and the global catalogs that are used to respond to Exchange and Outlook queries. This allows an administrator to easily control which GCs are used without having to hard code preferred GC settings into Exchange. You

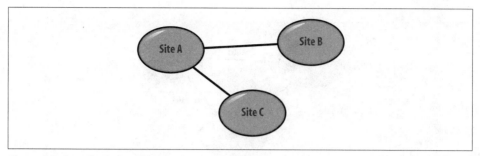

Figure 5-2. Sample site topology

can define the subnets as small as you need them, including down to a single IP address (32-bit subnet) to place servers in the proper site.

> It is no longer a recommended best practice to place Exchange 2007 servers in a separate site due to the changes in Exchange 2007's mail-routing behavior. If you are deploying Exchange 2007 in your environment you will need to work closely with your Exchange administrators to ensure you have enough global catalog capacity in the sites which support Exchange 2007.

Site Links

Site links allow you to define what sites are connected to each other and the relative cost of the connection. When you create a site link, you specify which sites are connected by this link and what the cost or metric of the connection is in a relative-costing model. For instance, three sites—A, B, and C—could be connected to each other, but because you understand the underlying physical network, you feel all traffic should be routed through the A site. This would require you to configure to two site links: A to B and A to C, as shown in Figure 5-2.

If at a later time, additional physical network connections are established between B and C, you could set up one more site link and connect B and C together. If you configure all three site links with an equal cost, say 100, traffic could flow across the B-to-C link instead of from B to A to C. This is because the total cost to use the B-to-C link would be 100 and the total cost to use the B-to-A-to-C route would be 200, which is more expensive. This scenario is demonstrated in Figure 5-3.

If you prefer that traffic to still flow through Site A, your total cost from B to A to C (and the reverse) should be lower than your cost from B to C. So, you would need to set the B-to-C link cost to something greater than 200—like 300, as shown in Figure 5-4. In this scenario, the B-to-C site link would only be used if the connection could not go through Site A for some reason.

Site links can come in two replication flavors: IP and SMTP. An IP site link actually represents an RPC-style replication connection. This is by far the most commonly used

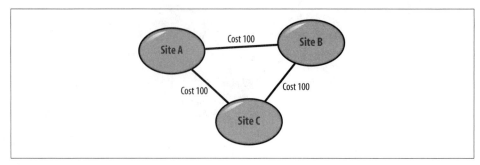

Figure 5-3. Sample site topology with equal costs

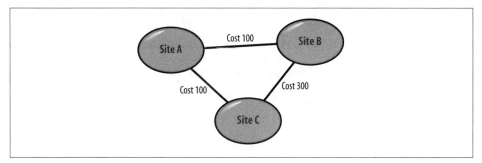

Figure 5-4. Sample site topology with unequal costs

type of site link and, in fact, the default site link created by Active Directory is an IP site link called *DEFAULTIPSITELINK*. The other site link type is an SMTP site link. SMTP site links are a special SMTP-based (think email) replication protocol. SMTP replication is used to communicate with sites that have very poor or unreliable network connections that cannot support an RPC replication connection. Due to security concerns, however, only certain naming contexts can be replicated across SMTP site links. Only the configuration NC, schema NC, and read-only global catalog NCs can be replicated via SMTP. This means that you must still replicate the domain NC via the more common IP replication protocol (with RPC).

Besides defining which replication protocols should be used and which sites should be replicating with what other sites, site links control domain controller and global catalog coverage of sites that do not have local DCs or GCs. This behavior is called *auto site coverage*.

Consider the diagram in Figure 5-5 showing Sites A, B, and C. Site A has domain controllers for Dom1 and Dom2, but Site B only has a DC for Dom1 and Site C has a DC for Dom2. How does a client decide which DC it should use for a domain that doesn't have a domain controller in the local site? Logically, you can look at it and say, "If someone needs to log on to Dom1 while in Site C, then the client should talk to Site A." Active Directory cannot make this intuitive leap; it needs to work with cold hard

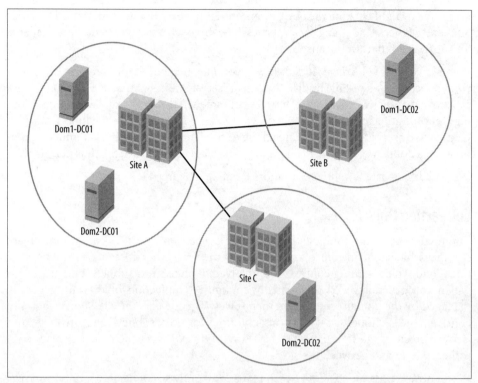

Figure 5-5. Sample site topology requiring auto site coverage

numbers, and that is what the site link metrics do: give the directory the information needed to make the calculations to determine which sites a given domain controller should cover in addition to its own site.

Active Directory will register the necessary covering DNS records for sites that do not have domain controllers automatically based on the site link topology. Active Directory and DNS is covered in detail in Chapter 6. For information on disabling auto site coverage, see *http://technet2.microsoft.com/windowsserver/en/library/e1199fad-9fd7-4f0f -b053-10d2e98aa3db1033.mspx?mfr=true*.

Site Link Bridges

By default, Active Directory assumes that the network paths between all of your sites are transitive. In other words, if you reference Figure 5-2, Active Directory assumes that domain controllers in Site C can talk *directly* to domain controllers in Site A. In some networks, this behavior is undesirable since the network does not permit this transitivity. Sometimes in the context of a networking discussion, people will refer to this scenario as the network not being *fully routed*. When you find yourself in this scenario, you may need to disable the *Bridge All Site Links* option for your forest. This option is accessible by right clicking the Sites\Inter-Site Transports\IP folder in Active Directory Sites and Services, and going to properties. The same setting is independently available for the SMTP replication transport.

If you have disabled *Bridge All Site Links*, you may need to define site-link bridges in your directory. A site-link bridge contains a set of site links that can be considered transitive. In other words, any of the sites contained in the site links that you are bridging can communicate directly. Referring to Figure 5-2 again, if the site links from A to C and A to B are bridged, then we are telling Active Directory that direct communication between a domain controller in Site C and a domain controller in Site B is permissible.

We will discuss site link bridges in more detail in Chapter 11.

Connection Objects

The final piece of the topology puzzle is the *connection object*. A connection object specifies which domain controllers replicate with which other domain controllers, how often, and which naming contexts are involved. Unlike sites, subnets, and site links, which you generally need to manually configure, connection objects are generally managed by the domain controllers themselves. The idea is that you should logically construct the site topology with good definitions for sites, subnets, and site links, and Active Directory can figure out the best way to interconnect the actual domain controllers within and between the sites.

It isn't always possible to allow AD to manage all of these connections, but it is a very good goal to work towards and you should endeavor not to modify or supplement connection objects unless you have no other choice. It is most often a problem that you have to tackle when you are dealing with very large Branch Office designs that involve hundreds or thousands of remote WAN sites connecting back to a network hub. If you find yourself in a situation where you think you need to make your own connections, it would probably be a good idea to download the Branch Office Guide whitepaper and be very familiar with its contents, because you can wreak havoc with Active Directory replication when you manually manipulate connection objects. You can download the Branch Office Guide whitepaper for Windows Server 2003 from the following Microsoft web site: *http://www.microsoft.com/downloads/details.aspx?FamilyId=9353A4F6 -A8A8-40BB-9FA7-3A95C9540112*. The Windows Server 2008 branch office guide was still being produced at the time of publication.

Knowledge Consistency Checker (KCC)

In all but the smallest deployments such as Small Business Server (SBS) or other single-site environments, administrators should create a site topology in Active Directory that maps closely to the physical network. Unfortunately, Active Directory is not intelligent enough to look at the network and build its own complex topologies to optimize replication and resource location for every company installing Active Directory—it needs your help. Creating a site topology is discussed in Chapter 11.

Once you have set up your site, subnet, and site link objects, an Active Directory process called the *Knowledge Consistency Checker* (KCC) takes that information and automatically generates and maintains the connection objects that describe which naming contexts should be replicated between what domain controllers as well as how and when. The KCC has two separate algorithms it uses to determine what connection objects are needed: intrasite and intersite.

The intrasite algorithm is designed to create a minimal latency ring topology *for each naming context* that guarantees no more than three hops between any two domain controllers in the site. As DCs, GCs, and domains are added and removed within a site, the KCC adds and removes connections between the domain controllers as necessary to maintain this minimal-hop topology. It is quite simple to visualize when dealing with a single domain and a small number of domain controllers, but gets extremely difficult to visualize as you add many domain controllers and additional domains.

The intersite algorithm, on the other hand, is not a minimum-hop algorithm; it simply tries to keep the sites connected via a spanning-tree algorithm so that replication can occur, and then simply follows the site link metrics for making those connections. It is quite possible for the KCC to generate a replication topology that forces a change to replicate through eight sites to get from one end of the topology to the other. If you are unhappy with the site connections made by the KCC for the intersite topology because they don't align with your network connections, it is almost certainly related to how the site links are configured. A well-designed site topology will help the KCC generate an intelligent and efficient collection of connection objects for replication.

We cover the KCC in greater depth later in Chapter 11.

Site and Replication Management Tools

Obviously, as more sites and connections are created, the replication topology can get very large. Microsoft provides the *Active Directory Sites and Services* MMC snap-in (*dssite.msc*) to help manage the topology. It allows you to drill down into the Sites Container, which holds all the site-topology objects and connection objects. The Sites Container is located directly under the Configuration Container. With Sites and Services, you can create new sites, subnets, links, bridges, and connections, as well as set replication schedules and metrics for each link and so on.

Other replication-related tools available in the Windows Support Tools are:

RepAdmin
   A command-line tool for administering replication. (Repadmin is available in the base Windows Server 2008 installation.)

ReplMon
   A graphical utility for managing and monitoring replication.

How Replication Works

Microsoft has introduced a number of new terms for Active Directory replication, and most of them will be completely unfamiliar to anyone new to Active Directory. To properly design your replication topology, you should understand the basics of how replication works, but you also need to understand how replication works using these new terms, which are used throughout both Microsoft's documentation and its management tools. As you read the rest of this chapter, refer as needed back to the definitions of the terms that are presented. Do not be disappointed if it doesn't all sink into your brain comfortably on your first or even fifth read of the material. Even experienced administrators have been known to debate how this all works, as well as what the proper terms are for the various structures and processes.

We will use the sample replication topology in Figure 5-6 for the discussion in this section.

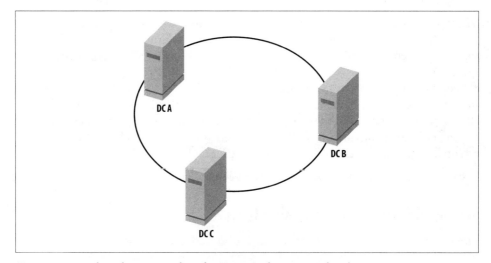

Figure 5-6. Sample replication topology for "How Replication Works" discussion

A Background to Metadata

Replication metadata is the data that governs the replication process. Active Directory replication enables data transfer between naming contexts on different domain controllers without ending up in a continuous replication loop or missing any data. To make this process work, each NC holds a number of pieces of information that specifically relate to replication within that particular NC. That means that the replication data for the Schema NC is held in the Schema NC and is separate from the replication data for the Configuration NC, which is held in the Configuration NC, and so forth. This is done this way because all replication is naming-context based. When a domain controller is pulling changes from another domain controller, it does so one naming context at a time in a serial fashion.

 Although time isn't used as the basis for replication in Active Directory, it is still incredibly important. All authentication between domain controllers for replication is Kerberos based, and Kerberos has a maximum time-skew requirement between hosts. In a default forest, if a domain controller deviates from the common time of all of the other domain controllers by more than five minutes, that domain controller will no longer be able to replicate with other domain controllers.

That means it is critically important for all domain controllers to have a consistent time, but, fortunately, it doesn't mean the time has to be correct. It is far better to have all domain controllers share an incorrect time than it is to have some domain controllers having the right time and some others being off by an hour. In this case, it is consistency that is important, not quality.

Thankfully, Microsoft has included a time synchronization service in all Windows machines since Windows 2000. Every machine in a forest except for the forest root PDC and its designated failover should not have a specific time server configured; that way, each machine will maintain time synchronization with the Active Directory forest. The forest root PDC (and its designated failover) should be configured to use some trustworthy NTP host. This could be a host inside or outside of your local network; the machines simply need to be able to occasionally contact it for updates. The time-server values can be viewed and modified with the NET TIME command.

Update Sequence Numbers (USN) and highestCommittedUSN

Each domain controller maintains its own separate *Update Sequence Number* (USN). Each time a change (new objects, updates, deletes, etc.) is made to an object in Active Directory, a transaction occurs. A USN is a 64-bit value that is assigned to each atomic update transaction, and it is meaningful only in relation to the domain controller the update was performed on. Each separate update transaction will generate an incrementing USN value. A single USN could represent the change of every attribute on an object or a single attribute on a single object. If we examined a domain controller's highest committed USN and discovered it was 1000 and then came back twenty minutes later and discovered the highest committed USN was now 1056, we would know that 56 transactions had occurred in the past twenty minutes on this domain controller.

While some directory systems use timestamps to control replication and what needs to be propagated from server to server, Microsoft chose to use USN values. The fact that these values increment sequentially completely avoids the issues of the domain controllers having their clocks set backwards or being out of synch with their replication partners. Each domain controller maintains its highest combined USN for all naming contexts in the `highestCommittedUSN` value of the `RootDSE`. See the sidebar "Querying RootDSE with Ldp" in Chapter 3 for steps to view the `highestCommittedUSN` value.

USNs are used to uniquely identify each update that has taken place in a naming context on a particular domain controller regardless of the update type. It is highly improbable that the same USNs will ever represent the same change on two different domain controllers. This means that you can request individual changes based on particular USNs from a specific domain controller, but does not allow for directory comparison between DCs based on similar USN values. The change of the description to "joe's computer" on a computer account named *Cerberus* may be USN 23865 on one domain controller, but could be USN 4078 on another and USN 673459234 on yet another.

Originating updates versus replicated updates

Replication distinguishes between two types of update:

Originating update (write)
> This term defines the point of origin for a particular update—i.e., on which domain controller the change initially occurred.

Replicated update (write)
> This term defines the opposite of an originating update—i.e., the change in question did not begin here; it was replicated from another domain controller.

If you use the Active Directory Users and Computers snap-in to create five users on DC A, then DC A's USN is incremented five times, once for each originating update. These changes are then replicated to DC B, incrementing its USN by five. If DC A receives a change from DC B, then DC A's USN is incremented once. This behavior is outlined in Table 5-1.

 If an Active Directory database transaction is aborted—i.e., fails to complete—the associated USN value is not assigned to any object or reused in any way. The USN continues incrementing as changes occur.

Table 5-1. USN increment example

Action	Naming context	Originating domain controller	Domain controller	USN
Initial USN value	Domain NC	N/A	DC A	1000
Initial USN value	Domain NC	N/A	DC B	2500
Create 5 new users (originating update)	Domain NC	DC A	DC A	1005
Receive 5 new users (replicated update)	Domain NC	DC A	DC B	2505
Modify user description attribute (originating update)	Domain NC	DC B	DC B	2506

Action	Naming context	Originating domain controller	Domain controller	USN
Receive modified user description attribute (replicated update)	Domain NC	DC B	DC A	1006

DSA GUID and Invocation ID

Each domain controller has a GUID called the *DSA GUID*. This DSA GUID is used to uniquely identify a domain controller and is the `objectGUID` of the *NTDS Settings* object viewable under the domain controller in Active Directory Sites and Services. This GUID does not change unless the domain controller is demoted and re-promoted.

The Active Directory database (*NTDS.DIT*) also has a GUID. This latter GUID is used to identify the server's Active Directory database in replication calls and is called the *Invocation ID*; it is stored in the `invocationId` attribute of the *NTDS Settings* object for the domain controller. The Invocation ID is changed any time Active Directory is restored on that DC or any time the DSA GUID is changed.

 This change of GUID makes sure that the other domain controllers on the network realize that this is a new database instance and that they create new high-watermark vector and up-to-dateness vector entries in their respective tables for it.

This allows changes that occurred after the backup to be replicated back to the newly restored database to bring it properly up to date. Without this step, any changes originated on the restored DC after the backup completed that had replicated out to the rest of the Directory would never replicate back to this DC once it was restored. This is because the replication partners would assume the DC already had those changes since it was the master of the changes in the first place.

Table 5-2 summarizes the DSA GUID and Invocation ID values.

Table 5-2. DSA GUID and Invocation ID summary

Object	Attribute	Description
NTDS Settings	`objectGUID`	Uniquely identifies the domain controller for its entire lifetime. This attribute value is referred to as the *DSA GUID*.
NTDS Settings	`invocationID`	Uniquely identifies the Active Directory database on the domain controller. This attribute value is referred to as the *Invocation ID*. The *Invocation ID* is reset when a domain controller is restored from a backup.

High-watermark vector (direct up-to-dateness vector)

The high-watermark vector (HWMV) is a table maintained independently by every domain controller to assist in efficient replication of a naming context. Specifically, it is used to help the domain controller determine where it last left off when replicating the naming context with a specific replication partner.

There is one table for every naming context the domain controller maintains a replica of, so at a minimum every domain controller would have at least three HWMV tables, that is, one each for the schema, the configuration, and domain NCs. Each table stores the highest USN of the updates the domain controller has received from each direct partner it replicates with for the given naming context. These USN values are used to determine where replication should begin with each partner on the next replication cycle. This allows the domain controller to request the most recent updates from a given replication partner for each naming context.

When the local domain controller initiates replication for a naming context with one of its partners, the highest USN for that partner from the domain controller's high-watermark vector for the naming context is one of the pieces of information sent to the replication partner. The replication partner compares that value with its current highest USN for the naming context to help determine what changes should be sent to the domain controller. This logic is further refined by the up-to-dateness vector, as described in the next section.

Continuing with our previous example, the HWMV tables of DC A and DC B are outlined in Tables 5-3 and 5-4.

Table 5-3. DC A's high-watermark vector table

Naming context	Replication partner	High-watermark vector (USN of last update received)
Domain NC	DC B invocation ID	2506
Domain NC	DC C invocation ID	3606

Table 5-4. DC B's high-watermark vector table

Naming context	Replication partner	High-watermark vector (USN of last update received)
Domain NC	DC A invocation ID	1006
Domain NC	DC C invocation ID	3606

Up-to-dateness vector

The up-to-dateness vector (UTDV) is a table maintained independently by every domain controller to assist in efficient replication of a naming context. Specifically, it is used for replication dampening to reduce needless replication traffic and endless replication loops.

There is one table for every naming context the domain controller maintains a replica of, so again, at a minimum, every domain controller will have at least three of these tables. Each table stores the highest originating update USN the domain controller has received from every other domain controller that has ever existed in the forest. In Windows Server 2003, an additional column of information was added to the table to represent the last time the domain controller last successfully completed a replication cycle with the given replication partner and naming context. This was added to assist in locating replication issues.

The up-to-dateness vector is used in conjunction with the high-watermark vector to reduce replication traffic. When the replication request for a naming context is passed to the replication partner, the destination domain controller's up-to-dateness vector for the naming context is also in the request. The source partner can then zero in on changes that it hasn't previously sent and then further filter out any changes that the destination may have already received from other replication partners. In this way, it guarantees that a single change is not replicated to the same domain controller multiple times; this is called *propagation dampening*.

Let's examine our sample replication scenario again; however, this time we will include DC C in the scenario. Table 5-5 shows the USN values as a result of each step.

Table 5-5. USN values including DC C

Action	Naming context	Originating domain controller	Domain controller	USN
Initial USN value	Domain NC	N/A	DC A	1000
Initial USN value	Domain NC	N/A	DC B	2500
Initial USN value	Domain NC	N/A	DC C	3750
Create 5 new users (originating update)	Domain NC	DC A	DC A	1005
Receive 5 new users (replicated update)	Domain NC	DC A	DC B	2505
Receive 5 new users (replicated update)	Domain NC	DC A	DC C	3755
Modify user description attribute (originating update)	Domain NC	DC B	DC B	2506
Receive modified user description attribute (replicated update)	Domain NC	DC B	DC A	1006
Receive modified user description attribute (replicated update)	Domain NC	DC B	DC C	3756

Once DC C receives the updates originated by DC A, it will attempt to replicate them to DC B; however, DC B has already received these updates from DC A directly. To prevent an endless replication loop, the up-to-dateness vector tables for DC B are checked by DC C, and it then knows not to send those updates.

Let's also look at the high-watermark vector table again now that DC C is included. Tables 5-6, 5-7, and 5-8 show the HWMV and UTDV tables for DC A, DC B, and DC C.

Table 5-6. DC A's high-watermark and up-to-dateness vector tables

Naming context	Replication partner	High-watermark vector (USN of last update)	Up-to-dateness vector
Domain NC	DC B invocation ID	2506	2506
Domain NC	DC C invocation ID	3756	3756

Table 5-7. DC B's high watermark and up-to-dateness vector tables

Naming context	Replication partner	High-watermark vector (USN of last update)	Up-to-dateness vector
Domain NC	DC A invocation ID	1006	1006
Domain NC	DC C invocation ID	3756	3756

Table 5-8. DC C's high watermark and up-to-dateness vector tables

Naming context	Replication partner	High-watermark vector (USN of last update)	Up-to-dateness vector
Domain NC	DC A invocation ID	1006	1006
Domain NC	DC B invocation ID	2506	2506

Notice that now each domain controller has an up-to-dateness vector for each domain controller that it replicates. When DC B goes to pull changes from DC C, it includes its up-to-dateness vector table in the request. DC C will then check this table and discover that DC B has already received the change from DC A. This functionality prevents the endless loop that would otherwise occur and also eliminates unnecessary replication traffic on the network.

Recap

The following list summarizes the important points of this section:

- Active Directory is split into separate naming contexts, each of which replicates independently.
- Within each naming context, a variety of metadata is held.

For each naming context on a given domain controller, a high-watermark vector is maintained that contains one entry for each of its replication partners for this naming context. The values in this table for the replication partners are updated only during a replication cycle.

For each naming context on a given domain controller, an up-to-dateness vector is maintained that contains one entry for every domain controller that has ever made an originating write within this NC. Each entry consists of three values: the Originating-DSA-GUID, Originating-USN, and a timestamp indicating the last successful replication with the originating domain controller. These values are updated only during a replication cycle.

How an Object's Metadata Is Modified During Replication

 To minimize the use of abbreviations, the terms DC and server are used interchangeably. The terms property and attribute are also used interchangeably in this section.

To see how the actual data is modified during replication, consider a four-step example:

1. An object (a user) is created on DC A.
2. That object is replicated to DC B.
3. That object is subsequently modified on DC B.
4. The new changes to that object are replicated back to DC A.

This four-step process is shown in Figure 5-7. The diagram depicts the status of the user object on both DC A and DC B during the four time periods that represent each of the steps.

Now use Figure 5-7 to follow a discussion of each of the steps.

Step 1: Initial creation of a user on Server A

When you create a user on DC A, DC A is the originating server. During the Active Directory database transaction representing the creation of the new user on DC A, a USN (1000) is assigned to the transaction. The user's uSNCreated and uSNChanged attributes are automatically set to 1000 (the USN of the transaction corresponding to the user creation). All of the user's attributes are also initialized with a set of data, as follows:

- The attribute's value(s) is/are set according to system defaults or parameters given during user creation.
- The attribute's USN is set to 1000 (the USN of this transaction).
- The attribute's version number is set to 1.
- The attribute's timestamp is set to the time of the object creation.
- The attribute's originating-server GUID is set to the GUID of DC A.
- The attribute's originating-server USN is set to 1000 (the USN of this transaction).

This information tells you several things about the user:

- The user was created during transaction 1000 on this domain controller (uSNCreated = 1000).
- The user was last changed during transaction 1000 (uSNChanged = 1000).

- The attributes for the user have never been modified from their original values (property version numbers = 1), and these values were set at transaction 1000 (attributes's USN = 1000).

- Each attribute was last set by the originating server, DC A, during transaction 1000 (originating-server GUID and originating-server USN).

The preceding example showed two per-object values and five per-attribute values being changed. While `uSNChanged` and `uSNCreated` are real attributes on each object in Active Directory, attributes of an object can only have values and cannot hold other attributes, such as a version number.

In reality, all of the per-attribute replication metadata (Property Version Number, Time-Changed, Originating-DC-GUID, Originating-USN, Property-USN) for every attribute of any given object is encoded together as a single byte string and stored as `replPropertyMetaData`, a non-replicated attribute of the object.

 Use the RepAdmin, adfind, ADSIEdit, or LDP tools to see a property's metadata. For an example of how to view replication metadata, see the sidebar "Viewing Replication Metadata," next.

COMMAND-LINE REFERENCE

Viewing Replication Metadata

Replication metadata is easily viewable with a number of tools and can be a key component of the troubleshooting process, particularly if you are trying to determine when and where data in Active Directory changed. In this example, we will use repadmin to display the replication metadata of the Administrator account.

Repadmin requires two arguments in this example:

- The domain controller to query the metadata on
- The distinguished name of the object to display metadata for
  `repadmin /showobjmeta`

```
"k8devdc01"
"CN=Administrator,CN=Users,DC=k8dev01,DC=brianlab,DC=local"
```

A partial version of the resulting output is shown below. You will notice that each replicated attribute stores the local and originating USNs, the originating domain controller, the date and time of the change, and the version number.

```
Loc.USN                          Originating DSA  Org.USN  Org.Time/Date
Ver Attribute
=======                          ===============  =========  =============
=== =========
   8194          Default-First-Site-Name\K8DEVDC01      8194 2008-03-24
21:27:24    1 objectClass
   8194          Default-First-Site-Name\K8DEVDC01      8194 2008-03-24
21:27:24    1 cn
```

```
    8194          Default-First-Site-Name\K8DEVDC01    8194  2008-03-24
  21:27:24   1 description
    8194          Default-First-Site-Name\K8DEVDC01    8194  2008-03-24
  21:27:24   1 instanceType
    8194          Default-First-Site-Name\K8DEVDC01    8194  2008-03-24
  21:27:24   1 whenCreated
    8194          Default-First-Site-Name\K8DEVDC01    8194  2008-03-24
  21:27:24   1 displayName
   12727          Default-First-Site-Name\K8DEVDC01   12727  2008-03-24
  21:53:46   2 nTSecurityDescriptor
    8194          Default-First-Site-Name\K8DEVDC01    8194  2008-03-24
  21:27:24   1 name
    8194          Default-First-Site-Name\K8DEVDC01    8194  2008-03-24
  21:27:24   1 userAccountControl
```

Step 2: Replication of the originating write to DC B

Later, when this object is replicated to DC B, DC B adds the user to its copy of Active
Directory as a replicated write. During this transaction, USN 2500 is allocated, and the
user's **uSNCreated** and **uSNChanged** attributes are modified to correspond to DC B's
transaction USN (2500).

From this we can learn several key points:

- The user was created during transaction 2500 on this server (**uSNCreated** = 2500).

- The user was last changed during transaction 2500 (**uSNChanged** = 2500).

- The attributes for the user have never been modified from their original values
  (property version numbers = 1), and these values were set at transaction 2500
  (attribute's USN = 2500).

- Each attribute was last set by the originating server, DC A, during transaction 1000
  (originating-server GUID and originating-server USN).

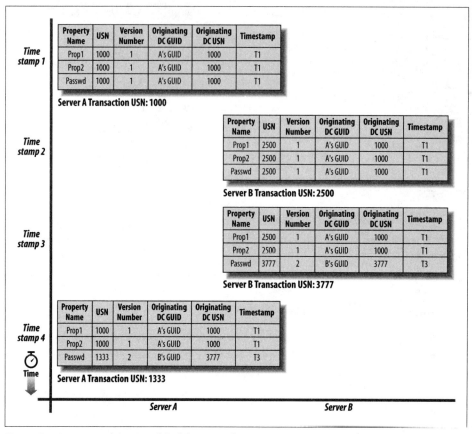

Figure 5-7. How metadata is modified during replication

Step 3: Password change for the user on DC B

Now an originating write (a password change) occurs on DC B's replicated-write user. Some time has passed since the user was originally created, so the USN assigned to the password-change transaction is 3777. When the password is changed, the user's uSNChanged property is modified to become 3777. In addition, the password attribute (and only the password attribute) is modified in the following way:

- The password value is set.
- The password's USN is set to 3777 (the USN of this transaction).
- The attribute's version number is set to 2.
- The attribute's timestamp is set to the time that transaction 3777 occurred.
- The attribute's originating-server GUID is set to the GUID of Server B.
- The attribute's originating-server USN is set to 3777 (the USN of this transaction).

Looking at the user object, you can now see that the object was last changed during transaction 3777 and that the transaction represented a password change that originated on DC B.

Step 4: Password-change replication to DC A

This step is similar to step 2. When DC A receives the password update during replication, it allocates the change transaction a USN of 1333.

 Remember that updates occur at the attribute level and not the object level, so only the password is sent and not the entire user object.

During transaction 1333, the user's uSNChanged attribute is modified to correspond to Server A's transaction USN.

From this, we can learn a number of things:

- The user was created during transaction 1000 on this server (uSNCreated = 1000).
- The user was last changed during transaction 1333 (uSNChanged = 1333).
- All but one of the attributes for the user have retained their original values (property version numbers = 1), and these values were set at transaction 1000 (property's USN = 1000).
- All but one of the attributes were last set by the originating server, DC A, during transaction 1000 (originating-server GUID and originating-server USN).
- The password was modified for the first time since its creation (password version number = 2) during transaction 1333 (password's USN = 1333), and it was modified on DC B during transaction 3777 (originating-server GUID and originating-server USN).

That's how object and property metadata is modified during replication. Let's now take a look at exactly how replication occurs.

If you are duplicating this step-by-step walkthrough on real domain controllers, you will have noticed two discrepancies.

The first is that after the replication from DC A to DC B, the cn attribute will actually show that the originated write came from DC B. This is a backend implementation detail impacting the RDN attribute for any given object, and it is the only case where this type of discrepancy occurs.

The second is that a password change actually updates several attributes, not just one. The attributes involved are dBCSPwd, unicodePwd, pwdLastSet, ntPwdHistory, and lmPwdHistory. This is another backend implementation detail. For most attributes, when you specifically update a single attribute, only that attribute gets modified and replicated; passwords are handled as a special case.

The Replication of a Naming Context Between Two Servers

In the following examples, there are five servers in a domain: Server A, Server B, Server C, Server D, and Server E. It doesn't matter what NC they are replicating or which servers replicate with which other servers (as they do not all have to replicate with one another directly), because the replication process for any two servers will be the same nonetheless. Replication is a five-step process:

1. Replication with a partner is initiated.
2. The partner works out what updates to send.
3. The partner sends the updates to the initiating server.
4. The initiating server processes the updates.
5. The initiating server checks whether it is up-to-date.

Step 1: Replication with a partner is initiated

Replication occurs between only two servers at any time, so let's consider Server A and Server B, which are replication partners . At a certain point in time indicated by the replication schedule on Server A, Server A initiates replication for a particular NC with Server B and requests any updates that it doesn't have. This is a one-way update transfer from Server B to Server A. No new updates will be passed to Server B in this replication cycle, as this would require Server B to initiate the replication.

Server A initiates the replication by sending Server B a request to replicate along with five pieces of important replication metadata, i.e., data relating to the replication process itself. The five pieces are:

- The name of the NC that Server A wishes to receive updates for
- The maximum number of object updates that Server A wishes to receive during this replication cycle

- The maximum number of values that Server A wishes to receive during this replication cycle
- USN for Server B from Server A's high-watermark vector for this NC
- Server A's up-to-dateness vector for this NC

The maximum object updates and property values are very important in limiting network bandwidth. If one server has had a large volume of updates since the last replication cycle, limiting the number of objects replicated out in one replication packet means that network bandwidth is not inordinately taken up by replicating those objects in one huge packet. Instead, the replication is broken down into smaller packets over the course of the replication cycle. Once a replication cycle has started for a naming context, it will replicate all changes regardless of how many packets are needed or how long it will take unless the connection between the domain controllers fails outright.

"Once a replication cycle has started for a naming context, it will replicate all changes regardless of how many packets are needed or how long it will take unless the connection between the domain controllers fails outright."

Whether you realize it or not, this implies that when you set up replication schedules for site links, you can specify when replication can start, but you *cannot* specify when it will stop. Replication will continue until it is completed or until the physical connection between the domain controllers is broken.

This is generally not an issue unless you have a very slow connection between a WAN site and a hub site, and you configure the site link to not replicate during normal business hours to conserve bandwidth for users. As long as the number and size of the changes do not exceed what can be replicated in the evening to the WAN site, you are fine; the moment you exceed that magic set of values, however, your replication cycle will take all night and continue into business hours regardless of the schedule.

This step is illustrated in Figure 5-8, which shows that while the initiation of the replication occurs from an NC denoted as xxxx on Server A (where xxxx could represent the Schema, the Configuration, an application partition, or any domain NC), the actual replication will occur later from Server B to Server A.

Step 2: The partner works out what updates to send

Server B receives all this metadata and works out which updates it needs to send back for this NC. First, Server B determines its own highest committed USN for its copy of the NC and then compares that to the USN Server A submitted from its high-watermark vector table. Assuming that there have been some updates, Server B instantly knows how many updates have occurred since Server A last replicated with Server B. This has

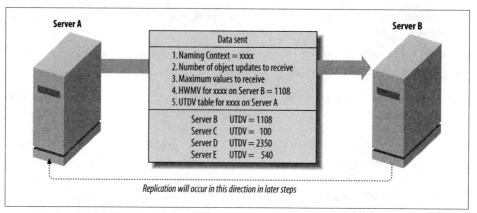

Figure 5-8. Initiating replication with Server B for NC xxxx

to be true, as Server A's HWMV would have been updated with Server B's highest committed USN for the NC during the last replication cycle. So, any difference between the two USNs must represent changes on Server B since the last replication, and Server B knows which individual USNs Server A is missing. Assuming also for now that the number of updates does not exceed the maximums specified by Server A in its metadata, Server B can supply all of the missing updates to Server A.

However, this entire set of updates may not need to go to Server A if Server A has had some of them replicated already from other servers. Server B now needs some way of knowing which updates Server A has already seen, so that it can remove those items from the list of updates to send. That's where the up-to-dateness vector comes in. For each update that could potentially be sent, Server B checks two pieces of data attached to the object that was updated: the DSA GUID of the server that originated the update (the Originating-DC-GUID) and the USN associated with that update (the Originating-USN) on the originating server. For example, a password change to a user may have been replicated to Server B and recorded as USN 1112, but it may in fact have originated on Server D as USN 2345. Server B cross-references the originating server's GUID with Server A's UTDV to find the highest originating write USN for the originating server. If the USN recorded in the UDTV for the originating server is equal to or higher than the USN attached to the update on Server D, Server A must have already seen the update. This has to be true, because Server A's UTDV is used to indicate the highest originating writes that Server A has received.

Let's say that Server B has four updates for Server A: one originating write (Server B USN: 1111) and three replicated writes (Server B USNs 1109, 1110, and 1112). The reason there are four is that 1112 is the last update made on Server B in this example, and the USN in Server A's HWMV for xxxx on Server B from Figure 5-7 is 1108. So, look for updates starting at 1109 up to the last update on Server B, which is 1112. The first two replicated writes (Server B USNs 1109 and 1110) originated on Server E (Server E USNs 567 and 788), and one (Server B USN 1112) originated on Server D (Server D USN 2345). This is shown in Table 5-9.

Table 5-9. *Potential updates to be sent*

Server B USN	Originating DC GUID	Originating DC USN
1109	Server E's GUID	567
1110	Server E's GUID	788
1111	Server B's GUID	1111
1112	Server D's GUID	2345

According to Figure 5-8, Server A already has Server D's 2345 update because the USN in Server A's UTDV for Server D is 2350. So, both Server A and Server B already have Server D's 2345 update, and there is no need to waste bandwidth sending it over the network again. The act of filtering previously seen updates to keep them from being continually sent between the servers is known as propagation dampening.

Now that you know how the high-watermark vector and up-to-dateness vector help Server B to work out what updates need to be sent, let's look at the exact process that Server B uses to work out what data is required.

When Server B receives a request for updates from Server A, the following steps occur:

1. Server B makes a copy of its up-to-dateness vector for Server A.

2. Server B puts the table to one side, so to speak, and does a search of the entire naming context for all objects with a uSNChanged value greater than the USN value from Server A's high-watermark vector entry for Server B. This list is then sorted into ascending uSNChanged order.

3. Server B initializes an empty output buffer to which it will add update entries for sending to Server A. It also initializes a value called Last-Object-USN-Changed. This will be used to represent the USN of the last object sent in that particular replication session. This value is not an attribute of any particular object, just a simple piece of replication metadata.

4. Server B enumerates the list of objects in ascending uSNChanged order and uses the following algorithm for each object:

    - If the object has already been added to the output buffer, Server B sets Last-Object-USN-Changed to the uSNChanged property of the current object. Enumeration continues with the next object.

    - If the object has not already been added to the output buffer, Server B tests the object to see if it contains changes that need to be sent to the destination. For each property of the current object, Server B takes the Originating-DC-GUID of that property and locates the USN that corresponds to that GUID from Server A's UTDV. From that entry, Server B looks at the Originating-USN. If the property's Originating-USN on Server B is greater than Server A's UTDV entry the property needs to be sent.

If changes need to be sent, an update entry is added to the output buffer. Server B sets Last-Object-USN-Changed to the uSNChanged property of the current object. Enumeration continues with the next object.

If no changes need to be sent, Server B sets the Last-Object-USN-Changed to the uSNChanged of the current object. Enumeration continues with the next object.

 During the enumeration, if the requested limit on object update entries or values is reached, the enumeration terminates early and a flag known as More-Data is set to true. If the enumeration finishes without either limit being hit, then More-Data is set to false.

Step 3: The partner sends the updates to the initiating server

Server B identifies the list of updates that it should send back based on those that Server A has not yet seen from other sources. Server B then sends this data to Server A. In addition, if More-Data is set to false, one extra piece of metadata is sent back as well. The returned information from Server B is:

- The output buffer updates from Server B
- Server B's Last-Object-USN-Changed value (i.e., the value for Server A to insert into the high-watermark vector for the NC for Server B)
- The More-Data flag
- Server B's up-to-date vector for this NC (sent only when More-Data set to false)

This is shown in Figure 5-9.

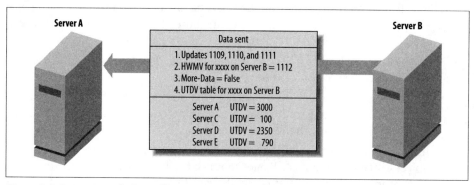

Figure 5-9. Server B sends the updates to Server A for NC xxxx

If Server B calculates that Server A is already up to date and requires no updates, only the last two pieces of metadata are returned to Server A. This can occur if the highest committed USN for the NC on Server B is identical to the HWMV entry passed by Server A, i.e., no updates have occurred since the last replication cycle. This also can occur if Server B's highest committed USN for the NC has changed, but Server A has already seen all of the originating updates through replication with other partners. In both cases, just the metadata is returned.

Step 4: The initiating server processes the updates

Server A receives the data. For each update entry it receives, Server A allocates a USN and starts a database transaction to update the relevant object in its own copy of the Active Directory database. The object's uSNChanged property is set to the USN of this transaction. The database transaction is then committed. This process continues for each update entry that was received.

After all the update entries have been processed, the USN in Server A's high-watermark vector for Server B is set to the Last-Object-USN-Changed received from Server B. In other words, Server A now knows that it is up-to-date with Server B, up to the last change just sent over.

The Last-Object-USN-Changed that Server A receives allows it to know the last update that Server B has made. This will be used in the next replication cycle. In the previous example, the highest update sent across to Server A is USN 1111. Server B's USN 1112 update is not actually sent since Server A has already seen it. However, the Last-Object-USN-Changed returned by Server B with the data would still be 1112 and not 1111.

Step 5: The initiating server checks whether it is up-to-date

Server A now checks the More-Data flag. If More-Data is set to true, Server A goes back to step 1 to start replication with Server B again and request more updates. If More-Data is set to false, every update must have been received from Server B, and finally Server A's up-to-dateness vector is itself updated.

The up-to-dateness vector allows Server A to identify which originating updates Server B has seen and thus, by replication, which originating updates it has now seen. Server A does not replace its up-to-dateness vector with the one it was sent. Instead, it checks each entry in the received table and does one of two things. If the entry for a server is not listed in its own UTDV, it adds that entry to the table. This allows Server A to know that it has now been updated to a certain level for a new server. If the entry for a server is listed in Server A's UTDV, and the value received is higher, it modifies its own copy of the table with the higher value. After all, it has now been updated to this new level by Server B, so it had better record that fact.

Table 5-10 shows Server A's up-to-dateness vector and high-watermark vector for the xxxx Naming Context before step 1 and after step 5.

Table 5-10. State of UTDV and HWMV for Server A before and after updates

	HWMV for Server B	Server B UTDV	Server C UTDV	Server D UTDV	Server E UTDV
Before step 1	1108	1108	100	2350	540
After step 5	1112	1111	100	2350	790

Recap

The following points summarize replication between naming contexts:

- The high-watermark vector is used to detect updates that need to be sent between replication partners.

- The up-to-dateness vector is used in propagation dampening to filter the updates so that only updates that the initiating server has not seen are transmitted from a partner.

- The uSNChanged property on each object is used to identify which objects might need to be sent out as updates to the initiating server.

 You can force manual replication of a particular NC on a DC if you choose, using the Sites and Services snap-in. Browse to the connection object that you want to replicate over, right-click it, and select Replicate Now. This can also be done from the command line with the `repadmin.exe` utility.

How Replication Conflicts Are Reconciled

While the replication process is usually fine on its own, there are times when conflicts can occur because two servers perform irreconcilable operations between replication cycles. For example, Server A creates an object with a particular name at roughly the same time that Server B creates an object with the same name under the same parent container. Both can't exist at the same time in Active Directory, so what happens to the two objects?

- Does one object get deleted or renamed?

- Do both objects get deleted or renamed?

- What about an administrator moving an object on Server D to an Organizational Unit while at the same time on Server B that Organizational Unit is being deleted?

- What happens to the soon-to-be orphaned object? Is it deleted along with the Organizational Unit or moved somewhere else entirely?

- Consider a final example: if an admin on Server B changes a user's password while the user himself changes his password on Server C, which password does the user get?

All of these conflicts need to be resolved within Active Directory during the next replication cycle. The exact reconciliation process and how the final decision is replicated back out depend on the exact conflict that occurred.

Conflict due to identical attribute change

This scenario is when an attribute on the same object is updated on two different domain controllers around the same time. During replication, each domain controller follows the following process to resolve the conflict:

1. The server starts reconciliation by looking at the version numbers of the two attributes. Whichever attribute has the higher version number wins the conflict.

2. If the property version numbers are equal, the server checks the timestamps of both attributes. Whichever attribute was changed at the later time wins the conflict.

3. If the attribute timestamps are equal, the GUIDS from the two originating servers are checked. As GUIDs must be unique, these two values have to be unique, so the server takes the attribute change from the originating server with the higher GUID as the winner of the conflict.

 All replication metadata timestamps for Active Directory are in Universal Time Coordinated (UTC), which is more commonly known as Greenwich Mean Time (GMT) or Zulu time.

Conflict due to a move or creation of an object under a now-deleted parent

This scenario is when an object is created on one server under a particular OU or container, for example, an OU called People. Meanwhile on another server at about the same time, the People OU is deleted.

This is a fairly easy conflict to resolve. In this case, the parent (the People OU) remains deleted, but the object is moved to the naming context's *Lost and Found* Container, which was specially set up for this scenario. The distinguished name of the Lost and Found Container for the *Mycorp.com* domain is:

```
cn=LostAndFound,dc=mycorp,dc=com
```

Conflict due to creation of objects with names that conflict

Recall that the relative distinguished name (RDN) for an object must be unique within the context of its parent container. This particular conflict occurs when two objects are created on two different servers with the same RDN. During replication, domain controllers follow the following steps to resolve this conflict:

1. The server starts reconciliation by looking at the version numbers of the two objects. Whichever object has the higher version number wins the conflict.

2. If the object version numbers are equal, the server checks the timestamps of both objects. Whichever object was changed at the later time wins the conflict.

3. If both object timestamps are equal, the GUIDs from the two originating servers are checked. The server once again takes the object change from the originating server with the higher GUID as the winner of the conflict.

In this case, however, the object that lost the conflict resolution is not lost or deleted; instead, the conflicting attribute is modified with a known unique value. That way, at the end of the resolution, both objects exist, with one having its conflicting name changed to a unique value. The unique name consists of the following format: *<:ObjectName><LineFeed>CNF:< ObjectGUID>*.

> This same logic is only used for the RDN naming value of the object (usually the cn attribute). It is not used for cleaning up other values that are normally required to be unique such as the sAMAccountName attribute that represents a user's username.

Replicating the conflict resolution

Let's say that Server A starts a replication cycle. First, it requests changes from Server B and receives updates. Then Server A requests changes from Server C and receives updates. However, as Server A is applying Server C's updates in order, it determines that a conflict has occurred between the updates recently applied by Server B. Server A resolves the conflict according to the preceding guidelines and finds in Server C's favor. Now, while Server A and Server C are correct, Server B still needs to be updated with Server C's value.

To do this, when Server B next requests updates from Server A, it receives, among others, the update that originated on Server C. Server B then applies the updates it receives in sequence, and when it gets to the update that originated on Server C, it detects the same conflict. Server B then goes through the same conflict resolution procedure that Server A did and comes to the same result. Server B then modifies its own copy of the object to accommodate the change.

Additional problems can occur when changes are made on a server and it goes down prior to replicating the changes. If the server never comes back up to replicate changes, those changes are obviously lost.

> Alternatively, if the server comes back up much later and attempts to replicate those changes back to Active Directory, there is a much greater chance of conflict resolution (with that server failing the conflict, if many of the changes that were made on that server have subsequently been made in Active Directory more recently on other servers). This isn't a problem, but is something you need to be aware of.

Summary

We have now looked at the importance of the site topology in Active Directory and how that relates to your physical network. We have also considered the metadata that governs the replication process, how the system keeps track of changes to objects and properties automatically, how data is replicated among servers including propagation dampening, and how conflicts are resolved.

In Chapter 11, we take this knowledge further and show you how Active Directory manages and automatically generates the replication connections that exist both within and between sites. With that knowledge, we can move on to the design principles for sites and links in Active Directory.

## CHAPTER 6

Active Directory and DNS

One of the big advantages of Active Directory over its predecessor, Windows NT, is the reliance on the *Domain Name System* (DNS) as opposed to the *Windows Internet Naming Service* (WINS) for name resolution. DNS is the ubiquitous, standards-based naming service used on the Internet. WINS, on the other hand, never garnered industry support and has become a red-headed stepchild on many enterprise networks.

The good news is that with Active Directory, the dependencies on WINS have been eliminated, but the potentially bad news is that Active Directory has many dependencies on the DNS infrastructure. It is only potentially bad based on the flexibility of your DNS environment. Often, the groups that manage DNS and Active Directory within an organization are different, and getting the two teams to agree on implementation can be difficult due to political turf battles or technology clashes.

 Although Active Directory doesn't need WINS or, more accurately, NetBIOS Name Resolution, many other Microsoft technologies, including Exchange 2000/2003, do need it. Implementing Active Directory doesn't necessarily guarantee that you won't be running WINS anymore.

The intent of this chapter is to provide you with a good understanding of how Active Directory uses DNS and a description of some of the options for setting it up within your organization. We will briefly touch on some DNS basics, but will not go into much depth on how to configure and administer the Windows DNS server. For more information on those topics, we highly recommend *DNS on Windows 2003* by Matt Larson, Cricket Liu, and Robbie Allen (O'Reilly).

DNS Fundamentals

DNS is a hierarchical name-resolution system. It is also the largest public directory service deployed. Virtually every company uses DNS for name-resolution services, including hostname to IP address, IP address to hostname, and hostname to alternate hostname (aliases). DNS is a well-documented standard that has been around since the early days of the Internet. The following RFCs cover some of the basics of DNS:

- RFC 1034, "Domain Names—Concepts and Facilities"
- RFC 1035, "Domain Names—Implementation and Specification"
- RFC 1912, "Common DNS Operational and Configuration Errors"
- RFC 1995, "Incremental Zone Transfer in DNS"
- RFC 1996, "A Mechanism for Prompt Notification of Zone Changes (DNS NOTIFY)"
- RFC 2181, "Clarifications to the DNS Specification"

There are three important DNS concepts that every Active Directory administrator must understand:

- Zones are delegated portions of the DNS namespace.
- Resource records contain name resolution information.
- Dynamic DNS allows clients to add and delete resource records dynamically.

Zones

A *zone* is a collection of hierarchical domain names, the root of which has been *delegated* to one or more name servers. For example, let's say that the *mycorp.com* namespace was delegated to the name server *ns1.mycorp.com*. All domain names contained under *mycorp.com* that *ns1.mycorp.com* was authoritative for would be considered part of the *mycorp.com* zone.

A subset of the *mycorp.com* zone could be delegated to another server; for example, *mycorp.com* could delegate *subdomain1.mycorp.com* to the name server *ns2.mycorp.com*. At that point, *subdomain1.mycorp.com* becomes its own zone for which *ns2.mycorp.com* is authoritative.

Resource Records

A *resource record* is the unit of information in DNS. A zone is essentially a collection of resource records . There are various resource record types that define different types of name lookups. Table 6-1 lists some of the more common resource record types.

Table 6-1. Commonly used resource record types

Record type	Name	Description
A	Address Record	Maps a hostname to an IPv4 address
AAAA	Address Record	Maps a hostname to an IPv6 address
PTR	Pointer Record	Maps an IPv4 address to a hostname
CNAME	Alias Record	Maps an alias to a hostname
MX	Mail Exchanger Record	Specifies a mail route for a domain
NS	Name Server Record	Specifies a name server for a given domain
SOA	Start of Authority Record	Contains administrative data about a zone, including the primary name server
SRV	Service Record	Maps a particular service (e.g., LDAP) to one or more hostnames

One important resource record to note is the SRV record type. SRV records are used extensively by domain controllers and Active Directory clients to locate servers that have a particular service. We will describe how Active Directory uses these records in more detail later in the chapter.

It is also important to note that SRV records are dependent upon A records. Each SRV record provides a variety of details about each service it represents (LDAP, for example), including the computers on which the services run. SRV records achieve this by maintaining a pointer to the fully qualified name of the A records that describe the computers running the service.

DDNS

Dynamic DNS, defined in RFC 2136, is a method for clients to send requests to a DNS server to add or delete resource records in a zone. Having this capability has greatly increased the supportability of DNS in large environments. Before DDNS, the primary means to update a zone was by either directly editing a text-based zone file or via a vendor-supported GUI, such as the Windows DNS MMC snap-in.

 RFC 2136 can be found at *http://www.ietf.org/rfc/rfc2136.txt*.

Active Directory takes full advantage of DDNS to ease the burden of maintaining the resource records it requires. Each domain controller can have anywhere from a few dozen to a few hundred associated resource records, depending on the size of the Active Directory site topology. Any time the site topology changes, one or more domain controllers may need to change some or all of the resource records previously registered. Because of this dynamic nature of Active Directory resource records, in a large environment it could easily take a person working full time to manually maintain all of the records. For more information about the security of dynamic DNS, see the sidebar "Securing Your Dynamic Updates."

Securing Your Dynamic Updates

The RFC that defined *Dynamic DNS*, RFC 2136, did not provide for a security model to secure updates from clients. As you might expect, this is a very serious limitation to wide-scale adoption. To address this problem, RFC 2137, "Secure Dynamic Update," was created. Unfortunately, RFC 2137 was not very practical in implementation and tended to be overly complex. Later, RFC 2535, "Domain Name System Security Extensions," defined a public key-based method for securing DNS requests, commonly known as DNSSEC. RFC 3007 was then created, which rendered RFC 2137 obsolete and updated RFC 2535 to provide a more flexible method to secure update requests. Many DNS server products have only recently started to provide support for these RFCs, and only time will tell whether they will become widely adopted. Check out the following for more information on RFC 2535 and 3007:

- *http://www.ietf.org/rfc/rfc2535.txt*
- *http://www.ietf.org/rfc/rfc3007.txt*

Although Windows Server 2008 provides support for some of the resource record types defined in RFC 2535, such as KEY, SIG, and NXT, it does not provide full compliance, such as message signing and verification.

The approach Microsoft takes to providing secure dynamic updates is by using access control lists (ACLs) in Active Directory. Zones that are Active Directory Integrated (described later in the chapter) store their DNS data in Active Directory. You can then set ACLs on the DNS-related objects in Active Directory to permit or deny security principals to add and/or update records. By default, authenticated computers in a forest can make new entries in a zone, but only the computer that created an entry is allowed to modify the data associated with that entry.

Global Names Zone

With each version of Windows since Windows 2000, Microsoft has continued to invest in making it more practical for some organizations to retire their WINS infrastructure. WINS is very useful in some organizations because it supports short name resolution or, in other words, unlike DNS you do not need to specify a hierarchical name to resolve (e.g., brian-server01 will resolve in WINS versus *brian-server01.briandesmond.com* resolving via DNS).

You can mitigate this with DNS by configuring DNS-suffix search orders on clients, and the DNS resolver on the client will attempt to resolve the short name by appending each DNS suffix, defined one at a time in the order listed. In a large organization with numerous DNS namespaces, this list of suffixes could be quite long and would be potentially quite difficult to maintain, and would also cause significant increases in network traffic when trying to resolve short host names.

Windows Server 2008 introduces new DNS server functionality called the *Global Names Zone*, which you can configure to support short name resolution via DNS without the DNS-suffix search-list requirements on your clients. Any client that supports DNS resolution can utilize the global name zones functionality without additional configuration. Windows Server 2008 DNS servers will first try to resolve the name queried in the local zone, and if that fails, they will then try to resolve it in the global name zone.

Global names zones may be particularly useful to you if you are looking to deploy IPv6 in your organization as WINS does not support IPv6 addressing. When evaluating whether or not to deploy a global names zone, consider the following:

- Are you retiring WINS or planning to?
- Are all of your DNS servers that clients contact running Windows Server 2008? Windows Server 2003 and earlier DNS servers do not implement the global names zone functionality.
- Are you able to manage the static registration of global names? Dynamic registration of records in the global names zones is *not* supported, so you will need to manage the registrations manually or with a script.

 While Windows Server 2008 does not support dynamic registration of records in the global names zone, it does check for uniqueness when clients register new records in other zones. If a client tries to register a new record for a hostname that is already defined in the global names zone, this registration will fail.

- Do you need the functionality global name zones offers? The feature has potentially increased management overhead, so you should consider whether you will benefit from it before investing the time in deploying it.

Deploying a global names zone is a three step process:

1. Create a forward lookup zone on a DNS server called **GlobalNames**.
2. Enable global names zone support on every DNS server that will host the GlobalNames zone:

    ```
    dnscmd ServerName /config /EnableGlobalNamesSupport 1
    ```
3. Configure replication of the GlobalNames zone. It is recommended that you use the ForestDnsZones application partition for this step.

If you have multiple forests and you want to maintain a single Global-Names zone, you will need to configure an SRV record in the _msdcs .otherforest.com zone in the other forests. This SRV record is called **_globalnames**, and it should point to the FQDN of a server hosting the actual GlobalNames zone.

You will need to perform step 2 on all of the DNS servers in the other forest in order for them to honor the _globalnames SRV record.

Once you have the zone created, you will need to populate it with records so that name resolution can occur. The recommended approach is to place CNAME records in the GlobalNames zone and alias them to the records for the specific server/name in the relevant forward lookup zone.

DC Locator

One of the fundamental issues for clients in any environment is finding the most optimal domain controller (DC) to authenticate against. The process under Windows NT was not very efficient and could cause clients to authenticate to domain controllers in the least optimal location. With Active Directory, clients use DNS to locate domain controllers via the DC locator process. To illustrate at a high level how the DC locator process works, we will describe an example where a client has moved from one location to another and needs to find a DC for the domain it is a member of:

1. A client previously located in Site A is moved to Site B.
2. When the client initially boots up, it thinks it is still in Site A, so it retrieves from the cache the last DC it used, most likely from Site A, and proceeds to contact it.
3. The DC in Site A receives the request, determines that the IP address is for Site B, and determines that the client should now be using a DC that services Site B. If the server does not service clients in Site B, it will return the client's new site in the reply and tell the client that it isn't the closest DC.
4. The client will then perform a DNS lookup to find all DCs that service Site B.
5. The client then contacts a DC servicing Site B. Three things can happen at this point:
   a. The DC servicing Site B can respond and authenticate the client.
   b. The DC might fail to respond (it could be down), at which point the client will attempt to use a different DC in Site B.
   c. All DCs servicing Site B fail to respond and the client then performs a DNS lookup to find all DCs that service the domain despite what sites they cover and uses any one of them to authenticate.

The two main things that are needed to support an efficient DC locator process are proper definition of the site topology in Active Directory and the presence of all the necessary Active Directory-related resource records in DNS. In the next section, we will describe the purpose of the resource records used in Active Directory.

 For a more detailed description of how the DC locator process works, including the specific resource records that are queried during the process, check out Microsoft Knowledge Base (KB) article 247811, "How Domain Controllers Are Located in Windows," and Microsoft KB article 314861, "How Domain Controllers Are Located in Windows XP," at *http://support.microsoft.com*.

Resource Records Used by Active Directory

When you promote a domain controller into a domain, a file containing the necessary resource records for it to function correctly within Active Directory is generated in *%SystemRoot%\System32\Config\netlogon.dns*.

The contents of the file will look something like the following for a DC named *moose .mycorp.com* in the *mycorp.com* domain with IP address 10.1.1.1. We've reordered the file a bit to group records of similar purpose together (note that some lines may wrap due to their length):

```
mycorp.com. 600 IN A 10.1.1.1
ec4caf62-31b2-4773-bcce-7b1e31c04d25._msdcs.mycorp.com. 600 IN CNAME moose.mycorp.
com.
gc._msdcs.mycorp.com. 600 IN A 10.1.1.1
_gc._tcp.mycorp.com. 600 IN SRV 0 100 3268 moose.mycorp.com.
_gc._tcp.Default-First-Site-Name._sites.mycorp.com. 600 IN SRV 0 100 3268 moose.
mycorp.com.
_ldap._tcp.gc._msdcs.mycorp.com. 600 IN SRV 0 100 3268 moose.mycorp.com.
_ldap._tcp.Default-First-Site-Name._sites.gc._msdcs.mycorp.com. 600 IN SRV 0 100
3268
moose.mycorp.com.
_kerberos._tcp.dc._msdcs.mycorp.com. 600 IN SRV 0 100 88 moose.mycorp.com.
_kerberos._tcp.Default-First-Site-Name._sites.dc._msdcs.mycorp.com. 600 IN SRV 0
100
88 moose.mycorp.com.
_kerberos._tcp.mycorp.com. 600 IN SRV 0 100 88 moose.mycorp.com.
_kerberos._tcp.Default-First-Site-Name._sites.mycorp.com. 600 IN SRV 0 100 88
moose.
mycorp.com.
_kerberos._udp.mycorp.com. 600 IN SRV 0 100 88 moose.mycorp.com.
_kpasswd._tcp.mycorp.com. 600 IN SRV 0 100 464 moose.mycorp.com.
_kpasswd._udp.mycorp.com. 600 IN SRV 0 100 464 moose.mycorp.com.
_ldap._tcp.mycorp.com. 600 IN SRV 0 100 389 moose.mycorp.com.
_ldap._tcp.Default-First-Site-Name._sites.mycorp.com. 600 IN SRV 0 100 389 moose.
mycorp.com.
_ldap._tcp.pdc._msdcs.mycorp.com. 600 IN SRV 0 100 389 moose.mycorp.com.
_ldap._tcp.97526bc9-adf7-4ec8-a096-0dbb34a17052.domains._msdcs.mycorp.com. 600 IN
SRV
0 100 389 moose.mycorp.com.
_ldap._tcp.dc._msdcs.mycorp.com. 600 IN SRV 0 100 389 moose.mycorp.com.
```

```
_ldap._tcp.Default-First-Site-Name._sites.dc._msdcs.mycorp.com. 600 IN SRV 0 100
389
moose.mycorp.com.
```

Although it may look complicated, it isn't. Let's go through what these records actually mean, splitting the records up into sections for ease of understanding. To start with, the first record is for the domain itself:

```
mycorp.com. 600 IN A 10.1.1.1
```

Each DC attempts to register an A record for its IP address for the domain it is in similar to the preceding record.

Next, we have the following record:

```
ec4caf62-31b2-4773-bcce-7b1e31c04d25._msdcs.mycorp.com. 600 IN CNAME
   moose.mycorp.com.
```

This is an alias or canonical name (CNAME) record. It is contained under the _msdcs subdomain, which is used by domain controllers to intercommunicate. The record is comprised of the GUID for the server, which is an alias for the server itself. DCs use this record if they know the GUID of a server and want to determine its IP address.

> CNAME records are aliases to other records. A CNAME can point to either another A record or even another CNAME. The benefit of using a CNAME is in the scenario where you need to point to one host with multiple names.
>
> For example, if your web server is accessible at *www.mycorp.com* and you also provide FTP services from your web server, then the IP addresses for the two services will always be the same. Instead of having two A records, www and ftp, you could have one A record, www, and a CNAME, ftp, that was aliased to www.
>
> The advantage here is that if the IP address of your server changes, you must only update it in one place.

Next, we have this A record:

```
gc._msdcs.mycorp.com. 600 IN A 10.1.1.1
```

This is registered only if the domain controller is also a Global Catalog server. You can query *gc._msdcs.mycorp.com* with `nslookup` to obtain a list of all the Global Catalog servers in the forest.

The remaining resource records are of type SRV. The SRV record type was defined in RFC 2052, "A DNS RR for Specifying the Location of Services (DNS SRV)." The full text can be found at *http://www.ietf.org/rfc/rfc2052.txt*. Simply put, SRV records allow you to specify server(s) on your network that should be used for specific protocols. These records also allow you to remap the port numbers for individual protocols or the priority in which certain servers are used.

Even if you change the port numbers for Active Directory specific SRV records, Active Directory will not honor these new port numbers.

A few more Global Catalog specific records are shown next:

```
_gc._tcp.mycorp.com. 600 IN SRV 0 100 3268 moose.mycorp.com.
_gc._tcp.Default-First-Site-Name._sites.mycorp.com. 600 IN SRV 0 100 3268 moose.
mycorp.com.
_ldap._tcp.gc._msdcs.mycorp.com. 600 IN SRV 0 100 3268 moose.mycorp.com.
_ldap._tcp.Default-First-Site-Name._sites.gc._msdcs.mycorp.com. 600 IN SRV 0 100
3268
moose.mycorp.com.
```

One interesting thing to note about SRV records is the 7th field, which designates the port used to contact the service on that host. In every case above, 3268 is used, which corresponds to the Global Catalog port. You may have also noticed the entries that contain Default-First-Site-Name. Each Global Catalog server registers site-specific records so clients can find the optimal Global Catalog based on their site membership. See the upcoming sidebar "Site Coverage" for more information.

The next few SRV records are for Kerberos authentication (port 88) and the Kpasswd process (port 464), which allows users to change passwords via Kerberos:

```
_kerberos._tcp.dc._msdcs.mycorp.com. 600 IN SRV 0 100 88 moose.mycorp.com.
_kerberos._tcp.Default-First-Site-Name._sites.dc._msdcs.mycorp.com. 600 IN SRV 0
100
88 moose.mycorp.com.
_kerberos._tcp.mycorp.com. 600 IN SRV 0 100 88 moose.mycorp.com.
_kerberos._tcp.Default-First-Site-Name._sites.mycorp.com. 600 IN SRV 0 100 88
moose.
mycorp.com.
_kerberos._udp.mycorp.com. 600 IN SRV 0 100 88 moose.mycorp.com.
_kpasswd._tcp.mycorp.com. 600 IN SRV 0 100 464 moose.mycorp.com.
_kpasswd._udp.mycorp.com. 600 IN SRV 0 100 464 moose.mycorp.com.
```

Site Coverage

You can create sites in the Active Directory site topology that do not have domain controllers located within the site. In this situation, the domain controllers that have the best connections as defined by the site links will "cover" for that site. This functionality is known as *automatic site coverage*.

When a DC covers for a site, it will add site-specific SRV records so that it will advertise itself as a DC that can handle queries for clients in the site. To see a list of the sites that a particular DC is covering for, run the following NLTEST command and replace *dc01* with the name of the DC you want to determine coverage for:

```
c:\> nltest /dsgetsitecov /server:dc01
```

In some scenarios you may find it necessary to disable the automatic site coverage behavior by toggling a registry value on your domain controllers. To disable automatic site coverage, create a registry value `AutoSiteCoverage` of type `REG_DWORD` under `HKLM\System\CurrentControlSet\Services\NetLogon\Parameters` and set it to `0`. Branch office deployments in particular are a common scenario for this. For more information on this configuration option, see *http://technet2.microsoft.com/windowsserver/en/li brary/e1199fad-9fd7-4f0f-b053-10d2e98aa3db1033.mspx?mfr=true*.

Just as with the Global Catalog SRV records, there may be more of the site-specific Kerberos records for any additional sites the DC covers.

The rest of the SRV records are used to represent a domain controller for a particular domain and site. One record to note is the *_ldap._tcp.pdc._msdcs.mycorp.com.* entry, which is registered by the DC that is acting as the PDC Emulator for the domain. No other FSMO roles are registered in DNS.

```
_ldap._tcp.mycorp.com. 600 IN SRV 0 100 389 moose.mycorp.com.
_ldap._tcp.Default-First-Site-Name._sites.mycorp.com. 600 IN SRV 0 100 389 moose.
mycorp.com.
_ldap._tcp.pdc._msdcs.mycorp.com. 600 IN SRV 0 100 389 moose.mycorp.com.
_ldap._tcp.97526bc9-adf7-4ec8-a096-0dbb34a17052.domains._msdcs.mycorp.com. 600 IN
SRV
0 100 389 moose.mycorp.com.
_ldap._tcp.dc._msdcs.mycorp.com. 600 IN SRV 0 100 389 moose.mycorp.com.
_ldap._tcp.Default-First-Site-Name._sites.dc._msdcs.mycorp.com. 600 IN SRV 0 100 389
moose.mycorp.com.
```

Based on all these records, you can obtain a lot of information about an Active Directory environment by doing simple DNS queries. Some of the information you can retrieve includes:

- All Global Catalog servers in a forest or a particular site
- All Kerberos servers in a domain or a particular site
- All domain controllers in a domain or a particular site
- The PDC Emulator for a domain

Overriding SRV Record Registration

There may be times when you do not want domain controllers or global catalogs publishing some or all of their records outside of the site they are in, or maybe you do not want them publishing any records at all. For example, you may have domain controllers that should be dedicated to an application like Microsoft Exchange that runs in the site where the domain controllers are located, or you might have domain controllers in branch offices, or you may have domain controllers that are dedicated to just replicating Active Directory for backups.

You have two options for configuring the SRV record registration behavior:

- Use the `DnsAvoidRegisterRecords` registry entry. For more details on configuring this option, see Microsoft KB article 306602 at *http://support.microsoft.com/kb/ 306602.*
- Use NetLogon system settings in the administrative templates of the group policy applied to domain controllers. For more details on configuring this option, see "DNS Support for Active Directory Tools and Settings" at *http://technet2.microsoft .com/windowsserver/en/library/4d8388e6-6ba0-4f08-b1d9-525bf949fa761033 .mspx?mfr=true.*

Regardless of which mechanism you choose, both give you the option of specifying which records should and shouldn't be registered. When determining which route to take, be sure to consider the manageability aspect in the event you need to change the settings later.

Delegation Options

Now that we've covered what Active Directory uses DNS for, we will review some of the options for setting up who is authoritative for the Active Directory-related zones. Ultimately, the decision boils down to whether you want to use your existing DNS servers or different servers, such as the domain controllers, to be authoritative for the zones. There are many factors that can affect this decision, including:

- Political turf battles between the AD and DNS teams
- Initial setup and configuration of the zones
- Support and maintenance of the zones
- Integration issues with existing administration software and practices

We will look at each of these factors as they apply to delegating the AD zones. Other slight variations of these options do exist, but we will discuss only the basic cases.

Not Delegating the AD DNS Zones

The first impulse of any cost-conscious organization should be to determine whether their existing DNS servers can be authoritative for the AD zones. That could entail manually populating all the necessary resource records required by each DC if the current DNS implementation doesn't support dynamic updates. While this sounds fairly trivial at first glance, it becomes decidedly less trivial once you begin to explore the requirements.

Political factors

By utilizing the existing DNS servers for the AD DNS zones, the Active Directory administrators will likely not have the same level of control as they would if the zones were delegated and managed by them. Although it does limit the scope of control for a crucial service used by Active Directory, some AD administrators may find it a blessing!

Initial setup and configuration

The initial population of the AD resource records can be burdensome depending on how you manage your resource records and how easy it will be for you to inject new ones. For example, domain controllers try to register their resource records via DDNS on a periodic basis. Many organizations do not allow just any client to make DDNS updates due to the potential security risks. For that reason, you'll need to configure your existing DNS servers to allow the domain controllers to perform DDNS updates. DNS administrators will need to configure DDNS to only allow domain controllers to update certain zones in order to mitigate security risks of allowing domain controllers to update any DNS record in the server. This should not typically be a problem, but depending on how paranoid the DNS administrators are, it could be a point of contention.

Support and maintenance

Assuming the existing DNS servers are stable and well supported (as they tend to be in most organizations), name resolution issues should not be a problem for domain controllers or other clients that are attempting to locate a DC via DNS.

Ongoing maintenance of the DC resource records can be an issue, as pointed out previously. Each time you promote a new DC in the forest, you'll need to make sure it is allowed to register all of its records via DDNS. The registration of these records could be done manually, but due to the dynamic nature of the AD resource records, they would have to be updated on a very frequent basis (potentially multiple times a day). In addition, promoting one DC could cause other DCs to update the records they need registered in DNS as well.

Yet another option is to programmatically retrieve the *netlogon.dns* file from each domain controller on a periodic basis and perform the DDNS updates from a script. In large environments, the manual solution will probably not scale, and either DDNS or a programmatic solution will need to be explored.

Integration issues

When Windows 2000 Active Directory was first released in 1999, this was more of a problem than it is today, but older versions of DNS server or administration software may not support SRV records or underscores in zone or record names (e.g., *_msdcs .mycorp.com*). Upgrading to the latest versions of your DNS server platform should be a priority in this case.

Figure 6-1 shows how the client request process is straightforward when the AD DNS zones are not delegated. Clients point at the same DNS servers they always have.

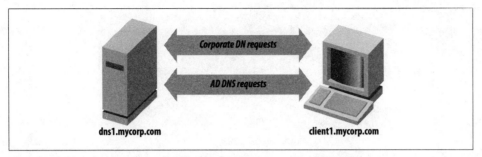

Figure 6-1. Client request flow when the AD DNS zones are not delegated

Delegating the AD DNS Zones

While at first glance it may seem pretty straightforward to support AD DNS zones in your existing DNS infrastructure, it can cause difficulties depending on your environment. Perhaps the most straightforward option is simply to delegate the DNS namespace(s) Active Directory will use to your domain controllers and allow them to host the DNS zones. If you use AD-integrated DNS zones, the maintenance becomes even easier. After you've done the initial creation of the zones by promoting a domain controller and adding the DNS service, the records are stored in Active Directory and distributed to the other domain controllers via replication.

Political factors

Frequently organizations will have a central DNS team that manages and supports name resolution. If you make the decision to delegate the AD DNS zones to domain controllers, for example, a significant part of name resolution for your clients will not be done on the existing corporate servers any more. This can make the DNS administrators uncomfortable, and rightly so. Note that Active Directory does allow you to delegate the management of records in an Active Directory integrated DNS zone to other administrators very easily.

Initial setup and configuration

The initial setup to delegate the AD DNS zones is straightforward. An NS record and any necessary glue records—for example, an A record for the server to which you're delegating—need to exist on the parent zone pointing to the servers that will be authoritative for the zones. The rest of the configuration must be done on the servers that are going to support the AD DNS zones. If those servers are one or more domain controllers running Active Directory integrated DNS, you will only need to add the DNS service and create the zone(s) on those servers.

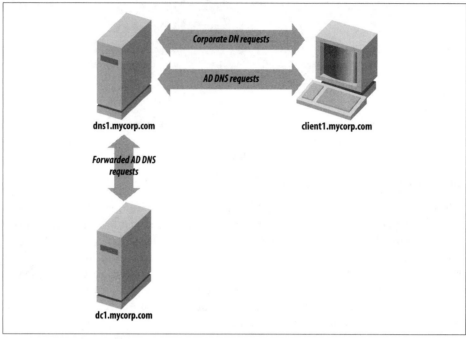

Figure 6-2. Client request flow when delegating the AD DNS zones

Support and maintenance

Ongoing support and maintenance of the AD DNS zones is very minimal, especially if you are using AD-integrated zones. In fact, since the domain controllers can use DDNS to update each other, this is one of the primary benefits of using this method.

Integration issues

Unless you already run Windows DNS Server, it is unlikely you'll be able to manage the AD DNS zones in the same manner as your existing DNS infrastructure. Figure 6-2 illustrates how, by delegating the AD DNS zones, you can still have clients point to the same DNS servers they do today. A variation of this approach would be to point the clients at the AD DNS servers and configure forwarding as described in the next section.

DNS for Standalone AD

Another scenario that is worth mentioning is creating a standalone Active Directory environment. By standalone, we mean an environment that can be set up without requiring your DNS administrators to either create or delegate zones on the corporate DNS servers. This is often needed when setting up lab or test forests, which may be short-lived. Figure 6-3 shows that the resolver for the clients must be pointed to the

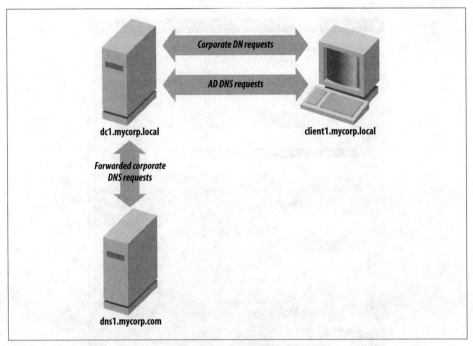

Figure 6-3. Client request flow in a standalone AD environment

AD DNS servers in this scenario or they will not be able to locate any domain controllers for the forest.

To set up a standalone environment, you simply need to install the DNS service on one or more domain controllers in the forest, add the DNS zones for the AD domains (for example, *mycorp.local*), and then configure the DNS server to forward unresolved queries to one or more of your existing corporate DNS servers. Figure 6-4 shows the screen from the DNS MMC snap-in for Windows Server 2003 that allows you to configure forwarders. Finally, you need to configure any clients of the *mycorp.local* forest to point their primary DNS resolver at the IP address of *dc1.mycorp.local*. When client1 makes a DNS request, it would first be sent to *dc1.mycorp.local*. If dc1 can resolve, it will return a response; if not, it will forward the query to *dns1.mycorp.com*. *Dns1.mycorp.com* will reply with an answer to dc1, who will then send the reply to client1. Windows Server 2003 introduced a much more powerful forwarding infrastructure called conditional forwarding. For more information about this, see the sidebar "Conditional Forwarding."

The great thing about this configuration is that it requires nothing to be set up on the existing DNS servers. Since you will need to modify the DNS resolvers that clients point to, you may want to look at using a Group Policy Object (GPO). In Windows Server 2003, you can configure client DNS settings through GPOs for Windows Server 2003 servers and Windows XP workstations. The new settings allow you to control things

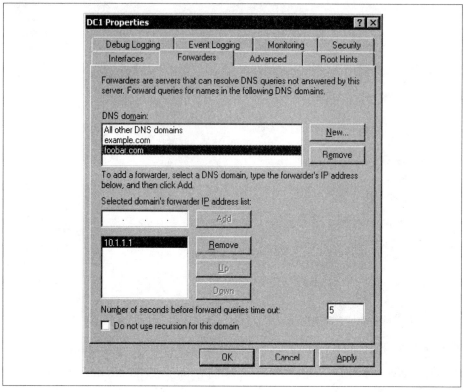

Figure 6-4. Forwarders configuration screen in the Windows Server 2003 DNS MMC snap-in

such as client DNS suffix, DNS resolvers, and DDNS behavior. While the functionality to configure DNS settings via group policy is available, it is generally advisable to rely on your DHCP infrastructure instead.

> In this scenario, if the clients do not point at *dc1.mycorp.local* as their first resolver, they will never be able to contact the *mycorp.local* forest. The reason is that the corporate name servers do not know about the *mycorp.local* namespace since it was not delegated.

Active Directory Integrated DNS

If you've decided to host your AD DNS zones on your domain controllers, you should strongly consider using AD-integrated zones. This section will explain some of the benefits of using AD-integrated DNS versus standard primary zones.

Conditional Forwarding

Conditional forwarding is a new feature available in Windows Server 2003 that gives administrators much more flexibility in how forwarding is handled than was available under Windows 2000. Figure 6-4 shows the forwarders configuration screen in the Windows Server 2003 DNS MMC snap-in. It allows you to set up one or more IP addresses to forward all requests that cannot be handled by the local DNS server. As you can see, we configured forwarding based on the domain name being queried:

- If the query is for *foobar.com*, forward to 10.1.1.1.
- If the query is for *example.com*, forward to 10.1.2.1.
- If the query is for any other zone, forward to 10.1.3.1.

Conditional forwarding allows you to create a more efficient resolution topology, particularly for corporate networks using disjointed namespaces, by sending queries directly to servers responsible for the individual zones instead of using only recursive queries to the Internet.

Windows Server 2008 greatly improves upon the conditional forwarders functionality by supporting the replication of conditional forwarder definitions via Active Directory. With Windows Server 2003, you need to configure conditional forwarders on every DNS server individually, which, in a large environment, is a tedious task that you will likely need to automate with a script.

The conditional forwarders configuration is now prominently available in the Windows Server 2008 DNS MMC console at the same level as the forward and reverse lookup zones folders exist. All of the conditional forwarders defined on the DNS server are shown here, and you can also create new conditional forwarders via the right-click context menu. Figure 6-5 shows the new conditional forwarder dialog. Notice the Active Directory replication scope option at the bottom of the screen.

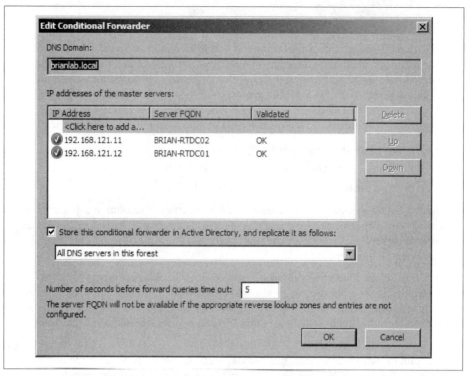

Figure 6-5. Managing a conditional forwarder in Windows Server 2008

In the normal world of DNS, you have two types of name servers: primary and secondary (a.k.a. slaves). The primary name server for a zone holds the data for the zone in a file on the host and reads the entries from there. Each zone typically has only one primary. A secondary gets the contents of its zone from the primary that is authoritative for the zone. Each primary name server can have multiple secondary name servers. When a secondary starts up, it contacts its primary and requests a copy of the relevant zone via zone transfer. The contents of the secondary file are then dynamically updated over time according to a set scheme. This is normally a periodic update or triggered automatically by a message from the primary stating that it has received an update. This is a very simplified picture, as each name server can host multiple zones, allowing each server to have a primary role for some zones and a secondary for others.

Each type of server can resolve name queries that come in for the zones that it hosts. However, if a change must be made to the underlying contents of the DNS file, it has to be made on the primary name server for that zone. Secondary name servers cannot accept updates.[*]

---

[*] This isn't strictly true. Although secondary servers cannot process updates, they can and do forward updates that they receive to the primary name server.

Another option available with Active Directory and Windows DNS server is to integrate your DNS data into Active Directory. Effectively, this means that you can store the contents of the zone file in Active Directory as a hierarchical structure. Integrating DNS into Active Directory means that the DNS structure is replicated among all DCs of a domain; each DC holds a writeable copy of the DNS data. The DNS objects stored in Active Directory could be updated on any DC via LDAP operations or through DDNS against DCs that are acting as DNS servers. This effectively makes the entire set of DCs act like primary name servers, where each DC can write to the zone and issue author-itative answers for the zone. This is a far cry from the standard model of one primary name server and one or more secondary name servers, which has the obvious downside of a single point of failure for updates to DNS.

There is a possible issue when using integrated DNS with Windows 2000 domain con-trollers called the DNS "island" issue. Active Directory requires proper DNS resolution to replicate changes, and when using integrated DNS, the domain controllers replicate DNS changes through Active Directory replication. This is the classic chicken-and-egg problem; it can be avoided with proper configuration. The issue occurs when a forest root domain controller configured as a name server points at itself for DNS resolution. If the DC changes its IP address, the DNS records will successfully be updated locally. However, unless the other DCs point at that same DC for their DNS resolution, they cannot resolve the DC's IP address, so replication fails and no other DC gets the IP address change. The forest root domain controller has effectively been segregated from the rest of the forest and becomes its own replication island. To avoid this issue, the forest root domain controllers that are name servers should be configured to point at root servers other than themselves.

Replication Impact

While AD-integrated DNS has many advantages, the one potential drawback is how DNS data gets replicated in Active Directory. Under Windows 2000, AD-integrated zones are stored in the System container for a domain. That means that every domain controller in that domain will replicate that zone data regardless of whether the domain controller is a DNS server or not. For domain controllers that are not DNS servers, there is no benefit to replicating the data. Fortunately, there is a better alternative in Windows Server 2003, using application partitions as described in the next section.

Background Zone Loading

A new feature in Windows Server 2008 DNS is background loading of DNS zones. Previous to Windows Server 2008, the DNS server service would not become available until it completed loading all of the zones it hosted from Active Directory. On a DNS server with large zones, loading all of the zones can take quite some time (hours in some cases). With background loading, the DNS server service no longer waits until every zone is loaded but instead loads them in the background and makes the zones available for query/update as they complete the loading process.

 This background loading behavior is only applicable to zones stored in Active Directory. Zones stored on the file system are still loaded serially prior to the service being available to service requests.

Using Application Partitions for DNS

Application partitions, as described in Chapter 3, are user-defined partitions that have a customized replication scope. Domain controllers that are configured to host replicas of an application partition will be the only servers that replicate the data contained within the partition. One of the benefits of application partitions is that they are not limited by domain boundaries. You can configure domain controllers in completely different domains to replicate an application partition, so long as they are in the same forest. It is for these reasons that application partitions make a lot of sense for storing AD-integrated DNS zones. No longer do you have to store DNS data within the domain context and replicate to every domain controller in the domain, even if only a handful are DNS servers. With application partitions, you can configure Active Directory to replicate only the DNS data between the domain controllers running the DNS service within a domain or forest.

When installing a new Windows Server 2003 Active Directory forest, the default DNS application partitions are created automatically. If you are upgrading from Windows 2000, you can manually create them by using the DNS MMC snap-in or the *dnscmd.exe* utility. There is one default application partition for each domain and forest. When configuring an AD-integrated zone in a Windows Server 2003 forest, you have several options for storing the DNS data. These options are listed in Table 6-2.

Table 6-2. Active Directory Integrated DNS zone storage options

Distinguished name	Replication scope
cn=System,*DomainDN* Example: cn=System,dc=amer,dc=mycorp,dc=com	To all domain controllers in the domain. This is the only storage method available under Windows 2000.
dc=DomainDnsZones, *DomainDN* Example: dc=DomainDnsZones,dc=amer, dc=my-corp,dc=com	To domain controllers in the domain that are also DNS servers.
dc=ForestDnsZones, *ForestDN* Example: dc=ForestDnsZones,dc=mycorp,dc=com	To domain controllers in the forest that are also DNS servers.
AppPartitionDN Example: dc=dnsdata,dc=mycorp,dc=com	To domain controllers that have been configured to replicate the application partition.

The final option in Table 6-2 highlights that you can define custom application partitions outside of the default DomainDnsZones and ForestDnsZones partitions. Some organizations elect to define additional application partitions to control the replication scope of other DNS zones. For example, your domain controllers might be hosting DNS zones specific to a certain building or campus, so, you might define an application partition called CampusDnsZones just to host these zones. You would, in turn, configure only the domain controllers at that campus to host this application partition, thereby limiting the replication scope of those zones.

Aging and Scavenging

One of the complexities of running a DNS infrastructure where clients can register their own records is that over time records will build up in your zones for clients that no longer exist, or perhaps have a new name. If you only have a small number of machines on your network, you could likely manage these records yourself through the MMC. On the other hand, if you have hundreds or even hundreds of thousands of machines participating in a single DNS zone, chances are you won't be able to manage the lifecycle of these records on your own.

Fortunately, since Windows 2000, Microsoft DNS has included a feature called scavenging. Scavenging is a background process that you configure on a per-DNS-server basis to scan all of the records in a zone and remove the records that have not been refreshed in a certain time period. Clients that register themselves with dynamic DNS will automatically refresh their DNS registrations periodically. Windows DNS will store this timestamp as an attribute of the DNS record. By default, Microsoft DNS clients update and refresh their DNS registrations once every 24 hours.

One of the scavenging configuration options is the "no-refresh interval," which defines how often the DNS server will accept the DNS registration refresh and update the DNS record. This functionality limits the amount of unnecessary replication for DNS record timestamp updates. For records that are manually created, the refresh timestamp is set to zero, which excludes the record from scavenging. You can also edit dynamically registered records to exclude them from scavenging.

Configuring Scavenging

Configuration of scavenging is a two step process:

1. Enable scavenging for a specific DNS zone and define the refresh intervals for that zone (see Figure 6-6).

 If you right-click on the DNS server node in the DNS MMC, there is an option "Set Aging/Scavenging for All Zones..." that will allow you to configure these two values once for all of the DNS zones hosted on that particular DNS server.

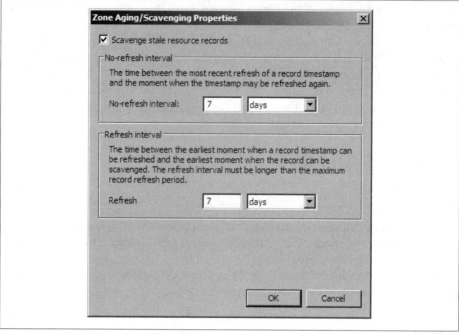

Figure 6-6. DNS zone scavenging settings

2. Enable scavenging on a DNS server and define how often the scavenging process runs.

Setting zone-specific options

The options to enable scavenging for a particular zone are accessible via the Aging button on the properties of the zone. As shown in the next section, "Enabling scavenging on the DNS server," there are two configuration items of interest:

No-refresh interval
    This is how often the DNS server will propagate a timestamp refresh from the client to the directory or filesystem. The default value is 7 days and is generally acceptable. The purpose of this setting is to reduce the amount of unnecessary replication or zone transfer activity that would be solely necessary for a timestamp update.

Refresh interval
    This is how long the DNS server must wait following a refresh for a record to be eligible for scavenging. The default value here is again 7 days. In practical terms, if you use the default values here, and a client refreshes its record on the 7th day of the month and then goes offline, the DNS server will scavenge the record no earlier than the 14th day of the month.

Enabling scavenging on the DNS server

The actual scavenging process must be enabled and configured on one or more DNS servers for scavenging to occur. It is a common misconception that the only scavenging configuration necessary is on the DNS zone itself.

The DNS server scavenging settings are accessible by accessing the properties of the DNS server in the DNS MMC, and accessing the advanced tab as shown in Figure 6-7. You will need to enable the scavenging process and define an interval for how often it runs. The default of 7 days is often acceptable; however, you can adjust it to run as frequently as every hour. Be careful that you don't set it to run so often that the DNS server is constantly running the scavenging process as this would be counterproductive.

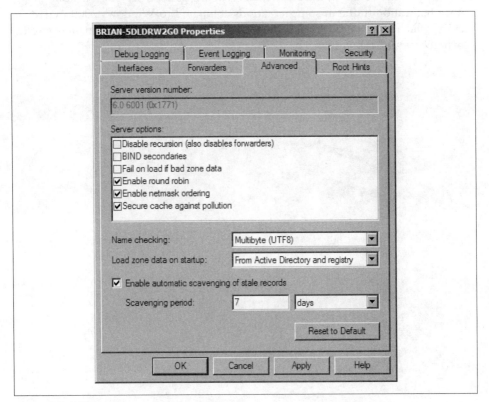

Figure 6-7. DNS server scavenging configuration

Summary

Active Directory relies heavily on DNS. In fact, Microsoft has shifted completely away from WINS for name resolution within the NOS in favor of standards-based DNS. The DC-locator process is a core DNS-based function used within Active Directory to help domain controllers and clients locate domain controllers that have certain properties, such as residing in a particular site or being a Global Catalog server or PDC emulator. Deciding how to manage the AD DNS zones can be a difficult decision, with each option having its own advantages and disadvantages. If you delegate the zones to domain controllers, AD-integrated zones can save a lot of time in maintenance and upkeep. In Windows Server 2003, you can use application partitions to replicate AD-integrated zones only to the domain controllers that are acting as DNS servers. This can greatly reduce replication traffic in some situations compared to Windows 2000 Active Directory, which replicated DNS data to every domain controller in a domain regardless of whether it was a DNS server.

## CHAPTER 7

Read-Only Domain Controllers

One of the most significant Active Directory features introduced in Windows Server 2008 was the *Read-Only Domain Controller* (RODC). Deploying domain controllers into untrusted locations has always been a substantial security risk for Active Directory deployments. The risk of a domain controller becoming physically compromised and having password hashes for that domain stolen or the risk of a database (*ntds.dit*) being modified offline and placed back on the network are both important risks to measure. The RODC brings the ability to mitigate both of these risks.

By default, RODCs do not store any passwords locally in their database. If a user authenticates to an RODC, the RODC will need to contact a writeable domain controller (sometimes called an *RWDC*) upstream in order to validate that user's password. This, of course, also applies to other objects with passwords, such as computer and trust accounts. Through the use of *Password Replication Policies*, you can define what passwords are allowed to be cached locally on an RODC. You can also examine a real-time view of what passwords are currently cached on an RODC.

In order to ensure that an RODC cannot impact the integrity of an Active Directory forest, all replication to RODCs is one way. This means that if someone manages to make a change, Active Directory will not replicate that change to other Domain Controllers. Figure 7-1 shows the replication paths in a network with RODCs deployed.

Generally speaking, there are a couple of scenarios where we see RODCs being deployed. The first scenario is in the branch office. Branch offices are typically smaller facilities that are connected by a WAN link to a datacenter or other central site. These WAN links vary greatly in speed and reliability. The second key characteristic of the branch office is the inability for the physical security of a domain controller to be guaranteed. Often times server rooms in branch offices are merely closets or other repurposed spaces that have limited provisions for managing who has access to the space. The majority of our discussion about RODCs in this book will be focused on the branch office.

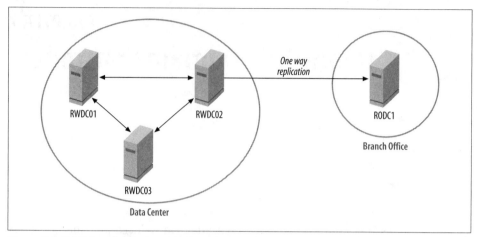

Figure 7-1. RODC replication

The second scenario is the concept of the RODC in the DMZ. The DMZ, or demilitarized zone, is a section of a network that is considered untrusted relative to the rest of the network. Many organizations place their servers that are Internet-facing in a DMZ network. In order for these servers to be joined to the domain, numerous ports must be opened through the firewall to the point that an analogy of comparing the firewall to Swiss cheese is often accurately used. Some organizations may elect to deploy RODCs into their DMZ to serve as domain controllers for the servers alongside them in the DMZ network.

As you read this section, keep in mind the guiding design principle behind the RODC. That principle is the core assumption that the RODC is compromised by default. If you're wondering why a feature of the RODC behaves in a certain way, take a moment to consider the scenario where the RODC is compromised.

Prerequisites

There are a few major prerequisites to deploying RODCs in to your Active Directory that you should take in to consideration before proceeding any further. The first is that your forest at a minimum be at the Windows Server 2003 forest-functional level. Next, you'll need to have a writeable Windows Server 2008 domain controller in a site that your RODC is connected to, as determined by the Active Directory site-link topology.

Consider Figure 7-2. If you have Bridge All Site Links enabled, RODCs can be more than one hop away from a Windows Server 2008 RWDC, and thus the RODC in *Site A* will be able to communicate with the Windows Server 2008 RWDC in *Site C*. If, however, you do not have bridge all site links enabled, you will either need to create a site-link bridge that includes site links *A - B* and *B - C*, or you will need to deploy a Windows Server 2008 RWDC in *Site B*.

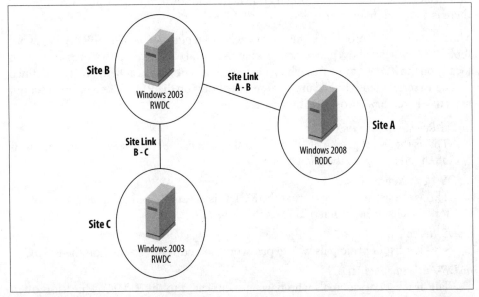

Figure 7-2. Sample RODC deployment topology

In addition to these Active Directory requirements, you should investigate deploying the RODC compatibility pack to your clients. This package is available for download (and described in) Microsoft Knowledge Base article 944043 at *http://support.microsoft .com/kb/944043*. There are a number of compatibility issues and bugs with Windows XP and Windows Server 2003 clients and domain controllers that you are likely to encounter, and this package solves many of them. We will make reference to situations where this package may be required throughout this chapter when appropriate.

> Throughout this chapter we will often reference situations where an RODC can specially request replication of a specific object. This functionality is known as *ReplicateSingleObject* or *RSO*. The replicate-single-object operation is initiated via a modification to the `replicateSingleOb ject` operational attribute of the `RootDSE` LDAP entry. For more information on this attribute, reference *http://msdn.microsoft.com/en-us/li brary/cc200527.aspx*.

Password Replication Policies

As we discussed briefly, RODCs don't cache passwords by default. This means that if an attacker were to get a copy of the Active Directory database from an RODC, they would not be able to compromise any passwords since there are none stored there. The downside of not storing any passwords is that the RODC will need to make a call to an RWDC, usually over the WAN, to authenticate a client. The value of the RODC diminishes when the WAN is down and clients cannot be authenticated even though there is a local domain controller.

The solution to this problem is the use of *password replication policies* (PRPs). Password replication policies allow you to define what user (and computer) passwords are cached locally on the RODC, as well as which passwords can never be cached. PRPs are defined through a series of four linked multivalued attributes on the RODC's computer account in Active Directory. Those attributes are:

msDS-RevealOnDemandGroup
> This is the list of principals that the RODC can cache the password for. This list is often referred to as the *allowed* list.

msDS-NeverRevealGroup
> This is the list of principals that the RODC is *never* allowed to cache the password for. This list is often referred to as the *denied* list.

msDS-RevealedList
> This is a list of principals whose passwords are currently cached on the RODC.

msDS-AuthenticatedAtDC
> This is a list of principals who have authenticated to the RODC. This list is often referred to as the *Auth-2* list.

In addition to these attributes, there are two new built-in groups that are added to Active Directory when you introduce the first RODC in the domain. These are the *Allowed RODC Password Replication Group* and the *Denied RODC Password Replication Group*. The allowed group is added to the `msDS-RevealOnDemandGroup` attribute by default, and the denied group is added to the `msDS-NeverRevealGroup` attribute by default. The allowed group has no members by default; however, the denied group has a number of members by default:

- Cert Publishers
- Domain Admins
- Enterprise Admins
- Enterprise Domain Controllers
- Enterprise Read-Only Domain Controllers
- Schema Admins
- Krbtgt account

In addition to these groups and accounts, there are a few groups that are added to the `msDS-NeverRevealGroup` attribute by default:

- Account Operators
- Administrators
- Backup Operators

- Denied RODC Password Replication Group
- Server Operators

In general, all of these groups generally contain highly trusted user accounts, so you would not want to risk compromising those passwords by caching them on an RODC. Thus we don't recommend that you remove these groups from the default denied replication group, or the msDS-NeverRevealGroup attribute.

In order for an RODC to issue a Kerberos service ticket without communicating with a writeable domain controller, the RODC will need to have the passwords cached locally for both the user account and the computer account involved. This is important to remember as you will need to plan for both user and computer account password caching. In addition to your users, you need to take into consideration any service accounts that are being used on servers or other machines at the site the RODC is located at.

As you plan your RODC deployment, you'll need to think carefully about how you setup your password replication policies. Depending on the route you take, you may need to invest in updating your user provisioning process to keep the password replication policies updated. There are three strategies we expect most organizations will take when planning their password replication policies:

No caching of passwords
> In this scenario, RODCs will not cache any passwords and will instead simply serve as read-only directories that are proxies in the authentication process. If you are considering deploying an RODC in the DMZ scenario, this is likely the route you will take when defining password replication policies for those RODCs.

Caching of almost all passwords
> If you are looking to reduce management overhead and provide the most tolerance for WAN failures, this is likely the scenario for your password replication policies. If you have physical security concerns about an RODC, we do not recommend that you opt for this strategy.

Limited caching of passwords
> In this scenario, you will define on a per-RODC basis which passwords can be cached by the RODC. This list will generally reflect the list of users and computers that are located at the site the RODC is servicing. You will need to devise a process to manage the lists for each of your RODCs in this situation. We recommend that you integrate this process with your user-provisioning process. In addition to your user-provisioning process, you will need to link in to a mechanism that manages your computer accounts.

Managing the Password Replication Policy

The Active Directory Users and Computers (ADUC) tool includes a new property page for managing an RODC's PRP, as well as for inspecting the revealed and authenticated

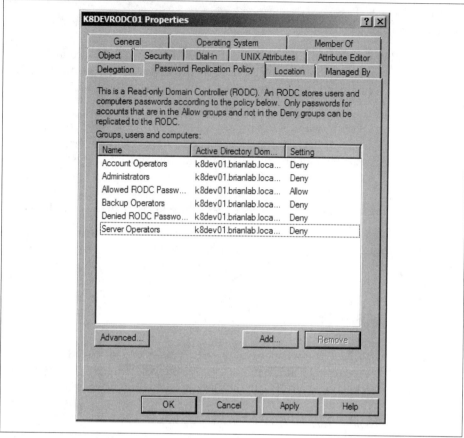

Figure 7-3. Password replication policy tab

to lists. Figure 7-3 shows the default settings for a new RODC. The list shown here is accessible via right-clicking the domain controller's computer account in ADUC and selecting Properties.

You can add users, groups, and computers to the list here by clicking Add. When you click Add, ADUC will prompt you to allow or deny replication for the selection as shown in Figure 7-4.

Clicking the Advanced button yields a dialog that allows you to inspect the msDS-RevealedList and msDS-AuthenticatedAtDC attributes. The drop-down list at the top of Figure 7-5 allows you to toggle between which attributes you want to display. *Accounts whose passwords are stored on this Read-only Domain Controller* displays the msDS-RevealedList attribute, and *Accounts that have been authenticated to this Read-only Domain Controller* displays the msDS-AuthenticatedAtDC attribute. If you click the Export button at the bottom of the dialog shown in Figure 7-5, you can save a CSV (comma-separated value) listing of the data shown.

Figure 7-4. Adding to the password replication policy lists

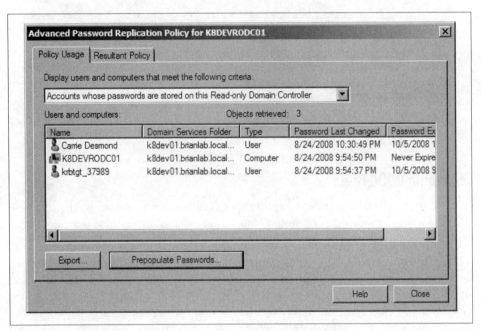

Figure 7-5. Viewing the revealed list

The Advanced dialog shown in Figure 7-5 also allows you to determine what accounts can have their passwords cached by an RODC. This is a useful feature when you're troubleshooting an account whose password caching behavior is unexpected. Figure 7-6 shows the Resultant Policy tab for a number of users.

There are a few different resultant policy settings that can be displayed for an account. An account that shows *Allow* is defined on the msDS-RevealOnDemandGroup list. An account that shows *Deny (explicit)* is defined on the msDS-NeverRevealGroup list. Finally, an account showing *Deny (implicit)* is not defined on either list and thus is not allowed to cache its password since the default behavior for an RODC is not to cache a given

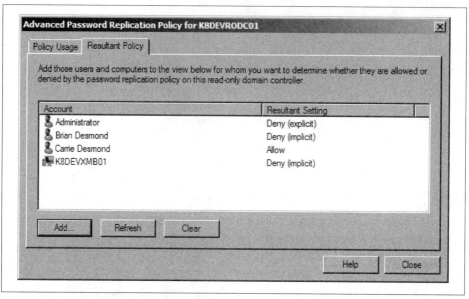

Figure 7-6. Resultant password replication policy

account's password. Notice that as shown in Figure 7-6, you can calculate resultant policy for both users and computers.

Managing RODC Theft

In the event an RODC is stolen or, more specifically, the drives holding the database are physically compromised or stolen, you should as a matter of best practice immediately reset the passwords that were cached on that RODC.

The ADUC user interface for performing this task is accessed by deleting the RODC's computer account from the Domain Controllers OU. If you attempt to delete the computer account, you'll be presented with the dialog shown in Figure 7-7. From this dialog, you can elect to reset the passwords for users, computers, or both. While the dialog only resets user passwords by default, keep in mind that computers are a special type of user account and they have passwords, too. An attacker could use a computer's account and password to authenticate to your domain.

While it's not required, we *highly* recommend that you export a CSV of the affected accounts so that you can follow up with your service desk and other support teams. Resetting user and computer passwords will undoubtedly cause substantial pain, so this is a scenario you should plan for as you plan your overall RODC deployment.

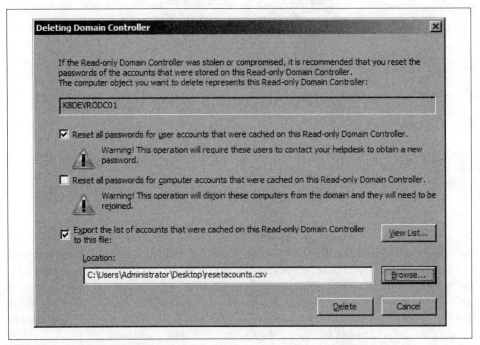

Figure 7-7. Deleting an RODC computer account

Be certain that you heed the warnings in Figure 7-7. Not resetting passwords is a security risk, so we don't recommend that you elect not to reset passwords in the name of convenience. We do, however, recommend that you pause to consider the implications of resetting all of the cached user passwords in a site. This will cause service desk calls for users who can't log in, and in the case of service account, services that can't start.

When you reset computer passwords, the computers will be disjoined from the domain. You will need to physically visit each workstation or script a solution using tools like netdom or nltest if you have the local administrator credentials for each machine available centrally.

The Client Logon Process

So far we've discussed the caching of passwords on RODCs and how to control the caching, but we have not looked at how the RODC actually gets passwords from a writeable domain controller and caches them locally. In this section we'll take a look not only at how passwords get cached locally, but also at the overall flow of communications between domain controllers and clients when an RODC is involved.

One key difference between RODCs and their writeable counterparts that you should keep in mind throughout this section (and that we will frequently point out) is that

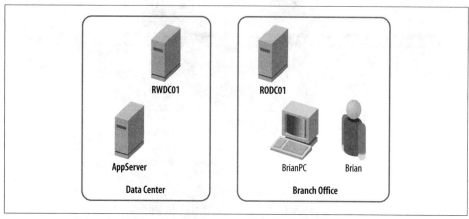

Figure 7-8. Sample network topology

each RODC has its own *krbtgt* account. The krbtgt accounts are the credentials that are used by domain controllers to encrypt Kerberos messages, and if you have access to these credentials, you have an endless degree of power over the forest. Consequently, each RODC maintains a separate *krbtgt* account that is named in the format *krbtgt_<number>*, where <number> is a unique number. The RODC stores only the password for its personal *krbtgt* account locally. Writeable domain controllers, however, store the passwords for each *krbtgt* account in their databases.

In order to determine what *krbtgt* account is associated with a given RODC, you can inspect the `msDS-KrbTgtLink` attribute on an RODC's computer account, or the `msDS-krbTgtLinkBL` attribute on the *krbtgt* account.

Let's consider the situation depicted in Figure 7-8 as our baseline for the rest of this discussion. Figure 7-8 has four players:

RWDC01
> This is our writeable domain controller in the datacenter.

RODC01
> This is our read-only domain controller in the branch office.

User Brian
> This is our user who will be logging on and accessing services.

Machine BrianPC
> This is the workstation for user Brian.

Let's assume that the first step is for our machine, *BrianPC*, to authenticate to the domain. The following are the steps that will take place:

1. First, *BrianPC* will contact *RODC01* and provide a Kerberos authentication service request (a `KRB_AS_REQ` packet).

2. When *RODC01* receives the `KRB_AS_REQ`, it will check its local database to see if it already has *BrianPC's* password cached locally. For this example, we'll assume that this is, in fact, not the case.

3. Since *RODC01* does not have the password cached locally, it must contact *RWDC01* and provide the `KRB_AS_REQ` it received.

4. *RWDC01* will generate a `KRB_AS_REP` (a Kerberos authentication service reply) and forward it back to *RODC01*.

5. *RODC01* will in turn provide this reply to *BrianPC*, completing the authentication request. *RWDC01* will also update *RODC01's* Auth-2 list (`msDS-Authenticate dAtDC`) to include *BrianPC* in that list.

   At this point, *BrianPC* has a valid Kerberos ticket-granting ticket (TGT) signed with the domain *krbtgt* account. Following step five, *RODC01* will initiate two additional steps to attempt to cache the password locally:

6. *RODC01* will submit a request to *RWDC01* to have *BrianPC's* credentials replicated to *RODC01*.

7. *RWDC01* will verify that the password replication policy permits *RODC01* to cache *BrianPC's* password and replicate the password to *RODC01*. *RWDC01* will also update *RODC01's* revealed list (`msDS-RevealedList`) to include *BrianPC*.

 You may be wondering why in step 7 *RWDC01* checks the password replication policy rather than assuming *RODC01* can cache the password since it requested it. The reason here is that we must assume that *RODC01* has been compromised and thus as part of that incident perhaps the local copy of the password replication policy on *RODC01* has been modified and additional accounts have been surreptitiously added to the PRP allowed list.

Let's now look at the process of user *Brian* logging in to his machine. We'll of course assume that the preceding seven steps have completed successfully. The following are the steps taken when Brian attempts to log in to his machine:

1. Brian presents his credentials to *BrianPC*, and *BrianPC* sends a `KRB_AS_REQ` to *RODC01* for user *Brian*.

2. When *RODC01* receives the `KRB_AS_REQ`, it will check its local database to see if it already has *Brian's* password cached locally. For this example, we'll assume that this is, in fact, not the case.

3. Since *RODC01* does not have the password cached locally, it must contact *RWDC01* and provide the `KRB_AS_REQ` it received.

4. *RWDC01* will generate a `KRB_AS_REP` and forward it back to *RODC01*.

5. *RODC01* will in turn provide this reply to *BrianPC*, completing the authentication request for user *Brian*. *RWDC01* will also update *RODC01's* Auth-2 list (msDS-AuthenticatedAtDC) to include user *Brian* in that list.

At this point, user *Brian* has a valid Kerberos ticket-granting ticket (TGT) signed with the domain *krbtgt* account. Following step five, *RODC01* will initiate steps six and seven from above, except this time *RODC01* will attempt to cache user *Brian's* password locally.

It is very important to realize, however, that the logon process for user *Brian* is not yet complete! Before user *Brian* can use his workstation, he must obtain a Kerberos service ticket (*TGS*) for *BrianPC*. Continuing with our example, when *BrianPC* sends a TGS to *RODC01* for user *Brian*, *RODC01* will be unable to decrypt user *Brian's* TGT because Brian's TGT was encrypted with the domain *krbtgt* account whose password is *never* cached on an RODC. The following steps show the process for *Brian* to obtain a TGS fo *BrianPC*:

1. *BrianPC* sends a KRB_TGS_REQ to *RODC01* for user *Brian* to access *BrianPC*. The KRB_TGS_REQ includes *Brian's* TGT from the previous example.

2. *RODC01* is unable to decrypt the TGT included in the TGS request since it is encrypted with the domain *krbtgt* account.

3. *RODC01* transmits the KRB_TGS_REQ to *RWDC01* who replies with a KRB_TGS_REP.

4. *RODC01* receives a valid KRB_TGS_REP. Rather than forwarding the KRB_TGS_REP to *BrianPC*, *RODC01* transmits an error to *BrianPC*.

> The specific Kerberos error that *RODC01* sends to *BrianPC* tells *BrianPC* that *Brian's* TGT has expired.

5. *BrianPC* prepares a new KRB_AS_REQ for user *Brian* and transmits it to *RODC01*.

6. Since *RODC01* now holds cached credentials for user *Brian*, *RODC01* is able to construct a new KRB_AS_REP locally (and thus a new TGT for *Brian*), encrypt it with *RODC01's* local *krbtgt* account, and transmit it to *BrianPC*.

7. *BrianPC* sends a new KRB_TGS_REQ to *RODC01* for user *Brian*, this time including the new TGT for *Brian*.

8. *RODC01* is able to decrypt the TGT in the KRB_TGS_REQ and construct a KRB_TGS_REP that includes a service ticket permitting user *Brian* to use *BrianPC*.

> You may be wondering what would happen if an RWDC receives a TGT that was encrypted by an RODC. Each RODC's *krbtgt* account is replicated to all of the RWDCs in the domain, so RWDCs can decrypt Kerberos packets encrypted by an RODC. The TGT includes unencrypted information in the header that allows an RWDC to determine which RODC's *krbtgt* account to use when decrypting the message.

After completing these steps, user *Brian* is able to use *BrianPC*. During subsequent logons by user *Brian* to *BrianPC*, the steps taken to obtain a service ticket (TGS) are much simpler:

1. *BrianPC* sends a `KRB_TGS_REQ` to *RODC01* for user *Brian* to access *BrianPC*. The `KRB_TGS_REQ` includes *Brian's* TGT, which has been encrypted by *RODC01*.

2. *RODC01* decrypts the TGT in the `KRB_TGS_REQ` and constructs a `KRB_TGS_REP` that includes a service ticket permitting user *Brian* to use *BrianPC*.

After reviewing these examples, you may have begun to notice the importance of caching both the user and computer passwords on the RODC. In order for a user authentication to succeed, the RODC must possess the passwords for both the user and the computer. If either of these is not present, the RODC will need to communicate with a writeable domain controller over the WAN. If the WAN is unavailable, the user logon will fail.

 The writeable domain controller that the RODC contacts must be running Windows Server 2008. If only Windows Server 2003 domain controllers are available, the logon request will fail.

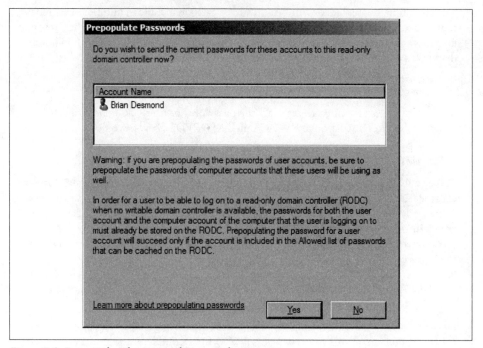

Figure 7-9. Password cache prepopulation confirmation

Populating the Password Cache

Since the success of a logon processed by an RODC can be entirely dependent on whether or not the WAN (or more specifically a Windows Server 2008 writeable domain controller) is available, you may want to prepopulate the RODC's password cache. You can prepopulate the password cache using the Prepopulate Passwords... button shown in Figure 7-5. When you click this button you will be able to search Active Directory for users and computers. After selecting the users and computers you wish to prepopulate the cache for, you will be shown a confirmation dialog similar to Figure 7-9.

If any errors occur, you will be shown a dialog similar to Figure 7-10 advising you of those errors. Any principals whose passwords are successfully prepopulated will appear in the list shown in Figure 7-5.

COMMAND-LINE REFERENCE

Managing Cached Passwords with Repadmin

The repadmin tool included with Windows Server 2008 includes a number of switches that you can use to manage an RODC's password cache. You can use the /rodcpw drepl switch to specify one or more users or computers that the RODC should immediately request replication of the password for. The syntax for this command is:

```
repadmin /rodcpwdrepl <RODC> <Hub DC> <user/computer distinguished name 1>
<[user/computer distinguished name 2]...>
```

If, for example, you wanted to replicate the password for user *bdesmond* to an RODC called *K8DEVRODC01* from a RWDC called *K8DEVDC01*, you would run

```
repadmin /rodcpwdrepl K8DEVRODC01 K8DEVDC01
cn=bdesmond,cn=users,dc=k8dev01,dc=brianlab,dc=local
```

You can also use *repadmin* to copy all of the users and/or computers in the msDS-Authen ticatedAtDC to a group that is in the msDS-RevealOnDemand list. In order to run this command, you must specify the RODC and group using this syntax: **repadmin /prp move <RODC> <Group Name>**. The group name attribute expects the sAMAccountName value for a group, and if that group is not found, it will be created below the Users container in the domain. If you wanted to move all the users on the Auth-2 list for *K8DEVRODC01* to a group called *RODC01-Allow*, you could run **repadmin /prp move K8DEVRODC01 RODC01-Allow**. If you want to add only users or computers, you could append the /users_only or /comps_only switches.

Nearly all of the other PRP management tasks we cover in this chapter can be completed using *repadmin*. You can run repadmin /prp /? for a complete listing of PRP related functions in *repadmin*.

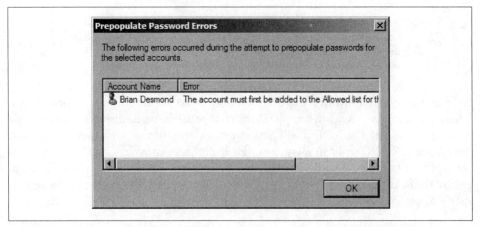

Figure 7-10. Password prepopulation errors

RODCs and Write Requests

RODCs have a great deal of special logic encoded in them to handle write requests they receive from clients. Perhaps the most obvious and common example of a write operation is a user or computer password change request. Other common examples are dynamic DNS registrations and updates to logon timestamp information.

User Password Changes

The behavior of an RODC when a user changes their password varies depending on what mechanism the user is using to change their password (such as Kerberos or LDAP), and the operating system of the client. Let's take the most common example of a user pressing Ctrl+Alt+Del on his workstation and selecting the change password option.

Clients running Windows Vista (and Windows Server 2008) will attempt to make the password change via Kerberos. When an RODC receives a Kerberos password change request, it will be forwarded to a writeable domain controller. The RODC will also immediately request that the RWDC replicate that user's password to the RODC. The RWDC will then follow the normal process discussed earlier for replicating a password to an RODC.

On a client running Windows XP or earlier (and server operating systems running Windows Server 2003 or earlier), the client will contact a writeable domain controller directly and the RODC will have no knowledge of the password change. Next time the RODC replicates with a writeable domain controller, it will erase its local copy of that user's password. The user authentication process discussed earlier will ensure the next time the user attempts to log on, and the RODC will again cache that user's password if permissible.

If you have loaded the RODC hotfix package discussed earlier in this chapter, the client will contact an RODC to change its password and the RODC will chain that request to an RWDC. The password will still not be requested for immediate replication, however.

If the user account password change request is made via LDAP (such as for the Outlook Web Access change password webpage), the change will be made directly on a writeable domain controller. The RODC will have no knowledge of the password change, and next time the RODC replicates with a writeable domain controller, it will erase its local copy of that user's password. The user authentication process discussed earlier will ensure the next time the user attempts to log on, and the RODC will again cache that user's password if permissible.

When an RODC erases its local copy of a password, the old password is still physically stored in the Active Directory database. The replication metadata for the user is updated such that when queried, the database reports that the password field is null.

Computer Account Password Changes

When a computer attempts to change its password, it will contact the RODC via its secure channel. The RODC will chain that password change request to a writeable domain controller and request that the RWDC replicate the new password to the RODC. The RWDC will then follow the normal process discussed earlier for replicating a password to an RODC.

The lastLogonTimeStampAttribute

The lastLogonTimeStampAttribute sometimes defies the conventional wisdom we've been saying all along in this chapter. If a user or computer's password is cached on the RODC, the RODC will locally write a new timestamp to the lastLogonTimeStampAttri bute for that user or computer if the RODC determines that an update to the lastLo gonTimeStampAttribute attribute is necessary. Simultaneously, the RODC will forward the lastLogonTimeStampAttribute update to a writeable domain controller. Since the forwarded lastLogonTimeStampAttribute is slightly newer, the RODC's lastLogonTimeStampAttribute value for the user or computer will be overwritten with a slightly later value via normal replication.

The lastLogonTimeStampAttribute update will not be forwarded if the WAN is unavailable or the RODC is unable to contact a writeable Windows Server 2008 domain controller

---

Last-Logon Statistics

If you have enabled tracking of last-logon statistics information as discussed in Chapter 13, the RODC will write updates to those attributes locally. However, unlike the lastLogonTimeStampAttribute, the RODC will *not* forward these updates to a writeable domain controller.

Logon Success/Fail Information

When an RODC processes a logon successfully, it will write new values for the lastLogon, logonCount, and badPwdCount attributes for the user or computer locally. As is the case with a writeable domain controller, these attribute changes will never be replicated or chained to a writeable domain controller. If an RODC processes a logon failure, it will update the badPwdTime and badPwdCount attributes. Likewise, these changes will never leave the RODC either by replication or chaining.

NetLogon Secure Channel Updates

Certain attributes of computer accounts, such as the computer's name, dNSHostName, and operating system information, that are stored in Active Directory are provided to domain controllers via a computer's NetLogon secure channel. When an RODC receives these updates, it will chain them to a writeable domain controller. The RODC will initiate a request for immediate replication of the computer object, and if the computer's password is permitted to be cached, that request will succeed.

Replication Connection Objects

The KCC on an RODC will locally write the connection objects an RODC requires to replicate to the RODC's database. These changes will never replicate and are not necessary outside of the RODC.

DNS Updates

RODCs leverage existing functionality in the DNS protocol in order to return a writeable domain controller to the client. When a client is ready to make a dynamic DNS update, it will first contact the DNS server (in this case, the RODC) and request an authoritative name server for the zone it is trying to update by way of accessing the zone's *SOA* (Start of Authority) record.

When an RODC generates the SOA record for a read-only DNS zone, it will attempt to locate a nearby Windows Server 2008 writeable domain controller that is a name server for the zone and that is also reachable. The RODC completes this process via a DC Locator call. In the event the RODC is unable to find a suitable Windows Server 2008 domain controller, it will randomly select, from the list of available name servers, a name server that is not the RODC itself. The name server that the RODC ultimately selects during this process will be specified as the master server in the SOA record.

In order to keep the RODC's local version of the DNS zone up-to-date, the RODC will queue a request for replicating the client's record from the master server that the RODC selected for placement in the SOA record. Enqueueing this replication request is best-effort, which means that if it fails, the RODC will not try again to queue a replication request for that DNS record. Instead, the RODC will receive the update during the next normal replication cycle.

If there is already an entry in the replication queue for the record in question, the RODC will not queue a second replication request.

By default the RODC will process the replication queue every five minutes and attempt to replicate a maximum of one hundred entries from the queue. For each entry in the queue, the RODC will verify that the entry is at least thirty seconds old, or else it will bypass it and attempt to replicate that entry during the next cycle. By default, when the queue depth reaches three hundred entries, no more entries will be enqueued until the queue depth is below three hundred entries.

The DsPollingInterval registry setting controls a number of activities in addition to the frequency of the DNS replication queue processing. These activities primarily include querying Active Directory for changes to Active Directory integrated DNS zones that are hosted on the DNS server. You should thus use caution when modifying this frequency.

There are five registry settings that you can use to control the RODC DNS service's attempts to replicate dynamically updated DNS records. All of these registry settings are located under HKLM\System\CurrentControlSet\Services\DNS\Parameters. Table 7-1 details each of the registry settings you can configure.

All of the registry settings in Table 7-1 are REG_DWORD values.

Table 7-1. Read-only DNS registry settings

Registry value	Description	Unit	Default value	Minimum value	Maximum value
DsPollingInterval	Controls the frequency of the polling thread that the DNS service uses to query Active Directory for all Active Directory-	Seconds	180	30	3600

Registry value	Description	Unit	Default value	Minimum value	Maximum value
	integrated DNS configuration settings.				
EnableRsoForRodc	Controls whether or not the special DNS record-replication behavior is enabled or disabled.	Boolean	TRUE	FALSE	TRUE
MaximumRodcRso-QueueLength	This is the maximum number of entries that can be in the replication queue at any given time.	Entries	300	1	1000000
MaximumRodcR-soAttemptsPerCycle	This is the maximum number of records that the RODC will attempt to replicate in any given pass of the queue.	Entries	100	1	1000000
DsRemoteReplicationDelay	This is the minimum number of seconds an RODC will wait between enqueuing a replication request for a DNS record and processing the request.	Seconds	30	5	3600

The primary purpose of the `MaximumRodcRsoAttemptsPerCycle` setting is to limit the potential for a denial-of-service attack on a writeable domain controller by way of flooding that domain controller with too many replication requests at once. Make sure to measure the impact on domain controller load if you increase this value.

In the event that you reach the maximum queue length (three hundred entries, by default), the RODC will log an event (event ID 4400, message "*The DNS server is experiencing high SOA query load. This may be caused by a large number of local client machines performing updates. Single object replication of DNS records corresponding to SOA queries is being throttled. This may delay replication of updates to this RODC DNS server, however scheduled replication will not be affected.*") in the DNS Server event log indicating this situation has occurred, and no further replication requests will be enqueued until the queue is processed and its depth is decreased. If you are encountering this situation frequently, you may need to increase the maximum queue length by modifying the `MaximumRodocRsoQueueLength` registry setting.

The event-log entry will be logged once per 24-hour period. If you restart the DNS server service, however, the event will be logged immediately following the next occurrence of the error condition.

The W32Time Service

As a rule, RODCs will synchronize time with writeable Windows Server 2008 domain controllers. In general, at no time will an RODC ever synchronize its time with another RODC.

When an RODC receives a request for time synchronization for a client, the manner in which the request is processed varies greatly depending upon whether or not the RODC has the client's password cached. If the RODC has the client computer's password cached locally, the RODC is able to process and sign the time-synchronization request as a standard writeable domain controller would. If, however, the RODC does not have the client's password cached, then a writeable domain controller must be involved.

When the RODC receives a time-synchronization request it cannot process, there are a number of steps involved:

1. The RODC forwards the request to a Windows Server 2008 writeable domain controller.
2. The writeable domain controller then processes the request and signs it using the client computer's password, and then returns the response to the RODC.
3. The RODC in turn receives the response and forwards it to the client, who processes the response.

In order to handle the forwarding of requests and responses, the RODC maintains a local table of client time-service requests that it has forwarded. This table is known as the chaining table. The table contains three fields:

- The client's IP address (either IPv4 or IPv6)
- The timestamp from the NTP request
- The client's RID

When an RODC receives a reply from the writeable domain controller, it searches the table for a matching request based on the RID and request timestamp. Once the RODC finds a match, the RODC forwards the response back to the source IP.

 In the event the RODC is unable to find a match in the table, the RODC assumes that it originated the request. If the request is signed with the RODC's computer account password, then the RODC updates its local clock as necessary. Otherwise, the RODC discards the response.

Any entry in the RODC's chaining table has a maximum lifetime of up to four seconds by default, and any given client (as defined by the client's IP address) can have a maximum of four entries in the chaining table at any given time. In total, the chaining table can contain a maximum of 128 entries by default. In the event either of these maximums is exceeded, new requests are simply discarded until the chaining table has additional room for them.

Each time a new entry is added to the chaining table, the RODC will examine the chaining table and determine if entries should be removed. RODCs will examine the chaining table for stale entries if more than 75% of the maximum number of entries is in use (96 entries by default). Any entry that is older than the maximum lifetime will be removed.

All of these defaults are configurable via a number of registry settings shown in Table 7-2. These registry settings are located under `HKLM\System\CurrentControlSet\Serv ices\W32Time\TimeProviders\NtpServer`.

Table 7-2. Chaining table configuration settings

Registry value	Description	Unit	Default value	Minimum value	Maximum value
ChainDisable	This controls whether the chaining of time requests by RODCs is enabled.	Boolean	0	0 (chaining enabled)	1 (chaining disabled)
ChainEntryTimeout	The maximum lifetime of an entry in the chaining table.	Seconds	4	4	16
ChainMaxEntries	The maximum number of entries in the chaining table.	Entries	128	128	1024
ChainMaxHostEntries	The maximum number of entries any given host can have in the chaining table.	Entries	4	4	16

 The purpose of controlling the size of the chaining table is to ensure that the chaining table does not exhaust memory resources on the RODC. If you increase `ChainMaxEntries`, take this warning into account.

If you disable the password chaining behavior on an RODC (by setting `ChainDisable` to `1`), the RODC will be able to communicate with Windows Server 2003 domain controllers in addition to writeable Windows Server 2008 domain controllers. In the event you make this configuration change, RODCs will no longer be able to process client time-synchronization requests.

Application Compatibility

Like any major change to your infrastructure, prior to large scale deployment of RODCs in your environment, you will need to perform significant testing in order to understand application behavior issues as they relate to RODCs.

Applications that attempt to write to Active Directory using LDAP will receive an LDAP referral from an RODC to a writeable domain controller. So long as the application is capable of *chasing* the referral, the write will succeed, and the next time the RODC replicates, that write will be reflected locally. In the event the WAN is down, the referral will fail. The application will need to be able to handle this situation.

 You can disable an RODC's ability to issue write referrals by setting the RODCMode registry value to 1. The RODCMode registry value is a REG_DWORD located at HKLM\System\CurrentControlSet\Services \NTDS\Parameters.

Another scenario where an application may fail is if it expects the results of a write to be immediately available on the local domain controller. One of the issues resolved by the RODC compatibility package is for a bug in the Windows print-spooler service. The print spooler publishes printers to Active Directory via LDAP (which would be referred to a writeable domain controller), and then immediately tries to read that published printer from the local domain controller. If the printer isn't present on the local domain controller (which is the case with a local RODC), then the spooler service determines that publication of the printer failed.

If an application is using legacy RPC calls to make changes to Active Directory, those RPC calls will fail if they are targeted to an RODC. The application must explicitly target a writeable domain controller in order for the writes to succeed. The RODC will replicate the changes through normal replication.

If you have added attributes to the Filtered Attribute Set (FAS), applications will need to be aware that those attributes will not be available from Active Directory on an RODC. If an application requires access to an attribute in the FAS, the application will need to communicate with a writeable domain controller. For more information on the filtered attribute set, see Chapter 4. Keep in mind that the FAS cannot be enforced in a multidomain forest until your forest is at the Windows Server 2008 functional level. This is because an RODC that is also a global catalog may replicate one of the global catalog naming contexts from a Windows Server 2003 domain controller. Windows Server 2003 domain controllers are unaware of the FAS, and as such they will include filtered attributes when replicating with an RODC. Filtering occurs at the replication source, not at the RODC, so the RODC will process inbound replication for filtered attributes and store them in its database.

In general, the most important thing you will need to do is test all of the applications in your environment that will potentially communicate with an RODC. You will likely find applications that require updates to their code or upgrades from the manufacturer. One application that you should be aware of is Microsoft Exchange. Exchange is unable to work with RODCs, and as such you should not collocate Exchange servers and RODCs in the same site.

 Microsoft has compiled a list of applications that are known to work with RODCs at *http://technet.microsoft.com/en-us/library/cc732790 .aspx*.

RODC Placement Considerations

When you place RODCs in your network, there are a few rules and considerations you should think about as you work on your design. The first rule to remember is that an RODC will never talk to another RODC.

If you're thinking of placing multiple RODCs in a given site, this is a very important rule to remember. Think of a situation where you have a branch office with two RODCs for the same domain. Let's call these RODCs *RODC01* and *RODC02*. Let's also assume we have a user *Brian* who works out of this site. On *RODC01, Brian's* password is cached; however, on *RODC02, Brian's* password is not cached. When the WAN becomes unavailable at this site and a writeable domain controller is unable to be contacted, *Brian* attempts to log on to his workstation. *Brian's* workstation contacts *RODC02*, and because the WAN is unavailable and *RODC02* does not have *Brian's* password cached, logon fails. *Brian's* workstation will not try to contact a different domain controller and will instead simply tell *Brian* his password is invalid. Having multiple RODCs in a site can provide redundancy where necessary, but it can also provide a great deal of unpredictability. If you are planning to deploy multiple RODCs to a site, we recommend you prepopulate each RODC's password cache.

When you create a trust between a given set of domains, a special type of object called a `trustedDomain` is created in Active Directory to represent that trust. The `trustedDomain` object includes a password that is used for communicating with the remote domain in the trust. RODCs will never cache trust passwords, which means that any time a user who is in a site serviced by an RODC wishes to communicate with a resource in a trusted domain, the RODC must go to a writeable domain controller to get the necessary Kerberos tickets. This is true even when the resources the user wishes to access are in the same site as the user. If the WAN is down, the user will be unable to access those resources since a writeable domain controller for the user's domain cannot be contacted.

If you place RODCs in your DMZ, you will need to pay special attention to applications that need to write to Active Directory as typically those writes will always fail. The assumption in this scenario is that you will close the firewall such that member servers in the DMZ cannot communicate with writeable domain controllers in the trusted network, since if you didn't do this, there would be no point in deploying RODCs in the DMZ to begin with. Applications will fail to write to Active Directory since the RODC will issue a write referral to a writeable domain controller that the client will be unable to contact. In this scenario we recommend you set the RODCMode registry setting discussed earlier to 1.

In order for dynamic DNS registrations to succeed for member servers in the DMZ, you will need to allow DMZ servers to contact writeable domain controllers on TCP and UDP port 53 in order for DNS registrations to succeed. Domain join operations will fail for member servers in the DMZ unless you pre-create the computer account on a writeable domain controller, ensure that the computer account is allowed to be cached by RODCs in the DMZ, and then prepopulate the RODC password caches with that computer account's password.

> In order for the prepopulation of the computer account's password to succeed, you will need to set it to a nonstandard value before you attempt to prepopulate the cache. In order to do this, you can run **net user <ComputerName>$ <Password>**, substituting the computer's name and a password where appropriate. Be sure to include the trailing $ in the computer name.

RODCs and Replication

One improvement that should greatly help with scalability when you are deploying branch offices is an RODC's ability to automatically load balance connections to bridgehead servers in the hub site without manual intervention. Each time the KCC executes on an RODC, the RODC will check and see if there are new potential replication bridgeheads in the hub site, and if necessary the RODC will automatically switch replication to a different bridgehead server for the purpose of load balancing replication connections.

Administrator Role Separation

One often-sought-after feature for domain controllers is the ability to separate administration of the domain controller hardware platform and operating system from administration of the Active Directory service. On a writeable domain controller, this is simply impossible since anyone who is an administrator on the domain controller can make changes that could elevate their privileges across the forest and lead to compromise of the forest. RODCs introduce the ability to delegate administrative control of the operating system to a third party, and we highly recommend that you do this as a best practice even if you are administering RODCs out of an Active Directory management team!

By delegating administrative rights to the RODC operating system to a group other than the *Domain Admins* group, you remove the need to ever log in to an RODC as a domain administrator. Keep in mind the paradigm of an RODC being compromised by default when you consider this recommendation. If you log in to a compromised RODC with an account with domain admin rights, you could be giving away your domain admin password, or perhaps the OS has been modified to run a login script under your domain administrator login that makes compromising changes to the directory via an RWDC.

You can configure a multitude of different local roles on an RODC; however, we expect the most common local role you will configure is the *Administrators* role. The list of available roles includes:

- Administrators
- Users
- Guests
- Remote Desktop Users
- Network Configuration Operators
- Performance Monitor Users
- Performance Log Users
- Distributed COM Users
- IIS_IUSRS
- Cryptographic Operators
- Event Log Readers
- Certificate Service DCOM Access
- Incoming Forest Trust Builders
- Terminal Server License Servers
- Pre-Windows 2000 Compatible Access
- Windows Authorization Access Group
- Server Operators
- Replicator
- Account Operators
- Backup Operators
- Print Operators

In order to configure the local *Administrators* role on an RODC, you can use either ntdsutil or the Active Directory Users and Computers (ADUC) tool. ADUC limits you to configuring the *Administrators* role by specifying a user or group on the managedBy

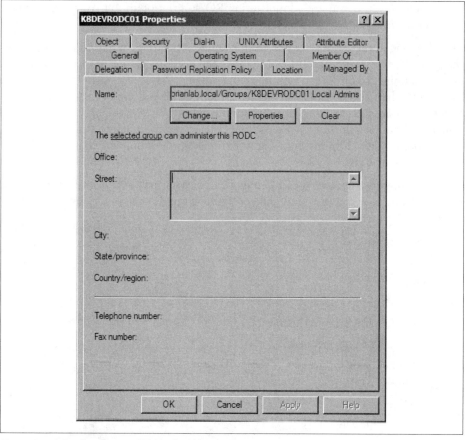

Figure 7-11. Configuring RODC local administrators in ADUC

attribute of the RODC's computer account. Figure 7-11 shows this configuration. This change will become effective on the RODC when the updated managedBy attribute replicates to the RODC.

If you want to configure a role other than the *Administrators* role or you prefer to complete this configuration via the command prompt, you will need to use *ntdsutil*. To add a group called *K8DEV01\RODC01-Admins* to the local *Administrators* role on RODC *K8DEVRODC01*, you would run these commands after launching *ntdsutil*:

1. local roles
2. connections
3. connect to server K8DEVRODC01
4. quit
5. add k8dev01\RODC01-Admins Administrators

The change will become effective immediately, and members of the *RODC01-Admins* group will be able to administer the RODC without concern that they will have administrative access to the domain or forest.

 Users who are members of the local *Administrators* role can modify the members of this role and other local roles.

We *highly* recommend that you define a domain group that has local *Administrators*-level access to each RODC in your environment. This group should contain accounts that do not have any elevated privileges in your environment (thus normal user accounts). You should use these accounts for performing all administrative functions on an RODC. If you need to perform an administrative task that requires domain-level administrative permissions, perform that task remotely as any attempt to logon interactively to the RODC either at the console or via Terminal Services could allow compromise.

Summary

This chapter has focused exclusively on the deployment of the read-only domain controller (RODC) into your environment. RODCs are a major feature in Windows Server 2008 Active Directory and are likely to play a key part in the Active Directory deployments of many organizations. RODCs mitigate key security risks around Active Directory with regard to domain controllers that are in physically insecure locations such as branch offices.

Over the course of this chapter, we took a look at changes in behavior between RODCs and their writeable counterparts. We explored the client logon process in depth and also discussed how RODCs handle write operations and time synchronization. We took a look at application compatibility testing requirements and known issues as well as important points to keep in mind when deploying RODCs within your Active Directory topology. We concluded our discussion with a look at the new administrative role separation functionality that RODCs enable, and stressed the importance of never logging in to an RODC with an account that has domain-level administrative privileges.

## CHAPTER 8

Group Policy Primer

Group Policy is a large topic that deserves a book in itself (and there are several of those) to be properly covered. We will discuss group policy as it applies specifically to the design and administration of an Active Directory in this book, but not Group Policy as it applies to the actual settings and operations on an Active Directory client.

The goal of policy-based administration is for an administrator to define the environment for users and computers once by defining policies, and then to rely on the system to enforce those policies. This chapter is an introduction to the Group Policy and how to manage it. Chapter 12 covers how to begin designing Group Policy and the OU structures in support of Group Policy.

The scope and functionality of Active Directory group policies encompasses a number of key points:

- They can be targeted to individual computers and users, sites, domains, and Organizational Units.
- They can apply to users, computers, or groups of either.
- They can set values and automatically unset them in specified situations.
- They can do far more than just a desktop lockdown.

With group policies, an administrator can define a large number of detailed settings to be enforced on users throughout the organization and be confident that the system will take care of things. Let's take an example from Leicester University. Administrators wanted the *Systems Administrator* toolset to be available on workstations they worked from. While they could install these tools on their own PCs, they also wanted the tools to follow them around the network and be available from any PC that they chose to log on from. However, they didn't want to leave these tools installed on that PC when they logged off. Prior to Active Directory, the administrators would have had to arrive at a client, log on, install the toolset, do whatever was required at a client, uninstall the toolset, and finally log off. This would be a considerable chore when working with a large number of machines. Active Directory group policies can be used to specify that the toolset is to be automatically installed on any client that an administrator logs on to. That way, an administrator could go straight to the Start menu and find the tools available. When the group policy goes out of scope, the same group policy would uninstall the toolset from the machine.

Let's take another example. Perhaps one of the most common uses of group policies is for deploying logon scripts. At Leicester University, a central logon script was used for every user. This is no different than under Windows NT. However, extra logon scripts for some sets of users were also applied based on which Organizational Unit the users were in. So, some users get more than one logon script depending on where in Active Directory their accounts reside. A logoff script was also specified to run when a user logged off the system. Workstations also can have scripts, but instead of executing at logon and logoff, these scripts run at startup and shutdown. So, rather than a single user logon script available for Windows NT, we now have multiple user logon/logoff scripts and multiple workstation startup/shutdown scripts, all of which can be customized using any of the data within Active Directory. And beginning with Windows XP clients, you can even use Windows Management Interface (WMI) filtering, which allows you to use most of the vast amount of data available in WMI to specify criteria for when group policies are applied. In addition, with the release of the Group Policy Preferences feature, you are able to set much more fine-grained filtering criteria on a per-setting basis than you ever could before.

With examples like these, it becomes quite easy to see the power of group policies. Now that we've covered a few examples, let's dive into the details of group policies.

 Group policy objects are normally referred to simply as GPOs.

Capabilities of GPOs

GPOs can be edited using the Group Policy Management Editor (GPME), formerly the Group Policy Object Editor (GPME), which is an MMC snap-in. The GPME is limited to managing a single GPO at a time and cannot be used to link a GPO. For this reason, Microsoft developed the Group Policy Management Console (GPMC) MMC snap-in, which was released around the same time as Windows Server 2003 as a web download from *http://www.microsoft.com/downloads/details.aspx?FamilyId=0A6D4C24-8CBD -4B35-9272-DD3CBFC81887*. The Group Policy Management Console was bundled with Windows starting with Windows Server 2003 R2 and is available on Windows Vista SP1 as a feature of the Remote Server Administration Tools (RSAT) download.

The GPMC provides a single interface to manage all aspects of GPOs, including editing (through the GPME), viewing the resultant set of policies (RSOP), and linking to domains, sites, and OUs. In general, the GPMC is a vastly superior interface to managing group policies via the Active Directory Users and Computers (ADUC) MMC snap-in. We will utilize the GPMC through all of the examples in this book.

There are three different policy areas that a GPO supports. These areas include registry settings, security settings, and software installation. Most registry settings in a GPO have three states: enabled, disabled, and unconfigured. By default, all settings in a GPO are unconfigured. Any unconfigured settings are ignored during application, so the GPO comes into play only when settings have actually been configured. In some cases, the setting needs no other parameters, while in other cases, a host of information must be entered to configure the setting; it all depends on what the setting itself does.

Enabling and disabling most settings is fairly straightforward. However, due to Microsoft's choice for the names of certain settings for GPOs, you actually can have the choice of enabling or disabling options with names such as "Disable Access to This Option." By default, this setting isn't in use, but you can disable the disable option (i.e., enable the option) or enable the disable option (i.e., disable the option). Be careful and make sure you know which way the setting is applied before you actually widely deploy the GPO.

GPOs can apply a very large number of changes to computers and users that are in Active Directory. These changes are grouped together within the GPME under the headings of Policies and Preferences. For more information on preferences, see the sidebar "Group Policy Preferences," next. There are two sets of these headings, one under Computer Configuration and one under User Configuration. The items under the two headings differ, as the settings that apply to users and to computers are not the same.

Group Policy Preferences

Microsoft acquired a company called DesktopStandard in September 2006. Desktop-Standard was known for their PolicyMaker and GPOVault products. PolicyMaker has been rebranded as Group Policy Preferences and is available with Windows Server 2008. You can use Group Policy Preferences on any Windows XP or newer client. In order to use Group Policy Preferences, you need to deploy a small client-side extension (CSE) that Microsoft provides in an update package for Windows.

There are countless new settings and options available via Group Policy Preferences that previously would have required scripting. Examples of things you can graphically configure include desktop shortcuts, mapped drives, printers, and start menu items.

For more information on Group Policy Preferences, see the whitepaper *Group Policy Preferences Overview* at *http://www.microsoft.com/downloads/details.aspx?FamilyID= 42e30e3f-6f01-4610-9d6e-f6e0fb7a0790&displaylang=en*.

You do not need to upgrade your domain to Windows Server 2008 in order to take advantage of Group Policy Preferences. You simply need the Windows Server 2008 version of the GPMC or the Windows Vista SP1 remote server administration tools (RSAT).

Group Policy Storage

Group Policies are stored as a number of components that collectively enable the Group Policy functionality both at the client side and for the administrator. This data is replicated using a number of methods depending on the component and platform. Throughout this section, we'll discuss the key components of group policies as well as the replication engines available and how to work with them.

ADM or ADMX files

Some of the settings under Administrative Templates might seem to make more sense if they were grouped in one of the other sections. However, the Administrative Templates section holds the settings that are entirely generated from the Administrative Template (ADM) files in the system volume; so, it makes more sense to include all the ADM data together. ADM files contain the entire set of options available for each setting, including explanations that are shown on the various property pages in the GPME.

Typically, a large portion of the disk space consumed by a domain's SYSVOL is the ADM files. ADM files don't play a part in the application of group policies, but rather they are there to populate the group policy object editor and GPMC reports. The Group Policy toolset that is included with Windows Server 2008 and Windows Vista SP1 with RSAT installed supports a new type of ADM file that has an ADMX extension. ADMX files serve the same purpose as ADM files; however, they are in a new XML format that cannot be interpreted by Windows Server 2003 and earlier Group Policy tools. Each ADMX file that Microsoft provides is accompanied by a language independent ADML file. In this way, localized strings for different languages can be stored in separate ADML files, which are referred to by the accompanying ADMX file. So, English-speaking users can see Administrative Template policy descriptions in English, whereas a French-speaking user, looking at the same GPO, will see those descriptions in French.

Microsoft has a free tool called the ADMX Migrator available for converting custom ADM files into the new ADMX format, as well as for graphically creating new ADMX files. You can get this tool at *http://www .microsoft.com/downloads/details.aspx?familyid=0F1EEC3D-10C4 -4B5F-9625-97C2F731090C.*

Windows Server 2008 also supports the concept of a central store for ADMX files. The central store eliminates the duplicate storage of ADM files within each group policy and instead stores them once per domain. You will need to create the central store manually in order to utilize this feature. Fortunately, creating the central store is quite straightforward:

1. Create a folder called PolicyDefinitions in the SysVol policies folder. If, for example, your domain was called *mycorp.com*, you would create PolicyDefinitions under *\\mycorp.com\sysvol\mycorp.com\policies*.

2. Copy the contents of the *%SystemRoot%\PolicyDefinitions* folder on a Windows Vista or Windows Server 2008 machine into the PolicyDefinitions folder you created in step 1. You should obtain the contents of the PolicyDefinitions folder from a Windows Vista or Windows Server 2008 machine with the latest service pack.

3. Restart any open Group Policy Management Editor sessions. The Group Policy editor as well as GPMC will automatically begin utilizing the central store.

Keep in mind that pre-Windows Vista SP1 and Windows Server 2003 or earlier group policy toolsets cannot leverage ADMX files or the central store, so in order to use the central store you must migrate to editing Group Policies with the newer tools. You do not need to have a Windows Server 2008 domain in order to use these tools or the central store.

 Once you have set up the central store, ADM files will not be cleaned up automatically. You will need to do this by hand.

For more information on the central store and ADMX files, visit *http://technet2.micro soft.com/WindowsVista/en/library/02633470-396c-4e34-971a-0c5b090dc4fd1033 .mspx?mfr=true*.

How GPOs are stored in Active Directory

GPOs themselves are stored in two places: Group Policy Configuration (GPC) data is stored in Active Directory, and certain key Group Policy Template (GPT) data is stored as files and directories in the system volume. They are split because while there is definitely a need to store GPOs in Active Directory if the system is to associate them with locations in the tree, you do not want to store all the registry changes, logon scripts, and so on in Active Directory itself. To do so could greatly increase the size of your DIT file. To that end, each GPO consists of the object holding GPC data, which itself is linked to a companion directory in the system volume that may or may not have GPTs stored within. The GPT data is essentially a folder structure that stores Administrative Template-based policies, security settings, applications available for software installation, and script files. GPT data is stored in the System Volume (SYSVOL) folder of DCs in the *Policies* subfolder.

Third-party developers can extend GPOs by incorporating options that do not reside in the normal GPT location.

The GPO objects themselves are held as instances of the `groupPolicyContainer` class within a single container in Active Directory at this location:

```
CN=Policies,CN=System,dc=mycorp,dc=com
```

Through a process known as linking, the GPOs are associated with the locations in the tree that are to apply the group policy. In other words, one object can be linked to multiple locations in the tree, which explains how one GPO can be applied to as many Organizational Units, sites, or domains as required.

Let's consider the `groupPolicyContainer` class objects themselves. Take a look at Figure 8-1; we are using one of the Windows Support Tools utilities, ADSI Edit, to show the view of the Policies container and its children.

Here you can see two `groupPolicyContainer` objects shown with a GUID as the `cn` field. The `displayName` attribute of these objects holds the name that administrators of Active Directory would see when using one of the normal tools to view these objects. Each GPO also has a `gPCFileSysPath` attribute that holds the full path to the corresponding directory in the system volume.

If you were to look under the Policies container on a default installation, you would find only two children. These children would correspond to the Default Domain Policy and the Default Domain Controllers Policy, the only GPOs created automatically by the system on installation. These GPOs have fixed names across all domains:

- {31B2F340-016D-11D2-945F-00C04FB984F9} is always the Default Domain Policy
- {6AC1786C-016F-11D2-945F-00C04fB984F9} is always the Default Domain Controllers Policy

Group Policy replication

Historically, the Sysvol container has replicated using the NTFRS (NT File Replication Service), which can perform multimaster replication of a file share. NTFRS has never been known for flexibility or even, in some cases, reliability. Windows Server 2008 introduces the ability to replicate the Sysvol folder hierarchy with DFS-R. DFS-R stands for Distributed File System-Replication and is a new file and folder replication technology that was introduced in Windows Server 2003 R2. DFS-R has substantially enhanced functionality and is much more reliable. It is in your best interest to migrate Sysvol replication when it becomes possible. For an extensive FAQ on DFS-R, visit *http://technet2.microsoft.com/windowsserver2008/en/library/f9b98a0f-c1ae-4a9f-9724 -80c679596e6b1033.mspx?mfr=true*.

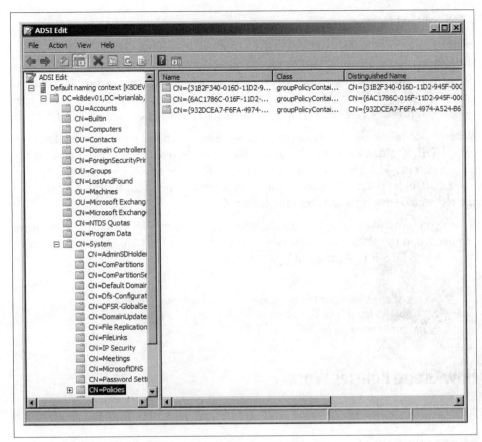

Figure 8-1. GPOs in the Policies container

Domains that are built starting with the Windows Server 2008 Domain Functional Level automatically use DFS-R to replicate the Sysvol container, but domains that are upgraded or built in a lower functional level will continue to use NTFRS. In order to migrate to DFS-R replication of Sysvol, the domain in question must be at the Windows Server 2008 Domain Functional Level. In order to move to DFS-R, you will use the dfsrmig utility.

The Microsoft Storage Team Blog has an extensive series on the process of migrating Sysvol to DFS-R replication, so rather than try to replicate this content; we will point you directly to the source: *http://blogs.technet.com/filecab/archive/2008/02/08/sysvol -migration-series-part-1-introduction-to-the-sysvol-migration-process.aspx*. Each of the subsequent blog posts in the series is linked at the bottom of the page. At a high level, there are four stages of the migration process:

1. Migration Start
2. Sysvol prepared state

3. Sysvol redirected state

4. Eliminated state

In the prepared state, new DFS-R objects get created in active Directory, and each domain controller creates a new *Sysvol_DFSR* folder into which it copies the contents of its *Sysvol* folder. The DFS-R service then begins initializing itself. Once all of your domain controllers have reached the prepared state, you can continue to step 3.

When you move to the redirected state, each domain controller updates its *Sysvol_DFSR* folder with any changes to the active Sysvol share since it entered the prepared state. The domain controller then modifies the Sysvol share so that the *Sysvol_DFSR* folder is shared out as Sysvol. Once all your domain controllers have reached the redirected state, you can continue to step 4.

When you move to the eliminated state, the NTFRS settings for replicating Sysvol are removed, and the old *Sysvol* folder is removed from the filesystem. At this point, your migration to DFS-R replication of Sysvol is complete.

 At any time prior to step 4, you can roll back one step or all the way back to step 1. Once you reach the Eliminated state, however, you cannot rollback to NTFRS.

How Group Policies Work

The remainder of this chapter takes an in-depth look at Group Policy Objects, focusing on two areas:

- How GPOs work in Active Directory
- How to manage GPOs with the Group Policy Object Editor and Group Policy Management Console

Group policies are very simple to understand, but their usage can be quite complex. Each GPO can consist of two parts: one that applies to a computer (such as a startup script or a change to the system portion of the registry) and one that applies to a user (such as a logoff script or a change to the user portion of the registry). You can use GPOs that contain only computer policies, only user policies, or a mixture of the two.

GPOs and Active Directory

Any GPO is initially created as a standalone object in Active Directory. Each object can then be linked one or more times to three different container types: Sites, Domains, and Organizational Units. GPOs for domains and Organizational Units are held in the domain relating to their application, but creating a GPO for a site stores that GPO in the forest root domain by default; administrators can change this if they wish.

You cannot link group policies to containers. Users and computers that are stored in a container will apply policies linked to the domain or their site, however.

In the normal state of affairs, an administrator would customarily browse to a Site, Domain, or Organizational Unit in GPMC, and then create a GPO and link it to that object. At this point, it appears that you have created a GPO at that location in the tree rather than what really happened, which was that the system created the GPO as a standalone object in the Policies container and then immediately linked it to that container.

To apply a GPO to a set of users or computers, you simply create a GPO in Active Directory and then link it to a Site, Domain, or Organizational Unit. Then, by default, the user portion of the GPO will apply to all users in the tree, and the computer portion of the GPO will apply to all computers in the tree.

Thus, if we were to create a policy and link it to a domain, all computers and users of that domain, respectively, would process the policy. If we were to create a policy and link it to an Organizational Unit, all users and computers in that Organizational Unit and all the users and computers within Organizational Units beneath that Organizational Unit (and so on down the tree) would process the policy.

To identify the links on a GPO, you simply look at the Scope tab of the GPO's properties in the Group Policy Management Console. Figure 8-2 shows the results of a scan for the locations in the domain where the Desktop Policy GPO has been linked. In this case, the Desktop Policy has been linked only to the Desktops OU.

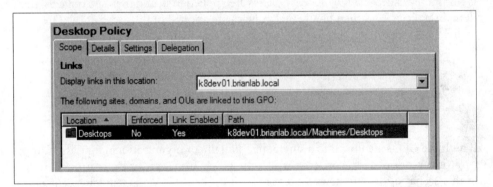

Figure 8-2. Identifying GPO links

We want to make three major points here:

- GPOs can be linked only to sites, domains, and organizational units.
- A single GPO can be linked to multiple locations in the tree.
- GPOs by default affect all of the users and computers in the linked scope.

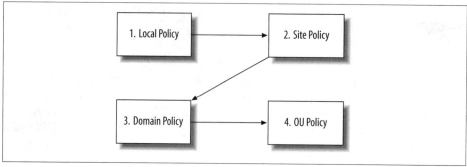

Figure 8-3. Order of policy application

This generates further questions. If multiple policies apply to different locations in a tree, can multiple GPOs apply to the same location, and if so, what takes precedence? Why would you want to apply one GPO to different parts of the tree? In addition, how can we stop the GPO from applying to the entire set of users and computers in the tree? Let's consider each of these questions to understand policies better.

Prioritizing the Application of Multiple Policies

Let's say that we create and link a GPO for all users in a site to run a logon script that loads an Intranet homepage local to that site. Let's also say that we create and link a domain GPO to set the *My Documents* folder location for each user in the domain. Finally, we have two user logon scripts that we need to run in a specific order for specific Organizational Units in that domain. GPOs are applied in a specific order; this order is commonly called *LSDOU*. Local policies are applied first, and then site policies, then domain policies, and then finally OU policies are applied in the order of the OU hierarchy. This order of application is illustrated in Figure 8-3.

If you are using legacy Windows NT system policies, these policies can be considered Step 0 in Figure 8-3 as they apply prior to local policies.

If multiple GPOs are linked to a single site, domain, or organizational unit, the administrator can prioritize the order in which the GPOs from that level are processed. So, in this scenario, the site news system runs first, then the My Document settings are applied, and finally the two logon scripts are applied in the order determined by the administrator.

To account for this, the GPOs for the site that the user resides in are applied first in prioritized order. No other sites have any influence over this. Then, the GPOs for the domain that the user resides in are applied in prioritized order. GPOs applied to parent domains in the domain tree have no influence on objects in domains lower down the tree. Domain trees do not impact GPO application at all. The Organizational Unit structure, however, has a significant bearing on what happens with GPOs. GPO links are inherited down an OU tree. So, while a child Organizational Unit can have its own GPOs linked to it, it also will inherit all of its parent's GPO links. These Organizational Unit GPOs are applied in order according to the Organizational Unit hierarchy once the site and domain GPOs have been processed.

 There are exceptions. You can block inheritance, force an override, and even define ACLs on objects. We'll cover all these topics later in this section.

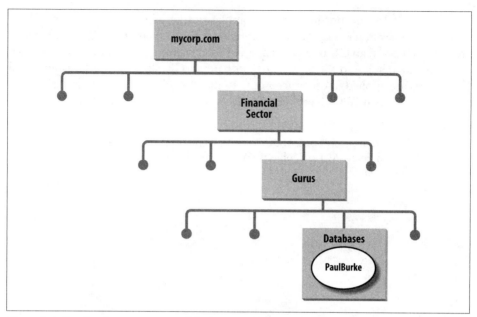

Figure 8-4. Graphical representation of the location of the Paul Burke user

For example, Paul Burke has the following DN to his account (see Figure 8-4):

```
cn=PaulBurke,ou=Databases,ou=Gurus,ou=Financial Sector,dc=mycorp,dc=com
```

The site GPOs are applied first, and the *mycorp.com* domain GPOs are applied next. Then come the GPOs on the Financial Sector Organizational Unit, the GPOs on the Gurus Organizational Unit, and the GPOs on the Databases Organizational Unit. From this, it's fairly easy to see how Organizational Unit hierarchy design has a significant effect on GPO precedence.

Remember that GPOs have a computer part as well as a user part. When a computer boots, any site GPOs that have computer settings are applied in prioritized order. This is followed by any domain GPOs with computer settings, and so on down the Organizational Unit hierarchy until any GPOs on the Organizational Unit that the computer resides in are applied. During boot up, the user portions of these GPOs are ignored. Later, when a user logs on, the same process applies, this time with the user settings. The computer settings are ignored during user logon.[*]

---

[*] This is the default case. There is a setting that you can use to force a different mode of operation. We'll explain this later when we cover loopback mode.

There are several policies that can only be set on a GPO linked at the domain. These policies are the ones that affect account settings for the domain users, such as the Kerberos policy, Lockout policy, Password Aging, and Complexity policy. No amount of blocking or priority setting will allow you to have different users in a single domain with different account policy settings. You can, however, set the lockout and password aging/complexity settings at the OU level to affect local machine user accounts on servers and workstations.

With Windows Server 2008 domains, you can control lockout policy, password aging and password complexity on a per-user basis with fine-grained password policies. Fine-grained password policies are discussed in detail in Chapter 9, but do not leverage Group Policy.

Standard GPO Inheritance Rules in Organizational Units

Any unconfigured settings anywhere in a GPO are ignored, and only configured settings are inherited. There are three possible scenarios:

- A higher-level GPO has a value for a setting, and a lower-level GPO does not.
- A GPO linked to a parent OU has a value for a setting, and a GPO linked to a child OU has a non-conflicting value for the same setting.
- A GPO linked to a parent OU has a value for a setting, and a GPO linked to a child OU has a conflicting value for the same setting.

If a GPO has settings configured for a parent organizational unit and the same policy settings are unconfigured for a child organizational unit, the child inherits the parent's GPO settings. That makes sense.

If a GPO has settings configured for a parent organizational unit that do not conflict with a GPO on a child organizational unit, the child organizational unit inherits the parent GPO settings and applies its own GPOs as well. A good example of this is two logon scripts; these scripts don't conflict, so both are run.

If a GPO has settings configured for a parent organizational unit that conflict with the same settings in another GPO configured for a child organizational unit, the child organizational unit does not inherit that specific GPO setting from the parent organizational unit. The setting in the GPO child policy takes priority.

While we only refer to parent organizational units in this section, the parent can be a site, domain, or local policy as well.

Blocking Inheritance and Overriding the Block in Organizational Unit GPOs

It is possible to force the settings of a GPO linked to an OU in the tree to be applied as the final settings for a child.

Blocking inheritance is a fairly simple concept. If you block inheritance to a specific Organizational Unit, GPOs linked to parent Organizational Units up the tree are not applied to objects in this specific Organizational Unit or its children.

    Local policies are processed even when Block Inheritance is checked.

Refer back to Figure 8-4. If we decide to block inheritance at the Databases organizational unit, Paul Burke will receive only GPOs directly defined on the Databases organizational unit. If we decide to block inheritance at the Gurus organizational unit, Paul Burke will receive only GPOs on the Databases organizational unit and those inherited from the Gurus organizational unit. The organizational unit that you block inheritance at stops any higher-level GPOs from applying to the branch starting at the blocked organizational unit. In fact, we can block inheritance on any of the organizational units within the *mycorp.com* domain. For example, blocking inheritance on the Financial Sector organizational unit makes sense if we want to block domain and site-level GPOs from applying.

This can cause problems if not carefully managed. For example, let's say that you have delegated control over an organizational unit branch to a group of administrators and allowed them access to manipulate GPOs on that branch. You may be applying GPOs to organizational units farther up the hierarchy that you wish this delegated branch to receive. However, your branch administrators have the ability to block inheritance of these parent organizational unit policies of yours. The branch administrators also have the ability to configure a setting that conflicts with one you set in a parent GPO; the branch administrator's child setting will take precedence in conflicts.

You can block inheritance by right-clicking a domain or organizational unit in the GPMC and selecting Block Inheritance as shown in Figure 8-5.

To prevent this, you can check the Enforced option on an individual GPO link. This allows administrators to force GPOs to be inherited by all children of an organizational unit. However, it has one further effect: it prevents GPO settings in child organizational units from overriding conflicting settings in a parent OU. The Enforced option is available by right-clicking on a group policy link in the GPMC and selecting Enforced as shown in Figure 8-6.

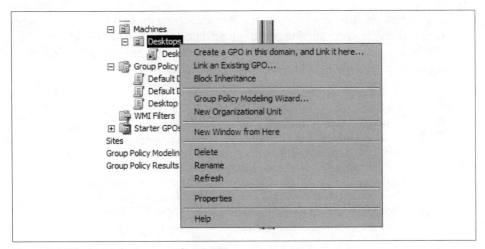

Figure 8-5. Blocking inheritance with GPMC

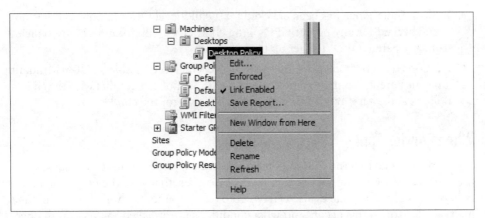

Figure 8-6. Group Policy Link Context Menu

 The Enforced setting is on a per-group policy link basis. You cannot set a given group policy object to be globally enforced through the domain.

Let's say that we change a registry setting using a GPO on the Financial Sector organizational unit. Unfortunately, another administrator then sets the same registry setting (among many others) to a conflicting value on the Gurus organizational unit and also blocks inheritance at the Databases organizational unit. By default, the registry setting will be correctly applied only to the Financial Sector organizational unit, as the Gurus organizational unit receives the different setting (child overrides parent on conflicts due to inheritance rules), and the Databases organizational unit doesn't inherit either policy. To fix both problems, we could set the original Financial Sector organizational unit

GPO link to Enforced. It then prevents the specific setting on the GPO on the Gurus organizational unit from modifying it without affecting any of the other GPO settings. Our GPO also is forced down past the Block Inheritance set up at the Databases organizational unit.

> If you perceive a trust issue in who can modify a given policy, it is suggested that you consider setting up an ACL on that policy to restrict the abilities of others to edit that GPO, leaving just a core group of administrators with the relevant permissions. This will ensure that the GPO is not changed without the knowledge of the core group. Of course, the fundamental issue is allowing anyone to have access to make any changes that you do not implicitly trust. Trying to secure bits and pieces from administrators you don't trust is a losing battle. If you do not trust someone to be an administrator, he shouldn't be one.

Summary

- If Block Inheritance has been checked for a child-level OU and Enforced has not been checked for any parent GPOs , the child GPO will not inherit any policies from any parent GPOs farther up the hierarchy.

- If Enforced has been checked for a parent-level GPO, the child-level OU will inherit all of the parent's configured policies, even if those policies conflict with the child's policies and even if Block Inheritance has been set for the child.

When Policies Apply

We've already said that the computer portion of a GPO applies during boot up and the user portion of a GPO applies during logon. However, that isn't the only time that a policy can apply. The policies also can be set to refresh periodically after a certain time interval. How often this occurs and what conditions are attached to this refresh operation are specified under the System\Group Policy key under the Administrative Templates section of the computer sections of a GPO.

Set the refresh value to 0 to have the policy continually apply every seven seconds. This is very useful for a test environment, but obviously not for a live service.

> For Windows 2000, you also can manually refresh policies on a client using the SECEDIT.EXE tool with the command `SECEDIT /refreshpolicy`. Windows XP, Vista, and Windows Server 2003 and newer have a utility called *GPUPDATE* that can accomplish the same thing. If any policies were modified that can only be applied at computer startup or user logon, *GPUPDATE* will ask if you want to reboot or logoff. Windows XP, Vista, and Windows Server 2003 and newer also have a tool to display details on what policies are applied called *GPRESULT*.

Refreshing is very useful for users who do not shut down their computers or log off from the system for days. In that case, GPOs apply in the normal way, but at very irregular intervals over long periods. Consequently, setting up policy refresh means that you can manage to apply those settings to such users at whatever interval you decide.

Group Policy refresh frequency

By default, Windows workstations and members servers refresh their policy every 90 minutes, and domain controllers refresh their policy every 5 minutes. In order to avoid having all machines retrieving the policy at once from the domain controllers, there is a random offset interval added to the refresh period on every machine. This offset interval, by default, is a random value up to 30 minutes on workstations and member servers, and 0 minutes on domain controllers. Both the refresh interval and offset interval are configurable. To modify these settings, you can modify the registry of a computer or you can edit a Group Policy Object that applies to the computer. The GPO settings are in the Group Policy section of the System portion of the Administrative Templates.

The registry entries for computer policy are under the `HKLM\Software\Policies\Micro soft\Windows\System` key. The specific values are listed in Table 8-1.

Table 8-1. Computer Group Policy refresh registry values

Registry value name	Description
GroupPolicyRefreshTime	REG_DWORD refresh interval for domain members. Valid range: 0–64,800 minutes.
GroupPolicyRefreshTimeOffset	REG_DWORD offset interval for domain members. Valid range: 0–1,440 minutes.
GroupPolicyRefreshTimeDC	REG_DWORD refresh interval for domain controllers. Valid range: 0–64,800 minutes.
GroupPolicyRefreshTimeOffsetDC	REG_DWORD offset interval for domain controllers. Valid range: 0–1,440 minutes.

The registry entries for user policy are under the `HKCU\Software\Policies\Microsoft \Windows\System` key. The specific values are listed in Table 8-2.

Table 8-2. User Group Policy refresh registry values

Registry value name	Description
GroupPolicyRefreshTime	REG_DWORD refresh interval for users. Valid range: 0-64,800 minutes.
GroupPolicyRefreshTimeOffset	REG_DWORD offset interval for users. Valid range: 0-1,440 minutes.

 While we provide the registry values here that Group Policy will configure, we do not recommend that you edit these registry values manually. Always use a Group Policy Object to configure these settings instead.

Combating Slowdown Due to Group Policy

Introducing Group Policy into your environment will slow down computer startup and user logon times to a degree. Exactly to what degree this occurs varies from environment to environment, and you will need to test in yours to come up with a representative figure. We do not recommend foregoing Group Policy in an effort to speed up your startup and logon times, but we do recommend being frugal when planning the number of policies that will apply to a given user or computer. There are some things you can take into consideration with regard to speed when planning your Group Policy deployment.

Limiting the number of GPOs that apply

Microsoft has its own take on designing your Active Directory for GPOs. They recommend that you should not have Organizational Unit structures more than 10 deep, so that policies do not take too much time during logon. Note that the issue isn't the number of OUs; it is the number of policies linked to the OUs. So, if you have 5 policies linked, it would be the same performance hit if these were linked over three OU levels or 10 OU levels.

Limiting cross-domain linking

It is possible for an administrator of one domain to create a GPO and for it to be applied to a site, domain, or organizational unit in another domain. For example, if the administrator of *child.mycorp.com* is given access to centralized setup GPOs within *my corp.com*, he can link the *mycorp.com* GPOs to domains or organizational units in the *child.mycorp.com* domain.

While this is a feasible setup, it is generally not recommended. In order for clients in the *child.mycorp.com* domain to apply policies from *mycorp.com*, they must contact a domain controller in *mycorp.com* in order to access the Sysvol share in *mycorp.com*. This will slow down logon and startup times, especially if the connectivity is slow. In lieu of linking policies between domains, we generally recommend that the policies be physically duplicated in each domain. Duplicating policies by way of import/export is discussed later in this chapter.

For more information about GPOs and WAN links, see the upcoming sidebar "How GPOs Work Across Slow Links."

Limiting use of site policies

Applying site policies has the same limitations as cross-domain linking if you are running in a multidomain environment. Site based policies are only stored on the domain controllers in the root domain of the forest by default. For clients to apply these policies, they must contact a domain controller in the root domain in order to retrieve the policy.

We generally recommend that organizations pursue alternatives to site-based policies when possible, unless they are running in a single domain environment. Site-based policies are often confusing for administrators to manage and troubleshoot as the administrator must remember to check the site, in addition to the domain and organizational units, for policies. Furthermore, site-based policies often require traversing one or more WAN links in order to retrieve the policy.

How GPOs Work Across Slow Links

GPOs and even user profiles can still work across slow links, and a lot of the configuration is left in the hands of the administrator. Administrators can specify what speed is used in the definition of a slow link. For computers and users, the following policy areas need looking at:

- Policies→Computer Configuration→Administrative Templates→System→ Group Policy→Group Policy Slow Link Detection
- Policies→User Configuration→Administrative Templates→System→ Group Policy→Group Policy Slow Link Detection

In both cases, the default setting is 500 KBps, but administrators can set any KBps connection speed time that they wish. This speed is used against a slow-link-detection algorithm; if the speed is above the value, the link is fast; a speed below the value indicates a slow link.

This is the algorithm in pseudocode prior to Windows Vista/Windows Server 2008:

```
Ping server with 0KB of data :
   Receive response#1 as a time in milliseconds (ms)
If response#1 < 10ms Then
   Exit as this is a fast link
Else
   Ping server with 2KB of data :
      Receive response#2 as a time in milliseconds
   Calculate Total-speed as response#2-response#1
End If
Ping server with 0KB of data :
   Receive response#1 as a time in milliseconds
If response#1 < 10ms Then
   Exit as this is a fast link
Else
   Ping server with 2KB of data :
      Receive response#2 as a time in milliseconds
   Calculate Total-speed as Total-speed + (response#2-response#1)
End If
Ping server with 0KB of data :
   Receive response#1 as a time in milliseconds
If response#1 < 10ms Then
   Exit as this is a fast link
Else
   Ping server with 2KB of data :
      Receive response#2 as a time in milliseconds
   Calculate Total-speed as Total-speed + (response#2-response#1)
End If
   'Average the total speed of (response#2-response#1)
```

```
Difference-in-milliseconds = Total-Speed/3
'If we know 2KB (16,384 bits) was moved in a certain number
'of milliseconds, then we need to calculate the number
'of bits moved per second (not per ms)
Bits-per-second-value = (16384 * 1000/Difference-in-milliseconds)
'Eight bits is a byte, so calculate bytes/second
bps-value = (Bits-per-second-value * 8)
'Calculate kilobytes/second to compare against GPO value
Kbps-value = bps-value / 1024
```

Windows Vista and Windows Server 2008 clients depend upon the Network Location Awareness client to determine if a link is slow.

The following GPOs are applied across slow links:

- When a user logs in using the "Logon using dial-up connection" checkbox on the logon screen, user policies are applied.
- When the computer is a member of the same domain as the RAS server or is in a domain with a trust relationship to the one the RAS server is in, both are applied.

GPOs are not applied:

- When the logon is done using cached credentials
- To computers that are members of a different domain

In all of these cases, security settings (i.e., IP security, EFS recovery, etc.) and Administrative Template settings are the only ones to be applied by default; folder redirection, disk quotas, scripts, and software installation policies are not applied. You can't turn off registry settings you have to apply. You can, however, alter the default state of any of the others, including the security settings, using the relevant sections of those GPOs.

Use simple queries in WMI filters

If you have a WMI filter applied to a GPO, a WMI query will be run before the GPO is applied to a user or computer, assuming the computer's operating system is Windows XP or newer. If the WMI query is very complex, it could significantly impact the time it takes to process the GPO. If you have multiple GPOs that contain a WMI filter, you need to pay special attention to the impact those queries will have.

Security Filtering and Group Policy Objects

As each GPO is an object in Active Directory and all objects have Access Control Lists (ACL) associated with them, it follows that it must be possible to allow and deny access to a GPO using that ACL. With ACLs, it is possible to allow and deny access to apply GPOs based on security group membership. It is also possible to go to an even finer-grained detail and set access control for an individual computer or user. Figure 8-7 shows that only one computer; XPCLNT01, can apply the policy pictured.

This is a significant feature of GPOs, and one that you can use heavily to your advantage. Let's take a simple example, in which we create a single GPO to roll out an internal

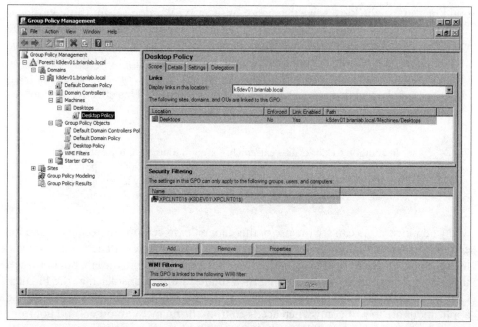

Figure 8-7. *Access control entries for a GPO*

application and link it to the Finance and Marketing Organizational Units in one domain. Now, all users in the Finance and Marketing Organizational Units will receive that application via the GPO on logon. Let's also say that certain users from both Organizational Units are not to receive this application. All we need to do is create a security group to hold that user subset, and set up an Access Control Entry (ACE) to the Application Deployment GPO and check the Deny Apply Group Policy checkbox in the ACL. Now, every user that we make a member of that new security group will not receive the policy

Deny always overrides Allow. Let's say a user or computer is a member of four security groups. If a GPO has an ACL that contains an ACE for the individual user or computer with Read and Apply rights, an ACE for three of the security groups that have Read and Apply rights, and an ACE for the fourth security group that has Apply rights denied, the GPO will not be applied.

Loopback Merge Mode and Loopback Replace Mode

Loopback mode is a special GPO option that allows you to apply the user portion of a GPO to a user, based on the computer that the user is logged in to. For example, imagine we have a suite of public kiosks in the foyer of our organization to give outsiders information about the company. Company employees can also use these devices if they want to check email quickly on their way in or out. Because literally anyone in the building can use the kiosks, we need a lot of security. We don't want those kiosks to allow company employees to have all the privileges and permissions that they normally would at their desktop devices; we want them to be able to use only email. What we can do is tie a set of user restrictions into the user portion of a GPO that sits on the Organizational Unit that holds the computer objects for the kiosk computers. Then employees are locked down at the kiosks and nowhere else. This effectively allows us to restrict what employees can do on a per-machine basis.

 In addition to kiosks, it is extremely common to use loopback processing of Group Policy objects on terminal servers. Using loopback policies here allows users to receive different settings when they log on to a terminal server as opposed to when they log on to their workstation.

Many administrators can see the use of this capability in certain environments and for certain situations. Take a lab of machines in a university where staff accounts are to be locked down like student accounts while the staff members are in the lab, but not when they are at their normal workstations. As a final example, consider that the Finance Organizational Unit users have a lot of deployed applications specific to Finance. These applications are to work only when accessed from the finance computers and not from anywhere else. So, you would put them as deployed applications into the computer section of GPOs that apply to the Finance Organizational Unit. However, if you also deployed to finance users (via the user portion of a GPO) applications that were supposed to roam with the users everywhere except in sales and marketing, you could use loopback mode to stop the applications from being advertised specifically in those two Organizational Units.

Loopback mode can be found in the Group Policy settings of the computer portion of any GPO ("Computer Configuration→Policies→System→Group Policy→User Group Policy loopback processing mode"). If you open that item, you get the dialog box shown in Figure 8-8, which allows you to switch between the two modes of loopback operation: merge mode and replace mode.

When a user logs on to a machine that uses loopback merge mode, the user policies are applied first as normal; the user portion of any GPOs that apply to the computer are applied in sequence, overriding any of the previous user policies as appropriate. Replace mode, by contrast, ignores the GPOs that would apply to the user and instead applies only the user portions of the GPOs that apply to the computers. Figure 8-9 illustrates this.

In Figure 8-9, the domain *mycorp.com* spans two sites, Main-Site and Second-Site. Marketing computers exist in Main-Site, and finance computers in Second-Site. Policy A applies to Main-Site only, Policy B applies to the entire domain, and C, D, E, and F apply to the Organizational Units as indicated. Policy G applies to Second-Site.

Figure 8-8. Setting loopback mode

Table 8-3 summarizes the position. When loopback is not turned on, the only real difference comes from the site policies (A or G) that are applied. When you turn merge mode on for all the GPOs, it becomes more obvious what will happen. In each case, the policy relating to the user is applied first in order, followed by the entire set of policy items that would apply to a user residing in the computer location. Take the example of a finance user logging on at a marketing computer in the main site:

- The user portion of the site policy that she is logging on from is applied (A).
- The user portion of the domain policy (B).
- The user portion of the Accounting Organizational Unit (E).
- The user portion of the Finance Organizational Unit (F).
- After this, the user portion of the site (A) is applied again.
- The user portion of the domain policy (B).
- The user portion of the Business Organizational Unit (C).
- Finally the user portion of the Marketing Organizational Unit (D).

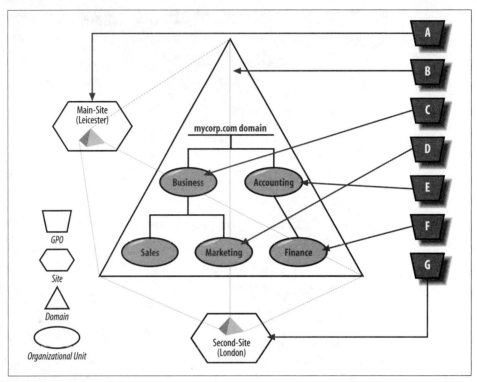

Figure 8-9. Loopback-mode processing

Table 8-3. Resultant set of policies for available loopback modes

Loopback mode in use	OU in which user resides	Where computer resides	Resultant set of policies
No	Marketing	OU=marketing (main site)	ABCD
No	Finance	OU=finance (second site)	GBEF
No	Marketing	OU=finance (second site)	GBCD
No	Finance	OU=marketing (main site)	ABEF
Merge	Marketing	OU=marketing (main site)	ABCDABCD
Merge	Finance	OU=finance (second site)	GBEFGBEF
Merge	Marketing	OU=finance (second site)	GBCDGBEF
Merge	Finance	OU=marketing (main site)	ABEFABCD
Replace	Marketing	OU=marketing (main site)	ABCD
Replace	Finance	OU=finance (second site)	GBEF
Replace	Marketing	OU=finance (second site)	GBEF
Replace	Finance	OU=marketing (main site)	ABCD

Remember that later policies can override earlier policies, so the user portion of the policies applying to the location of the computer will always override previous policies if there is a conflict. With policy order ABEFABCD, D can override C, which can override B, which can override A, which can override F, and so on. Also, in all these cases, if any of the computer GPOs do not have any defined settings in the user portion, the policy is ignored.

Loopback replace mode is used when the user portion of the GPOs that apply to a computer are to be the only ones set. For the finance user logging on to a computer in marketing in the main site, the only policies that get applied to that user are ABCD, the user portions of the GPOs that apply to the marketing computer.

Administrators must be aware that loopback mode can impose a significant amount of extra load on the processing at the client, especially when using loopback in its merge mode.

WMI Filtering

Microsoft has added a powerful new GPO filtering option in Windows Server 2003 Active Directory called Windows Management Interface (WMI) filtering. With WMI filtering, you can associate a WMI query with a GPO, which will run for each user and computer that the GPO applies to. A WMI filter can utilize any WMI-based information that is accessible from the client's machine, including computer hardware and configuration, user profile, and environment settings. This presents a lot of options for targeting GPOs to clients that have certain properties.

WMI filters will only run on Windows XP and newer operating systems. If a policy with a WMI filter attached applies to a Windows 2000 computer, the WMI filter will be ignored.

For example, let's say you want to apply a certain GPO if a client is accessing your network over a Virtual Private Network (VPN) connection. Depending on which VPN software the client is running, your WMI query could check for the existence of a process or service or even an IP address range. If the query returns true, the GPO will be applied; if it returns false, it will not be applied.

Summary of Policy Options

That's a lot of information on GPOs. Let's summarize what we've covered about the workings of GPOs so far:

- GPOs exist in a split state. The configuration data for the GPO, known in shorthand form as GPC data, is held in the AD object itself. The template files and settings that tell the GPO what its capabilities are, known in shorthand form as GPT data, are stored in the SYSVOL.

- Individual GPOs can be linked to multiple sites, domains, and Organizational Units in Active Directory as required.

- GPOs can contain policies that apply to both computers and users in a container. The default operation of a GPO on a container is to apply the computer portion of the GPO to every computer in that container during boot up and to apply the user portion of the GPO to every user in that container during logon. GPOs can also be set to refresh periodically.

- Multiple GPOs linked to a particular container in Active Directory will be applied in a strict order according to a series of priorities. The default-prioritized order corresponds to the exact order in which the GPOs were linked to the container. Administrators can adjust the priorities as required.

- While GPOs exist only in a domain environment due to their dependence on Active Directory, individual domain or workgroup computers can have local GPOs, known as LGPOs, defined for them.

- Windows NT 4.0 system policies can also apply to standalone Windows NT or later clients.

- GPOs are inherited down the Organizational Unit hierarchy by default. This can be blocked using the properties of an OU, domain, or site. Administrators can also set a checkbox that allows a policy to override all lower settings and bypass any blocks.

- Loopback mode allows the administrator to specify that user settings can be over-ridden on a per-machine basis. Effectively, this means that the user parts of policies that normally apply only to computers are applied to the users as well as (merge mode) or instead of (replace mode) the existing user policies.

- A new feature in Windows Server 2003 Active Directory called WMI filtering allows you to configure a WMI query that can be used as additional criteria to determine whether a GPO should be applied. If the filter evaluates to true, the GPO will continue to be processed; if it evaluates to false, the GPO will not be processed. This is a powerful feature because you have the vast amount of WMI data available to determine whether GPOs should be applied.

- A number of things can slow down processing on a client, including attempting to process many policies one after the other. Use of loopback mode, especially in merge mode, can significantly impact performance. Attempting to apply GPOs across domains can also lead to slowdowns depending on the network speed between the domains. Finally, complex queries in WMI filters can also have a negative impact on GPO processing.

- Policies are applied in a strict order known as 4LSDOU. This notation indicates that Windows NT 4.0 system policies are applied first, followed by any LGPO policies, followed by site GPOs, domain GPOs, and finally any Organizational Unit GPOs hierarchically down the tree. At each point, the policies are applied in prioritized order if multiple policies exist at a location.

- When policies are to be applied to a client, the system identifies the entire list of policies to be applied before actually applying them in order. This is to determine whether any blocking, overriding, or loopback has been put in place that could alter the order or application of the policies.

- ACLs can be used to limit the application of GPOs to certain individual users or computers or groups of users or computers. Specifically setting up the ACLs on a GPO to deny or allow access means that you can tailor the impact of a policy from the normal method of applying the GPO to all users or computers in a container.

- Finally, both user profiles and policies can be applied across a slow link, but the speed that the system uses to determine whether a link is slow is configurable by the administrator within an individual GPO. In addition, while security settings and administrative templates normally are applied by default, the exact settings that will apply across a slow link when one is detected are configurable by the administrator as well. The only exception is that administrative templates will always be applied; the administrator has no control over this.

Managing Group Policies

The Microsoft tools available to manage GPOs under Windows 2000 were pretty limited, consisting of the Group Policy Object Editor (formerly Group Policy Editor) and built-in support in the Active Directory Users and Computers and Active Directory Sites and Services snap-ins. While these tools could get the job done, they did not provide any support for viewing the Resultant Set of Policy (RSoP), viewing how GPOs had been applied throughout a domain, or backing up or restoring GPOs.

Directly after the release of Windows Server 2003, Microsoft released the Group Policy Management Console (GPMC) as a separate web download. The GPMC is a much-needed addition to Microsoft's GPO management tools and provides nearly every GPO management function that an organization might need, including scripting support.

The other new feature available in the Windows Server 2003 Active Directory administrative tools and in GPMC is support for viewing the RSoP for a given computer based on certain criteria. RSoP allows administrators to determine what settings will be applied to a user and can aid in troubleshooting GPO problems. RSoP will be described in more detail in the section on debugging group policies.

 The Windows Server 2008 version of the Active Directory administrative tools no longer includes RSoP. You must instead use the GPMC.

Using the Group Policy Management Console (GPMC)

The GPMC is a one-stop shop for all your GPO management needs. You can browse a forest and see where GPOs are applied; you can create and link GPOs; you can import and export, backup and restore, delegate control, and view RSoP reports, all from the GPMC. Not only does the GPMC have a bunch of new functionality not available in any of the previous standard tools, it also integrates the existing tools—such as the GPME for editing GPOs.

GPOs and the PDC Emulator

When you are editing GPOs, the GPMC and GPME connect to and use the FSMO PDC role owner by default. This ensures that multiple copies of the GPME on different machines are all focused on the same DC. This behavior may be overridden in two cases.

If the PDC is unavailable for whatever reason, an error dialog will be displayed, and the administrator may select an alternate DC to use. An administrator can also manually target a different domain controller in the GPMC.

If GPOs are edited on multiple DCs, this could lead to inconsistencies because the last person to write to the GPO wins. For this reason, you should use caution when multiple administrators regularly administer policies.

Figure 8-7 shows what the GPMC looks like when viewing a GPO. As you can see in the left pane, you can browse through the domains in a forest down to specific Organizational Units. If you right-click on an Organizational Unit, you'll get many of the same options, as shown in Figure 8-6.

In Figure 8-7, the Desktops organizational unit has been expanded to show that the Desktop Policy GPO has been linked to it (i.e., icon with a shortcut/arrow symbol). A virtual Group Policy Objects container is expanded, which shows all of the GPOs that have been created in the domain. There is also a virtual WMI Filters container that holds any WMI filter objects that have been created. Note that the Group Policy Objects, WMI Filters, and Starter GPOs containers are virtual. This was done so that instead of requiring drilling down into the System container to locate GPOs, they would be readily available directly under a domain.

 You can also browse the GPOs that have been linked to a site by right clicking on the Sites container and selecting Show Sites. You have an option of which sites to display.

If we take a look at Figure 8-7 again, we can see that the Desktop Policy was selected in the left pane, and several options and settings are displayed in the right pane. The following list is a summary of each tab:

Scope

Under the Scope tab, you can view the domains, sites, or Organizational Units that have been linked to the GPO and delete them if necessary. You can also view what security groups the GPO applies to, and add and remove groups from the list. Finally, you can set the WMI filter that should be associated with the GPO.

Details

The Details tab contains information about who created the GPO, the date it was created and last modified, and the current user version and computer version. The only thing that can be set on this page is beside GPO Status, which defines whether the user and/or computer settings are enabled.

Settings

The Settings tab provides a nice shortcut to view which settings have been configured in a GPO. Unlike the GPME, in which you have to drill down through each folder to determine which settings have been configured, you can view the Settings tab for a GPO in the GPMC to see only the options that have been set.

Delegation

The Delegation tab is similar to the Delegation of Control wizard, but it's specifically for GPOs. We'll cover this screen in more detail later in the chapter.

One last feature that is worth mentioning is the Group Policy Modeling and Group Policy Results. Group Policy Modeling is very similar to the RSoP option, which is described later in this chapter. Group Policy Results is very similar to the Group Policy Modeling/RSoP, except that it is not a simulation. The results are returned from the client, not simulated on a domain controller. Group Policy Results will only work on a computer running Windows XP, or Windows Server 2003 or newer.

Group Policy Modeling

While the Group Policy Results Wizard allows you to see the effective settings for a user and/or computer, it is dependent on that user having logged into the computer in question before. The GPMC includes a second wizard which is helpful for generating "what-if" reports for various scenarios. You can specify a specific user and computer to model or specific locations in the OU hierarchy as shown in Figure 8-10.

The wizard will allow you to simulate conditions such as slow links, loopback processing, or site membership as shown in Figure 8-11. You can also simulate a change to the user or computer's security group membership if, for example, you were testing changes to security filtering for a policy. Figure 8-12 shows the report that is created by GPMC. The Summary and Settings tabs are similar to the results reports, and the query tab displays a summary of the parameters you specified during the modeling wizard.

Much like the Group Policy Results reports, you can rerun and export modeling reports as well as view the RSoP MMC by using the "Advanced View" option.

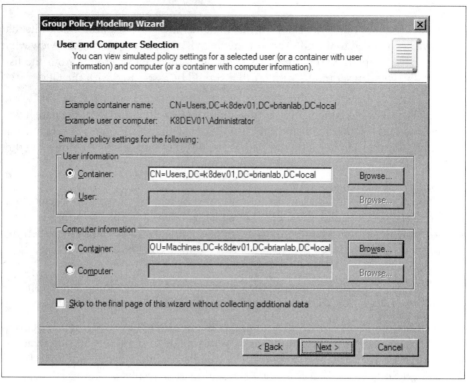

Figure 8-10. Group Policy Modeling Wizard

Delegation and Change Control

When planning your group policy deployment, you have to work out how you will maintain firm control over GPOs once you start deploying them. Specifically, you need to consider who will be managing your GPOs and how you will keep control over the wide-ranging changes they can make.

The importance of change-control procedures

The best way to keep track of GPOs in your organization is through a series of change-control procedures. These work well whether your GPO administrators are domain administrators or not. The complexity of the change-control system used for group policy varies from organization to organization. Some organizations opt to manage all of their group policies in their configuration management database (CMDB); others implement simpler systems such as Word documents or Excel spreadsheets. It is important that you test any group policy changes in the lab before applying them in production, due to the potential for disrupting service if a faulty policy change is applied.

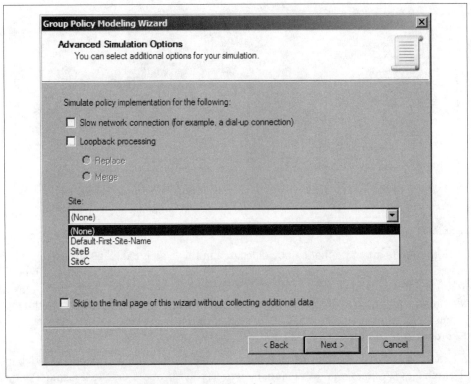

Figure 8-11. Simulating network conditions and loopback processing

Designing the delegation of GPO administration

There are three types of permission that can be considered here:

- The permission to allow sets of users to link policies (and manage the block inheritance setting) to a domain or an Organizational Unit branch
- The permission to allow sets of users to create GPOs
- The permission to allow sets of users to change the GPOs themselves

Link delegation can be easily accomplished using the Delegation of Control Wizard[†] that you get by right-clicking an Organizational Unit, domain, or site in Active Directory and choosing Delegate Control. You'll want to use the "Manage Group Policy Links" task. Here you are actually delegating read and write access to the gPLink[‡] attribute of objects.

---

† This wizard is discussed more fully in Chapter 13.

‡ The GPC data part of a GPO is an object in Active Directory. This object, like all others, has attributes.

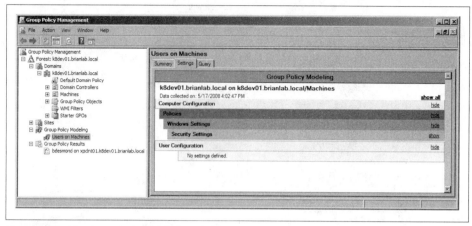

Figure 8-12. The Group Policy Modeling report

The other GPO attribute that can be delegated in this way is called `gPOptions`. As discussed earlier and shown in Figure 8-6, this deals with the area of blocking inheritance. If you're interested in how these attributes work, set up a few GPOs in your Active Directory. Then use ADSI Edit from the Windows Support Tools to examine the attributes of the newly created GPOs in this location `CN=Policies,CN=System,dc=windows,dc=mycorp,dc=com`.

Creation of GPOs is limited to those accounts indicated in the upcoming sidebar "Default GPO Permissions" by default. However, you can add users to the Group Policy Creator Owners security group, which allows members of that group to create new GPOs.

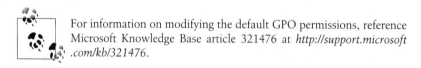 For information on modifying the default GPO permissions, reference Microsoft Knowledge Base article 321476 at *http://support.microsoft .com/kb/321476*.

If a member of Group Policy Creator Owners creates a GPO, that user is set as the Creator Owner[§] of the GPO and can continue to manage it. The Creator Owner of a GPO can manage the GPO even if the user is removed from all groups that give GPO management privileges.

[§] When administrators create GPOs, the Domain Admins group becomes the Creator Owner.

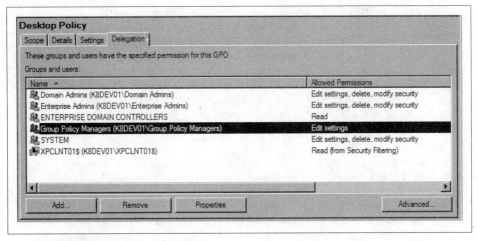

Figure 8-13. GPO delegation in the GPMC

GPC data in Active Directory (i.e., the actual Active Directory object itself) will never inherit security permissions from parents up the tree. There is a special block in place that prevents this in Active Directory, so that all GPO ACLs have to be modified from within the Group Policy tools.

You can delegate edit access to new GPOs, as long as the people creating those GPOs are the ones who will be editing them, by placing those users into the Group Policy Creator Owners group. If you also want to delegate edit access to more people or to GPOs that a user is not the Creator Owner of, use the GPMC. Navigate to the *Group Policy Object* folder under the domain in which the GPO you want to edit is contained. Click on the GPO you want to delegate and select the Delegation tab in the right pane, as shown in Figure 8-13. Click the Add button; this will bring up the object picker, which allows you to select which users or groups you want to have access. Next you'll need to pick the permission you want to grant. You have three options:

- Read
- Edit settings
- Edit settings, delete, modify security

Finally, click OK and the delegation will be applied.

A word of warning before we finish up here: correctly applied, GPOs are fundamental to the well-being of your Active Directory. Policies incorrectly applied to the root of the domain could lock down the Administrator account or disallow logons at domain controllers. This is obviously a worst-case scenario, but there are some mistakes that are much more likely to occur: a mistyped registry value that forces users to an invalid proxy server and thus stops Internet Explorer from working, forgetting to clear a checkbox and thus applying a policy down an entire branch of the tree (the default) when it was only to apply to the root of the branch, and so on.

These changes have the potential to affect all users or computers throughout the tree, so we would caution you to keep GPO administrators to a very select subset. If you allow non-administrators the ability to create, change, and delete GPOs, they have to be able to take responsibility for and be accountable for their actions. Users who are already administrator-equivalent will automatically be able to administer GPOs and should already be held accountable.

Default GPO Permissions

Any user, computer, or group needs both Read and Apply Group Policy to apply a policy. Active Directory ships with certain permissions already in existence for GPOs. These are:

- Authenticated Users group has Read and Apply Group Policy.
- Creator Owner has Full Control without an explicit Apply Group Policy.
- Local System group has Full Control without an explicit Apply Group Policy.
- Domain Admins group has Full Control without an explicit Apply Group Policy.
- Enterprise Admins group has Full Control without an explicit Apply Group Policy.
- Group Policy Creator Owners group has Full Control without an explicit Apply Group Policy.

Administrators in the latter three groups are also authenticated users and so inherit the Read permission from that group. If you don't want administrators to have the user parts of GPOs applied on logon, set the Apply Group Policy setting to Deny for Domain Admins, Enterprise Admins, and possibly Creator Owner as well.

Using Starter GPOs

One of the new features for Group Policy in the Windows Server 2008 toolset is Starter GPOs. Starter GPOs allow you to define a template GPO that can then be duplicated in the GPMC. Starter GPOs are stored and replicated alongside normal Group Policies in the Sysvol container in a new folder called *StarterGPOs*.

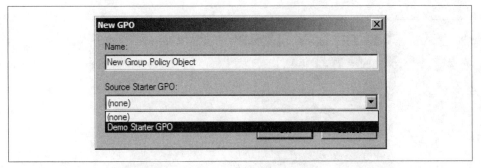

Figure 8-14. New GPO with Starter GPO

 The settings you can define in Starter GPOs are limited to the settings in the Administrative Templates section of the GPME.

Creating a Starter GPO is nearly identical to creating a normal GPO. Simply right-click the Starter GPOs virtual container in the GPMC and click New.

You may have noticed that the New GPO dialog has an additional selection for the Starter GPO as shown in Figure 8-14.If you select a Starter GPO at this time, the settings from that Starter GPO will be imported into your new GPO providing a baseline to start with.

Group Policy Backup and Restore

Restoring the Sysvol container from a system-state backup of a domain controller is an involved and somewhat painful process. Fortunately, with the introduction of the GPMC, there is an easy GUI and script-based mechanism for backing up and restoring some or all of your group policies. To back up all of the group policies in the domain with GPMC, right-click on the Group Policy Objects virtual container and select the Backup All option. You will be presented with a dialog similar to Figure 8-15. You must provide the GPMC with a path to an empty folder to backup all of the GPOs to, and optionally a comment to include in the backup. Once the wizard completes, you can zip the target folder and have a portable and easy-to-work-with backup.

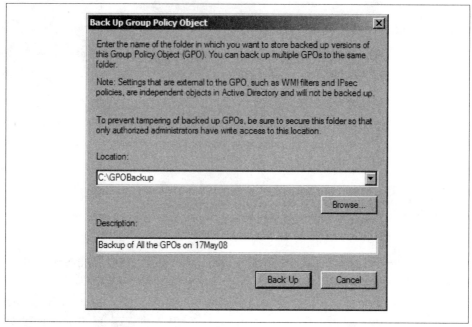

Figure 8-15. Group Policy backup

If you want to back up an individual policy, simply right-click it under the Group Policy Objects container and select Back Up. GPMC only supports restoring policies on a per-policy basis. To restore a policy, right-click it under the Group Policy Objects container and select Restore From Backup. The wizard will prompt you for the path to the backup. You must point the wizard to the *parent* folder of the backup. If you are restoring from the backup created in Figure 8-15, you would point the restore wizard to C:\GPOBackup.

If you need to restore all of the GPOs in a backup at once, you can use the RestoreAllGPOs.wsf script that is included in the GPMC sample scripts discussed in the "Scripting Group Policies" section of this chapter. You can conversely use the BackupAllGPOs.wsf script to backup all of the GPOs in a domain. There are individual group policy backup-and-restore scripts called BackupGPO.wsf and RestoreGPO.wsf, respectively.

You can also use the GPMC backup and restore functionality to copy Group Polices between domains, or perhaps between a test environment and production. The GPMC includes a Migration Table Editor tool that will be invoked when you need to modify references to security principals in the source domain so that the policy will continue to function in the target domain. For more information on migrating Group Policies, see the whitepaper *Migrating GPOs Across Domains with GPMC* at:

http://download.microsoft.com/download/1/9/f/19f1728a-6314-4d29-a60d
-ea9cadcd2c16/MigGPOs.doc

 If you're looking for a more robust Group Policy backup-and-restore solution, take a look at GPExpert™ Backup Manager for Group Policy from SDM Software. For more information, visit *http://www.sdmsoft ware.com/group_policy_backup*.

Scripting Group Policies

Another hurdle to efficiently managing GPOs with the initial release of Active Directory was the lack of scripting support. Not having the ability to automate the creation or maintenance of GPOs meant that administrators had to spend a lot of time manually managing GPOs. Fortunately, the GPMC also provides scripting capabilities. Whenever you install the GPMC, it registers several COM-based objects that can be used to automate most of the tasks you'd need to do with GPOs. The word "most" is used because the GPMC COM objects do not allow you to configure any GPO settings; you still have to do that manually. On the other hand, you can copy or import a GPO and its settings, so if you have a template GPO or a GPO you want to create in multiple domains, you can conceivably create it once, then use the COM objects to copy it to other domains

There are a number of useful sample scripts (over thirty) for working with the GPMC that Microsoft distributes freely on their website at *http://www.microsoft.com/down loads/details.aspx?familyid=38c1a89b-a6d2-4f2a-a944-9236999aee65*. Once you download and run the installer, the scripts will be stored in %ProgramFiles%\Microsoft Group Policy\GPMC Sample Scripts.

The following is a partial list of some of the tasks you can perform via scripts with the GPMC objects:

- Create a GPO with the default settings
- Copy a GPO
- Import GPO settings
- Set GPO permissions
- Delete a GPO
- Search for GPOs
- List GPOs
- Retrieve GPO information
- Back up GPOs
- Restore GPOs
- Generate a RSoP report for GPOs

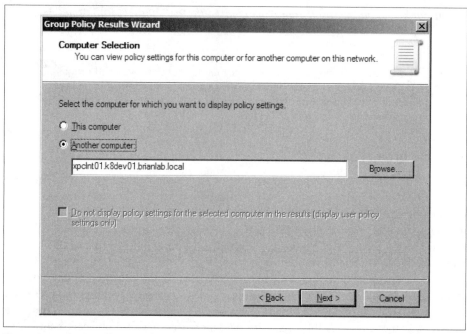

Figure 8-16. Group Policy Results Wizard target selection

You can also work with Group Policy via Windows PowerShell if you leverage third-party snap-ins. For more information on this, check out Chapter 31. If you want to jump right in, you can download the free cmdlets from *http://www.sdmsoftware.com/freeware*.

Troubleshooting Group Policy

If, at any point, you need to debug group policies, there are couple of available options. The first is new as of Windows Server 2003 and is called the Resultant Set of Policy, which some people may be familiar with if you've used tools like Full Armor's Fazam 2000. The Resultant Set of Policy (RSoP) allows you to specify certain user, computer, group, and GPO criteria to determine what GPOs will be applied. Another option is to enable some extra logging that can help point out GPO processing problems.

Group Policy Results Wizard

The Group Policy Results Wizard is a frontend for the Resultant Set of Policy (RSoP) tool. RSoP is a very powerful tool that will identify what GPO settings have been applied to a user or computer. Before RSoP, administrators were left to do their own estimates as to what GPOs took precedence and what settings were actually applied to users and computers. RSoP removes much of the guesswork with an easy-to-use wizard interface.

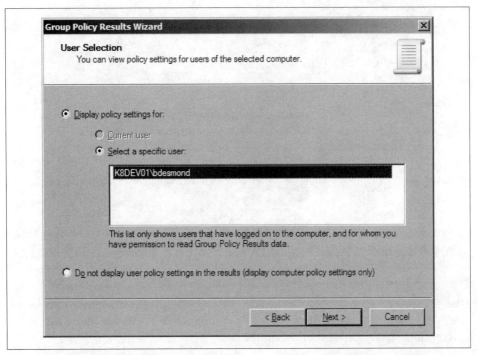

Figure 8-17. Target-user selection

To start the Group Policy Results wizard, open the GPMC, and right click the *Group Policy Results* folder and launch the "Group Policy Results Wizard." Figure 8-16 shows the initial screen where you will be prompted to select a target machine to run the RSoP session on.

The next screen, as shown in Figure 8-17, allows you to optionally specify what user to run the RSoP session in the context of. If you only need computer settings, you can skip this step. The wizard will only display users who have logged on to the target machine successfully in the past.

Once you finish the wizard, the GPMC will create a report similar to the one shown in Figure 8-18. This report is divided into three sections:

- The summary view gives a high-level overview of which policies were applied, filters that were executed, and so forth.
- The settings view allows you to view every setting that was applied and the GPO this setting originated from.
- The policy events tab is new in Windows Server 2008 and allows you to view a consolidated view of event log entries related to group policy processing.

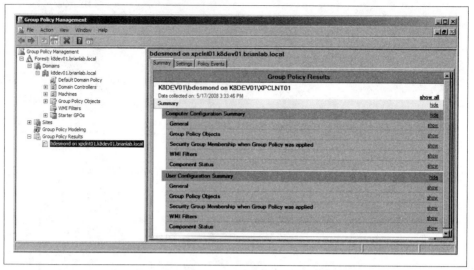

Figure 8-18. Group Policy Results report

One of the nice features of the Group Policy Results tool is that the reports are saved, so you can reference them later. You can also right-click the report in the tree at left and rerun the query or export the report.

You can also run an RSoP session from the command line. See the upcoming sidebar "Using the GPRESULT Tool."

 If you are looking for the Resultant Set of Policy view rather than the HTML report style pictured in Figure 8-18, right-click the report and select "Advanced View..."

COMMAND-LINE REFERENCE

Using the GPRESULT Tool

The GPRESULT tool can be run from any system to export the group policy results for the current session or a target machine and/or user to a text file. GPRESULT has been available since Windows XP.

To export the group policy settings for the current session, use this command:

gpresult /v

If you would like to target a different user, run:

gpresult /v /USER *otherusername*

To target a different machine, run:

gpresult /v /S *othercomputer*

You can also combine these switches to target a different user and computer.

Vista SP1 and Windows Server 2008 added the **/H** switch, which allows you to export an HTML report similar to the one found in the GPMC console.

For additional options, run **gpresult /?**.

Forcing Group Policy Updates

Sometimes when troubleshooting an issue, you may not want to wait for a policy to refresh in the normal time period. Beginning with Windows XP, there is a command-line tool to do this called gpupdate. You can simply run gpupdate to update the group policy settings; however, there are other options available that are documented if you run **gpupdate /?**.

Enabling Extra Logging

You can turn on verbose logging in the event log for group policy-related events simply by setting a registry key. Once the key exists with the correct value, logging is done automatically; a reboot is not necessary for the new value to take effect. The value, a REG_DWORD, is called RunDiagnosticLoggingGroupPolicy and needs to be created with a value of 1 in the HKLM\Software\Microsoft\Windows NT\CurrentVersion\Diagnostics key.

The value of 1 sets the logging to verbose mode; setting the value to 0 is the same as having the key absent and is known as normal logging. In other words, the key makes a difference only when set to a value of 1. It's really as simple as that.

 This key is actually one of four currently supported keys that you can use at this location. You also can create the following:

- RunDiagnosticLoggingIntellimirror
- RunDiagnosticLoggingAppDeploy

If the verbose logging in the event log is not providing enough information, another option is to enable debug logging for policy and profile processing. To do so, create a value called UserEnvDebugLevel as a REG_DWORD in the HKLM\Software\Microsoft\WindowsNT\CurrentVersion\Winlogon key. Assign UserEnvDebugLevel the value 10002 in hexadecimal format. Restart the computer, and from then on, extensive logging information will be recorded on the machine in the file *%SystemRoot%\Debug\UserMode\Userenv.log*. For more information, check out Microsoft Knowledge Base Article 221833, which can be found at: *http://support.microsoft.com/kb/221833*.

The UserEnv debug log file is extremely dense, so chances are you will need to search for keywords such as "error" if you are not used to reading the log. Keep in mind that some errors are normal even though they are flagged as errors. Be sure to disable the `UserEnvDebugLevel` setting once you are finished with it.

 For a comprehensive listing of group policy logging settings, check out the free ADM file available for download at *http://www.gpoguy.com/FreeTools/FreeToolsLibrary/tabid/67/agentType/View/PropertyID/84/Default.aspx*.

Group Policy Diagnostic Best Practices Analyzer

Microsoft has a free tool available from their website called the Group Policy Diagnostic BPA. BPA stands for Best Practices Analyzer, and it's a breed of tool Microsoft has been releasing for various tools and products over the past several years. The Group Policy Diagnostic BPA can help with troubleshooting. To get the Group Policy Diagnostic BPA, go to *http://support.microsoft.com/kb/940122* to get the most appropriate version.

Third-Party Troubleshooting Tools

Independent software vendor SDM Software has developed a group policy trouble-shooting toolset that can visually report on group policy processing health on clients, as well as visually analyze many of the logging options discussed earlier in this chapter. For more information, visit *http://www.sdmsoftware.com/group_policy_troubleshoot*.

The *www.gpoguy.com* community website is also an excellent resource for Group Policy information. There is also an email discussion list for Group Policy topics hosted at *www.gpoguy.com*.

Summary

One of the big selling points of Active Directory has always been group policy, and in Windows Server 2008 Active Directory, Microsoft greatly extended the functionality and management of GPOs. In this chapter, we covered the details of how group policies are stored in Active Directory, how GPOs are processed by clients, the GPO precedence order, the effect of inheritance, and the role ACLs play.

With Windows Server 2003, Microsoft introduced several new tools to help manage and troubleshoot GPOs. Perhaps the most important is the Group Policy Management Console (GPMC), which is a one-stop shop for all your GPO needs. With the GPMC, you can perform virtually any function you need to do from a single interface, as opposed to using three or four separate tools as was necessary with the Windows 2000 tools. Another benefit of the GPMC is that it installs several COM objects that allow you to script many of your GPO management functions.

There are a number of troubleshooting and diagnostic tools available for discerning what happened when things go wrong that we introduced in this chapter as well.

## CHAPTER 9

Fine-Grained Password Policies

Undoubtedly, one of the most exciting new features in Windows Server 2008 Active Directory is the introduction of a feature called fine-grained password policies (FGPPs). Prior to FGPPs, domain account policies (password and lockout policies, specifically) could only be set on a per-domain basis. If you had a requirement to have separate password-complexity requirements for two sets of users, you could either deploy a third-party password filter or deploy a second domain. Fine-grained password policies solve both of these issues within a single domain and are immediately available once your domain is running at Windows Server 2008 domain functional level.

Understanding Password Setting Objects

Fine-grained password policies you create are represented by Password Setting Objects (PSOs) within Active Directory. PSOs are standard Active Directory objects and are stored under the System container in the domain partition.

Fine-grained password policies functionality is new to Windows Server 2008 and, as such, Windows Server 2003 and earlier versions of Windows domain controllers are not capable of enforcing the functionality. FGPPs become available once the domain has been promoted to Windows Server 2008 Domain Functional Level. While you can create and manage PSOs before your domain is running at the Windows 2008 Domain Functional Level, the policies will have no effect on users.

Unfortunately, Microsoft did not include a dedicated toolset to manage Password Setting Objects in Windows Server 2008. In order to manage PSOs with the out-of-the-box toolset, you'll need to use ADSI Edit or an LDIF file. ADSI Edit was enhanced in Windows Server 2008, so at least you will not need to convert values to the special underlying formats required by Active Directory to create the PSOs. An alternative to the built-in tools is a freely available tool called PSOMgr. PSOMgr is a command-line interface designed specifically for managing PSOs. You can get PSOMgr at *http://www .joeware.net/freetools/tools/PSOMgr/*. Since PSOMgr is so much easier to use, we will use it throughout this chapter.

Scenarios for Fine-Grained Password Policies

Nearly all of the settings that you could historically only define in the Default Domain Policy for the entire domain can be configured with Password Setting Objects. The exceptions to this rule are the Kerberos settings that must still be defined on a per-domain basis via Group Policy.

 If you are using one or more custom password filters in your domain, you can continue to utilize these filters in addition to fine-grained password policies.

Each of the settings in question is stored as an attribute of the `msds-PasswordSettings` schema class that was added with the Windows Server 2008 schema extensions. These attributes are outlined in Table 9-1.

Table 9-1. Mandatory Password Setting Object attributes

Attribute	Description
cn	The name of the PSO
msDS-PasswordSettingsPrecedence	The order of precedence of the PSO in the event multiple PSOs apply to a user
msDS-PasswordReversibleEncryptionEnabled	Toggles storing the password with reversible encryption
msDS-PasswordHistoryLength	The number of previous passwords stored in Active Directory
msDS-PasswordComplexityEnabled	Toggles password complexity checking
msDS-MinimumPasswordLength	The minimum length of the password
msDS-MinimumPasswordAge	The minimum interval before the password can be reset
msDS-MaximumPasswordAge	The maximum age of the password before it must be reset
msDS-LockoutThreshold	The number of failed login attempts necessary to trigger a lockout
msDS-LockoutDuration	The number of minutes to lock the account out
msDS-LockoutObservationWindow	The time window during which the lockout threshold is maintained

Defining Password Setting Objects

When you define your strategy for using password setting objects, you will need to determine the number of separate PSOs you will require to implement your strategy, as well as the relevant values for each PSO. All of the settings for a given user will come from a single PSO as the settings from multiple PSOs are not merged. This may mean that you will need to duplicate some common settings across multiple PSOs.

Generally speaking, you should endeavor to have as few PSOs defined as possible in order to implement your password policies. PSOs add additional management overhead and thus each additional PSO will add complexity to your environment. We will discuss the delegation options for PSOs in depth later in this chapter, but keep in mind that, generally speaking, the team that runs the domain will probably be responsible for managing the PSOs; however, the helpdesk staff also needs to be aware of them so that they can respond correctly to questions from users, such as "What are the rules for the password that I should enter?" Some organizations may elect to delegate this responsibility to an information security group instead.

 As you begin to build your plan for deploying fine-grained password policies, keep in mind that as a general best practice you should aim to limit the number of PSOs in a domain to the minimum number you really need.

Defining PSO precedence

Password setting objects are associated with users either directly or via group membership. The `msDS-PSOAppliesTo` attribute of each PSO is a forward link that can be linked to either users or global groups. Since the `msDS-PSOAppliesTo` attribute is multivalued, a single PSO can be applied to multiple users or groups simultaneously. The `msDS-PSOApplied` attribute is a back-linked attribute of users and groups that defines which PSOs are linked to it. Since `msDS-PSOApplied` is a back link, it is also multivalued, and thus a mechanism must exist to determine which PSO actually applies to a given user.

Each PSO also has an attribute `msDS-PasswordSettingsPrecedence`. This is an integer attribute that must be defined on each PSO and that controls the precedence of the PSO in the event multiple PSOs apply to a given group. Any integer greater than or equal to 1 and less than or equal to 2,147,483,646 is a valid value, and it is recommended that you define a unique precedence value for each PSO in your domain. The lowest precedence value always wins a conflict.

Every user object has an additional constructed attribute called `msDS-ResultantPSO`. When this attribute is returned, it will return the PSO that ultimately applies to the user.

 Since `msDS-ResultantPSO` is a constructed attribute, you cannot directly query it in an LDAP filter. If you try to do so, you will receive an error specifying that you used the wrong matching operator.

Domain Controllers use the following logic to compute the resultant PSO when multiple PSOs apply:

1. Is a PSO linked directly to the user? This will override any PSOs linked to the user's groups.

If multiple PSOs are linked directly to the user, the PSO with the lowest GUID will win. Linking a PSO to a user should be an exception to the general PSO assignment rule, and thus a user with multiple PSOs linked directly to her should be considered an error condition.

2. Does a PSO apply to any of the user's global security group memberships? If so, the PSO with the lowest precedence wins.

 If multiple PSOs with the same precedence are found to apply in step 2, the PSO with the lowest GUID wins the conflict.

3. If no PSOs were matched in steps 2 and 3, the Default Domain Policy settings are applied.

Creating Password Setting Objects

Now that we've discussed the basics of password setting objects, we'll go ahead and provision a PSO in the domain in order to walk through the process.

Password Setting Objects are stored in the *Password Settings Container* under the *System* container at the root of your domain as shown in Figure 9-1. You will need to select View→Advanced Features in Active Directory Users and Computers in order to view the contents of the *System* container.

PSO Quick Start

One useful feature of PSOMgr is its ability to get you started with a copy of your domain password policy (as defined via Group Policy), as well as some common PSO templates. For the sake of simplicity, we'll be working with the common PSO templates PSOMgr creates throughout most of this chapter. In order to create these PSOs, you'll need to run this command: **PSOMgr /quickstart /forreal**. In any case where PSOMgr is going to make changes to your environment, you must specify the /forreal switch as a confirmation. If you don't do this, PSOMgr will simply print out the changes it would make in the event you specify /forreal. Figure 9-1 shows the results of running the /quickstart option.

Building a PSO from Scratch

While the quick-start examples PSOMgr makes are excellent, chances are you may want to define one or more PSOs with custom settings. In this section, we're going to walk through creating a PSO with the settings defined in Table 9-2 both with the GUI and with PSOMgr.

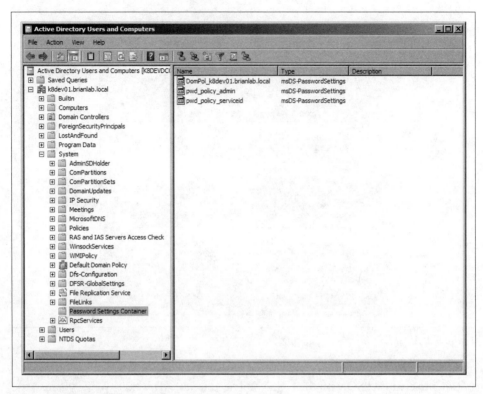

Figure 9-1. Password Settings Objects

Table 9-2. Custom PSO settings

Setting	Value	ADSI Edit formatted value
Name	CustomPSO1	CustomPSO1
Precedence	11	11
Reversible Encryption Enabled	No	FALSE
Password History Length	10 passwords	10
Password Complexity Enabled	Yes	TRUE
Minimum Password Length	8 characters	8
Minimum Password Age	1 day	1:00:00:00
Maximum Password Age	90 days	90:00:00:00
Account Lockout Threshold	15 failed logons	15
Account Lockout Window	30 minutes	00:00:30:00
Account Lockout Observation Window	30 minutes	00:00:30:00

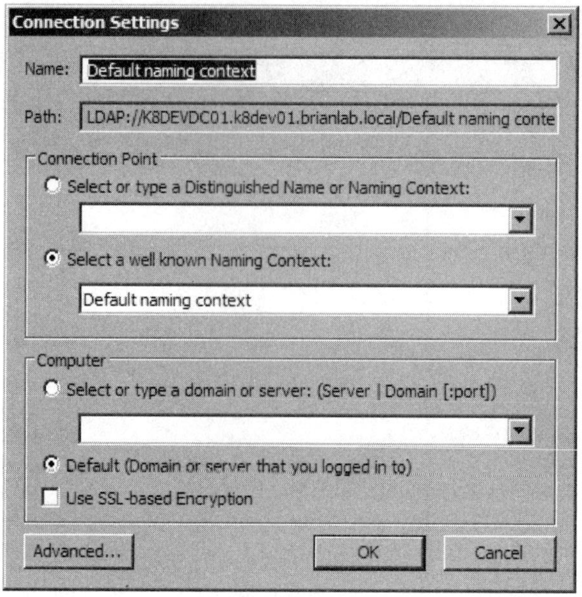

Figure 9-2. ADSI Edit Connection Settings

Creating a PSO with ADSI edit

In order to create a PSO with the GUI, we'll need to use ADSI Edit. While you can use Windows Server 2003 and earlier versions of ADSI Edit, the logic to make entering some of the values in a PSO (specifically the durations) significantly less painful is only available in the Windows Server 2008 version of ADSI Edit. You can launch ADSI Edit by going to Start→Run→adsiedit.msc. When you launch ADSI Edit for the first time, you'll need to connect to a partition. In our case we want to connect to the Domain NC for the domain we're currently logged in to. To do this, go to Action→Connect To. The Connection Settings dialog, shown in Figure 9-2, gives you the option to specify a domain and/or server to connect to.

Once you've connected, browse to Default Naming Context→DC=domain, DC=com→CN=System→CN=Password Settings Container. ADSI Edit uses a wizard style format to create the PSO. To launch this wizard, right click and select New→Object. You will be prompted to choose the class of the new object as shown in Figure 9-3. We only have one choice in this case, `msDS-PasswordSettings`.

The wizard will then walk you through specifying values for each of the mandatory attributes. You will be prompted in the same order as the values are laid out in Tables 9-1 and 9-2. Note that in Table 9-2, we've provided the "ADSI Edit Formatted Value" for each attribute. ADSI Edit takes some of the legwork out of converting the input into the underlying data formats, but it requires that you provide input in a specific format.

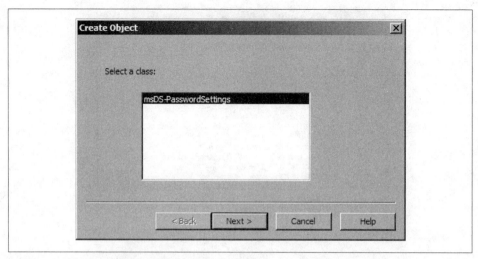

Figure 9-3. Selecting the object class

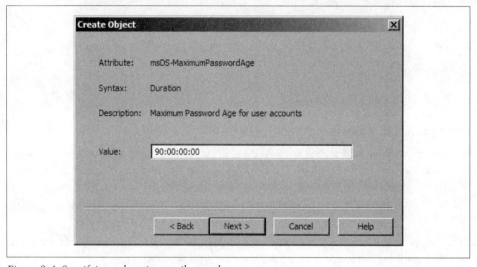

Figure 9-4. Specifying a duration attribute value

Figure 9-4 shows specifying a time-duration attribute value for the maximum password age. ADSI Edit expects these inputs in the format of dd:hh:mm:ss. Figure 9-4 shows specifying a duration of 90 days.

If you enter data in an invalid format or specify an invalid value, you will receive an error similar to Figure 9-5. The error shows the attributes that did not pass validation, and you can return to them in the wizard to make corrections.

Figure 9-5. Invalid attribute values error

 DSIDs like those in Figure 9-5 and many other Active Directory error messages are a specially constructed value that Microsoft can decode to determine precisely where in the Active Directory source code the error occurred.

Creating a PSO with PSOMgr

Now that we've created a PSO with ADSI Edit, we'll walk through creating the same PSO specified in Table 9-2 with PSOMgr. There are a number of different ways to specify the same data to PSOMgr. Some of them are easier to read than others, so we'll opt for one of the wordier permutations as opposed to trying to be as succinct as possible.

You can view the full usage screen for PSOMgr by running **PSOMgr -help**, but the switches we'll be using and their arguments are:

- `add name::precedence`
- `lockout threshold:duration:observation`
- `pwdage max:min`
- `pwdlen minlength`
- `pwdhist historycount`
- `pwdcomplex (true|false)`
- `pwdreverse (true|false)`

- forreal

The command to create the PSO from Table 9-2 is:

```
PSOMgr -add CustomPSO1::11 -lockout 15:30:30 -pwdage 90:1 -pwdlen 8
-pwdcomplex true -pwdreverse false -pwdhist 10 -forreal
```

You should, in turn, receive output similar to following:

```
PSOMgr V01.00.00cpp Joe Richards (joe@joeware.net) April 2007

WARN: Using name CustomPSO1 for displayName.

Using host: Chicago\K8DEVDC01.k8dev01.brianlab.local
Retrieving PSOs...
Checking existing policies...

Creating new PSO: CN=CustomPSO1,CN=Password Settings Container,CN=System,DC=k8de
v01,DC=brianlab,DC=local
PSO successfully created.

    Type               : Policy Settings Object
    Domain             : k8dev01.brianlab.local
    Policy Precedence  : 11
    DN          : CN=CustomPSO1,CN=Password Settings
Container,CN=System,DC=k8dev01,DC=brianlab,DC=local
    Name               : CustomPSO1
    Canonical Name     :
    Display Name       : CustomPSO1
    Lockout Threshold  : 15
    Lockout Duration   : 30
    Lockout Observation: 30
    Min Pwd Age        : 1
    Max Pwd Age        : 90
    Min Pwd Length     : 8
    Pwd History        : 10
    Pwd Complexity     : TRUE
    Pwd Reversible     : FALSE

The command completed successfully.
```

 If you use PSOMgr to create a PSO with a precedence value that is already in use, it will succeed, but will output a warning to the console similar to the following:

```
WARN: A policy setting object already exists with the
same precedence.
  WARN: Policy Setting object -
DomPol_k8dev01.brianlab.local
  WARN: (CN=DomPol_k8dev01.brianlab.local,CN=Password
Settings
Container,CN=System,DC=k8dev01,DC=brianlab,DC=local)
  WARN: When a single user has two policies assigned
with the same
  WARN: precedence at the same scope (i.e. directly
applied or
```

If you want to edit an existing PSO with PSOMgr, you can substitute the -mod switch in lieu of -add. The rest of the switches have the exact same behavior.

Managing Password Settings Objects

As noted earlier, Microsoft doesn't have a comprehensive tool for managing PSOs, so we're forced to go to a few different places to get the information we need. If you're comfortable with the command line, PSOMgr will do all of the tasks in this section. In some cases, we can use Active Directory Users and Computers (ADUC) or ADSI Edit to manage PSOs, though. This section focuses on managing existing PSOs and the application of them to users.

Strategies for Controlling PSO Application

There are a few strategies for managing which PSO applies to your user population, and you'll have to decide on which strategy works best based on your organization. The first strategy is to define a global security group for each PSO and apply the PSO to that group. You can, in turn, place users (or nest additional global groups) in the group. The second strategy is to apply PSOs directly to users or existing groups. Of course, the third strateogy here is to mix application to groups and users where necessary.

Applying PSOs to groups

Applying your PSOs primarily to groups is likely to be the most scalable strategy for many organizations. The strategy here is that you create a global group for each PSO and place the users who the PSO will apply to in this group. While you can reuse existing global security groups, we recommend that you create new groups dedicated just to application of PSOs. This ensures that you will not affect users inadvertently by adding or removing them from a group that controls PSOs or resource access.

It is important to remember that only global security groups are applicable for applying a PSO to a user. While you can link a PSO to a universal or domain local group, it will not actually be considered for application to the user in the resultant PSO calculation.

If multiple PSOs apply to a user by virtue of being a member of multiple groups linked to different PSOs, the PSO with the lowest precedence will win and in the case of multiple PSOs with the same precedence, the PSO with the smallest GUID will win.

Applying PSOs to users

If you have a small organization or intend to manage your PSO application with an automated tool, it may be feasible to apply PSOs directly to users. Note that the application of a PSO to a user is controlled by whoever has access to modify the PSO, not the user. Keep in mind that if you have multiple PSOs applied to a user, then the PSO with the smallest GUID will apply. This is not a condition you want to be in, so if you opt to link PSOs against users directly, the process should be very tightly managed.

Mixing group application and user application

Taking a hybrid approach to applying PSOs to users and groups may be the recipe for success in your case. Remember that if a user has PSOs applied to him by groups and directly to his user object, the PSO applied to the user object will always win. With this in mind, you can define exceptions to the rule where the standard PSO for users is implemented with a group, and exception users are linked directly to an exception PSO.

Managing PSO Application

You can manage PSO application with ADSI Edit, Active Directory Users and Computers, or PSOMgr. You control PSO application by editing the msDS-PSOAppliesTo attribute. We will quickly go over linking a PSO to a group with each of these tools.

Applying a PSO with ADSI Edit

Open the PSO you wish to apply in ADSI Edit by browsing to it under Default Naming Context→DC=domain,DC=com→CN=System→CN=Password Settings Container or the similar applicable location in your environment. If you do not see msDS-PSOAppliesTo in the attribute list, click Filter and uncheck "Show only attributes that have values."

When you edit msDS-PSOAppliesTo, a dialog like the one shown in Figure 9-6 appears. This dialog, which was added to ADSI Edit for Windows Server 2008, allows you to either manually enter a distinguished name (which was the only option in prior versions) or to search for a user or group using the standard Active Directory object search dialog. Use the "Add Windows Account" button to search Active Directory.

Once you click OK and apply your changes, they will take effect immediately (factoring in replication, of course).

You can remove a user or group from the scope of a PSO using this same process and selecting the user or group and clicking Remove.

Applying a PSO with Active Directory users and computers

Microsoft added the ADSI Edit attribute editor property page to the Windows Server 2008 version of Active Directory Users and Computers (ADUC). In order to see the attribute editor in ADUC, check View→Advanced Features. Once you browse to System→Password Settings Container under your domain, you will be able to open a PSO and edit it in the exact same manner as in ADSI Edit.

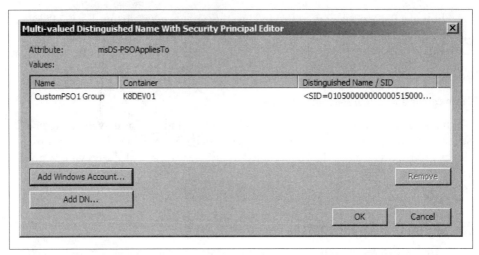

Figure 9-6. ADSI Edit linked value editor

Applying a PSO with PSOMgr

pSOMgr has a versatile syntax for applying and unapplying a PSO. You can specify a username (sAMAccountName), user principal name (UPN), or distinguished name of the object to apply the policy to. As in the previous examples, we will apply our CustomPSO1 PSO to a group called "CustomPSO1 Group." The switches we will use to accomplish this are:

- `applyto (samname|upn|dn)`
- `pso psoname`
- `forreal`

`psomgr -applyto "custompso1 group" -pso custompso1 -forreal` is the syntax to apply the PSO in this scenario. After running this command, you should get output similar to the following:

```
PSOMgr V01.00.00cpp Joe Richards (joe@joeware.net) April 2007

Using host: Chicago\K8DEVDC01.k8dev01.brianlab.local
Retrieving PSOs...
Applying PSO cn=custompso1,cn=password settings
container,cn=system,dc=k8dev01,dc=brianlab,dc=local
to object CN=CustomPSO1 Group,CN=Users,DC=k8dev01,DC=brianlab,DC=local
PSO successfully updated.

The command completed successfully.
```

If you want to unapply a PSO, the syntax is nearly identical, simply substituting `-unapplyto` for `-applyto`:

```
psomgr -unapplyto "custompso1 group" -pso custompso1 -forreal
```

Viewing the effective PSO

The easiest way to view the effective PSO for a given user is to use PSOMgr. Since the msDS-ResultantPso attribute is computed, it won't be displayed in a standard listing of all the attributes of a user. Active Directory will only return the value of a computed attribute when it is asked for it explicitly in a search. There is only one switch necessary for viewing the resultant PSO:

```
-effective (samname|upn|dn)
```

psomgr -effective bdesmond is the syntax to view the resultant PSO for user bdesmond. After running this command, you should get output similar to the following:

```
PSOMgr V01.00.00cpp Joe Richards (joe@joeware.net) April 2007

Using host: Chicago\K8DEVDC01.k8dev01.brianlab.local

User: bdesmond | bdesmond@k8dev01.brianlab.local | CN=Brian
Desmond,CN=Users,DC=k8dev01,DC=brianlab,DC=local
Applied PSOs:
  CN=DomPol_k8dev01.brianlab.local,CN=Password Settings
Container,CN=System,DC=k8dev01,DC=brianlab,DC=local
Effective PSO: CN=DomPol_k8dev01.brianlab.local,CN=Password Settings
Container,CN=System,DC=k8dev01,DC=brianlab,DC=local
     Type               : Policy Settings Object
     Domain             : k8dev01.brianlab.local
     Policy Precedence  : 20
     DN                 : CN=DomPol_k8dev01.brianlab.local,CN=Password Settings
Container,CN=System,DC=k8dev01,DC=brianlab,DC=local
     Name               : DomPol_k8dev01.brianlab.local
     Canonical Name     : k8dev01.brianlab.local/System/Password Settings
Container/DomPol_k8dev01.brianlab.local
     Display Name       : PSOMGR: Copy of Domain Policy for k8dev01.brianlab.local
     Lockout Threshold  : 0
     Lockout Duration   : 30
     Lockout Observation: 30
     Min Pwd Age        : 1
     Max Pwd Age        : 42
     Min Pwd Length     : 7
     Pwd History        : 24
     Pwd Complexity     : TRUE
     Pwd Reversible     : FALSE

The command completed successfully.
```

The first part of the output shows each of the PSOs that apply to the given user, and then the second part shows all of the details of the PSO that is effective. You can also view the resultant PSO by accessing the Attribute Editor tab of the properties of a user in Active Directory Users and Computers. In order to access the Attribute Editor, you must ensure View→Advanced Features is checked. Additionally on the Attribute Editor tab, you should check Filter→Constructed. This will show the msDS-ResultantPSO attribute in the listing.

Delegating Management of PSOs

One of the decisions you will likely need to make when planning your implementation of fine-grained password policies is who will manage the PSOs. It is likely that this will fall into the hands of a few different groups or tools depending on the organization. One possibility is that the Active Directory team will manage the PSOs in which case this section is somewhat irrelevant. Another possibility is that the PSOs will be controlled by an information security team. A third is that PSOs will be managed indirectly by an identity management/provisioning system.

In the event that the Active Directory team owns PSOs end-to-end, you likely will not need to perform any delegation of security rights to accomplish the management of PSOs. In the event a separate team such as an information security group controls PSOs, you will need to delegate the necessary rights. In this case, it is likely there will be three ways you can handle the delegation:

Delegate access to only application groups
> In this scenario you would strictly employ a design of applying password policies based on security groups with no exceptions. The information security group would be delegated access to these groups and be responsible for managing the membership of the groups. When a new PSO is deemed necessary, they will need to engage the Active Directory team to create it. This model creates a system of checks and balances to ensure that growth in the number of PSOs is managed. This model would also require that the Active Directory team be engaged to modify the settings on a PSO.

Delegate access to modify PSOs and application groups
> In this case you would delegate access to modify existing PSOs and also to manage the membership of application groups. The information security group would be able to modify the specific settings on a PSO and control where the PSO is applied. If you feel that you will often need to implement exceptions where PSOs are linked directly to users, this model will enable this to be done independent of the Active Directory team. While chances are that the frequency of changes to PSO settings should be rare, this model also mitigates the need to engage the Active Directory team for those changes. The system of checks and balances for creating new PSOs still exists here.

Delegate access to modify and create PSOs and application groups
> Here we take the previous model one step further and delegate to the information security team the ability to both modify and create new PSOs. If you have a frequent need to create PSOs, this may be the ideal route. Keep in mind that this removes the checks and balances we created earlier, so the potential for the number of PSOs to grow without bound could come into play.

If you are going to use your identity management system or provisioning tool to manage PSOs, you will need to delegate the account that tool runs under the necessary rights to manage the PSO application. This delegation may involve either allowing the tool to edit the `msDS-PSOAppliesTo` attribute directly, and/or allowing the tool to manage the membership of the application groups for the PSOs.

 For more information about implementing Active Directory permissions and delegations, see Chapter 13.

Summary

Fine-grained password policies are an important and long-awaited new feature in Windows Server 2008. FGPPs allow administrators to define Password Settings Objects and apply different password and account lockout policies to different sets of users in the domain. PSOs can be applied either to global security groups that users are members of, or directly to users.

Managing PSOs is possible either with the ADSI Edit GUI or with the free PSOMgr command-line tool. The PSOMgr tool offers a number of enhanced features that any administrator who is planning to deploy FGPPs should at least investigate.

Due to the manner in which PSOs are implemented in Active Directory, you will need to consider the management and delegation model of those PSOs as it applies to your organization. Applying PSOs to groups provides flexibility in delegating this responsibility.

## PART II

Designing an Active Directory Infrastructure

## CHAPTER 10

Designing the Namespace

The emphasis of this chapter is on reducing the number of domains that you require for Active Directory while gaining administrative control over sections of the Active Directory domain namespace using Organizational Units. The purpose of this chapter is to help you create a domain namespace design. That includes all the domains you will need, the forest and domain-tree hierarchies, and the contents of those domains in terms of Organizational Units and even groups.

When designing a forest, remember that there are often multiple good answers to forest design for any given company. There is no "best" design for all situations. Microsoft has provided great flexibility in what can be done, which can turn around and bite you with indecision on how you should implement. It isn't unusual for two engineers to have two very different designs for the same company that are both good for completely different reasons. Simply document all recommended designs and let the decision makers decide together which one will be the best for long-term operations. Overall, the best solutions are usually the simplest solutions. In most cases, you will want to choose single-forest designs over multiforest designs, single-tree designs over multitree designs, and single-domain designs over multidomain designs. The design example shown here is simply that: an example. The company in question could have designed their Active Directory infrastructure in a number of ways, and this is one of them.

There are a number of restrictions that you have to be aware of when beginning your Active Directory design. We will introduce you to them in context as we go along, but here are some important ones:

- The forest, not the domain, is the security boundary for Active Directory. Anyone with high-level access rights on any writeable domain controller in any domain can negatively impact or take control of any other DC or domain in the forest.

- Under Windows 2000, you cannot rename a domain once it has been created. Fortunately, with Windows Server 2003, this limitation has been removed given specific caveats, although the rename process is tedious. You can even rename forest root domains once you've reached the Windows Server 2003 forest functional level. If you are running Exchange, however, there are additional considerations and limitations for domain renames. In general, domain renames are not a recommended endeavor, so you should aim to never need to perform one.

- You can never remove the forest root domain without destroying the whole forest in the process. The forest root domain is the cornerstone of your forest.

- The Schema Admins and Enterprise Admins groups exist in the forest root domain only. So, if you are migrating from a previous version of NT with an in-place upgrade, be cognizant of the fact that the administrators of the first domain you migrate have immediate control over these groups and over Active Directory.

- Multiple domains cannot be hosted on a single DC. Imagine three child domains under a root domain located in the United States, each of which corresponds to one of three business units. Now imagine that you have a small office of 15 people in Eastern Europe or Latin America with a slow link to the United States offices. These 15 users are made up of three sets of 5; each set of 5 users belongs to one of the 3 business units/domains. If you decide that the intersite link is too slow and you would like to install a local domain controller for these three domains at the remote site, you will need to install and support three separate domain controllers, one for each domain. While this could be virtualized, that is still three additional domain controllers to manage, patch, and monitor.

- Too many Group Policy Objects (GPOs) means a long logon time as the group policies are applied to sites, domains, and Organizational Units. This obviously has a bearing on your Organizational Unit structure, as a 10-deep Organizational Unit tree with GPOs applying at each branch will incur more GPO processing than a 5-deep Organizational Unit tree with GPOs at each branch. However, if 10-deep and 5-deep OU structures both contained only two levels with GPOs, they would both incur the same GPO processing.

The Complexities of a Design

Active Directory is a complex service, and designing for it isn't easy. Take a look at a fictitious global company called PetroCorp, depicted in Figure 10-1.

Here you can see a huge network of sites linked with various network connections across wide area networks. A variety of domains seems to exist for *othercorp.com* and *petrocorp.com*, and as each one of those square boxes represents a single domain controller, you can see that some of the servers will need to replicate data across those WAN links. *petrocorp.com*, for example, seems to need to replicate to all the major sites, since it has domain controllers (DCs) in each of those sites.

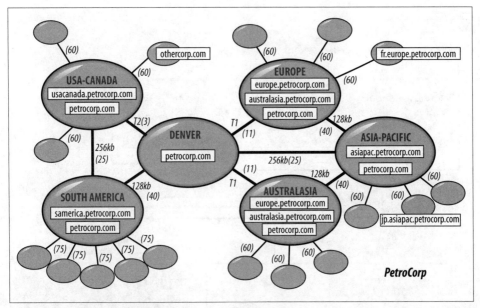

Figure 10-1. The sites and servers of a company called PetroCorp

Take a look at Figure 10-2, which shows a much more complex hierarchy.

It's possible to see the users and computers in all the Organizational Units in this view, and the structure seems to be set up so that Group Policy Objects (represented by trapezoids) can be applied to various portions of the tree. The following is a discussion of the principles and processes that will help you create complicated designs like these to mirror the complexities in your own organization.

Where to Start

Before you sit down to make your design, you will need to obtain some important pieces of information. At a minimum, you will need:

- A copy of your organizational structure, since this is effectively the document that explains how your organization's business units fit together in the hierarchy.

- A copy of the geographical layout of your company. This includes the large-scale picture in continents and countries and also the individual states, counties, or areas in which you have business units.

- A copy of the network diagram(s), indicating the speeds of connection between the various sites.

- A copy of any diagrams and information on any systems that will need to interface to Active Directory, such as existing X.500 and LDAP directories, so that you can take them into account.

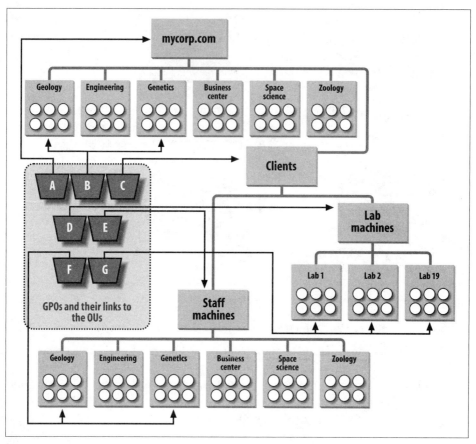

Figure 10-2. A complex domain tree showing GPOs

Once you've gathered the information, you can sit down and plan your design.

Overview of the Design Process

The namespace design process takes place in two stages:

Design of the domain namespace
    During the first stage, you deal with the namespace design itself. That means calculating the number of domains you need, designing the forest and tree structure, and defining the naming scheme for workstations, servers, and the network as a whole.

Design of the internal domain structure
    During the second stage, you need to concentrate on the internal structure of each domain that you have previously noted. Here you also need to use your business

model as a template for the internal structure and then move on to consider how administration and other rights will be delegated. The internal structure can also be modified depending on how you intend to use Group Policy Objects; this will be covered in Chapter 12.

 When you are finished with your design, you can implement it by setting up a test forest in a lab environment. This will enable you to get a better feel for how the design actually works and whether there is anything you have failed to consider. We can't stress enough the importance of a test environment.

When working on the budget for your production forest, include time, money, and resources for the test environment as well. This up-front expenditure will likely save you considerable back-end mistakes and uncertainty on a continual basis.

Domain Namespace Design

The first stage in your design is to work out the domain, domain tree, and forest configuration of your network. The best way to do this is to make a first pass at designing the domains and then structure them together into a single tree or a series of trees. Before we start, however, let's take a look at our objectives for this part of the design.

Objectives

There are two objectives for the design of the domain namespace:

- Designing Active Directory to represent the structure of your business
- Minimizing the number of domains by making much more use of the more flexible Organizational Units

Represent the structure of your business

When designing your Active Directory, you should aim to make it both match the structure of your business, and also be managed by whatever management model your IT organization operates under. Typically, organizations fall into one of three or four common models for managing their IT infrastructure:

Centralized administration
In this model, your entire IT infrastructure is centrally managed by one team.

Decentralized administration
In this model, your IT infrastructure is typically managed either locally at each location or on an organizational basis, perhaps by department or division. It is difficult to deploy a common Active Directory forest in this model as standards are often lax or nonexistent and Active Directory doesn't lend particularly well to being

administered by a large group from an infrastructure (e.g., domain controllers and forest-level configuration) perspective.

Hybrid centralized/decentralized administration

In a large organization this is likely to be the most common model. Certain components of the Active Directory are managed centrally, such as the domain controllers and enterprise-wide configuration, while other components such as objects stored in OUs are managed by distributed IT staff.

Outsourced administration

In this model, a third party manages your IT organization for you to some extent. The scope of outsourcing varies from organization to organization, but oftentimes architecture and engineering decisions are retained and not given to the outsourcer to handle.

When Active Directory first came to market in Windows 2000, it was common to deploy multiple domains to mimic the existing NT4 deployment or for other various reasons, and most large companies today who deployed Active Directory early on have this model. There is nothing wrong with the early best practices such as empty root domains or regional domains, but conventional wisdom today in the Windows Server 2008 timeframe says that you should endeavor to have the fewest number of domains possible. By no means are we recommending that you endeavor to collapse domains created early on unless you can achieve cost or management savings that exceed the cost of this restructuring.

One of the most common justifications that will be made for an additional domain in the forest is a purely political requirement to separate administration. In reality, a determined administrator of any domain in a forest could elevate his privileges to the Enterprise Admin level without too much work. Instead of creating a separate domain in this situation at a relatively high cost (with practically no benefit), use organizational units over which you can delegate the necessary permissions

As you go through the process in this chapter, keep in mind that, especially in large organizations, businesses frequently reorganize. Develop a design that you feel can survive multiple reorganizations without substantial investment in changes to your Active Directory design.

Step 1: Decide on the Number of Domains

Start by imagining that every object is to be stored in one domain. This will give you a much simpler layout for administration. It doesn't matter what the domain is called for now; just label it as your organization's main/sole domain.

Now expand the number of domains that you have by adding other domains that you can give specific justification for. While the number of objects and delegation of administration are not good reasons for creating new domains, there are three main reasons that would require more domains:

- The need to isolate replication
- A requirement for disparate Kerberos domain policies
- A requirement for keeping a Windows NT domain for something other than as a security boundary (the domain is not a security boundary) such as for an application or some other technical reason

If you can match any of these criteria, write down a new domain for that area.

 There are good reasons to add domains to the design, but there are also good reasons to not add domains. You should weigh these against the requirements listed previously to determine which are most important.

Some reasons to not deploy an additional domain include:

Forest complexity
Each domain requires more DCs and more policy management.

Application complexity
Applications may only be able to search a single domain for information. Many Unix- and Java-based LDAP applications are generally written to have a single simple hierarchy and may not be able to be configured to work with a multidomain forest without serious work.

Exchange issues
Microsoft Exchange has several issues with multidomain forests around user and group object updates. The protocols used in Exchange/Outlook just weren't designed for proper multidomain operation.

Isolated replication

While we discuss replication in the next chapter, you should begin to consider it from a high level at this point as it can have a substantial impact on the domain design you settle upon. Many large organizations have elected to deploy domains in a regional fashion that matches major divisions in WAN topology. Such models often include domains such as *Americas, AsiaPacific*, and *EMEA* (EMEA is a common acronym for Europe, Middle East, and Africa). The reasoning for this is to segment replication at a high level. Environments with large domains often cannot bear the replication overhead of replicating all of the contents from an Americas domain to a remote site in Asia, for example.

Since Windows 2000, replication has improved greatly with respect to compression in particular, and also WAN links have gotten faster in some regions. As you explore design options, you will need to consider whether or not your WAN could be impacted by the replication overhead of a large domain and if limiting this replication would be beneficial. Keep in mind that even if you segment your domains on a regional basis, there will still be some interregional replication for the global catalog.

Unique domain policy

In Chapters 8 and 12, we explain the basics of group policies and how to properly design them. For now, the important thing to understand is that policies are Active Directory objects that reference a number of settings that can be applied to users or computers. These settings are things like a fixed desktop, a certain core set of applications, the ability of users to perform a shutdown, and so on. If you create an Organizational Unit called Finance and then decide that it needs special settings, you can create a GPO and assign it to the OU. Then the computer settings and user settings in the GPO will be applied to all computers and users under the Finance OU.

We now need to look at what settings have to be applied on a domain-by-domain basis. Here's a list of what types of settings can be set only on a domain-wide basis:

- Kerberos policies.
- Encrypted filesystem recovery policies.
- Public key encryption policies.
- Certificate authorities.

If a special department or geographical area needs special encryption, security safeguards, certificates, and so on, you may need a separate domain.

 Domains that are not operating at the Windows Server 2008 functional level can only have one password policy per domain. For more information about fine-grained Password Policies, see Chapter 9.

In-place upgrade of current domain

Some organizations still have existing Windows NT infrastructures and will be planning to migrate at some point. During the design of your migration to Active Directory, you will need to consider the option of merging old Windows NT domain hierarchies into single domains. This is known as collapsing old domain structures. However, even though AD usually requires fewer domains than Windows NT since it can accommodate more objects and allow delegation of administration without domains, organizations may wish to retain some of their current domains.

Final notes

You now should have your first draft of the list of domains that you think you will need. There is one more very important point on this subject. Domains are very inflexible and unforgiving, and due to the fact that you can host only a single domain on a domain controller, each domain means at least one more domain controller you have to support. Depending on how many domain controllers you would have to deploy for a domain, you can greatly decrease your total cost of ownership (TCO) for Active Directory by limiting the number of domains you support.

For fault tolerance, you should always deploy new domains with at least two domain controllers. If you only have a single domain controller for a given domain and the domain controller fails, you will be forced to restore from backup. This is easily avoided by deploying a second domain controller.

Step 2: Design and Name the Tree Structure

Now that you have the domains listed, you need to consider what sort of hierarchy to put them in. It is easiest to start with one domain, the one that will become the forest root.

Choose the forest root domain

There are two ways to go about choosing the forest root domain. The first model is to deploy an empty root domain. The empty root simply contains a small number of domain controllers and accounts for the Active Directory administrators for the forest. The empty root is the most common model you're likely to see in large environments that have had Active Directory deployed for some time. The second model is to simply choose a domain that you know will be required for the lifetime of the forest as the forest root domain, which can never be removed. If you are deploying a single domain forest, this decision is simple. If you are deploying multiple domains, you should keep in mind your namespace requirements as you design the hierarchy such that the forest root domain is actually at the root of the tree.

 The security concerns that led many organizations to deploy an empty root have since been proven to be a nonissue. While the empty root model is perfectly valid, you should not choose to deploy a forest with an empty root solely with the goal of protecting the enterprise-wide groups (such as *Enterprise Admins* and *Schema Admins*).

Design the namespace naming scheme

As each domain has a DNS name to identify it, you need to consider what names you are going to choose. You can use any of the RFC 1123 standard characters:

- A–Z
- a–z
- 0–9
- - (dash character)

Microsoft's DNS supports a wider range of characters, such as the Unicode character set, but if you need compatibility with other DNS flavors, be very careful allowing these.

There are currently two schools of thought on how to pick the DNS names for your Active Directory network: root zone or subzone. The root zone method says that you name your root Active Directory domain based on the root zone for your organization. For the Mycorp Corporation, this would be *mycorp.com*. The subzone method suggests that you pick a new subdomain from your root zone and make that the base of your Active Directory namespace. For Mycorp, this could be *ad.mycorp.com*.

If you choose the root zone method and wish to have a non-Windows DNS, you will need to either enable dynamic updates or manually register a number of records in the DNS, as discussed in Chapter 6. If you choose the root zone method and wish to have a Windows DNS server at your root, you will need to migrate your existing entries, if you have any, to the new DNS servers. Both methods are fine, but they require configuration or migration at the root. A less invasive procedure would be to choose a new subzone for your Active Directory network and run your network from that. With this setup, you still have two choices, but they are less disruptive to any existing structure and you won't have to affect the main root zone. Arguably, the easiest solution is to let two servers on your network run Windows DNS server and manage this DNS zone. This allows you to have a root that doesn't allow dynamic updates and a subdomain that does. The alternative would allow a non-Windows DNS to manage the zone.

Another common extension of the root zone method is to choose a parallel namespace, such as *mycorp.net* for your Active Directory. This allows you to have a root level namespace and not need to migrate existing DNS entries or manage a split-DNS model if *mycorp.com* is also your external namespace.

As an example, Leicester University had a very large existing DNS infrastructure branching down from the root domain that they didn't want to change with this new Active Directory infrastructure. The main DNS servers, while being dynamic update-capable, did not have dynamic update turned on for specific reasons. So they set up two domain controllers to run the Windows DNS service and gave those name servers a subdomain to host. Then they delegated that subdomain on the main DNS servers and specified which servers had authority for the new zone. Then DHCP was modified to point all new client workstations at the two new Windows DNS servers and configured the DNS servers to pass any queries that they could not resolve back to the main campus DNS servers. Clients could update the Windows DNS servers without affecting the main campus servers. However, external queries were still resolved by passing those queries to the main campus servers for resolution.

To continue with the planning process, start with the forest root and assign a DNS name to the domain, writing the name inside or beside the triangle on the paper. You should choose the name very carefully for two reasons. First, while renaming a domain is possible beginning with Windows Server 2003 Active Directory, it is a highly invasive process and is not generally recommended unless absolutely necessary. Second, you can never remove the forest root domain from Active Directory. You must destroy your entire forest and start again.

Create additional trees

Having created and named your forest root, you need to consider your other domains. If you have two distinct business units or companies, some analysts may think that they will require noncontiguous names to match the structure. This means that you will need two trees coming from a domain root. Think long and hard on this decision, as multiple domain trees in a forest add complexity and often cause support and application confusion for no real benefit. Some common examples that people will use to indicate a perceived need for multiple trees are different email address suffixes, different UPN suffixes, resource separation, and security separation. However, separate trees aren't actually required to implement any of these requirements.

If you still conclude that you need multiple trees, draw all the other tree root domains that you think you will need as separate triangles at the same horizontal level on the paper and assign them valid DNS names. These domains are all tree root domains, but should not be confused with "the" forest root domain. A real-world example is the Microsoft brand name and the MSN brand name. Both *msn.com* and *microsoft.com* could be separate trees in the same forest. They couldn't be in the same tree without giving them a hierarchical link, i.e., *msn.microsoft.com*. However, the only real benefit for having an *msn.com* and *microsoft.com* in the forest instead of an *msn.microsoft.com* is how it all looks on a PowerPoint presentation.

 If we think that Mycorp's finance department needs a separate domain, we will make a subdomain and call it *finance.mycorp.com*. Within Active Directory we could make *finance.mycorp.com* a separate tree in its own right, but since hierarchical and transitive trusts exist throughout a forest, we would gain absolutely nothing by doing this. The only differences come in choosing finance to be a new domain (which we did) or a new forest in itself. Making it a new tree gains absolutely nothing.

Create additional forests

So far, we've been considering domains that will exist in the same forest, but you may have business units that will require two entirely separate forests. How do you know if that is the case? If you have business units in an organization that are independent and in fact wish to be isolated from each other, then you must not combine them in a single forest. If you simply give each business unit its own domain, these business units can get the idea that they are autonomous and isolated from each other. However, in Active Directory, this level of isolation can be achieved only through separate forests. This is also the case if you need to comply with regulatory or legal isolation requirements.

The first and most common reason may be political: certain business units may decide that they want to be as autonomous as possible. It may be that, politically, the finance department has to be completely separate, so you end up making a second forest with *finance.mycorp.com* as the second forest's forest root domain. In effect, you are treating this business unit as a separate, autonomous, and noncontiguous part of the tree.

The second reason you may need two forests involves having two businesses that must be separately maintained for regulatory or other legal reasons. Similarly, if you have a business that may be divested or sold in the future, it will be much easier to separate if this business exists in its own forest.

The third reason is one born out of necessity. Remember from Chapter 2 that certain aspects of a namespace are forest-wide in scope. If you want to isolate a separate schema or configuration partition, your only solution is to create a separate forest.

The fourth reason, which is becoming more common, is the need for a separate forest for Microsoft Exchange. Exchange is very tightly integrated into Active Directory and does not easily allow for a clean separation of duties through delegation. Additionally, Exchange can have serious management issues with multidomain deployments in a single forest. These two reasons can often result in a single-domain resource forest being implemented for Exchange, with trusts configured to the appropriate domains in the NOS forest or to the NOS forest itself.

 The delegation capabilities of Exchange have been substantially improved in Exchange 2007. For more information, reference Chapter 19.

If any of these reasons are true, you need to create a second forest root domain and give it a unique DNS name, as you did for the first forest root domain. In effect, you need to separate your designs and do each forest individually. The best thing to do now is to figure out how many forests you need and which domains from your list are going to be the forest root domains. Once you have determined this, you will name these root domains and then use a separate piece of paper to draw each forest. Maintain separate lists of domains for each forest. You're now doing *x* designs, where *x* is the number of forests you have.

There is one other important point that you need to be aware of. While domains and trees in a forest maintain automatic trust relationships, it is possible to set up manual trust relationships with domains external to a forest. You can therefore set up manual trust relationships between forests. These relationships can be one-way trusts (A trusts B but B does not trust A) or two-way trusts (A trusts B and B trusts A).

If you require a limited trust situation (in the Windows NT/2000 sense), in which you wish to give access to your forest to vendors and partners, you can do this manually. If you have two forests that you wish to link, you have several options: establish an explicit one-way trust or create a transitive forest trust.

The first option allows other domains that are members of another domain tree in a different forest or that do not support Kerberos authentication to have limited access to a domain in the forest. Only resources in the domain will be visible; no other resources in the tree are available for access.

The second option is new to Windows Server 2003 Active Directory. Under Windows 2000, if you wanted all domains in one forest to trust all domains in a second forest, you had to create individual trusts to and from each domain. With the new forest trust, you can simply create a single transitive trust between two forests, and all domains in both forests will trust each other.

Arrange subdomain hierarchy

You now have a forest root domain with a valid DNS name. You may have other domains that act as the roots of separate trees in the same forest; you may even have extra forest root domains representing separate forests entirely. Now you need to lay out the domain tree hierarchies. If you have a number of remaining domains listed on your sheet of paper from step 1, these are the subdomains that will form your domain-tree hierarchy.

Start with the first forest. Representing each domain with a triangle on the paper, arrange the domains in a hierarchical fashion beneath one of the domain tree roots in the forest. Name the domain appropriately, according to its position in the hierarchy. Repeat this process for all domains in this forest, then move on to the next forest and repeat.

For example, if we have *mycorp.com* as a tree root, and finance, marketing, and sales all need separate domains, we call them *finance.mycorp.com*, *marketing.mycorp.com*, and *sales.mycorp.com*. If the sales domain needed separate domains for pre-sales and post-sales, we arrange these two domains beneath sales, as *pre.sales.mycorp.com* and *post.sales.mycorp.com*.

Step 3: Design the Workstation and Server-Naming Scheme

You now have one or more forests of domain trees. Each tree is uniquely named in a hierarchical fashion. You can now consider the naming scheme for the servers and workstations.

 While we are considering the naming scheme here, the exact placement of machines in Active Directory is covered in Chapter 12 on designing GPOs. That is because GPOs can impact clients based on machine location.

Each client workstation or server in an Active Directory network must have a computer account somewhere in the forest to let users log on via that client. When a workstation is added to a domain in a forest, the computer account is created in Active Directory, and a trust relationship is set up between the client and the domain so that the client is recognized as a valid member of the domain.

Where a client is placed in the forest determines part of the name. Member servers are usually placed in the domain that hosts most of the users that use the server, and DCs are located by their very nature in the individual domains that they host. Clients can be placed anywhere, but they are usually placed in the domain that the primary users of that client will normally log on to.

Under Windows NT 4.0, if you had a single-master or multimaster domain model in which multiple resource domains had one-way trusts to one or more master user domains that held the accounts, the workstations were normally placed in the resource domains. This enabled the workstations to log on to both the resource domain and the user domain. Putting the clients only in the user domain would have meant that the clients could not be used to access the resources in the resource domains, as no trust existed in that direction.

> Cast this completely out of your mind in Active Directory. Each domain within a single forest has a hierarchical and transitive trust between it and every other domain in that forest, so from that perspective, it no longer makes any difference where the clients are located.

All hosts are named *computer.domain*. For example, a server called *moose* in *mycorp.com* would usually be called *moose.mycorp.com*; a server called *moose* in the finance domain would usually be called *moose.finance.mycorp.com*.

> It isn't normally discussed, but the naming of the machines in a domain does not strictly need to have a DNS domain name that matches the Active Directory Domain Name. This is one example of a disjoint namespace, and it is a supported configuration by Microsoft. This is most common in larger Enterprise class organizations that have large distributed DNS configurations. You may find, for example, a server with the name *moose.manton.michigan.us.company.com*, which is a member of the AD Domain *na1.company.com*.

Deploying Active Directory does not force you to change the names of any existing hosts that you have. However, if you are planning to consolidate a number of separate domains, you need to ensure that all hostnames are unique within the domain they exist in or throughout the entire company if WINS is being used with full mesh replication. You can easily make use of ADSI (discussed in Part III) to script a query for a list of computers from every one of your domains and then check the lists via a second script for duplicate names.

If you don't already require a consistent naming scheme for your clients and servers, now is the time to create one. Fully Qualified Domain Names must be unique across the entire forest; this is achieved by appending the domain component onto the computer name. That leaves you to worry about the prefix, meaning that computer names have to be unique only domain-wide.

To maintain backwards compatibility, names cannot be longer than 15 characters. This is because Active Directory still has some legacy support for NetBIOS names, and the hostname that you choose will be incorporated as the NetBIOS name on the client. NetBIOS names are limited to 15 characters.

You need to work out a forest-wide naming scheme, determining how you will name the clients within the 15-character limit. We can't help you much here; the choice of your naming scheme is up to you.

Design of the Internal Domain Structure

Having designed the domain namespace, you can now concentrate on the internals of each domain. The design process itself is the same for each domain, but the order is mostly up to you. The first domain that you should design is the forest root domain. After that, iterate through the tree, designing subdomains within that first tree. Once the tree is finished, go on to the next tree and start at the root as before.

In a tree with three subdomains called Finance, Sales, and Marketing under the root, you could either design the entire tree below Finance, then the entire tree below Sales, and so on, or you could design the three tier-two domains first, then do all the subdomains immediately below these three, and so on.

When designing the internals of a domain, you need to consider both the hierarchical structure of Organizational Units and the users and groups that will reside within those Organizational Units. Let's look at each of those in turn.

 When we refer to a hierarchy, a tree, or the directory tree, we mean the hierarchical Organizational Unit structure within a domain. We are not referring to the hierarchy of domain trees in a forest.

Step 4: Design the Hierarchy of Organizational Units

Earlier, when we discussed how to design domains, we spoke of how to minimize the number of domains you have. The idea is to represent most of your requirements for a hierarchical set of administrative permissions using Organizational Units instead.

Organizational Units are the best way to structure your data because of their flexibility. They can be renamed and easily moved around within and between domains and placed at any point in the hierarchy without affecting their contents. These two facts make them very easy for administrators to manage.

There are four main reasons to structure your data in an effective hierarchy:

To represent your business model to ease management

Partitioning your data into an Organizational Unit structure that you will instantly recognize makes managing it much more comfortable than with every user and computer in one Organizational Unit.

To delegate administration

Active Directory allows you to set up a hierarchical administration structure that wasn't possible with Windows NT. If you have three branch locations, and the main administrator wants to make one branch completely autonomous with its own administrator but wants to continue to maintain control over the other two branches, it's easy to set up. In a way, most of the limitations that you come up against when structuring Active Directory are limits that you set for yourself: political necessities, organizational models, and so on. Active Directory really won't care how you structure your data.

To apply policies to subsets of your users and computers

As group policies can be applied to each individual Organizational Unit in the hierarchy, you can specify that different computers and users get different policies depending on where you place them in the tree. For example, let's say that you want to place an interactive touch-screen client in the lobby of your headquarters and allow people to interact with whatever applications you specify, such as company reports, maps of the building, and so on. With Active Directory, if you lock down a certain Organizational Unit hierarchy using policies, you can guarantee that any computer and user accounts that you create or move to that part of the tree will be so severely restricted that hacking the network from the client will be far more difficult.

To replace Windows NT resource domains

If you have a previous Windows NT installation with a master or multimaster domain model, you can replace your resource domains with Organizational Units in a single domain. This allows you to retain all the benefits of having resource domains (i.e., resource administration by local administrators who do not have account administration rights) without forcing you to have multiple domains that you don't really want or need.

Let's take Leicester University as an example. The university is a large, single site with mostly 10/100 MB links around campus and 2 MB links to some outlying areas a couple of miles away. The domain model was multimaster under Windows NT, but under Active Directory, it moved to a single domain and so it is much simpler than before. Administration is centrally managed, which means that delegation of administration was of little concern during design. We had a departmental organizational model for the Organizational Unit structure holding our accounts. We created a flat structure with more than a hundred Organizational Units directly off the root and almost no lower Organizational Units at all. Each Organizational Unit corresponded to one department, and it held all the users from that department. We also had an Organizational Unit hierarchy for the computer accounts separate from the department Organizational

Units. This was due to our requirement for group policies; we'll discuss this in more detail in Chapter 12.

When creating Organizational Units, you need to ask:

- How will the Organizational Units be used?
- Who are the administrators and what sets of administrator permissions should they have?
- What group policies will be applied?

The hierarchy should organize information in a manner pleasing to your administration and allowing you to delegate administration to various parts of the tree.

> You should not nest user or computer accounts in an Organizational Unit structure in such a way that the group policies that apply to the accounts create a slowdown during the logon process. Microsoft recommends nesting no more than 10 Organizational Units deep, but in fact, to a much greater extent, it's the application actions of group policies that you need to consider when designing your OU structure. This prevents slowdown on booting (policies applied to the computer account on boot up) or logon (policies applied to the user account on logon).
>
> If your users are in a 10-tier structure but only four policies were applied to the users, you shouldn't have a problem with logons. You can break this rule, but boot-up and/or logon will slow down as a result. By how much is a relative question and the easiest answer is to test it on your network to get your own feel for the delay if this becomes a problem. We cover this item in much more depth in Chapter 12 when we discuss GPOs. All you need to be aware of here is that this can be a problem.
>
> Nesting OU structures excessively also has a tendency to lead to substantially increased administrative overhead due to the additional complexity of the model.

Recreating the business model

The easiest way to start a design is to consider the business model that you sat down with when creating these designs. You now need to recreate that structure in Active Directory using Organizational Units as the building blocks. Create a complete Organizational Unit structure that exactly mirrors your business model as represented by that domain. In other words, if the domain you are designing is the Finance domain, implement the finance organizational structure within the Finance domain. You don't create the entire organization's business model within each Organizational Unit; you create only the part of the model that would actually apply to that Organizational Unit. Draw this structure out on a piece of paper. Figure 10-3 shows the Organizational Unit structure of *mycorp.com*'s domain. We've expanded only the Finance Organizational Unit here for the example.

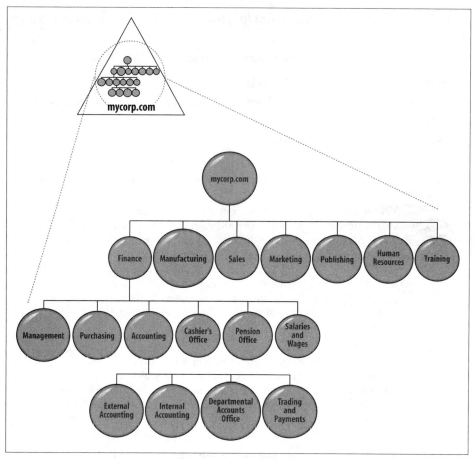

Figure 10-3. The Mycorp domain's internal Organizational Unit structure

Once you have drawn an Organizational Unit structure as a template for your Active Directory hierarchy within the domain, you can begin to tailor it to your specific requirements. The easiest way to tailor the initial Organizational Unit design is to consider the hierarchy that you wish to create for your delegation of administration.

Delegating full administration

First, identify any areas of your hierarchy where you need to grant administrators autonomous access over their branch of the tree. These Organizational Units should have at least two administrators who will look after that Organizational Unit. These administrators will look after the structure below that Organizational Unit, creating whatever Organizational Units, users, groups, and so on that they desire. They will not, however, have administrative access to any other part of the tree.

You need to note two pieces of information about each of the Organizational Units that you identify:

- Who will be the administrators?
- Which branch of the tree will they administer?

 You must ensure that delegated administrators take responsibility and can be held accountable. This cannot be stressed too strongly. It is possible for an administrator of a low-level Organizational Unit to make changes which affect other people. The best way to highlight this is with user accounts. Remember, user accounts are visible forest-wide and so in some sense must be unique forest-wide. In much the same way as with computers, the domain component normally is used here in an attribute of the user object called the userPrincipalName (UPN). While the normal username only has to be unique domain-wide, the UPN attribute ensures forest-wide uniqueness. Let's concentrate on the domain-wide part.

If a low-level Organizational Unit administrator creates a user with a username that someone else wants to create in the future in another Organizational Unit, that's tough. Only one account with a given username can exist (in this case, we are referring to the sAMAccountName attribute). We deal with creating a naming scheme for administrators to follow later in step 5.

If you do not have a company policy in this area, you need to create one and document it.

Delegating other rights

Having noted the two pieces of information for all Organizational Units that need full administrative access, you next need to identify those Organizational Units that require some users to have a more restricted set of permissions. You may want to set up account administrators that have the ability to create and delete user accounts, as well as setting passwords and account details. We're interested in rights only in general terms at the moment, so just note the following:

- What the access rights are
- Which branch of the tree the access rights will be applied to
- Which users or groups (in general terms) will have these access rights

It is possible to set access rights of any sort down to the individual property level on a specific object if you require. That means you can allow a user named Richard Lang to change the password or telephone number of a user named Vicky Launders (and only that user) if you wish. Obviously the more minute the access, the more complex things can get, especially since permissions are inherited down a tree by default. To make things easier, Microsoft provides a simple Delegation of Control wizard that allows you to set these access rights in a fairly easy manner. All this information on permissions to Active Directory is covered in much greater depth in Chapter 13. However, all we're concerned with at this stage in the design is delegation of control at the Organizational Unit level. From experience, we can tell you that assigning access rights at the Organizational Unit level is always much simpler to manage than tracking permissions to individual objects and properties.

 Perhaps the most important thing to remember when designing your organizational unit structure is to make it consistent and repeatable. If you are creating an OU structure by location, write a script to create that standard structure (and any applicable delegations) for each of your locations. Managing OU structures that are all independently designed will quickly become extremely difficult if not impossible to do efficiently in a large environment.

Step 5: Design the Users and Groups

Before starting this section, we must make clear the distinction between groups and Organizational Units. Organizational Units are containers for objects that allow the objects to be represented in a hierarchical structure within a domain. Placing objects in such a hierarchy allows delegation of administration to those Organizational Units on a selective basis. We've seen all this already. Groups, on the other hand, have only users or computers as members and can be used in assigning permissions or rights to the members collectively. Let's say that we have 50 users contained in an Organizational Unit called FinanceOU, and the users are also members of a group called FinanceGrp. When we want to grant these 50 users read permissions to a share or restricted access to certain parts of a domain's hierarchy, we assign the permissions to the FinanceGrp. The fact that they are in the Organizational Unit makes no difference when you wish to assign permissions to objects contained inside the Organizational Unit. However, if we wish to delegate someone to have permission to manage those 50 accounts, we place the administrative delegation onto the Organizational Unit. Here we'll be talking about how to effectively design user accounts and the groups those users belong to.

Naming and placing users

When you are designing users, the only thing you really have to worry about is the username or user identifier that the client logs on with. Each username (the sAMAccountName property of a user object) must be unique throughout each domain. Arguably, if you have decided to delegate administration within your organization, you need to create a naming scheme to which each administrator will adhere so that unique usernames are generated for all users throughout your forest. That way, if you ever collapse the existing domains, you never need to rename the users if there are any conflicts. Naming groups is important, too.

Another name that you should give to all Active Directory users is known as the user principal name (the userPrincipalName property of the user object). This property looks like an RFC 2822 email address, i.e., *username@here.there.somewhere.com*. In fact, this property is not the email address but is a unique identifier for the user in the entire forest. It has to be unique as it uniquely identifies a user across an entire forest. So, while the users AlistairGLN in *mycorp.com* and AlistairGLN in *finance.mycorp.com* are perfectly valid, their UPNs must be different. The normal way to create a UPN is simply to append an @ symbol and the domain onto the end of the username. This ensures uniqueness because the username was unique in the domain, and appending the domain forces a unique forest-wide UPN. This makes *AlistairGLN@mycorp.com* and *AlistairGLN@finance.mycorp.com* the UPNs for the two users in the example.

However, while it is conventional to construct the UPNs in this way, you can in fact make the UPN of a user anything you wish as long as it follows the format specified in RFC 2822. We could, for example, append the *@mycorp.com* to all our users, eliminating the need to rely on domains at all. If we do that though, we should make sure that our usernames (sAMAccountName) are unique not only domain-wide, but also forest-wide. In the previous example, we can't have two users with the username AlistairGLN. For such a scheme to work, a central database or allocating authority needs to be set up to uniquely generate and allocate names. Leicester University has maintained a separate database from the early 1980s for this purpose, as have many other universities and companies. If this database or authority can generate unique usernames via a reliable algorithm, you can make use of a much simpler UPN.

Just because we chose *@mycorp.com* as the suffix does not mean we are limited to a forest or domain name. We could just as easily have chosen *@moosebanana.com*, which has no relation to the domains or the forest. The UPN simply has to be unique for every user in the forest.

Just as the suffix doesn't have to match the forest or domain name, the username portion doesn't have to match the sAMAccountName. Beginning with Windows Server 2003, you can create a user without specifying a sAMAccountName. This will auto-generate a sAMAccountName that looks something like $KJK000-H4GJL6AQOV1I, which really isn't a friendly logon name. However, you could then set the UPN to be *joe@mycorp.com* and that could be used to logon.

UPNs are very important. Imagine a user sitting down at a client anywhere in a forest and being presented with the logon dialog box. Here she can type in her username (sAMAccountName), password, and domain, and be authenticated to the forest. However, it is perfectly valid to authenticate with the UPN. If the user, presented with the same logon dialog box, instead types a UPN in the first field, the domain box becomes grayed out and inaccessible. In other words, a UPN and a password are all that is needed to authenticate to Active Directory. This makes sense since the UPN is unique forest-wide; apart from a password, nothing else should be needed. You now should be able to see that even with a very large and complex set of domains in a forest, you can use a simplified UPN form that does not contain a domain component and then simply instruct users to log on with a UPN and a password. This means that users never need to care about what domain they are in.

 Many organizations choose to use their users' email addresses as UPNs as well. The benefit to this strategy is twofold. The first benefit is that users can be instructed to login with their email address and thus be required to remember one less piece of information. The second benefit is that email addresses are a unique identifier, so UPNs will be too.

Your choice of where you place the user accounts in each domain's hierarchy is really affected only by who is to administer the accounts and what GPOs will be applied on the Organizational Unit the account is in. Other than that, it makes little difference.

Naming and placing groups

Groups need unique names, too, so a naming scheme for groups should also be laid out in the design. Where you put groups is less important. In effect, groups can go almost anywhere in the hierarchy. The GPOs that determine your placement of users, for example, do not apply to groups. However, as the groups available to you will differ based on the mode or functional level of your forest, the only way you can do a proper design is to know roughly how long you intend to stay in mixed or interim mode before upgrading.

If you are planning to wait a while on mixed/interim mode before upgrading for whatever reason, you need to do two sets of group designs: what the groups will be prior to the upgrade and what you will convert them to after the upgrade. Of course, the two designs may be the same.

 Going native in one domain does not have to affect the mode of another domain. There is nothing wrong with *apac.ad.mycorp.com* going native while *ad.mycorp.com* is mixed mode or vice versa. Remember that mixed mode and native mode affect only the use of Windows NT BDCs in a domain, not the use of Windows NT clients or member servers.

Creating proper security group designs

If your organization is based on a single site (in the sense of being a "fast interconnected set of subnets," which is detailed in the next chapter), you can use universal security groups entirely. You don't have to, but for the purposes of design, it will make very little difference in the long run that you choose.

Based on the tables in Chapter 2, for large complex organizations with many different sets of permissions to many individual resources, we would suggest using two sets of security groups. One set of security groups has permissions to local resources on a particular server, and the other set of security groups contains the users. You then can add one set of security groups to another to control access. In this manner, you are maintaining a fine-grained control over the access permissions for groups while not having to add users many times over to multiple groups.

In mixed mode, we would use Domain Local Security groups for access to local resources and add users to Domain Global Security groups or even Universal Distribution groups. In native mode, we would do one of three things:

- Continue as before, but now allow Universal Security groups to be members of Domain Local Security groups.

- Convert the Domain Local Security groups to Universal Security groups with the same membership as before, because this is now allowed under native mode.

- Convert the Domain Local Security groups and Domain Global Security groups to Universal Security groups, understanding the impact this will have on the GC and the potential for token explosion when converting Global groups.

 Group use and "what scope is best for what configuration" are topics that spawn endless debate in newsgroups and any time administrators get together to talk about securing resources. In the end, it comes down to what you want and how you want to secure your infrastructure, whether this is through the use of the old NT mechanism called UGLy (Users into Global, Global into Local, Local get permissions) or simply using all groups from a single scope and placing users directly in them. The point is that Microsoft has offered up multiple paths to do the same thing; you are free to choose the path that most appeals to you.

Step 6: Design the Application Partition Structure

Another namespace design issue to consider is the application partition structure for your forest. As described in Chapter 3, application partitions, which are new to Windows Server 2003 Active Directory, are user-defined partitions that have a customized replication scope. Application partitions can be especially helpful in branch office deployment scenarios where you have to deploy a lot of domain controllers. Often you'll have applications that want to store data in Active Directory, but that data is not pertinent or used frequently enough to warrant replicating to all domain controllers, especially in the branch offices. With application partitions, you can configure a new partition to hold application data that replicates data only among your hub domain controllers. The other great thing about application partitions is that you are not restricted by domain boundaries. If you want to replicate data globally and have domain controllers geographically located, you can create an application partition that replicates data between your geographically dispersed domain controllers regardless of which domain they reside in.

Application partitions have an impact on your namespace design because they are named very much like domains. For example, say you wanted to create an application partition in the *mycorp.com* forest; you could name it dc=apps, dc=mycorp, dc=com. In fact, application partitions have the same implications on the namespace and to DNS as do regular domains. So, in the dc=apps, dc=mycorp, dc=com example, the *apps.mycorp.com* DNS domain will be populated with the standard SRV records, just like a domain.

You can also nest application partitions. For example, if you had a specific application you wanted to create a partition for, you could host it directly off the apps partition we just mentioned. We could name it dc=MyApp, dc=apps, dc=mycorp, dc=com.

The most common example of using application partitions is the Windows DNS service. Active Directory Integrated DNS zones can be stored in an application partition with a custom replication scope. For more information on application partitions as they relate to DNS, see Chapter 6.

 Don't forget you also have the option to use Active Directory Lightweight Directory Services (AD LDS, formerly Active Directory Application Mode [ADAM]) instead of application partitions in Active Directory. See Chapter 20 for more details on AD LDS.

Other Design Considerations

In many cases, you may need to revise your namespace designs a number of times. Certainly GPOs will make a difference as to how you structure your users and computer objects, so we do not assume that one pass through a design process will be enough.

Once you have a basic design, there is nothing stopping you from putting that design to one side and working on identifying a perfect design for your Active Directory network, one that you would like to implement in your organization, ignoring all Active Directory-imposed design constraints. You then can work out how difficult it will be to move to that perfect design from the practical one that you worked out using the preceding steps. You can look at the feasibility of the move from one to the other and then rationalize and adjust your final design to take into account the factors you have listed. You can then use this as an iteration tool so that your final design is much closer to the perfection you are aiming for.

Apart from GPOs, which we cover in Chapters 8 and 12, there are other aspects of Active Directory design that we have not and will not be covering. For example, you are quite likely to want printers advertised in Active Directory so that they can be accessed easily using a simple search of Active Directory (which the Add Printer wizard now uses as the default option). The Distributed File System (DFS) that allows you to organize disjointed and distributed shares into a single contiguous hierarchy is a fine example of this. When you reference a share held by the DFS, the DFS uses the Active Directory site topology to automatically redirect your request to the closest share replica. There is also the matter of designing your own objects and attributes that you want to include. However, there are two points that you should consider:

- As a general rule, Active Directory should hold only static or relatively static data. At the very least, the lifetime of the data has to be greater than the time to replicate to all DCs throughout the organization. When considering which objects to add, don't consider adding objects with very short life spans. Dynamic data—that is, data with a relatively short lifespan—is more suited for storage in an application partition or an ADAM instance. Windows Server 2003 introduces the ability to host data with a short lifespan through the use of dynamic objects.

- Any object that you include will have attributes that are held in the global catalog. For every type of object that you seek to store in Active Directory, check the schema definition for that object to find out what attributes will be stored in the global catalog.

Design Examples

Having covered the design of the namespace, some real-world example designs are in order. We have created three fictitious companies that will serve as good models for demonstrations of the design process. We will also use these three companies in the following chapters. The companies themselves are not fully detailed here, although there is enough information to enable you to make a reasonable attempt at a namespace design. In the chapters that follow, we will expand the relevant information on each company as required for that part of the design.

We used a number of criteria to create these companies:

- The companies were set up to represent various organizations and structures.

- While each corporation has a large number of users and machines, the design principles will scale down to smaller organizations well.

- In these example corporations, we are not interested in how many servers each company has or where those servers are. These facts come into play in the next chapter on sites. We are interested in users, groups, machines, domains, and the business and administration models that are used.

TwoSiteCorp

TwoSiteCorp is an organization that employs 50,000 people using 50,000 desktop computers. The organization spans two sites connected with a 128 KB dedicated link. The London site has 40,000 clients and 40,000 employees, while the new expansion at the Leicester site has 10,000 clients and 10,000 employees. TwoSiteCorp's business model is based on a structure in which users are members of one of three divisions: U.K. Private Sector, U.K. Public Sector, and Foreign. No division is based entirely at one site. Various other minor divisions exist beneath these as required for the management structure. Administration is handled centrally from the major London site by a team of dedicated systems administrators.

Step 1: Set the number of domains

While TwoSiteCorp's 128 KB link between its two physical locations is slow for site purposes, there is no need to split the two sites into two domains. No particular part of the organization has a unique policy requirement, because the administrators decided that they will implement one set of policies for all users. Finally, the sites already have two Windows NT domains installed. However, management has no desire to maintain either, so both will be rationalized into one domain. Thus, TwoSiteCorp will end up with one domain.

Step 2: Design and name the tree structure

TwoSiteCorp's single domain will be the forest root domain. The designers decide to name the domain *twositecorp.com* after their DNS domain name. With only one domain, they do not have to worry about any other trees or forests or the domain hierarchy.

Step 3: Design the workstation- and server-naming scheme

TwoSiteCorp decides that each machine name will be made up of four strings concatenated together. The first string is three characters representing the location of the machine (e.g., LEI or LON). The next string holds two or three letters indicating the type of machine (e.g., DC, SRV, or WKS). Finally, the last string is a six-digit numeric string that starts with 000001 and continues to 999999. The following are example machine names:

- LEIDC000001
- LEIDC000002
- LONWKS000183

This appears to be such a small step, but it can spawn huge wars and cause design meetings to stretch out over long periods of time. Here are a couple of recommendations for things to keep in mind:

- Consider using pieces of information that will not change or will not change often. If you are spinning up, shutting down, or renaming sites all of the time, using a site in the name may not be wise, as the machine names would have to be changed each time the site is renamed or servers are moved. That being said, some really good namespace designs have been based on using the site code for the first part of the machine name.

- Be careful of allowing resource administrators to just choose whatever names they want. This can turn out badly because words not generally associated with professional directories may end up getting used. In addition, you can end up with the same server name in multiple domains because different administrators like the same name. In a very large organization, for example, it would not be surprising to find multiple servers named WEB or WWW in various NT domains that needed to be collapsed into a single Active Directory domain.

- Try to use numbers as much as possible, especially in global organizations. It is much easier to understand numbers spoken in various languages over the phone versus letters.

- *Be consistent!* A bunch of random names pulled out of the blue at the point in time you build the server confuses support techs. If you use a consistent naming system, it will be familiar to the techs and they can put brain energy into other issues. It is probably more comforting to new support techs to see BBQ00001, FNT00001, and WHQ00001 as server names versus Athena, Vern, Vader, and Nikki, especially if all servers starting with FNT are in some special grouping, such as a site, function, or realm of administrative control.

Step 4: Design the hierarchy of Organizational Units

TwoSiteCorp needs three major Organizational Units (U.K. Private Sector, U.K. Public Sector, and Foreign) based on its business model of divisions. The second and succeeding tiers of Organizational Units can then be created according to the lower-level management structure if required. There is no necessity to do so in this scenario, although it would make the structure easier to manage visually. In fact, this domain could be completely flat with all users and machines in one Organizational Unit, but then you aren't gaining much from Active Directory's ability to structure the data in a useful manner for administration. Speaking of administration, since it is handled centrally, there is no need to delegate administration for the three top-tier Organizational Units to any specific group of administrators, although there is room for expansion should that become necessary. Nor does TwoSiteCorp need to delegate any other permissions to the Organizational Unit structure. Now TwoSiteCorp has a fairly simple hierarchy that perfectly maps their domain.

Step 5: Design the users and groups

TwoSiteCorp has two Windows NT domains at present using a variety of global groups and local groups. During the migration, the company will have a mixed-mode domain. However, their ultimate aim is to move to native mode very quickly and reap the added benefits of universal groups. The design, therefore, needs to cover what universal groups the company would like for its resources. The existing global and local groups can be moved to Active Directory during migration, allowing the current setup to work with the new system. Once the switchover to native mode goes ahead, either the groups can be converted to universal groups and rationalized to fit into the new design, or they can be left as they are and new universal groups created according to the design to take the place of the old groups.

Step 6: Design the application partition structure

Because TwoSiteCorp has only two sites to replicate, they do not need to create any application partitions.

Recap

This is a very simple system that maintains a good level of administration based on the structure of the organization while managing to maintain control over its expansion in the years to come.

RetailCorp

RetailCorp is a global, multibillion-dollar retail organization that has more than 600 stores spread throughout the world under four different store names. There are around 60,000 staff members in the company, with about 25,000 in the central office based in Leicester in the United Kingdom. Each store is connected to the central HQ via 64 KB leased lines. Each store has a number of Windows-based point-of-sale workstations running database software and one or more large database servers in the back room. The database servers replicate the day's transactions down the links each evening to the central HQ.

RetailCorp is very centralized with almost no administrators at the stores themselves. The only special requirement that the company has is that it would like the administrators to be able to easily hide the operating environment from staff working at the checkout registers at each branch. Changes to checkout registers should be possible on an individual branch or global level.

Step 1: Identify the number of domains

RetailCorp has no need to isolate replication or do any in-place upgrades. The part about policies is a little tricky: do they need new domains for every branch in case policy changes need to be applied to one branch specifically? The answer is no. The administrators need to be able to apply policies to certain branches or all branches, but these policies have to do with the user interface and thus fall into the area of GPOs rather than separate domains. That effectively leaves them with one domain.

Step 2: Design and name the tree structure

RetailCorp, having only one domain, makes that the forest root domain. The namespace has the *retailcorp.com* global name that is already in use.

Step 3: Design the workstation- and server-naming scheme

RetailCorp uses a central database to register machines, which automatically produces a 15-character name based on a machine's location and purpose (i.e., client, database server, file and print server). Every time a machine is moved or its function changes, the name is updated in the central database, and the machine is renamed.

Step 4: Design the hierarchy of Organizational Units

It is decided to make each store an Organizational Unit, so that central administrators can delegate control over individual stores and their objects as required. However, to make things even easier to manage and delegate on a countrywide or regional basis, RetailCorp creates a series of country Organizational Units under the base. Each of these country Organizational Units contains either the shop Organizational Units directly (for countries with only a handful of stores) or a series of regional Organizational Units that themselves contain the store OUs.

Step 5: Design the users and groups

RetailCorp uses a central database to generate its own unique usernames and group names as needed. It has done this for many years, and the database produces a changes file on an hourly basis. A script picks up the changes file and applies it to Active Directory in the same manner that it does with all other systems.

Step 6: Design the application partition structure

Because RetailCorp is using a centralized deployment model and has no special replication requirements, there is no need to create any application partitions.

Recap

This example shows how a geographically-based company can do its own design. It's not particularly difficult, although this design does not take into account the slow links between the stores and the HQ. That is left until the next chapter, when we revisit RetailCorp from a physical-layer perspective.

PetroCorp

PetroCorp (refer back to Figure 10-1) is a global multibillion dollar petrochemical organization that has more than 100,000 people and machines at about 100 sites around the world. The business has its global headquarters in Denver. There are five major sites that link to the HQ and to which the smaller 94 smaller branch offices link. The major sites or hubs represent Asia-Pacific, Australasia, USA-Canada, South America, and Europe. The small sites link to the five hubs via 64 KB links; the hubs themselves connect to the HQ via T1, 256 KB, and 128 KB links. Some of the hubs are also interconnected. Management structure is geographic, with each geographical unit running itself as an independent business as part of the global whole. The top level of the management structure is at HQ, which sits above the five hubs. Even though Denver could be considered within the USA-Canada area, the organization is not structured that way. In fact, Denver oversees the hubs in terms of selecting the administrators and how the

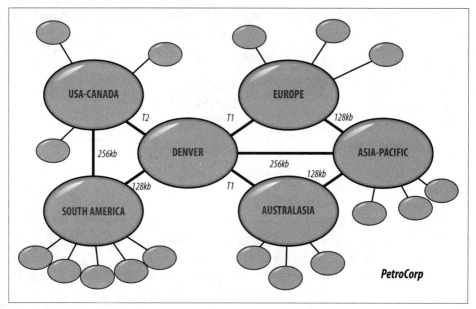

Figure 10-4. PetroCorp's wide area network

network is to be structured. Corporate policy dictates that branches that have more than 500 people have their own administrator, backup support, and helpdesk staff locally. Branches with fewer than 500 people have to be managed by the administrators of the hub to which they connect (see Figure 10-4).

Other considerations include the following:

- Due to special company policies, public-key encryption and different language settings are used in each of the hubs (and their branches). So Europe and its branches have different settings from those in Australasia and its branches.

- Japan has a database system running on Windows NT 4.0 that must stay in its own domain.

- PetroCorp recently acquired OtherCorp, a Canadian company that has a strong brand name that PetroCorp would like to maintain. OtherCorp is solely based in a new branch in Canada.

- The links between the eight South American branches and the hub are very unreliable.

- The branch in France needs to maintain a number of Windows NT BDCs and member servers running legacy applications and services that will not run under Windows 2000. This requirement may exist for a few years.

- The Asia-Pacific 128 KB link to Europe is severely congested at all times.

Step 1: Set the number of domains

There is a wrong way and a right way to look at PetroCorp:

The wrong way

PetroCorp starts off with five domains representing the hubs because each requires different public-key security settings.[*] As the branch offices are part of the domain at each hub, the hub's settings will apply to the branch offices as well because the settings are domain-wide. So extra domains are not needed, although they are needed for each branch office for Japan and OtherCorp. As France cannot upgrade, whatever domain France is in must remain in mixed mode. Management could make the Europe domain mixed mode, but would like it to be native mode to make use of the features. So, a special domain for France makes a total of eight domains.

The right way

PetroCorp starts off with one domain: the one representing Denver, the HQ of PetroCorp. The organization then needs to create a separate domain for each of the five hubs for the public-key security settings. As the branch offices are part of the domain at each hub, the hub's settings will apply to the branch offices as well, due to the settings being domain-wide. Now an extra domain each is needed for Japan and OtherCorp. France cannot upgrade, so whatever domain France is in must remain in mixed mode. Management could make the Europe domain mixed mode, but would like it to be native mode so that they can make use of the Active Directory features. A special domain for France makes a total of nine domains.

Both solutions can seem valid, although you may feel that the first is not as valid as the second. The first solution would result in problems during later parts of the design process. That there are different sites with different link speeds is not really an issue here. The issue revolves around the major HQ that is separate from but which oversees the five hubs in an administrative capacity. In the wrong design, one of these domains must become the forest root domain with the relevant authority that confers. USA-Canada is the natural choice. Then HQ administrators would effectively be running the USA-Canada domain, which conflicts with the initial company notes that each hub, as well as the HQ, has its own administrators. Consequently, the second design is better.

While each domain may have its own administrators, all of them would need to be fully trusted as if they were Enterprise Admins. This reflects the fact that *the domain is not a security boundary*—the forest is. If the trust in the administrators does not exist across the domains, this design must suddenly become a multiforest design.

---

[*] That they also require different language settings is a red herring: Windows 2000 and newer can support different language settings on a per-client basis rather than a per-domain basis like Windows NT.

Step 2: Design and name the tree structure

PetroCorp chooses the Denver domain as the forest root domain. The forest root domain is to be called *petrocorp.com*.

When it comes to choosing a naming scheme for the domains corresponding to the hubs, the administrators choose a simple one. The domains will be called:

- *europe.petrocorp.com*
- *usacanada.petrocorp.com*
- *samerica.petrocorp.com*
- *asiapac.petrocorp.com*
- *australasia.petrocorp.com*

The domain representing OtherCorp will be called *othercorp.com*. They could have merged OtherCorp into PetroCorp's structure and just used multiple DNS names for the web servers and so on. However, the company may be sold for a profit in the future, and management wants to keep it politically separate.

There are obviously now two distinct trees. We'll put them in the same forest so that resources can be shared. The subdomain hierarchy is fairly easy to follow from now on. The domains for France and Japan will follow ISO 3166 country codes and be called *fr.europe.petrocorp.com* and *jp.asiapac.petrocorp.com*. Figure 10-5 shows the forest view of the domain trees.

Step 3: Design the workstation- and server-naming scheme

PetroCorp has decided that it specifically does not want to use any parts of its naming scheme to duplicate data that can be obtained elsewhere. For example, PetroCorp does not want to use country, city, or building information, as this can be gathered from the exact Active Directory site that the client is in. For example, there's no point in including the data UK, London, Building 3 if the site that the computer resides in is called UK-London-Building3. They also do not want to include indications of the operating system or version, as they will be using Microsoft Systems Management Server (SMS) to inventory each device; the required information can be retrieved directly from SMS's own database. They do, however, want to include the department that the client is installed in.

They also decide to use this name as part of the worldwide asset-registering system under development, so that they can institute a worldwide rolling-update program of older devices. Thus, they need to include the year the client was purchased and when the client was introduced to the network.

To do this, they decide to borrow a trick from the FSMO RID Master's book and use a central pool of values at their HQ for the naming of machines. Names of machines

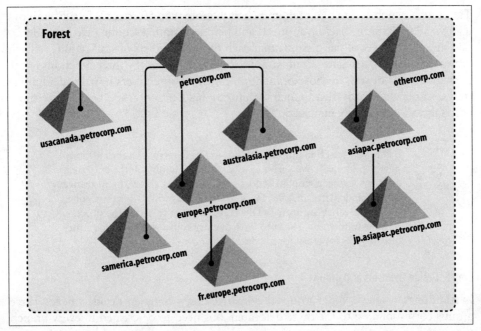

Figure 10-5. PetroCorp's forest domain tree hierarchies

will start with a department code of seven or fewer letters, followed by a two-digit year code and a number consisting of six or fewer digits, allocated from the central pool.

When a client is to be installed, the user doing the installation goes to a web page on PetroCorp's intranet and provides his ID and the department and two-digit year for the machine. The web page (which is connected to a database) allocates that user the next central value in the list. In this manner, the central database maintains an exact note of which department a machine is in, what year it was purchased, when it was installed, what its full name is to be, and who installed it.

Step 4: Design the hierarchy of Organizational Units

As far as the internal structure of the hub domains goes, each domain is to be broken down into a number of Organizational Units based on its branches. Every branch gets an Organizational Unit created, which will contain its servers, users, and groups.

We don't have enough information to specify the internal structure of the HQ, the Japanese domain, and the OtherCorp domain. However, that doesn't matter, since we do know that local administrators at all three will manage their respective domains. That means we do not have to worry about delegating administration of internal parts of those domains to particular administrators. So effectively we have carte blanche to do what we wish with those designs.

The company notes state that each branch with more than 500 people locally employs its own administrator, backup support, and helpdesk staff. Assuming we have identified the standard set of permissions that each of the three sets of staff require at each branch, we need to delegate administrative responsibility for the three functions to the relevant groups of staff in those branches. Branch staff members now have administrative responsibility for their branch Organizational Unit only, and branches without any staff will be centrally managed.

 Before you start building all of this in Active Directory Users and Computers, pull the *Active Directory Cookbook* (O'Reilly) off the bookshelf and put together a script to build the OU structures, three administrative groups, and all permissions. Since the structures will all be very similar, the best mechanism to maintain consistency is to script the process. Administrators don't want to be data entry clerks, so building a structure like this is perfect for a script.

Step 5: Design the users and groups

In addition to whatever other groups the organization's designers decide it needs, three groups corresponding to the three delegated jobs need to be created in every branch that is to have autonomous control. These three groups will be used when delegating responsibility.

Any domains intending to stay on Windows NT (i.e., France) can run in mixed mode, with other domains going native as soon as is feasible. Domain Global Security and Domain Local Security will be mainly used, although a scattering of Domain Universal Security groups will be used in the native-mode domains as soon as conversion takes place.

Step 6: Design the application partition structure

PetroCorp has several corporate applications that need to store data in Active Directory. Since everyone in the company uses these applications, placing the data in a single domain would not be sufficient. For this reason, an application partition should be created and replicated to a domain controller in each major geographic location.

Recap

This example shows how a global company can create its own design and maintain a large degree of control. It also shows how laws in the real world can wreak havoc with a good design!

These are only examples; there are multiple ways each of these cases could have been designed. Do not feel that because you saw these designs documented here, they are the way you have to do your designs. It is definitely useful to start with them, but make sure it makes sense for your network.

Designing for the Real World

It's very easy to get bogged down in the early stages of the namespace design without actually progressing much further. The stumbling block seems to be that it feels conceptually wrong to have only one domain, yet administrators can't put their finger on what the problem is. If you follow the guidelines in the initial steps of the namespace design, you quite possibly could end up with one domain to start with.

This is partly a conceptual problem: a set of domains with individual objects managed by different teams can feel more secure and complete than a set of Organizational Units in a single domain containing individual objects managed by different teams. It's also partly an organizational problem and, possibly, a political problem. Putting in an Active Directory environment is a significant undertaking for an organization and shouldn't be taken lightly. This change is likely to impact everyone across the company, assuming you're deploying across the enterprise. Changes at that level are likely to require ratification by a person or group who may not be directly involved on a day-to-day basis with the team proposing the change. So, you have to present a business case that explains the benefits of moving to Active Directory.

Identify the Number of Domains

Following our advice in this chapter and Microsoft's official guidelines from the whitepapers, TechNet, or the Resource Kit will lead most companies to a single domain for their namespace design. It is your network, and you can do what you want. More domains give you better control over replication traffic but may mean more expense in terms of hardware and administrative overhead. If you do decide to have multiple domains but have users in certain locations that need to log on to more than one domain, you need DCs for each domain that the users need in that location. This can be expensive. We'll come back to this again later, but let's start by considering the number of domains you need.

If the algorithm we use to help you determine the number of domains gives you too small a figure in your opinion, here's how you can raise it:

- Have one domain for every single-master and multimaster Windows NT domain that you have. If you are using the Windows NT multimaster domain model, consider the entire set of multimasters as one domain under Active Directory (use Organizational Units for your resource domains).

- Have one domain per geographical region, such as Asia-Pacific, North America, Europe, and so on.

- Have extra domains whenever putting data into one domain would deny you the control over replication that you would like if you used Organizational Units instead. It's all very well for us to say that Organizational Units are better, but that isn't true in all situations. If you work through the algorithm and come up with a single domain holding five Organizational Units, but you don't want any of the replication traffic from any of those Organizational Units to go around to certain parts of your network, you need to consider separate domains.

 It isn't unusual for very large organizations to go from hundreds or even thousands of domains to just a few domains.

Design to Help Business Plans and Budget Proposals

There are two parts to this: how you construct a business case itself for such a wide-reaching change and how you can show that you're aiming to save money with this new plan.

Simply stated, your business case should answer two main questions:

- Why should you not stay where you are now?
- Why should you move to Active Directory?

If you can sensibly answer these two questions, you've probably solved half your business case; the other half is cost. Here we're talking about actual money. Will using Active Directory provide you with a tangible business cost reduction? Will it reduce your total cost of ownership? It sure will, but only if you design it correctly. Design it the wrong way, and you'll increase costs.

Imagine first that you have a company with two sites, Paris and Leicester, separated by a 64 KB WAN link. Now imagine you have one domain run by Leicester. You do not have to place a DC in Paris if it is acceptable that when a user logs on, the WAN link uses bandwidth for items like these:

- Roaming user profiles
- Access to resources, such as server-based home directories
- GPOs
- Application deployment via Microsoft Installer (MSI) files

If authentication across the link from Paris would represent a reasonable amount of traffic, but you do not want profiles and resources coming across the slow link, you could combat that by putting a member server in Paris that could service those resources. You could even redirect application deployment mount points to the local member server in Paris. However, if GPOs themselves won't go across the link, you need to consider a DC in Paris holding all the local resources. That gives you two sites each with at least one DC, and one domain.

Now let's expand this to imagine that you have a company with 50 WAN locations; they could be shops, banks, suppliers, or whatever. These are the Active Directory sites. Next, imagine that the same company has 10 major business units: Finance, Marketing, Sales, IS, and so on. You really have three choices when designing Active Directory for this environment:

- Assuming everything else is equal, create a single domain with a DC in whichever sites require faster access than they would get across any link. Now make the business units Organizational Units under the single domain. The pros and cons of this choice are as follows:

  Pros

  > Everything is in one domain.

  > You need as many DCs as you have sites with links that you consider too slow. If you want to count a rough minimum, make it 1 DC per site with more DCs for larger sites; that is a rough minimum of 50 DCs. This is a low-cost solution.

  > With one forest and one domain, any user can log on quickly anywhere because authentication is always to a local DC.

  Con

  > Every part of the domain is replicated to every other part of the domain, so you have no granularity if you don't want objects from one business unit replicating to DCs everywhere.

- Create multiple domains representing the 10 major business units. Place DCs for each business unit in whichever sites require faster access than they would get across any link.

  Pro

  > This means more domains than the previous solution, but replication can now be better controlled on a per-business unit basis between sites.

  Con

  > Active Directory cannot host multiple domains on a single DC. This can make for an extremely high cost due to the large number of DCs that you may need. If you need to be able to log on to each of the 10 business unit domains from every site, you need 10 DCs per site, which makes 500 DCs. That's a much more costly solution.

  Pro/Con

  > With one forest and multiple domains, any user can log on quickly at any site that has a local DC for her domain; otherwise, she would have to span a WAN link to authenticate her logon and send down her data.

- Create multiple domains representing geographical regions that encompass the 50 sites. Make these geographical regions the domains and have each domain hold Organizational Units representing business units that contain only the users from that region.

  Pros

  > Even if you end up with 10 geographic regions, the DCs for each region are placed only in the sites belonging to that region. So if there were five sites per region (to make the math simple), each of the five needs only 1 DC. As the namespace model is a geographic model, you need to place a DC for Europe in the Asia-Pacific region only if the Asia-Pacific region ever has visiting users from Europe who need to authenticate faster than they would across the WAN link from Asia-Pacific to Europe. So, the number of DCs that you need is going to be smaller.

  > Domain replication traffic occurs now only within a region and between regions that has DCs hosting the same domain.

  Con

  > You end up duplicating the business units in all the domains ... or maybe not, if some don't need all business units—you get the idea.

  Pro/Con

  > With one forest and multiple domains, any user can log on quickly at any site that has a local DC for his domain; otherwise, he would have to span a WAN link to authenticate his logon and send down his data.

We hope this illustrates that while it is easy to map a simple and elegant design on paper, there can be limitations on the feasibility of the design based on replication issues, DC placement, and cost.

Recognizing Nirvana's Problems

Arguably, there are a number of "best" ways to design depending on whom you talk to. We propose an iterative approach with Active Directory, and this is probably going to happen anyway due to the nature of the many competing factors that come into play. On your first pass through this chapter, you'll get a draft design in hand for the namespace. In Chapter 11, you'll get a draft site and replication design. Then you'll come up against the issue that your namespace design may need changing based on the new draft sites and replication design, specifically on the issues of domain replication and server placement that we have just covered. After you've revised the namespace design, you can sit down and look at the GPO design (using Chapters 8 and 12) in a broad sense, as this will have an impact on the Organizational Unit structure that you have previously drafted in your namespace design. And so it goes.

While this is the way to design, you will come up against parts of your organization that do not fit in with the design that you're making. The point is to realize that your job is to identify a very good solution for your organization and then decide how to adapt that solution to the real world that your company lives in. One domain may be ideal but may not be practicable in terms of cost or human resources. You have to go through stages of modifying the design to a compromise solution that you're happy with.

Summary

In this chapter, we presented seven steps toward effective namespace design:

1. Decide on the number of domains.
2. Design and name the tree structure.
3. Design the workstation- and server-naming scheme.
4. Design the hierarchy of Organizational Units.
5. Design the users and groups.
6. Design the Global Catalog.
7. Design the application partition structure.

Following these seven steps allows you to solve the two main objectives of this chapter:

- Come up with an Active Directory namespace design to represent the structure of your business.
- Minimize the number of domains by making much more use of the more flexible Organizational Units.

Although we've shown you how to start to design your Active Directory, there is still a long way to go. Designing the namespace of domains, trees, and forests and the internal Organizational Unit hierarchy according to the guidelines given here means that you should have a structural template that represents your business model within the preceding restrictions. Hopefully this design makes sense in terms of your organization and will be simpler to manage.

The rest of the design still needs to be completed. You need to look at the low-level network links between sites and how they will affect your replication decisions. You then need to tackle the subject of how to revise the initial namespace design based on Group Policy Objects, security delegation and auditing, schema changes, and so on. Next we'll move on to designing the physical site topology that the DCs use when communicating with one another.

## CHAPTER 11

Creating a Site Topology

As we mentioned in Chapter 5, there are two aspects to replication:

- How data gets replicated around an existing network of links between domain controllers
- How the *Knowledge Consistency Checker* generates and maintains the replication links between domain controllers, both *intrasite* and *intersite*

We covered the former in Chapter 5, and we'll cover the latter here, leading to an explanation of how to properly design a representation of your organization's network infrastructure within Active Directory.

Intrasite and Intersite Topologies

Two distinct types of replication connections exist with Active Directory sites: intrasite (within sites) and intersite (between sites). An Active Directory service known as the Knowledge Consistency Checker (KCC) is responsible for automatically generating the replication connections between intrasite DCs. The KCC will create intersite connections automatically for you as well, but only when an administrator has specified that two sites should be connected via a *site link*. Every aspect of the KCC and the connection objects that are created is configurable, so you can manipulate what has been automatically created and what will be automatically created via manipulation of the various options.

Note that there is a large distinction between the KCC (the process that runs every 15 minutes and creates the replication topology) and the replication process itself. The KCC is not involved in the regular work of replicating the actual data in any way. Intrasite replication along the connections created by the KCC uses a notification process to announce that changes have occurred—each domain controller is responsible for notifying its replication partners of changes. If no changes occur at all within a six-hour period, the replication process is kicked off automatically just to make sure that nothing was missed. Intersite replication, on the other hand, does not use a notification process by default. Instead, intersite replication relies on a schedule to transfer updates, using compression to reduce the total traffic size.

The KCC and the topologies it generates were dramatically improved in Windows Server 2003 Active Directory. With Windows 2000 Active Directory, when there were more than 200 sites with domain controllers, it could take the KCC longer than 15 minutes to complete and would also drive up CPU utilization. Since the KCC runs every 15 minutes, it could get backlogged as a result or not finish at all. Typically when faced with this situation, administrators had to disable the KCC and manually create connection objects. With Windows Server 2003, Microsoft has stated that the new limit is closer to 5,000 sites when running a forest at the Windows Server 2003 forest functional level, which is a vast improvement. In fact, the KCC was largely rewritten in Windows Server 2003 and became much more scalable and efficient.

The KCC

Domain controllers within sites have connections created between them by the KCC. These connections use a random GUID as the unique identifier and are represented in Active Directory as *connection objects*. When domain controllers between sites must be connected, the Intersite Topology Generator (ISTG) automatically creates connection objects in Active Directory between these domain controllers. Within each site, an ISTG is designated to generate the intersite topology for that particular site via the KCC process.

The ISTG depends upon the presence of site links in your Active Directory in order to create the connections between domain controllers in different sites. Site links are an administratively defined construct that generally represents the network topology on top of which an Active Directory deployment exists. We will cover site links in detail later in this chapter. There are two reasons that the ISTG cannot automatically create links between two sites. First, the ISTG has no idea which sites you will want to connect. Second, the ISTG does not know which replication transport protocol you will want to use.

The KCC runs locally every 15 minutes on each DC. The default time period can be changed, and it can be started manually on demand if required. To force the KCC to run manually, see the sidebar "Triggering the KCC and ISTG," next. If we create two domain controllers called Server A and Server B in a new domain, the KCC will run on each server to create links. Each KCC is tasked with creating a link to define incoming replication only. The KCC on Server A will define an incoming link from Server B, and Server B's KCC will define an incoming link from Server A. The KCC creates only one incoming link per replication partner, so Server A will never have two auto-generated incoming links from Server B, for example.

The KCC does not create one topology for all naming contexts (NCs) or one topology per NC. The Configuration and Schema NCs share one replication topology, so the KCC creates a topology for these two together. The KCC also creates another topology on a per-domain/naming context basis. Because the Schema and Configuration are forest-wide in scope, the KCC needs to replicate changes to these items across site links. The KCC needs to maintain a forest-wide topology spanning all domains for these two NCs together. However, unless a domain is set up to span multiple sites, the topology for a particular domain will be made up of only intrasite connections. If the domain does span sites, the KCC needs to create a replication topology across those sites.

Automatic Intrasite Topology Generation by the KCC

For each naming context, the KCC builds a bidirectional ring of replication connections between the domain controllers in a site. However, while upstream and downstream connections are created between partners around a ring, the KCC can also create additional connections across the ring as well. These connections are created on the basis of a single rule: that no DC in the site can be more than three replication hops from any other DC in the same site. The KCC does this to maintain a guaranteed theoretical maximum convergence time within a site for a NC. In a site with Windows 2000 domain controllers, this convergence time is approximately 15 minutes. In a site with only Windows Server 2003 or newer domain controllers, this convergence time is approximately 1 minute. For example, as you add new DCs for a domain to a site, they will just get inserted into the ring. Due to the three-hop rule, when you put in your eighth

DC, the KCC must add at least one cross-ring connection. Let's take a look at this process in more detail.

 There were quite a few administrators who weren't happy about the default intrasite convergence time in Windows 2000, without realizing that it is fully configurable. The related registry values are located under the `HKLM\SYSTEM\CurrentControlSet\Services\NTDS\Parameters` registry key. The specific values are:

Replicator notify pause after modify (secs)
How long to wait before notifying the first change-notification partner of an originating write. Windows 2000 default: 300 seconds. Windows Server 2003 and newer default: 15 seconds.

Replicator notify pause between DSAs (secs)
How long to wait after notifying each additional change-notification partner of an originating write. Windows 2000 default: 30 seconds. Windows Server 2003 and newer default: 3 seconds.

 These registry modifications also work in Windows Server 2003 and newer AD; however, the timings can also be modified by changing the following attributes on the cross-reference objects for the specific NCs:

- `msDS-Replication-Notify-First-DSA-Delay`
- `msDS-Replication-Notify-Subsequent-DSA-Delay`

This will impact all domain controllers replicating the NC so it isn't as targeted as the registry settings.

Two servers

In the case of two domain controllers, we start off with one DC, Server A. When Server B is promoted as the second DC for the domain, the DCPROMO process uses Server A as its source for Active Directory information for the domain, Schema and Configuration naming contexts on Server B. During the promotion process, the Configuration Container is replicated from Server A to Server B, and the KCC on Server B creates the relevant incoming connection object representing Server A. Server B then informs Server A that it exists, and Server A correspondingly creates the incoming connection object representing Server B. Replication now occurs for all NCs using the connection objects. While replication occurs separately for each NC, the same connection objects are used for all three at this moment.

Three servers

The DCPROMO process is later started on Server C. Server C then uses a DNS lookup and picks one of the existing DCs to use as a promotion partner. For now we'll say that it picks Server B. During the promotion process, the Configuration container is repli-

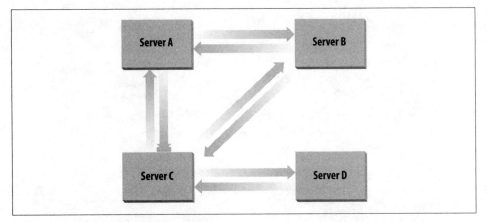

Figure 11-1. Adding a fourth DC to a site

cated from Server B to Server C, and Server C creates the relevant incoming connection object representing Server B. Server C then informs Server B that it exists, and Server B correspondingly creates the incoming connection object representing Server C. Replication now occurs for all NCs using the connection objects.

At present, you have two-way links between Server A and Server B, as well as between Server B and Server C. We have no links between Server A and Server C, but the KCC must create a ring topology for replication purposes. So as soon as Server B does a full replication to Server C, Server C knows about Server A from the Configuration NC. Server C's KCC then creates an incoming connection object for Server A. Server A now finds out about Server C in one of two ways:

- Server A requests updates from Server B and identifies a new DC.
- Server C requests changes from Server A, and this allows Server A to identify the new DC.

Server A now creates an incoming connection object for Server C. This completes the Server A to Server B to Server C to Server A loop.

Four servers

Server D comes along, and the promotion process starts. It picks Server C to connect to. Server D ends up creating the incoming connection object for Server C. Server C also creates the incoming connection object for Server D. You now have the loop from the previous section, plus a two-way connection from Server C to Server D. See Figure 11-1 for this topology.

Server D's KCC now uses the newly replicated data from Server C to go through the existing topology. It knows that it has to continue the ring topology, and as it is already linked to Server C, Server D has to create an incoming connection object for one of Server C's partners. It chooses Server B in this case. So Server D's KCC creates an

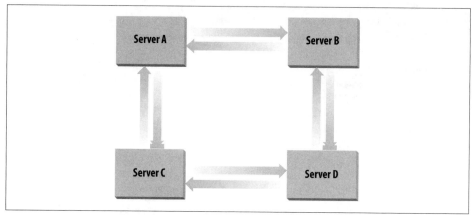

Figure 11-2. Ring of four DCs

incoming connection object for Server B. Server D then requests changes from Server B. The rest of the process can happen in a number of ways, so we'll just play out one scenario.

Server B now knows about Server D. Server B's KCC runs and realizes that it doesn't need the link to Server C, so it deletes that connection and creates a new one directly to Server D itself. Finally, as replication takes place around the ring along the existing links, Server C notes that it has a now defunct incoming link from Server B and removes it. You now have a simple ring, as depicted in Figure 11-2.

Eight servers

Once you hit eight servers connected together, you need more links across the ring if you are to maintain the three-hop rule. If you look at Figure 11-3, you will see this demonstrated. If the cross-ring links did not exist, some servers would be four hops away from one another. The KCC figures out which servers it wishes to link by allowing the last server to enter the ring to make the initial choice. Thus, if Server H is the new server in the ring, it knows that Server D is four hops away and makes a connection to it. When Server D's KCC receives the new data that Server H has linked to it, it reciprocates and creates a link to Server H.

However, this doesn't completely solve the problem. Consider Server B and Server F: they're still four hops away from each other. Now the KCC creates a link between these pairs to maintain the three-hop rule.

Now what?

We've now gone through the mechanism that the KCC uses for intrasite link generation between DCs. However, that's not the whole story. Remember that Active Directory can have multiple domains per site, so what happens if we add *othercorp.com* (a new

---

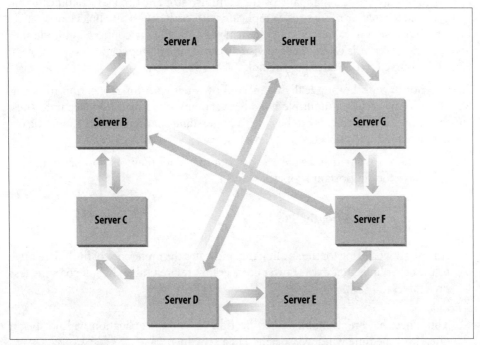

Figure 11-3. Eight servers and the extra KCC-generated links

domain in the same forest) to the same site or even *sales.mycorp.com* (a new child domain)? What happens then? The answer is the same for both, and it is based on NCs:

- The Schema and Configuration replicate across the enterprise, and they share a replication topology. Although they replicate separately, it is along the same links.

- Each domain replicates only domain-wide, so the domain topologies for both domains stay in the same ring formation that they previously had.

Once the two domains integrate, the KCC-generated topologies for *mycorp.com* and the other domain stay the same. However, the KCC-generated Configuration/Schema replication topology that exists separately on both domains will form itself into its own ring, encompassing both domains according to standard KCC rules.

To summarize, when you have multiple domains in a site, each domain has its own KCC-generated topology connecting its DCs, but all the DCs in the site, no matter what domain they come from, connect in a separate topology representing Schema/Configuration replication.

Site Links: The Basic Building Blocks of Intersite Topologies

Having sites is all well and good, but you need to be able to connect them if you are ever going to replicate any data. An intersite connection of this type is known as a *site link*. Site links are created manually by the administrator and are used to indicate that it is possible for two or more sites to replicate with each other. Site links can connect more than two sites if the underlying physical network already connects multiple sites together; however, it is often easier to visualize and control replication connections if you limit yourself to two sites per site link.

Sites do not have to be physically connected by a network for replication to occur. Replication can occur via multiple links between any two hosts from separate sites. However, for Active Directory to be able to understand that replication should be occurring between these two sites, you have to create a site link between them.

We've mentioned that site links have a cost, but that's not their only property. In fact, site links have four important properties:

Name
>   An identifying name for the site link.

Cost
>   An integer weighting for the site link that indicates the preference of the link relative to the other links that exist. Lower costs are more preferable; higher costs are less *preferable*.

Schedule
>   The times that are available for replication to begin. Replication will not begin outside of the time windows specified in a schedule.

Transports
>   The protocols that are used for replication along this link.

Cost

As each link has a cost, it is possible to calculate the total cost of traveling over any one route by adding up all the costs of the individual routes. If multiple routes exist between two disparate sites, the KCC will automatically identify the lowest cost route and use that for replication. If only a single route exists between any two sites, then the site link costs are irrelevant.

Schedule

The schedule on a link represents the time period that replication is allowed to be initiated across that link. Domain Controllers also maintain times that they are allowed to replicate. Obviously, if two DCs and a link do not have times that coincide, no replication will ever be possible.

Between the scheduled start and stop times for replication on a site link, the server is available to open so-called windows for replication to occur. As soon as any server that replicates through that link becomes available for replication, a replication window is opened between the site link and that server. As soon as two servers that need to replicate with each other have two windows that coincide, replication can occur. Once a server becomes unavailable for replication, the window is removed for that server. Once the site link becomes unavailable, all windows close.

 Schedules only define when replication can *begin*. Once replication has begun, it will not stop until it completes regardless of the schedule defined on the site link.

Transport

Site links can currently replicate using two transport mechanisms:

- Directory Service Remote Procedure Call (DS-RPC)
- Inter-Site Mechanism Simple Mail Transport Protocol (ISM-SMTP)

A site link using DS-RPC means that servers wishing to replicate using that site link can make direct synchronous connections using RPC across the link. As the transport protocol is synchronous, the replication across the connection is conducted and negotiated in real time between two partners. This is the normal sort of connection for a real-time link. In some scenarios, certain sites may have unpredictable availability or they may have a very unreliable or highly latent WAN connection. In these scenarios, SMTP replication can be appropriate.

The SMTP connector, as a site link using the ISM-SMTP transport is called, allows partner domain controllers to encrypt and email their updates to each other. In this scenario, Active Directory assumes that you already have an underlying SMTP-based connection mechanism between these two sites. If you don't, you'll have to set one up for this to work. If a connection is in place, the SMTP Connector assumes that the existing underlying mail routing structure will sort out how mail is transferred. To that end, a site link using the SMTP Connector ignores the scheduling tab, as it will send and receive updates automatically via the underlying system whenever the email system sends and receives them itself.

SMTP Connector messages are encrypted using certificates, so to encrypt the messages you need to install special certificates on the domain controllers which will participate in SMTP replication. You can automatically request and install these certificates if you have an Enterprise Certification Authority (CA) running on Windows in your organization. Otherwise, reference *http://support.microsoft.com/kb/321051* for instructions on requesting and installing certificates from a third party CA.

 The SMTP replication protocol cannot be used for domain NC replication. It can, however, be used to replicate global catalog, schema, and configuration information. This means that multisite domains with slow links will be required to use RPC for domain replication.

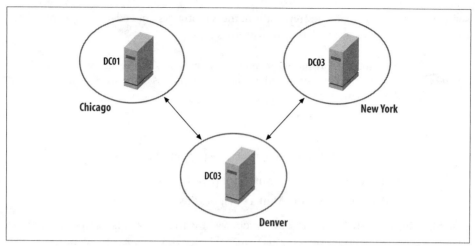

Figure 11-4. Site link bridging scenario

When the ISTG becomes involved

In order to generate the intersite replication topology, the ISTG actively uses site link costs to identify which routes it should be using for replication purposes. If a stable series of site links exists in an organization, and a new route is added with a lower cost, the ISTG will switch over to use the new link where appropriate and delete the old connection objects. The network of connections that the KCC creates is known as a minimum-cost spanning tree.

Site Link Bridges: The Second Building Blocks of Intersite Topologies

Site link bridges are only necessary in scenarios where you have disabled the "Bridge All Site Links" options in Active Directory. We discussed an example of when a site link bridge may be necessary in Chapter 5. To summarize, site link bridges are necessary when you wish to tell the KCC that it can create a direct replication connection between two domain controllers who are not directly connected according to the topology information in Active Directory.

Consider the sample topology in Figure 11-4 and pretend that for the purposes of this discussion, "Bridge All Site Links" is disabled in the sample topology and that the underlying network allows communication between Chicago and New York. Given this information, Chicago and New York cannot replicate directly with one another. Instead, Chicago must replicate with Denver, and New York must replicate with Denver as well. In the event the Denver domain controller (DC02) goes down, there will be no replication between Chicago and New York. If you define a site link bridge that includes the Chicago-Denver and New York-Denver site links, then Active Directory will be able to create a replication connection directly between Chicago and New York in the event that the Denver domain controller becomes unavailable.

Now that you've seen the site links and site link bridges, let's look at how to design your sites and their replication links.

Designing Sites and Links for Replication

There is only one really important point that is the overriding factor when designing a replication strategy for your network: how much traffic and over what period will you be replicating across the network? However, replication isn't the only reason for creating sites. Sites also need to exist to group sets of machines together for ease of locating data, finding the nearest DC to authenticate with, finding the nearest DFS share mount point, or routing email in Exchange 2007 organizations.

Step 1: Gather Background Data for Your Network

Before you sit down to design your site and WAN topology, you need to obtain the map of your existing network infrastructure. This map should contain all physical locations where your company has computers, along with every link between those locations. The speed and reliability of each link should be noted.

If you have an existing IP infrastructure, write down all the subnets that correspond to the sites you have noted.

Step 2: Design the Sites

From the network diagram, you need to draw your site structure and name each site, using a one-to-one mapping from the network diagram as your starting point. If you have 50 physical WAN locations, you have 50 sites. If only 30 of these will be used for Active Directory, you may not see a need to include the entire set of sites in Active Directory. If you do include the entire set, however, it is much easier to visualize your entire network and add clients or servers to those locations later.

 When drawing Active Directory topologies, sites normally are represented by ovals.

Remember that a site is a well-connected set of subnets ("well-connected" tends to mean about 10 Mbps LAN speed). A site does not have to have a domain controller in it; it can be composed entirely of clients. If you have two buildings (or an entire campus) that is connected over 10/100 Mbps links, your entire location is a single site.

This is not a hard-and-fast rule. By the normal rules, two locations connected over a 2 Mbps link represent two distinct sites. You can, however, group networks together into single sites if you want to. You have to appreciate that there will be more replication than if you had created two sites and a site link, because DCs in both physical locations will maintain the intrasite replication ring topology. If you had created two sites and a site link, only two bridgehead servers would replicate with each other.

To summarize, we would suggest that, by default, you create one site per physical location on your WAN unless you do not feel a need to segregate replication between two physical locations.

Step 3: Plan the Domain Controller Locations

Planning for placement of domain controllers is fairly easy, but the number of DCs to use is a different matter entirely.

Where to put domain controllers

Each workstation in a domain exists in a single site that it knows about. When a user tries to log on to the domain at that workstation, the workstation authenticates to a DC from the local site, which it originally locates via a DNS query. If no DC is available in the local site, the workstation finds a remote site by way of the site topology, and by a process of negotiation with a DC in that site, either authenticates with that DC or is redirected to a better domain controller.

This consideration governs the placement of DCs. You should place one DC for authentication purposes per domain in all sites that meet any of the following criteria:

- The site has links that are not fast enough for logon purposes to a particular domain.
- The site has links that may be fast enough for logon, but you do not wish to authenticate across them for a particular domain.
- An application that requires fast responses from a domain controller (such as Exchange) exists in the site.
- You have overarching business requirements to ensure authentication in that site will always be available regardless of the WAN link status.
- Under Windows 2000, if you made heavy use of universal groups, you needed to place a Global Catalog at a site if you did not want to impact logons due to a network failure. But as of Windows Server 2003 Active Directory, you can enable universal group membership caching so that this is no longer a requirement.

The first and second points also need to be considered in light of the number of users and workstations at the sites. If there are enough workstations at the site to generate logon traffic that will utilize a large percentage of the available WAN bandwidth, then you will probably be forced to place a local domain controller at the site.

How many domain controllers to have

Deciding how many DCs to place at a site is never easy. If you have a Windows server that's already serving 500 heavy users and is close to its load limit, could it authenticate 100 additional users quickly enough at the same time? Powerful servers can authenticate hundreds or thousands of users simultaneously, but even these servers will balk if they are already heavily loaded.

There are some things that are tough to accurately assess, such as LDAP-based applications using the DCs. Often you do not know the specifics of how any given application uses the directory, so you end up taking a "wait and see" stance in terms of how many DCs will be needed and hoping that the usage levels aren't so high that users will notice any performance problems.

 Exchange is an example of an application that ships with best practice guidelines for how many global catalog servers are required. Exchange defines these best practices in terms of a ratio of Exchange CPU cores to Global Catalog CPU cores.

For more information on Exchange and Active Directory best practices, see Chapter 19.

The only way to definitively decide on how many domain controllers are required in a site is often to try the best practice and recommended guidelines, and then adjust the actual count to meet your reality as patterns become clear. That way, you should be able to judge for yourself how many DCs you may need for authentication and other purposes.

It is important that you define up front when planning for your domain controller deployment as to what criteria you will use to justify an additional domain controller in a site. This usually depends on such performance metrics as average CPU utilization or disk utilization.

Placing a domain controller in more than one site

Any domain controller that you promote will belong to one site only. However, there can be instances in which you may want to configure a domain controller to cover multiple sites. For example, you might want to make sure that workstations from a number of sites all authenticate using one DC. Domain controllers perform a behavior by default called automatic site coverage, which registers the necessary DNS records for a domain controller to service multiple sites.

Automatic site coverage is important when you have sites without domain controllers as clients in those sites will still need to authenticate and access Active Directory. In branch office scenarios, it is often ideal to modify this behavior so that domain controllers in branch offices don't cover other sites. You can find more information on configuring this behavior in Chapter 4 of the Windows 2003 Branch Office Deployment

Guide available at *http://www.microsoft.com/downloads/details.aspx?FamilyId= 9353A4F6-A8A8-40BB-9FA7-3A95C9540112*. It is no longer necessary to configure this behavior for Windows Server 2008 Read-Only Domain Controllers.

 You can manually configure domain controllers to service multiple sites by modifying a registry value. To do this, edit the registry on the server that will be covering multiple sites and add a REG_MULTI_SZ value called SiteCoverage to the HKLM\SYSTEM\CurrentControlSet\Services\Netlo gon\Parameters key. Add the names of the sites to this value. If you're using *RegEdit* or *RegEdt32*, use Shift-Enter to add the data for multiple lines.

Generally speaking, you should plan to rely on automatic site coverage; however, this manual functionality exists in case you need to make an exception.

Step 4: Decide How You Will Use the KCC to Your Advantage

There are really three ways to use the KCC to your advantage over intersite links:

- Manually create all the connection objects and turn off the KCC for intersite replication. This isn't something we recommend unless you know exactly what you're doing.

- Let the KCC generate your entire topology for you automatically. This is the default and what Microsoft recommends as standard. You still need to create all site links manually, but if you leave the Bridge All Site Links option enabled, the KCC will not need you to create extra site links to replicate data via sites that do not have the relevant DCs. Site link bridges are not necessary in this scenario.

- A mixture of the two can be had by forcing the KCC to make decisions based on certain key information that you provide. For example, if you disable Bridge All Site Links, the KCC will be able to replicate only across site links that actually exist. You then can make use of site link bridges to force the KCC to use certain routes for replication.

You can leave this step until after you have designed the site links if you are not sure what to do.

Step 5: Create Site Links

Now that you have all the sites down on paper, you need to think about the links. In this step, we identify how sites are connected and to what degree we need to replicate the physical topology in Active Directory. Additionally, we identify any site links that will require nonstandard replication schedules and the frequencies at which site links replicate.

The first thing to consider is how you will name your site links. We recommend that you limit yourself to two sites per site link, and to adopt a naming convention that makes it easy to identify the sites involved in a site link. One strategy that works well is to place the two sites involved in both the name and description attributes, reversing the order. For example, you might make the name of the site link "SiteA-SiteB" and the description "SiteB-SiteA." This makes it easy to sort on either field in Active Directory Sites and Services and see which site links involve a given site.

When applying costs to your site links, you should make every effort to use a standardized system for the cost values you choose across the entire deployment. There are multiple ways to implement this costing model, and there isn't necessarily a "right" way to do it either. Some organizations choose to assign link costs categorically such that links between hub sites have a certain costs, and then links between hubs and spokes have another cost, and links between two spokes have a third cost. Other organizations choose to associate the site link costs with the speed of the underlying WAN connection. Remember that either way, if there is only one path to a site, the cost is irrelevant.

For a discussion of using WAN speeds to populate site link cost values, see *http://briandesmond.com/blog/archive/2007/11/29/active-directory -site-links-naming-costing.aspx*. This blog post also includes a spreadsheet that provides the costs of many common WAN link speeds.

The frequency is simply how often replication will occur over the site link. This value is specified in minutes and can range from 15 minutes to 1 week. You should choose this value based on the requirement for how up-to-date Active Directory data is at either end of the site link, and also with respect to how much load replication will place on the underlying WAN link. If you do not have enough change volume to generate a significant amount of replication traffic, then it will likely not be beneficial to you to make the frequency intervals very long.

Schedule is the final configurable option on site links. The site link schedule defines during what time windows replication is allowed to *begin*. "Begin" is an important word here as once replication starts, it will not stop until it concludes regardless of the site link schedule. Site link schedules are very helpful when working around WAN links that are saturated or unavailable during certain time periods.

Step 6: Create Site Link Bridges

If you elect to disable the Bridge All Site Links option, you will need to examine whether your topology requires site link bridges to help the ISTG generate your intersite topology. In many hub/spoke topologies, this step ends up being unnecessary but you will need to examine yours to be sure.

Examples

Having considered the 6 steps, let's take another brief look at the three examples from the previous chapter and see what they will need in terms of sites.

TwoSiteCorp

TwoSiteCorp has two locations split by a 128 Kbps link. This means creation of two sites separated by a single site link, with DCs for domain authentication in each site. The site link cost is not an issue, as only one route exists between the two sites; whether the link cost is set to 1 or 500, you get the same result. Here the only issue is scheduling the replication, which depends on the existing traffic levels of the link. For a slow link like this one, it is best to schedule replication during the least busy times. If replication has to take place all the time, as changes need to be propagated rapidly, it may be time to consider increasing the capacity of the link.

RetailCorp

RetailCorp has a large, centralized retail organization with 600 shops connected via 64 Kbps links to a large centralized 10/100 Mbps interconnected headquarters in London. In this situation, you have one site for HQ and 600 sites for the stores. RetailCorp also uses a DC in each store. They then have to create 600 high-cost site links, each with the same cost. RetailCorp decides this is one very good reason to use ADSI (discussed in Part III) and writes a script to automate the creation of the site link objects in the configuration. The only aspect of the site links that is important here is the schedule. Can central HQ cope with all of the servers replicating intersite at the same time? Does the replication have to be staggered? The decision is made that all data has to be replicated during the times that the stores are closed; for stores that do not close, data is replicated during the least busy times. There is no need to worry about site link bridges or site link transitiveness as all links go through the central hub, and no stores need to intercommunicate. The administrators decide to let the KCC pick the bridgehead servers automatically.

PetroCorp

PetroCorp has 94 outlying branch offices. These branch offices are connected via 64 Kbps links to five central hub sites. These 5 hubs are connected to the central organization's HQ in Denver via T2, T1, 256 Kbps, and 128 Kbps links. Some of the hubs also are interconnected. To make it easier to understand, look at PetroCorp's network again (see Figure 11-5).

Initially, you need to create 100 sites representing HQ, the hubs, and the branch offices. How many servers do you need per site? From the design we made in Chapter 10, we decided on nine domains in the forest. Each of those distinct domains must obviously

---

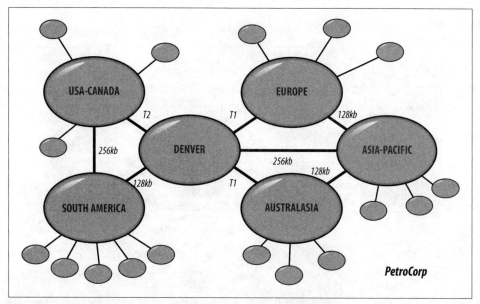

Figure 11-5. PetroCorp's network connections

have a server within it that forms part of the single forest. However, although the description doesn't say so, there is very little cross-pollination of clients from one hub needing to log on to servers from another hub. As this is the case, there is no need to put a server for every domain in every hub. If a user from Denver travels to the *asiapac .petrocorp.com* domain, the user can still log on to *petrocorp.com* from the Asia-Pacific hub, albeit much more slowly. PetroCorp sees that what little cross-pollination traffic it has is made up of two types of user:

- Senior *petrocorp.com* IT and business managers traveling to all hubs.

- Groups of Europe and Australasia users regularly staying at the alternate hub for periods during joint research. This means that *europe.petrocorp.com* users need to log on in the Australasia hub and *australasia.petrocorp.com* users need to log on in the Europe hub.

Although the senior managers' use is infrequent, these key decision makers need to log on as rapidly as possible to access email and their data. Money is found to ultimately place *petrocorp.com* servers for authentication purposes in each of the five hubs. The second requirement means that servers for each domain need to be added to the alternate hub. Due to this limitation, only enough money is found to support *petrocorp .com* from outside its own Denver location and the Europe/Australasia hubs hosting each other's domains (see Figure 11-6).

While domains are normally represented by triangles in diagrams, here the rectangular borders around a domain name represent servers that host that domain. Each domain is hosted by multiple servers represented by a single rectangle, although you could run

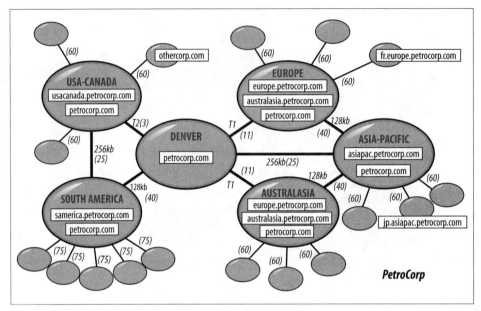

Figure 11-6. PetroCorp's sites and servers

this structure using only one server per rectangle. You can see that *petrocorp.com* is hosted in Denver, as well as in all other hubs.

Regarding intrasite KCC topology generation, PetroCorp has decided to let the KCC automatically generate intradomain server links. If this causes a problem, local administrators should be able to handle it.

The site links are depicted in Figure 11-6 with parentheses to indicate the costs. They can also be described as follows:

- Create one low-cost (3) DS-RPC site link for the T2 connection.
- Create two medium-cost (11) DS-RPC site links representing the T1 connections.
- Create high-cost DS-RPC site links for the five remaining interhub connections of 256 Kbps (25) and 128 Kbps (40).

What about the branches? All links are stable except the links between the eight South America branches and the hub, which are very unreliable. In this case, you have two choices: you can either let the clients in those eight sites authenticate across the less-than-reliable links or you can place domain controllers in those branches so that authentication is always possible even when the link is down. PetroCorp opts for the latter and places domain controllers in each of the eight branches.

Step 6 was left until now on purpose, since the administrators wanted to wait until the site links were designed to see whether site link bridging should be turned off and whether bridging routes might help. Now you can easily see that transitivity is important between the Europe and Australasia hubs. If you don't turn on transitiveness by default, you need to create a site link bridge in Denver that allows the Europe and Australasia hub sites to replicate across the two T1 links even though they have no direct links.

Now look at the diagram again, and consider that site link bridging is enabled. This means any site can use any connection to any other site based on the lowest cost. So, if you leave site link bridging enabled and let the KCC create the intersite connection objects and bridgehead servers, replication traffic between Denver and South America is likely to route through USA-Canada, as the total cost across those two links (28) is lower than the direct link (40). This also is true for Asia-Pacific to either Europe (40) or Australasia (40). All traffic is likely to route through Denver (36) because of that. All that means is that the slow 128 Kbps links will not have their bandwidth used up by replication; instead, the 256 Kbps links will absorb the overflow. In the eastern link, you have potentially added two lots of bidirectional replication traffic across the 256 Kbps link. Whether this is a problem is up to PetroCorp to decide. They have four main choices:

- Turn off transitiveness throughout the network. This forces the KCC to use only directly connected routes to replicate. This forces the use of the 128 Kbps links by default. Now add the site link bridge at Denver as mentioned previously, then add any other site link bridges to enforce using certain routes when the directly connected routes are not to be used for replication.

- Turn off transitiveness throughout the network. This forces the KCC to use only directly connected routes to replicate, which forces the use of the 128 Kbps links by default. Add the site link bridge at Denver as mentioned previously, and add any other site link bridges to enforce use of certain routes when the directly connected routes are not to be used for replication. Finally, turn off the KCC intersite topology generation in key sites where the bridgehead servers are handpicked from the available DCs and then create the connection objects manually.

- Leave transitiveness turned on throughout the network, automatically bridge all site links of the same DS-RPC transport, allow the KCC to choose the lowest cost routes, and accept the routes it chooses, controlling it with schedules.

- Leave transitiveness turned on throughout the network, automatically bridge all site links of the same DS-RPC transport, and turn off the KCC intersite topology generation in key sites where the bridgehead servers are handpicked from the available DCs, creating the connection objects manually.

Which of these options is chosen depends entirely on the traffic use of the links, the requirements on those links, and how much use the administrators wish to make of the KCC. PetroCorp decides that it wants the KCC to make the most of the connections but still wants to retain the greatest control and the potential to force the KCC to use certain routes. To that end, they select the second option.

In the end, the company chooses to bridge South America to Denver via USA-Canada to free up the 128 Kbps link for other traffic. They also choose to bridge Europe to Asia-Pacific via Denver to free up what is currently a congested link. The KCC automatically routes all traffic via Denver, as this bridge cost is lower than the single site link. Finally, the administrators allow the KCC in the Denver site to generate the eight intersite site links (four connections, each with two site links for redundancy) and then turn off intersite generation for that site. They then modify the connection objects created (deleting some and creating others) because they have a number of DCs that they do not want to use for replication purposes within Denver that the KCC picked up and used.

This is a fairly complicated site problem, but one that wasn't difficult to solve. There are many other viable solutions. Many options are available to you as well. That's why a design is so important.

Additional Resources

Microsoft has produced an outstanding guide for customers setting up a branch office deployment. A branch office deployment is a deployment with a large number of WAN sites that need to host local copies of Active Directory. One example of a branch office deployment is a large retail outlet that has a central office and hundreds of retail outlets that are all tied together into the same forest. If you have to deploy this kind of infrastructure, you absolutely need to review the Windows Server 2003 Active Directory Branch Office Guide; you can find it on the Microsoft web site at *http://www.microsoft .com/downloads/details.aspx?FamilyId=9353A4F6-A8A8-40BB-9FA7 -3A95C9540112*.

Bridgehead load balancing is an area that Microsoft greatly improved in Windows Server 2003. Although Windows Server 2003 will better distribute the replication load across multiple domain controllers, the new load-balancing algorithm will only work with new connections that are established; so, when you add a new domain controller, it will be underutilized for replication connections. Windows 2000, on the other hand, will not spread the load at all, which can create a topology that results in overloaded bridgehead servers in hub sites. Microsoft produced a tool to help with both of these issues. The tool is called the Active Directory Load Balancer (ADLB) and will look at the connection objects for a specified site and evenly spread those connections across all of the DCs in the site that can be used as bridgeheads. ADLB is part of the Windows Server 2003 Resource Kit Tools and is available for download from *http://www.micro soft.com/downloads/details.aspx?FamilyID=9d467a69-57ff-4ae7-96ee-b18c4790cffd*.

Summary

Based on this chapter, you should have a good understanding of how to go about designing the site topology for your Active Directory deployment and also how to determine if a domain controller is necessary in any given site. Site topologies are leveraged by Active Directory for replication and also by various other applications such as DFS and Exchange Server 2007. Clients also rely on the site topology to locate a domain controller for authentication.

The Knowledge Consistency Checker (KCC) is the process that runs automatically on each domain controller to generate the underlying replication connections. Intersite replication connections are generated on one domain controller in a site that is designated the Intersite Topology Generate (ISTG) for that site.

Planning your site topology requires a good understanding of the underlying network as you apply it to your requirements for sites, site links, and site link bridges. Sites represent disparate network locations that you want to segregate replication and authentication traffic between. Site links represent the connectivity between sites, and site link bridges provide the KCC with hints about transitivity between site links for generating the necessary connections for replication to occur.

The next chapter deals with how to update your designs to reflect your requirements for Group Policy Objects in your organization.

## CHAPTER 12

Designing Organization-Wide Group Policies

This chapter takes an in-depth look at Group Policy Objects (GPOs), focusing on how to structure your Active Directory effectively using Organizational Units and groups so that you can make the best use of the GPOs required in your organization.

Using GPOs to Help Design the Organizational Unit Structure

In Chapter 10, we described the design of the Active Directory Organizational Unit hierarchy. We also explained that other items have a bearing on that design. You see, there are two key design issues that affect the structure of your Organizational Units: permissions delegation and GPO placement. If you decide that your Active Directory is to be managed centrally rather than in a distributed fashion and that you will employ only a few GPOs that will be implemented mostly domain-wide (rather than many GPOs on many Organizational Units), your Organizational Unit structure can be almost any way that you want it to be. It shouldn't make much difference whether you have 400 branches coming off the root or one container with every item inside it. However, if permissions over specific objects do need to be delegated to specific sets of administrators, it will make more sense to structure your domain Organizational Units in a manner that facilitates that administration. This doesn't have to be the case, but it makes it much easier to use Organizational Units.

For example, if we have 1,000 users and 10 managers who each manage 100 users, we could put the 1,000 users in one Organizational Unit and give the 10 administrators permission to modify only their 100 users. This is a slow and daft way to run systems administration. It would be better to create 10 Organizational Units and put 100 users in each, giving each administrator permissions over his particular Organizational Unit. This makes much more sense, as the administrator can be changed very easily, it is easier to report on access, and so on. Sense and reducing management overhead are the overriding keys here. Either solution is feasible; one is just easier to implement and maintain.

Permissions delegation is covered in more detail in Chapter 13.

The same fundamental facts apply to GPOs. If you are going to need to apply multiple policies to multiple sets of users, it makes more sense and will be easier to manage if you set up multiple Organizational Units. However, this isn't always possible, for example, if the Organizational Unit structure that you have as an ideal conflicts with the one that you will need for permissions delegation, which again conflicts with the one you would like for GPO structuring.

Identifying Areas of Policy

We will assume that within your organization, you will be writing a document that describes your plan for the security features you wish to use in your Active Directory environment and exactly how those features will be implemented. Part of this document will relate to other security features of AD such as Kerberos, firewalls, permissions, and so on, but here we're concerned with GPOs.

First you need to identify the general policy goals that you wish to achieve with GPOs. There's no need to go into the exact details of each GPO setting and its value at this moment. Instead, you're looking at items such as "Deploy financial applications" and "Restrict desktop settings." As you identify each general policy area, you need to note whether it is to apply to all computers or users in a site, to all computers or users in a single domain, or to a subsection of the user and computer accounts. If you aren't sure for some items, put the items in more than one category. You end up with items such as "Deploy financial applications to accountants in France" and "Restrict desktop settings in southern Europe."

Once you have the general policy areas constructed, you need to construct an Organizational Unit structure that facilitates implementation of this policy design. At this point, you start placing computers and users in various Organizational Units, deciding if all objects in each container are to receive the policy or whether you will restrict application to the policy via ACLs. There are a number of questions you can ask yourself during this stage. To help with this, a loose set of guidelines follows the example in the next section.

Ultimately the document will need to specify exactly which GPO settings are to be applied, which groups you will set up for ACL permission restrictions, and what the Organizational Unit structure is going to be. It helps to explain justifications for any decisions you make.

To make the guidelines more meaningful, we'll show how you can structure a tree in different ways using a real-world example.

How GPOs Influenced a Real Organizational Unit Design

Leicester University needed an Organizational Unit structure that represented its user and computer population. The system needed to allow users from every department to roam anywhere on campus and log on to the system. User accounts were fairly generic across the system, with the main differences resulting only from membership in certain groups indicating the type of account the user had (staff, undergraduate, and so on). The main distinction came in the two sorts of machines that we maintain on campus: staff devices that exist in a number of staff member's offices, and open devices that exist in areas known as open-area labs, which anyone could use. While staff machines always exist within a department, labs exist in certain locations and buildings throughout the university campus.

Having full Internet and drop-in access, we needed to make sure that these open-area client devices were as secure as they could possibly be. This security had to extend to all users who logged on at the machines, whether they were staff or student. However, we also wanted to make sure that staff accounts were not locked down in their own departments. In other words, we wanted the user profiles of the staff users to be much more locked down only in the open-area labs and nowhere else.

In terms of policies, we needed to apply quite a few. While the specifics aren't important here, we needed a number of policies to apply to different areas:

Area	Policies to apply to
A	All computers and users in the domain
B	Users in specific departments
C	All clients (not servers)
D	All open-area clients
E	All staff clients
F	Staff clients in specific departments
G	Open-area clients in specific labs

With these requirements, we came up with a design. This was a lengthy process, but we'll try to break it down so that it makes sense. Let's take a look at the users themselves to start with.

Users were always members of a specific department, and this was how the university was structured in terms of its business, so it seemed logical to name the Organizational Units after the university departments. We should add, by the way, that Leicester University needed only one domain, the forest root domain in a single forest, for its organization; the Organizational Unit structure was much more important than the domain structure in this case. The overall Organizational Unit structure came out something like that shown in Figure 12-1. Each department is joined directly to the

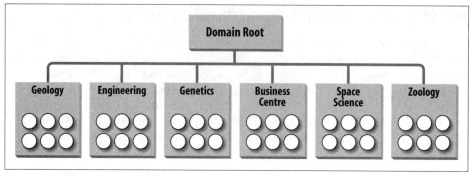

Figure 12-1. OU structure to hold user objects

root of the domain, with the users (represented by the circles) being children of the departmental containers.

Next, we needed an Organizational Unit structure that represented the distinct divisions of computers that existed throughout the university. There's no necessity to presume that your computers should go in the same Organizational Unit structure as your users, and that's how we approached the concept at Leicester. Initially, based on the policy areas, it seemed sensible to us to create an entirely new client tree that held only the machine accounts. This hierarchy ended up looking like the one in Figure 12-2.

Here you can see the branch solely for the computer accounts, with two children that each hold lab locations or departments themselves. Notice how the staff machine branch of the tree looks remarkably like the user structure diagram from Figure 12-1. We'll come back to that in a minute. For now, let's see if we can successfully apply the policies properly to this hierarchy. Take a look at Figure 12-3, where the policies are shown using the letter notation from the earlier table. This screen looks very cluttered, but it simply depicts each policy area with indications of where the policy area is linked. The trapezoid is Microsoft's symbol for a GPO.

Not every department and lab is listed in this screen. In a similar vein, we've linked the GPOs to only some of the Organizational Units, since that would be the case in reality. After all, if every department or lab were to receive a policy, you might as well link the GPO to the parent.

The merits of collapsing the Organizational Unit structure

We've created a structure that is understandable and perfectly represents the business that we operate. That's a good achievement from this design. The next step is to consider whether the domain would be easier to manage if we merged the duplicated staff organizational units.

Take a look at Figure 12-4. This is the hierarchy if we do away with all the staff machine Organizational Units and put the staff computers directly into the departmental Organizational Units. Policy areas A and B stay the same. Policy area C has to apply to all

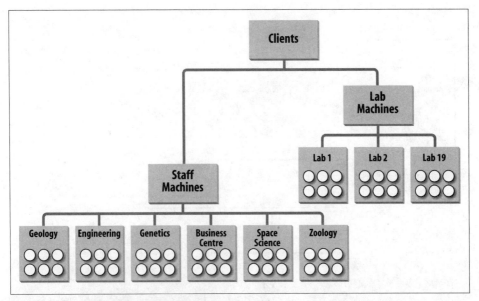

Figure 12-2. OU structure to hold computer objects

clients, so we can't use the Clients Organizational Unit any more. We have two choices: link the policy to the domain and have it apply to all Organizational Units containing computers beneath the root, or link the policy to each Organizational Unit under the root by hand. The latter solution also requires us to link the GPO to any new Organizational Units that we create under the root, if they are to receive the policy.

The former is the easier solution to manage, so let's run with it and link policy area C to the domain root. Unfortunately, this means that the GPO is going to apply to any computer objects in the domain, including Organizational Units that we store servers in, such as the Domain Controllers Organizational Unit that exists under the root of the domain. We don't want this, so the only way forward here is to block policy inheritance at these server Organizational Units. You may see where this is going now. We've not only blocked policy area C from being inherited by these Organizational Units that contain servers, we've also blocked any other policies that may need to apply as part of policy area A. My only solution to fix this is to use my ability to force an override of policy area A down the tree. So much for a simpler solution; we now have at least one block in place (for the domain controllers Organizational Unit) and policies from area A overriding all blocks down the tree to make sure they get past the blocks we just set up. While this is a solution, it's starting to feel more complex than the one before. Isn't there a better way?

Yes, there is—by making use of security groups. Forget about the blocks and inheritance for now and consider that instead we put all the computers that are not to get policy area C in a security group. We can then deny the Apply Group Policy permission to this particular security group, so that no members of the group ever have that policy

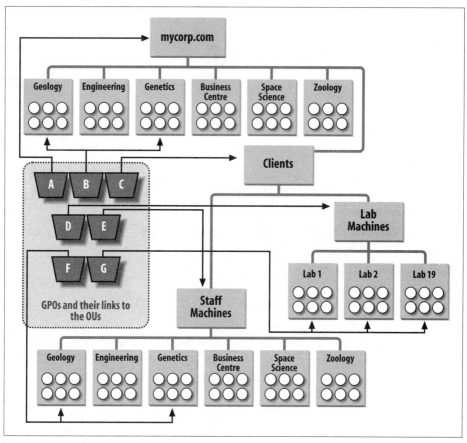

Figure 12-3. GPOs applied to the entire OU structure

applied to them. This is a much easier solution. However, it does mean that the administrators must remember that if a new computer is created and is not to receive the policy, it must be added to the group.

Policy areas D and G can still apply as they did before. Policy area F applies only to certain Organizational Units, so we just link F to the various departments under the root and carry on as before. However, we have more problems with E. Again, the choices are similar to the previous predicament: we could apply E to the department Organizational Units individually (remembering to do this for each new department we create), we could apply the policy to the domain root and use block inheritance-force override as before, or we could use groups again. The use of groups seems simpler, so let's go with that option. If we create a group for all the staff machines, we can just give the group permission to apply group policy to policy E in addition to removing the default permission for authenticated users to apply group policy. Now all users won't run the policy by default, but members of the staff machines group will.

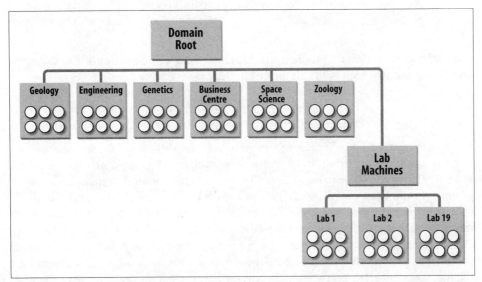

Figure 12-4. Another solution to the OU structure

This is a different solution that now achieves the same goal. The solution that Leicester chose (the first design) required fewer groups and allowed a computer's or user's location in the hierarchy to dictate which policies were applied. The new solution that we've just worked through collapses the tree structure, but instead makes more use of groups to indicate which policies are to be applied.

In fact, this tends to be a rule: as you collapse a structure where a number of GPOs apply, you need greater control via groups or the use of block inheritance and overrides.

A bridge too far

We could go one stage further and remove the lab machines' Organizational Unit entirely. That would cause the same problems with policy area D that we had with E. The simpler solution is to add all lab machines into a group and allow only members of that group to access the policy.

You can continue on in this manner, removing Organizational Units and creating more groups until you actually end up with all objects in a single Organizational Unit under the domain. At that point, all the GPOs are applied to that Organizational Unit, and you control access to the Organizational Units via groups. Prioritization of the order that the multiple GPOs would be applied might be more of a nightmare in this situation.

We hope you can see that there are a number of options open to you when designing your Organizational Unit structure for GPOs. It doesn't really matter which method you choose, as long as you're happy with it. The Organizational Unit structure that Leicester adopted requires less maintenance, because you don't have to put an object in a group after creation; you just create it in the place in the tree that it is to receive policies from. That's less of an issue with the capabilities of ADSI, since the code to bind to the parent group and add the newly created object to that group is just two extra lines.

We also created some other Organizational Units for specific functions. For example, one Organizational Unit holds all the groups that we ever created. That way, when we want to find a group, we know where it is. We also created a test Organizational Unit so that we could roll out policies and do testing with users and computers within the domain without affecting the existing user setup.

It may appear that Leicester doesn't make much use of groups to control access to GPOs, but that's not the case. Just because they set up the Organizational Unit structure in a way that made sense to them doesn't mean that they shouldn't make good use of groups as well. For example, look back at Figure 12-3. Policy areas D and G actually consist of a number of completely different and opposing GPOs that can affect all lab machines (D) or machines in specific labs (G). One group of settings entirely locks down the workstations in those labs from access to the hard disk and various control panels, and places other security measures. Another raft of settings serves to unlock the machines entirely; in other words, this GPO is the complete opposite of the first. Further sets of GPOs allow them to put the lab into a mixture of the two states, with some areas locked down and others remaining unlocked. These policies are applied as required to the specific lab Organizational Units, so that if all were to apply at the same time, it would be a complete fiasco. Instead, they use global security groups, one for access to each GPO, and make the computers from that lab members of each group.

To gain access to the policies, they move the computers from one group into another. If a client needs to be unlocked entirely, they move it to the unlocked group and reboot or wait until the policy refreshes. Similarly, if a user from zoology decides that he wants his machine locked down, they can apply the relevant GPOs to the zoology Organizational Unit, then place that machine in the global group that allows access to the GPO.

If they had a situation in which the client was either locked down or not locked down, they could have used just one group and had a lockdown state by default, with membership in the group implying an unlocked state or vice versa.

Loopback mode

One important aspect of Leicester's GPO design that hasn't been mentioned until now is loopback mode. Leicester needs to use loopback mode to lock down both staff and students while they are in a lab environment. To do this successfully requires that the computer policies be separate from the user policies. When you add this requirement to the equation, it makes more sense to keep the lab part of the tree separate in some way from the other part of the tree. This ensures that the user sections of the computer policies do not apply to any user accounts except during loopback mode. Both Figures 12-1 and 12-2 have structures that will happily accommodate the requirement.

Guidelines for Designing GPOs

In this section, we provide guidelines that help you toward two critical design goals:

- All policies should be applied quickly, so that users do not feel a significant impact due to policy processing.
- All policies should be as easy as possible to administer and maintain.

With these two concepts in mind, let's take a look at the guidelines:

Design in a way that you feel comfortable with
As shown in the example in the last section, it can be easier to do large designs by considering the user Organizational Unit and computer Organizational Unit structures separately. If you want to do them together and have a small enough network that you can do so easily, that's fine. If not, try it the way we first did.

Restrict as best you can the number of policies that apply
In a perfect world, this wouldn't be important. But in the real world, the more policies you have, the more processing the client has to do in addition to its normal logon/boot up, and the longer it takes to complete the process.

If you have multiple policies applying to an object from the same location in a tree, consider collapsing them into a single object, since this will process faster than multiple policies will. If the number of policies you are applying during a logon/boot up is larger than you can effectively get out to the client across the network or, more importantly, larger than you can get the client to process, you need to consider reducing or collapsing the policies. If you need to apply a significantly large set of policies with many settings that extends logon to five minutes, but you feel that is acceptable to achieve this level of policy, that's fine.

When it comes down to it, only you know what you can accept, and you will need to do your own testing in this area to satisfy your constraints. If you have to have a client logged on in less than four seconds, you have to work within that constraint. Microsoft likes to recommend no more than 10 Organizational Units deep to make sure that you don't use too many GPOs. As we know, this isn't very helpful. Having one GPO applying at a site, one at the domain, and one at each of five Organizational Units means only seven GPOs. Applying 10 at each level is 70. So it's not only how deep you nest your Organizational Unit structure that matters, but it's also how many policies you can apply. The unfortunate part, of course, is that it always comes back to how many settings you are applying in each policy.

The simple answer is that a faster machine with more RAM can apply more policies in less time than a slower PC with less RAM; consequently, for a network of heterogeneous clients, you need to do testing on your own network to see how fast application of policies is and how much bandwidth they take up.

Use security groups to tailor access
While you can set up ACLs to allow or deny application of policy to an individual user or computer, it makes more sense to use groups to do this whenever you can.

If you use groups, it lets you keep all policy access in one object, and it can make complex systems much more manageable.

Limit the use of block/force inheritance

You should be very cautious of blocking inheritance at locations in the tree unless you are quite sure that this is the right way to solve your problem. The repercussions from a simple blocking of inheritance can spiral quickly as you encounter areas of policy that need to override the block. Your well-designed system can become quite difficult to maintain if you block and override regularly. This is not to say that you should never use them; just exercise caution in their use.

Collapse the Organizational Unit design

If you wish, you can collapse your Organizational Unit design and make more use of groups (or even block inheritance/force override) to govern access to specific policies. These are both perfectly valid solutions, and you should use whichever one you are more comfortable with. Remember the axiom that the more you collapse the Organizational Unit structure while maintaining or increasing the number of GPOs, the greater need for control via groups or block inheritance/force override.

Avoid using cross-domain GPO links

If you link GPOs across domains, the entire set of *SYSVOL* data as well as the object information itself for the relevant GPOs needs to transfer over from the source domain whenever a user or computer needs to access it. So unless you have very fast links between the two domains with enough available bandwidth, you should duplicate the functionality of the GPO in the target domain instead of cross-domain linking unless the domain controllers for each domain are collocated on the same network.

Prioritize GPOs

Remember that it is possible to prioritize applications of multiple GPOs at the site, domain, or Organizational Unit level. This ordering of the application of policies allows you to add useful options to the administrator's toolkit. For example, if you need a group of users to reverse specific settings that are being applied by default as part of a larger set, create a new GPO with ACLs for this group that apply in the priority list to unset all the previous settings. This solution allows you to override a selection of previous settings without creating two GPOs, one with settings for everyone and one for just this group. The former solution allows you to add in settings to the main GPO and still have them apply to everyone, without needing to add them to the second GPO of the latter solution. Prioritizing GPOs can be very useful.

Increase processing speed

The main ways to increase processing speed are to reduce the number of GPOs that you apply, disable the computer or user portion of a GPO if it is not needed, or limit the use of block inheritance, force override, cross-domain linking, and loopback mode. All of these place an extra processing load on the client to some degree. A really bad mistake would be to use combinations of them.

Be cautious with loopback mode

Loopback mode is a very useful tool, but is another technology that you need to approach with caution. As a completely different set of policies (replace mode) or a very large number of policies (merge mode) will be applied to your users, and since there are no Resultant Set of Policy (RSoP) tools in existence as we write this, you need to take great care to ensure that the policy received by a user is the one you expect.

In most cases, loopback merge mode will incur significant extra processing load on the client PC and extra bandwidth on the network. That's not to say it isn't useful, but you have to be very aware of the delays that could occur after its introduction. Loopback replace mode imposes less of a processing load, but it can still be a problem. If you are contemplating loopback mode, ensure adequate stress testing of user impact.

Limit how often GPOs are refreshed

You should also carefully control the policy refresh interval. You have to ask yourself if you really need to refresh policy every 10 minutes when every 24 hours might be sufficient.

Thoroughly test WMI filters

If you are using WMI filters, be sure to test the queries thoroughly before releasing in production. If you use an inefficient query or one that is very resource-intensive, it could cause significant delays during GPO processing. Creating a simple script or even using the new WMI tool called WMIC can help facilitate the testing.

Restrict blocking of domain GPOs

You should not block domain GPOs to specifically use LGPOs on a domain client without very good reasons. If you do choose to apply LGPOs only to a client, you need to be aware of the management overhead because each client needs to be managed individually. If you have 20 orphaned clients using LGPOs and you need to make a change, you need to make it 20 times, once per client. The whole concept behind GPOs was to aid centralized management and administration of distributed resources, not distributed management of distributed resources. Think carefully before going down this path.

Use test GPOs

We always recommend creating test GPOs and linking them to a branch of test Organizational Units set up for this purpose. No GPO should ever be applied to users or computers unless it has been fully tested. And with the new tools, such as GPMC or the Resultant Set of Policies (described in more detail shortly), it is much easier to assess the impact GPOs will have on your client base.

Choose monolithic or segmented GPOs

While we would recommend keeping similar settings—or all settings relating to a particular item—in the same GPO, there is nothing stopping you from having only a few huge GPOs as opposed to a number of smaller GPOs. If you go for the monolithic approach, you process fewer GPOs, which is obviously faster; however, delegation is not as easy due to the fact that the policy contains so many settings. Segmented GPOs allow easier delegation, but can impact performance. Mix and match the two to a level that you are comfortable with and that works for your network.

Summary

One of the big selling points of Active Directory has always been group policy, and in Windows Server 2003 Active Directory, Microsoft extended the functionality and management of GPOs greatly. In this chapter, we expanded on the information presented in Chapter 8 to cover strategies for designing your Group Policy deployment.

## CHAPTER 13

Active Directory Security: Permissions and Auditing

Permissions can be set in Active Directory in much the same way they are set for files. Although you may not care that everyone in the tree can read all your users' phone numbers, you may want to store more sensitive information and restrict that access. Reading is not the only problem, of course. You also have create, modify, and delete privileges to worry about, and the last thing you need is a disgruntled or clever employee finding a way to delete all the users in an Organizational Unit.

None of this should be new to system managers who already deal with Windows NT Access Control Lists and Access Masks, Novell eDirectory Trustee Lists and Inherited Rights Masks, and Unix access permissions in file masks. In fact, Microsoft has carried the NT terminology from file permissions forward to Active Directory, so if you already know these terms, you're well ahead. If you are not familiar with them, don't worry. Terminology in permissions can seem confusing at first, so we'll go through it all in detail.

Managing the permissions in Active Directory doesn't have to be a headache. You can design sensible permissions schemes using guidelines on inheritance and complexity that will allow you to have a much easier time as a systems administrator. The GUI that Microsoft provides is fairly good for simple tasks but more cumbersome for complex multiple permissions. In Windows Server 2003, the GUI was enhanced to provide an "effective permissions" option that lets you determine the effective permissions a user or group has on the container or object. Also, Active Directory permissions are supported by ADSI, which opens up a whole raft of opportunities for you to use scripts to track problems and manipulate access simply and effectively. Finally, the DSACLS utility allows administrators to manage permissions from a command line if you prefer an alternative to the GUI.

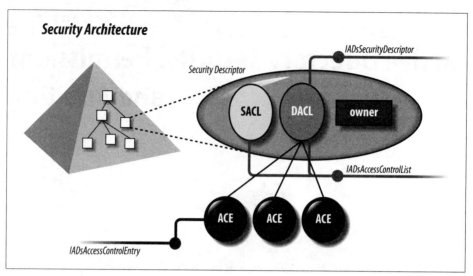

Figure 13-1. Active Directory security architecture

Yet permissions are only half the story. If you allow a user to modify details of every user in a specific branch below a certain organizational unit, you can monitor the creations, deletions, and changes to objects and properties within that branch using auditing entries. In fact, you can monitor any aspect of modification to Active Directory using auditing. The system keeps track of logging the auditing events, and you can then periodically check them or use a script or third-party tool to alert you quickly to any problems.

Windows Server 2008 introduces numerous new security features in Active Directory including the ability to protect objects from being deleted accidentally, completely revamped auditing, interactive display of the last time a user logged on, and more. We cover all of these new features in this chapter.

Permission Basics

Figure 13-1 shows the basics. Each object stores a value called a *Security Descriptor*, or SD, in the `nTSecurityDescriptor` attribute. This attribute holds all the information describing the security for that object. Included with the information are a flag indicating whether or not the security descriptor is protected against inheritance, as well as two important collections called Access Control Lists, or ACLs, that hold the relevant permissions.

The first ACL, called the *System* ACL or *SACL*, defines the permission events that will trigger both success and failure audit messages. The second, called the Discretionary ACL or DACL, defines the permissions that users have to the object, its properties, and its children. Each of the two ACLs holds a collection of *Access Control Entries* (ACEs) that correspond to individual audit or permission entries.

Audit and permission ACEs can apply to the object as a whole or to the individual properties of the object. This allows an administrator to control all aspects of access and auditing. Audit ACES are discussed further in Chapter 25, but we will briefly document some of the information in the following section so that other permission topics discussed later in this chapter are more readily understood.

Permission ACE

Each permission ACE is made up of several pieces of information:

Trustee
> SID of the user or group to which the ACE applies, such as the SID for the group Mycorp\Domain Admins.

ACE Type
> Determines whether the ACE is a Grant or a Deny.

Object Type
> `schemaIDGUID` for the attribute or object class that the ACE applies to. Alternatively, the `rightsGuid` for the property set, validated write, or extended right that the ACE applies to such as the `member` attribute, `Personal Information` property set, `Change Password` extended right, or `user` objects. For delete or create child objects permissions, the `objectType` should be configured to the `schemaIDGUID` of the object class delegated.

Inherited Object Types
> `schemaIDGUID` for the object types that the ACE applies to when an attribute, property set, or validated right is specified or when the ACE is inherited—e.g., `user` objects.

Access Mask
> A bit flag that describes the type of access, such as Read, Write, List, Create, Delete, Control Access, etc. See Table 25-3 for more detail.

Flags
> There are actually two different fields for flags. The flags specify inheritance settings such as ACE is inherited, ACE is allowed to be inherited, ACE is not inheritable, etc.

Every permission granted in Active Directory is based on these ACE structures as described above. Objects and properties are only revealed to users who have the appropriate permissions on the object. Any attribute that doesn't have an ACE specifically granting the requested access to a trustee is implicitly denied. The security descriptor also allows an administrator to specifically deny access with a deny ACE, but this isn't needed unless you are attempting to override another more generic ACE that is granting access.

This permission mechanism allows different users or groups of users to have completely different and very granular access to an object. For example, all users might be granted read access to the telephone number and email properties, but only a subset will have access to modify the description.

Property Sets, Validated Writes, and Extended Rights

Microsoft introduced several new "tools" that are not present in the NTFS ACLs. These tools are called property sets, validated writes, and extended rights. Instead of inserting the `schemaIDGUID` into the object type field of an ACE, you would insert the `rightsGuid` attribute of the property set, validated write, or extended right object. These objects are all stored in the extended-rights subcontainer of the configuration container.

> Property sets, validated writes, and extended rights are all *controlAccessRight* objects. You can determine what specific type of `controlAccessRight` they are by looking at the `validAccesses` attribute of the object with any utility that allows viewing of all attribute values on an object such as *LDP* or *ADSIEDIT*. Property sets have a value of 48, validated writes have a value of 8, and extended rights have a value of 256. For more information, reference *http://msdn.microsoft.com/en -us/library/ms675747(VS.85).aspx*.

Property sets are collections of attributes that can be referenced in a single permission ACE. The big win here is that you could assign one ACE to a SD and have it grant access to 5, 10, 20, or more attributes. The savings in SD size should be immediately obvious: a single ACE that can substitute for 20 different ACEs is a good data reduction ratio. There are several predefined property sets in a default forest; some of these are `Personal Information`, `Public Information`, `Web Information`, and `Account Restrictions`. You can also add your own property sets as desired. Exchange 2007 adds a number of property sets to ease delegation, including `Exchange-Personal-Information` and `Exchange-Information`.

While property sets are a great boon to securing the directory in a manner that is simpler than could otherwise have been achieved, the implementation does suffer a major shortcoming. *An attribute can only be part of a single property set.* Unfortunately, many of the base schema attributes are already included in existing property sets; while most of these can be successfully removed from the property sets or moved to other property sets, you can never be sure doing so won't break some application. It is generally much safer to stick to managing property sets comprised of your own custom attributes that you add to the directory.

> Property sets cannot be modified in Windows 2000 Active Directories. In Windows Server 2003 and newer, you are prevented from modifying the property set memberships of SAM attributes such as `sAMAccountName`, etc.

Validated writes are writes that go through additional verification. You cannot modify these validated writes nor create your own; what comes with AD is what you get. The only validated writes that are currently defined are:

- `Validated Write of Service Principal Name`
- `Validated Write of DNS host name`
- `Add/Remove self as member`

Extended rights are the mechanism used to delegate special operations such as Password Changes or Password Resets. While you can add additional extended rights to the directory, you cannot create extended rights that are enforced by the directory. Any new extended rights that you create will simply be additional permissions that can control an application you write that knows how to use the permissions. Your primary use of these extended rights will generally be to delegate to admins the right to set passwords on `user` objects with the `Reset Password` extended right.

Inherited Versus Explicit Permissions

Many Windows administrators everywhere are used to quoting the mantra "Deny overrides everything." Fortunately (or maybe unfortunately, depending on what you are trying to accomplish), Active Directory ACLs are a little more complicated than that. You need to specifically be aware of inherited versus explicit permissions. Explicit permissions are permissions that are directly applied to an object. Inherited permissions are permissions that are applied at some level of the tree above the object and "flow down" to the object and its children. When working with inherited and explicit permissions on an object, *a deny doesn't necessarily override a grant.*

The rules for what access will result from a set of inherited and explicit ACEs are easiest to understand when taken in steps:

1. Deny ACEs override grant ACEs of the same type (inherited versus explicit) and application point in the directory tree.
2. Explicit ACEs override inherited ACEs.
3. Inherited ACEs are hierarchical (e.g., an inherited deny applied to a container will be overridden by an inherited grant applied to containers nested below in the same tree).

Most simply, the closest ACEs to the object will dictate the access for the object. If you use an inherited deny to prevent access to some attribute on objects in an OU and the deny isn't effective, look for inherited grant permissions applied further down the branch or for explicit grant permissions applied on the objects themselves.

Default Security Descriptors

Every object defined in the schema has the attribute `defaultSecurityDescriptor`. This attribute is the *Security Descriptor Definition Language (SDDL)* format of the object's default SD. It will be applied to any object created without a SD specified during the object creation. These default permissions are rather extensive in Active Directory and are composed entirely of explicit ACEs so that they override any inherited denies (This tends to make denying access to specific attributes a little more challenging than it probably should be.) The DACL defined by the default security descriptor for the user object is listed in Table 13-1.

Table 13-1. DACL for Default Security Descriptor on user objectClass

Trustee	Permission
Domain\Domain Admins	Full Control
Builtin\Account Operators	Full Control
System	Full Control
Self	Read Permissions
	List Contents
	Read Property
	List Object
	Read/Write Personal Information
	Read/Write Phone and Mail Options
	Read/Write Web Information
	Change Password
	Send As
	Receive As
Authenticated Users	Read Permissions
	Read General Information
	Read Public Information
	Read Personal Information
	Read Web Information
Domain\RAS and IAS Servers	Read Account Restrictions
	Read Logon Information
	Read Group Membership
	Read Remote Access Information
Domain\Cert Publishers	Read/Write userCertificate
Builtin\Windows Authorization Access Group	Read tokenGroupsGlobalAndUniversal

Trustee	Permission
Builtin\Terminal Server License Servers	Read/Write terminalServer
Everyone	Change Password

Permission Lockdown

You can see from the information above that in a default Active Directory installation Authenticated Users have access to quite a bit of information. There is even more information available if you have Pre-Windows 2000 Compatible Access enabled, which allows Authenticated Users to see all properties of groups, users, and inetOrgPerson objects. Open access to this information is a sore spot for many companies who don't want employees to have quite that much information available to them; maybe they want to restrict access to employee phone numbers, or addresses, or other personal information.

Removing the ability to see the information can be difficult to accomplish, especially the items granted through explicit property set ACEs. In addition, any modification you make needs to be thoroughly tested to verify it doesn't break any of your line of business applications. Microsoft Exchange is particularly sensitive to permission lockdowns, and if you take away Authenticated Users access to some attributes, you may need to re-grant the permissions back to the Exchange servers. ADSI is another common tool that is very sensitive to changes to the default permissions. You may find ADSI calls fail with inexplicable errors if assumed permissions have been removed.

 You cannot permanently lock down the directory from Domain Admins. At any point, anyone from that group can take ownership of any object (if they don't already have it) and rewrite the Security Descriptor to include Domain Admins or any other security principal in the access. There should be very few Domain Admins in your forest, preferably five or less, even for Fortune 10-class companies.

Once you have decided to proceed with the lockdown, your next step is to decide how to accomplish the lockdown. The "how" and the resulting workload and impact depends entirely on the attribute in question and how the access is being granted.

By far, the simplest case is when the access is granted through inheritance. You can either remove the inherited grant if it is just the one attribute or you can add an inherited deny for the attribute or attributes you want protected. An example of an inherited permission you may want to remove is read access to the employeeID property. Authenticated Users are granted read access to employeeID through an ACE applied to the root of the domain that gives access to read all properties of users for the Pre-Windows 2000 Compatible Access group. Inserting an inheritable deny read ACE on the root of the domain or other container for Authenticated Users will effectively block the inherited grant read access to this attribute. Read access can be re-added further down the tree beneath the deny ACE if desired with either an additional explicit or inherited grant read access ACE.

If the access is granted through an explicit ACE, locking down is considerably more involved and may actually be so difficult it isn't feasible. There are several mechanisms available for locking down explicitly granted access:

- If the access is granted through a property set, modify the membership of the property set involved.

- Change the default security of the object class definition in the schema to remove the explicit Authenticated Users permissions or alternatively add a deny ACE for the specific attribute and then "fix" the ACLs on every instance of the object in existence in the directory. Any new objects will be created with the new security descriptor.

- Strip the explicit grant ACE from every instance of the object in the directory. You will need to keep doing this as new instances of the object are created, or if someone resets the ACL to schema defaults on any of the objects.

- Add an explicit deny ACE on every instance of the object in the directory. Like the previous solution, this requires "fixing" new instances of the objects that are created or reset to schema defaults.

- If all of your domain controllers are at least at Windows Server 2003 Service Pack 1 or better, you may be able to use the confidentiality bit. This new capability is described in the following section.

 If you use the GUI to set granular permissions, you should double-check the actual ACEs written to the ACL with *DSACLS* or a script. The GUI has an annoying habit of trying to figure out what you want instead of just doing what you tell it. The result can be an inefficient ACL with far more ACEs than necessary. This happens most often when adding deny ACEs.

Confidentiality Bit

After five years of customers wrestling with the directory lockdown difficulties previously outlined, Microsoft finally tried to fix the problem. The result, more a workaround than a fix, in Windows Server 2003 Service Pack 1 is called "confidential attributes." Microsoft has defined a new searchFlags bit called the confidentiality bit; this is bit 7, which has the value 128. When the bit is enabled, the attribute is considered to be confidential on any domain controller running Windows Server 2003 Service Pack 1 or newer. Only users with both Read Property permission *and* Control Access permission for the attribute on an object can view the attribute. This would mean anyone with Full Control or All Extended Rights (Control Access for object) or Control Access for the specific attribute. Assuming default permissions, this would mean access would be granted to:

- Builtin\Administrators (inherited FC)
- Builtin\Account Operators (explicit FC)
- NT Authority\System (explicit FC)
- Domain\Domain Admins (explicit FC)
- Domain\Enterprise Admins (inherited CA)

As you can see, this would appear to give us a great new solution to the issues mentioned previously with explicit permissions. You could simply mark any troublesome attributes as confidential, and then normal users can no longer see them. This is a great plan, but there is a great big kink in the plan: you cannot set the confidentiality bit on category-one attributes, which are more generically known as base-schema attributes. So, many of the attributes companies are trying to lock down can't be locked down with this capability.

Officially, as mentioned previously, you can't lock down category-one attributes with the confidentiality bit. Unofficially, there is a back door that is available to accomplish this. However, you are taking things into your own hands if you use it, and if you have a problem, Microsoft will most likely tell you what you have done is unsupported.

Since this capability was released in Windows Server 2003 Service Pack 1, the verification of which attributes can have the bit set only applies to servers running that version of the OS or better. This means that if you make the schema modification of the `searchFlags` attribute on a pre-SP1 machine, nothing will prevent you from modifying any attribute you choose to modify, including category-one attributes.

If you choose to do this, it is highly recommended that you avoid the attributes that have bit 1 (value 2) set in `systemFlags`. The attributes with that flag set are very sensitive attributes such as `sAMAccountName`, `nTSecurityDescriptor`, `objectCategory`, `objectClass`, `servicePrincipal Name`, and many others that are core to Active Directory functions. Manipulating their visibility could be quite disastrous to a forest.

In addition to the category-one attribute shortcoming, there are some other issues with this new capability. It may seem obvious, but only domain controllers running Windows Server 2003 Service Pack 1 or better will prevent display of confidential attributes to users without Control Access rights. So, if you have Windows 2000 domain controllers or Pre-SP1 Windows Server 2003 domain controllers in the domain, any queries sent to those DCs will return the information that is supposed to be confidential. This also applies to any Global Catalogs if the attributes you have made confidential are partial attribute set (PAS) attributes.

Another issue is that Microsoft seems to have forgotten to give a tool with Windows Server 2003 Service Pack 1 to easily grant granular permissions to allow delegation of who can see confidential attributes. The GUI dialogs in Active Directory Users and

Computers and ADSIEDIT will only allow you to grant Full Control or Control Access of the entire object, which is also known as All Extended Rights. The command-line tool DSACLS does nothing to help either. This is a lot of access to grant to allow someone to see one or two attributes. Currently, the only mechanism available to grant granular Control Access permission to a single attribute on an object is to write a script to configure the delegation. Once delegated, the GUI cannot properly display the permission, but DSACLS can.

 Windows Server 2008 (and also R2 ADAM and ADAM SP1) has an updated version of LDP that has the most flexible GUI-based ACL Editor available in Windows. This tool will allow you to set Control Access for a specific property. You need to be aware, however, that you can set any number of incorrect ACEs with the tool, as it doesn't perform ACE validation that is done with ADUC, DSACLS, and other ACL Editor tools.

Protecting Objects from Accidental Deletion

A common problem Active Directory administrators have faced is when an object or an entire OU tree is accidentally deleted. Usually this happens because of a careless mistake made with the Active Directory Users and Computers tool. The ensuing recovery process often involves authoritative restores and business downtime. Windows Server 2008 introduces a checkbox in the Active Directory Users and Computers MMC "Protect from Accidental Deletion." Behind the scenes, this checkbox simply adds an ACE to the ACL for the object it is applied to and prevents deletion. Consequently, this will prevent a tree from being deleted since its parent cannot be deleted. In order to delete that object or tree, the administrator must first uncheck the checkbox or remove the ACE manually.

In order to see the Protect from Accidental Deletion checkbox, you must first select View→Advanced Features in ADUC. Once you have done this, you can right click an object in the directory and select Properties, and then access the Object tab. Figure 13-2 shows the Cool People OU being protected.

If you try to delete an object that is protected from accidental deletion, you will receive an error similar to the one in Figure 13-3. In order to delete the object, you must go back in the properties and uncheck the Protect from Accidental Deletion checkbox.

Figure 13-4 shows the ACE that was added to the ACL for the Cool People OU in order to protect it. Notice that the well-known Everyone security principal has been denied the rights to delete the object or the subtree.

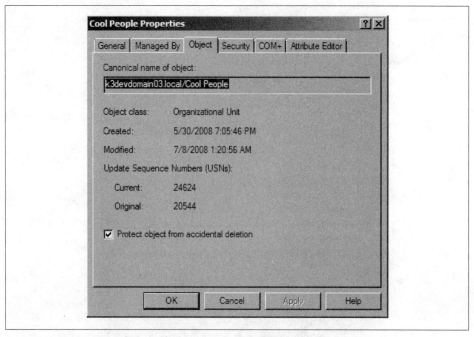

Figure 13-2. Protecting Cool People from accidental deletion

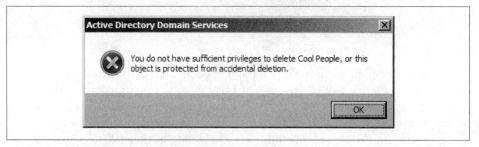

Figure 13-3. Error message when trying to delete a protected object

Using the GUI to Examine Permissions

To access the permissions for any object, select the Active Directory Users and Computers MMC and right-click on it. Choose Properties from the drop-down menu and select the Security tab of the properties window that is displayed.

 To make the Security tab visible, you need to select View→Advanced Features. If you reopen the properties window of the object to which you wish to assign permissions, you should see a Security tab.

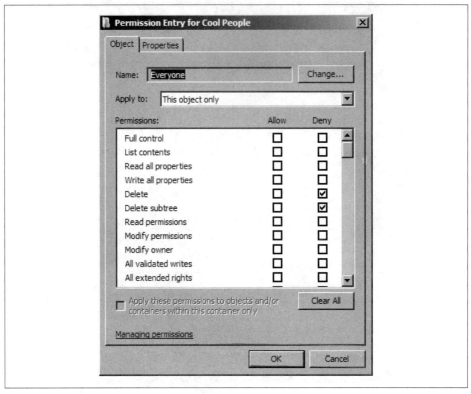

Figure 13-4. ACE created by protecting Cool People

The window in Figure 13-5 is your first point of contact for permissions. The top area contains a complete list of all groups and users who have permissions to the object whose properties we are looking at. The Permissions section below this list displays which general permissions are allowed and denied for the highlighted user or group. The general permissions listed are only those deemed to be the most likely to be set on a regular basis. Each general permission is only an umbrella term representing a complex set of actual implemented permissions hidden underneath the item. Consequently, the general permission called Read translates to specific permissions like Read All Properties and List Contents, as we will show later. Below the Permissions section are three important parts of this window:

Advanced button

> The Advanced button allows you to delve further into the object, so that permissions can be set using a more fine-grained approach.

Text display area

> The second part of this area of the window is used to display a message, such as that shown in Figure 13-5. The text shows that the permissions for the current

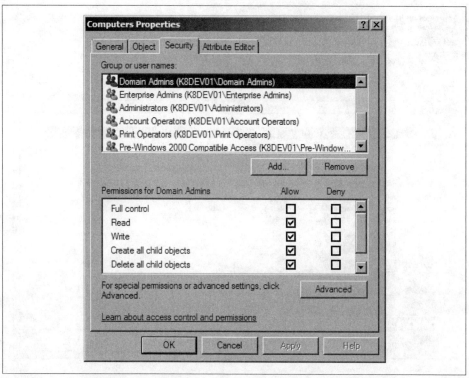

Figure 13-5. Security properties of an object

object are more complex than can be displayed here. Consequently, we would have to press the Advanced button to see them.

Inheritance checkbox (Windows 2000 only; not shown in Figure 13-5)

The "Allow inheritable permissions from parent to propagate to this object" option protects or blocks the object from inheriting Access Control Entries from its parent. When you clear the checkbox on the security properties or Access Control Settings windows mentioned later, the system pops up a Yes/No/Cancel dialog box that asks if you want to convert your inherited entries to normal entries. If you click Cancel, the operation aborts. Clicking No removes all inherited entries and protects the object or branch. Clicking Yes converts the current inherited entries to standard entries and protects the object from any new inherited permissions applied to the parent or higher branch. All normal permission entries for the object are unchanged by whatever choice you make. We will cover this in more detail later in the book. For Windows Server 2003 and newer, this checkbox is located on the Advanced screen. Clicking the Advanced button actually displays the same users and groups again, but in slightly more detail. Figure 13-6 shows this window, known as the Advanced Security Settings for the object.

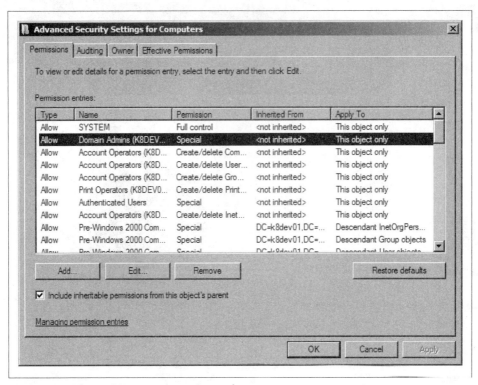

Figure 13-6. Advanced Security settings for an object

While the Advanced Security Settings window gives only slightly more information than the previous window, it serves an important purpose: it is a gateway to some of the lowest, most granular, permissions. The Advanced window allows you to view the globally set permissions from Figure 13-5 as well as a brief summary of the advanced permissions that may be set for each object. While the Name and Permission columns effectively duplicate information from Figure 13-5, the Type field shows whether the permissions to the object for this user or group are Allow or Deny. If a group has some allow and some deny permissions, two entries are recorded in this window. The Inherited From field was a new addition in Windows Server 2003 that allows you to see what object, if any, the permission was inherited from. The Apply To column usefully indicates what the permission applies to. This could be to this object only, the object and all sub-objects, or just to an individual property, say telephoneNumber, of a user object.

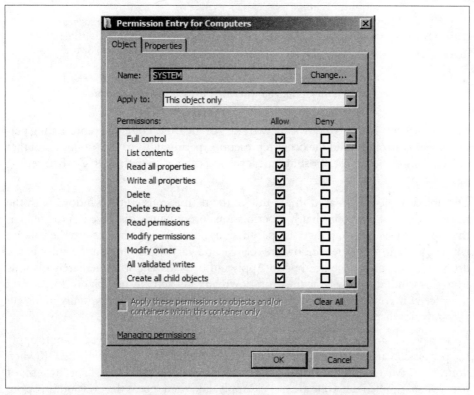

Figure 13-7. Permission Entry for an object

The permission dialog boxes have quite a lot of information and are usually too small to see the information comfortably. This makes it painful to look at permissions because you are constantly resizing the individual columns or scrolling the dialog back and forth. Unfortunately, there is no way to modify these dialog boxes to better fit the information they contain.

You now have two choices to view the atomic permissions. You can click Add, which pops up a window allowing you to add a new user or group to those with permissions set on this object. Alternatively, you can highlight an existing user or group and click the Edit button (or View/Edit on Windows 2000). If you highlight a user or group or add one from the pop-up window, the next screens you see are the Permissions Entry (PE) windows, shown in Figures 13-7 and 13-8.

Until you know exactly what you are doing with permissions, we suggest that you use a test forest to play with permissions settings. The last thing you want to do is make a simple mistake with a built-in group or user and deny yourself access to the tree. If you create two test users and three test groups, put each user in a separate group, and then put both users in the third group, you will have the basis of a test system.

The permissions editor windows are two sides of the same coin, one representing permissions to the object and the other representing permissions to the properties of that object. This is the lowest, most atomic level you can get to with ADUC when setting permissions.

The object name is displayed in the title of the permissions editor window, with the name of the user or group that has permissions prominently displayed in the field at the top. The user or group then has permissions allowed and denied from the column entries. The entries in the window are relative and vary depending on the entry in the drop-down list under the heading of Apply Onto. What is not immediately obvious from this window is how large the drop-down box can actually get. Figure 13-9 shows this nicely. If you look at the scroll bar, you will get an idea of how many items are currently not displayed.

To set a permission from the permissions editor window, pick where you want to apply the permission and then click the relevant Allow and Deny boxes, selecting OK when done. Since Microsoft has not provided an Apply button, you cannot specify a set of permissions applied onto one area, click Apply, and then repeat the cycle until you are done with this user and group. You have to click OK, which means the window closes, whereupon you then have to click Add again, and so on. This is a tiresome problem if you are implementing multiple changes from a set of prepared designs, but one you have to live with if you choose to use the GUI to set permissions.

Reverting to the Default Permissions

In Figure 13-6, you may have noticed the Restore Defaults button at the bottom. This is a new feature as of Windows Server 2003 that allows you to revert the current permission set to the default security as defined in the schema for the objectClass of the object. If you click Restore Defaults for an object you have not modified the permissions on, you may notice that the list still changes. If you look closer, you'll see that the inherited permissions were the ones removed. That is because inherited permissions are not defined as part of the default security of an object and will be removed. Even if you then click OK to apply the permissions, as long as the Allow Inheritable Permissions box is checked, the inherited permissions will still apply. Having the ability to apply the default permissions is a useful feature, especially for administrators who are trying to determine what changes have been made from the default installation.

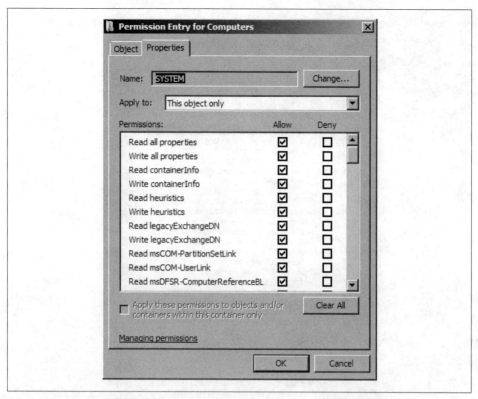

Figure 13-8. Permission Entry for an object's properties

Viewing the Effective Permissions for a User or Group

Another feature added in Windows Server 2003 is Effective Permissions, which is available from the Advanced button when viewing the security for an object. The Effective Permissions screen allows you to select a user or group and determine its effective (or actual) permissions to the object, taking into account group membership and permission inheritance. Figure 13-10 shows the results of the effective permissions for Authenticated Users on the EMEA domain object. As you can see, Authenticated Users have List Contents, Read All Properties, and Read Permissions. All objects in the forest will inherit these permissions unless inheritance has been blocked. As you might guess, this is a significant feature that allows for much easier troubleshooting of permission problems. There are some limitations to be aware of, however.

The Effective Permissions tool is only an approximation of the actual permissions a user or group has and does not take into account many of the well-known security principals such as Anonymous Logon and Network. Another potential issue to be mindful of is that the user running the Effective Permissions tool must have the rights to read the group membership of the target user or group. By default, Authenticated Users has this right.

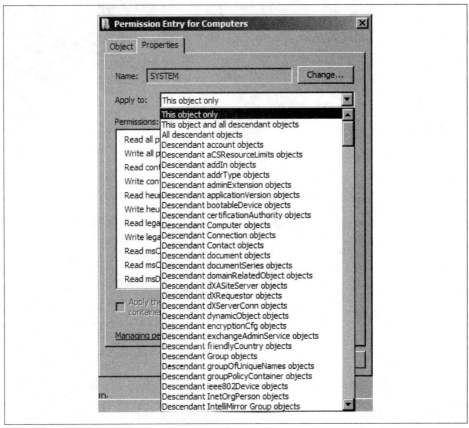

Figure 13-9. Permission Entry window showing the large number of targets to which permissions can be applied

Using the Delegation of Control Wizard

To help with delegating permissions for objects in Active Directory, Active Directory Users and Computers comes with a wizard called the *Delegation of Control* wizard. It is intended to allow administrators to delegate management of certain types of objects to key individuals or groups in the organization. It is activated by right-clicking almost any container in the tree and selecting the wizard from the pop-up menu. Builtin and LostAndFound are the two containers for which it does not work by default.

The wizard is useful only when you need to clearly apply general allow permissions to one or more object types below a container. It is not useful if you want to specify deny permissions (which it doesn't support), remove previously delegated control, delegate control over individual objects, or apply special permissions to branches of the tree. The wizard's great strength is its ability to set permissions and apply them to multiple users and groups at the same time. We use the wizard to set these sorts of permissions,

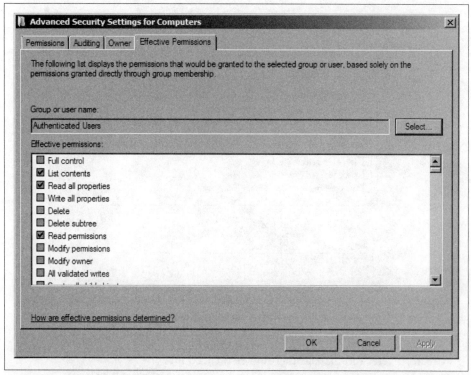

Figure 13-10. Viewing the effective permissions for authenticated users on the EMEA domain object

although much less regularly than we do the standard GUI, since it is much more limited in what it can do. Scripting with ADSI also provides a solution here that is more adaptive to an administrator's own needs.

The wizard provides several screens for you to navigate through. The first is the welcome screen, which tells you what the wizard does. The second is an object picker for you to select which users or groups to delegate to. The third screen asks what task you wish to delegate control for in that container. Figure 13-11 shows this window.

The default is to delegate control for a specific task, and there are several to choose from. In fact, several new tasks were added in Windows Server 2003. Since the list scrolled off the screen in Figure 13-11, we'll list them here:

- Create, delete, and manage user accounts
- Reset user passwords and force user change password at next logon
- Read all user information
- Modify the membership of a group
- Manage Group Policy links
- Generate Resultant Set of Policy (Planning)

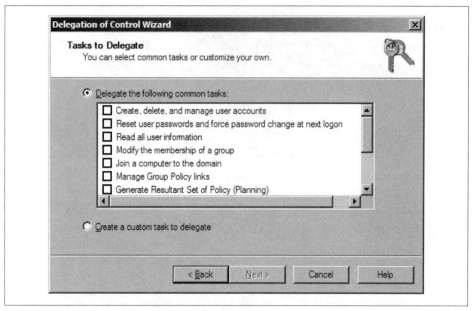

Figure 13-11. Delegation of Control wizard—object type selection

- Generate Resultant Set of Policy (Logging)
- Create, delete, and manage inetOrgPerson accounts
- Reset inetOrgPerson passwords and force password change at next logon
- Read all inetOrgPerson information

If you choose the Custom radio button and click Next, an extra page opens, allowing you to specify individual objects. Figure 13-12 shows this.

If you want to delegate certain permissions to computer or user objects in a specific container or branch, you can do it from here. The next screen of the wizard allows you to specify what permissions you wish to assign for the selected users/groups. Figure 13-13 shows this screen.

When the window opens initially, only the first checkbox is checked. As you click each of the other boxes, the list of specific permissions that you can delegate becomes very large as it encompasses all of the permissions that you could potentially delegate. Finally, the last screen of the wizard summarizes the previous answers and allows the user to go back, cancel, or finish and grant the permissions.

However, just as the permissions listed in the security properties for an object (Figure 13-5) can change, so can the permissions listed in the access rights box, depending on the object(s) to which permissions are being applied. A good demonstration of this is to open up the security permissions for any user and scroll through the displayed list

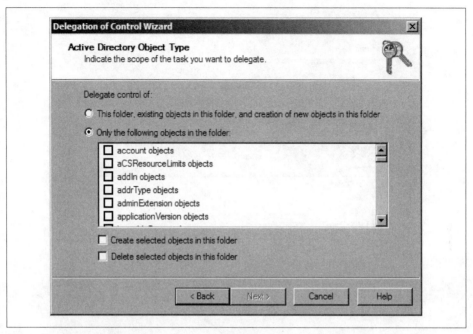

Figure 13-12. Delegation of Control wizard—choosing objects to delegate

of permissions. Next, open up the wizard on any container and specify Custom Task (see the screen shown in Figure 13-11) and only user objects (see Figure 13-12). The screen shown in Figure 13-13 should then display the same list that the screen in Figure 13-5 does. This makes sense since they should be the same; available permissions for one user should be the same as the available permissions for all users. It is still nice to see the correlation and appreciate it in the flesh, so to speak.

Using the GUI to Examine Auditing

Examining auditing entries is almost identical to viewing permissions entries. If you go back to the screen shown in Figure 13-6 and click on the Auditing tab, a screen similar to that in Figure 13-14 is displayed.

This window shows the list of *Auditing Entries* (AEs) that have been defined on the object. This object has one AE, and it's not very helpful viewing it from here since the detail is too limited. So just as you would do with permissions, you can click the Edit button (or View/Edit with Windows 2000), drill down, and view the individual AE itself.

Figure 13-15 shows the successful and failed items that are being audited. The items are grayed out because this entry is inherited from further up the tree, i.e., it is not defined directly on this object but instead further up the hierarchy.

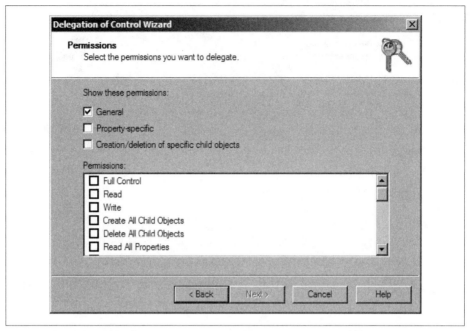

Figure 13-13. Delegation of Control wizard—access rights selection

Figure 13-16 shows an example auditing entry window for successful and failed auditing of properties. Here you are auditing only property writes.

Designing Permission Schemes

Having worked through many designs for different domain structures, we have come up with a series of rules or guidelines you can follow to structure the design process effectively. The idea is that if you design your permissions schemes using these rules, you will be more likely to create a design with global scope and minimum effort.

The Five Golden Rules of Permissions Design

This list is not exhaustive. We are sure you will be able to think of others beyond these. If, however, these rules spark your creative juices and help you design more effectively, they will have done their job.

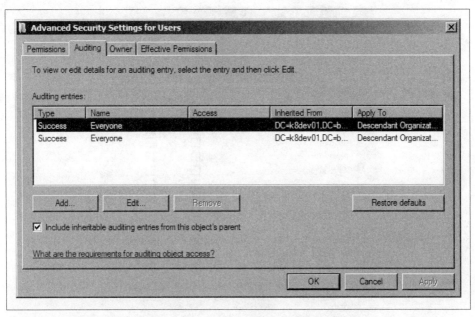

Figure 13-14. Advanced Settings window showing auditing entries

The rules are:

1. Whenever possible, assign object permissions to groups of users rather than individual users.

2. Design group permissions so that you have a minimum of duplication.

3. Manage permissions globally whenever possible.

4. Allow inheritance: do not protect sections of the tree from inheritance.

5. Keep a log of every unusual change that you have made to the tree, especially when you have protected sections of it from inheritance or applied special rights to certain users.

Let's look at these rules in more detail.

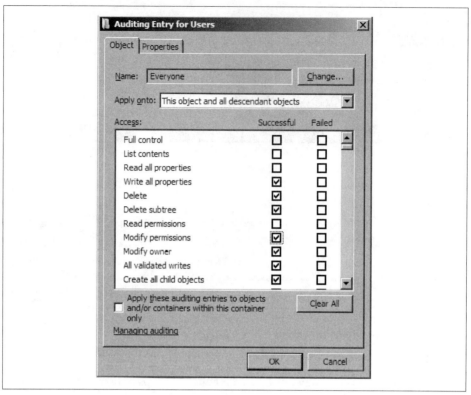

Figure 13-15. Auditing entry for an object

Rule 1: Apply permissions to groups whenever possible

By default, you should use groups to manage your user permissions. At its simplest, this rule makes sense whenever you have more than one user for whom you wish to set certain permissions.

Some things need to be made very clear about how groups are different between Windows NT and Active Directory:

- Active Directory supports the concept of two types of group: security and distribution. A distribution group is simply a group that is not Windows Security-enabled. A security-enabled group is a group that is used in calculating access rights to objects. The SID from security groups a user is a member of will be added to the user's security token when they authenticate. Distribution groups are most often used for mailing lists; however, they can be used for other basic "group" tasks as well, such as instant messaging lists or even security for LDAP-based applications not using Windows security.

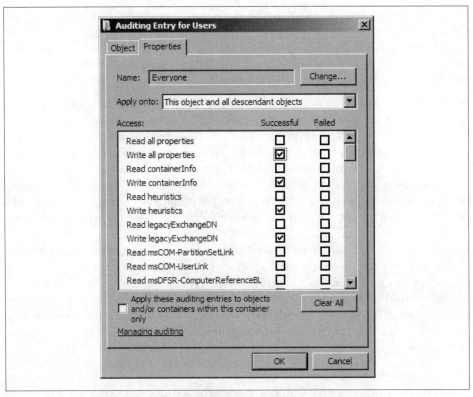

Figure 13-16. Auditing entry for an object's properties

- Windows 2000 mixed-mode and Windows Server 2003 Interim domains natively support Security groups that have two types of scope: Global or Local. These correspond to the Windows NT 4.0 Global and Domain Local groups.

- Windows 2000 native-mode or better domains have access to a third scope, universal. Universal security groups can contain other groups and have permissions assigned to them.

More detailed information on the differences between Windows NT groups and Active Directory groups and how Active Directory groups differ in the various modes and functional levels can be found in Chapter 2.

Under Windows 2000 mixed-mode and Windows Server 2003 Interim functional level, the paths you can choose are clear. You either follow the method outlined in the "Global Group and Local Group Permissions Under Windows NT 4.0" sidebar, or you choose to assign permissions in some other manner of your own choosing.

When you convert your domain to native mode, you have a more difficult decision: do you choose "Domain users go into universal groups, universal groups go into universal groups, universal groups are assigned resources"? Or do you move to "Domain users go into universal groups, universal groups are assigned resources"? Or do you assign permissions in a manner of your own choosing?

We're not advocating the use of one group or two, as we'll explain in more detail in the next section on how to plan permissions. We are advocating that whichever way you choose to implement group permissions, you should add users to groups and apply permissions to groups, even if the group initially contains only one user. This removes organizational dependence on one particular account. Time after time, we have seen organizations in which individual users with a whole raft of permissions to various objects suddenly leave or change roles. The new administrator then has to go in and unravel differing permissions settings from this account. We have even seen one administrator, who looked in anguish at the tangled mess of a recently departed administrator's account, delete his own account and rename the departed user's account just so that he could get the correct permission set without having to figure out the mess! If the old administrator had been a member of, say, five different groups, each with the relevant permissions, the new administrator could simply have replaced the group memberships of the old account with his new account. This is a much simpler approach, and we are sure that none of the preceding common sense is very new to systems administrators.

Global Group and Local Group Permissions Under Windows NT 4.0

Under Windows NT 4.0, Microsoft's preferred method of applying file and directory permissions was to create two sets of groups: Domain Local Groups, which had permissions, and Global Groups, which contained users.

The Local Group would exist on the server that had the resource, and the relevant permissions were assigned to that. Local groups were allowed to contain both users and groups. Domain Users were then placed in Domain Global Groups, which themselves were placed in the Local Groups on each server. Domain Global Groups were allowed to contain only users and not other groups. This may sound complicated, but it worked well in practice. A good way of demonstrating this is through an example.

Consider an NT 4.0 domain called Mycorp containing a Global Domain Group called Marketing. This group has four members. Within Mycorp are two servers, called Server1 and Server2, each of which has published a share. Each server also has a Local Group SH_USERS, which contains the Global Group Marketing as a member. Each SH_USERS group has read access to the relevant share on the same server.

You use global groups in this scenario because it is faster to deal with a large number of users as one group than it is to deal with them individually. In a similar vein, it makes sense to keep control over permissions to resources by creating Local Groups, each with a relevant set of permissions. That way, if you ever need to modify the permissions for a particular set of users, you need to modify only the Local Group's permissions.

So if we decide that Keith and Sue should have full permissions to the share on Server1, we could create a Local Group on Server1 with full permissions and add a newly created Global Group, say MKTG_ADMIN, to it with Keith and Sue as members. Future users who need full permissions are added to this Global Group.

Rule 2: Design group permissions so that you have minimum duplication

It makes much more sense to create groups with simple permission sets than it does to create multiple groups with overlapping permissions. If you decide that some of your users need, say, create and modify, while others need modify and delete, and a third set needs just modify, it makes much more sense to create three separate groups with create, delete, and modify, than it does to make three groups with the permissions sets described. Let's consider an example. We will call the three groups CRE_MOD, MOD_DEL, and MOD. Let's now say we add 10 users to each group. If the only modifications ever to happen to these groups are occasional membership changes, this solution fits adequately. However, let's say that as with every large organization, the permissions requirements change over time. If Dave Peace, a member of CRE_MOD, now needs delete, what do we do? Do we make a special case of Dave's account and add the delete permission to his account only? Arguably, that is the simple solution, but according to Rule 1, we really should create a group to manage the permission. Do we create a DEL group and add Dave's account or create a CRE_MOD_DEL group and move his membership from CRE_MOD to the new group? Both are valid solutions.

Let's say we go with the former and create a DEL group, adding Dave as a member of that group. Things change again, and Mark Newell joins. Mark needs to be a member of groups giving him both MOD and DEL, so do we add him to MOD_DEL or MOD and DEL? Either way, we now have potential confusion. Whenever we have to check for members who can modify and delete, we have to check three groups, not one.

If we'd taken the second approach and chosen to create CRE_MOD_DEL rather than the DEL group, Mark is added to MOD_DEL when he joins, and things seem to be working fine. Paul Burke now moves from another team and requires create only, so a CRE group is created and his account added to that. Later, three others join the CRE group, but Paul now needs create and delete, so CRE_DEL is created, and he is moved to this group. Now we have six groups: CRE, MOD, CRE_DEL, CRE_MOD, MOD_DEL, and CRE_MOD_DEL. Unfortunately, if we ever have to check who has create and modify permission, we have to check the three groups: CRE, MOD, and CRE_MOD.

The minimum ACEs and groups required solution is to have one group for each permission granted, CRE, MOD, and DEL. Users are added to the groups as needed. If you prefer a more "role"-based approach, you could create role-based groups such as the CRE_MOD and the others and nest it in the CRE and MOD groups that have the actual permissions in the directory.

This example was heavily contrived. However, we hope it serves to show that duplication will occur whenever you have users requiring separate permissions to an object or property and users requiring combinations of those permissions. It is for this very reason that we suggest creating separate groups for the lowest common-denominator permissions that you need to set. Keep possible future enhancements and role redefinitions in mind because you don't usually want to be changing permissions in the directory in an ad-hoc manner any time new requirements pop up.

If you have users who always need read, list, and create but require different combinations of delete and modify, it may not make sense to have the three groups—one each for read, list, and create. You could instead create one group with the read, list, and create permissions assigned to it, one group for delete, and one for modify. Then you would use multiple group memberships to assemble the group permissions as you require them. Of course, if later on you now have a requirement to only give read or create, you end up separating out the permissions anyway. Try to think ahead.

The most important point to note is that we are talking about minimizing and simplifying the number of ACEs applied to the directory. If you need only CRE_MOD_DEL to an object, you probably don't want to create three groups. But don't necessarily rule out this approach if you think the requirements are apt to change.

If, after you have created a group with multiple permissions, you find that you now need groups with individual permissions, you can always create the smaller groups and migrate the users. Active Directory is flexible enough to allow you to operate like this, but it can be considerable work to clean up after the fact and must be done in a slow painstaking way to avoid impacting the users.

Rule 3: Manage Advanced permissions only when absolutely necessary

(Please note that this says "permissions" and not "auditing." Auditing entries can be accessed only from the Advanced tab, so this rule makes less sense for auditing entries.)

Whenever you right-click an object to view its properties, the Security Properties window that appears has an Advanced button on it. This was shown in Figure 13-1 in the previous section. The Security Properties window itself typically has the following allow and deny options as General Permissions:

- Full control
- Read
- Write
- Create all child objects
- Delete all child objects

In Windows 2000, this screen also allows you to specify whether the object inherits permissions from its parent. In other words, it allows you to protect the object ACL from inheriting ACEs from its parent.

The general permissions are not limited to those five in the previous list, and indeed they change depending on the object you are looking at. For example, the security properties for any user object display additional general permissions, such as Reset Password, Modify Web Information, and Send As. While these general permissions make sense for the user object, they are not all appropriate for other objects. This rule suggests that you manage permissions for objects from the Security Properties window as often as you can. You should choose the Advanced button only when you wish to allow or deny a permission to one aspect of an object rather than the whole object. An example would be manipulating the permission to a user object's telephone number rather than the whole account details.

While there is nothing wrong with managing atomic permissions to objects and properties, permissions are much easier to manage from a higher level. The main permissions that administrators might want to set were put here for this express purpose, so that users and groups can easily manage the tree without having to worry about the large amount of individual properties.

If you choose to get very granular with permissions, you will want to look at using DSACLS at the command line for setting the permissions. DSACLS does a better job of showing all of the permissions and in some situations is more intelligent about ACEs that are applied than ADUC. Finally, DSACLS can be used in scripts for consistent results.

Rule 4: Allow inheritance; do not protect sections of the domain tree from inheritance

If you allow or deny permission for a group or user to all objects of a certain type in a container, by default the permissions are applied recursively to all objects of that type in all the child containers down the tree. It is possible to block inheritance, but we recommend leaving inheritance in place (the default) and protecting branches on an individual basis only when there are good justifications for doing so. The reason is simple: if you specify that children do not inherit permissions from their parents, you are adding additional complexity to your Active Directory. There are several examples of inheritance blocking found in every default domain. You can simply look at any administrative ID or alternatively drill down into the system container, then the policies container, and look at any of the `groupPolicyContainer` objects.

The administrative IDs are protected from inheritance due to the possible security issue of moving the user object into a container that would give a non-admin user rights to manipulate the admin ID. These IDs are actually a special case because there is functionality built into Active Directory called `AdminSDHolder` functionality. This is named after the `AdminSDHolder` object, which has the permissions that should be applied to admin user objects. Once an hour, the PDC loops through all admin user objects and makes sure the permissions are set to be the same as what is on the `AdminSDHolder` object.

If you want to configure the AdminSDHolder process, review the `HKLM\System\CurrentControlSet\Services\NTDS\Parameters\AdminSDPro tectFrequency` registry value. The default is 60 minutes; it can be set to any whole value between 1 and 120 minutes.

By default, this includes disabling inheritance. This functionality can confuse some administrators and block delegations they purposefully try to configure, so it is often discovered accidentally. Please see Microsoft Knowledge Base articles 232199 at *http://support.microsoft.com/kb/232199* and 817433 at *http://support.microsoft.com/kb/817433* for more information about `adminSDHolder`.

Microsoft has changed the definition of the administrator groups protected by this functionality in various hot fixes, services packs, and OS revisions. The original list of protected groups consisted of `Enterprise Admins, Schema Admins, Domain Admins`, and `Administrators`. After the hotfix available from *http://support.microsoft.com/kb/817433*, Windows 2000 SP4, or Windows Server 2003, several groups were added, including `Account Operators, Server Operators, Print Operators, Backup Operators`, and `Cert Publishers`. In addition to those groups, the `Administrator` and `Krbtgt` user objects are also specifically protected. You have a little control over the groups that are protected with a `dsHeuristics` setting that can be configured; see Microsoft Knowledge Base article 817433 at *http://support.microsoft.com/kb/817433* for details.

The `groupPolicyContainer` objects are protected for similar security reasons. As discussed in Chapter 12, these objects contain information about security policies applied to the domain. Microsoft rightfully decided to protect these objects from being accidentally impacted by permission delegations higher up in the directory. You will not generally have to manipulate these objects directly, so you could manage Active Directory for years and never notice these objects; the complexity involved with protecting them won't directly impact you.

Ultimately, there is nothing wrong with protecting objects or sections of the tree from inheritance. It is important to remember that every time you do it, you are possibly creating more work and possible confusion for yourself and other administrators. As an administrator, you should keep track of these changes in a log, so that you can easily reference your special cases when required.

Rule 5: Keep a log of unusual changes

This may sound like an obvious statement, but it is surprising how many administrators overlook such a simple requirement. Simply put, it is always wise to keep a log of custom changes that you make to a default installation so that you and others have something to refer back to. There will be times when you may not be available and this sort of information is required. The following list shows the relevant fields of a basic Active Directory ACL log:

- Unique name of object or LDAP location of object in tree
- Object class being modified
- Object or property being modified
- User or group to whom permissions are being assigned
- Permissions being assigned
- Notes on reasons why this change is being made

Some additional items outside of ACL changes worth logging are schema default security descriptor changes, property set modifications, attribute index changes, and attribute confidentiality changes.

Let's now look at how you can put these rules into practice in your own designs.

How to Plan Permissions

There are a number of Active Directory Users and Computers permission sets that administrators may need to implement in their organizations. Some examples are:

- A set of centralized teams, each with responsibility for certain areas. Users can be members of more than one area: account modifiers, printer managers, computer account managers, publishing managers, and so on.
- A manager for each individual major Organizational Unit under a domain.
- Again, a manager for each individual major Organizational Unit under a domain, but this time each manager is also able to delegate responsibility for lower Organizational Units.
- An administrator of the top-level domain is given permission to every subdomain by each subdomain's administrators.

While we could go through each of the preceding settings and show how to design permissions in each case, every organization is different. For that reason, it seems better to try to show what we consider to be the best method to use when designing Active Directory permissions for all types of organizations.

First, create two documents, one called Allow and the other called Deny. On each document, label two sections, one called Global Tree Permissions and the other Specific Tree Permissions. Place two subheadings under each of the two sections, calling one General Permissions and the other Special Permissions. You should end up with three columns for each general and special heading: "LDAP path," "What to set," and "To whom."

The first six columns relate to permissions that will apply throughout the whole tree; the last six relate to permissions that will apply to specific locations in the tree. The latter is likely to be the much larger of the two. The General columns relate to permissions that can be set without needing to use the Advanced button, such as read access to all objects below an Organizational Unit. The Special columns relate to those permissions that you have to manually bring up a permission editor window for, such as allowing read access to all telephone numbers of user objects below a particular Organizational Unit. The last three columns relate to the LDAP path to the object that is to have properties set, the permissions that are being set, and the group or user to whom the permissions are being assigned.

The LDAP path under Global Tree Permissions is, strictly speaking, unnecessary, since these columns relate to permissions applied to the domain as a whole. If, however, you have a special need to apply permissions to a large number of Organizational Units directly below the root, you could use this column for this purpose.

Now you should go through your Active Directory design and begin to populate both the Allow and Deny tables. For a first pass, you should concentrate on a thorough design, listing all the permissions that you think you will need. Print out a number of copies of the table. Once you have a list in front of you, you can start amalgamating identical permissions into groups. It is likely that you will need to go through much iteration of these designs until you get a pared-down list that you are happy with. As you go through the design, you will start identifying groups of users to which you need to apply permissions. When designing the groups, you have two choices, as previously discussed under Rule 2. You can either create a single group to which permissions are applied and which contains users, or you can create two groups, one to apply permissions to and one to hold users that is nested in the first group.

The decision on whether to go for single or dual groups is not necessarily an easy one. My preference is to use single groups as often as possible, unless we need extra flexibility or have a lot of permissions to assign to many groups. In order to help you to make a bit more sense of the decision, a few reasons why you would want to consider one or the other are shown in Table 13-2.

Table 13-2. When to consider user groups and permission groups or combined groups

You should consider one group if	You should consider two groups if
You want to keep the number of groups to a minimum.	You want greater flexibility. Having one group for applying permissions and one for users means that you are always able to manage the system with a minimum of fuss.
You have only a small or simple tree, where it would be fairly easy to track down problems.	You have a large or complex tree, in which you need to be able to identify any problems quickly.
You need to assign only a few simple permissions.	You need to assign a large number of permissions.
You have very little change in the membership of groups and very few changes to permissions.	You have regular changes in your group membership or permissions.

You should consider one group if	You should consider two groups if
You have little cross-membership of groups.	You have major cross-membership of groups, where a user could exist in more than one group with conflicting permissions. (Two groups make it easier to debug problems in a large environment.)
You very rarely need new groups.	You regularly need new groups with subsets of your existing users who have been assigned to some task.
You very rarely have to split user groups so that each user group subset has different permissions than the original group had.	You regularly have to split an existing group into more than one group, because each requires a different set of permissions than the old group used to have.

One last point: if you are creating permission groups and user groups, remember to name them sensibly from the outset. Maybe use something such as res_Finance_User-Mod for a resource group granting user modification on the Finance OU and role_Finance_UserAdmin for the user admin role over the Finance OU. It makes it easier when managing and scripting if you can easily identify which type of groups are which.

Bringing Order Out of Chaos

We've had people ask what we would recommend to someone arriving at a new company where the previous directory services administrator had left a tree with no proper permissions design or consistency. In this situation, start by analyzing what the organization requires and work from there. You also should analyze what permissions Active Directory currently has assigned, although concentrating solely on this could be detrimental. After all, if the last administrator was not competent or knowledgeable enough to set up a sensible permissions scheme from the start, he may not have accurately implemented the permissions required by the organization.

When analyzing Active Directory, you need to start by identifying the members of the built-in groups on the server, such as Domain Administrators, Backup Operators, and so on. Now do the same for the other groups that are specific to the organization. Once this is done, using the previously described tables, you need to list the permissions on the root of the first domain in the tree you are responsible for. From there you should look at the permissions for the first container or Organizational Unit in that list. Then navigate the branch represented by that container, looking sequentially at the child containers, continually recursing through the tree. Once this first branch of the root is mapped out for the container permissions, you may be getting an idea of what permissions are required. Now go through all the objects in that branch, including printers, users, shares, and so on. This is time-consuming and annoying, but after a while you may start getting an idea of what is going on. All of this is just a sensible approach to going through Active Directory, not a quick-fix solution. You still have to continue throughout the domains you are responsible for to complete the process. It is also often helpful to use a script to iterate through Active Directory and display all of the ACLs for an object. For help on this, consult Chapter 25.

Your first main goal should be to move the individual user permissions to groups with users assigned to them as often as possible, thus making Active Directory simpler to manage and comprehend. These groups should be sensibly named for what they do rather than whom they contain (after all, you are looking to understand Active Directory first). Ideally, you can start consolidating users with identical permissions into the same group.

Your second goal is to remove permissions that users or your newly created groups should not have. This may, of course, mean that your new groups need to have their members split into two or more separate extra groups. For example, a group that has Read All Properties and Write All Properties to an object may actually need three groups with permissions instead: one to have Read All Properties, one to have Write All Properties, and one to have selected Write rather than complete Write access. This may be evident from your Active Directory analysis, or it may come out of discussions with users or their managers, with whom you should at least confirm the changes before implementing them just to make sure your analysis is correct.

Ultimately, your third goal, having rationalized the array of Active Directory permissions, is to try to limit the inheritance blocking of objects and branches and to try to move as many advanced permissions to general permissions as you can. You might think that it makes more sense to do this earlier, and in some cases, this is true. However, if you complete the first two goals, you will have an Active Directory tree that you understand and that has been brought back into line with sensible rules. It is much easier to attempt to fix problems with inheritance blocking and advanced permissions once you have a manageable and rationalized tree. You may end up going back and changing groups or permissions that you already sorted out in attaining the first two goals, but consider how much more difficult it would be to attempt to do these concurrently. After all, you are trying to make the best of an already annoying task. There is no sense in trying to do everything at once. As you go through the tree checking for inheritance blocking, you should document the blocked objects and branches, as specified in Rule 5, just as if you had set up the blocking from scratch yourself. That way, you can use the tables to analyze and keep track, crossing off those that are of no use as you rationalize the tree.

This whole section can be boiled down to two simple words: simplify and secure. You want to end up with the simplest, least delegated model you can attain while meeting the requirements at hand resulting in the most locked-down directory you can live with.

Designing Auditing Schemes

Designing auditing schemes, in contrast to permissions, is a relatively easy process. Imagine the circumstances in which you may need to check what is happening in Active Directory, and then set things up accordingly.

 You must remember that every Active Directory event that is audited causes the system to incur extra processing. Having auditing turned on all the time at the root for every modification by anyone is a great way to get all DCs to really slow down if a lot of Active Directory access occurs on those DCs.

That point bears repeating. Auditing changes to any object in the domain Naming Context (NC) will propagate domain-wide and cause logging to the security event log on every DC that services the Domain NC. Auditing changes to the Configuration NC or Schema NC will cause all DCs in a forest to begin auditing to their security event logs. You must have tools in place to retrieve logs from multiple DCs if you wish to see every security event that occurs. After all, if you have 100 DCs and are logging Configuration NC changes, then because changes can occur on any DC, you need to amalgamate 100 security event logs to gather a complete picture.

Here are a few examples where designing auditing schemes could come in handy:

- Someone complains that user details are being set to silly values by someone else as a joke.
- You notice that new objects you weren't expecting have been created or deleted in a container.
- The Active Directory hierarchy has changed and you weren't informed.
- You suspect a security problem.

Although the preceding reasons are all great reasons for enabling auditing, they are better reasons for removing native update access rights to the directory and pushing updates through some sort of provisioning system such as Microsoft's Identity Lifecycle Manager tool (ILM, formerly known as MIIS), Quest's Active Roles Directory Management tool, or even home-grown web-based tools. With these kinds of tools, you can implement good solid features sorely missing from Active Directory, such as the following:

Centralized logging
All information concerning all requested changes easily deposited in one location with no additional work.

Business rules
Allows you to force naming standards or specifically allow/disallow values in attributes.

Triggers

Send notifications to various individuals when certain things are requested, such as notifying the asset management group of a new computer added to Active Directory.

Custom authorization levels

Could allow you, for example, to specify that a data admin could create no more than five users a day.

Prevent bad things from happening versus trying to chase the occurrences through auditing

Auditing the directory for things that shouldn't have happened is reactive; securing the directory so those things can't happen in the first place is proactive and considerably less work in the long run.

In all of these scenarios, you will need to set auditing options on a container or a leaf object. These auditing entries do not have to exist all the time, so you could write them up and then code them into a script that you run at the first sign of trouble. That way, the system is immediately updated and ready to monitor the situation. This can happen only if you are prepared.

You need to analyze the scenarios that you envisage cropping up and then translate them into exact sets of auditing entry specifications. After you have written up each scenario and an emergency occurs, you will be able to follow the exact instructions that you previously laid down and set up a proper rapid response, which is what auditing is all about.

Implementing Auditing under Windows Server 2008

Windows Server 2008 introduces a completely new Active Directory auditing capability that greatly improves upon the capabilities in Windows Server 2003. Prior to Windows Server 2008, if you enabled the *Audit Directory Services Access* setting, a generic event was logged each time a user succeeded or failed to access an object with a System Access Control List (SACL) defined. From a practicality standpoint, this functionality was of limited value and could easily flood the security logs on your domain controllers.

Windows Server 2008 allows you to audit changes to the directory on a granular level as well as to view previous and current values when changes occur. Figure 13-17 shows an example of an attribute-modify audit event. A number of new auditing events have been created that will be logged to the Security log when changes occur. See Table 13-3 for a listing of these events.

Table 13-3. Windows Server 2008 auditing events

Event ID	Change Type	Description
5136	Modify	Logged anytime an attribute on an audited object is changed when the relevant *Write Property* audit is set in the SACL
5137	Create	Logged anytime an object is created under a parent with the *Create Child* audit is set in the SACL

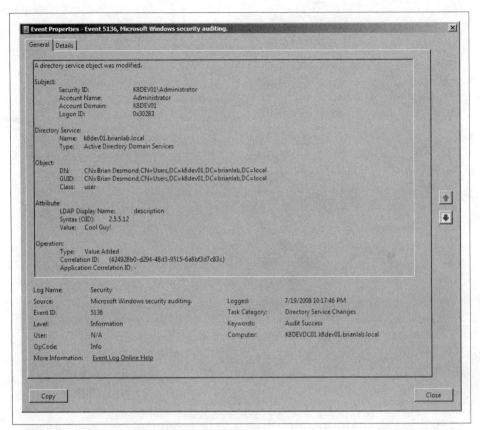

Figure 13-17. Attribute change audit in Windows Server 2008

Event ID	Change Type	Description
5138	Undelete	Logged anytime an object is reanimated under a parent with the *Create Child* audit is set in the SACL
5139	Move	Logged anytime an object is moved to a parent with the *Create Child* audit is set in the SACL
5141	Delete	Logged anytime an object with the *Delete Self* audit is set or the parent *Delete Child* audit is set in the SACL

 The Directory Service Access event 566 that was logged under Windows Server 2003 and Windows 2000 is still present in Windows Server 2008; however, the event ID has changed to 4662.

Enabling the new auditing functionality is a three or four step process:

1. Enable *Audit Directory Service Access* Group Policy setting.
2. Use `auditpol` to configure specific auditing settings on each domain controller.
3. Configure auditing in the SACL of objects in the domain.

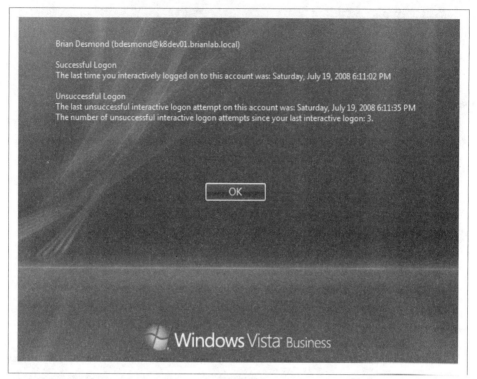

Figure 13-18. Displaying last interactive logon statistics

4. Exclude attributes from auditing forest-wide by modifying the attribute's definition in the schema.

In order to enable the *Audit Directory Service Access* setting, you should browse to it under `Computer Configuration\Policies\Windows Settings\Security Setting\Local Policies\Audit Policy` inside of a Group Policy that applies to your domain controllers, and audit *Success* attempts.

Next, you'll need to use `auditpol` to configure the new auditing subcategories in Windows Server 2008. Once you enable Audit Directory Service Access, all of the new settings are enabled by default. You can view these settings by running `auditpol /get /category:"DS Access"` from a command prompt. To disable success auditing for Directory Service Access auditing, for example, you would run `auditpol /set /subcategory:"Directory Service Access" /success:disable`. You will need to configure these settings individually on each domain controller in your domain.

 To view all of the auditing settings you can configure, run `auditpol /list /category`. In order to view the individual subcategories under each category, run `auditpol /list /subcategory:"<category>"`.

In order for change audits to be logged, you will need to configure the SACL on the objects to be audited as discussed earlier in this chapter. Make sure to enable the correct auditing entries as outlined in Figure 13-16.

Change auditing can be disabled globally for attributes by modifying the `searchFlags` attribute on the `attributeSchema` object in the Active Directory schema. The `search Flags` attribute is a bitmask, and auditing is managed by the ninth bit. To disable auditing for the `info` attribute using *adfind* and *admod*, you would run the following command: `adfind -sc s:info systemFlags -adcsv | admod systemFlags::{{.:SET: 256}} -upto 1`. To enable auditing for the info attribute, run this command: `adfind -sc s:info systemFlags -adcsv | admod systemFlags::{{.:CLR:256}} -upto 1`. You must be a member of Schema Admins to modify this attribute.

For more information about the new auditing features in Windows Server 2008, visit *http://technet2.microsoft.com/windowsserver2008/en/library/a9c25483-89e2-4202 -881c-ea8e02b4b2a51033.mspx?mfr=true*.

Tracking Last Interactive Logon Information

Windows Server 2008 supports a series of attributes that when enabled store the date and time of the last successful and failed control-alt-delete logons in the directory as well as the hostname of the machine they occurred on. These attributes are part of the user class in the directory. You may be wondering how this is different from the `lastLogonTimeStamp` attribute. The `lastLogonTimeStamp` attribute uses special functionality to limit the update frequency to an infrequent (every 10 to 14 days, roughly) interval, and it does not store the hostname of the logon. These new attributes are updated immediately.

There are a number of limitations to this feature that you should keep in mind when considering whether or not it is appropriate for your environment. The first is that this functionality only tracks interactive logons. In other words, only logons that occur when a user presses *Control+Alt+Delete* on a Windows Vista or newer machine are tracked. In order for the tracking to occur at all, the user's domain must be running at the Windows Server 2008 functional level, and a registry setting must be enabled on the client and on the domain controllers.

The registry setting is a `REG_DWORD` called `DisplayLastLogonInfo` located at `HKLM\Sotware \Microsoft\Windows\CurrentVersion\Policies\System`. If, on a domain controller, you set `DisplayLastLogonInfo` to `1`, it will begin storing logon statistics in Active Directory. If you set this value to `1` on a client, the client will begin reporting last logon statistics similar to Figure 13-18 when a user logs in.

In lieu of setting a registry setting, we recommend that you instead use the corresponding Group Policy setting for this feature. The Group Policy setting is available under `Computer Configuration\Policies\Administrative Templates\Windows Components\Win dows Logon Options`. The particular setting you want to enable is *Display information*

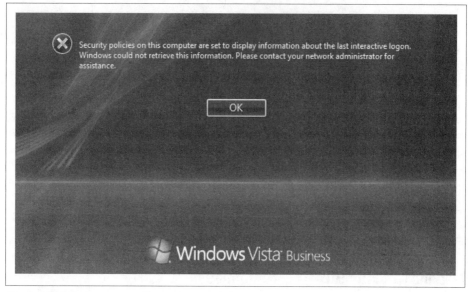

Figure 13-19. Last interactive logon statistics failure

about previous logons during user logon. This setting needs to be enabled in policies that apply to both domain controllers and clients in order to enable storage and display of logon statistics, respectively.

If you enable this setting on clients that have users logging into domains not in the Windows Server 2008 functional level, clients will receive an error similar to Figure 13-19 and be unable to log in. You will also receive the error in Figure 13-19 if this setting is enabled on clients, but not domain controllers.

There are four attributes that are used to provide this additional logon information functionality in the directory:

msDS-LastSuccessfulInteractiveLogonTime
> The time of the last successful Control+Alt+Delete logon.

msDS-LastFailedInteractiveLogonTime
> This is the last time a failed Control+Alt+Delete logon occurred.

msDS-FailedInteractiveLogonCount
> This is the number of logon failures that have occurred since the feature was enabled.

msDS-FailedInteractiveLogonCountAtLastSuccessfulLogon
> The number of failed Control+Alt+Delete logons since the last successful Control +Alt+Delete logon.

Unlike the `lastLogonTimeStamp` attribute, there is no update frequency safeguard for these attributes. If you enable this feature, keep in mind that every single time these attributes are update, they will replicate in the next cycle. There could potentially be thousands of updates a day to these attributes in a busy domain. There is no guarantee that the values shown to the user similar to Figure 13-19 are in fact the most accurate values in an environment with more than one domain controller in the domain since these attributes replicate like any other change to the directory.

 If you have deployed Read-Only Domain Controllers, they will update these attributes locally, but the changes will not be replicated to the rest of the domain.

The implementation of the last interactive logon statistics feature discussed in this section was designed primarily for compliance with Common Criteria (*http://www.com moncriteriaportal.org*). Unless you have a business need for this feature or you are enabling it in a small (e.g., single site) domain, we do not recommend that you enable it.

Real-World Examples

It now seems appropriate to put what we have laid out earlier into practice. We will use a series of tasks that could crop up during your everyday work as an administrator. The solutions we propose probably are not the only solutions to the problems. That is often the case with Active Directory; there are many ways of solving the same problem.

Hiding Specific Personal Details for All Users in an Organizational Unit from a Group

In this example, an Organizational Unit called Hardware Support Staff contains the user accounts of an in-house team of people whose job is to repair and fix broken computers within your organization. Whenever a user has a fault, he rings the central faults hotline to request a support engineer. An engineer is assigned the job, which is added to the end of her existing list of faults to deal with. The user is informed about which engineer will be calling and approximately when she will arrive. As with all jobs of this sort, some take longer than others, and users have discovered how to find the mobile or pager number of the engineer they have been assigned and have taken to calling her to get an arrival-time update rather than ringing the central desk. Management has decided that they want to restrict who can ring the pager or mobile, but they do not want to stop giving out the engineer's name as they feel it is part of the friendly service. Consequently, they have asked you to find a way of hiding the pager and mobile numbers in Active Directory from all users who should not have access.

The solution that we will use is to remove the default ability of every user to see the pager and mobile properties of the Engineer objects by default. The first thing we need to find out is how the permissions are currently granted to the users. We look at the ACL on a user object and we do not see either attribute listed specifically. We do however see an inherited Read Property (RP) access for the entire object granted to the

Pre-Windows 2000 Compatible Access group. We also see explicit RP access for several Property Sets granted to Authenticated Users.

Next we look at the schema definition for the two attributes and we see that both have the attributeSecurityGUID set with {77B5B886-944A-11D1-AEBD-0000F80367C1}, which means the attributes are in a property set. We scan through the extended-rights container and determine that the property set these attributes are in is the Personal Information property set. We look at the ACL again and see that the Personal Information property set is one of the property sets that has RP access granted to Authenticated Users. We know that the domain has Pre-Windows 2000 Compatible Access enabled, so users are getting access to the pager and mobile attributes through two different ACES, both explicit and inherited. If you recall from the earlier Permission Lockdown section, you know that the explicit property set ACE is the more difficult of the two to deal with. We will focus on that one initially.

The first thing we will do is create a sub-OU under Hardware Support Staff called Engineers and move all of the engineer user objects into that OU. We could try to individually lock down the engineer user objects in the parent OU, but that is a layer of complexity that isn't needed and should be avoided. Now that all of the engineers are isolated in their own OU, we need to decide which mechanism previously discussed is appropriate to lock down access to the pager and mobile attributes. Again, these options are:

1. Remove the pager and mobile attributes from the Personal Information property set.

2. Change the defaultSD of the user object class to remove Personal Information property set.

3. Strip the Personal Information ACE from each of the engineer objects and add inherited deny ACES for the mobile and pager attributes.

4. Add an explicit deny ACE for mobile and pager attributes on each engineer object.

Options 1 and 2 could be used, but we would have to go back through the rest of the forest and add inherited ACEs granting RP to the pager and mobile attributes for Authenticated Users. All of this extra work would be needed to attain the net effect of a permission change only on the targeted OU. If you think that you will be locking these attributes down for more OUs or maybe all users in the forest, these options would become more palatable.

With option 3, you target only the engineer objects. When you strip the Personal Information ACE, not only will access to the mobile and pager attributes be affected, but also every other attribute in the Personal Information property set, which includes 46 attributes in the default Windows Server 2008 forest.

For all three of these options, if the domain is in Pre-Windows 2000 Compatible mode, users will still have access to all attributes through the inherited ACE granted to the Pre-Windows 2000 Compatible Access group. In order to lock down the two targeted attributes, we would also need to add an inherited deny ACE for each attribute on the Engineers OU. This would work great and everyone would be happy until later on, maybe a year or two down the road after you forgot all about this change, when you decide "We don't need to be in Pre-Windows 2000 Compatible mode anymore" and remove the `Authenticated Users` group from the `Pre-Windows 2000 Compatible Access` group. As soon as you do this, the permissions removed for steps 1, 2, and 3 would quite suddenly impact you by disallowing access to all attributes that are in the `Personal Information` property set. Obviously this could be quite a surprise! You could think it was because you still needed to be in Pre-Windows 2000 Compatible mode, but it would actually just be a delegation issue.

The last option, option 4, would target just the engineer user objects, plus there would be no unintended side effects later with other domain changes. This is probably the best solution in this case, though there is a good amount of initial work plus ongoing maintenance as new engineer users are added. It is best if a script was built strictly for doing this work.

You may wonder, "Wouldn't this be a great place to use the confidential bit capability in Windows Server 2003 Service Pack 1?" Unfortunately no, this isn't a good example because it would impact all users in the forest and, more importantly, both the `mobile` and `pager` attributes are category 1 attributes, so you can't modify them to make them confidential.

Allowing Only a Specific Group of Users to Access a New Published Resource

The Finance department created a new share called *Budget_Details* and published it in the tree. The permissions to the share itself allow only the correctly authorized staff to read and view the contents, but everyone by default can see the `volume` object describing the share in the tree. The Finance department does not want the share visible in Active Directory to anyone who is not a member of the Finance group.

Again, the first thing we need to determine how the permissions are currently granted to the users. We look at the ACL on a `volume` object, and the only permission granted to normal users is a Generic Read ACE for `Authenticated Users`. Since this is a single object, it probably doesn't make sense to create a whole OU for it, so we will open up the permission editor window for the `volume` object and remove the `Authenticated Users` group entry. We then add an entry for the Finance group and assign Read and List permissions.

Restricting Everyone but HR from Viewing Social Security Numbers with Confidential Access Capability

Let's say after much discussion, it is decided that Social Security numbers will be moved from a proprietary database and inserted into Active Directory. There is quite a bit of concern about the visibility of the attribute, as only the HR department and domain admins should be able to see the attributes by default. Luckily, you just installed Windows Server 2003 Service Pack 1 or later on all of your domain controllers, so you now have the capability to use the Confidential Access capability.

You extend the schema with a new Social Security number attribute and you set the searchFlags attribute to 128 to indicate that the attribute should be protected. Now you simply have to create a new group called HR-Confidential and assign a single inheritable ACE at the root of each domain that grants Control Access to the Social Security number attribute on user objects.

Later, if someone decides they want to secure the attribute from Domain Administrators as well, you will need to go through and apply an explicit deny ACE to every single object for that group. However, trying to deny access to data in the directory to Domain Administrators is not actually enforceable. At any point that a Domain Admin would like to get access to the attribute again, she can simply modify the ACL herself. If you absolutely cannot allow Domain Administrators access to the data, you need to find someplace else to put the data using third-party encryption or on a machine that isn't in the domain and therefore in some way under the control of the Domain Administrators.

Summary

Security is always important, and when access to your organization's network is concerned, it's paramount. We hope this chapter has given you an understanding of how permission to access can be allowed or denied to entire domains or individual properties of a single object. Auditing is also part of security, and having mechanisms already designed—so that they can be constantly working or dropped in when required—is the best way to keep track of such a system.

Assigning permission and auditing entries to an object appears to be a simple subject on the surface. However, once you start delving into the art of setting permissions and auditing entries, it quickly becomes obvious how much there is to consider. Global design is the necessary first step.

Although expanding your tree later by adding extra containers is rarely a problem, in a large tree it makes sense to have some overall guidelines or rules that allow you to impose a sense of structure on the whole process of design and redesign. Ideally, the golden rules and tables that we created should allow you to plan and implement sensible permissions schemes, which was the goal of the chapter.

## CHAPTER 14

Designing and Implementing Schema Extensions

For Active Directory to hold any object, such as a user, it needs to know what the attributes and characteristics of that object are. In other words, it needs a blueprint for that object. The Active Directory schema is the blueprint for all classes, attributes, and syntaxes that can potentially be stored in Active Directory.

The following considerations should be kept in mind when you contemplate extending your schema:

- Microsoft designed Active Directory to hold the most common objects and attributes you would require. Because they could never anticipate every class of object or every specific attribute that a company would need, Active Directory was designed to be extensible. After all, if these objects and properties are going to be in everyday use, the design shouldn't be taken lightly. Administrators need to be aware of the importance of the schema and how to extend it. Extending the schema is a useful and simple solution to a variety of problems, and not being aware of this potential means that you will have a hard time identifying it as a solution to problems you might encounter.

- Designing schema extensions is very important, in part because any new class or attribute that you create in the schema is a permanent addition. Under Windows Server 2003, you can disable or redefine schema extensions, but you can never remove them completely.

- Although it is easy to extend Active Directory, it's surprising how many companies are reluctant to implement schema extensions due to concerns over the impact to Active Directory. One of the biggest impediments in Windows 2000 was that anytime the partial attribute set was extended (i.e., an attribute added to the Global Catalog), a full resync had to be done for all Global Catalog servers. Fortunately, Microsoft resolved this in Windows Server 2003, and a full resync is no longer performed.

This chapter takes you through the process of extending the schema, from the initial design of the changes through the implementation, and discusses how to avoid the pitfalls that can crop up. We then talk about analyzing the choices available and seeing whether you can obtain the required design result some other way. We obviously cover how to implement schema changes from first principles, but before that we identify the steps in designing or modifying a class or attribute. Finally, we cover some pitfalls to be aware of when administering the schema.

We won't spend much time introducing a large number of specific examples. This is mainly because there's no way we can conceive of every sort of class that you will require. Consequently, for examples we use only one new generic class as well as a few attribute extensions to the default user object. When giving examples of modifying a class, we extend the user object class.

Let's first look at how you would design the changes you may wish to make in an enterprise environment.

 If you have not done so already, we highly recommend you review Chapter 4 for an in-depth discussion of the Active Directory schema. This chapter is dependent on the concepts discussed there.

Nominating Responsible People in Your Organization

If you don't already have a central person or group of people responsible for the Object Identifier (OID) namespace for your organization, you need to form such a group. This OID Managers group is responsible for obtaining an OID namespace, designing a structure for the namespace that makes sense to your organization, managing that namespace by maintaining a diagram of the structure and a list of the allocated OIDs, and issuing appropriate OIDs for new classes from that structure as required. Whenever a new class or attribute is to be added to your organization's schema, the OID Managers provide a unique OID for that new addition. This is then logged by the OID Managers with a set of details about the reason for the request and the type of schema extension that it is to be used for. All these details need to be defined by the OID Managers group.

The Schema Managers, by comparison, are responsible for designing and creating proper classes in the schema for a forest as well as for handling schema extensions required by third party applications. They are responsible for actually making changes to the schema via requests from within the organization, and for ensuring that redundant objects doing the same thing are not created, that inheritance is used to best effect, that the appropriate objects are indexed, and that the partial attribute set contains the right attributes.

If you are designing code that will modify some other organization's schema, the documentation accompanying that code should make it explicitly clear exactly which classes and attributes are being created and why. The documentation also should explain that the code needs to be run with the privilege of a member of the Schema Admins group, since some organizations may have an Active Directory in which the Schema Admins group is empty most of the time.

A better solution to programmatically processing schema changes is to supply organizations with the LDIF files for the schema modifications. This allows the organizations to review the actual changes and incorporate them into a batch update process with other schema modifications, which allows for easier testing and production implementation. Some large organizations have extensive schema change control procedures that require LDIF format files describing all changes. Failure to supply the required LDIF file results in the update being rejected.

Note that while the membership of OID Managers does not necessarily coincide with that of Schema Managers, it is a possibility.

Thinking of Changing the Schema

Before you start thinking of changing the schema, you need to consider not just the namespace, but also the data your Active Directory will hold. After all, if you know your data, you can decide what changes you want to make and whom those changes might impact.

Designing the Data

No matter how you migrated to Active Directory, at some point you'll need to determine exactly what data you will add or migrate for the objects you create. Will you use the `physicalDeliveryOfficeName` attribute of the user object? What about the `telephonePager` attribute? Do you want to merge the internal staff office location list and telephone database during the migration? What if you really need to know what languages each of your staff speaks or qualifications they hold? What about their shoe size, their shirt size, number of children, and whether they like animals? The point is that some of these already exist in the Active Directory schema and some don't. At some point, you need to design the actual data that you want to include. This is an important decision, since not all data should necessarily be added to Active Directory. While it may be nice to have shoe size in the directory, it may not make much business sense. You need to ask, "Is this data needed on all domain controllers for a given domain or all global catalogs in the forest?" It is possible that an application partition, Active Directory Lightweight Directory Services (AD LDS), or even a SQL Server database may be a better store for this information. Keep in mind that every piece of data that gets added to the directory needs to be replicated. This has significant impact on network traffic, storage needs, and the time required to build new domain controllers.

Let's consider MyUnixCorp, a large fictional organization that for many years has run perfectly well on a large mainframe system. The system is unusual in that the login process has been completely replaced in-house with a two-tier password system. A file called *additional-passwd* maintains a list of usernames and their second Unix password in an encrypted format. Your design for the migration for MyUnixCorp's system has to take account of the extra login check. In this scenario, either MyUnixCorp accepts that the new Active Directory Kerberos security mechanism is secure enough for its site, or it has to add entries to the schema for the second password attribute and write a new Active Directory logon interface that incorporates both checks.

This example serves to outline that the data that is to be stored in Active Directory has a bearing on the schema structure and consequently has to be incorporated into the design phase.

To Change or Not to Change

When you identify a deficiency in the schema for your own Active Directory, you have to look hard into whether modifying the schema is the correct way to proceed. Finding that the schema lacks a complete series of objects along with multiple attributes is a far cry from identifying that the `person-who-needs-to-refill-the-printer-with-toner` attribute of the printer object is missing from the schema. There's no rule, either, that says that once you wish to create three extra attributes on an existing object, you should modify the schema. It all comes down to choice.

 There is one useful guideline: you should identify all the data you want to hold in Active Directory prior to considering your design. If you consider how to implement each change in Active Directory one at a time, you may simply lose sight of the overall picture.

To help you make that choice, you should ask yourself whether there are any other objects or attributes that you could use to solve your problem.

Let's say you were looking for an attribute of a user object that would hold a staff identification number for your users. You need to ask whether there is an existing attribute of the user object that could hold the staff ID number, which you are not planning to use. This saves you from modifying the schema if you don't have to. Take Leicester University as an example: we had a large user base that we were going to register, and we needed to hold a special ID number for our students. In Great Britain, every university student has a so-called University and Colleges Administration System number, more commonly known as the UCAS number; this is a unique alphanumeric string that UCAS assigns independent of a student's particular university affiliation. Students receive their UCAS numbers when they first begin looking into universities.

The numbers identify students to their prospective universities, stay with students throughout their undergraduate careers, and are good identifiers for checking the validity of students' details. By default, there is no schema attribute called UCAS-Number, so we had two choices. We could find an appropriately named attribute that we were not going to use and make use of that, or we could modify the schema.

Since we were initially only looking to store this piece of information in addition to the default user information, we were not talking about a huge change in any case. We simply looked to see whether we could use any other schema attributes to contain the data. We soon found the `employeeID` user attribute that we were not ever intending to use, and that seemed to fit the bill, so we decided to use that. While it isn't as appropriately named as an attribute called UCAS-Number would be, it did mean that we didn't have to modify the base schema in this instance.

The important point here is that we chose not to modify the schema, having found a spare attribute that we were satisfied with. We could just as easily have found no appropriate attributes and decided to go through making the schema changes using our own customized attributes.

 This example of repurposing the `employeeID` attribute is one where the data it was repurposed to hold is closely aligned with the original intent implied by the name `employeeID`. It is not at all advisable to repurpose attributes that are included in the base schema for purposes that are not remotely related to their original intent. It is entirely possible that a later version of Active Directory may begin using an attribute in the base schema for its original intent, or a third party application may make this assumption. If you have elected to repurpose the attribute, you will then need to migrate the data out of this attribute and update all of the applications that depended upon it.

If you've installed Microsoft Exchange into the forest, there is also a set of attributes available to use for whatever you need. These are known as the extension or custom attributes and have names like extensionAttribute1, extensionAttribute2, and so on. These are not generally used by the operating system[*] and have been left in for you to use as you wish. There are 20 created by default, thus giving you spare attribute capacity built right into Active Directory. So, if we wanted to store the number of languages spoken by a user, we could just store that value inside extensionAttribute1 if we chose. You can see how these attributes have been designed by using the Active Directory Schema MMC.

Making use of extension attributes and making use of unused attributes works well for a small number of cases. However, if there were 20, 30, or more complex attributes

---

[*] It is possible that `extensionAttribute10` may be used for `NTDSNoMatch` information during an Exchange 5.5 to Exchange Server 2000 or Exchange 2003 Server migration. See Microsoft Knowledge Base article 274173 at *http://support.microsoft.com/kb/274173*.

each with a specific syntax, or if we needed to store 20 objects with 30 attributes each, we would have more difficulty. When you have data like that, you need to consider the bigger picture.

The Global Picture

So you have a list of all your data and suspect either that the schema will not hold your data or that it will not do so to your satisfaction. You now need to consider the future of your organization's schema and design it accordingly. The following questions should help you decide how to design for each new class or attribute:

- Is this class or attribute already in the schema in some form? In other words, does the attribute already exist by default or has someone already created it? If it doesn't exist, you can create it. If it does already exist in some form, can you make use of that existing attribute? If you can, you should consider doing so.

   If you can't, you need to consider modifying the existing attribute to cope with your needs or creating a second attribute that essentially holds similar or identical data, which is wasteful. If the existing attribute is of no use, can you create a new one and migrate the values for the existing attribute to the new one and disable the old one? These are the sorts of questions you need to be thinking of.

- Is this a class or attribute that is to be used only for a very specific purpose, or could this object potentially be made of use (i.e., created, changed, and modified) by others in the organization? If the class or attribute is for only a specific purpose, the person suggesting the change should know what is required. If the class or attribute may impact others, care should be taken to ensure it is designed to cope with the requirements of all potential users, for example, that it can later be extended if necessary without affecting the existing object instances at the moment the schema object is updated.

   For an attribute, for example, you should ask whether the attribute's syntax and maximum/minimum values (for strings or integers) are valid or whether they should be made more applicable to the needs of many. Specifically, if you created a CASE_INSENSITIVE_STRING of between 5 and 20 characters now and later you require that attribute to be a CASE_SENSITIVE_STRING of between 5 and 20 characters, you would need to create a new attribute and migrate the data as the syntax of an attribute cannot be changed once the attribute is created.

- Are you modifying an existing class by adding an attribute? If so, would this attribute be better if it were not applied directly to the object, but instead added to a set of attributes within an auxiliary class?

- Are you adding an attribute to an existing class that you normally manage through the standard GUI tools such as Active Directory Users and Computers? The new attribute will not automatically show up in the GUI and will require changing the tool being used or extending the tool if it is possible. You must be aware of the impact that your changes may have on existing tools and ones that you design yourself.

Basically, these questions boil down to four much simpler ones:

- Is the change that needs to be made valid and sensible for all potential uses and users of this object?
- Will my change impact any other changes that may need to be made to this and other objects in the future?
- Will my change impact anyone else now or in the future?
- Will my change impact any applications that people inside or outside the company are developing?

 In a similar fashion to getting a valid OID namespace, make sure that the classes and attributes are created with sensible names. These names should have a unique company prefix for easy identification and be capitalized words separated by hyphens. For specific examples, see Chapter 26.

The Schema Managers group needs to sit down with all groups of people who would potentially like to make changes to the schema, brief them on how the schema operates, and attempt to identify the sorts of changes that need to be made by these groups. If a series of meetings is not your style, consider creating a briefing paper, followed by a form to request schema updates, issued to all relevant department heads. If you allow enough time, you will be able to collate responses received and make a good stab at an initial design. You can find attributes that may conflict, ways of making auxiliary classes rather than modifications to individual attributes, and so on. This gives the Schema Managers a good chance to come up with a valid initial design for the schema changes prior to or during a rollout.

An important rule of thumb is to never modify default system attributes. This makes sure that you never conflict with anything considered a default by the operating system, which might eventually cause problems during upgrades or with other applications such as Exchange. Adding extra attributes to classes is fine, but avoid modifying existing attributes.

Creating Schema Extensions

There are three ways to modify the schema: through the Active Directory Schema MMC, using LDIF files, or programmatically using ADSI or LDAP. We will not cover the use of the Active Directory Schema MMC very heavily here since it is fairly straightforward to use, although we will cover its use in managing the Schema Master FSMO role. Typically, you should not use the Active Directory Schema MMC to extend the schema and instead use LDIF files or ADSI. Most vendors provide LDIF files, which contain the schema extensions that you can run at your leisure. We cover extending the schema with ADSI in Chapter 26.

Running the Schema Manager MMC for the First Time

The Schema Manager MMC is not available from the Administrative Tools menu like the other Active Directory snap-ins. To use it, you need to first register the Dynamic Link Library (DLL) file for the MMC snap-in by typing the following command at the command prompt:

```
regsvr32.exe schmmgmt.dll
```

You can then start the Active Directory Schema console by creating a custom MMC and adding the Active Directory Schema snap-in to it. To create a console, go to the Run menu from the Start button, type mmc.exe, and click OK. Then in the empty MMC, go to File→Add/Remove Snap-in.... From here, you can click the Add button and select Active Directory Schema as the item. If you then click the Add button, followed by Close, and then the OK button, that will give you an MMC hosting the Schema Manager snap-in for you to use and later save as required.

Allowing the Schema to Be Modified on Windows 2000

Under Windows 2000, there was a safeguard you had to bypass for the Schema Master FSMO owner to allow you to modify the schema. First, the user who is to make the changes has to be a member of the Schema Admins group, which exists in the forest root domain. Second, you need to make a change to the registry on the domain controller that you wish to make the changes on.

On the schema master itself, open up the registry using *regedt32.exe* or *regedit.exe* and locate the following key: HKLM\SYSTEM\CurrentControlSet\Services\NTDS\Parameters.

Now, create a new REG_DWORD value called Schema Update Allowed and set the value to 1. That's all you need to do. You now can edit the Schema on that domain controller.

Another alternative method for making the change is to copy the following three lines to a text file with a REG extension and open it (i.e., execute it) on the DC where you wish to enable schema updates. This will automatically modify the registry for you without the need to open the registry by hand:

```
REGEDIT4
[HKEY_LOCAL_MACHINE\SYSTEM\CurrentControlSet\Services\NTDS\Parameters]
"Schema Update Allowed"=dword:00000001
```

Once you've modified the registry on a particular domain controller and placed the user account that is to make the changes into the Schema Admins group, any changes you make to the schema on that domain controller will be accepted.

The Schema Cache

Each domain controller maintains a copy of the entire schema in memory. This is known as the schema cache. It is used to provide a very rapid response when requesting a schema object OID from a name.

The schema cache is actually a set of hash tables of all the classSchema and attribute Schema objects known to the system, along with specific indices (attributeID and lDAPDisplayName for attributeSchema objects and governsID, lDAPDisplayName, and mapiID for classSchema objects) for fast searching.

The objects are loaded into the schema cache when the domain controller is booted and then five minutes after an update. However, if you need the schema cache to be updated immediately for some reason, say after the creation of a new object or attribute class, you can force an immediate reload of the cache.

As we said, the system holds a copy in memory solely to aid in searches that require quick and regular access to the schema. If the system were to keep both the cache and the actual Active Directory schema in synch, it could be costly in terms of performance; making changes to the schema is an intensive process due to the significant checking and setting of object defaults by the system upon creation of new objects. Consequently, there is a time delay between changes made to the underlying schema and the cached copy. Typically, the schema tends to be updated in bunches. This is likely to be due to applications creating multiple classes for their own purposes during an installation or even normal operation. If classes are still being created after five minutes, the system updates the cache in five-minute increments after the first five-minute update has completed. This continues for as long as schema class updates continue.

During the intervening five-minute period, when the underlying schema has been modified but the cache has yet to be updated, instances of objects or attributes of the new classes cannot be created. If you try to create an object, the system will return an error. This is due to the fact that object creations refer to the cache and not the underlying schema. To get around this problem, you can force an immediate reload of the cache by updating a special operational attribute on the RootDSE. We'll cover this later when we consider how to use the Schema Manager interface to create and delete classes. In a similar vein, if you mark an object as defunct, this will not take effect until the cache is reloaded.

Although you cannot create new instances of new object types that you have created until the schema cache refreshes, you can add new attributes or classes that you have created to other classes that you are creating. For example, if you create a new attribute, you can immediately add it to a new class. Why? Because the attribute or class is added using an OID, and the system thus doesn't need to do any lookups in the schema cache. While all system checks by Active Directory confirming that the data is valid (covered in detail a couple of sections later) will still be performed, the checks are performed on the schema in Active Directory, not in the cache. If this weren't the case, you would have to wait for at least five minutes before any new attributes that you created could be added to new classes, and that would be unacceptable.

The Schema Master FSMO

The Schema Master FSMO is the domain controller where changes to the schema take place so that multiple users or applications cannot modify the schema on two or more different domain controllers at the same time. When Active Directory is installed in an enterprise, the first server in the first domain in the forest (the forest root domain) becomes the nominated Schema FSMO. Later, if changes need to be made to the schema, they can be made at the current master.

You can transfer the role from an existing Schema Master in three ways: via the Schema Manager MMC, via the NTDSUTIL tool, or via code that makes use of ADSI or LDAP.

Using the Active Directory Schema MMC to transfer the role is easy. First you need to connect to the server that is to be the new master (*dc2.mycorp.com*), and then you need to force the role to change to the server to which you are now connected. To start the process, simply run the MMC and right-click Active Directory Schema in the left hand scope pane. From the context menu that drops down, select Change Active Directory Domain Controller.

You can now select a new server to connect to. You should transfer any FSMO roles (not just the Schema Master) to a new server before shutting down a server for an extended period, such as for maintenance. Once you have connected to the intended target for the Schema Master FSMO role, right-click on Active Directory Domains Schema in the scope pane and select Operations Master from the context menu. A dialog box will appear, showing the current DC holding the Schema FSMO role, as well as an option to change the role to the currently connected server. Figure 14-1 shows this dialog box. Click the Change button and change the schema role.

In the event the schema master role owner becomes permanently unavailable (due to hardware failure, operating system corruption, or so forth), you will need to seize the schema master role on another domain controller. In order to seize a FSMO, you must use the `ntdsutil` command-line utility. For more information about seizing FSMO roles, see Chapter 15.

If you are writing ADSI scripts to manipulate the schema, just connect to the Schema FSMO directly and make the changes there, rather than worrying about checking to see if the server you wish to make the changes on is the Schema FSMO. We'll show you how to do that in Chapter 26.

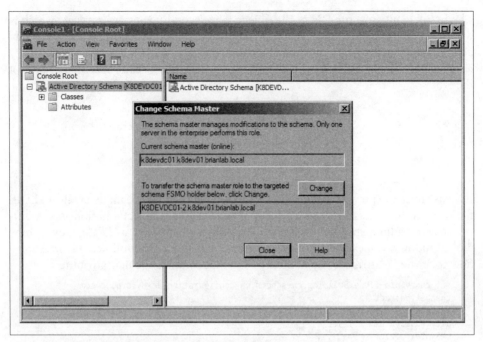

Figure 14-1. Transferring the Schema Master FSMO

Using LDIF to Extend the Schema

One of the most commonly used ways to extend the schema is with LDIF. The LDAP Data Interchange Format was defined in RFC 2849 (*http://www.ietf.org/rfc/rfc2849.txt*) and provides a way to represent directory data via a human-readable text file. You can export data from Active Directory in LDIF format, and you can also add, modify, and delete data with LDIF. The LDIFDE program comes installed as part of any Windows Server and can be used to import and export LDIF data. To import the contents of an LDIF file, run the following command:

```
c:> ldifde -v -i -f import.ldf
```

Replace *import.ldf* with the name of the LDIF file you want to import.

LDIF files contain one or more entries, with each entry containing one or more attributes that should be added, replaced, or removed. The format is straightforward, but very strict. The following is an LDIF that would add a group object to the Users container:

```
dn: cn=mygroup,cn=users,dc=mycorp,dc=com
changetype: add
objectclass: group
description: My Group
member: cn=administrator,cn=users,dc=mycorp,dc=com
member: cn=guest,cn=users,dc=mycorp,dc=com
```

The first line must be the DN of the object. The second line is changetype:, which is one of add, modify, modrdn, or delete. When using add as in this case, we must specify all the mandatory attributes for the object. For group objects, we need to specify only objectClass. The cn attribute is not required because it is already specified as part of the DN.

 Windows 2000 Active Directory also requires the sAMAccountName attribute to be specified for new users and groups.

It is easy to create portable schema extensions using LDIF files. Simply create an LDIF file with all the necessary classSchema or attributeSchema object additions or modifications, and administrators using any LDIF-based client (such as *ldifde*, which ships with Windows) can easily import it into Active Directory. The following LDIF shows how to create an attribute and auxiliary class that contains the new attribute:

```
dn: cn=myCorp-ITUserBuilding,cn=schema,cn=configuration,dc=mycorp,dc=com
changetype: add
attributeID: 1.2.3.4.111.1
attributeSyntax: 2.5.5.1
oMSyntax: 127
isSingleValued: TRUE
lDAPDisplayName: myCorp-ITUserBuilding
objectClass: attributeSchema

dn:
changetype: modify
add: schemaUpdateNow
schemaUpdateNow: 1
-

dn: cn=myCorp-ITUser,cn=schema,cn=configuration,dc=mycorp,dc=com
changetype: add
objectclass: classSchema
description: Class for MyCorp Employees
lDAPDisplayName: myCorp-ITUser
governsID: 1.2.3.4.111.2
objectClassCategory: 3
subClassOf: top
mayContain: myCorp-ITUserBuilding
dn:
changetype: modify
add: schemaUpdateNow
schemaUpdateNow: 1
-
```

As we mentioned before, all mandatory attributes for attributeSchema and classSchema objects must be specified. The order of the additions is also important. Because we wanted to add the new attribute to the class, we needed to create it first. We also needed to reload the schema cache before attempting to reference the new attribute by lDAPDisplayName or a failure would have occurred. To accomplish that, we perform a modify operation against the RootDSE (i.e., blank DN) and write to the schemaUpdateNow attribute.

We could have skipped the schema cache refresh after the attribute creation if we had used the attributeID OID 1.2.3.4.111.1 in place of the lDAPDisplayName myCorp-ITUserBuilding in the mayContain attribute of the myCorp-ITUser class. Since we used the lDAPDisplayName in this example, it required the schema cache to be reloaded because a lookup to retrieve the proper OID had to be performed.

The benefits of using LDIF to implement schema extensions are two-fold. First, since LDIF is human-readable with a well-defined syntax, it is easy for those who need to implement the extensions to see what is going to be done. If you use a program that the administrator cannot see the source for, they will not have as much visibility into what changes are made. Along the same lines, LDIF files provide a crude documentation mechanism for schema extensions. Because LDIF files are just text-based files, schema administrators can archive the files on a server and have instant access to exactly what changes were made for certain applications.

Checks the System Makes When You Modify the Schema

When you create a new class or attribute, the system performs some basic checks within Active Directory to see if the data is valid, in addition to any checks you provide. The checks for attributes are shown in Table 14-1, and those for new classes are shown in Table 14-2.

Table 14-1. System checks made when creating new attributes

Attribute	System check performed
lDAPDisplayName	Must be unique in Active Directory.
attributeId	Must be unique in Active Directory.
mapiId	If present, must be unique in Active Directory.
schemaIDGUID	Must be unique in Active Directory.
attributeSyntax	Must correlate with oMSyntax.
oMSyntax	Must correlate with attributeSyntax.
rangeLower	If rangeUpper is present as well, the following should be true: rangeUpper > rangeLower.
rangeUpper	If RangeLower is present as well, the following should be true: rangeUpper > rangeLower.
linkID	Must be unique in Active Directory. Back links must have corresponding forward links.
searchFlags	Ambiguous Name Resolution (ANR) attributes must be Unicode or Teletex.

Table 14-2. System checks made when creating new classes

Attribute	System check performed
lDAPDisplayName	Must be unique in Active Directory.
governsId	Must be unique in Active Directory.
schemaIDGUID	Must be unique in Active Directory.
subClassOf	Checks to make sure that the X.500 specifications are not contravened, (i.e., that an auxiliary class cannot inherit from a structural class, and an abstract class can only inherit from another abstract class). All classes defined in this attribute must already exist.
rDNAttID	Must have a Unicode string as its syntax.
mayContain	Before you can specify a class in the mayContain attribute, it must already be defined in the schema.
systemMayContain	All classes defined in this attribute must already exist.
mustContain	All classes defined in this attribute must already exist.
systemMustContain	All classes defined in this attribute must already exist.
auxiliaryClass	All classes defined in this attribute must already exist and must have an objectClassCategory indicating either 88-Class or Auxiliary.
systemAuxiliaryClass	All classes defined in this attribute must already exist and must have an objectClassCategory indicating either 88-Class or Auxiliary.
possSuperiors	All classes defined in this attribute must already exist and must have an objectClassCategory indicating either 88-Class or Structural Class.
systemPossSuperiors	All classes defined in this attribute must already exist and must have an objectClassCategory indicating either 88-Class or Structural Class.

Making Classes and Attributes Defunct

Microsoft does not currently allow you to delete objects from the schema. If your forest is running at Windows 2003 functional level, you can redefine or disable classes and attributes. This is a new feature in Windows 2003, which allows you to correct potential mistakes you may have made or to repurpose classes or attributes you are no longer using.

If you create a class or attribute of some sort and decide that you don't want it any more, you can simply disable it, which is otherwise known as making it defunct. This is achieved by setting the isDefunct attribute on the schema object to True. For this to succeed for an attribute, the system makes sure that the attribute is not a mandatory or optional attribute of any non-defunct class and is not the RDN attribute (rDNAttID) for any class. For this to succeed for a class, the system makes sure that the class is not a parent of any other non-defunct class, is not an auxiliary class to any other non-defunct class, and is not a possible superior of any other non-defunct class. If you later decide that you want to use the schema object again, set the value of isDefunct to False. The checks that occur when doing this are the same as for creating a new schema object of the appropriate type in the first place.

When a schema object is defunct, attempts to create instances of it fail as if it doesn't exist. The same applies to modifying existing instances, whether an attribute on an object or an object itself, as they will appear not to exist. You can, however, delete objects that are instances of defunct classes. Searches for objects that are instances of defunct classes will happily succeed, as will searches on non-defunct classes that contain defunct attributes. All attributes, defunct or not, can be read. This is all required to enable the administrator or application author to clean up and remove the now-defunct object instances and all values from now-defunct attributes.

> Even though a schema object is defunct, it still exists in terms of its distinguishedName, OID, and lDAPDisplayName. You cannot create a second schema object that has these values, but in most cases, you can change them when running Windows 2003 forest functional level. The exception to this is that for attributes used as the RDN attribute for an objectClass, you cannot reuse the OID.

Summary

Carefully designing the changes that you make to the Active Directory schema cannot be stressed highly enough for large corporations or application developers. Selecting a team of Schema Managers and OID Managers and creating documentation to accompany and justify changes will smooth that process. Whether you are a small company or a large multinational, creating sensible structures should mean that you rarely make mistakes and almost never have to make objects defunct.

Hopefully we have shown you not only the perils and pitfalls of modifying the schema, but also why the schema is necessary and how it underpins the entire Active Directory. While you should be cautious when modifying Active Directory, a sensible administrator should have as little to fear from the Active Directory schema as he does from the Windows Registry.

## CHAPTER 15

Backup, Recovery, and Maintenance

A very important though often overlooked aspect of maintaining Active Directory is having a solid disaster recovery plan in place. While the reported incidents of corruption of Active Directory have been minimal, it has happened and is something you should be prepared for regardless of how unlikely it is to occur. Restoring accidentally deleted objects is much more likely to happen than complete corruption, and thus you should be equally prepared for this as well. Do you have a plan in place for what to do if a domain controller that has a FSMO role suddenly goes offline, and you are unable to bring it back? All the scenarios we've just described typically happen under times of duress. That is, clients are complaining or an application is no longer working correctly and people aren't happy. It is during times like this that you don't want to have to scramble to find a solution. Having well-documented and tested procedures to handle these issues is critical.

In this chapter, we will look at how to prepare for failures by backing up Active Directory. We will then describe how you can recover all or portions of your Active Directory from backup. We will then cover how to recover from FSMO failures. Finally, we will look at other preventive maintenance operations you can do to ensure the health of Active Directory.

Backing Up Active Directory

Backing up Active Directory is a straightforward operation. It can be done using the NT Backup utility provided with Windows 2000 and 2003, the Windows Server Backup utility provided with Windows Server 2008, or with a third-party backup package such as Veritas NetBackup. Fortunately, you can back up Active Directory while it is online, so you do not have to worry about taking outages just to perform backups like you do with some other systems.

To back up Active Directory, you have to back up the System State of one or more domain controllers within each domain in the forest. If you want to be able to restore any domain controller in the forest, you'll need to back up every domain controller.

On a Windows 2000 or Windows Server 2003 domain controller, the System State contains the following:

Active Directory
> This includes the files in the NTDS folder that contains the Active Directory database (*ntds.dit*), the checkpoint file (*edb.chk*), transaction log files (*edb*.log*), and reserved transaction logs (*res1.log* and *res2.log*).

Boot Files
> The files necessary for the machine to boot up.

COM+ Class Registration Database
> The database for registered COM components.

Registry
> The contents of the registry.

SYSVOL
> This is the *SYSVOL* share that contains all of the file-based GPO information as well as the *NETLOGON* share, which typically contain user logon and logoff scripts.

Certificate Services
> This applies only to DCs that are running Certificate Services.

 Although most backup packages allow you to perform incremental or differential backups, with Active Directory you can only perform full backups of the system state.

Windows Server 2008 domain controller system-state backups include practically every operating system file in addition to the components listed previously. Consequentially, you will notice a substantial increase in the size of system-state backups on Windows Server 2008.

The user that performs the backup must be a member of the Backup Operators group or have Domain Admins equivalent privileges.

Due to the way Active Directory handles deleted objects, your backups are only good for a certain period of time. When objects are deleted in Active Directory, initially they are not removed completely. A copy of the object still resides in Active Directory for the duration of the tombstone lifetime. The tombstone lifetime value dictates how long Active Directory keeps deleted objects before completely removing them. The tombstone lifetime is configurable and is defined in the `tombStoneLifetime` attribute on the following object:

```
cn=Directory Services, cn=WindowsNT, cn=Services, cn=Configuration, <ForestDN>
```

The default value for `tombStoneLifetime` is 60 days prior to Windows Server 2003 Service Pack 1 and 180 days after that for new forests. This value can be modified, so you should check the `tombStoneLifetime` attribute to see what the value is for your forest. That means deleted objects are purged from Active Directory several months after they are initially deleted. As far as backups go, you should not restore a backup that is older than the tombstone lifetime because deleted objects will be reintroduced. If, for whatever reason, you are not able to get successful backups within the `tombstoneLifetime`, consider increasing the value.

Another issue to be mindful of in regard to how long you keep copies of your backup has to do with passwords. Computer accounts change their passwords every 30 days by default. Domain Controllers will accept the current password as well as one previous password, so if you restore computer objects from a backup that is older than 60 days, those computers will more than likely have to be reset. Trust relationships can also be affected. Like computer accounts, the current and previous passwords are stored with the trust objects, but unlike computer accounts, trust passwords are changed every seven days. That means if you authoritatively restore trust objects from a backup that is older than 14 days, then you may need to reset the trust.

 Disk imaging is specifically not supported for domain controller backups. This covers all instances of imaging from backup of virtual hardware disks to using disk image software like Ghost to special imaging available in various attached storage products. Active Directory is a distributed system running across multiple domain controllers, which each domain controller maintains state for other domain controllers. Imaging various pieces of the distributed system and recovering them separately can have catastrophic results on the consistency of the directory as a whole. Some of the possible issues are USN rollback, lingering objects, and SID rollback.

The only safe way to use disk imaging is to shut down every domain controller in the forest and then image the disks. When you need to restore, you again shut down every domain controller and roll each domain controller back to the same point in time. Even though this is a safe way to do it, it still isn't supported by Microsoft and should only be used in a test environment.

See MS Knowledge Base article 875495 at *http://support.microsoft.com/ kb/875495* for more details.

Using the NT Backup Utility

The NT Backup utility is installed on all Windows 2000 and Windows Server 2003 machines. It is available by going to Start→All Programs→Accessories→System Tools→Backup. You can also start it up by going to Start→Run, entering `ntbackup`, and clicking OK. Figure 15-1 shows the first screen of the NT Backup utility under Windows Server 2003.

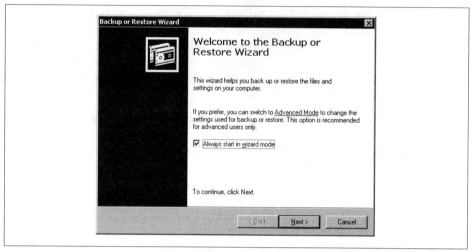

Figure 15-1. NT Backup Wizard

The NT Backup utility can be used to back up the system and also to perform a restore. We will cover restores in the next section. If you click on the "Advanced Mode" link in the first screen, you'll then see a screen such as that in Figure 15-2.

In this case, we clicked on the Backup tab and then selected the box beside System State. We could also back up any of the other drives if we wanted, but the System State is all that is required when doing a basic restore of Active Directory.

By clicking the "Start Backup" button, we can kick off the backup. In Figure 15-2, we configured the *D:* drive to be the location where the backup file gets stored. This could have been to a remote file server or other backup media if we wanted.

We can also schedule a backup to run at an interval of our choosing by clicking the "Start Backup" button and then the "Schedule" button. After that, we click the "Properties" button and the screen shown in Figure 15-3 pops up.

In this case, we've configured the backup to run once a day at 7:30 A.M. The screen in Figure 15-3 is actually part of Scheduled Tasks, which is the job scheduling system available in Windows 2000 and Windows Server 2003.

Using Windows Server Backup

Windows Server 2008 introduces a completely revamped backup and restore utility. If you're used to NT Backup, you'll have some adjusting to do as the tool has been completely redesigned and has some significant new limitations. In the interest of space, we'll only discuss the functionality specific to backing up and restoring Active Directory in this book. For a full introduction to Windows Server Backup, visit *http://technet2 .microsoft.com/windowsserver2008/en/library/00162c92-a834-43f9-9e8a -71aeb25fa4ad1033.mspx*.

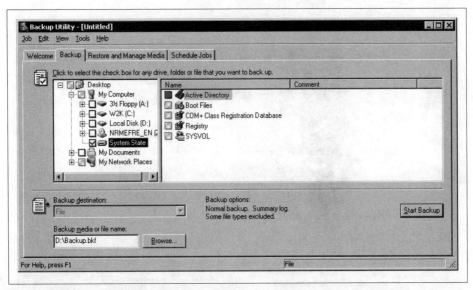

Figure 15-2. Advanced mode NT backup

Windows Server Backup is not installed by default. In order to use Windows Server Backup, you must install the feature using Server Manager.

In order to launch Windows Server Backup (WSB), look under Administrative Tools on the Start menu for Windows Server Backup. The tool has been converted to an MMC as shown in Figure 15-4.

You can launch WSB directly by going to Start→Run→wbadmin.msc in lieu of browsing for it on the Start menu.

Unfortunately, the Windows Server Backup GUI does not support generating a system-state backup, but instead only full-volume backups. In order to generate a system-state backup, you'll need to use the `wbadmin` command-line utility.

Windows Server Backup must backup to a volume that does not contain any components of the system state backup. This means that you cannot select a volume that contains the system files, Active Directory database (ntds.dit), Sysvol, Active Directory transaction logs, and so forth. The backup will be created in a directory structure on the drive specified under *<Drive>:\WindowsImageBackup\<HostName>\SystemState Backup*. For information about working around this limitation, see the upcoming side-bar "Allowing System-State Backups to Any Volume." If you do not have this setting

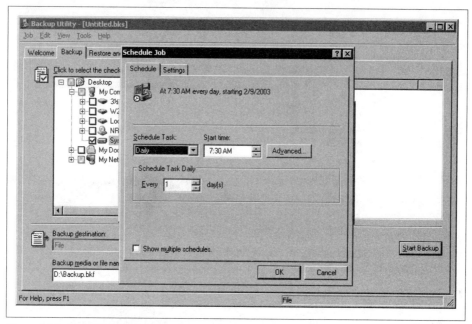

Figure 15-3. Scheduling NT Backup

enabled and you don't specify a volume that is not in scope for the backup, you will receive an error similar to Figure 15-5. You can alternatively specify a network path to backup to. Windows Server Backup will always overwrite the previous backup of the machine at the given network path.

Allowing System-State Backups to Any Volume

By default you cannot create a system-state backup on a volume that includes files that are part of the backup. There is, however, a registry value you can set to work around this. Keep in mind that the risk of using this registry value is that if the backup data is modified during the backup, the backup will fail. You will also need to use twice the amount of space as volume shadow copy will create a shadow copy of the backup.

To enable this functionality, create a REG_DWORD called **AllowSSBToAnyVolume** under *HKLM\SYSTEM\CurrentControlSet\Services\wbengine\SystemStateBackup*. Set the value of AllowSSBToAnyVolume to **1** to enable system state backups to a volume that is included in the backup.

For more information on this registry setting, see *http://support.microsoft.com/kb/944530*.

Due to the risks of making this change, we recommend that if you are going to use Windows Server Backup on your domain controllers that you setup your partition scheme specifically to have a separate volume to store backups on.

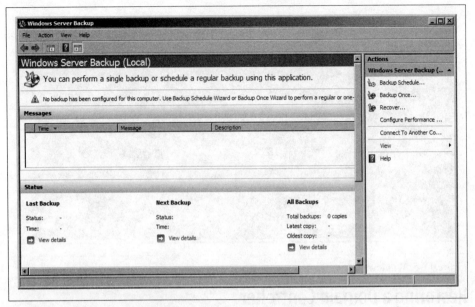

Figure 15-4. Windows Server Backup

The command to create a system state backup stored on the E: drive is: **wbadmin start systemstatebackup -backuptarget:E: -quiet**. If you don't specify **-quiet**, you will be prompted to continue before the backup completes. On our test systems with a freshly created Active Directory forest on Windows Server 2008 Enterprise, the total system state backup size was about six gigabytes (6GB).

In order to schedule backups of Windows Server 2008 domain controllers, you'll need to use the Windows Task Scheduler to create a scheduled task that calls **wbadmin** at the appropriate time. While the system state backup will include the contents of any Active Directory Integrated DNS zones, it will not include any standard primary/secondary zone files that are stored on the filesystem. In order to back these zone files up, you will need to back up the volume that contains the DNS zone files. Windows Server Backup does not support backing up specific files/folders on a drive like NT Backup did, so there is substantial overhead involved in this option. The alternative is to include in your backup script a step that copies the DNS zone files to the backup destination. One such script which can backup and restore DNS zones is available courtesy of Dean Wells at *http://www.briandesmond.com/ad4/dnsdump.txt*.

> For more information on Windows Server Backup and Active Directory, see the *Step-by-Step Guide for Windows Server 2008 AD DS Backup and Recovery* at *http://technet2.microsoft.com/windowsserver2008/en/li brary/778ff4c7-623d-4475-ba70-4453f964d4911033.mspx*.

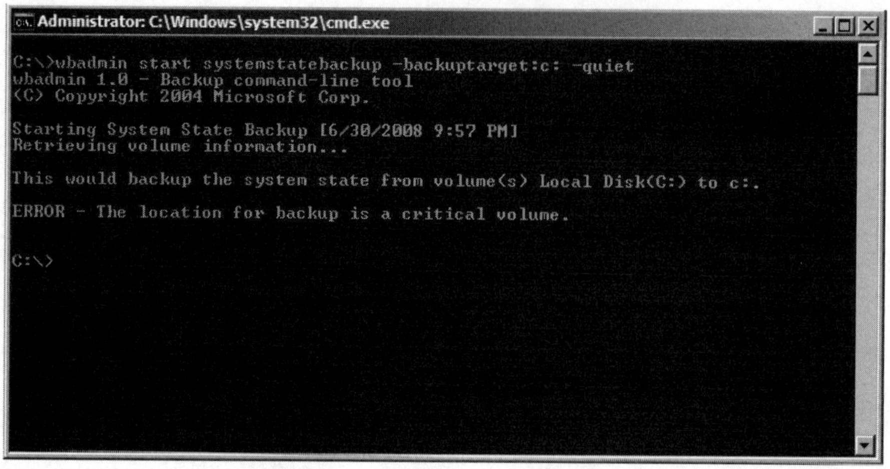

```
Administrator: C:\Windows\system32\cmd.exe                                    _ □ ×

C:\>wbadmin start systemstatebackup -backuptarget:c: -quiet
wbadmin 1.0 - Backup command-line tool
(C) Copyright 2004 Microsoft Corp.

Starting System State Backup [6/30/2008 9:57 PM]
Retrieving volume information...

This would backup the system state from volume(s) Local Disk(C:) to c:.

ERROR - The location for backup is a critical volume.

C:\>
```

Figure 15-5. Windows Server Backup error

Restoring a Domain Controller

One of the benefits of Active Directory is built-in redundancy. When you lose a single domain controller, the impact can and generally should be insignificant. With many services, such as DHCP, the architecture dictates a dependency on a specific server. When that server becomes unavailable, clients are impacted. Over the years, failover or redundancy has been built into most of these services, including DHCP. With Active Directory, the architecture is built around redundancy. Clients are not dependent on a single DC; they can failover to another DC seamlessly if a failure occurs.

When a failure does occur, you should ask yourself several questions to assess the impact:

Is the domain controller the only one for the domain?
> This is the worst-case scenario. The redundancy in Active Directory applies only if you have more than one domain controller in a domain. If there is only one, you have a single point of failure. You could irrevocably lose the domain unless you can get that domain controller back online or restore it from backup.

Does the domain controller own a FSMO role?
> The five FSMO roles outlined in Chapter 2 play an important part in Active Directory. FSMO roles are not redundant, so if a FSMO role owner becomes unavailable, you may need to seize the FSMO role on another domain controller. Check out the FSMO recovery section later in this chapter for more information.

Is the domain controller a Global Catalog server?
> The Global Catalog is a function that any domain controller can perform if enabled. But if you have only one Global Catalog server in a site and it becomes unavailable,

it can impact users' ability to log in. As long as clients can access a Global Catalog, even if it isn't in the most optimal location, they will be able to log in. If a site without a Global Catalog for some reason loses connectivity with the rest of the network, it would impact users' ability to log in. With Windows Server 2003 and newer, you can enable universal group caching on a per-site basis to limit this potential issue, but only if the user is not using a `userPrincipalName` for authentication.

Is the domain controller necessary from a capacity perspective?

If your domain controllers are running near capacity and one fails, it could overwhelm the remaining servers. At this point, clients could start to experience login failures or extreme slowness when authenticating.

Are any other services, such as Exchange, relying on that specific domain controller?

Exchange is a heavy consumer of Active Directory Services, especially AD Global Catalogs. Failure of a domain controller that Exchange is using can cause considerable issues in the mail environment depending on the versions of the Outlook and Exchange being used. More recent versions of Exchange and Outlook (2003 and newer) handle outages better than older versions. During the outage period, mail delivery could be impacted along with client lookups. Exchange is just one example, but it illustrates that you have to be careful of this when introducing Active Directory-enabled services into your environment.

These questions can help you assess the urgency of restoring the domain controller. If you answered no to all of the questions, the domain controller can stay down for some period without significant impact.

When you've identified that you need to restore a domain controller, there are two options to choose from: restoring from replication or restoring from a backup.

Restore from Replication

One option for restoring a domain controller is to bring up a freshly installed or repaired machine and promote it into Active Directory. You would use this option if you had a single domain controller failure due to hardware and either did not have a recent backup of the machine or you didn't want to go through the process of restoring the DC from a backup. This method allows you to replace the server in AD by promoting a newly installed machine and allowing replication to copy all of the data to the DC. Here are the steps to perform this type of restore:

1. Remove the failed DC from AD. The old remnants of the domain controller must be removed from Active Directory before you promote the freshly installed server. We describe the exact steps to do this shortly.

2. Rebuild OS. Reinstall the operating system and any other applications you support on your domain controllers.

3. Promote server. After you've allowed time for the DC removal process to replicate throughout the forest, you can then promote the new server into AD.

4. Configure any necessary roles. If the failed server had any FSMO roles or was a global catalog or a DNS server, you can configure the new server to have these roles.

 One possible best practice is to keep a spare server that already has the OS and any other software installed ready-to-ship or onsite at all locations. That way, if you have a major failure with one of your domain controllers, you can use the spare server without needing to stress over getting the hardware replaced immediately in the failed machine. Alternatively, just have additional domain controller capacity in the primary sites that failures would be most painful for, especially for Exchange. This alternative strategy is generally much more common than keeping spare hardware in every location.

The biggest potential drawback with this method is the restore time. Depending on the size of your DIT file and how fast your network connections are between the new DC and the server it will replicate with, the restore time could be several hours or even days. Restore time can be dramatically reduced with a new option in Windows Server 2003, called Install from Media. It allows you to take files from a system-state backup from one domain controller and use them to quickly promote another domain controller. It may possibly be faster to compress and then copy these backup files over the network to the remote site or ship the files on some other media to the site versus trying to replicate the entire DIT over the WAN. For more information on this, see the section "Install from Media," later in this chapter.

Manually removing a domain controller from Active Directory

One of the key steps with the restore-from-replication method is removing the objects that are associated with the domain controller before it gets added to AD again. Windows Server 2008 allows you to remove a failed domain controller using the Active Directory Users and Computers GUI. Select the computer object representing the failed domain controller and delete it. You will receive a prompt similar to Figure 15-6 asking you to confirm that the domain controller is, in fact, permanently offline. Once you confirm this, the metadata cleanup steps will be performed automatically.

Under Windows Server 2003, this is a three-step process. The first step is to remove the associated metadata with the *ntdsutil* utility. The following example shows the commands necessary to remove the DC3 domain controller, which is in the RTP site, from the *emea.mycorp.com* domain:

```
C:\>ntdsutil
ntdsutil: metadata cleanup
metadata cleanup: connections
```

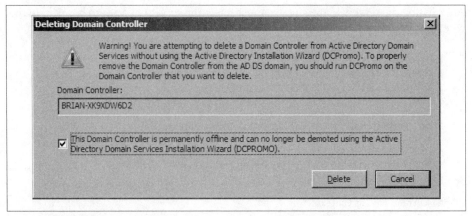

Figure 15-6. Windows Server 2008 removing a failed domain controller

Next, we need to connect to an existing domain controller in the domain that contains the domain controller you want to remove. In this case, we connect to DC2:

```
server connections: connect to server dc2
Binding to dc2 ...
Connected to dc2 using credentials of locally logged on user.
server connections: quit
metadata cleanup: select operation target
```

Now we need to select the domain the domain controller is in. In this case, it is *emea .mycorp.com*:

```
select operation target: list domains
Found 2 domain(s)
0 - DC=mycorp,DC=com
1 - DC=emea,DC=mycorp,DC=com
select operation target: select domain 1
No current site
Domain - DC=emea,DC=mycorp,DC=com
No current server
No current Naming Context
```

Next we must select the site the domain controller is in. In this case, it is the RTP site:

```
select operation target: list sites
Found 4 site(s)
0 - CN=Default-First-Site-Name,CN=Sites,CN=Configuration,DC=mycorp,DC=com
1 - CN=RTP,CN=Sites,CN=Configuration,DC=mycorp,DC=com
2 - CN=SJC,CN=Sites,CN=Configuration,DC=mycorp,DC=com
3 - CN=NYC,CN=Sites,CN=Configuration,DC=mycorp,DC=com
select operation target: select site 1
Site - CN=RTP,CN=Sites,CN=Configuration,DC=mycorp,DC=com
Domain - DC=emea,DC=mycorp,DC=com
No current server
No current Naming Context
```

After listing the servers in the site, we must select the server we want to remove. In this case, it is DC3:

```
select operation target: list servers in site
Found 3 server(s)
0 - CN=DC1,CN=Servers,CN=RTP,CN=Sites,CN=Configuration,DC=mycorp,DC=com
1 - CN=DC2,CN=Servers,CN=RTP,CN=Sites,CN=Configuration,DC=mycorp,DC=com
2 - CN=DC3,CN=Servers,CN=RTP,CN=Sites,CN=Configuration,DC=mycorp,DC=com
select operation target: select server 2
Site - CN=RTP,CN=Sites,CN=Configuration, DC=mycorp,DC=com
Domain - DC=emea,DC=mycorp,DC=com
Server - CN=DC3,CN=Servers,CN=RTP,CN=Sites,CN=Configuration,DC=mycorp,DC=com
    DSA object - CN=NTDS Settings,CN=DC3,CN=Servers,CN=RTP,CN=Sites,
CN=Configuration,DC=mycorp,DC=com
    Computer object - CN=DC3,OU=Domain Controllers,DC=emea,DC=mycorp,DC=com
No current Naming Context
select operation target: quit
```

 This process has been considerably simplified in Windows Server 2003 Service Pack 1; however, you need to know the distinguishedName of the Domain Controller's server object in the configuration container. It is recommended that you simply follow the preceding directions for removing dead domain controllers, as there is less possibility of a mistake.

The last step removes the metadata for the selected domain controller:

```
metadata cleanup: remove selected server
```

At this point, you should receive confirmation that the DC was removed successfully. If you receive an error that the object could not be found, it might have already been removed if you tried to demote the server with *dcpromo*.

If you are performing this procedure on a domain controller that is running a version of Windows prior to Windows Server 2003 SP1, you will then need to manually remove a few more objects from Active Directory. See MS Knowledge Base article 216498 at *http://support.microsoft.com/kb/216498* for details on this. You will need to manually remove the server object under the site in the configuration partition regardless of which version of Windows you are running.

Restore from Backup

Another option to reestablish a failed domain controller is to restore the machine using a backup. This approach does not require you to remove any objects from Active Directory. When you restore a DC from a backup, the latest changes will replicate to make it current. If time is of the essence and the backup file is immediately available, this will be the quicker approach because only the latest changes since the last backup, instead of the whole directory tree, will be replicated over the network.

Here are the steps to restore from backup:

1. Rebuild OS. Reinstall the operating system and any other applications you support on your domain controllers. Leave the server as a standalone or member server.

2. Restore from backup. Use your backup package—e.g., NT Backup—to restore at least the System State onto the machine. In the next section, we will walk through the NT Backup and Windows Server Backup utilities to show how this is done.

3. Reboot server and allow replication to complete. If the failed server had any FSMO roles or was a GC, you can configure the new server to have these roles.

It is also possible to restore the backup of a machine onto a machine that has different hardware. Here are some issues to be aware of when doing so:

- The number of drives and drive letters should be the same.

- The disk drive controller and configuration should be the same.

- The attached cards, such as network cards, video adapter, and processors, should be the same. After the restore, you can install the new cards, which should be recognized by Plug and Play.

- The *boot.ini* from the failed machine will be restored, which may not be compatible with the new hardware, so you'll need to make any necessary changes.

- If the Hardware Abstraction Layer (HAL) is different between machines, you can run into problems. For example, if the failed machine was single processor and the new machine is multiprocessor, you will have a compatibility problem. The only workaround is to copy the *Hal.dll*, which is not included as part of System State, from the old machine and put it on the new machine. The obvious drawback to this is it will make the new multiprocessor machine act like a single processor machine.

Because there are numerous things that can go wrong with restoring to different hardware, we highly suggest you test and document the process thoroughly; refer to MS Knowledge Base article 263532 at *http://support.microsoft.com/kb/263532*. The last thing you want to do is troubleshoot hardware compatibility issues when you are trying to restore a crucial domain controller.

Install from Media

One of the challenges of working with Active Directory in a highly distributed environment is often the impact of replicating the initial copy of the database when a new domain controller is promoted. Over a slow WAN link with a large database, this operation can easily take days or weeks. While this is running it can also put an unmanageable load on WAN links that may already be fully utilized without the burden of replicating a full Active Directory database.

Windows Server 2003 introduced a new feature called *Install from Media* (IFM) that allows domain controllers to be promoted from a backup of another domain controller

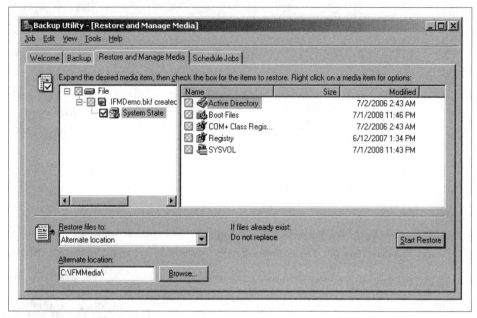

Figure 15-7. Restoring to an alternate location

in the domain. The only replication that will take place in order for the promotion to complete is the changes that have occurred since the backup was taken. The backup image can be either copied to the domain controller via SMB or another protocol, or shipped out of band using a commercial courier. Shipping the backup this way substantially lessens the burden on the WAN for promotion of the domain controller and in some scenarios can substantially speed up the promotion process.

The process for promoting a domain controller from IFM media varies substantially between Windows Server 2003 and Windows Server 2008 domain controllers. On Windows Server 2008 you must create the IFM media using `ntdsutil` and then pointing the dcpromo wizard at the folder `ntdsutil` creates. Windows Server 2003 domain controllers require that you restore a system state backup taken with NT Backup to an "alternate location" and then point the dcpromo wizard at this folder.

Creating and using IFM media on Windows Server 2003

Working with IFM on Windows Server 2003 is very similar to doing so on Windows Server 2008. There are a few key differences that we've highlighted here:

- You must create the IFM using a system state backup from NT Backup.
- To use the backup, you must restore it on the target system using the "Restore files to Alternate Location" option shown in Figure 15-7.
- Dcpromo must be started directly in advanced mode by running `dcpromo /adv`.

Creating and using IFM media on Windows Server 2008

Creating the IFM media is a straightforward process as shown in the following example. You will be given the choice of which type of media you'd like to create:

- Full writeable domain controller (without sysvol)
- Full writeable domain controller (with sysvol)
- Read-only domain controller (without sysvol)
- Read-only domain controller (with sysvol)

The difference between full domain controller and read-only domain controller media is that the latter does not contain any passwords or other secrets. While you can include the contents of sysvol, the dcpromo wizard will not use it during promotion to seed the local sysvol share:

```
ntdsutil: activate instance ntds
Active instance set to "ntds".
ifm: create full c:\ifmmedia
Creating snapshot...
Snapshot set {f15b79ab-9b0b-4845-9583-eb6c7a49bee9} generated successfully.
Snapshot {b1681552-114b-44b9-b547-9a1b15104907} mounted as C:\$SNAP_200807012230
_VOLUMEC$\
Snapshot {b1681552-114b-44b9-b547-9a1b15104907} is already mounted.
Initiating DEFRAGMENTATION mode...
     Source Database: C:\$SNAP_200807012230_VOLUMEC$\Windows\NTDS\ntds.dit
     Target Database: c:\ifmmedia\Active Directory\ntds.dit

            Defragmentation  Status (% complete)

     0    10   20   30   40   50   60   70   80   90   100
     |----|----|----|----|----|----|----|----|----|----|
     ..................................................

Copying registry files...
Copying c:\ifmmedia\registry\SYSTEM
Copying c:\ifmmedia\registry\SECURITY
Snapshot {b1681552-114b-44b9-b547-9a1b15104907} unmounted.
IFM media created successfully in c:\ifmmedia
```

In the preceding example, we've created IFM media for promoting a full writeable domain controller excluding the contents of the sysvol. Figure 15-8 shows the contents of *c:\ifmmedia*.

You can use IFM media created on a 32-bit domain controller to promote a 64-bit domain controller and vice versa. You cannot, however, use RODC media to promote a full domain controller.

Once you have created the IFM media you can copy it to the new/target domain controller using whatever means are most convenient. In order to utilize the media, you

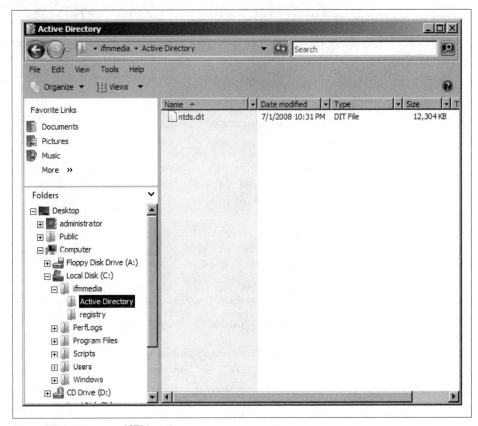

Figure 15-8. Contents of IFM media

will need to start dcpromo in advanced mode. Advanced mode is accessible via checking the "Advanced Mode" checkbox on the first page of the wizard as shown in Figure 15-9. You can also run `dcpromo /adv`.

As you proceed through the wizard, you will be shown a wizard page similar to Figure 15-10 that gives you the option to use the IFM media.

Once the wizard completes it will modify the backup of the ntds.dit database from the source domain controller and then replicate any changes since the backup of the database was created.

Restoring Active Directory

No one ever wants to be in a position where you have to restore Active Directory, but nevertheless you should prepare for it. Restoring Active Directory comes in a few different flavors, which we'll cover now.

Figure 15-9. Starting dcpromo in advanced mode

Non-Authoritative Restore

A non-authoritative restore is a restore where you simply bring a domain controller back to a known good state using a backup. You then let replication resync the contents of the latest changes in Active Directory since the backup. The restore-from-backup method we described earlier to handle DC failures is an example of a non-authoritative restore. The only difference between that scenario and the one we'll describe here is that previously we assumed that the failed server you rebuilt or replaced was not a domain controller yet. There may be some circumstances when you want to perform a similar restore, but the server is already configured as a domain controller. One ex-ample might be if some changes were made on a particular domain controller that you wanted to take back. If you were able to disconnect the domain controller from the network in time before it replicated, you could perform a non-authoritative restore to get it back to a known state before the changes were made. This would effectively nullify the changes as long as they didn't replicate to another server.

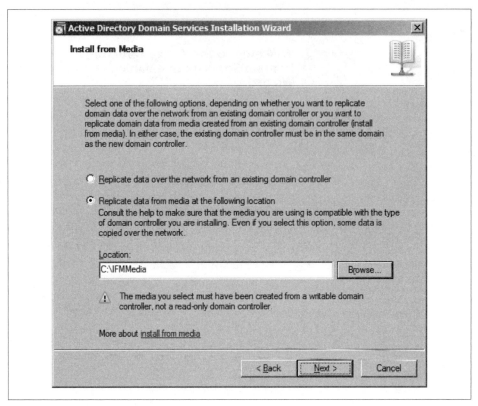

Figure 15-10. Using install from Media

 You cannot restore "null" values from a backup. If you erroneously populate a series of attributes on a domain controller that were not previously populated and then perform a restore, those attributes will not become null once again. This is because Active Directory does not store null values in the database, and thus it is impossible to recover them because they're not there.

A non-authoritative restore simply restores Active Directory without marking any of the data as authoritative. This means that any changes that have happened since the backup will replicate to the restored server. Also, any changes that were made on the server that had not replicated will be lost.

To perform a non-authoritative restore of a domain controller, you need to boot the DC into "Directory Services Restore Mode." The reason you have to do this is that when a domain controller is live, it locks the Active Directory database (*ntds.dit*) in exclusive mode. That means that no other processes can modify its contents. To restore over the *ntds.dit* file, you must boot into DS Restore Mode, which is a version of Safe

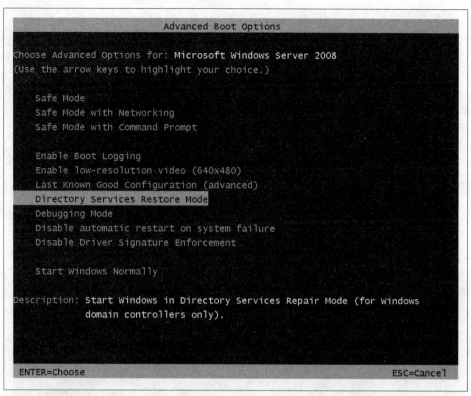

```
                    Advanced Boot Options

Choose Advanced Options for: Microsoft Windows Server 2008
(Use the arrow keys to highlight your choice.)


    Safe Mode
    Safe Mode with Networking
    Safe Mode with Command Prompt

    Enable Boot Logging
    Enable low-resolution video (640x480)
    Last Known Good Configuration (advanced)
    Directory Services Restore Mode
    Debugging Mode
    Disable automatic restart on system failure
    Disable Driver Signature Enforcement

    Start Windows Normally

Description: Start Windows in Directory Services Repair Mode (for Windows
            domain controllers only).




ENTER=Choose                                              ESC=Cancel
```

Figure 15-11. Directory Services Restore Mode

Mode for domain controllers. If you try to restore a live domain controller, you'll get an error and be unable to continue.

You can get into DS Restore Mode by hitting the F8 key during the initial system startup. After doing so, you'll see the screen shown in Figure 15-11.

Once you receive a logon prompt, you have to log in with the DS Restore Administrator account and password. You set the password for this account when you initially *dcpromo* the machine into Active Directory. Since Active Directory is offline in DS Restore Mode, you have to log in with the local Administrator account that is stored in the local SAM and that can only be used in this mode.

Restoring with NT Backup

After logging into the system, you'll need to bring up the NT Backup utility or other backup software. We will walk through how to do the restore using NT Backup. After clicking Next at the initial wizard screen, you'll see the screen shown in Figure 15-12.

Select Restore Files and Settings and click Next. You'll now be brought to a screen to select what to restore. You should restore at least the System State, but you can also

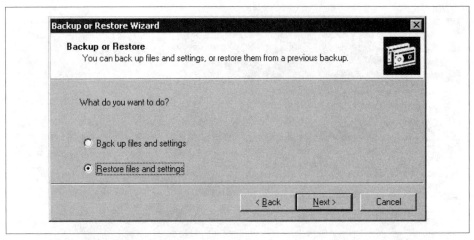

Figure 15-12. Backup or restore options

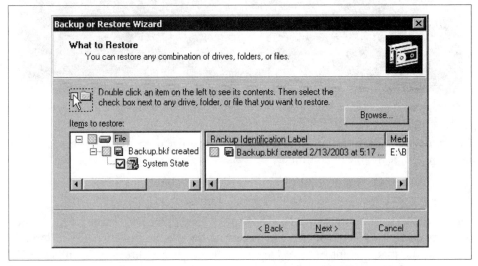

Figure 15-13. Restore selection

restore the System Drive and other drives if necessary. Figure 15-13 shows the selection screen.

After you've made your selection and clicked Next, the summary screen will be displayed, showing what will be restored. Before finishing, you need to click the Advanced button and walk through the advanced screens to ensure that junction points will be restored, as shown in Figure 15-14.

Click Finish to kick off the restore. After the restore is complete, you'll need to reboot into normal mode. At this point, the domain controller will replicate the latest changes

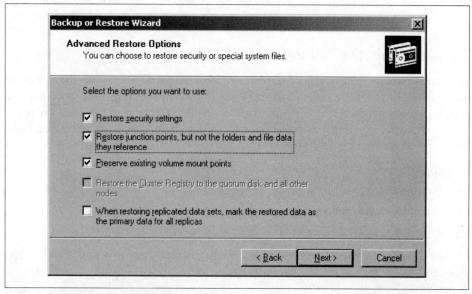

Figure 15-14. Restore junction points

with its replication partners. Give time for the replication to complete and then monitor the server and check the event logs to make sure it is functioning correctly.

Restoring with Windows Server Backup

Much like creating the system state backup, restoring a system state backup under Windows Server Backup requires the use of the command-line utility wbadmin in lieu of the GUI. Once you have started in DS Restore Mode, the first step is to list the available backup versions for restore by running **wbadmin get versions**:

```
wbadmin 1.0 - Backup command-line tool
(C) Copyright 2004 Microsoft Corp.

Backup time: 6/30/2008 8:25 PM
Backup target: Fixed Disk labeled E:
Version identifier: 07/01/2008-01:25
Can Recover: Application(s), System State
```

Once you have identified the backup you need to restore, you will need to provide the version identifier to the wbadmin startsystemstaterecovery command. In this case, we will restore the 07/01/2008-01:25 backup and run the command:

wbadmin startsystemstaterecovery -version:*07/01/2008-01:25*

If you need to perform an authoritative restore of the SYSVOL as well, you should include the -authsysvol switch as well.

Once the restore has completed, reboot the server into normal mode and monitor the event logs to ensure correct functionality.

Partial Authoritative Restore

In some situations, you may need to restore data in Active Directory. In the examples we've shown so far of restoring a domain controller and performing a non-authoritative restore, we simply wanted to get the domain controller back up and running. There are certain situations, though, in which you may need to do an authoritative restore. Here are a few examples:

- Accidental deletion of important objects
- Accidental deletion of a subtree
- Corruption of objects or the entire directory
- Reversing certain object additions or modifications

In all of these scenarios, you can do a partial authoritative restore to reverse the changes. If the entire directory gets corrupted, you'll need to do a complete authoritative restore, which we will touch on shortly.

 You cannot authoritatively restore the schema naming context.

You have two options for doing an authoritative restore. You can either find a domain controller that has the data it is supposed to, perhaps because the changes haven't replicated to it yet, or you can restore the data from a backup. In either case, you need to boot into DS Restore Mode as described in the previous section. Again, this is necessary due to the fact that the Active Directory database is locked when the DC is live, and no modifications can be made. Once you are in DS Restore Mode, you can restore from backup if necessary, as described earlier.

At this point we need to mark the data we want restored as authoritative in our offline Active Directory database. This is done with the *ntdsutil* utility. There are several options to choose from under the `authoritative restore` menu shown here:

```
ntdsutil: authoritative restore
authoritative restore: ?
    ?                              - Show this help information
    Create ldif file(s) from %s    - Creates ldif file(s) using specified
                                     authoritatively restored objects list
                                     to recreate back-links of those objects.
    Help                           - Show this help information
    List NC CRs                    - Lists Partitions and cross-refs.  You need
                                     the cross-ref of a Application Directory
                                     Partition to restore it.
    Quit                           - Return to the prior menu
```

```
Restore database                  - Authoritatively restore entire database
Restore database verinc %d        - ... and override version increase
Restore object %s                 - Authoritatively restore an object
Restore object %s verinc %d       - ... and override version increase
Restore subtree %s                - Authoritatively restore a subtree
Restore subtree %s verinc %d      - ... and override version increase
authoritative restore:
```

When doing a partial restore, you can use either the **restore object %s** subcommand to restore a single object or the **restore subtree %s** subcommand to restore an entire subtree of objects. In the following example, we will restore the jsmith user object:

```
authoritative restore: restore object cn=jsmith,ou=sales,dc=mycorp,dc=com
Opening DIT database... Done.
 The current time is 08-10-05 00:15.25.
Most recent database update occured at 08-09-05 21:48.51.
Increasing attribute version numbers by 100000.
 Counting records that need updating...
Records found: 0000000001
Done.
  Found 1 records to update.
 Updating records...
Records remaining: 0000000000
Done.
Successfully updated 1 records.
 The following text file with a list of authoritatively restored
objects has been created in the current working directory:
        ar_20050810-001525_objects.txt
 One or more specified objects have back-links in this domain.
The following LDIF files with link restore operations have
 been created in the current working directory:
        ar_20050810-001525_links_ad.loc.ldf
 Authoritative Restore completed successfully.
authoritative restore: quit
```

As you can see, *ntdsutil* increases the object's version number by 100,000. This is how it is marked as authoritative in the database. After you reboot into normal mode, the domain controller will check with its replication partners and determine that the jsmith user object has a higher version than its partners have. It will then replicate this out to them, and likewise, all other objects that have been updated on the partner will be replicated to this server.

 If, for whatever reason, the auto-increment of 100,000 is not enough for the object(s), you can use the alternate subcommand of **restoreobject %s verinc %d** where %d is the version increase to increment.

Depending on the version of *ntdsutil*, you could see different results than what you see here. The utility had some major changes incorporated in Windows Server 2003 Service Pack 1 version. New in this version, you will notice that it has created an LDF file. This file will contain any linked attribute values attached to the object in the same domain; this allows for recovery of group membership and other linked attributes.

Complete Authoritative Restore

Restoring the entire Active Directory database is similar in concept to restoring individual objects or subtrees, except you are restoring all of the objects, with the exception of the schema. This should be done with caution and only under the most extreme situations. We highly recommend that you test this out in a lab environment to ensure you have the process correctly documented and you actually have experience with doing restores.

Again, to run the restore command, you have to be in DS Restore Mode, and you need to have restored the system from backup, as described previously in this chapter. The following is example output from the **restore database** subcommand:

```
authoritative restore: restore database
Opening DIT database... Done.
   The current time is 08-10-05 00:39.46.
Most recent database update occured at 08-09-05 21:48.51.
Increasing attribute version numbers by 100000.
 Counting records that need updating...
Records found: 0000001725
Done.
   Found 1725 records to update.
 Updating records...
Records remaining: 0000000000
Done.
   Successfully updated 1725 records.
 The following text file with a list of authoritatively
restored objects has been created in the current working directory:
        ar_20050810-003946_objects.txt
 One or more specified objects have back-links in this domain.
 The following LDIF files with link restore operations have
 been created in the current working directory:
        ar_20050810-003946_links_ad.loc-Configuration.ldf
        ar_20050810-003946_links_ad.loc.ldf
 Authoritative Restore completed successfully.
 authoritative restore: quit
```

If you have to perform a complete authoritative restore, the assumption is that something catastrophic happened on a domain controller that caused some form of global irreparable Active Directory corruption. The safest thing may in fact be to restore one domain controller per domain and rebuild the rest. You would need to manually remove each of the rebuilt domain controllers from Active Directory and then re-promote each. Again, this is only a suggestion, and each situation must be thoroughly thought out before taking such drastic measures. If you have a thorough understanding of the processes and procedures involved and practice them, you will certainly be better prepared to tackle such an eventuality. For the Microsoft documentation on Active

Directory Forest Recovery best practices, see *http://technet2.microsoft.com/windows server/en/library/c5db2957-b932-4f55-b7fd-9f1e2442fde61033.mspx*.

Working with Snapshots

One of the new features for Active Directory in Windows Server 2008 is the notion of *snapshots*. With snapshots, you can make a point in time copy of the Active Directory database. This feature uses the Volume Shadow Copy (VSS) service to create the snapshot. Once you have created a snapshot, you can mount it using the `dsamain` command-line utility and browse it like the live Active Directory database using `ldp` or Active Directory Users and Computers.

The benefits of this new capability are endless, but some ideas include:

- Looking at permissions or other settings prior to modification in case you need to rollback
- Exporting objects or values that were inadvertently modified and then importing them back to your production directory
- Determining which backup to perform a restore from
- Restoring a complete object with a third-party tool

 A free third-party tool for restoring objects from a snapshot is available at *http://www.one-identity.net/tools/snapshot/*.

Creating the snapshot is a straight forward process using the `ntdsutil` command-line utility:

```
C:\>ntdsutil
ntdsutil: snapshot
snapshot: activate instance ntds
Active instance set to "ntds".
snapshot: create
Creating snapshot...
Snapshot set {e73b71cd-7e2b-40ee-8871-69575f4b1e66} generated successfully.
```

Once you have created a snapshot, you can mount it and make it available to LDAP clients. Mounting the snapshot consists of either specifying the GUID generated in the previous step or selecting the snapshot from a list. In this example, we select the snapshot from a list:

```
snapshot: list all
 1: 2008/06/30:22:44 {e73b71cd-7e2b-40ee-8871-69575f4b1e66}
 2:    C: {c8bc59c0-f20b-4bac-a12a-ab6eab737f0c}

snapshot: mount 1
```

```
Snapshot {c8bc59c0-f20b-4bac-a12a-ab6eab737f0c} mounted as
C:\$SNAP_200806302244_VOLUMEC$\
```

Once the snapshot has been mounted in the filesystem, you can use the dsamain utility
to mount the snapshot version of the Active Directory and make it accessible via LDAP.
Dsamain requires that you provide the path to the database to mount as well as a port
number to listen on. If you only specify the LDAP port, dsamain will automatically use
the subsequent three ports for LDAPS, Global Catalog, and Global Catalog SSL. Thus
if you specify port 10389, ports 10390, 10392, and 10393 will also be used. The command to mount the database in this scenario is:

```
dsamain -dbpath C:\$SNAP_200806302244_VOLUMEC$\Windows\NTDS\ntds.dit -ldapport 10389
```

You can then use LDP or any LDAP client to connect to port 10389 as shown in
Figure 15-15.

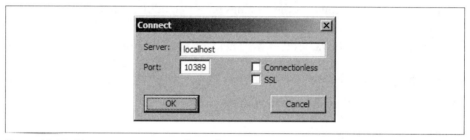

Figure 15-15. Connecting to a mounted snapshot

You can also connect to mounted snapshots using Active Directory Users and Computers (ADUC):

1. Launch ADUC.

2. Right click the domain and select Change Domain Controller...

3. Select This Domain Controller or AD LDS instance.

4. Click <Type a Directory Server name[:port] here>.

5. Enter the name of a domain controller or the localhost as shown in Figure 15-16
   and click OK.

Once you're done with a snapshot, you need to stop the dsamain instance and unmount
the snapshot. To stop the dsamain instance, simply press Ctrl+C in the command window and it will exit. Unmounting the snapshot is similar to mounting it:

```
C:\>ntdsutil
ntdsutil: snapshot
snapshot: list all
 1: 2008/06/30:22:44 {e73b71cd-7e2b-40ee-8871-69575f4b1e66}
 2:    C: {c8bc59c0-f20b-4bac-a12a-ab6eab737f0c} C:\$SNAP_200806302244_VOLUMEC$\

snapshot: unmount 1
Snapshot {c8bc59c0-f20b-4bac-a12a-ab6eab737f0c} unmounted.
```

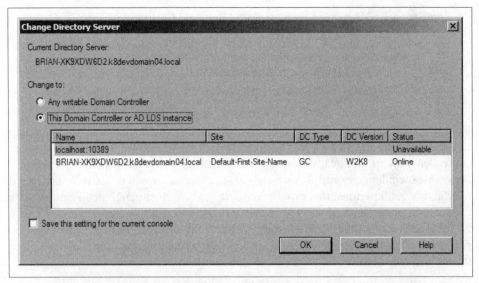

Figure 15-16. Connecting to a mounted snapshot with ADUC

In summary, Active Directory snapshots allow you to take a point-in-time copy of the Active Directory database on a domain controller and mount it for parallel access via LDAP. For more information on this functionality, check out the step-by-step guide at *http://technet2.microsoft.com/windowsserver2008/en/library/778ff4c7-623d-4475 -ba70-4453f964d4911033.mspx*.

FSMO Recovery

The FSMO roles were described in Chapter 2. These roles are considered special in Active Directory because they are hosted on a single domain controller within a forest or domain. The architecture of Active Directory is highly redundant, except for FSMO roles. It is for this reason that you need to have a plan on how to handle FSMO failures.

While it would be a really nice feature if domain controllers could detect that they are being shut down and gracefully transfer any FSMO roles to other domain controllers, this isn't reality. Without having the graceful FSMO role transfer, you have to perform manual transfers. Manually transferring a role is pretty straightforward. You bring up the appropriate Active Directory snap-in, bring up the FSMO property page, select a new role owner, and perform the transfer. Here is a list of the FSMO roles and the corresponding snap-in that can be used to transfer it to another domain controller:

- Schema Master: Active Directory Schema
- Domain Naming Master: Active Directory Domains and Trusts
- RID Master: Active Directory Users and Computers
- PDC Emulator: Active Directory Users and Computers

- Infrastructure Master: Active Directory Users and Computers

 You can use the command-line tool NETDOM to query all FSMOs for a given domain with a single command:

```
netdom query fsmo /domain:domainname
```

When a FSMO role owner goes down and cannot be brought back online, you no longer can transfer the role; you instead have to "seize" it. Windows Server 2008 domain controllers will automatically seize the roles held by a domain controller when you perform a metadata cleanup. If you wish to specify exactly where the roles are seized to, you must still perform this task by hand, though. Unfortunately, you cannot seize FSMO roles using the Active Directory snap-ins as you can to transfer them. To seize a FSMO role, you will need to use the *ntdsutil* utility. We will now walk through the *ntdsutil* commands that are used to seize a FSMO role. Note that due to the width of the output, some of the text wraps to the following line.

We first start off by getting into the *ntdsutil* interactive mode and looking at the options for the **roles** command:

```
C:\> ntdsutil
ntdsutil: roles
fsmo maintenance: ?
 ?                              - Show this help information
 Connections                    - Connect to a specific domain controller
 Help                           - Show this help information
 Quit                           - Return to the prior menu
 Seize domain naming master     - Overwrite domain role on connected server
 Seize infrastructure master    - Overwrite infrastructure role on connected server
 Seize PDC                      - Overwrite PDC role on connected server
 Seize RID master               - Overwrite RID role on connected server
 Seize schema master            - Overwrite schema role on connected server
 Select operation target        - Select sites, servers, domains, roles and
                                   naming contexts
 Transfer domain naming master - Make connected server the domain naming master
 Transfer infrastructure master - Make connected server the infrastructure master
 Transfer PDC                   - Make connected server the PDC
 Transfer RID master            - Make connected server the RID master
 Transfer schema master         - Make connected server the schema master
```

We must now connect to the domain controller to which we want to seize the role. In this case, we will connect to DC1.

```
fsmo maintenance: connections
server connections: connect to server dc1
Binding to dc1 ...
Connected to dc1 using credentials of locally logged on user.
server connections: quit
```

At this point, we can transfer and seize any available FSMO role to the DC1 domain controller. In the next example, we will attempt to seize the Schema Master. The current

Schema Master is DC2. If we tried to perform a seizure and DC2 was operational, we would effectively do a graceful transfer of the role to DC1. If DC2 is not available then, a seizure will take place, as shown in the following output (note that some lines may wrap due to their length):

```
fsmo maintenance: seize schema master
Attempting safe transfer of schema FSMO before seizure.
ldap_modify_sW error 0x34(52 (Unavailable).
Ldap extended error message is 000020AF: SvcErr: DSID-03210300, problem 5002
(UNAVAILABLE), data 1753
 Win32 error returned is 0x20af(The requested FSMO operation failed. The currentFSMO
holder could not be contacted.)
)
Depending on the error code this may indicate a connection,
ldap, or role transfer error.
Transfer of schema FSMO failed, proceeding with seizure ...
Server "dc1" knows about 5 roles
Schema - CN=NTDS
Settings,CN=DC1,CN=Servers,CN=RTP,CN=Sites,CN=Configuration,DC=mycorp,DC=com
Domain - CN=NTDS Settings,CN=DC1,CN=Servers,CN=RTP,CN=Configuration, DC=mycorp,DC=com
PDC - CN=NTDS Settings,CN=DC1,CN=Servers,CN=RTP,CN=Sites,CN=Configuration,
DC=mycorp,DC=com
RID - CN=NTDS Settings,CN=DC1,CN=Servers,CN=RTP,CN=Sites,CN=Configuration,
DC=mycorp,DC=com
Infrastructure - CN=NTDS Settings,CN=DC1,CN=Servers,CN=RTP,CN=Sites,CN=Configuration,
DC=mycorp,DC=com
```

Note that a connection is first attempted to the current role owner, and if it cannot be reached, *ntdsutil* does the seizure.

One of the nice features of the quirky *ntdsutil* command is that it can be run in interactive mode as we just showed, or it can be run from a single command line. To accomplish the same seizure using a single command line, the command would look as follows:

```
C:\> ntdsutil roles conn "co to ser dc1" q "seize schema master" q q
```

Depending on your needs, you could write a batch script to prompt for the role you want to seize and the DC to transfer or seize the role to. This could help when it gets down to crunch time and you need to seize the role quickly, and you do not want to thumb through this book trying to find all of the commands.

Restartable Directory Service

Windows Server 2008 introduces the ability to start and stop Active Directory like a normal Windows service. This allows you to perform most offline operations without restarting the domain controller. While Active Directory is stopped, it will not respond to logon requests. If the domain controller is hosting Active Directory Integrated DNS zones, it will also not respond to queries for these zones. While the Active Directory service is stopped, you can perform all of the offline tasks outlined in this chapter with the exception of restoring a backup. Restoring still requires that you boot into Directory Services Restore Mode.

Once you have stopped the Active Directory service, you can log in to the domain controller with domain credentials if another domain controller is available to service the request. If another domain controller is not available to service the request, then you will not be able to log in. If you want to continue to have the option of using the Directory Services Restore Mode Password, you must modify a registry value. This configuration change is outlined in the sidebar, "Modify the DSRM Logon Behavior," next.

Modify the DSRM Logon Behavior

By default, you must use a domain account to log on to a domain controller that has the Active Directory service stopped or is booted in Directory Services Restore Mode.

To change this behavior, you need to create or modify the REG_DWORD DSRMAdminLogon Behavior registry value under HKLM\System\CurrentControlSet\Control\Lsa.

There are three possible values for this registry value as outlined in Table 15-1.

If you only have one domain controller in the domain or expect there will be situations where you will not be able to contact another domain controller, you must set this registry value to 1 or you will not be able to log in to a domain controller in DS Restore Mode. In general, we recommend that you use a value of 1 for all deployments.

Table 15-1. DSRMAdminLogonBehavior values

Value	Description
0	You can only log on to the domain controller with a domain account, which requires that another domain controller be available to service the request.
	This is the default setting.
1	You can login to the domain controller with a domain account or the Directory Services Restore Mode account only when the Active Directory service is stopped.
	This is the default setting in Windows Small Business Server 2008 and Windows Essential Business Server 2008.
2	You can login to the domain controller with the Directory Services Restore Mode account regardless of whether the Active Directory service is stopped or started.

 If you are trying to log in to a Windows Server 2008 domain controller where the directory service is stopped, and login is failing when you try to use the DSRM credentials, make sure that you are not attempting to login to the domain. If you need to explicitly specify the local administrator account, click Switch User on the logon screen, and specify a username of .\administrator.

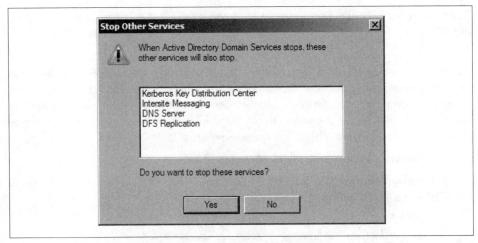

Figure 15-17. Stopping the Active Directory service

In order to stop the Active Directory service, open the Services MMC by going to Start→Run→Services.msc, right-clicking Active Directory Domain Services, and selecting to Stop. You will be prompted to also stop dependent services as shown in Figure 15-17. You can also stop Active Directory from the command prompt by running `net stop ntds`.

In order to restart the Active Directory service, you will need to manually start each of these dependent services once you have started the Active Directory Domain Services service.

DIT Maintenance

Using the *ntdsutil* utility, you can check the integrity and semantics of the Active Directory database and reclaim whitespace, which can dramatically reduce the size of the DIT. Also, just as you should rotate the password for the Administrator accounts in the forest, you should also change the DS Restore Mode Administrator password as well. You may even need to do this more frequently depending on whether you have people who leave your team and should no longer know the password.

Unfortunately, to accomplish all these tasks (with the exception of changing the DS Restore Mode Administrator password) on Windows Server 2003 and earlier domain controllers, you have to boot the domain controller into DS Restore Mode. That means you will have to have schedule downtime for the machine. Also, to use DS Restore Mode, you need console access, either through being physically at the machine or with out-of-band access, such as with an HP Integrated Lights Out (iLO) connection. There is one other option: using Terminal Services. You can modify the *boot.ini* file on the domain controller to automatically start up in DS Restore Mode. You can then use a

Terminal Services connection to log in to the machine. For more information, check out MS Knowledge Base article 256588 at *http://support.microsoft.com/kb/256588.*

The majority of the offline maintenance tasks discussed in this section can be performed without rebooting Windows Server 2008 domain controllers into DS Restore Mode as discussed earlier in the section "Restartable Directory Service." However, if you need to set a Windows Server 2008 domain controller to automatically boot into DS Restore Mode, you'll need to use the `bcdedit` command-line utility to reconfigure the domain controller's boot settings. This is a three step process:

1. `bcdedit /copy {current} /d "DC-DS Restore Mode"`

   The tool will output a GUID response similar to this: `The entry was successfully copied to {49fa7976-5065-11dd-ae21-000c291a8e6c}.`

2. `bcdedit /set {49fa7976-5065-11dd-ae21-000c291a8e6c} safeboot dsrepair`

3. `bcdedit /default {49fa7976-5065-11dd-ae21-000c291a8e6c}`

When you restart the domain controller, it will boot into DS Restore Mode. In order to change the domain controller's default boot option back to the original setting, you will need to use bcdedit to change the default back. This is a two step process:

1. `bcdedit /enum`

   This will output a list of all the boot manager options. Find the GUID of the normal Windows instance.

2. `bcdedit /default <guid of normal Windows instance>`

Checking the Integrity of the DIT

There are several checks you can perform against the DIT file to determine whether it is healthy. The first we'll show checks the integrity of the DIT file. The integrity check inspects the database at a low level to determine whether there is any binary corruption. It scans the entire file, so depending on the size of your DIT file, it can take a while to complete. While the speed varies greatly based on a number of factors, we've seen some estimates that state it can check around 2 gigabytes per hour, so allocate your change notification accordingly.

To start the integrity check, run the *ntdsutil* command from within DS Restore Mode. The `integrity` subcommand can be found within the `files` menu:

```
C:\> ntdsutil
ntdsutil: files
file maintenance: integrity
Opening database [Current].
Executing Command: C:\WINDOWS\system32\esentutl.exe /g"C:\WINDOWS\NTDS\ntds.dit" /o
Initiating INTEGRITY mode...
        Database: C:\WINDOWS\NTDS\ntds.dit
    Temp. Database: TEMPINTEG1752.EDB
Checking database integrity.
                    Scanning Status (% complete)
```

```
           0   10  20  30  40  50  60  70  80  90 100
           |----|----|----|----|----|----|----|----|----|----|
           .................................................
Integrity check successful.
Operation completed successfully in 11.766 seconds.
Spawned Process Exit code 0x0(0)
If integrity was successful, it is recommended
 you run semantic database analysis to ensure
 semantic database consistency as well.
file maintenance: quit
```

The integrity check looks at the database headers to make sure they are correct and also checks all database tables to make sure they are working correctly. If the database integrity check fails or encounters errors, you must restore the database from backup.

If the integrity check succeeds, you should then run a semantics check. Whereas the integrity check examines the database as a whole, the semantics check will examine the database to determine whether it is healthy as it pertains to Active Directory semantics. Some of the things the semantics check looks at include security descriptors, reference counts, distinguished name tag (DNT) consistency, and deleted objects.

To start a semantics check, run the go subcommand from the semantic database analysis menu:

```
ntdsutil: semantic database analysis
semantic checker: ?
 ?                         - Show this help information
 Check Quota               - Integrity-check quota-tracking table
 Get %d                    - Get record info with given DNT
 Go                        - Start Semantic Checker with No Fixup
 Go Fixup                  - Start Semantic Checker with Fixup
 Help                      - Show this help information
 Quit                      - Return to the prior menu
 Rebuild Quota             - Force asynchronous rebuild of quota-tracking table
 Verbose %s                - Turn verbose mode on/off
 semantic checker: go
Fixup mode is turned off
Opening database [Current].......Done.
 Getting record count...3115 records
Getting security descriptor count...82 security descriptors
 Writing summary into log file dsdit.dmp.0
SDs scanned:            82
Records scanned:      3115
Processing records..Done.
 semantic checker: quit
```

If any errors are reported, you can then run go fixup, which will attempt to repair any problems.

If you have to run the repair or go fixup commands after you boot back into normal mode, you should perform a backup as soon as possible and be sure to indicate on the backup that a repair was performed. If, for some reason, you need to restore the domain controller at a later point, and if you restore from a backup prior to the repair, you'll need to perform the same commands to fix the database again. Alternatively, if you start experiencing problems immediately after the repair, you want to know where the last backup was before the repair occurred and restore that copy.

Reclaiming Space

If your domain controllers are running low on disk space or if you have deleted a lot of objects since you promoted your domain controllers, you may want to perform an offline defragmentation of the DIT file. You've probably seen the online defragmentation events that get logged to the Directory Service Event Log. This includes event 700, which states that an online defrag is about to begin, and event 701, which states that the online defrag completed. The online defrag process by default runs twice a day and consolidates free space within the DIT file. The online defrag process does not reclaim any disk space used by the DIT file. To do that, you must perform an offline defragmentation. For information on determining how much free space is available in the DIT, see the upcoming sidebar "Configuring Logging of Available Database Space."

 If you perform an in-place upgrade of Windows 2000 domain controllers to Windows Server 2003, your ntds.dit may develop a substantial amount of free space in it. This is because of an improvement in Windows Server 2003 that stores unique security descriptors once in the entire database versus each time they are used. Some Active Directory administrators have seen as much as a 40% reduction in the size of their Active Directory database following this upgrade. If you want to reclaim this space on disk, you will need to perform an offline defragmentation of the ntds.dit.

An offline defragmentation must be done while the domain controller is in Directory Service Restore Mode. You can then use the `ntdsutil` command to compact—that is, defrag—the *ntds.dit* file. This process actually creates a copy of the *ntds.dit* file in an alternate location. You can then overwrite the existing DIT file with the new compacted version.

Configuring Logging of Available Database Space

If you are wondering how much free space exists in the ntds.dit, you can set a registry value which will cause Active Directory to log an additional event—event 1646—when an online defragmentation pass is complete.

Figure 15-18 shows this event on a Windows Server 2008 domain controller. In this scenario, the Active Directory database is 12MB in size and has 1MB of free space in the database file. You can use this information to help decide if there will be any benefit to performing an offline defragmentation of the database.

To enable this logging, set registry the REG_DWORD value 6 Garbage Collection under HKLM\System\CurrentControlSet\Services\NTDS\Diagnostics to 1. You do not need to reboot for this change to take effect.

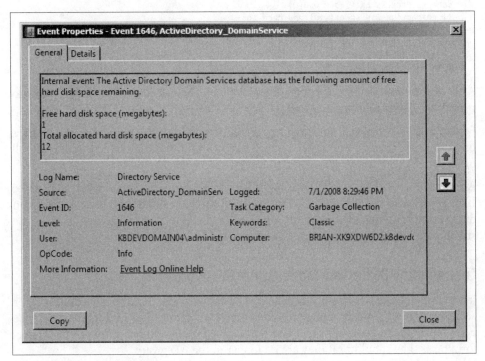

Figure 15-18. Available space in the database

The following shows how to perform an offline defragmentation using *ntdsutil*. After you enter the files menu, you'll need to issue the compact to *directorypath* command. The *directorypath* should be the directory the new compacted *ntds.dit* file would be created in. If the directory does not exist, it will be created automatically.

```
ntdsutil: files
file maintenance: compact to c:\windows\ntds\compact
Opening database [Current].
Creating dir: c:\windows\ntds\compact
Executing Command: C:\WINDOWS\system32\esentutl.exe /d"C:\WINDOWS\NTDS\ntds.dit"
 /t"c:\windows\ntds\compact\ntds.dit" /p /o
Initiating DEFRAGMENTATION mode...
            Database: C:\WINDOWS\NTDS\ntds.dit
      Temp. Database: c:\windows\ntds\compact\ntds.dit
              Defragmentation Status (% complete)
          0    10   20   30   40   50   60   70   80   90  100
          |----|----|----|----|----|----|----|----|----|----|
          ...................................................
Note:
```

```
    It is recommended that you immediately perform a full backup
    of this database. If you restore a backup made before the
    defragmentation, the database will be rolled back to the state
    it was in at the time of that backup.
Operation completed successfully in 20.961 seconds.
Spawned Process Exit code 0x0(0)
If compaction was successful you need to:
    copy "c:\windows\ntds\compact\ntds.dit" "C:\WINDOWS\NTDS\ntds.dit"
and delete the old log files:
    del C:\WINDOWS\NTDS\*.log
file maintenance: quit
```

After you've completed the compaction, you can then decide whether you want to overwrite your current *ntds.dit* file.

Performing an offline defrag of a machine affects only that machine. To reclaim space on your other domain controllers, you'll need to follow the same procedures for all other servers.

After you do an offline defrag, you should also make sure a backup is taken soon after. If for some reason you have to do a restore, and you have not done a backup since you did the offline defrag, the *ntds.dit* file on the domain controller will go right back to the size it was prior to the defrag.

Changing the DS Restore Mode Admin Password

It is a good practice to periodically change the password for your domain Administrator accounts. This should be done so that the password does not find its way to more people than it should, and so that you don't have former administrators trying to perform tasks they shouldn't if they are no longer in the AD group.

The domain administrator account should not be the only one you are concerned about. The DS Restore Mode Administrator account is just as important and can be used to do very damaging things, such as directly modifying the contents of the Active Directory database. For this reason, you should also periodically rotate the DS Restore Mode Administrator password.

Unfortunately, with Windows 2000 pre-Sp2, the only way to change the DS Restore Mode Administrator password was by booting into DS Restore Mode. When Windows 2000 Service Pack 2 was released, a new utility called setpwd was released that allowed an easy way to update the password without entering DS Restore Mode. Windows Server 2003 saw the addition of a command added to the ntdsutil utility to allow changing the password even when a domain controller is live. The reset password on server%s subcommand can be used from the set dsrm password menu, where %s is the name of the server to target. Leave %s blank if you want to change the password on the local machine. In the following example, we set the password for the DC1 domain controller:

```
ntdsutil: set dsrm password
Reset DSRM Administrator Password: reset password on server dc1
Please type password for DS Restore Mode Administrator Account: **********
Please confirm new
password: **********
Password has been set successfully.
Reset DSRM Administrator Password: quit
```

 You cannot use *ntdsutil* to set the DS Restore Mode administrator password if the target machine is currently in DS Restore Mode.

In a large environment with many hundreds of domain controllers, the methods Microsoft made available for setting the DS Restore Mode password are still sadly lacking. A technical reviewer of the third edition of this book, Dean Wells, has kindly helped out with this problem. Dean wrapped a batch file around *setpwd* to allow you to easily change all passwords in a forest, making a possibly enormous problem into a very simple task. You can get it from *http://www.briandesmond.com/ad4/dsrmreset.txt*.

 This script will work on Windows Server 2003 and newer domain controllers. In order to use it, you will need to obtain the setpwd.exe utility from a Windows 2000 Server.

Summary

In this chapter, we reviewed all the elements necessary to develop a disaster recovery plan. We covered how to back up Active Directory and some of the gotchas related to the tombstone lifetime and password-change cycles. We then discussed the various options for restoring Active Directory, including restore by replication, authoritative restores, and nonauthoritative restores. We discussed the FSMO transfer process and what is needed to seize FSMO roles. Finally, we delved into some of the maintenance tasks that can be done with the Active Directory DIT files.

## CHAPTER 16

Upgrading to Windows Server 2003

The first version of Active Directory with Windows 2000 was surprisingly stable and robust. That said, since Active Directory is such a complex and broad technology, there was still much room for improvement. There were some issues with scalability, such as the infamous 5,000-member soft limit with groups or the 300-site soft limit, which may have imposed artificial limitations on how you implemented Active Directory. Both of these issues were resolved in Windows Server 2003. The default security setup with Windows 2000 Active Directory out-of-the-box was not as secure as it should have been. Signed LDAP traffic and other security enhancements have since been added into service packs, but they are provided by default as of Windows Server 2003. Finally, manageability was another area that needed work in Active Directory. Windows Server 2003 added numerous command-line utilities along with some significant improvements to the administrative snap-ins.

We have highlighted a few key areas where Active Directory was improved in Windows Server 2003, and we'll describe more new features in the next section. If you already have a Windows 2000 Active Directory infrastructure deployed, your next big decision will be when to upgrade. At the time of publication, chances are you should be thinking of when to upgrade to Windows Server 2008 rather than Windows Server 2003. We still recommend you read the chapters on upgrading to Windows Server 2003 and R2 prior to reading about upgrading to Windows Server 2008 as these chapters build upon each other. Fortunately, the transition to Windows Server 2003 (and 2008) is evolutionary, not revolutionary as with the migration from Windows NT to Active Directory. In fact, Microsoft's goal was to make the move to Windows Server 2003 as seamless as possible, and for the most part they have accomplished this. You can introduce Windows Server 2003 domain controllers at any rate you wish into your existing Active Directory environment; they are fully compatible with Windows 2000 domain controllers.

Before you can introduce Windows Server 2003 domain controllers, you must prepare the forest and domains with the ADPrep utility, which primes the forest for new features that will be available once you raise the functional level of the domain or forest. Functional levels are similar in nature to domain modes in Windows 2000 Active Directory. They allow you to configure different levels of functionality that will be available in the domain or forest based on which operating systems are running on the domain controllers.

Before we cover the upgrade process to Windows Server 2003, we'll first discuss some of the major new features in Windows Server 2003 and some of the functionality differences with Windows 2000. Since Windows 2000 entered the extended support phase of its lifecycle in mid-2005, you should be thinking seriously about eliminating any remaining Windows 2000 servers.

New Features in Windows Server 2003

While the release of Windows Server 2003 is viewed as evolutionary, there are quite a few new features that make the upgrade attractive.

 By "feature," we mean new functionality that is not just a modification of the way it worked in Windows 2000. In this sense, a feature is something you have to use or implement explicitly. Functionality differences with Windows 2000 are covered in the next section.

We suggest you carefully review each of these features and rate them according to the following categories:

- You would use the feature immediately.
- You would use the feature eventually.
- You would never use the feature or it is not important.

Rating each feature will help you determine how much you could benefit from the upgrade. The following is the list of new features, in alphabetic order:

Application partitions
    You can create partitions that can replicate to any domain controller in the forest.
Concurrent LDAP binds
    Concurrent LDAP binds do not generate a Kerberos ticket and security token and are therefore much faster than a simple LDAP bind.
Cross-forest trust
    This is a transitive trust that allows all the domains in two different forests to trust each other via a single trust defined between two forest root domains. This requires Windows Server 2003 Forest Functional Level.

Domain controller rename

The rename procedure for domain controllers requires a single reboot.

Domain rename

Domains can now be renamed, but not without significant impact to the user base (e.g., all member computers must be rebooted twice). For more information, check out the following whitepaper: *http://technet.microsoft.com/en-us/windowsserver/ bb405948.aspx*. This requires Windows Server 2003 Forest Functional Level.

Dynamic auxiliary classes

There is now support for the standards-based implementation of dynamic auxiliary classes. Under Windows 2000, auxiliary classes are considered "static" because they are statically linked to structural classes in the schema. With dynamic auxiliary classes, you can link one when creating an object (or add after the creation) without it being defined in the schema as an auxiliary class for the object's objectClass. This requires Windows Server 2003 Forest Functional Level.

Dynamic objects

Traditionally, objects are stored in Active Directory until they are explicitly deleted. With dynamic objects, you can create objects that have a time to live (TTL) value that dictates when they will be automatically deleted unless refreshed. Dynamic objects do not remain as a tombstone when they are deleted due to expiration. This requires Windows Server 2003 Forest Functional Level.

Install from Media

A much-needed feature allows replica domain controllers to be promoted into a forest using a backup from another domain controller. This can greatly decrease the amount of time it takes to promote domain controllers in large domains.

Last logon timestamp attribute

A classic problem in a NOS environment is trying to determine the last time a user or computer logged in. The new `lastLogonTimeStamp` attribute is replicated, which means you can use a single query to find all users or computers that have not logged in within a certain period of time. By default, this attribute is updated approximately every 10 days. This requires the domain be operating in Windows Server 2003 Functional Level. For more information on this attribute, visit *http://blog .joeware.net/2007/05/01/864/*.

MMC and CLI enhancements

The Active Directory Users and Computers (ADUC) tool has been enhanced to allow multiselect of objects; other tools such as repadmin and netdom also have new options.

New DS CLI tools

A new set of command-line tools provides greater flexibility with managing Active Directory from a command line. These tools include dsadd, dsmod, dsrm, dsget, and dsquery.

Group Policy RSoP

Resultant Set of Policy (RSoP) has been built into ADUC and can be fully utilized with the Group Policy Management Console (GPMC). RSoP allows administrators to determine what settings of GPOs will be applied to end users and computers.

objectClass change

You can change `user` objects to `inetOrgPerson` objects and `inetOrgPerson` objects to `user` objects. This requires Windows Server 2003 Forest Functional Level.

TLS support

With Windows 2000, only SSL was supported to encrypt traffic over the wire. TLS, the latest standards-based approach for encrypting LDAP traffic, is now also supported.

Quotas

In Windows 2000, if users had access to create objects, they could create as many as they wanted, and there was no way to limit it. Quotas allow you to define how many objects a user or group of users can create. Quotas can also dictate how many objects of a certain objectClass can be created.

Query-based groups

Used for role-based authorization, the new Authorization Manager allows you to create flexible groups based on information stored with users (e.g., department). This requires Windows Server 2003 Forest Functional Level.

Redirect users and computers

You can redirect the default location to store new users and computers with the *redirusr* and *redircmp* commands, respectively.

Schema redefine

You can defunct and then redefine attributes and classes in the schema. This requires Windows Server 2003 Forest Functional Level.

Universal group caching

You can eliminate the requirement to have a global catalog server present during login for Universal group expansion by enabling universal group caching. This is enabled at the site level and applies to any clients that log on to domain controllers in the site. Global Catalogs are still needed for `userPrincipalName` authentications.

WMI filtering of GPOs

In addition to the OU, site, domain, and security group criteria that can be used to filter GPOs, you can now use WMI information on a client's machine to determine if a GPO should be applied. This functionality only works for Windows XP/2003 and newer clients.

WMI providers for trust and replication monitoring

These new WMI providers provide the ability to query and monitor the health of trusts and replication programmatically.

Differences with Windows 2000

Even though Active Directory was scalable enough to meet the needs of most organizations, there were some improvements to be made after several years of real-world deployment experience. Many of the functionality differences with Windows 2000 are the direct result of feedback from AD administrators.

As with the new features, we suggest you carefully review each of the differences and rate them according to the following categories:

- It would positively affect my environment to a large degree.
- It would positively affect my environment to a small degree.
- It would negatively affect my environment.

The vast majority of differences are actually improvements that translate into something positive for you, but in some situations, such as with the security-related changes, the impact may cause you additional work initially.

Account lockout enhancements
: Several bugs have been fixed that erroneously caused user lockouts in Windows 2000.

Changes with Pre-Windows 2000 Compatible Access
: To enhance security, the *Everyone* security principal no longer means all unauthenticated and authenticated users. It instead represents only authenticated users. To grant the equivalent of anonymous access in Windows Server 2003, the *Anonymous Logon* account should be added to the Pre-Windows 2000 Compatible Access group.

Distributed Link Tracking (DLT) service disabled by default
: The DLT service can be the source of thousands if not millions of `linkTrackOMTEn try` objects that are nested within the System container of a domain. By default, the DLT service is disabled on Windows Server 2003 domain controllers.

Faster global catalog removal
: With Windows 2000, whenever you disabled the global catalog on a domain controller, the global catalog removal process could only remove 500 objects every 15 minutes. This has been changed so that the process is much quicker.

Improved event log messages
: There are several new event log messages that will aid in troubleshooting replication, DNS, FRS, etc.

Intrasite replication frequency changed to 15 seconds
: The previous default was 5 minutes, which has now been changed to 15 seconds. This requires Windows Server 2003 Forest Functional mode for any Domain Controllers upgraded from Windows 2000.

ISTG and KCC scalability improvements

The algorithms used to generate the intersite connections have been greatly improved to the point where the previous soft limit of 300 to 400 sites has been raised to support roughly 3,000 to 5,000 sites. This new replication mechanism requires Windows Server 2003 Interim mode or Windows Server 2003 Forest Functional Level.

Link value replication (LVR)

Replication in Active Directory is done at the attribute level. That is, when an attribute is modified, the whole attribute is replicated. This was problematic for some attributes, such as the member attribute on group objects, which could only store roughly 5,000 members. LVR replication means that certain attributes, such as member, will only replicate the changes within the attribute and not the contents of the whole attribute whenever it is updated. This requires Windows Server 2003 Interim mode or Windows Server 2003 Forest Functional Level.

No global catalog sync for PAS addition

With Windows Server 2003, whenever an attribute is added to the partial attribute set (PAS), a global catalog sync is no longer performed as it was with Windows 2000. This was especially painful to administrators of large, globally dispersed Windows 2000 domains. This functionality is automatically in place on any new Windows Server 2003 domain controllers. It is not dependent on Forest Functional Level.

Signed and Sealed LDAP traffic

Instead of sending LDAP traffic, including usernames and passwords, over the wire in plain text with tools such as ADUC and ADSIEdit, the traffic is signed and also encrypted.

Single instance ACL storage

Unique security descriptors are stored once no matter how many times they are used, as opposed to being stored separately for each instance. This alone can save upwards of 20%–40% of the space in your DIT after upgrading. Note that an offline defragmentation will have to be performed to reduce the DIT size on upgraded domain controllers.

If you find that more than two or three of these would benefit your environment significantly, and less than one or two would have a negative effect, that is another good indication that an upgrade to Windows Server 2003 would benefit you enough to start in the near-term. This is by no means a hard-and-fast rule, since some features or differences may be more important than others. For example, if you have over 300 or 400 sites with domain controllers, the improvements in the KCC could potentially help you out significantly. Likewise, if you see the need to add attributes to the partial attribute set in the future, and you have large geographically disperse global catalog servers, then the no-global-catalog-sync behavior could save you some long weekends babysitting replication. You may view other features, such as the MMC enhancements, as beneficial, but not to the same degree as the other two just described. You'll have to weigh the priorities of each when you are considering them.

Functional Levels Explained

Now that you are sufficiently excited about the new features with Active Directory and improvements since Windows 2000, we will cover how you can actually enable these features in Windows Server 2003. If you've already deployed Windows 2000 Active Directory, you are most certainly familiar with the domain mode concept. With Windows 2000 Active Directory, you had mixed and native-mode domains. Domain mode simply dictated what operating systems were allowed to run on the domain controllers and nothing more. New features were enabled with the move to native mode, including universal security groups and enhanced group nesting to name a couple. Think of functional levels like domain modes, but taken a step further.

Windows Server 2003 functional levels are very similar to Windows 2000 domain modes from the standpoint that they dictate what operating systems can run on domain controllers, and they can only be increased or raised and never reversed. One common misunderstanding with domain modes, which hopefully will not be carried over to functional levels, is that they have virtually no impact on clients and what operating systems your clients run. For example, you can have Windows 9x clients in mixed or native-mode Windows 2000 domains and also in domains that are at the Windows 2000 or Windows Server 2003 domain functional level.

 For information about which operating systems domain controllers can run at the various functional levels, check out Chapter 2.

An important difference with functional levels is that they apply both to domains and at the forest level. The reason for this is that some features of Windows Server 2003 Active Directory require either that all the domain controllers in a domain are running Windows Server 2003 or that all the domain controllers in the entire forest are running Windows Server 2003.

To illustrate why this is necessary, let's look at two examples. First, let's look at the new "last logon timestamp attribute" feature. With this feature, a new attribute called lastLogonTimeStamp is populated when a user or computer logs on to a domain, and it is replicated to all the domain controllers in a domain. This attribute provides an easier way to identify whether a user or computer has logged on recently than using the lastLogon attribute, which is not replicated and therefore must be queried on every domain controller in the domain. For lastLogonTimeStamp to be of use, all domain controllers in the domain need to know to update it when they receive a logon request from a user or computer. Domain controllers from other domains only need to worry about

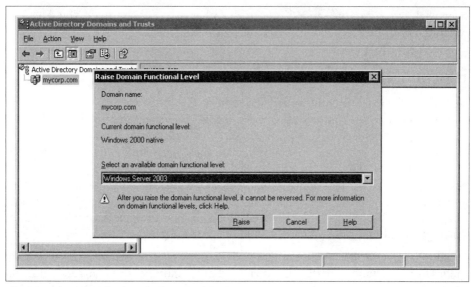

Figure 16-1. Raising the domain functional level

the objects within their domain, so for this reason this feature has a domain scope. Windows 2000 domain controllers do not know about `lastLogonTimeStamp` and do not update it. Therefore, for that attribute to be consistently updated and truly useful, all domain controllers in the domain must be running Windows Server 2003. All the domain controllers must know that all the other domain controllers are running Windows Server 2003, and they can do this by querying the functional level for the domain. Once they discover the domain is at a certain functional level, they start utilizing features specific to that function level.

Likewise, there are times when all domain controllers in the forest must be running Windows Server 2003 before a certain feature can be used. A good example is with the replication improvements. If some of the ISTGs were using the old site topology algorithms and others were using the new ones, you could have replication chaos. All domain controllers in the forest need to be running Windows Server 2003 before the new algorithms are enabled. Until then, they will use the legacy Windows 2000 algorithms.

How to Raise the Functional Level

To raise the functional level of a domain or forest, you can use the Active Directory Domains and Trusts MMC snap-in. To raise the functional level of a domain, open the snap-in, browse to the domain you want to raise, right-click on it in the left pane, and select Raise Domain Functional Level.... You will then see a screen similar to that in Figure 16-1.

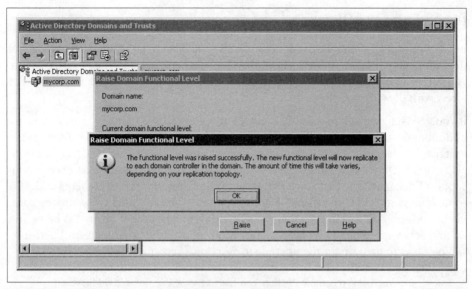

Figure 16-2. The result of raising the domain functional level

Select the new functional level and click the Raise button. You will then get a confirmation that it was successful or an error stating why it couldn't be raised. Figure 16-2 shows the message returned after successfully raising the functional level. Follow the same procedure to raise the functional level of a forest, but right-click on Active Directory Domains and Trusts in the left pane and select Raise Forest Functional Level....

You can determine the functional level of a domain or forest two other ways. First, you can look at the msDS-Behavior-Version attribute on the Domain Naming Context (e.g., dc=mycorp,dc=com) for domains or the Partitions container in the Configuration Naming Context (e.g., cn=partitions,cn=configuration,dc=mycorp,dc=com) for the forest. A value of 0 indicates Windows 2000 functional level, 1 indicates Windows 2003 Interim functional level, 2 indicates Windows Server 2003 functional level, and 3 indicates Windows Server 2008 functional level.

Alternatively, you can view this information by simply looking at the RootDSE for a domain controller. On Windows Server 2003 domain controllers, the RootDSE contains two new attributes that describe the current functional level:

domainFunctionality
    This value mirrors the msDS-Behavior-Version value on the Domain Naming Context.

forestFunctionality
    This value mirrors the msDS-Behavior-Version value on the Partitions container.

Preparing for ADPrep

Before you can start enabling functional levels, you have to go through the process of upgrading your existing infrastructure to Windows Server 2003. The first step before you can promote your first Windows Server 2003 domain controller is to prepare the forest with the ADPrep utility.

If you've installed Exchange 2000 or newer into your Active Directory forest, you are undoubtedly familiar with the Exchange setup.exe /forestprep and /domainprep switches. These switches are run independently from the Exchange server install to allow Active Directory administrators to take care of the AD-related tasks necessary to support Exchange. The Exchange /forestprep command extends the schema and adds some objects in the Configuration Naming Context. The Exchange /domainprep command adds objects within the Domain Naming Context of the domain it is being run on and sets some ACLs. The ADPrep command follows the same logic and performs similar tasks to prepare for the upgrade to Windows Server 2003.

Microsoft recommends that you have at least Windows 2000 Service Pack (SP) 2 installed on your domain controllers before running ADPrep. There are a number of fixes that you should ensure you have if you are still running SP2. More details on these are available at *http://support.microsoft.com/kb/331161*.

While the minimum is SP2, we recommend that you have SP3 at a minimum on your Windows 2000 domain controllers.

The ADPrep command can be found in the \i386 directory on the Windows Server 2003 CD. The ADPrep command depends on several files in that directory, so it cannot simply be copied out and put on a floppy or CD by itself. To run the ForestPrep, you would execute the following:

    X:\i386\adprep /forestprep

where *X*: is a CD drive or mapped drive to a network share containing the Windows Server 2003 CD. Similarly, to run DomainPrep, you would execute the following:

    X:\i386\adprep /domainprep

Finally, you would execute the following command:

    X:\i386\adprep /domainprep /gpprep

You can view detailed output of the *ADPrep* command by looking at the log files in the *%SystemRoot%\system32\debug\adprep\logs* directory. Each time ADPrep is executed, a new log file is generated that contains the actions taken during that particular invocation. The log files are named based on the time and date ADPrep was run.

Now we will review what ForestPrep and DomainPrep do.

ForestPrep

The `ADPrep /forestprep` command extends the schema with quite a few new classes and attributes. These new schema objects are necessary for the new features supported by Windows Server 2003. You can view the schema extensions by looking at the *.ldf* files in the \i386 directory on the Windows Server 2003 CD. These files contain LDIF entries for adding and modifying new and existing classes and attributes.

 Microsoft warns against manually extending the schema with the AD-Prep LDIF files. You should instead let `ADPrep` do it for you.

ForestPrep hardens some default security descriptors and modifies some of the ACLs on the containers in the Configuration NC. New `displaySpecifier` objects are added and some existing ones modified to support new features within the Active Directory administrative snap-ins. A NTDS Quotas container is added at the root of the Configuration container. This is a new container that hosts the quota objects that dictate how many objects a user or group of users can add within a container or OU.

One of the clever aspects of `ADPrep` is that it stores its progress in Active Directory. This is useful because it can gracefully recover from failures halfway through execution. It also provides a quick way to determine whether all of the necessary operations have completed and whether `ADPrep` was successful. Another benefit of storing the operations in Active Directory is in case you encounter problems and need to call Microsoft Product Support Services (PSS). You can look at this container and list out all of the operations that have been successful. PSS would then be able to look up which operation is failing.

A `ForestUpdates` container is created directly under the Configuration container. Within the `ForestUpdates` container are two other containers, one called Operations and the other called Windows2003Update . The Operations container contains additional containers, each one representing a certain task that `ADPrep` completed. For example, one operation might be to create new `displaySpecifier` objects. The operation container names are GUIDs, and the objects themselves do not contain any information that would be of interest. There should be a total of 36 of these operation containers after ForestPrep completes.

The other object within the `ForestUpdates` container is called `Windows2003Update`. This object is created after `ADPrep` finishes. If that object exists, it signifies that `ADPrep` completed ForestPrep successfully. If you are interested to find out when ForestPrep completed in a forest, simply look at the `whenCreated` attribute on the Windows2003Update object. Figure 16-3 shows what these containers look like with the ADSI Edit snap-in from the Windows Support Tools.

You only need to execute ForestPrep once. You can run it multiple times, but due to the fact that it keeps track of its progress in Active Directory under the `ForestUpdates`

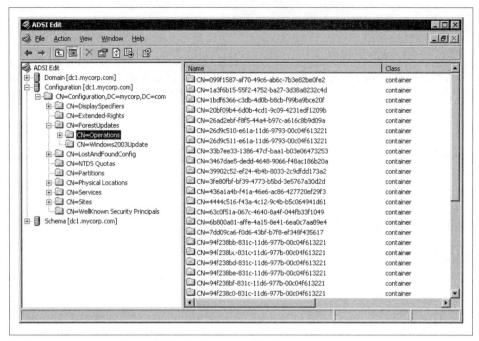

Figure 16-3. ADPrep forest update operations

container, it will only do something if it determines that an operation did not complete previously.

Because the schema is extended and objects are added in several places in the Configuration NC, the user running ForestPrep must be a member of both the Schema Admins and Enterprise Admins groups. In addition, you should run the command directly on the Schema Master for the forest. Importing the schema extensions is fairly resource-intensive, which is why it is necessary to run it from the Schema Master. Also, if you have large domains containing a lot of objects, ForestPrep may take a while to complete. ForestPrep indexes several attributes, which requires a lot of processing while it updates the AD database.

DomainPrep

Before you can run `ADPrep /domainprep`, you must be sure that the updates from ForestPrep have replicated to all domain controllers in the forest. DomainPrep must be run on the Infrastructure Master of the domain and under the credentials of someone in the Domain Admins group. If you try to run DomainPrep before ForestPrep has been run or before it has replicated all its changes out, you will get an error message. Again, if you are unsure about the error, check the ADPrep logs in the *%SystemRoot%\system32\debug\adprep\logs* directory for more information.

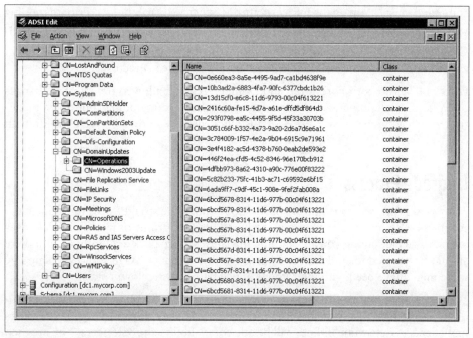

Figure 16-4. ADPrep domain update operations

DomainPrep creates new containers and objects, modifies ACLs on some objects, and changes the meaning of the Everyone security principal.

Unlike the ForestPrep command, which was fairly resource-intensive, DomainPrep completes quickly. The changes in comparison to ForestPrep are relatively minor. Two new top-level containers are created, one called NTDS Quotas, just like what ForestPrep added in the Configuration container, and another container called Program Data. This is intended to be a starting point for applications to store their data instead of each vendor coming up with their own top-level OU structure.

Just like ForestPrep, DomainPrep stores the status of its completion in Active Directory. Under the System container, a DomainUpdates container is created. Within that container, two other containers are created, called Operations and Windows2003Update. The same principles apply here as did for ForestPrep. Each of the operations that Domain-Prep performs is stored as an individual object within the Operations container. For DomainPrep, there are 52 operations. After all the operations complete, the Windows2003Update object is written, which indicates DomainPrep has completed. Figure 16-4 shows an example of what this container structure looks like using ADSI Edit.

GPPrep

The last step before you can begin upgrading your domain controllers to Windows Server 2003 is to run ADPrep /domainprep /gpprep. Much like DomainPrep, this command must be run on the Infrastructure Master FSMO role holder. Prior to running GPPrep, you must have successfully run DomainPrep, or the tool will exit with an error.

GPPrep updates the access control lists (ACLs) on the group policy folders in the SysVol container as well as the policy definitions stored in Active Directory.

Once you've run both ForestPrep and DomainPrep and allowed time for the changes to replicate to all domain controllers, you can then start upgrading your domain controllers to Windows Server 2003 or installing new Windows Server 2003 domain controllers.

Upgrade Process

The upgrade process to Windows Server 2003 should be straightforward for most deployments. No forest restructuring is required, no user profile or workstation changes are necessary assuming you are running the latest service pack and hotfixes, and there should be no need for political turf battles over namespace usage and ownership like there might have been with your initial Active Directory deployment.

We are going to outline five high-level steps that you should follow to upgrade to Windows Server 2003. They include performing an inventory of your domain controllers and clients to determine if there will be any compatibility showstoppers. You are then ready to do a trial run and perform extensive testing to see what impact the upgrade may have on functionality. Next, you have to prepare your forest and domains with ADPrep, which we've already discussed in some depth. Finally, you'll upgrade your domain controllers to Windows Server 2003. In the Post-Upgrade Tasks section of this chapter, we will describe what to do after you've upgraded your domain controllers as far as monitoring, raising functional levels, and taking advantage of new features goes.

 Prior to running your adprep process, fully read and understand Microsoft Knowledge Base Article 555040 at *http://support.microsoft.com/kb/555040*. It details all of the known issues with the adprep process. Also review KB article 309628 at *http://support.microsoft.com/kb/309628*, which details the operations adprep performs.

Inventory Domain Controllers

A good first step before you start the upgrade process is to do a complete inventory of all the hardware and software that is on your domain controllers. You'll then want to contact your vendors to determine whether they've already done compatibility testing and can verify support for Windows Server 2003. The last thing you want to do is start the upgrade process and find out halfway through that a critical monitoring application or backup software that runs on your domain controllers does not work correctly. Much of this testing can be done in your own labs, but it is always good to check with the vendors and get their seal of approval. After all, if a problem does arise, you'll want to make sure they are supporting the new platform and won't push back on you.

Next you'll want to ensure you have all the necessary hotfixes and service packs installed. A good overview of Microsoft's recommendations is documented in Microsoft Knowledge Base Article 331161 at *http://support.microsoft.com/kb/331161*.

After you are sure that your hardware and software is fully up-to-date and will work under Windows Server 2003, you'll then want to do a very thorough check of your current domain controllers and make sure they are running without error. Go through the event logs and resolve any errors and warnings that may be occurring. The *dcdiag* and *netdiag* commands are useful for identifying potential issues. Also, if you don't already trend CPU and memory statistics, you'll need to start. The reason for collecting all this data is that if problems occur after the upgrade to Windows Server 2003, you'll want to narrow it down to whether it was previously a problem or if it is new, most likely as a result of the upgrade. If you don't collect this data, you are setting yourself up for trouble.

A good compatibility test is to run the /checkupgradeonly switch with the Windows Server 2003 installer (*winnt32.exe*):

```
X:\> i386\winnt32.exe /checkupgradeonly
```

This command will go through the steps as if you were upgrading, but it will check only the applications you have installed and the status of the forest. If you have not run ADPrep yet, it will return an error about that.

At this point, you'll also want to check the status of your backups. Before you run ADPrep, you should have successful backups for at least two domain controllers in every domain in the forest and every FSMO role owner. You should also ensure that your disaster recovery procedures are well documented and have been tested.

Inventory Clients

The good news as far as clients go is that there aren't a lot of requirements for them to work in a Windows Server 2003 forest. In fact, there are no changes required for Windows Vista, XP, and 2000 machines. For NT 4.0 clients, you should have at least Service Pack 3, and Microsoft recommends Service Pack 6a. For Windows 98 and Windows 95 clients, they will need the DS Client installed.

Other than that, your clients are fine as is. That said any wise AD administrator would make sure the clients are thoroughly tested before starting the upgrade.

Trial Run

Although we can go on all day about how easy the upgrade process is, the proof is in the proverbial pudding. We consider it a mandatory step that before you upgrade your first production domain controller to Windows Server 2003, you go through extensive testing in a "production-like" Active Directory forest. So what do we mean by "production-like"? That depends on how much time and resources you have. Perhaps the best way to simulate your production environment is to actually take a production domain controller from each domain in the forest off the network and put it on a private network. You can then build up the forest on the private network, and all the data that is in production is now in the test environment you just set up. Your other alternative is to populate the test forest with as much of the data from production as possible. If you already have provisioning scripts or a metadirectory that feeds your production Active Directory environment, you may be able to utilize a similar process to populate the test forest.

Once you have a test forest that simulates production up and running, you should add as many clients as possible that represent your users and the various operating systems you support. If you are running Exchange, you should also install it, along with any other directory-enabled applications. Sound tedious? It is necessary to cover your bases no matter how trivial Microsoft says the upgrade will be. The last thing you want to happen is a major blow-up and then having to explain to your CIO that you didn't do very extensive testing because Microsoft said the upgrade was easy.

The key with the trial run is to document everything thoroughly. If you see anomalies, be sure to document them and follow up to determine whether it is going to be a problem. By the time you are done with the trial-run period, you should have an end-to-end document that describes how you are going to upgrade, how long you plan to wait before you raise functional levels, and in what priority you are going to enable new features.

Prepare the Forest and Domains

As we outlined earlier, before you can promote the first Windows Server 2003 domain controller into your forest, you have to run the ADPrep command. After you've done the DC and client inventories and determined there are no showstoppers to moving forward, you should run ADPrep.

First, you must run ADPrep /forestprep, and after the changes have replicated throughout the forest, you need to run ADPrep /domainprep and ADPrep /domainprep /gpprep in every domain which you will be upgrading to Windows Server 2003. You must run ADPrep /forestprep on the schema master FSMO owner and ADPrep /domainprep (and /gpprep) on the infrastructure master role owner for each domain.

Exchange 2000

If you've installed Exchange 2000 into the forest before running ADPrep, you have to correct some mistakes that were made in the Exchange 2000 schema extensions. Specifically, both ADPrep and Exchange 2000 define labledURI, houseIdentifier, and secretary attributes, but Exchange 2000 does not use the correct LDAP display names (lDAPDisplayName) as defined in RFC 2798. If you run ADPrep after Exchange 2000 has been installed without fixing these attributes, you can end up with duplicate schema objects with different lDAPDisplayName attributes. To solve the problem, you must run the *inetorgpersonfix.ldf* file that is located in *\support\tools\support.cab*. This LDIF file fixes the lDAPDisplayName attributes of the three attributes.

First, save the *inetorgpersonfix.ldf* file then import it using the *ldifde* utility. Here is an example where we will be importing into the *mycorp.com* forest:

```
ldifde.exe /i /f inetOrgPersonFix.ldf /c "DC=X" "DC=mycorp,DC=com"
```

Note that *inetorgpersonfix.ldf* uses DC=X as the forest path, which is why we needed to use the /c switch to replace it with our own forest path.

SFU 2.0

If you've installed Microsoft Services for UNIX (SFU) 2.0 in your Windows 2000 forest, you can run across a similar to issue as the one just described with Exchange 2000. The problem again comes back to an incorrectly defined attribute. In this case, it is the uid attribute. Microsoft has developed a hotfix for this issue, which is described in Microsoft Knowledge Base Article 293783 at *http://support.microsoft.com/kb/293783*.

This applies only to SFU 2.0. If you are running SFU 3.0, you will not encounter this problem.

Tweak Settings

Prior to upgrading domain controllers, you'll want to tweak any settings that you discovered during your testing that are set differently than what you want or what you have configured previously. Of special interest should be the settings related to security and account lockout. If you need to disable SMB Signing, you can do so via Group Policy in the Domain Controller Policy→Windows Settings→Security Settings→Local Policies→Security Options→Digitally Sign Communications. If this policy is not set in the Domain Controllers policy the local policy on Windows Server 2003 servers will apply which enables SMB signing. This can result in inconsistencies in clients connecting to different domain controllers based on their operating system.

A common pain point for Windows 2000 Active Directory administrators was account lockouts. All of the bug fixes that were incorporated into Service Packs 2 and 3 are included in Windows Server 2003. You may want to revisit your account lockout settings. Microsoft's recommendations are included in their Security Template file located at *%SystemRoot%\security\templates\SECUREDC.INF* on a Windows Server 2003 domain controller.

If you had to hardcode any settings on domain controllers in the Registry, you should reevaluate those settings to see whether you still need them. For example, many people increased the intrasite replication frequency from 5 minutes to 15–60 seconds. With Windows Server 2003, the default frequency has changed to 15 seconds.

Upgrade Domain Controllers

Now comes the easy part. You may be wondering how we could possibly say that doing the upgrade is the easy part. Perhaps we should preface it with this: if you've done all your homework, this will be the easy part. All of the hard work comes from doing the DC and client inventory, checking for compatibility issues, monitoring, checking event logs, getting a representative baseline, performing mock upgrades, etc. By the time you get the point of actually doing the upgrades in production, it should be second nature to you.

You can proceed with the upgrade process as slowly or as quickly as you want. Windows Server 2003 domain controllers are fully compatible with Windows 2000 domain controllers. They can also serve any role in a forest, including acting as a global catalog server, any FSMO master, ISTG, or Bridgehead server.

You can either promote new Windows Server 2003 servers into the forest, or you can perform in-place upgrades of existing Windows 2000 domain controllers. We recommend that whenever possible you use fresh installations of Windows Server 2003 so that your domain controllers are as clean as possible.

Post-Upgrade Tasks

After you've upgraded one or more of your domain controllers to Windows Server 2003, you need to do some additional tasks to fully complete the migration. First and foremost, you need to monitor the domain controllers every step of the way and especially after they have been upgraded. You are setting yourself up for failure if you are not adequately monitoring Active Directory.

Monitor

The criticality of monitoring cannot be overstated. If you are not monitoring, how can you determine whether something broke during the upgrade? Here are several things you should check after you upgrade your first domain controller in a domain, any FSMO role owner, and after all DCs have been upgraded:

Responds to all services
Query LDAP, Kerberos, the global catalog (if applicable), and DNS (if applicable) and be sure authentication and login requests are being processed. The *dcdiag* command can run many of these tests.

Processor and memory utilization
Trend processor and memory utilization for some period before you do the upgrade so you can compare to the numbers after the upgrade.

DIT growth

The growth of the DIT should not be significant. If you performed an in-place upgrade of Windows 2000 domain controllers, you may in fact want to do an offline defrag after the upgrade to reclaim any space due to single-instance store of ACLs.

Event logs

This is a no-brainer, but you should always check the event logs to see whether any errors are being logged.

DC resource records registered

Ensure that all of the SRV, CNAME, and A records for the domain controllers are registered. The *dcdiag* command can perform these checks.

Replication is working

Run `repadmin /showreps` and `repadmin /replsum` and watch for anything out of the ordinary.

Group policies are being applied

You may want to add a new setting to an existing GPO or create a new GPO and see if the settings apply on a client that should be receiving it.

NETLOGON and SYSVOL shares exist

This can consist of opening an Explorer window and browsing the available shares on the domain controller.

FRS is replicating correctly

You can test this out by placing a test file in the SYSVOL share on a domain controller and waiting for it to replicate to the other domain controllers.

This is not a comprehensive list of everything you should possibly monitor, but it is a good start. If everything checks out over a period of a week, you can feel pretty comfortable that the upgrade was successful. If nothing else, as long as you keep a close eye on the event logs, you should be able to catch the majority of problems.

Raise Functional Levels

After you feel comfortable that the upgrades have completed successfully, your next step should be to start raising the functional levels. If you've only upgraded the domain controllers in a single domain, you can raise the functional level for only that domain to Windows Server 2003. If you've upgraded all the domain controllers in the forest, you can also proceed to upgrade the Forest Functional Level to Windows Server 2003.

If you want to err on the side of caution and you support multiple domains, you may want to raise the functional level of a single domain and repeat the monitoring steps over a week before raising the Forest Functional Level.

After you raise the functional level of a domain or forest, you should add some additional steps to what you monitor to include testing out new features in Windows Server 2003. For example, to test the Windows Server 2003 domain functional level, you should log on to a domain controller and view the `lastLogonTimestamp` attribute of your user object that we discussed earlier in the chapter. This is a new replicated attribute that will contain your logon time. If after a period of time, you don't see that attribute getting populated, you'll need to dig deeper to determine what is going on.

Perhaps the easiest test to determine whether a functional level has been set for a domain or forest is to query the `RootDSE` and look at the `forestFunctionality` and `domainFunctionality` attributes. A value of 2 indicates the domain or forest is at the Windows Server 2003 functional level.

Start Implementing New Features

After you've upgraded your domain controllers and raised the functional level of a domain or forest, you are ready to start taking advantage of the new features. You can start utilizing some of them, such as the MMC and CLI enhancements, immediately. With others, such as quotas, you'll want to think out exactly how to implement them and have them properly documented and communicated before you start using them. If you are using AD-integrated DNS zones, you should look at converting to application partitions to store DNS data. This is a fairly easy conversion that can be done with the DNS MMC snap-in. In some cases, you may need to completely rethink your current processes. For example, if you start using the "Install from Media" feature, you may change how you build and deploy domain controllers.

Summary

In this chapter, we covered the new features in Windows Server 2003 and some of the differences with Windows 2000, most of which were instigated by real-world deployment issues. We then went over how you can enable new features with the use of functional levels and why they are necessary. Next we discussed the aDPrep process and how that must be done before the first Windows Server 2003 domain controller can be promoted. Once you have your forest and domains prepared, you can start the upgrade process. We described some of the important issues to be aware of when upgrading, and finally what to do after you've completed the upgrade.

## CHAPTER 17

Upgrading to Windows Server 2003 R2

Windows Server 2003 has been available to the public since March 2003. Since its release, Microsoft has also released several feature packs that add additional functionality to the base operating system, and there has also been a substantial update in the form of Service Pack 1. Because the release dates for Windows Server 2008 were pushed further and further out, as well as for a number of other reasons, Microsoft decided to release a new version of Windows Server 2003 called R2. This is the gold version of Windows Server 2003 with Service Pack 1, and it includes the previously released to web (RTW) feature packs, as well as some new feature packs that were not previously released.

Windows Server 2003 Service Pack 1 should not be considered an *optional* update; however, R2 can certainly be considered optional. Service Pack 1 for Windows Server 2003 is comparable to Service Pack 2 for XP in terms of the amount of security changes implemented across the OS. There are also a few additions to the Active Directory Services that this chapter will focus on. If you have already installed Service Pack 1 and do not want or need any of the feature packs on the R2 CD, then you will not need to install R2, though you should still consider running the R2 `ADPrep` to upgrade the schema to the latest Microsoft schema revision.

Before you can introduce Windows Server 2003 R2 domain controllers, you must prepare the forest with the `ADPrep` utility, which is like the `ADPrep` utility needed to upgrade Windows 2000 forests to Windows Server 2003 forests. `ADPrep` primes the forest for new platform interoperability features available in R2. This schema update is one of the reasons that R2 is a "new" server release instead of simply a rollup or Service Pack.

Before diving into the process to upgrade to Windows Server 2003 R2, the discussion will focus on some of the new Active Directory features included in R2, as well as Service Pack 1, and some of the functionality differences with the original Windows Server 2003 release to manufacturing (RTM) edition. Based on this information, you should be able to prioritize the importance of how quickly or even *if* you should start migrating to R2.

New Active Directory Features in Windows Server 2003 Service Pack 1

On January 15, 2002, Bill Gates, Chief Software Architect for Microsoft, sent the now-famous Trustworthy Computing email memo to all Microsoft employees disclosing the new Microsoft direction. It outlined a direction toward security and a trusted computing base. As the first major project out of the gate after this milestone event, Windows Server 2003 was a valiant step in the right direction, but the momentum and technical acumen wasn't fully built up by the time of its release.

Microsoft truly started to hit its security stride with the release of Windows XP Service Pack 2 in August 2004. Then in March 2005, Windows Server 2003 Service Pack 1 was released as the comparable service pack for the server OS. As you may well expect, both service packs are packed full of security fixes, new technology, and coding techniques to help counter unknown future security holes. For this reason, these service packs should *not* be considered optional updates.

On top of the security fixes and other non-AD related hotfixes, there are quite a few new Active Directory features and updates that make Service Pack 1 attractive to any Active Directory administrator. We list the Active Directory specific SP1 updates and features in this section. If upgrading from Windows 2000 to Windows Server 2003 SP1, you should also refer to Chapter 16 for benefits gained when upgrading from Windows 2000 to Windows Server 2003.

 By "feature," we mean new functionality that is not just a modification of the way it worked in Windows Server 2003.

We suggest you carefully review each of these features and rate them according to the following categories:

- I would use the feature immediately.
- I would use the feature eventually.
- I would never use the feature or it is not important.

Rating each feature will help you determine how much you could benefit from the upgrade. The following is the list of new features, in alphabetical order:

Confidential attributes
> Ability to mark attributes as confidential so they cannot be read without additional permissions granted. By default, any attribute marked "confidential" can only be read by administrators; however, this can be delegated.

Directory service backup reminders
 Special messages logged to the Directory Service event log if directory partitions are not backed up in a timely manner.

Drag and drop changes in Active Directory Users and Computers Console
 Ability to disable drag-and-drop functionality in ADUC and display confirmation dialogs when initiating a move operation.

Virtual Server support
 Official support for running domain controllers within Virtual Server 2005. This includes additional protection against directory corruption due to improper backup and restoration procedures.

Differences with Windows Server 2003

As with the new features, we suggest you carefully review each of the differences and rate them according to the following categories:

- It would positively affect my environment to a large degree.
- It would positively affect my environment to a small degree.
- It would negatively affect my environment.

The vast majority of differences are actually improvements that translate into something positive for you, but in some situations, such as with the security-related changes, the impact may initially cause you additional work:

Additional replication security and fewer replication errors
 Replication metadata is now removed for domain controllers that are removed from the domain. This enhances directory security and eliminates replication error messages related to the deleted domain controllers.

Install from Media improvements for installing DNS Servers
 New option to include application directory partitions in the backup media eliminates requirement for network replication of DomainDNSZone and Forest-DNSZones application directory partitions before the DNS Server is operational.

Updated tools
 Newer versions of DcDiag, NTDSUtil, AdPrep, and other tools to aid in management, updates, and troubleshooting.

Extended storage of deleted objects
 Tombstone lifetime on new forests increased from 60 to 180 days. Existing forests are not modified.

SID History attribute retained on object deletion
 The SID History attribute has been added to the default list of attributes retained on an object tombstone. When the object is undeleted, the attribute will be restored along with the object.

Operations master health and status reporting
>   Operations that require a FSMO domain controller that cannot be performed will generate Directory Service event log messages.

New Active Directory Features in Windows Server 2003 R2

Windows Server 2003 R2 includes all of the aforementioned Service Pack 1 upgrades, as well as some additional feature packs. There are only a few features in R2 that are specific to Active Directory; these are listed below.

We suggest you carefully review each of these features and rate them according to the following categories:

- I would use the feature immediately.
- I would use the feature eventually.
- I would never use the feature or it is not important.

Rating each feature will help you determine how much you could benefit from the upgrade. The following is the list of new features, in alphabetical order:

Active Directory Application Mode (AD/AM or ADAM)
>   Standalone LDAP service that is Active Directory with the NOS-specific components and requirements stripped out. This feature does not require your domain controllers or your schema to be updated to R2; you can just upgrade the standalone or member server on which you want to run R2 ADAM.

Active Directory Federated Services (ADFS)
>   Standards-based technology that enables distributed identification, authentication, and authorization across organizational and platform boundaries. This feature does not require your domain controllers or your schema to be updated to R2; you can just upgrade the standalone or member server on which you want to run ADFS.

Identity Management for UNIX (IMU or IdMU)/Subsystem for UNIX Applications (SUA)
>   Manage user accounts and passwords on Windows and Unix via NIS. Automatically synchronize passwords between Windows and Unix.

Preparing for ADPrep

Before you can install your first R2 domain controller, you have to go through the process of upgrading your existing schema to Windows Server 2003 R2 with the ADPrep utility. If you've upgraded from Windows 2000 to Windows Server 2003 AD, you are undoubtedly familiar with the adprep.exe /forestprep switch. If not, please review Chapter 16. This switch is run independently from the domain controller promotion to allow Active Directory administrators to take care of the AD-related tasks necessary to support Windows Server 2003 R2 Active Directory. The R2 ForestPrep process extends the schema to include the objects and attributes necessary for the R2 Feature Packs, primarily the Unix interoperability functions.

Unlike the Windows 2000 to Windows Server 2003 upgrade, you do not have to run `adprep.exe /domainprep` or `adprep.exe /domainprep /gpprep` for the Windows Server 2003 to Windows Server 2003 R2 Upgrade, as there are no domain-level changes that need to be implemented.

If you are upgrading from Windows 2000 to Windows Server 2003 R2, however, you do need to run `adprep.exe /domainprep` and `adprep.exe /domainprep /gpprep`. See Chapter 16 for details; the process is the same as it is under the initial version of Windows Server 2003.

Windows Server 2003 Service Pack 1 is required to load R2.

The `ADPrep` command can be found in the *\CMPNENTS\R2\ADPREP* directory on Windows Server 2003 R2 disk 2. The `ADPrep` command depends on several files that reside in that directory, so it cannot simply be copied out and put on a floppy or CD by itself. To run the ForestPrep, you would execute the following:

```
X:\CMPNENTS\R2\ADPREP\adprep /forestprep
```

where *X:* is a CD drive or mapped drive to a network share containing the Windows Server 2003 R2 CD.

Windows Server 2003 R2 comes with two CDs. The version of *AD-Prep* specific to R2 is on CD2. If you are upgrading from Windows 2000 to Windows Server 2003 R2, you only need to run *ADPrep* from CD2. The version of *ADPrep* on CD1 does not contain any of the R2 changes.

You can view detailed output of the `ADPrep` command by looking at the log files in the *%SystemRoot%\system32\debug\adprep\logs* directory. Each time `ADPrep` is executed, a new folder with the current date is generated that contains files with information concerning the actions taken during that particular invocation of `ADPrep`. The folders are named based on the time and date `ADPrep` was run.

ForestPrep

The `ADPrep /forestprep` command extends the schema with quite a few new classes and attributes. These new schema objects are necessary for the new features supported by Windows Server 2003 R2. You can view the schema extensions by looking at the *.ldf* files in the *\CMPNENTS\R2\ADPREP* directory on the Windows Server 2003 R2 CD. These files contain LDIF entries for adding and modifying new and existing classes and attributes.

Microsoft warns against manually extending the schema with the AD-Prep LDIF files. You should instead let ADPrep do it for you.

You only need to execute ForestPrep once when upgrading from Windows Server 2003 to R2. You can run it multiple times, but due to the fact that it updates only the schema, it will only apply schema changes that did not complete previously.

Because the schema is being upgraded, the user running ForestPrep must be a member of the Schema Admins group. In addition, you should run the command directly on the Schema Master for the forest.

 When running the R2 ForestPrep against a Windows 2000 forest, you *must* be at Windows 2000 SP2 or later with hotfix 265089 (*http://support .microsoft.com/kb/265089*) installed on all domain controllers. Failure to adhere to this requirement could cause domain controller corruption. For more information, see Microsoft KB 331161 at *http://support.micro soft.com/kb/331161*.

Service Pack 1 Upgrade Process

The upgrade process to Windows Server 2003 Service Pack 1 is similar to any service pack upgrade—test, test, test, test, and test some more before introducing changes to production. You need to test all aspects of your business requirements and management tools against a domain with domain controllers that have been upgraded. This upgrade will not require you to make any Active Directory changes. However, there are non-Active Directory-related changes, specifically security changes, in SP1 that could impact your line of business applications and management capabilities.

 One non-AD-related change in Windows Server 2003 Service Pack 1 that has caused a significant number of issues in managing domains and servers is a change to the Discretionary Access Control List (DACL) of the Service Control (SC) Manager. This change locks down the ability to remotely enumerate installed services to administrators. Previously, an administrator could delegate to a non-administrator the ability to stop and start services. This delegation will break under SP1 if the tool used to manage the services enumerates the services on the remote server. You must either re-open the DACL access on the SC Manager using the Support Tool SC.EXE or use a tool that doesn't enumerate the services prior to managing the delegated service.

The Service Pack 1 installation files can be downloaded directly from the Microsoft Website; see Microsoft Knowledge Base Article 889101 at *http://support.microsoft.com/ kb/889101* for the Service Pack release notes and the download location.

Once you have determined through testing that loading Service Pack 1 on your domain controllers will create no obvious dangers to your business or your ability to manage your environment, you should back up any systems to be upgraded. Make sure that the backup includes the system state to capture Active Directory and SYSVOL information, and then deploy the Service Pack into production. Don't forget to verify that your Line of Business apps, monitoring, and management software are all working properly after the upgrade.

R2 Upgrade Process

The R2 upgrade process is quite simple, and because there is no change in the function of the operating system, there is no real concern of possible issues with the exception of the schema update processed in the ForestPrep. Even if there are issues during the schema update, they are not usually terribly difficult to overcome, especially with the schema defunct capability in Windows Server 2003 Active Directory. The ForestPrep only has to be run once, so after that is completed, the rest of the R2 rollout should be quite smooth.

 During the beta of R2, there were cases reporting failures during the ForestPrep process due to preexisting schema attributes colliding with the new attributes in various ways. All of these cases were corrected by defuncting and/or redefining the old attributes causing the collisions.

Prepare the Forest

As we outlined earlier, before you can promote the first Windows Server 2003 R2 domain controller into your forest, you have to run the ForestPrep procedure. Log in to the Schema FSMO role holder and run `ADPrep /forestprep`. When the process has successfully completed, you will be greeted with a heartening success message:

```
The command has completed successfully.
ADPrep successfully updated the forest-wide information.
```

If you run into errors, messages will be provided that should give an indication of the problem. Assuming your prerequisites are in order, any errors will be concerning preexisting schema definitions. If you have been particular about your schema updates, it is unlikely you will encounter issues.

Upgrade Domain Controllers

Now comes the easy part, really. The installation of R2 will copy a few files to the server and add some menu items to the Add/Remove Windows Components of the Add or Remove Programs dialog. These additional menu picks will allow you to later install the various feature packs as needed. The Active Directory-specific feature packs, including ADAM, ADFS, and IMU, are available under the Active Directory Services pack.

That's it, all done, nothing else to do for the upgrade. The hard part was the SP1 upgrade and ForestPrep procedure mentioned previously.

If you do not need any of the new features on your domain controllers from R2, such as ADAM, ADFS, or IMU, there is no need to perform this step.

 Creating a new R2 forest is as simple as building a new Windows 2000 or Windows Server 2003 forest. Configure DNS for the forest root domain enabling dynamic updates, and then DCPROMO an R2 server (standalone or domain member) to domain controller status. There are no ForestPrep or other upgrade processes necessary.

Summary

In this chapter, we covered the new Active Directory features in Windows Server 2003 SP1 and Windows Server 2003 R2. Further, we mentioned that while Windows Server 2003 Service Pack 1 is an important, if not critical, upgrade, R2 is optional and should only be done if you need one or more of the feature packs included in the release. Next, we discussed the processes involved with upgrading from a Windows Server 2003 Active Directory and domain controllers to Windows Server SP1 and then R2. Finally, we discussed the ForestPrep process and how that must be completed prior to introduction of the first R2 domain controller.

## CHAPTER 18

Upgrading to Windows Server 2008

The process for upgrading to Windows Server 2008 from Windows 2000 or Windows 2003 Active Directory is relatively straightforward. If you've completed the upgrade from Windows 2000 to Windows Server 2003, you should have all the skills necessary to embark upon upgrading to Windows Server 2008. If not, we recommend that you review the previous two chapters on upgrading to Windows Server 2003 as we will not be rehashing the content already covered there.

The goal of this chapter is to provide an at a glance overview of the new Active Directory features you will be able to leverage as you begin and complete your migration to Windows Server 2008. We will also discuss the upgrade process with specific attention to the additional steps necessary to deploy new Windows Server 2008 features.

New Features in Windows Server 2008

While the release of Windows Server 2008 is viewed as evolutionary, there are quite a few new features that make the upgrade attractive.

 By "feature," we mean new functionality that is not just a modification of the way it worked in Windows Server 2003. In this sense, a feature is something you have to use or implement explicitly. Functionality differences with Windows Server 2003 are covered in the next section.

We suggest you carefully review each of these features and rate them according to the following categories:

- I would use the feature immediately.
- I would use the feature eventually.
- I would never use the feature or it is not important.

Rating each feature will help you determine how much you could benefit from the upgrade. The following is the list of new features, in alphabetic order:

Administrative role separation
> Users who are not domain administrators can be securely delegated administrative control of RODCs without providing access to the writeable Active Directory (e.g., they cannot modify anything but the RODC).

ADMX repository
> Upgraded Group Policy template files can be stored once per domain in the Sysvol, thus greatly reducing the size of the Sysvol for many organizations.

Database snapshots
> Point-in-time snapshots of the Active Directory database can be taken as a basis for disaster recovery and other object restore and comparison operations.

DNS Server features
> Support for new locator options, automatic configuration during install, background zone loading, and multicast DNS support.

DFS-R Sysvol replication
> Sysvol can now be replicated with the new DFS-R replication engine, which is much more reliable and scalable when compared to NTFRS.

Fine-Grained Password Policies
> Password policies can now be defined on a per-user basis.

GlobalNames DNS zone
> A new type of DNS zone that can help pave the way to migrating away from WINS by resolving unqualified hostnames.

Group Policy Preferences
> A product Microsoft purchased from Desktop Standard, Group Policy Preferences allow you to control numerous settings and Windows features that were previously only accessible via scripts.

Last-logon statistics
> Windows Vista and Windows Server 2008 clients can store detailed last-logon success and failure information directly on user objects in the directory. This feature was implemented for Common Criteria compliance.

Owner Access Rights
> An additional well-known security principal representing the owner of an object is now available.

Phonetic name indexing
> The `displayName` attribute is phonetically sortable on Japanese locale domain controllers.

Read-only DNS
> RODCs can host dynamic DNS zones and refer any updates to writeable domain controllers.

Read-only domain controllers (RODCs)
> RODCs do not allow local writes and any compromise of the directory will not replicate to writeable domain controllers in the domain. They also do not store passwords and other secrets by default. This feature adds a great deal of security to domain controllers in locations with questionable physical security.

Restartable Directory service
> Active Directory can be stopped to allow for certain offline operations to be performed without restarting the domain controller in Directory Service Repair Mode.

Server Core support
> Domain controllers can now run on a version of the Windows Server 2008 operating system that is substantially lighter and thus more secure. Components such as the Explorer shell, Internet Explorer, and other items not essential to server operations have been removed from Server Core.

Starter Group policies
> Group Policy templates can be defined that administrators can base new policies on.

Differences with Windows Server 2003

Even though Active Directory was scalable enough to meet the needs of most organizations, there were some improvements to be made after several years of real-world deployment experience. Many of the functionality differences with Windows Server 2003 are the direct result of feedback from AD administrators.

As with the new features, we suggest you carefully review each of the differences and rate them according to the following categories:

- It would positively affect my environment to a large degree.
- It would positively affect my environment to a small degree.
- It would negatively affect my environment.

The vast majority of differences are actually improvements that translate into something positive for you, but in some situations, such as with the security-related changes, the impact may cause you additional work initially:

Active Directory user interface enhancements
> The core Active Directory GUI tools have been improved so that they can connect to mounted snapshots as well as AD LDS instances, in addition to various cosmetic features and enhancements. In addition, the attribute editor allows editing of any object attribute in the GUI, and Active Directory Sites and Services supports searching for servers.

Auditing and logging infrastructure enhancements
> Auditing of Active Directory access and changes as well as various other actions have been updated substantially.

Delegated DCPromo
> Domain controller promotion can be broken up into a two-step process allowing delegation of the physical hands-on portion of *dcpromo* to users other than domain administrators such as local site support technicians.

Domain DFS scalability enhancements
> Domain-based DFS roots can host more than 5,000 links and can also leverage Access Based Enumeration.

DNS user interface enhancements
> Various usability enhancements to the MMC such as storing conditional forwarders in Active Directory.

ESE single bit error correction
> The JET database engine that Active Directory uses is now capable of detecting single bit errors and correcting them, and thus reducing incidences of database failure due to corruption.

Group Policy user interface enhancements
> Numerous improvements to the GPMC and GPO Editor tools such as searching for settings and filtering displays.

Kerberos AES key length upgrade
> The maximum key length supported by Kerberos for Advanced Encryption Standard has been lengthened from 128 bits to 256 bits.

Preparing for ADPrep

Before you can install your first Windows Server 2008 domain controller, you have to go through the process of upgrading your existing schema to Windows Server 2008 with the `ADPrep` utility. If you've upgraded from Windows 2000 to Windows Server 2003 AD, you are undoubtedly familiar with the `adprep.exe /forestprep` switch. If not, please review Chapter 16. This switch is run independently from the domain controller promotion to allow Active Directory administrators to take care of the AD-related tasks necessary to support Windows Server 2008 Active Directory. The Windows Server 2008 process extends the schema to include the objects and attributes necessary for the new Windows Server 2008 features.

You will need to run `adprep.exe /domainprep` in each domain you plan to deploy Windows Server 2008 domain controllers to. See Chapter 16 for details; the process is the same as it is under the initial version of Windows Server 2003. If you are upgrading from Windows 2000, you will also need to run `adprep.exe /domainprep /gpprep` in each domain you plan to deploy Windows Server 2008 domain controllers to.

If you intend to deploy read only domain controllers (RODCs) in your environment, you will need to run `adprep /rodcprep` once per forest.

The ADPrep command can be found in the *\SOURCES\ADPREP* directory on Windows Server 2008 DVD. The ADPrep command depends on several files that reside in that directory, so it cannot simply be copied out and put on a floppy or CD by itself. To run the ForestPrep, you would execute the following:

```
X:\SOURCES\ADPREP\adprep /forestprep
```

where *X:* is a DVD drive or mapped drive to a network share containing the Windows Server 2008 DVD.

You can view detailed output of the ADPrep command by looking at the log files in the *%SystemRoot%\system32\debug\adprep\logs* directory. Each time ADPrep is executed, a new folder with the current date is generated that contains files with information concerning the actions taken during that particular invocation of ADPrep. The folders are named based on the time and date ADPrep was run.

ForestPrep

The ADPrep /forestprep command extends the schema with quite a few new classes and attributes. These new schema objects are necessary for the new features supported by Windows Server 2008. You can view the schema extensions by looking at the *.ldf* files in the *\SOURCES\ADPREP* directory on the Windows Server 2008 DVD. These files contain LDIF entries for adding and modifying new and existing classes and attributes.

Microsoft warns against manually extending the schema with the AD-Prep LDIF files. You should instead let ADPrep do it for you.

Forestprep also updates a number of ACLs in the configuration naming context and creates additional well-known security principal objects.

You only need to execute ForestPrep once when upgrading to Windows Server 2008. You can run it multiple times, but it will only make changes that did not succeed previously.

Because the schema is being upgraded, the user running ForestPrep must be a member of the Schema Admins group. In addition, you should run the command directly on the Schema Master for the forest.

When running the Windows Server 2008 ForestPrep against a Windows 2000 forest, all of your Windows 2000 domain controllers must be running service pack 4.

RODCPrep

If you intend to have RODCs in your environment, you'll need to run `ADPrep /rodc prep`. RODCPrep modifies the ACLs on any application partitions (such as for DNS) in your environment in order to allow RODC replication. You will need to be an enterprise admin in order to run RODCPrep.

Unlike ForestPrep, RODCprep will complete quickly as the changes it makes are relatively minor. If there is an error, check the ADPrep logs in the *%SystemRoot%\system32\debug\adprep\logs* directory for more information.

There are two common errors some administrators are encountering when they run RODCPrep. These errors are similar to the following:

```
Adprep could not contact a replica for partition DC=DomainDnsZones,DC=mycorp,DC=com
Adprep failed the operation on partition DC=DomainDnsZones,DC=mycorp,DC=com
Skipping to next partition.


Adprep failed the operation on partition DC=ForestDnsZones,DC=MyCorp,DC=com
Skipping to next partition.
Adprep completed with errors. Not all partitions are updated.
```

There are two possible causes for this error. The first is that an application partition is defined in the forest that is no longer replicated to any domain controllers. To correct this problem, perform a metadata cleanup of that partition using *ntdsutil*. Launch *ntdsutil* and run the following commands:

1. **domain management**
2. **connections**
3. **connect to server** *dc1*
4. **quit**
5. **delete nc** *DC=OldAppPart,DC=MyCorp,DC=com*

This will remove the reference to the application partition that no longer exists. The path specified in step five should be the distinguished name given in the error message from Adprep.

 Make certain that you actually want to remove the application partition in question before running these commands. If the application partition is still replicated to domain controllers, this will delete the contents of the application partition!

The second cause of this error is that the infrastructure master owner for the application partition has not been maintained. While the infrastructure master has no operational purpose for application partitions, it is used as a single point to perform critical operations such as RODCPrep. Microsoft knowledge base article 949257 at *http://support .microsoft.com/kb/949257* provides a script for updating the Infrastructure Master

---

owner for a given application partition. It simply modifies the `fSMORoleOwner` attribute of the `Infrastructure` object at the root of the application partition. You can modify this attribute yourself and point it to a domain controller hosting this application partition as well.

DomainPrep

Before you can run `ADPrep /domainprep`, you must be sure that the updates from ForestPrep have replicated to all domain controllers in the forest. DomainPrep must be run on the Infrastructure Master of the domain and under the credentials of someone in the Domain Admins group. If you try to run DomainPrep before ForestPrep has been run or before it has replicated all its changes out, you will get an error message. Again, if you are unsure about the error, check the ADPrep logs in the *%SystemRoot%\sys tem32\debug\adprep\logs* directory for more information.

DomainPrep creates new containers and objects and modifies ACLs on some objects.

Unlike the ForestPrep command, which was fairly resource-intensive, DomainPrep completes quickly. The changes in comparison to ForestPrep are relatively minor. One new top-level container called `Password Settings Container` is created; this container provides a location for storage of Fine-Grained Password Policies.

GPPrep

The last step is only required if you are upgrading from Windows 2000. If you are, you must run `ADPrep /domainprep /gpprep` before you can begin upgrading your domain controllers to Windows Server 2008. Much like DomainPrep, this command must be run on the Infrastructure Master FSMO role holder. Prior to running GPPrep, you must have successfully run DomainPrep, or the tool will exit with an error.

GPPrep updates the access control lists (ACLs) on the group policy folders in the Sysvol container as well as the policy definitions stored in Active Directory.

Once you've run both ForestPrep and DomainPrep and allowed time for the changes to replicate to all domain controllers, you can then start upgrading your domain controllers to Windows Server 2008 or installing new Windows Server 2008 domain controllers.

Windows Server 2008 Upgrade Process

As with any major upgrade, the first step when beginning your Windows Server 2008 upgrade is to test the upgrade in a representative lab environment. Your lab should model applications that connect to Active Directory, as well as clients. If you are planning to deploy RODCs, you will need to pay particular attention to how applications interact with RODCs.

Once you have completed your testing, you will need to perform the forestprep, domainprep, and optionally rodcprep processes outlined earlier in this chapter. Then you can begin deploying Windows Server 2008 domain controllers. While it is supported to simply upgrade an existing domain controller in place to Windows Server 2008, we recommend that you always perform clean installations.

Once you have upgraded all of the domain controllers in a domain to Windows Server 2008, you can upgrade the domain to the Windows Server 2008 functional level to begin taking advantage of new Windows Server 2008 Active Directory features. Once all of the domains are at the Windows Server 2008 functional level, you can upgrade the forest functional level as well.

Summary

In this chapter, we covered the new features in Windows Server 2008 and some of the differences with Windows Server 2003. We then went over how you can enable new features with the use of functional levels and why they are necessary. Next we discussed the aDPrep process and how that must be done before the first Windows Server 2008 domain controller can be promoted. Once you have your forest and domains prepared, you can start the upgrade process. We described some of the important issues to be aware of when upgrading, and finally what to do after you've completed the upgrade.

## CHAPTER 19

Integrating Microsoft Exchange

Microsoft Exchange[*] has been the driving reason behind many companies move to Active Directory. Starting with Exchange 2000, Exchange requires an Active Directory infrastructure, and the dependencies it places on Active Directory are not small. In fact, the Exchange schema extensions roughly double the size of the default Active Directory schema. There are also restrictions on the location of your domain controllers relative to the Exchange servers. For these reasons and the critical nature of email, calendar, and collaboration services, all of which Exchange can provide, it is clear that Exchange can be one of the most significant applications you integrate into Active Directory.

In this chapter, we will briefly touch on some of the important issues regarding the integration of Exchange with Active Directory. We'll also cover how to prepare the forest for Exchange and describe some of the changes this causes.

A Quick Word about Exchange/AD Interaction

Here are a few key points to note about Active Directory, Exchange Server 2000, Exchange Server 2003, and Exchange Server 2007:

- Exchange 2000 can run only on Windows 2000.
- Exchange Server 2003 can run on Windows 2000 (with reduced functionality) and Windows Server 2003.
- Exchange Server 2007 SP1 can run Windows Server 2003 or Windows Server 2008.
- Exchange 2000 can run in a Windows Server 2003 or Windows 2000 Active Directory forest.

 If you are running Exchange 2000 in a forest that is running at the Windows Server 2003 forest functional level, you must review Microsoft Knowledge Base article 831809 at *http://support.micro soft.com/kb/831809*.

---

[*] The word "Exchange" signifies Exchange 2000, Exchange 2003, or Exchange 2007 unless specified.

- Exchange 2000 SP3 servers cannot exist in an Active Directory site that also contains Windows Server 2008 domain controllers unless you hardcode DSAccess to ignore these domain controllers.

- Exchange Server 2003 can run in a Windows Server 2003 or Windows 2000 Active Directory forest.

 Be sure to review Microsoft Knowledge Base article 903291 at *http://support.microsoft.com/kb/903291* before upgrading a forest to Windows Server 2003 functional level.

- Exchange Server 2003 SP2 (and newer) can run in a Windows Server 2008 Active Directory forest.

 For more information on Windows Server 2008 and Exchange, visit *http://msexchangeteam.com/archive/2007/08/16/446709.aspx*.

- Exchange Server 2007 can run in a Windows Server 2003 or Windows Server 2008 Active Directory forest.

Preparing Active Directory for Exchange

Before you can install the first Exchange server in Active Directory, you have to prepare your forest and domains. The Exchange 2000 and 2003 setup programs provided two options called /forestprep and /domainprep that perform various tasks such as extending the schema, creating groups, creating containers for Exchange, and setting permissions on those containers. Exchange Server 2007 has revamped this process significantly and now requires a series of setup commands:

- /PrepareLegacyExchangePermissions
- /PrepareSchema
- /PrepareAd
- /PrepareDomain

Due to the extent of changes caused by running these commands and the elevated privileges required to do so, it is imperative that Active Directory administrators have a thorough understanding of what the commands do.

Setup Prerequisites

Exchange Server 2007 is available in 32-bit and 64-bit versions. While it is not supported to run the 32-bit version of Exchange 2007 in production, you can use the 32-bit version for testing, management, and for preparing your Active Directory.

In order to run the Exchange 2007 setup tool, you will need to load Windows Power-Shell. On Windows Server 2008, PowerShell is a feature that you can install using Server Manager. Alternatively, you can run **ServerManagerCmd -i PowerShell** from a command prompt to install PowerShell. On Windows Server 2003, you will need to download PowerShell from Microsoft's website. Reference *http://support.microsoft.com/kb/926139* for download links and installation instructions.

On Windows Server 2008, you must also install the Remote Server Administration Tools (RSAT) for Active Directory Domain Services. You can either install these tools via the Add Features Wizard in Server Manager, or by running **ServerManagerCmd -i RSAT-ADDS** from a command prompt. This feature includes the *ldifde* utility that Exchange setup uses to extend the Active Directory schema.

 In our experience, a server reboot may be necessary after installing the RSAT-ADDS feature.

The machine on which you are running setup from must be a member of an Active Directory site. More specifically, the machine's IP address must match a valid subnet definition in Active Directory that is associated with an Active Directory site.

PrepareLegacyExchangePermissions

If you have an existing Exchange organization in your forest, the first step when adding Exchange 2007 servers to your forest is to update the existing Exchange permissions. If you don't do this, the Recipient Update Service (RUS) may fail to work correctly on your existing Exchange 2000 and Exchange 2003 servers. You need to run this command against every domain in the forest that contains the *Exchange Enterprise Servers* or *Exchange Domain Servers* groups.

If you have multiple domains, you can either run this command once to prepare all of the domains in the forest, or you can run it once per domain. If you want to prepare all of the domains at once, you must be a member of the Enterprise Admins group. Run this command to make the changes:

```
setup /PrepareLegacyExchangePermissions
```

If you want to update domains individually, you must be a member of the Domain Admins group in the relevant domain, and you must have been delegated Exchange Full Administrator rights using the Exchange System Manager delegation wizard. To prepare a specific domain, run this command:

```
setup /PrepareLegacyExchangePermissions:<fqdn of domain to prepare>
```

Before proceeding to the next step, allow enough time for these changes to replicate throughout your environment.

For more information on this step, reference *http://technet.microsoft.com/en-us/library/aa997914(EXCHG.80).aspx*.

PrepareSchema

Regardless of whether or not you have deployed Exchange before, you will need to extend the Active Directory schema to include the Exchange classes and attributes.

Exchange Server 2007 SP1 requires a schema update. If you are currently running Exchange 2007, you will need to update the schema again. If you are deploying Exchange 2007 for the first time, be sure to use Exchange 2007 SP1 media when updating the Active Directory schema so that you do not have to update it twice.

This extension will add attributes to the partial attribute set (PAS), modify existing Active Directory classes and attributes, add property sets, and index attributes.

If you still have Windows 2000 domain controllers in your forest at this step, they will completely resynchronize the global catalog after this schema extension is put in place since attributes are added to the PAS.

If you would like to examine the changes in detail, all of the relevant LDIF files are stored under \Setup\Data on the Exchange 2007 installation DVD. In order to import the LDIF files and make the schema changes, you must use the Exchange setup tool as importing the schema modifications directly is not supported by Microsoft.

In order to complete this step, you must be a member of the Enterprise Admins group as well as the Schema Admins group. The Schema Master FSMO role holder must be accessible in order to make the changes. To extend the Active Directory schema for Exchange, run this command:

```
Setup /PrepareSchema
```

Once the schema updates have replicated, you can continue to the next step. If you would like to check the version of the Exchange schema on a given domain controller, you can check the `rangeUpper` value on the `msExchSchemaVersionPt` attribute, which is added to the Active Directory schema as part of the Exchange schema extensions. Figure 19-1 shows this value in the Active Directory Schema MMC snap-in. Table 19-1 describes the possible values.

Table 19-1. Exchange schema versions

rangeUpper value	Exchange server version
4397	Exchange 2000
6903	Exchange 2003

rangeUpper value	Exchange server version
10637	Exchange 2007
11116	Exchange 2007 SP1

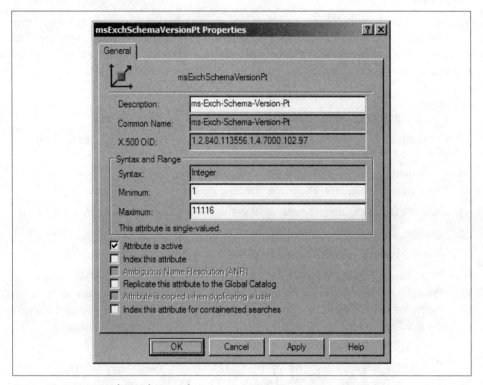

Figure 19-1. Viewing the Exchange schema version

Before proceeding to the next step, allow enough time for these changes to replicate throughout your environment.

 If you run **PrepareSchema**, you *must* run **PrepareAD**, which is detailed next. If you do not run **PrepareAD**, you will leave the permissions in your forest in an inconsistent state, which will prevent you from reading certain attributes on user objects.

For details on the Exchange 2007 schema changes, reference the following links:

- Exchange 2007—*http://msdn.microsoft.com/en-us/library/aa581540(EXCHG.80) .aspx*

- Exchange 2007 SP1—*http://msdn.microsoft.com/en-us/library/bb799744(EXCHG .80).aspx*

- Exchange 2003—*http://msdn.microsoft.com/en-us/library/aa581270(EXCHG.80).aspx*

PrepareAD

The scope of the `PrepareAD` steps varies depending on whether or not you are upgrading an existing Exchange organization in your forest or if you are deploying a new one. The `PrepareAD` step creates and/or updates the Exchange configuration data in the configuration partition as well as key objects in the forest root domain.

The changes made during this step include:

- Importing the extended rights Exchange requires to operate
- Creating the new Microsoft Exchange Security Groups OU and groups in the forest root domain
- Creating objects under the Microsoft Exchange System Objects container in the forest root domain (and the corresponding container if it does not exist)
- Creating the Exchange configuration container and a number of objects inside it
- Creating the Exchange Organization in Active Directory if it does not already exist
- Creating the Exchange 2007 administrative and routing groups

In order to run `PrepareAD`, you will need to be a member of the Enterprise Admins group. You will need to run the setup program from a machine that is in the same domain as the schema master as well as in the same site as the schema master. The setup program will also need to contact one domain controller in each domain in the forest.

 You can transfer the schema master FSMO to a domain controller that is not in the forest root domain. This may be more convenient than joining a machine to your forest root domain to run setup if you do not have one available.

In order to run `PrepareAD`, run this command: **setup /PrepareAD**. If you are installing Exchange for the first time in the forest, you must also specify an Exchange organization name: **setup /PrepareAD /OrganizationName: "<OrganizationName>"**. The name you pick at this step is permanent and cannot be changed. You can only have one Exchange organization per forest.

Before proceeding to the next step, allow enough time for these changes to replicate throughout your environment.

For more information on this step, reference *http://technet.microsoft.com/en-us/library/bb125224(EXCHG.80).aspx*.

PrepareDomain

The final step of preparing your Active Directory for Exchange is to run the `PrepareDomain` command. This command updates the permissions in the domain and creates a number of objects required by Exchange. `PrepareDomain` must be run in every domain that will contain Exchange servers or contain mail enabled objects.

> If you only have one domain in your forest or will only be hosting Exchange servers or mail enabled objects in the domain you ran `PrepareAD` in, you do not need to run `PrepareDomain`.

The changes taken during this step include:

- Creation of objects under the Microsoft Exchange system Objects container (and the corresponding container if it does not exist)
- Changes to permissions for Exchange servers and administrators at the domain level
- Granting Exchange servers the *Manage Auditing and Security Log* right (`SeSecurityPrivilege`) on domain controllers (via modifying the domain controller GPO)

In order to run `PrepareDomain`, you must be a member of the Domain Admins group. If the domain was created after you ran `PrepareAD`, you must also be a member of the Exchange Organization Administrators group.

To run `PrepareDomain`, run this command: **setup /PrepareDomain**. This will prepare the domain you are logged in to. If you want to prepare all of the domains in your forest at once, run **setup /PrepareAllDomains**. You will need to be a member of the Enterprise Admins group.

Before proceeding to the next step (installing Exchange servers), allow enough time for these changes to replicate throughout your environment.

For more information on this step, reference *http://technet.microsoft.com/en-us/library/bb125224(EXCHG.80).aspx*. For a general reference on Exchange setup and Active Directory permissions, reference *http://technet.microsoft.com/en-us/library/bb310770(EXCHG.80).aspx* and the whitepaper at *http://technet.microsoft.com/en-us/library/bb288907(EXCHG.80).aspx*.

Active Directory Site Design and Domain Controller Placement

If you did not plan for Exchange in your initial Active Directory design, consider a whiteboard discussion to review your entire design with Exchange in mind. It is possible and even likely there are aspects of your design that are not optimal for Exchange and will cause issues unless redesigned. Exchange is not very tolerant of Active Directory issues; it is much less tolerant than, for instance, the client logon process. Exchange can have a negative effect on other applications and client access to Active Directory if not planned for properly, and if Active Directory is not performing to par for Exchange, mail users will undoubtedly notice very quickly. As an Active Directory Administrator, you need to understand Exchange's requirements and best practices and how it uses, or in some cases abuses, Active Directory. If you simply try to install Exchange into the forest as-is, you could be in for a rough time with lots of troubleshooting and heartache.

A common practice in Exchange 5.5 environments was to load Exchange 5.5 onto domain controllers to speed up authentication. This is not at all recommended with Exchange 2000 and newer since the directory has been separated from the application. Normally if Exchange is experiencing slow or failed responses from a domain controller, it will start using another domain controller. When Exchange is loaded on a domain controller, this failover capability is disabled. Domain controllers should, of course, by design be just domain controllers, so loading Exchange and all of the additional components it requires completely defeats this design.

Site topology

When you implement Exchange, keeping the Active Directory site topology up to date becomes even more important. The Exchange installation process will abort if the server does not have a subnet defined in Active Directory that maps to a site in the topology. Each Exchange server uses the site topology to build a list of domain controllers to use for server queries and to assign to clients for their queries. Starting with Exchange 2007, Exchange now uses the Active Directory site topology for mail routing. While previous versions of Exchange used routing groups, this has been abandoned in Exchange 2007. Consequentially, you will need to work closely with messaging administrators to ensure that the site link topology is suitable for mail routing. You will also need to advise messaging administrators of any changes that could affect mail routing.

Every site that contains an Exchange Mailbox or Unified Messaging server must also contain an Exchange Hub Transport server. All mail between sites is relayed by Hub Transport servers. Hub Transport servers rely on the site link topology in Active Directory in order to determine the best path to route mail. Unless you manually configure site links using the `set-adsitelink` command, Hub Transport servers will respect the cost configured on the site link. You can customize site links to retain an Exchange specific cost using `set-adsitelink`.

 You can also use the `set-adsitelink` command to configure maximum message sizes for specific site links.

When a Hub Transport server needs to send mail to a different site, by default mail is sent directly to the Hub Transport server closest to the final destination of the message.

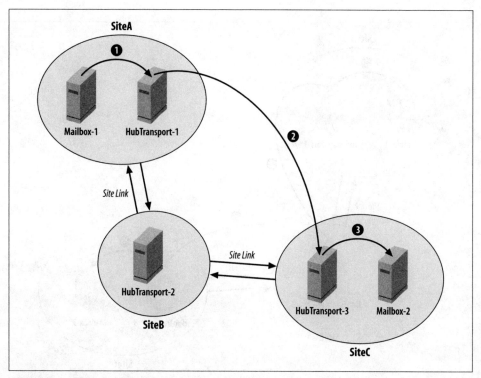

Figure 19-2. Direct mail routing

This applies even if there are intermediate hub transport servers along the path. Figure 19-2 shows this.

If you want to configure this differently such that mail is relayed between intermediate hub transport servers, you must use the `set-adsite` command to configure the necessary intermediate site(s) as hub sites. In general, you most likely only want to do this if there are firewalls along the path that do not permit direct SMTP traffic. Figure 19-3 shows this behavior where SiteB has been marked as a hub site.

For more information on Exchange and its dependencies on the Active Directory site topology, visit *http://technet.microsoft.com/en-us/library/aa996299(EXCHG.80).aspx*. For a more in depth discussion, review *http://technet.microsoft.com/en-us/library/aa998825(EXCHG.80).aspx*.

A common practice in larger organizations is to place Exchange servers and domain controllers dedicated to Exchange in a single Active Directory site together. This practice isolates Exchange servers from using domain controllers that are servicing user traffic or other applications, and it isolates those domain controllers from the additional load Exchange will place upon them. This recommendation is not always considered best practice anymore with Exchange 2007. The reason is that the site topology now influences mail routing, so adding this additional hop could negatively affect the

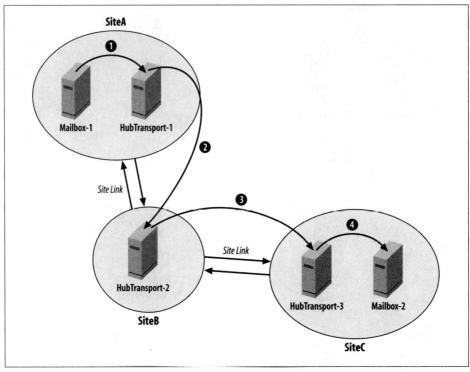

Figure 19-3. Mail routing with a hub site

topology used for message routing. You will need to examine your topology and determine if this is the case.

Domain controller impact

Perhaps the most significant impact of Exchange on Active Directory is the dependencies it creates in regard to domain controller location. The general best-practice recommendation is to have domain controllers in the same datacenter or computer room as your Exchange servers. Exchange is specifically very dependent on global catalog availability. Exchange servers will fail to operate correctly if they do not have ready access to a global catalog server that is responsive. As a general rule of thumb, Microsoft recommends that you have a 1:8 ratio of global catalog processor cores to Exchange mailbox server processor cores in a given site if you meet the following criteria:

- You are running Exchange 2007
- Your domain controllers are running a 64-bit version of Windows
- Your domain controllers have enough memory to cache the entire *ntds.dit* database in memory

In all other cases, Microsoft recommends that you maintain a 1:4 ratio of global catalog processors to Exchange processors in a given site. For more information on sizing global catalogs for Exchange, visit *http://msexchangeteam.com/archive/2007/03/28/437313.aspx*.

Exchange 2003 and 2000 servers have a process called the Recipient Update Service (RUS), which is responsible for the majority of the Active Directory changes when you mail-enable or mailbox-enable an object. This process is asynchronous whereby an administrator sets a number of attributes directly on an object that the RUS, in turn, detects and uses to complete the operation. There is typically one "Enterprise" RUS instance, as well as at least one RUS instance per domain running in the Exchange organization.

The Enterprise RUS is responsible for processing server objects and global types of changes, such as the permission modifications that may be required by the Exchange Delegation Wizard. Each domain RUS is responsible for dealing with stamping and modifying recipient objects such as users and contacts. It can be useful to have multiple domain RUS setups in case one of the domain controllers is offline for an extended period of time. It is important that you work with your messaging administrators to understand the domain controllers they are required to target the RUS to. This is to ensure that there are adequate resources available for Exchange to perform the required operations in a reasonable period of time. Exchange 2007 has done away with the RUS and the entire process of mail or mailbox enabling an object is now synchronous. All of the necessary attributes in Active Directory are set at the time the proper calls are made to Exchange to enable that object.

Other Considerations

Microsoft went the route of splitting up the install process for Exchange, but you have the option of doing it all at the same time. If the user account you used to install Exchange for the first time is a member of the Enterprise Admins and Schema Admins group, you can simple run `setup /PrepareAD` followed optionally by `setup /PrepareAll Domains` if necessary.

The global-catalog-to-Exchange-server ratio guideline put forth by Microsoft best practices is simply a guideline. Since this is a guideline, you may find that your Exchange deployment requires more or less global catalog processors per Exchange processor than the guideline. This is something that you will need to monitor performance counters and historical trending to understand. If you are unsure and are designing a new environment, the guideline is a good rule of thumb.

Unfortunately, there are no guaranteed signs to tell you when you need more global catalog capacity. Generally, when your DSACCESS performance counters start reporting slow LDAP lookups, it is a sign that you may need more domain controller capacity. However, it could also signify network issues or that your distribution lists have too many individual users in them and you need to start placing fewer users in groups and nesting the groups together, or any number of other things.

Deploying Exchange in a multidomain forest almost guarantees that you will need to use universal groups for Exchange permissioning and distribution lists. Exchange is more dependent on global catalogs than on domain controllers, which means that resolution of a distribution list could occur on any global catalog in the forest, and if the distribution list isn't a universal group, there is a good chance the group will not be able to be expanded to its full membership. There are mechanisms that can be employed to counteract this; however, it adds additional overhead and possible break points. If you intend to use Exchange distribution lists or secure Exchange with groups in a multidomain forest, use universal groups to do so.

Historically, in a single forest implementation, creating a "split permissions model" to separate Active Directory administrators and Exchange administrators is extremely difficult to accomplish, and if you are completely honest, actually impossible. If having this separation is mandatory due to security concerns or legal ramifications, then you absolutely must look into a dedicated Exchange resource forest model. In that model, Exchange is not installed in the NOS forest; instead, it has its own single domain resource forest that is entirely managed by the Exchange administrators. This resource forest will trust the NOS forest (or individual domains) and is run very much like Exchange 5.5 was run in large organizations. There is additional work required when provisioning and de-provisioning users, but this model offers a true security boundary and actually can solve other painful multidomain issues that are otherwise present in Exchange.

Exchange 2007 greatly simplifies this and adds a number of property sets to the Active Directory schema that can be used to delegate management of the Exchange attributes. The Exchange Management Console (EMC) and Shell both include functionality to delegate administration of recipients as well as a number of other roles. The delegations can be managed by accessing the root of the Organization Configuration pane in the EMC as shown in Figure 19-4. You can access the Add Exchange Administrator dialog by right-clicking Organization Configuration or using the Action Pane. Figure 19-5 shows the Add Exchange Administrator dialog.

Mail-Enabling Objects

In order for an object such as a user or group to be able to receive mail, you must mailbox-enable or mail-enable the object. This process sets all of the necessary attributes on the object so that Exchange knows how to handle mail for that object. In order

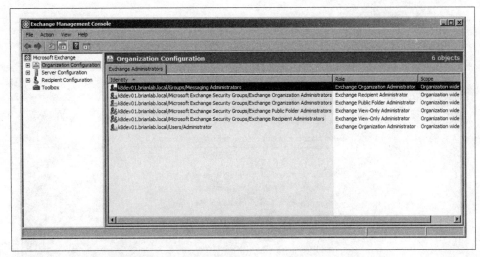

Figure 19-4. Exchange permissions management

to carry out this process, you'll need to either use the Exchange Management Console GUI or the PowerShell cmdlets that ship with Exchange 2007. If you're running Exchange 2003 or Exchange 2000, you'll need to use the wizards that are integrated with Active Directory Users and Computers.

Using the Exchange Management Console

The Exchange Management Console (EMC) is a complete replacement for the duo of Exchange System Manager and Active Directory Users and Computers, which were used in versions of Exchange previous to Exchange 2007. The EMC is a frontend to Windows PowerShell, and anytime you run a wizard that executes a PowerShell command, the GUI will actually tell you the PowerShell command that was just run. In this section, we will walk through mailbox-enabling an existing user with the EMC as well as mail-enabling a group.

Mailbox-enabling a user

The EMC is capable of either modifying existing user objects or creating new ones and mailbox-enabling them at the same time. Managing end-user mailboxes is accomplished in the Mailbox pane under Recipient Configuration in the console. You can either right click and select New Mailbox, or use the Action Pane.

Figure 19-6 shows the choices presented when you run the New Mailbox wizard. We will only discuss creating a user mailbox and briefly a linked mailbox. For more information on the various types of mailboxes and recipients, visit *http://technet.microsoft.com/en-us/library/bb201680(EXCHG.80).aspx*.

Figure 19-7 shows the screen that you can elect to create mailboxes for existing users or to create new users. You can add to the list as many existing users as you want to

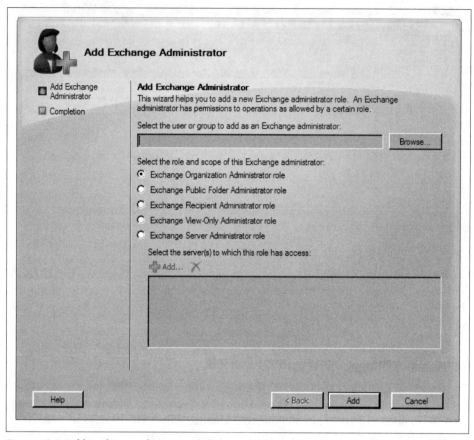

Figure 19-5. Add Exchange Administrator dialog

create mailboxes for; however, you can only select one set of settings for all of these users (such as mailbox database and policy settings).

When you click the Add button, you will see a dialog similar to the one shown in Figure 19-8; the dialog allows you to browse for users. By default, every user in the domain who does not have a mailbox will be shown. This can be difficult to work with in large domains. You can change the scope of this view by going to Scope→Modify Recipient Picker Scope. You will likely find it is far more efficient to use PowerShell for these tasks in a large environment.

Once you complete the wizard, a status pane will be displayed; this status pane includes the PowerShell command run by the wizard, as shown in Figure 19-9. As a rule, every wizard in the Exchange Management Console shows the PowerShell command(s) that were run to execute the tasks you used the wizard for. This is an excellent way to learn the various Exchange PowerShell commands.

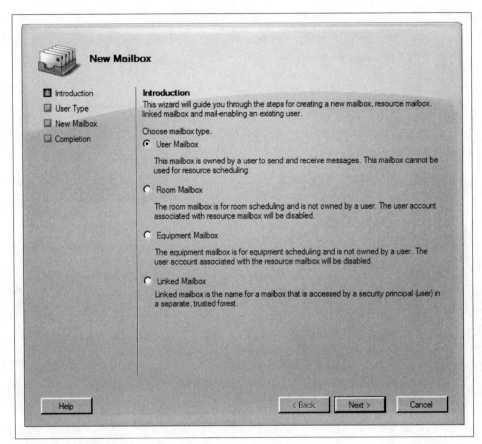

Figure 19-6. New Mailbox wizard

Linked mailboxes

Linked mailboxes are useful if you are running Exchange in a dedicated resource forest or are providing mailboxes for users in a remote, trusted domain or forest. When you create a linked mailbox, a dummy account is used in the forest hosting Exchange to represent the mailbox. The dummy account is a disabled user account that contains additional entries in the account's ACL pointing to the actual user account in the trusted domain. Exchange also stores the SID of the actual user account as an attribute of the trusted account.

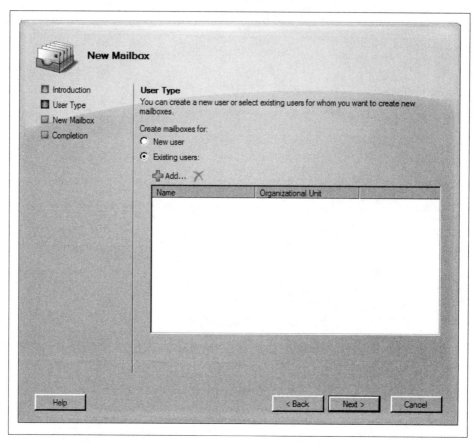

Figure 19-7. Selecting users to create mailboxes for

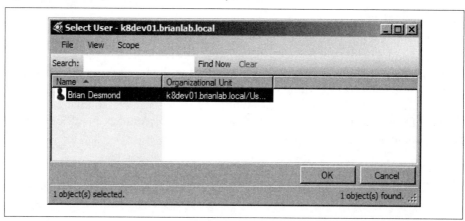

Figure 19-8. Recipient picker

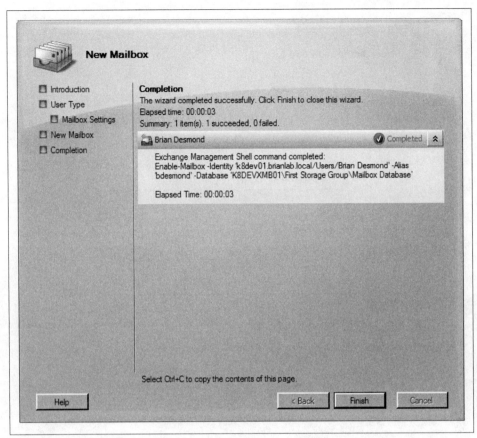

Figure 19-9. Completing the New Mailbox wizard

Mail-enabling a group

Creating a mail-enabled distribution group is a very similar process to creating a mailbox for a user. The EMC can create new group objects and mail-enable them, or mail-enable an existing group. To do this, go to the Distribution Group pane under Recipient Configuration in the EMC and either right-click or use the Action Pane. Figure 19-10 shows the dialog for mail-enabling an existing group called Brian's Friends.

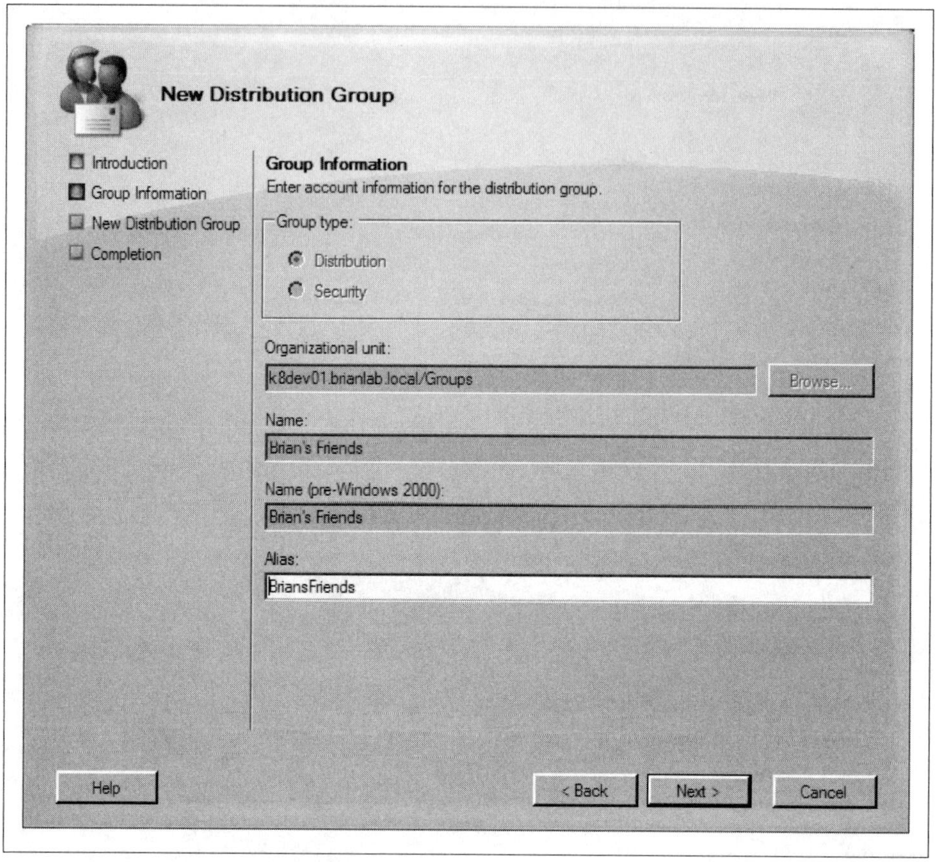

Figure 19-10. Mail enabling a distribution group

Exchange also supports a type of group called a dynamic distribution group. Dynamic distribution groups get their membership via an LDAP query instead of having the membership specified as an attribute of the group like normal distribution and security groups. The EMC allows you to create dynamic distribution groups in the same place as normal distribution groups; however, the wizard is very limited in functionality. You can only select certain attributes and then the wizard will build the LDAP filter for you. In Exchange 2003, dynamic distribution groups were called query-based distribution groups.

Using PowerShell

Exchange 2007 is the first version of Exchange to have a Microsoft-supplied command-line management toolset. The entire command-line experience is known as the Exchange Management Shell (EMS), which is built on top of Windows PowerShell. We provide an introduction to Windows PowerShell in Chapter 30 and cover various Exchange PowerShell tasks in Chapter 33, including the examples from the previous section.

Summary

The importance of Exchange in the enterprise is ever increasing. Exchange has steadily eaten away at the messaging market to the point where it is currently the market leader. In fact, the initial driving force behind the move to Active Directory for many organizations is the need to deploy Exchange. Integrating Exchange into Active Directory is no small feat due to its heavy reliance on AD.

Exchange setup has a number of steps that are necessary to prepare Active Directory to support Exchange, and all of these steps will need to be performed by an Active Directory administrator who has elevated access to the directory. The Exchange Management Console (EMC) and Exchange Management Shell (EMS) are a completely new management experience in Exchange 2007 and provide an end-to-end environment for managing both the Exchange infrastructure as well as objects in the directory that are mail-enabled.

Exchange may be the most significant application you'll integrate with Active Directory. Knowing this, as an Active Directory administrator you should come to the table with a basic understanding of Exchange, and we covered the principles of Exchange we think you'll find most useful in this chapter.

Active Directory Lightweight Directory Service (a.k.a. ADAM)

Shortly after Microsoft released Windows 2000 Active Directory, developers and administrators started asking for a standalone Microsoft LDAP service that was similar to Active Directory, but didn't have the baggage of Active Directory such as DNS requirements, the FRS requirements, Group Policy, and other domain pieces like Kerberos and the legacy SAM stuff—basically, something light and easy to set up and play with, and then tear back down as required. While you can do this with Active Directory, there tends to be additional clean-up and configuration required, and things unrelated to the LDAP functionality can get confused and cause it all to malfunction.

In November 2003, shortly after Windows Server 2003 Active Directory was released, Microsoft released Active Directory Application Mode (ADAM) V1.0 to the web (RTW). This was the product that the developers and administrators had been asking for: Active Directory Lite. ADAM allows developers and administrators to play with Active Directory on Windows XP (in the case of ADAM V1.0) or Windows Server 2003 and newer servers without promoting the local host to a full domain controller. The only DNS requirement is resolution of the hostname. There is no FRS, no Kerberos, no group policy, and no extra domain stuff. In fact, ADAM runs nicely as a regular Windows application that can leverage any Windows Domain authentication or local machine authentication that is available, as well as offering up its own authentication that is completely application specific. It is just as happy in a domain as it is on a standalone machine.

Over the last couple of years, companies large and small (including Microsoft) have been building and deploying ADAM-based applications. Due to the fact that ADAM was released after the security push and didn't have any legacy requirement baggage other than being programmatically compatible with Active Directory, it is, by default, considerably more locked down. Where Active Directory followed the "on or enabled or open by default" mentality, ADAM followed the new "off/disabled/closed by default" approach. From a security standpoint, this is great. Another huge benefit is that many experienced Active Directory administrators and developers will be able to get familiar with ADAM quickly, which will benefit administration, management, monitoring, and application development since ADAM is so similar to Active Directory.

With all of that going for it, you may wonder why you may not have heard more about ADAM, since it certainly hasn't received nearly the amount of press that Active Directory has. One reason for this is that ADAM was initially only released to the web; this tends to put some people off as they may think the support is not quite what the support is for a product officially released on a CD. That is a reason why ADAM is now being packaged with Windows Server 2003 R2 and newer. Instead of going out to the web to download ADAM, you simply install it as a feature on Windows Server.

This chapter is meant to serve as an introduction to ADAM, not an all encompassing guide. An entire book could be written on ADAM: the cool tools available for it and how it can be used both with and without Active Directory. There is a considerable amount of information available concerning ADAM on the Microsoft website; if you find this chapter insufficient for what you need to do, visit *http://www.microsoft.com/adam*.

With the release of Windows Server 2008, Microsoft updated ADAM and renamed it the Active Directory Lightweight Directory Service (AD LDS). Throughout this chapter we will use the terms ADAM and AD LDS interchangeably.

ADAM Terms

There are several terms used throughout this chapter; here are some simple definitions to help understand the concepts:

Instance
> An instance is a single installation of ADAM on a server. Each server can have multiple instances of ADAM installed; they would all be independently managed and use different LDAP and LDAPS ports.

Configuration set
> A collection of ADAM instances that replicate with each other and share a common schema and configuration container. Application partitions can be shared amongst the instances that make up the configuration set as well.

Replica
> An instance of ADAM that is part of a configuration set and replicates with other ADAM instances.

Partition/naming context
> Unique namespace named after the root DN. ADAM will have at least two partitions per instance: the configuration and schema partitions. ADAM can also have multiple application partitions.

Application partition
> Type of partition that contains application data. ADAM can have multiple application partitions per instance.

Configuration partition
> Type of partition that contains configuration data for the instance or configuration set.

Schema partition
> Type of partition that contains the class and attribute mappings.

Bindable object
> An object instantiated from an objectClass that has `msDS-BindableObject` listed as a static auxiliary class in the schema definition for the `objectClass`. The most common bindable object is the `user` class. Objects of this type are authenticated by ADAM directly.

Bindable proxy object
> An object instantiated from an objectClass that has `msDS-BindProxy` listed as a static auxiliary class in the schema definition for the objectClass. The most common Bindable proxy object is the `userProxy` class. Objects of this type are authenticated by ADAM by proxying the authentication request to Windows.

Differences Between AD and ADAM V1.0

ADAM and AD are quite similar, but obviously there are differences or else there would be nothing to talk about. This section isn't intended to be a comprehensive listing of all differences, but rather an attempt to catch the major changes and popular "gotchas."

Standalone Application Service

The most obvious difference is that ADAM is set up to run as a standalone application service; it isn't part of the system-level service NETLOGON. This means that instead of the LDAP functions being handled by the *LSASS.EXE* process, they instead run from the *DSAMAIN.EXE* process. The not-so-obvious upshot of this is that ADAM can be stopped or started on demand without having to reboot the machine. It also means ADAM can be updated as needed, again without rebooting the machine. Anytime you had to go anywhere near the LDAP functionality of a domain controller, you were pretty much guaranteed a reboot and had concerns of it restarting properly and users being impacted. All of these concerns are dramatically reduced now because Active Directory in Application Mode is just an application.

In addition to the benefit of stopping and starting on command, the new service implementation allows you to set up multiple instances of ADAM on a single machine, each under a different service. So instead of having a single Active Directory instance on a machine responding to requests on port 389, you can have multiple ADAM instances on a machine listening on various ports, with each instance having an entirely different schema.

Configurable LDAP Ports

Another difference is that with ADAM you can actually control what ports the LDAP Service is listening on. Active Directory seemed to have some registry entries you could change to specify what ports it listened on. Unfortunately, it was just a dirty trick: the ports were really hardcoded in the binaries so that you could modify them in the registry, but it didn't do anything. This is silly because the DNS SRV records have a field describing what port the service is listening on, but it just wasn't used by the DC Locator functions.

No SRV Records

ADAM doesn't register SRV records in DNS like Active Directory does; unfortunately, even registering your own SRV records on behalf of ADAM doesn't make it so the DC location API calls will work for finding ADAM instances. A network trace shows two reasons for this. The first reason is that the DC Locator services don't look at the port field of the SRV record, so if ADAM is running on a different port, the DC Locator service can't connect to it. The second reason is that the DC Locator services send a special UDP LDAP ping to the host, and ADAM doesn't know how to respond to that request. This, of course, all makes sense since ADAM isn't a domain controller, but it would be nice to have that functionality to make use of ADAM a trifle more seamless for applications.

Instead of SRV records, ADAM can publish `serviceConnectionPoint` (SCP) objects in Active Directory for resource location. These are objects in Active Directory that are usually published under the computer object that the service is installed on (this is configurable). The `serviceConnectionPoint` objects maintain key pieces of information about the ADAM installation in the `keywords` and `serviceBindingInformation` attributes. An example of this information is listed in Example 20-1.

Example 20-1. ADAM SCP example

```
>keywords: partition:DC=joeware,DC=net
>keywords: 1cf21445-f4f5-4451-bff2-d32f511c478b
>keywords: 42eca3c5-ee95-48c8-ab7d-7524ae887239
>keywords: partition:DC=domain,DC=com
>keywords: 9549ae64-a3ee-461a-918f-828f522b0382
>keywords: partition:CN=newpart
>keywords: 450d8cf9-19de-4c3c-817d-d5443fb968f5
>keywords: partition:CN=user
>keywords: partition:DC=test,DC=etherpunk,DC=local
>keywords: 7547aa81-51ad-416f-9ee6-7bfd1f88853d
>keywords: partition:DC=mytest,DC=com
>keywords: c4d69674-b673-45f9-ad14-b1e488d4a0c8
>keywords: 0a891bbf-1be6-4fe4-9406-3f21355e144e
```

```
>keywords: partition:DC=set-con,DC=org
>keywords: 81b58144-7068-410b-bd93-8248109a329b
>keywords: partition:DC=etherpunk,DC=local
>keywords: partition:CN=Configuration,CN={E28AE3C2-1228-4F6B-917C-56B9757DB796}
>keywords: 47abf207-536a-4ea4-9295-9ef3c7f1fb8c
>keywords: fsmo:naming
>keywords: fsmo:schema
>keywords: instance:ADAM1
>keywords: site:Default-First-Site-Name
>keywords: 1.2.840.113556.1.4.1791
>keywords: 1.2.840.113556.1.4.1851
>keywords: 14b5dcce-8584-4100-8d5b-139b1e8a95b1
>serviceBindingInformation: ldaps://adamserver.mycorp.com:636
>serviceBindingInformation: ldap://adamserver.mycorp.com:389
```

As you can see in the example, the serviceBindingInformation attribute shows the actual hostname and ports in use:

```
>serviceBindingInformation: ldaps://adamserver.mycorp.com:636
>serviceBindingInformation: ldap://adamserver.mycorp.com:389
```

In the keywords attribute, there is more good info. Here are some of the more useful pieces of info about the partitions that are available:

```
>keywords: partition:DC=joeware,DC=net
>keywords: partition:DC=domain,DC=com
>keywords: partition:CN=newpart
>keywords: partition:CN=user
>keywords: partition:DC=test,DC=etherpunk,DC=local
>keywords: partition:DC=mytest,DC=com
>keywords: partition:DC=set-con,DC=org
>keywords: partition:DC=etherpunk,DC=local
>keywords: partition:CN=Configuration,CN={E28AE3C2-1228-4F6B-917C-56B9757DB796}
```

Here are the FSMOs held by this instance:

```
>keywords: fsmo:naming
>keywords: fsmo:schema
```

the site the instance is in:

```
>keywords: site:Default-First-Site-Name
```

the instance name that maps to the actual service name on the host:

```
>keywords: instance:ADAM1
```

and some OIDs describing functionality of the instance:

```
>keywords: 1.2.840.113556.1.4.1791
>keywords: 1.2.840.113556.1.4.1851
```

If you choose, you can add additional keywords to help your applications select the proper instance or naming context. For more on using the serviceConnectionPoint objects for ADAM, see the following:

- Understanding ADAM service publication: *http://technet2.microsoft.com/Windows Server/en/Library/80e08d70-0eb5-4ee7-aee6-cdc3c968c87b1033.mspx*
- Service Connection Points for Replicated, Host-Based, and Database Services: *http: //msdn.microsoft.com/en-us/library/ms677946(VS.85).aspx*

No Global Catalog

Active Directory has the global catalog in order to easily query for objects across the entire forest hierarchy. You send a standard LDAP query to a special port, and you have access to a subset of attributes for all objects in the forest. A single query will allow you to search across the configuration container, the schema, and every default domain partition in the forest. ADAM has multiple partitions, but it doesn't have the matching global catalog functionality. Fortunately, the Windows LDAP server accepts a special LDAP control setting that allows you to use one single query that will scan across all of the partitions (or a subset of the partitions like DC=com) of an ADAM instance. Unfortunately, this functionality is not available to ADSI scripts and programs, only from the LDAP API-based applications.

There is an option that could work for ADSI and any third-party applications that don't implement the proper LDAP control. It involves implementing GC functionality yourself by setting up another top-level application partition and synchronizing certain objects and attributes from the other application partitions. You then grant read-only access to applications and users that need to query the entire instance, and full control to the syncing application. If you are simply looking for a quick lookup of a DN for an object based on a couple of public attributes like sAMAccountName, this option might work for you.

 We just described the LDAP_SERVER_SEARCH_OPTIONS_OID server control. This control, combined with the SERVER_SEARCH_FLAG_PHANTOM_ROOT flag, enables the special full instance search functionality. The control is also available for Active Directory, but generally isn't required due to the global catalog functionality. For more information, see *http://msdn.mi crosoft.com/en-us/library/aa366988(VS.85).aspx*.

The loss of the global catalog also impacts a special protocol used by Outlook and Exchange, primarily used for Address Book functionality. The Name Service Provider Interface (NSPI) and the backend Address Book (AB) support functionality are only provided in the Global Catalog code. Stripping out the GC functions also strips out the NSPI and AB functions.

Top-Level Application Partition Object Classes

In Active Directory, application partitions must all be objectclass `domainDNS` objects. ADAM allows application partitions to be of any objectclass, as long as it is a container-type object. This means that you can have application partitions that are of many different types, including `organizationalUnit`, `container`, `o`, `c`, `l`, or even `user`.

Group and User Scope

The scope of an ADAM group or user is limited to the partition in which it exists; e.g., a group or user created in partition 1 can neither be used to assign permissions on objects in partition 2 nor added to a group in partition 2. You can, however, add Windows security principals and ADAM security principals from the configuration partition to the groups in other partitions.

FSMOs

In an Active Directory forest, you have two FSMOs for the entire forest (Schema and Domain Naming) and three FSMOs (PDC, RID, and Infrastructure) for each domain. A single domain forest would have a total of five FSMOs, a two domain forest would have 8 FSMOs, etc. ADAM, on the other hand, only has two FSMO roles regardless of the number of partitions or the number of replicas. The two FSMOs are the Naming FSMO and the Schema FSMO, whose roles map to the Active Directory Domain Naming FSMO and Schema FSMO. Just like with Active Directory, if you want to add a new partition, you must contact the Naming FSMO, and if you want to update the Schema, you must contact the Schema FSMO.

The missing FSMOs are generally not too surprising when you think of the functional changes between AD and ADAM. However, the lack of the RID FSMO may confuse some administrators because ADAM still uses Security Identifiers (SIDs), and SIDs need to be unique to be of value. The RID FSMO is used in an Active Directory domain to make sure that each security principal that is created has a unique SID value to uniquely identify it within the domain. This was handled in a well-known way in Active Directory as it followed the basic mechanism used for NT4, where RIDs were incremented as they were passed out. ADAM has changed this process so that a RID Master is no longer needed.

Instead of using RIDs, Microsoft has an algorithm in place based on the GUID generation algorithm to generate unique SIDs. Instead of the SIDs having just a unique RID, the last four sub-authorities in the SID are all generated for each user. While one or more of those sub-authorities may match other groups or users, there shouldn't be a collision with all four values because ADAM tries to enforce the uniqueness. This means a RID master is not needed.

What's in a Security Identifier (SID)?

Most every Windows administrator knows what a SID is: a unique, variable-length identifier used to identify a trustee or security principal. However, few understand what components a SID is comprised of. A little bit of time spent understanding how SIDs are composed can possibly help an administrator understand the underpinnings of Windows security.

A Windows SID is generally composed of two fixed fields and up to 15 additional fields, all separated by dashes like so:

```
S-v-id-s1-s2-s3-s4-s5-s6-s7-s8-s9-s10-s11-s12-s13-s14-s15
```

The first fixed field (**v**) describes the version of the SID structure. Microsoft has never changed this, so it is always 1.

The second fixed field (**id**) is called the identifier authority. In Windows domains and Windows computers, it uniquely identifies the authority involved such as NULL (0), World (1), Local (2), NT Authority (5), etc.

The next 15 fields (**s1-s15**) are not required for every SID and, in fact, most SIDs only have a few of these fields populated. These additional fields are called sub-authorities and help uniquely identify the object being referenced. The last sub-authority on most SIDs is generally called the RID. This is the value that a domain or computer increments to create unique SIDs.

With that information, you can now look at a SID such as S-1-5-10 and determine that it is a version 1 SID issued by the NT Authority. This SID is special and is called a well-known SID, representing NTAUTHORITY\SELF. Another well-known SID is S-1-1-0, which is a version 1 World SID; it represents Everyone.

There are several other well-known SIDs with various values. They are easily identifiable because they don't fit the format of normal computer and domain SIDs. These normal SIDs usually look like this:

```
S-1-21-xxx-yyy-zzz-r
```

where the values for *xxx, yyy*, and *zzz* are randomly generated when the computer or domain is created. The RID value **r** could either be a consecutive number issued by the RID generation routine or a well-known RID assigned to certain security principals that exist in every domain. An example of a well-known RID is 500, which translates to the built-in administrator account.

ADAM changed the use of the SID fields for ADAM Trustees and Security Principals slightly. The new format looks like this:

```
S-v-id1-id2-r1-r2-r3-r4
```

The first fixed field (**v**) still describes the version of the SID structure. Although the use of the various fields has been slightly modified, the binary format of the SID structure is identical; Microsoft didn't change the version, and it is still always 1.

The second and third fixed fields (`id1-id2`) are the identifier authority and are specific to the directory partition. Each partition in an ADAM instance will have a unique combination of these values.

The next four fields (`r1-r4`) are not required for every SID. The built-in groups will only have `r1` populated, and they will be populated with well-known RID values. The built-in groups are Readers (**514**), Users (**513**), and Administrators (**512**). Any other objects created that need SIDs will have `r1-r4` populated with unique combinations of randomly generated values.

It is possible to encounter Windows SIDs inside of ADAM. They are easily identified because they follow the Windows SID format instead of the ADAM format. These Windows SIDs are used to either identify Windows Trustees or grant permissions inside of ADAM to Windows Trustees. For example, you will add the SID for a Windows user to the Administrators group of any partition in order to grant that Windows user administrator rights over the partition.

Schema

The default ADAM schema is a very light-weight schema in comparison to the default AD Schema. Initially, it only has 44 classes and 268 attributes, which is quite sparse. Microsoft supplies a couple of LDIF files with ADAM so you can initially build up the schema to instantiate some Microsoft standard objects, such as `inetOrgPerson` and `user` objects. Extension of the schema beyond this is fully supported and similar to the process used to extend the AD Schema.

Another difference with the schema is that you can have multiple schemas on a single machine with ADAM. Each instance of ADAM can have its own schema, and you can install multiple instances.

Service Account

AD runs in the LSASS process on domain controllers as `LocalSystem`. The ADAM service runs as `NT AUTHORITY\NetworkService` or you can specify any normal Windows user ID.

Configuration/Schema Partition Names

ADAM, like AD, has both configuration and schema partitions. Unlike AD, there is no root domain or root partition, so the names of these critical partitions are based on a randomly generated GUID and have nothing to do with the application partitions that exist in the instance—for example:

```
CN=Configuration,CN={E28AE3C2-1228-4F6B-917C-56B9757DB796}
```

Default Directory Security

The default security in Active Directory is extremely open. By default, any user that is from the domain or any trusted domain can look at most attributes of most every object. Attempts to lock down AD can be met with frustration, confusion, and applications blowing up. ADAM completely reversed this. By default, normal users do not have read access to anything but the schema. The only Access Control Entries (ACEs) defined on the application partitions are read permissions for the readers group, full control for administrators, and minimal permissions for replication for the instances group used for replicas.

User Principal Names

Active Directory user principal names follow RFC822 email address formatting rules. ADAM has no so such limitation; instead of using *joe@mycorp.com*, you can simply use *joe* for the UPN. While Active Directory doesn't enforce `userPrincipalName` values, ADAM does in fact enforce this uniqueness.

Authentication

There are a few differences that must be mentioned in the area of authentication. To start with, there is some good news. You aren't locked into the type of objects that you can bind with. Any object can be used for binding, as long as it is derived from a class that includes the `msDS-BindableObject` auxiliary class in the schema definition and has a valid password value set for `unicodePwd`.

The next difference, unfortunately, is that ADAM V1.0 bindable objects can only use simple bind authentication. This means that if you want secure binding with ADAM users or other ADAM bindable objects, you must set up a certificate and encrypt the communication channel using SSL. In order to use secure authentication without SSL, you have to use simple authentication and security layer (SASL) binds with either Windows local or domain users. By default, an ADAM user can be authenticated over the standard LDAP port with a clear-text simple bind. You can override this and force an SSL requirement by setting `RequireSecureSimpleBind=1` in the `msDS-Other-Settings` attribute of the `Directory Service` attribute.

The last difference to mention here is bind redirection. ADAM allows you to configure a bindable proxy object, which links to a Windows user. The user can use a simple bind to ADAM, which then proxies the authentication request to Windows in a secure manner. This is used when an application cannot use the Windows security principals directly or possibly if you want to disguise the backend Windows account. Unlike ADAM user simple-bind authentication, the default for using a simple bind for `userProxy` objects is to require an SSL connection. This can be overridden by setting `RequireSecureProxyBind=0` in the `msDS-Other-Settings` attribute of the `Directory Service` attribute.

ADAM R2 Updates

There were several changes in the ADAM R2 release. Unless otherwise noted, these changes apply both to ADAM R2 and the Service Pack 1 release for RTW ADAM V1.0. Most of these changes are directly related to feedback from administrators and developers who took the time to post in the various Active Directory newsgroups or submit requests to Microsoft. The Microsoft Directory Services group is very responsive to feedback; if you have suggestions for improvement or have found issues, be sure to document the ideas and post them in the Active Directory newsgroups.

Users in the Configuration Partition

ADAM now allows you to create `user` and `userProxy` objects in the configuration partition. These users can then be added to any group in any partition. So, you could add the user to the configuration partition's administrators group, which is nested in the administrators group of all application partitions. The change allows an ADAM user to administrate an ADAM instance instead of having the requirement to use a Windows user. To enable this new capability, set:

```
ADAMAllowADAMSecurityPrincipalsInConfigPartition=1
```

in the `msDS-Other-Settings` attribute of the Directory Service object to enable this new capability.

Password Reset/Change Chaining to Windows

Password change requests to bindable proxy objects (such as `userProxy`) are now chained directly to Windows. Previously Windows user passwords needed to be managed within Windows, and any requests sent to ADAM returned an error. No configuration changes are required to enable this.

Virtual List View (VLV) Searching

ADAM gets the VLV searching capability available in Windows Server 2003 Active Directory. VLV allows you to display a subset of the result set without returning every entry. No configuration changes are required to enable this.

 Although there isn't anything you have to enable to get VLV to work with ADAM, it is likely that you will want to make some changes to better support it. By default, VLV is not efficient when used against an ADAM directory. Also, due to how VLV is implemented in ADAM, you can actually have LDAP query failures if too many objects match the query filter. See the upcoming section "ADAM Schema" for more details.

Confidentiality Bit

The confidentiality bit functionality added to Active Directory in Windows Server 2003 Service Pack 1 was also added to ADAM. You don't really need the confidentiality bit in the context of ADAM since the security baseline permissions in ADAM are so much better.

New and Updated Tools

One of the biggest initial complaints with ADAM V1.0 was a lack of tools. Microsoft helped out in this area by creating new tools like ADSchemaAnalyzer and ADAMSync and updating older tools like LDP by giving a better ACL Editor.

Installation

The installation process for ADAM R2 has matured and is updated to reflect its integration into the base media. Instead of running a separate installation executable, you now select ADAM to be installed from the Add/Remove Windows Components from the Add/Remove Programs dialog. In addition, if you want to add a new instance, you have a Start Menu selection to do so. You no longer have to rerun the entire installation executable.

Authentication

The R2 and ADAM SP1 have added support for Digest authentication of native ADAM principals; this resolves the previous requirement to use SSL for binding with ADAM principals.

R2 ADAM for R2 Server Only

The R2 version of ADAM can only be loaded on Windows Server 2003 R2 servers. This could be a bit of a surprise to some since ADAM V1.0 could be loaded and used on Windows XP or Windows Server 2003. Another change here is that ADAM V1.0 could be redistributed with your applications; this is not the case with ADAM R2. Fortunately, ADAM SP1 can run on XP and be redistributed; you simply need to install it (or upgrade an existing install) as you did with the original V1.0 product.

Active Directory Lightweight Directory Services Updates

Windows Server 2008 brings an updated version of ADAM that has been renamed to AD LDS. AD LDS is now available as a role under Windows Server 2008. Many of the new Active Directory features in Windows Server 2008 are also available under AD LDS.

GUI Tools

The major Active Directory GUI tools, including the Active Directory Schema MMC and Active Directory Sites and Services, are now capable of connecting to AD LDS instances. You can now manage AD LDS replication the same way as you manage Active Directory replication.

In order to connect to an AD LDS instance with the GUI tools, you'll need to right-click and select Change Domain Controller, and then enter the name and port number of the AD LDS instance (e.g., to connect to an AD LDS instance running on port 389 on server k8devlds01.brianlab.local, you would specify k8devlds01.brianlab.local: 389).

Availability on Server Core

AD LDS instances can be hosted on Server Core installations of Windows Server 2008.

Support for Install from Media

You can install AD LDS replicas from media now (IFM) similar to Active Directory. In order to see the IFM step in the AD LDS setup wizard, you will need to run it from the command line. To do this, run `%windir%\ADAM\adaminstall.exe /adv`. For more information on Install from Media, see Chapter 15.

Support for Snapshots and the Database Mounting Tool

You can now create snapshots of AD LDS instances and mount them in the same way as with Active Directory domains. For more information about snapshots, see Chapter 15.

Support for Enhanced Auditing Features

AD LDS supports the enhanced directory modification auditing that was introduced to Active Directory in Windows Server 2008. This functionality allows you to log changes to attribute values as well as their previous values. For more information about auditing, see Chapter 13.

AD LDS Installation

A Windows Server 2008 server does not automatically load AD LDS. In order to use it, you must first install it. Fortunately, the installation routine is a rather trivial process that you can complete in short order. Microsoft also delivers on the promise of reduced reboots in that you will not need to reboot after installing AD LDS.

The AD LDS installation is broken up into two main pieces: installation of the base components and installation of new instances. The base component installation only needs to occur once per server while new instance installations will occur every time you want to install a new instance or replica of an existing instance.

Installing Components

Base component installation is as simple as opening up Server Manager, selecting Roles, clicking Add Roles, checking the Active Directory Lightweight Directory Services checkbox, and hitting Next a couple of times.

Installing a New ADAM Instance

Now that you have the component installation completed, you will probably want to actually install a new instance of ADAM. This process is also quite simple, though not as trivial as the component install. When you install a new instance, you need to have answers to the questions listed in Table 20-1.

Table 20-1. New instance installation questions

Question	Description	Example
Unique instance or replica? (Figure 20-2)	Do you want to replicate the configuration and schema with an existing instance, or do you want a completely new instance?	Unique instance
Instance name? (Figure 20-3)	This value is appended to the string "ADAM_" to specify the ADAM service name running this instance and listed in the Add/Remove Programs dialog.	AddressBook
LDAP port number? (Figure 20-4)	The TCP port you should listen on for standard LDAP requests.	389
SSL port number? (Figure 20-4)	The TCP port you should listen on for SSL-based Secure LDAP (LDAPS) requests.	636
Create application directory partition? (Figure 20-5)	Select whether you would like to have the instance creation process create an application partition. This is recommended when you first set up ADAM.	Yes
Partition name? (Figure 20-5)	The name to use for the initial application partition, only needed if you decide to have ADAM create the initial partition during instance installation.	CN=addressbook
Datafile location? (Figure 20-6)	Where do you want the ADAM datafiles located?	E:\ADAM\AddressBook\data
Data recovery files? (Figure 20-6)	Where do you want the ADAM log files located?	E:\ADAM\AddressBook\data
Service account? (Figure 20-7)	Service account to use for running this ADAM instance. Network Service is recommended unless the server is member of NT4 Domain or in a workgroup and you need replicas.	Network Service

Question	Description	Example
Initial administrator? (Figure 20-8)	What group or user should be initially assigned administrative rights over this instance?	Currently logged on user
Import LDIF files? (Figure 20-9)	Specifies whether or not you would like to import some of the basic MS schema definitions for user, userProxy, inetOrgPerson, and Authorization Manager.	Import
Files to import? (Figure 20-9)	Select which of the displayed LDIF files you would like to import.	MS-InetOrgPerson.LDF MS-User.LDF MS-UserProxy.LDF

When you are prepared with responses to all of the questions in Table 20-1, you initiate the instance installation by selecting the Active Directory Lightweight Directory Services Setup Wizard menu pick (see Figure 20-1).

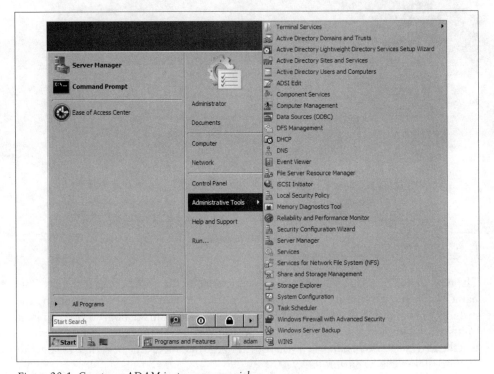

Figure 20-1. Create an ADAM instance menu pick

You can also run `%windir%\ADAM\adaminstall.exe` to launch this wizard.

This will launch a normal Windows installation wizard. The first dialog of consequence (see Figure 20-2) asks about whether you want to install a unique instance of ADAM or if you would like to create a replica of an existing instance. (Replicas will be covered in the section "Installing an ADAM Replica.") When you install a unique instance, you are creating an instance that has no connection to any other ADAM instance and that has a fresh ADAM schema and all default configuration settings. You will not be able to configure this instance to replicate with any other instances that currently exist, though you could create another new instance and install it as a replica to this instance. The default selection in this dialog is "A unique instance."

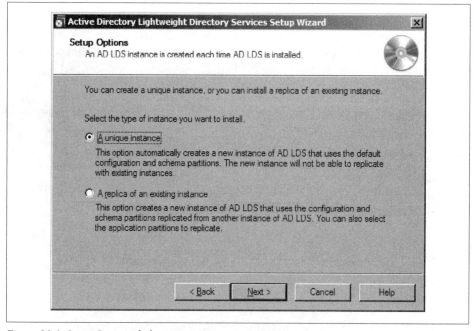

Figure 20-2. Setup Options dialog

The next dialog (see Figure 20-3) allows you to specify the name of the instance. This name is appended to the string ADAM_ and used for the name of the service running the instance. The name is also used in the Add/Remove Programs dialog, so you can later uninstall this instance if necessary. The default instance name for the first instance installed on a server is *Instance1*. If you use the name Instance1, the next time the default instance name will be *Instance2*, etc.

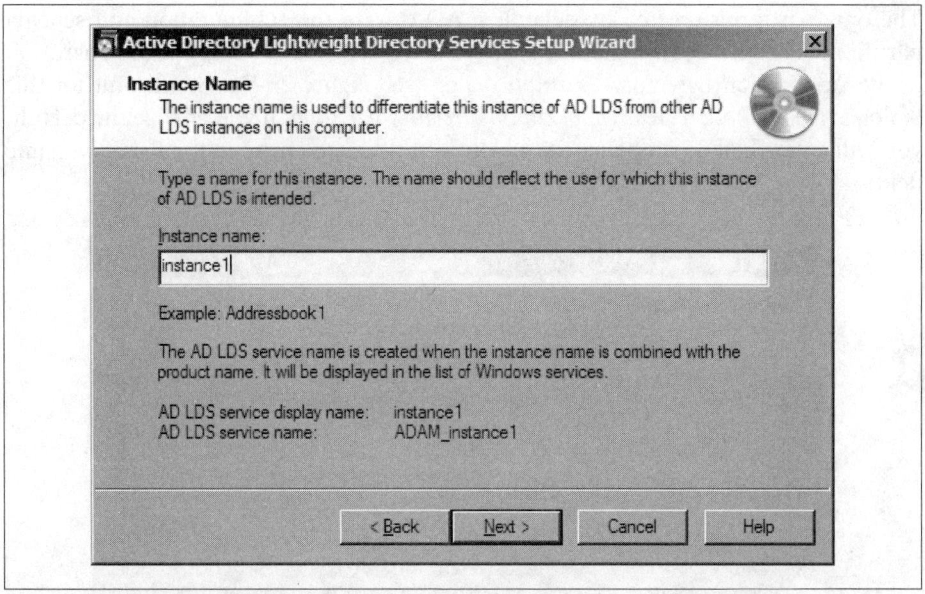

Figure 20-3. Instance Name dialog

After you choose your instance name, you will be presented with a dialog (see Figure 20-4) that allows you to specify the ports to use both for standard LDAP and LDAPS. The default ports are 389 and 636; you should stick with these ports unless you know that your applications are flexible enough to allow you to specify different ports.

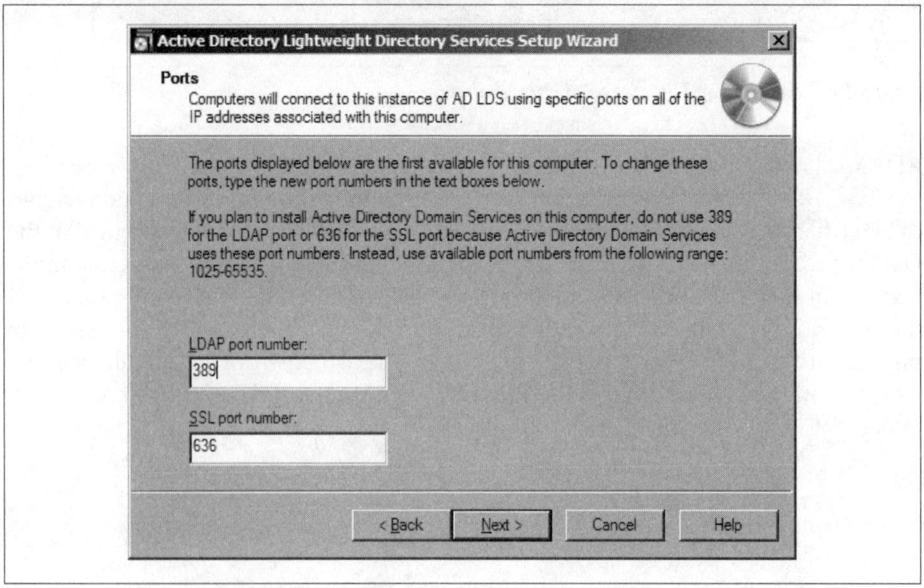

Figure 20-4. LDAP/LDAPS port selection

The only partitions created by default in ADAM are the configuration and schema partitions. The instance installation allows you to create one initial application partition in the Application Directory Partition dialog (see Figure 20-5). The default for this dialog is *No, do not create an application directory partition*. If you change the default, you will enter the DN of the partition you would like to create in the Partition name field.

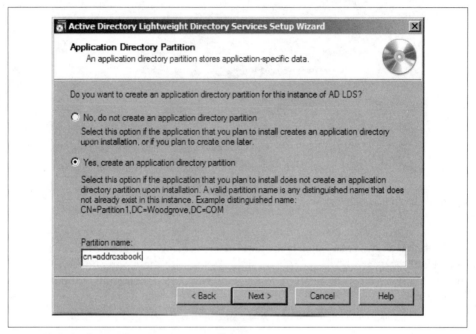

Figure 20-5. Application Directory Partition dialog

ADAM allows you to choose where to place your database and log files (see Figure 20-6). The database file location is specified in the "Data files" field and includes the DIT file, as well as the EDB and CHK files. The log file location is specified in the Data recovery files field and includes the log files that hold the ESE transaction information. In high-performance configurations, depending on the disk configuration of the server, it is usually recommended to split up these two sets of files onto separate physical drives. At the very least, you will want to move them from the default location, which is on the system drive in the *Program Files\Microsoft ADAM\<instancename>* folder.

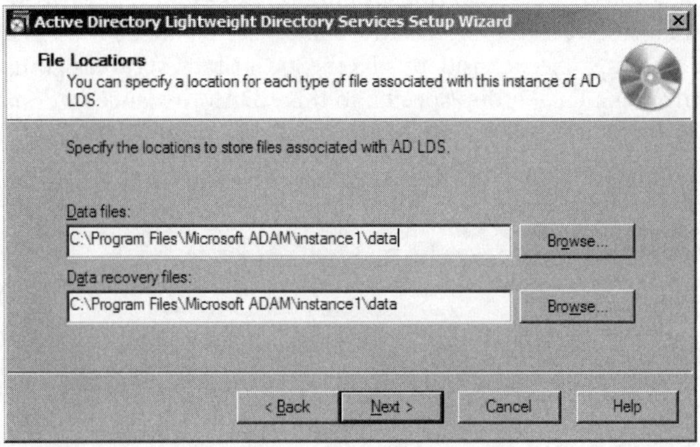

Figure 20-6. ADAM File Location dialog

Microsoft has written ADAM so that, by default, it runs as the Network Service account. This is a very good thing, and you should stick with this default. However, if you do not want to run as Network Service, you have the option to change the security context to any Windows user you choose (see Figure 20-7). You should only need to make this change if you are running in a Windows NT4 domain or Workgroup mode and want to have replicas. In that case, ADAM will need to use a Windows account to enable replication.

Figure 20-7. Service Account Selection dialog

The next dialog you encounter is critically important; it is the dialog where you specify the initial administrator(s) of the ADAM instance (see Figure 20-8). The default is the user installing the instance; consider using the local **Administrators** group instead or, better yet, creating a local group specific to this ADAM instance or domain group if you intend to configure a configuration set.

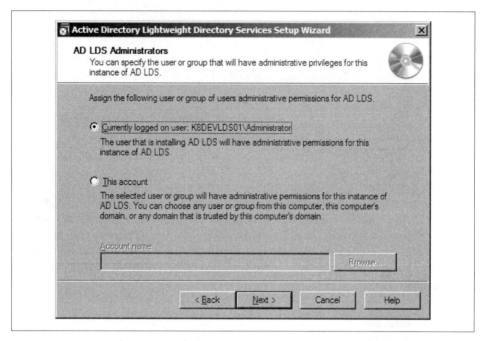

Figure 20-8. ADAM Administrators dialog

Quite unlike most other Windows application, the server's **Administrators** group has no control over ADAM's internal data or configuration unless the group is specifically added to the configuration container's Administrators group (or role if you prefer). This is great from a security standpoint, unless you somehow lose access to the users placed in that group; if that happens, you have lost control of the instance.

The final dialog that requires a decision, shown in Figure 20-9, concerns what LDIF files ADAM should import. The default is that no files should be imported, which gives you the ADAM base schema only. However, if you want to add the functionality gained through these LDIF files, you should allow the installation to import them. If you decide at a later time you would like to incorporate any of these schema updates, simply use *ldifde.exe* to import them. The LDIF files are located in the folder *%windir%\ADAM*. See Table 20-2 for a description of these LDIF files.

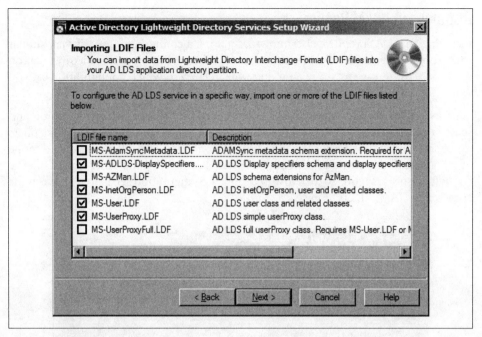

Figure 20-9. ADAM LDIF import dialog

Table 20-2. ADAM instance installation LDIF files

Filename	Description
MS-AdamSyncMetadata.LDF	Metadata schema extensions that are required to utilize ADAM Sync.
MS-ADLDS-DisplaySpecifiers.LDF	Display specifiers schema and data required to use the GUI tools with AD LDS.
MS-AZMan.LDF	Objects and attributes needed for Microsoft Authorization Manager (AZMan). Framework for roles-based access control.
MS-InetOrgPerson.LDF	inetOrgPerson object definition.
MS-User.LDF	Active Directory user definition. Bindable object class, trustee exists in ADAM.
MS-UserProxy.LDF	ADAM userProxy definition. Bindable object class, trustee exists in Windows (either local or domain).
MS-UserProxyFull.LDF	ADAM userProxy definition with additional attributes from the user class. Bindable object class, trustee exists in Windows (either local or domain).

After completing the LDIF file dialog, you will be presented with a Ready to Install dialog listing the choices made. Click Next if you accept the choices; the ADAM instance will be created, and you will be rewarded with a dialog indicating that you successfully completed the ADAM Setup Wizard. Click on Finish to complete the installation process.

Installing an ADAM Replica

Installing an ADAM replica, also known as joining a configuration set, is very similar to creating a new unique ADAM instance. In addition to the unique instance installation questions, you must answer several questions related to which configuration set you would like to join and what to replicate.

When you join a configuration set, you are choosing to share the configuration and schema partitions with another ADAM instance (or replica) just like domain controllers in the same forest. In addition, you have the option to replicate all, some, one, or none of the application partitions with all, some, one, or none of the other replicas in the configuration set. Figure 20-10 shows a complex configuration set shared between the servers *R2ADAM, LJ*, and *Tiny2*.

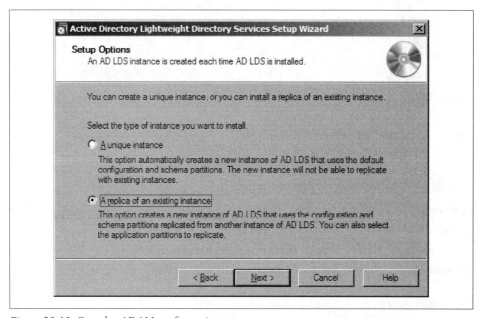

Figure 20-10. Complex ADAM configuration set

This may seem very complicated, but it is actually quite simple to configure. You need a plan of what partitions should go where; then you simply install each replica one-by-one, setting up the proper application partitions for replication.

The additional questions you need to respond to when installing a replica into a configuration set are listed in Table 20-3.

Table 20-3. Replica installation questions

Question	Description	Example
Source server? (Figure 20-12)	FQDN of any server in the configuration set to replicate initial configurations from.	k8devlds01
Source server LDAP port? (Figure 20-12)	LDAP port of instance to join.	389
Configuration set administrative credentials? (Figure 20-13)	Credentials of user with administrative permissions in configuration set.	MYCORP\administrator
Application partitions to replicate? (Figure 20-14)	Which application partitions, if any, you want to replicate to this specific replica.	cn=addressbook

Once you are ready with the responses for the questions in Tables 20-1 and 20-3, you start the instance creation process just as you did when you created a new instance. When you get to the Setup Options dialog, you want to select "A replica of an existing instance" (see Figure 20-11).

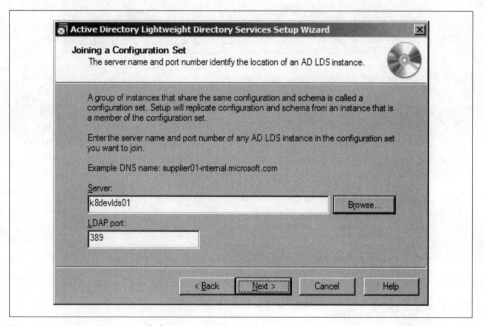

Figure 20-11. Setup Options dialog

The wizard will continue on the same path as when installing a unique instance, presenting the dialogs from Figures 20-3 and 20-4. After that, the wizard will start presenting some new dialog boxes. The first new dialog allows you to specify the connection information for an ADAM instance that is part of the configuration set you want to join (see Figure 20-12). You will need to specify both the fully qualified domain name (FQDN) of the server, as well as the port the instance is listening on for LDAP connections.

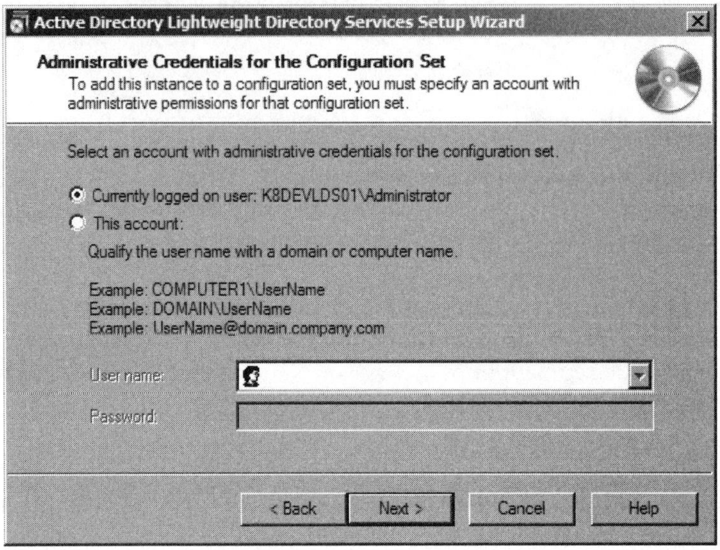

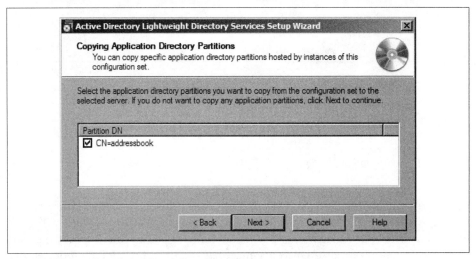

Figure 20-12. Configuration set instance information

After you have specified the configuration set instance connection information, you will need to specify some administrative credentials for that configuration set; see Figure 20-13. Obviously, this is so you can actually add a new ADAM instance into the configuration set. It wouldn't be very secure if it just let anyone add new instances.

Figure 20-13. Credentials for the configuration set join

The last new dialog that will be presented, Figure 20-14, is where you get to choose which application partitions, if any, you want this specific replica to maintain a copy of. If you refer back to Figure 20-11, you can see that you have the option to select any number of the application partitions that exist in the configuration set. In a very simple configuration set, there may only be one application partition, and that partition is shared amongst every replica. In a very complex configuration set, you could have any number of replicas that are or aren't replicating any number of the partitions. Again, the configuration of a complex configuration set is quite simple; monitoring and management, on the other hand, could be another story.

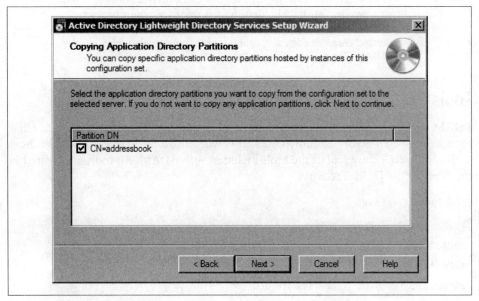

Figure 20-14. Application partitions to add to the replica

After this dialog, you will return to the normal unique instance installation procedure with the next dialog being the File Locations dialog, shown in Figure 20-6. Walk through the rest of the wizard dialogs, and after you click Finish at the end of the wizard, you will have a new replica.

ADAM has a couple of installation options not previously mentioned. You have the ability to run an unattended install, as well as install applications from media. These options can be specified when you launch the install process from the command line with *adaminstall.exe*. Type **adaminstall /?** or see the ADAM help file for more information.

After you have configured a replica, you will often notice that the replica immediately has replication connections to the instance you specified in the Join a Configuration Set dialog, but none of the other replicas have replication connections to the new replica. This is perfectly normal; it can take some time for the news of the new replica to circulate throughout the configuration set and the necessary replication topology to be built up with the new replica inserted into it.

If you would like to speed up this process, you can use the REPAD-MIN.EXE command-line tool to generate the connections. Specifically, you want the addrepsto switch. Help for this switch is available if you type **repadmin /experthelp**. Repadmin is one of the most useful tools available for determining how healthy you are from a replication stand-point and correcting any sore spots you encounter. This applies equally to ADAM and AD.

Tools

ADAM introduces several new tools and other updated tools that should be familiar to most Active Directory administrators. It is worth loading ADAM just to get these tools. Table 20-4 shows all of the tools included with ADAM. All tools are located in the *%windir%\ADAM* directory.

Table 20-4. ADAM tools

Filename	New	Description
ADAM-adsiedit.msc	Yes	View/modify AD and ADAM objects.
ADAM-schmmgmt.dll	Yes	View/Modify ADAM schema objects. This tool will only work on ADAM not AD.
adaminstall.exe	Yes	ADAM instance installer.
adamsync.exe	Yes	Synchronize data from Active Directory to ADAM.
adamuninstall.exe	Yes	ADAM instance remover.
ADSchemaAnalyzer.exe	Yes	Schema comparison to assist with schema differencing/synchronization. Works with AD and ADAM.
csvde.exe	No	CSV directory object import/export. Works with AD and ADAM.
dsacls.exe	No	View/Modify AD and ADAM object ACLs.
dsdbutil.exe	Yes	ADAM instance database management tool.
dsdiag.exe	Yes	Directory diagnosis to assist in directory troubleshooting. Compare with Active Directory DCDiag tool.
dsmgmt.exe	Yes	ADAM instance configuration management tool.
ldifde.exe	No	LDIF directory object import/export. Works with AD and ADAM.
ldp.exe	No	GUI LDAP query tool. Works with AD and ADAM. Great new ACL editor.
repadmin.exe	No	AD and ADAM replication management tool plus much more.

ADAM ADSIEDIT

The ADAM-ADSIEDIT GUI tool is similar to ADSIEDIT for Active Directory with some slight upgrades to support ADAM. The primary difference is in data entry forms that allow modification of group membership to insert Windows or ADAM Security principals, as well as the ability to connect to ADAM instances.

ADAM Schema Management

The ADAM Schema Management GUI tool is similar to the Schema Management tool for Active Directory with some slight upgrades to support ADAM. The primary difference is in connection dialog and lack of Default Security tab to update the `defaultSD` attribute for the object. This generally isn't much of an issue as there aren't any classes in the base ADAM schema that have any ACEs defined in their `defaultSD`. If you import `user` and `userProxy` classes, they both have a `defaultSD` with an ACE granting the ability for `SELF` to change the password.

ADAM Install

ADAM Install is the GUI tool launched by the Create an ADAM Instance menu selection. You have the option to launch the application directly to enable the advanced installation dialogs, which allow you to install an application partition from a file. You can also specify an unattended installation answer file if you would like to automate the ADAM instance installation.

ADAMSync

This is a command-line tool that offers basic synchronization functions to populate ADAM information from AD. This is made available to administrators who only need a one-way feed and don't need the overhead of *Identity Integration Feature Pack* (IIFP) or *Microsoft Identity Lifecycle Manager* (ILM), both of which allow two-way synchronization.

ADAM Uninstall

This tool allows you to remove ADAM instances from a server at the command line.

AD Schema Analyzer

This is an extremely useful GUI tool that will analyze two schemas (live or from LDIF files) and graphically display differences between them or "deltas." The tool can create an LDIF file with all of the deltas between the two schemas so that you could import the LDIF file to synchronize them. The AD Schema Analyzer is helpful to use with applications that modify the schema where the vendor didn't supply an LDIF file showing the changes for you to easily review.

CSVDE

CSVDE is a command-line tool used to import or export Active Directory objects in CSV format. Unfortunately, the tool will not update objects that already exist. There are no apparent differences in the version of CSVDE released with Windows Server 2003 and ADAM.

DSACLS

This command-line tool should be familiar to every Active Directory administrator. It is the most accurate Microsoft supplied tool for displaying ACLs on AD objects. The updates to DSACLS are to allow it to properly connect to and manipulate ACLs in ADAM instances, including allowing DNs to be specified for the grant, deny, and revoke switches.

DSDBUTIL

The DSDBUTIL command-line tool has a subset of the functionality present in the Active Directory NTDSUTIL tool. It is specifically configured to be used with ADAM and cannot be used with Active Directory. You use this tool for all low-level database management such as authoritative restores, compacting files, integrity checks, etc.

DSDiag

This command-line tool is the ADAM equivalent of the DCDiag tool. It is used for identifying and troubleshooting directory issues. If you have a problem with replication, this is one of the first tools you should run. In addition, you should run it occasionally to verify current status, in case there are errors or issues you are not currently aware of.

DSMgmt

The DSMgmt command-line tool has a subset of the functionality present in the Active Directory NTDSUTIL tool. It is specifically configured to be used with ADAM and cannot be used with Active Directory. You use this tool for controlling various ADAM configuration settings, metadata cleanup of retired ADAM instances, and creating and deleting naming contexts.

LDIFDE

LDIFDE is a command-line tool used to import or export Active Directory objects in LDIF format. Unlike CSVDE, LDIFDE can be used to update as well as create and delete objects in ADAM or Active Directory. LDIF is a standard format used for all LDAP-based directories and is usually the format that you receive schema update information in for applications that need schema modifications. It is important for AD and ADAM administrators and developers to be familiar with the LDIF format in general and the LDIFDE tool in particular.

LDP

This is a GUI tool used to browse, search, or update AD or ADAM . You have the ability to view the directory in a tree hierarchy or construct a standard LDAP query. LDP allows you to check in nearly any LDAP client or server control to enable capability to find deleted objects or other items that require special queries. This version of LDP is significantly updated from its Windows Server 2003 predecessor; if you use LDP on a regular basis, it is worth loading ADAM just to get the new version of this tool. Microsoft has done a great job of reworking the various data dialogs for inputting information, as well as adding a great new ACL editor interface.

RepAdmin

The base function of the REPADMIN command-line tool is to display and manage the replication topology of a set of directory servers. But the more you use repadmin, the more things you find that it can do, from displaying object metadata to updating SPNs to displaying trusts to translating time stamps, etc. Once you have figured out everything it can do with the switches displayed when you run `repadmin /?`, you can then start investigating the additional switches that are displayed when you run `repad min /experthelp`.

ADAM Schema

As mentioned previously, the initial ADAM schema is a small subset of the Active Directory schema. The ability to extend the schema is the same as in Active Directory, so you can fully expand the schema to be the same as the AD Schema. Because of this, ADAM is a great place to test schema modifications that you want to make in Active Directory. The fact that the extensions work the same and you can quickly destroy and recreate ADAM instances means that you can quickly test new extensions, changing the definitions until you get exactly what you want. You can even have multiple instances on the same computer running at the same time, each with a different version of the schema so you can easily compare and contrast them. For details on working with the schema, AD and ADAM, see Chapters 4 and 14.

Virtual List View (VLV) Index Support

ADAM supports an additional type of index that is not currently supported by Active Directory. The index is a subtree container index and was specifically added to better support VLV operations. Microsoft first introduced this change for ADAM V1.0 as the hotfix for Microsoft Knowledge Base Article 832474 and was only available upon request. The hotfix is now included with ADAM SP1 and newer for everyone's benefit.

Creating this index allows any VLV operations using a particular attribute as the sort key to be handled in a significantly more efficient manner. It can also prevent a common failure that causes a VLV query to terminate with a "Critical extension unavailable" error in larger directories. By default, when a VLV query is processed, the directory executes the query and stores the result set in a special internal table called the temp table so it can be sorted. This table can vary in size, but can be no larger than the value specified in the `MaxTempTableSize` setting of the `Default Query Policy`. The value for that setting, by default, is only 10,000 records. If the query result set exceeds the size of the current temp table, you will get the Critical extension unavailable error instead of the results. Enabling the subtree container index allows ADAM to avoid using the temp table, which significantly increases performance and avoids the issue of exceeding the temp table size.

Configuring this index is usually done when you use ADAM as an Address Book for Microsoft Outlook. Outlook, by default, supports VLV Address Book access. If you use an ADAM instance for an Address Book and it returns a result set of more than 10,000 records for the query (`&(mail=*)(cn=*)`), then it is likely you will experience the Critical extension unavailable error mentioned in the previous paragraph. You can quickly correct this problem by setting up the subtree container index for the cn attribute, which is the sort key for the query. You can also correct this by disabling the VLV capability in Outlook; Microsoft has a hotfix to disable this capability.

To enable this index for an attribute, you need to set bit 6 (value 64) and bit 0 (value 1) in the `searchFlags` attribute of the targeted attribute's schema definition. Generally, this means setting a value of 65, but if there are other bits already set, the value could vary. Bit 0 enables the index for the attribute, and bit 6 specifies that the directory should create a subtree container index. If you set bit 6, but fail to set bit 0, no index will be created.

Here is a simple example showing the process to enable the cn attribute to have the subtree container index. Create an LDIF file called *cn_vlv.ldf* with the following contents:

```
# VLV enable cn
dn: CN=Common-Name,DC=X
changetype: modify
replace: searchFlags
searchFlags: 65
-
```

Once you have created the LDIF file, run the following command:

```
> ldifde -i -f cn_vlv.ldf -s <server>:<ldap_port> -c DC=X #schemaNamingContext
```

 A question that may come to mind is, "If ADAM needs this, how come Active Directory doesn't need it as well?" The information on this is sparse, but it appears from various public newsgroup posts written by Microsoft employees that Active Directory is specially configured to handle some special case VLV queries that are common for Exchange/Outlook in an optimal manner. This seems to be tied to some special Address Book functionality that exists in Active Directory, but has been stripped from ADAM. If a customer needed better performance for any generic VLV queries against Active Directory like she gets with ADAM, she would need to contact Microsoft and submit a Design Change Request (DCR) to have that index capability added to Active Directory.

Default Security Descriptors

Quite unlike the Active Directory schema, the base ADAM schema `classSchema` objects do not have ACEs defined in their `defaultSD` attributes. This causes objects to be created without any explicit ACEs, unless a security descriptor with explicit ACEs is specified during the object creation. The obvious benefit of this is that all of your default security is based on inherited ACEs. As you will recall from Chapter 13's discussion of Active Directory security, this makes it far easier to configure delegation. Although you are not required to follow this model for any classes you add to ADAM, you are *strongly* encouraged to do so. You should have very great reasons to deviate from this practice.

Bindable Objects and Bindable Proxy Objects

As previously mentioned, any `objectClass` you import into ADAM can be configured to allow bind functionality in ADAM. The two types of bind functionality are covered by bindable objects and bindable proxy objects. A bindable object is an object that is actually authenticated directly by ADAM; an example would be an ADAM user. A bindable proxy object is an object that is actually authenticated by Windows. ADAM simply proxies the authentication request to Windows; an example would be a `userProxy`.

In order to make it possible to instantiate a bindable object or bindable proxy object of a given `objectClass`, you must statically associate either the `msDS-BindableObject` or `msDS-BindProxy` classes as an auxiliary class of the given `objectClass`. If you associate both classes to the given `objectClass`, `msDS-BindableObject` takes precedence.

Note that you cannot configure existing `classSchema` objects to have either of the auxiliary classes; these classes must be specified when the class is initially defined in the ADAM Schema. The limitation is due to not being able to add mandatory attributes to an existing class definition.

Using ADAM

Now that you have an overview of what ADAM is, some of the differences, and how to install it, you are probably sitting there with an empty ADAM wondering, "What next?" This section will walk you through some common simple tasks, including creating an application partition and populating it with some data. These examples assume you have installed an ADAM instance with the *MS-User.LDF* and *MS-User Proxy.LDF* files. All of the examples will use LDIF files and *ldifde.exe* for making the updates because it is available with every server and requires no scripting knowledge. If you are familiar with scripting or other LDAP applications, they could be used as well.

 If you prefer command-line tools over GUI based tools, point your web browser at *http://www.joeware.net* and download the ADMOD and ADFIND freeware utilities. These command-line tools are specifically optimized to work with Active Directory and ADAM and have several built-in capabilities that take advantage of special features that aren't available through ADSI.

Creating Application Partitions

Generally, the first thing you need to do with ADAM to add data to it is to create an application partition to house that data. If you had an application partition created during the instance install, then you don't have to worry about this step unless you would like to create an additional application partition within the same instance.

ADAM will allow you to use any container class as an application partition root. If you want the application partition root to be a `container`, `domainDNS`, `organizationalUnit`, `c`, `o`, or even a `user`, you can easily set it up. You only have to specify three pieces of data to create an application partition: the distinguished name (DN), the `object Class`, and `instanceType`. The `instanceType` attribute must always be 5, so that just leaves you with two attributes you have to figure out: the DN and `objectClass`.

The distinguished name is the full qualified name for the root of the partition. This is the value you will use any time you want to access the application partition. The `objectClass` is the type of object you want the root object to be, and the choice will impact the DN of the root. For instance, if you choose `organizationalUnit`, you know the DN will start with `OU=`.

The following example will create several application partitions with different object classes. If you want to create a single partition, only copy the application partition type you would like to use.

Create an LDIF file called *create_app_parts.ldf* with the following contents:

```
# Container type application partition
dn: cn=AddressBook
changetype: add
```

```
objectClass: container
instanceType: 5
 # Organizational Unit type application partition
dn: ou=products
changetype: add
objectClass: organizationalUnit
instanceType: 5
 # Domain DNS type application partition
dn: dc=mycorp,dc=com
changetype: add
objectClass: domainDNS
instanceType: 5
 # Organization (X.500) type application partition
dn: o=mycorp,c=us
changetype: add
objectClass: organization
instanceType: 5
```

Once you have created the LDIF file, run the following command:

```
> ldifde -i -f create_app_parts.ldf -s <server>:<ldap_port>
```

You can also use *dsmgmt.exe* to create application partitions.

Creating Containers

Creating containers in ADAM is identical to creating containers in Active Directory. The following example will create a several containers under the *AddressBook* application partition root.

Create an LDIF file called *create_containers.ldf* with the following contents:

```
# Users container
dn: cn=users,cn=AddressBook
changetype: add
objectClass: container
 # User proxies container
dn: cn=userproxies,cn=AddressBook
changetype: add
objectClass: container
 # Groups container
dn: cn=groups,cn=AddressBook
changetype: add
objectClass: container
```

Once you have created the LDIF file, run the following command:

```
> ldifde -i -f create_containers.ldf -s <server>:<ldap_port>
```

Creating Users

Creating users in ADAM is similar to creating users in Active Directory. A rather obvious difference is that ADAM users do not have the **sAMAccountName** attribute. Although the attribute could be defined and linked to the **user** class, it will not have the same special properties as it does in Active Directory, such as enforced uniqueness.

The following example will create several users under the previously created *users* container.

Create an LDIF file called *create_users.ldf* with the following contents:

```
dn: cn=d.m.sauter,cn=users,cn=AddressBook
changetype: add
objectClass: user
userPrincipalName: DMSauter
mail: Diane_Sauter@mycorp.com
displayName: Sauter, Diane
telephoneNumber: 456.555.3452
userPassword: SecureInitialPassword1!
 dn: cn=d.v.sauter,cn=users,cn=AddressBook
changetype: add
objectClass: user
userPrincipalName: DVSauter
mail: Dawn_Sauter@mycorp.com
displayName: Sauter, Dawn
telephoneNumber: 456.555.3453
userPassword: SecureInitialPassword1!
 dn: cn=k.cinco,cn-users,cn=AddressBook
changetype: add
objectClass: user
userPrincipalName: KCinco
mail: Kristen_Cinco@mycorp.com
displayName: Cinco, Kristen
telephoneNumber: 456.555.3455
userPassword: SecureInitialPassword1!
 dn: cn=s.nelson,cn=users,cn=AddressBook
changetype: add
objectClass: user
userPrincipalName: SNelson
mail: Shannon_Nelson@mycorp.com
displayName: Nelson, Shannon
telephoneNumber: 456.555.3454
userPassword: SecureInitialPassword1!
```

Once you have created the LDIF file, run the following command:

```
> ldifde -i -f create_users.ldf -s <server>:<ldaps_port>
```

> By default, creating enabled users in Active Directory with *ldifde.exe* requires a 128-bit SSL connection and Base64 encoding of the Unicode version of the password enclosed in quotes. See *http://support.microsoft.com/kb/263991* for more information.

For ADAM, Microsoft enabled the `userPassword` attribute to function as a write-alias for `unicodePwd` and removed the requirement for the special formatting `unicodePwd` required. This allows your LDIF files to have clear-text passwords specified; however, you still have the SSL requirement unless you have relaxed the requirement for secure connections for password operations with *dsmgmt*.

Windows Server 2003 Active Directory and newer has the ability to also use the `userPassword` attribute instead of `unicodePwd`; you must enable that capability though the `dsheuristics` attribute. See *http://msdn.microsoft.com/en-us/library/ms675656(VS.85).aspx*.

The `userPassword` attribute can only be used for set operations in ADAM and AD; if you need to execute a change password operation instead, then you must use `unicodePwd`, as mentioned at *http://support.microsoft.com/kb/263991*.

Passwords are far easier to deal with using ADSI scripts, *ldp.exe*, or command-line tools, such as the previously mentioned freeware tool admod.exe.

Creating User Proxies

The `userProxy` `objectClass` is new to ADAM. These objects are similar to users in that they represent trustees that can be authenticated; they are different in that they are only a reference to a Windows user instead of the direct representation of a user. The `userProxy` object points at a Windows user via the `objectSID` attribute on the object; that attribute can only be set on object creation.

When someone authenticates with a `userProxy`, by default, they must perform a simple bind over SSL against ADAM with the DN or UPN of the `userproxy` object. First ADAM accepts the userProxy DN/UPN and password, and then the SID is retrieved from the object and resolved to a Windows user (and domain if necessary); finally, a secure `LogonUser` API call is executed with the user's SAM name (and NetBIOS domain name if necessary) and password to authenticate the user. If the user successfully authenticates, his security token is generated and he has any access to the directory that is delegated to any of the following security principles:

- `userProxy` object
- Any groups the Windows userid is a member of
- Any groups the userProxy is a member of

The following example will create a `userProxy` object under the previously created *userproxies* container.

Create an LDIF file called *create_userproxies.ldf* with the following contents:

```
dn: cn=joeproxy,cn=userproxies,cn=AddressBook
changetype: add
objectClass: userProxy
objectSID: S-1-5-21-2571958876-650952397-806722693-1108
userPrincipalName: joeproxy
```

Once you have created the LDIF file, run the following command:

```
> ldifde -i -f create_userproxies.ldf -s <server>:<ldap_port>
```

In this example, the objectSID for the user MyCorp\$joe is specified in the objectSID attribute for joeproxy. Any time the joeproxy user is used for binding to ADAM, it will proxy that authentication through LogonUser to Windows.

Special considerations

The userProxy object can use any Windows user that can be authenticated through the trust channels of the server the ADAM instance is running on. This includes local computer users, domain users, and trusted domain users. If you choose to use local users, you need to keep in mind that only the computer that the user exists on will be able to authenticate the user. This has obvious implications with replicated instances of ADAM; only a single instance of the configuration set would be able to authenticate the user. Possibly this is what you are looking to do in the case of only allowing access to a single replica, but overall this would be confusing and difficult to troubleshoot if someone who wasn't familiar with this special configuration had to get involved.

Another special consideration with userProxy objects concerns object creation. If a Windows user's SID has already been added to the ADAM instance as a foreignSecurityPrincipal, you will not be allowed to create a userProxy object with the same SID. The directory modification will be rejected with an Unwilling to Perform error.

 Microsoft recommends against the use of userProxy and other Bindable Proxy objects. ADAM fully supports Windows users through secure bind, and this capability should be used if possible. The bind proxy functionality was made available for legacy applications or other specific cases where it is not possible to use secure binding.

Renaming Users

A common task in any address book or other application that has user information is rename operations. People are out there getting married, divorced, or just changing their names for some other reason, and one of the things they generally want is to see that change reflected in directories that contain their names.

The following example will rename a couple of users previously created.

Create an LDIF file called *rename_users.ldf* with the following contents:

```
dn: cn=d.v.sauter,cn=users,cn=AddressBook
changetype: modify
replace: userPrincipalName
userPrincipalName: DVSimon
-
replace: mail
mail: Dawn_Simon@mycorp.com
```

```
    -
    replace: displayName
    displayName: Simon, Dawn
    -
     dn: cn=d.v.sauter,cn=users,cn=AddressBook
    changetype: modrdn
    newrdn: d.v.simon
    deleteoldrdn: 1
     dn: cn=k.cinco,cn=users,cn=AddressBook
    changetype: modify
    replace: userPrincipalName
    userPrincipalName: KNiemiec
    -
    replace: mail
    mail: Kristen_Niemiec@mycorp.com
    -
    replace: displayName
    displayName: Niemiec, Kristen
    -
     dn: cn=k.cinco,cn=users,cn=AddressBook
    changetype: modrdn
    newrdn: k.niemiec
    deleteoldrdn: 1
```

Once you have created the LDIF file, run the following command:

```
> ldifde -i -f rename_users.ldf -s <server>:<ldap_port>
```

Each rename consists of two LDAP operations. The first operation is to replace several of the attributes that house the old name, specifically **userPrincipalName**, **mail**, and **displayName**. The second operation is the rename of the relative distinguished name (RDN) of the object. This update forces a change of the **cn**, **name**, and **distinguishedName** attributes for **user** objects.

Creating Groups

Creating groups in ADAM is similar to creating groups in Active Directory. As with creating users, you do not have a **sAMAccountName** attribute to be concerned with, so you can ignore that attribute.

The following example will create several groups in the previously created *groups* container.

Create an LDIF file called *create_groups.ldf* with the following contents:

```
dn: cn=group1,cn=groups,cn=AddressBook
changetype: add
objectClass: group
 dn: cn=group2,cn=groups,cn=AddressBook
changetype: add
objectClass: group
 dn: cn=group3,cn=groups,cn=AddressBook
changetype: add
objectClass: group
```

```
dn: cn=group4,cn=groups,cn=AddressBook
changetype: add
objectClass: group
```

Once you have created the LDIF file, run the following command:

```
> ldifde -i -f rename_users.ldf -s <server>:<ldap_port>
```

Adding Members to Groups

Adding members to groups with *ldifde.exe* is similar to the process followed for Active Directory. You have two options:

- Specify the DN of the user, group, or other object in an update to the member attribute of the group.
- Specify the SID of the user, group, or other object as a Base64-encoded string with the format <SID=S-1-xxx-yyyy...>.

Unfortunately, at the present time, a Windows user must be specified in the SID format unless it has already been added to the ADAM application partition as a userProxy or foreignSecurityPrincipal. Once added as one of these objects, the Windows user can be referenced by the DN of the object.

The following example will add users and groups as members to the groups previously created.

Create an LDIF file called *add_ users.ldf* with the following contents:

```
dn: cn=group1,cn=groups,cn=AddressBook
changetype: modify
add: member
member: cn=d.v.simon,cn=users,cn=AddressBook
-

dn: cn=group2,cn=groups,cn=AddressBook
changetype: modify
add: member
member: cn=d.v.simon,cn=users,cn=AddressBook
member: cn=d.m.sauter,cn=users,cn=AddressBook
-

dn: cn=group3,cn=groups,cn=AddressBook
changetype: modify
add: member
member: cn=group2,cn=groups,cn=AddressBook
member: cn=k.niemiec,cn=users,cn=AddressBook
member: cn=s.nelson,cn=users,cn=AddressBook
-

dn: cn=group4,cn=groups,cn=AddressBook
changetype: modify
add: member
member: CN=Administrators,CN=Roles,CN=AddressBook
-
```

Once you have created the LDIF file, run the following command:

```
> ldifde -i -f add_users.ldf -s <server>:<ldap_port>
```

Removing Members from Groups

Removing members from groups with *ldifde.exe* is similar to the process followed for Active Directory. You simply specify the DN of the user, group, or other object that is currently a member that you would like to remove.

The following example will remove members from the groups previously created.

Create an LDIF file called *remove_ users.ldf* with the following contents:

```
dn: cn=group1,cn=groups,cn=AddressBook
changetype: modify
delete: member
member: cn=d.v.simon,cn=users,cn=AddressBook
-

dn: cn=group2,cn=groups,cn=AddressBook
changetype: modify
delete: member
member: cn=d.v.simon,cn=users,cn=AddressBook
member: cn=d.m.sauter,cn=users,cn=AddressBook
-

dn: cn=group3,cn=groups,cn=AddressBook
changetype: modify
delete: member
member: cn=group2,cn=groups,cn=AddressBook
member: cn=k.niemiec,cn=users,cn=AddressBook
member: cn=s.nelson,cn=users,cn=AddressBook
-

dn: cn=group4,cn=groups,cn=AddressBook
changetype: modify
delete: member
member: CN=Administrators,CN=Roles,CN=AddressBook
-
```

Once you have created the LDIF file, run the following command:

```
> ldifde -i -f remove_users.ldf -s <server>:<ldap_port>
```

Deleting Objects

Deleting objects with *ldifde.exe* is generally pretty straightforward. As long as you have permissions to delete the object in question and it has no children, you should have no issues with the deletion.

The following example will remove various group and container objects previously created.

Create an LDIF file called *remove_ objs.ldf* with the following contents:

```
dn: cn=group1,cn=groups,cn=AddressBook
changetype: delete
 dn: cn=group2,cn=groups,cn=AddressBook
changetype: delete
 dn: cn=group3,cn=groups,cn=AddressBook
changetype: delete
 dn: cn=group4,cn=groups,cn=AddressBook
changetype: delete
 dn: cn=groups,cn=AddressBook
changetype: delete
```

Once you have created the LDIF file, run the following command:

```
> ldifde -i -f remove_objs.ldf -s <server>:<ldap_port>
```

Deleting Application Partitions

Programmatically deleting an application partition in ADAM is not an intuitive process. When you created a partition, you specified the DN, `objectClass`, and `instanceType`, and that was all that was required. When you need to delete an application partition, you have to look at the objects in the `cn=partitions,cn=configuration,cn={instance GUID}` container. Locate the object with the `nCName` that matches the application partition you want to delete and copy the DN into your LDIF file that has the delete operations.

The following example will delete the `cn=AddressBook` application partition previously created.

Create an LDIF file called *remove_app_part.ldf* with the following contents:

```
#>nCName: CN=AddressBook
dn:
  CN=45d599d5-9bd4-41be-9604-b8209db3f866,CN=Partitions,
  CN=Configuration,CN={92B82A0E-CEC4-4720-9035-D0CA9632C20E}
changetype: delete
```

Once you have created the LDIF file, run the following command:

```
> ldifde -i -f remove_app_part.ldf -s <server>:<ldap_port>
```

 You can also use *dsmgmt.exe* to delete application partitions.

Summary

ADAM is an extremely exciting product that is certainly going to find heavy use for both Microsoft and other applications in the enterprise environment. The flexibility it offers allows an Active Directory administrator to say "We can do that" more often now in order to support line of business applications and other functions that they would have never allowed near their domain-based Active Directory. Knowledge and understanding of AD LDS will become more and more important to all Active Directory administrators going forward as more and more applications start to leverage it.

In this chapter, basic AD LDS concepts, as well as some more advanced concepts, were discussed and explored. Next, differences between AD LDS and Active Directory as well as updates in the Windows Server 2008, Windows Server 2003 R2 and Windows Server 2003 SP1 versions of AD LDS/ADAM were discussed. A complete walkthrough of the installation of the core components of AD LDS was provided, as well as walk-throughs for the installations of a standard unique instance and a replica instance with screenshots and tables illustrating decision points. Readers were also introduced to the new and updated tools that ship with AD LDS. Finally, many *ldifde.exe* examples showing most aspects of creating and deleting objects and partitions were provided and discussed to help a new AD LDS administrator quickly get up and running with a new AD LDS instance.

The management tools for AD LDS are sparse at the moment, but expect a great number of currently existing and all new tools to become available as it becomes more and more widely accepted. Look to AD LDS to give a hint as to possible future modifications and strategic direction of Active Directory.

## PART III

Scripting Active Directory with ADSI, ADO, and WMI

## CHAPTER 21

Scripting with ADSI

This chapter covers the basics of ADSI and VBScript so that even inexperienced programmers and system administrators can understand how to write useful Active Directory scripts. In Chapter 23, we show you how to use ADO to search Active Directory and retrieve sets of records according to the search conditions that you impose. Other chapters take this knowledge and extend it so that you can manipulate other aspects of Active Directory, such as permissions and auditing (Chapter 25) and modifying the schema (Chapter 26). In Chapter 29, we make an introduction to the .NET Framework and programming Active Directory with it. In Chapter 30, we apply the .NET Framework skills to build a web application using ASP.NET to manage Active Directory objects. Finally, in Chapter 31 we discuss using PowerShell to manage Active Directory. Chapter 30 covers basic PowerShell constructs.

What Are All These Buzzwords?

First, let's take a look at some of the underlying technologies that you'll use when developing scripts.

ActiveX

ActiveX, the base component of a number of these technologies, enables software components to interact with one another in a networked environment, regardless of the language in which they were created. Think of ActiveX as the method developers use to specify objects that the rest of us then create and access with our scripts in whatever language we choose. Microsoft currently provides a number of hosts that run scripts to manipulate ActiveX objects including the Internet Information Server (IIS) web server, the Internet Explorer (IE) web browser, and the Windows Scripting Host (WSH). IIS allows scripts called from HTML pages to run on the host server, and IE runs scripts called from HTML pages on the client. WSH allows scripts to run directly or remotely on a host from a command-line or GUI interface. WSH is an integral part of the Windows operating system.

Windows Scripting Host (WSH)

WSH is an important technology for a number of reasons:

- You need no other software to start scripting.

- The development environment for WSH has no special requirements to build or compile programs; your favorite text editor will do.

- You can execute any WSH script with a VBS, JS, or WSF extension just by double-clicking it.

- You can actually execute scripts from the command line, directing window output to that command line. This is possible because WSH has two interpreters, one called *wscript.exe*, which interprets scripts in the GUI Windows environment, and one called *cscript.exe*, which interprets scripts in the command-line environment of a *cmd.exe* session. By default, if you double-click a script called *myscript.vbs*, the system passes that script to *wscript.exe*, just as if you had manually typed `wscript.exe myscript.vbs`. The default interpreter can be changed globally or on a per-script basis along with other settings.

- WSH comes with a series of procedures that allow you to script interactions with the target machine. There are procedures for running programs, reading from and writing to the registry, creating and deleting files and shortcuts, manipulating the contents of files, reading and writing environment variables, mapping and removing drives, and adding, removing, and setting default printers. These procedures are native to WSH, meaning that only scripts executing under WSH can access them. Being able to access these settings is very useful when configuring users' environments, since you can now write logon scripts using VBScript or JScript if you wish.

Active Server Pages (ASPs)

When a VBScript is wrapped inside an HTML page and executed at the server, it is called an Active Server Page (ASP) because it can contain dynamic (or active) content. This means that the web page displayed to the user differs depending on the results of a script incorporated as part of that web page. Imagine a web server connected to a database. You can write ASPs to contain server-side scripts that query the database and return the results to the user. You can also include client-side scripts to gather information from the user to pass with the query.

Active Directory Service Interface (ADSI)

In February 1997, Microsoft released a set of generic interfaces, called the Active Directory Service Interface (ADSI), to access and manipulate different directory services. ADSI is a collection of classes and methods that allow developers using any language that supports COM to access and manipulate objects on a server or in a directory service. Contrary to its name, it was written to be generic and extensible rather than specific to Active Directory. This means that developers can write code to access objects on various directory servers without the need to know vendor-specific library routines. ADSI is also extensible, so developers of other directory services can write the underlying Dynamic Link Library (DLL) code that will allow ADSI to interact with their systems. This is possible because Microsoft publishes the specifications that a directory service provider (code that implements the ADSI spec for a particular directory service) must meet to work correctly with ADSI. This means that whenever you call an ADSI procedure or reference any object via ADSI against a valid provider, you can guarantee that the procedure performs according to ADSI's formal documentation no matter who the provider is. Although there are several directory service provider-specific extensions, ADSI also supports Lightweight Directory Access Protocol (LDAP), which provides the majority of functionality that most directory vendors need.

LDAP is a network protocol that is the primary mechanism for accessing directory services over TCP/IP, and it has become the de facto standard for directory service access on the Internet. A directory server simply has to support LDAP 2.0 or later, and ADSI can instantly access the directory service without a provider-specific DLL.

Natively supporting LDAP in ADSI means that the list of directory services that can be accessed is very large. For the older directories such as NT4, several vendors have written providers to support ADSI. The list of supported directory services includes the following:

- Active Directory
- Microsoft Exchange Server 5.5
- Windows NT 4.0 and NT 3.51 systems
- NetWare 3.x's bindery-based system
- NetWare and IntraNetware 4.x's and 5.x's Novell Directory Service (NDS)
- Netscape Commerce Server
- Netscape iPlanet/Sun ONE
- OpenLDAP
- IBM's Lotus Notes
- Microsoft's Internet Information Server (IIS) objects
- Microsoft Commercial Internet System's (MCIS's) Address Book Server
- Microsoft Site Server

 If you are using ADSI on Windows XP or Windows Server 2003 clients and you have deployed Read Only Domain Controllers, you may need the hotfixes described at *http://support.microsoft.com/kb/944043*.

ActiveX Data Objects (ADO)

In the same way that ADSI is a general set of interfaces to access and manipulate data in any directory service, ActiveX Data Objects (ADO) is a generic interface that allows developers to write scripts and applications to query and manipulate data held in a database server. For a database server to work with ADO, the database server vendor must develop an OLE DB provider. This is relevant to Active Directory because Microsoft wrote an OLE DB provider for ADSI. This allows developers to access Active Directory, or indeed any other directory service, via ADO. This provider effectively considers Active Directory a database and provides fast and powerful searching capabilities. For example, using ADO, you can search Active Directory for all computers whose names begin with CF or all users whose accounts are disabled and get back the distinguished name of each one using a SQL-based query language or a standard LDAP filter. While it is possible to search and retrieve sets of records using standard ADSI calls, you would have to write your own set of routines to iterate through a directory service. When the developers of ADSI came to this requirement, they developed a provider so that the database searching algorithms that already existed in ADO could be leveraged for use by ADSI.

There is, however, one important caveat for ADO use with ADSI: the ADSI OLE DB provider is read-only even as of Windows Server 2008, so many of the useful ADO methods for updating data aren't available.

Windows Management Instrumentation (WMI)

The Windows Management Instrumentation (WMI) API was developed by Microsoft in 1998 in response to the ever-growing need for developers and system administrators to have a common, scriptable API to manage the components of the Windows operating system. Before WMI, if you wanted to manage some component of the operating system, you had to resort to using one of the component-specific Win32 APIs, such as the Registry API or Event Log API. Each API typically had its own implementation quirks and required way too much work to do simple tasks. The other big problem with the Win32 APIs is that scripting languages such as VBScript could not use them. This really limited how much an inexperienced programmer or system administrator could do to programmatically manage systems. WMI changes all this by providing a single API that can be used to query and manage the Event Log, the Registry, processes, the filesystem, or any other operating system component. For more information on WMI, check out Chapter 27.

.NET and .NET Framework

Unless you've been hiding in a cave in recent years, you've undoubtedly heard of Microsoft's initiative called .NET. .NET is the basis for a new programming platform, including a completely new set of APIs, called the .NET Framework, to manage

Microsoft-based products and develop Windows applications. Microsoft even released a new programming language in conjunction with .NET called C# (C-sharp).

The .NET Framework is a new programming model that Microsoft developed with the intention of replacing the old Win32 and COM APIs. A major design goal for the .NET Framework was to make programming in a Windows environment simpler and more consistent. The .NET Framework has two major components: the common language runtime (CLR) and the .NET Framework class library. For information on these technologies, check out Chapter 29.

Writing and Running Scripts

The third part of this book is dedicated to showing you techniques to access and manipulate Active Directory programmatically. It contains a plethora of useful scripts that you will be able to adapt for use in your organization, as well as a lot of information on how you can write your own scripts to access Active Directory to do whatever you need. Let's take a quick look at how to get started writing and running scripts.

A Brief Primer on COM and WSH

Since the release of Windows 2000, each operating system Microsoft has produced comes with a technology called the Windows Scripting Host, more commonly known as WSH, which allows scripts to execute directly on the client. WSH-based scripts can open and read files, attach to network resources, automate Word and Excel to create reports and graphs, automate Outlook to manipulate email, change values in the registry, and so on. The reason these scripts can be so versatile is that WSH supports scripting access to all Component Object Model (COM) objects installed on the client.

COM is a Microsoft technology that allows programmers to automate and manipulate virtually anything you require on a host by defining each host component as a set of objects. When someone needs to create or manage a new component on a Windows-based host, she creates a COM interface, which can be thought of as the definition of the object and the entire set of operations that can be performed on that object. Interfaces normally are stored in DLL files.

For example, if you want to manipulate a file, you actually need to manipulate a file COM object. The file COM object definition is stored in an interface held in a DLL. The interface also holds all of the operations, such as creating the file, deleting the file, writing to the file, and so on. The interface also defines a series of properties of the object, such as the filename and owner, that can be accessed and modified. Procedures that operate on an object are known as methods, whereas the properties of an object are known simply as properties.

In addition to methods and properties provided by interfaces, each scripting language that you use has a series of defined functions, such as writing to the screen or adding two numbers together.

Figure 21-1. Output from a very simple script

You can write scripts that execute using WSH and access any COM objects available to you using the methods and properties defined in the interface for that object and any functions in your chosen scripting language. By default, you can use Microsoft VBScript or Microsoft JScript (Microsoft's version of JavaScript). WSH is fully extensible, so other language vendors can provide installation routines that update WSH on a client to allow support for other languages. A good example is PerlScript, the WSH scripting language that provides support for the Perl language.

How to Write Scripts

WSH scripts are simple to write. The following example is a very simple script written in VBScript and called *simple.vbs*:

```
MsgBox "Hello World!"
```

All you have to do is open up your favorite text editor type in the command, then save the file with a specific filename extension (VBS for VBScript or JS for JScript). Then you can double-click the script and it will run using WSH. Figure 21-1 shows the output of the script, which is a simple dialog box with a text string in it. The script uses the VBScript MsgBox function.

Now let's take a look at a slightly more complex script called *simpleadsi.vbs*. This script makes use of ADSI to display the description of a user.

```
Option Explicit
Dim objUser 'A variable representing my user
Set objUser = _
GetObject("LDAP://cn=Richard Lang,ou=Pre-Sales,ou=Sales,dc=mycorp,dc=com")
MsgBox objUser.Description
Set objUser = Nothing
```

The first line is an interpreter directive. The purpose of Option Explicit is to require that all variables used in our script are declared before they are first used.

The second line is a variable declaration. We are declaring that objUser is the name for an object we are going to retrieve from Active Directory. The Dim keyword is used to declare a variable, and the apostrophe (') indicates that everything following it is a comment that will not be executed.

The third line is too long to print on the page, so we have broken it into two lines with an underscore (_) line continuation character at the end of the line. It tells the interpreter that it should read the next line as if it were joined to the end of the first. The entire line, ignoring the underscore, uses the `objUser` variable to hold a reference to a user object via a call to VBScript's `GetObject` function, passing the distinguished name of the user.

The fourth line simply uses the VBScript `MsgBox` function again to print out the description of the Richard Lang user object. The dot signifies that we are accessing a property method available for the specific type of object we are accessing, which in this case is a user.

The last line simply discards the reference to Richard Lang, and `objUser` becomes empty again. Strictly speaking, at the end of a script, the system discards all references anyway, but we are including it for completeness.

As you can see, printing out properties of objects in Active Directory isn't very hard at all.

WSH File Formats

WSH supports two types of file formats. The first is the traditional text-based script file with no markup language. These files contain pure VBScript or JScript and have a language-specific file extension (e.g., *.vbs*). The second is Windows Script File (WSF), which has a *.wsf* extension.

WSF is actually an Extensible Markup Language (XML) file with the scripting code embedded inside <script> ... </script> tags, which is then embedded in <job> ... </job> tags. The following example shows how the *simple.vbs* example would look using the WSF format:

```
<job>
<script language="VBScript">
 MsgBox "Hello World"
 </script>
</job>
```

The XML defines that the file contains a single script (a job) and that the script to be run is written in VBScript. At its simplest, to write WSF scripts instead the traditional script files, all you have to do is prefix your code with the first two lines and end your code with the last two lines, as shown here:

```
<job>
<script language="VBScript">
 Option Explicit
 Dim objUser 'A variable representing my user
 Set objUser = _
 GetObject("LDAP://cn=Richard Lang,ou=Pre-Sales,ou=Sales,dc=mycorp,dc=com")
 MsgBox objUser.Description
 Set objUser = Nothing
 </script>
</job>
```

To keep the examples straightforward and the focus on scripting Active Directory, only the code necessary to make a WSF file will be shown throughout the remainder of this book. Tags will not be included. You can then decide whether you want to utilize the WSF format or just use the traditional script file.

We also encourage you to find out more about WSH in order to fully utilize its capabilities. For more information on WSH and scripting in general, check out the TechNet Script Center at *http://www.microsoft.com/technet/scriptcenter/default.mspx*. The Script Center has an extensive library of documentation, articles, tools, and sample scripts in the Script Repository.

ADSI

Before you can start writing scripts that use ADSI, you first need to understand the basic COM concept of interfaces and the ADSI concepts of namespaces, programmatic identifiers (ProgIDs), and ADsPath.

Objects and Interfaces

A COM interface defines the properties associated with an item, how to access those properties, and how to access specific functionality of the item, more commonly referred to as an object. For example, WSH has a number of objects that represent files, shortcuts, network access, and so on. ADSI provides a specification for interfaces that each directory service provider must implement to maintain uniformity. Each ADSI interface normally supports methods that can be called to perform a specific action, and properties (or property methods) to retrieve information about the object.

A method is a procedure or function that is defined on an object and interacts with the object. An interface to access Active Directory group objects would have `Add` and `Remove` methods, so that members could be added or removed from a group. Methods are normally represented as `Interface::MethodName` when referenced, and this is the form we adopt in this book. Objects also have properties that are retrieved using the `IADs::Get` or `IADs::GetEx` methods, and set or replaced using the `IADs::Put` or `IADs::PutEx` methods.

Each ADSI object supports an IADs interface that provides six basic pieces of information about that object:

Name
    Relative name for the object (RDN in the case of Active Directory)

ADsPath
    Unique identifier for object

GUID
    128-bit Globally Unique Identifier of object

Class

Objectclass of the object

Schema

ADsPath to the objectclass of the object

Parent

ADsPath to the parent object

If you wanted to retrieve the `objectGUID` property of an object, you would use the following:

```
strGUID = objX.Get("objectGUID")
```

You can see that we are calling the `IADs::Get` method on the object called `objX`; the dot (.) indicates the invocation of a property or method. The `IADs::Get` method takes as its one parameter the property to retrieve, which in this case is the `objectGUID`, and passes it out to a variable that we have called `strGUID`. So that you do not have to use the `IADs::Get` method for the most common properties, certain interfaces define these common properties with property methods. In these specific cases, you use the dotted method notation to retrieve the property by using the property method with a similar name, GUID. In the previous GUID example, the `objectGUID` attribute has a property method of the same name (i.e., `IADs::GUID`). We could therefore retrieve the GUID with:

```
strGUID = objX.GUID
```

We won't go into the interfaces in any more depth here; we just want to give you a feel for the fact that methods and properties can be accessed on an object via ADSI interfaces. Although an object can support more than one interface without a problem, each object supports only the interfaces that are relevant to it. For example, the user object does not support the interface that works for groups. The other interfaces, of which there are around 40, begin with the prefix IADs. Interfaces can relate to many different types of objects, including objects that reside in directory services (e.g., `IADsUser` and `IADsGroup`), transient objects that don't exist in a directory service (e.g., `IADsPrintJob`), and security-related objects (e.g., `IADsOpenDSObject` and `IADsAccessControlList`). Note that not all objects have a specific IADs interface that applies its objectclass (e.g., `IADsUser`), so in those cases you have to use the more generic `IADs` or `IADsContainer` interfaces.

Because each directory service is slightly different, not every ADSI interface method and property works in every directory service. If you make a method call to a directory service that doesn't support that method, you'll receive an error message specifying that the provider doesn't support that method. According to the ADSI specification, each service provider must reject inappropriate calls with the correct ADSI error message.

Namespaces, ProgIDs, and ADsPath

To reference different types of servers (e.g., Windows NT 4.0, NetWare) with ADSI, you must use the namespaces that correspond to the ADSI providers used by that directory service. ADSI uses a unique prefix called a ProgID to distinguish between these namespaces. Each ProgID is synonymous with a particular namespace and directory provider.

In a script, you specify the ProgID, which is used behind the scenes to correctly connect and bind to the corresponding directory service. For example, you specify WinNT:// to access individual Windows NT domains and Windows NT or newer machines directly; you use LDAP:// to access Active Directory and other LDAP directories. When ADSI encounters the ProgID, ADSI loads an appropriate ADSI-provider DLL to correctly process the bind request and method invocations.

 ProgIDs are case-sensitive. WinNT:// will work, whereas WINNT:// will not.

Since each ProgID is synonymous with a particular namespace, the term ProgID is usually dropped. For example, individual systems are accessed using the ProgID WinNT:. However, conventionally, this namespace is referred to as the *WinNT namespace* rather than the *WinNT ProgID*. This is the convention adopted in the book.

The following example references JoeB, a user on computer MOOSE in WORKGROUP:

    WinNT://WORKGROUP/MOOSE/JoeB

This references JoeB, a user on computer MOOSE:

    WinNT://MOOSE/JoeB

Each namespace has a unique format for the ADsPath string, so you need to make sure that you're using the correct ADsPath notation. For example, each of these ADsPath references a unique object.

The following ADsPath references JoeB, a user in DOMAIN:

    WinNT://DOMAIN/JoeB, User

This next one references JoeB, a user in the Finance Organizational Unit (OU) within the Mycorp organization of the IntraNetWare tree called MyNetWareTree:

    NDS://MyNetWareTree/O=MYCORP/OU=FINANCE/CN=JoeB

This one references JoeB, a NetWare 3.x or 4.x (bindery services) user that exists on server *MYSERVER:*

    NWCOMPAT://MYSERVER/JoeB

Finally, this one references the first website of the WWW service component of IIS running on the local host:

```
IIS://localhost/w3svc/1
```

In the preceding examples, NDS: refers to IntraNetWare 5.x and 4.x. (Because Intra-NetWare 5.x is LDAP-compliant, you also can use LDAP paths with it.) NWCOMPAT: refers to NetWare 4.x, 3.2, 3.12, and 3.11 servers in bindery-emulation mode. IIS: refers to metabase paths on a host running IIS 3.0 or later.

One of the most commonly used namespaces is the LDAP namespace. You can use LDAP with ADSI to access a variety of directory services, including Active Directory. Although you can use the WinNT namespace to access Active Directory, you need to use the LDAP namespace to fully utilize all of ADSI's methods and properties. For this reason, our primary focus will be on the LDAP namespace.

You can use several formats to refer to LDAP directories. For example, all the following ADsPath reference the Administrator object within the Users container of the *moose* directory server in the *mycorp.com* zone:

```
LDAP://cn=administrator,cn=users,dc=mycorp,dc=com
LDAP://moose.mycorp.com/cn=administrator,cn=users,dc=mycorp,dc=com
LDAP://moose/cn=administrator,cn=users,dc=mycorp,dc=com
LDAP://DC=com/DC=mycorp/CN=Users/CN=Administrator
LDAP://moose.mycorp.com/DC=com/DC=mycorp/CN=Users/CN=Administrator
```

In these examples, CN stands for common name, and DC stands for domain component. These examples show that you can specify the LDAP namespace ADsPath going down or up the hierarchical Directory Information Tree (DIT). Most people have adopted the naming style used in the first three examples, where the most specific element of an object is used first. Also note that you can specify either a NetBIOS name or a fully qualified Domain Name System (DNS) server name after LDAP://, using a forward slash character (/) to separate the DNS server name from the rest of the path.

 If you don't specify the name of a server in the ADsPath, ADSI will use DC Locator to find the nearest domain controller. Generally speaking, you should not hardcode a server name in a script unless you have a specific reason for doing so.

If a name includes some unusual characters, such as a forward slash or a comma, you can use double quotation marks ("/") or a single backslash (\/) to specify that the character should be interpreted as part of the ADsPath itself. For example, if you have a user called AC/DC on the server, this is wrong:

```
LDAP://cn=ac/dc,cn=users,dc=amer,dc=mycorp,dc=com
```

This will interpret the path using cn=ac, followed by dc, followed by cn=users, and so on. As dc on its own is not a valid part of the path, the ADsPath is invalid. Here are the correct paths:

```
LDAP://cn=ac\/dc,cn=users,dc=amer,dc=mycorp,dc=com
LDAP://"cn=ac/dc",cn=users,dc=amer,dc=mycorp,dc=com
```

Obviously, as the backslash is a special character, you would need to do the following for an object called cn=hot\cold:

```
LDAP://cn=hot\\cold,cn=users,dc=amer,dc=mycorp,dc=com
LDAP://"cn=hot\cold",cn=users,dc=amer,dc=mycorp,dc=com
```

The first specifies that the character following the first backslash is to be interpreted as part of the name, and the latter says to specify that the whole first name is a valid string.[*]

Retrieving Objects

Now that you know how to use ADsPath to distinguish between different namespaces, we'll demonstrate how to establish a connection and authenticate to the server containing the directory service you want to access. Authenticating a connection isn't always necessary; some directories, such as Active Directory, can allow anonymous read-only access to certain parts of the directory tree if you configure it that way. In general, allowing anonymous access is not a good practice. It can make things much more difficult to troubleshoot if you discover that one of your domain controllers is being impacted by an overzealous client. When using ADSI, if authentication is not done explicitly, the credentials of the account the script is running under will be used. If the account running the script is not part of either the Active Directory you want to query or in a trusted domain, you will not be able to do very much. If you just want to use the current account's credentials to bind to a directory server to get a reference to an object, use the GetObject function.

The code begins by declaring two variables with VBScript Dim statements. The first variable, strPath, is an ADsPath. The prefix str specifies that this ADsPath is a text string; see the sidebar about typical VBScript naming conventions. The second variable, objMyObject, is a pointer to the object in the directory that the ADsPath represents. The prefix obj specifies that the variable is an object.

Next, we assign the strPath variable to the path of the directory server we want to bind to—in this case, LDAP://dc=amer,dc=mycorp,dc=com. You need to enclose this path in quotation marks, because it is a text string.

Finally, we use VBScript's Set statement with the GetObject method to create a reference between the variable we declared and the existing object we want to interact with. In this case, we're creating a reference between objMyObject and the existing object that the ADsPath LDAP://dc=amer,dc=mycorp,dc=com represents (i.e., the domain object of the *amer.mycorp.com* domain). After we've established this reference, we can use other IADs-based interfaces to interact with that object:

---

[*] Unfortunately, the latter, while valid, will not work with VBScript's GetObject function due to the extra quotation marks ("/").

```
Dim strPath        'path to the directory server
Dim objMyObject    'root object of the directory
strPath = "LDAP://dc=amer,dc=mycorp,dc=com"
Set objMyObject = GetObject(strPath)
```

When to Use the LDAP and WinNT Namespaces

Contrary to popular belief, the fact that the WinNT namespace is used to access Windows NT servers does not mean it is useless for Windows 2000 and Windows Server 2003. Actually, while the LDAP namespace is used to access Active Directory, the WinNT namespace is typically used to access users, groups, and other objects on individual computers utilizing the Security Accounts Manager (SAM) registry-based directory. Active Directory objects only exist on DCs in your forest. If you have a server or client that is a member of a workgroup or domain, that machine also has objects on it. These could be local users such as Administrator or Guest, printers, shares, and so on. Obviously, these objects are not part of Active Directory if they are stored on the local machine. As individual machines do not support direct access via LDAP, you have to use the WinNT namespace.

To explicitly authenticate to a directory server, use the IADsOpenDSObject interface, which contains only one method: OpenDSObject, which takes four parameters (also known as arguments):

- ADsPath to authenticate to
- User DN or UPN to bind as
- User's password
- Additional security setting(s)

The following listing shows how to use IADsOpenDSObject::OpenDSObject to authenticate to a directory server. We begin by declaring three string variables (strPath, strUsername, and strPassword) and two object variables (objNamespaceLDAP and objMyObject):

```
Option Explicit
Dim strPath           'path to authenticate to in the directory service
Dim strUsername       'DN of the username
Dim strPassword       'plain text password
Dim objNamespaceLDAP  'ADSI namespace object
Dim objMyObject       'root object of the directory
strPath = "LDAP://dc=amer,dc=mycorp,dc=com"
strUsername = "cn=Administrator,cn=Users,dc=amer,dc=mycorp,dc=com"
strPassword = "the password goes here in plain text"
Set objNamespaceLDAP = GetObject("LDAP:")
Set objMyObject = objNamespaceLDAP.OpenDSObject(strPath, strUsername, strPassword, 0)
```

We then assign the appropriate ADsPath, username, and password strings to the strPath, strUsername, and strPassword variables. The username string can take several formats: Distinguished Name (DN), User Principal Name (UPN), and SAM Format. DN references the username's exact location in the directory. UPN typically has the format of *username@ForestDnsName* (e.g., *administrator@mycorp.com*). The SAM format is the standard Windows NT format of username or domain\username (e.g., administrator or mycorp\administrator).

Variable Prefix Conventions

You can use whatever name you like for a variable. However, the consensus is to use a prefix with a descriptive name. The prefix, which represents the type of data, typically contains one lowercase character or three lowercase characters. Commonly used three-character prefixes include:

- `str` = string
- `int` = integer
- `b` = boolean
- `obj` = object
- `arr` = array
- `lng` = long integer
- `sng` = single precision value
- `dbl` = double precision value

In the descriptive name, you capitalize the first letter of each word, but don't put hyphens between words—for example, `strMyPassword`.

The `strPath` is used to bind to a specific point in Active Directory if you wish. This can be used if the user authenticating does not have permission to work at the root and has to bind further down the tree.

Next, we use a `Set` statement with `GetObject` to create a reference for the variable called `objNamespaceLDAP`. Notice that we're using "LDAP:" rather than `strPath` as an argument to `GetObject`. Using the LDAP namespace might seem unusual, but it is necessary so that in the next line, you can call the `IADsOpenDSObject::OpenDSObject` method on the LDAP namespace that ADSI returns. The last `IADsOpenDSObject::OpenDSObject` argument is to specify any security settings that should be applied to the connection. When set to 0 or left blank, no security is enabled for the connection. That is typically not the optimal choice, considering that all traffic between client and server will be sent in plain text over the network.

The following two constants are important to use if at all possible:

ADS_SECURE_AUTHENTICATION (0x1)
> Negotiates with the server to use the most secure authentication possible. For the WinNT provider, NT LAN Manager (NTLM) will be used. For Active Directory, Kerberos is the first option with NTLM being used if Kerberos isn't available.

ADS_USE_ENCRYPTION/ADS_USE_SSL (0x2)

Encrypts the data between client and server. SSL must be available on the target domain controller.

You use multiple constants by adding them together—e.g., (ADS_SECURE_AU-THENTICATION + ADS_USE_ENCRYPTION)—as they represent integer values. While these are defined constants, they cannot be used by name from VBScript. The entire set of values from the ADS_AUTHENTICATION_ENUM enumerated type can be found in the MSDN Library at *http://msdn.microsoft.com/en-us/library/aa772247 .aspx.*

 We want to emphasize the importance of using encryption. If encryption is not used, anyone using a network sniffer such as NetMon or Wireshark on the network might be able to see the information being passed, including, possibly, the username and password specified in the `IADsOpenDSObject::OpenDSObject` call.

The following code is slightly modified from the previous example to show how to enable ADS_SECURE_AUTHENTICATION and ADS_USE_ENCRYPTION for a connection:

```
Option Explicit
Const ADS_SECURE_AUTHENTICATION = 1
Const ADS_USE_ENCRYPTION        = 2
Dim strPath             'path to authenticate to in the directory service
Dim strUsername         'DN of the username
Dim strPassword         'plain text password
Dim objNamespaceLDAP    'ADSI namespace object
Dim objMyObject         'root object of the directory
strPath = "LDAP://dc=amer,dc=mycorp,dc=com"
strUsername = "cn=Administrator,cn=Users,dc=amer,dc=mycorp,dc=com"
strPassword = "the password goes here in plain text"
Set objNamespaceLDAP = GetObject("LDAP:")
Set objMyObject = objNamespaceLDAP.OpenDSObject(strPath, _
                        strUsername, strPassword, _
            ADS_USE_ENCRYPTION + ADS_SECURE_AUTHENTICATION)
```

While securing the connection to the domain controller is an important precaution to take, including an administrator's password in a script can obviously be pretty insecure. If you don't want to include plain-text passwords, you have several options. The first option is to assign a value to `strPassword` from the VBScript `InputBox` function. The following listing shows this:

```
Option Explicit
Const ADS_SECURE_AUTHENTICATION = 1
Const ADS_USE_ENCRYPTION        = 2
Dim strPath             'path to authenticate to in the directory service
Dim strUsername         'DN of the username
Dim strPassword         'plain-text password
Dim objNamespaceLDAP    'ADSI namespace object
```

```
Dim objMyObject          'root object of the directory
strPath = "LDAP://dc=amer,dc=mycorp,dc=com"
strUsername = "cn=Administrator,cn=Users,dc=amer,dc=mycorp,dc=com"
strPassword = InputBox("Enter the Administrator password","Password entry box")
Set objNamespaceLDAP = GetObject("LDAP:")
Set objMyObject = objNamespaceLDAP.OpenDSObject(strPath, _
                               strUsername, strPassword, _
           ADS_USE_ENCRYPTION + ADS_SECURE_AUTHENTICATION)
```

When you run the script, the InputBox prompts you to enter the administrator's password. However, the InputBox echoes the password in plain text while you type it into the password entry box, so this approach isn't terribly secure either. Windows XP and Windows Server 2003 include a COM object available for securely collecting a password from the command prompt. The following listing shows how to collect the password from the user:

```
Option Explicit
Dim objPw
Set objPw = WScript.CreateObject("ScriptPW.Password")
WScript.StdOut.Write "Enter a password: "
Dim password
password = objPw.GetPassword
WScript.StdOut.WriteLine 'line break
WScript.Echo "Password: " & password
```

If you want to authenticate a connection but have already logged on to the directory, you can use the default credentials for your existing connection. You simply use the VBScript vbNullString constant in both the username and password fields, as the following listing shows:

```
Option Explicit
Dim strPath              'path to authenticate to in the directory service
Dim objNamespaceLDAP     'ADSI namespace object
Dim objMyObject          'root object of the directory
strPath = "LDAP://dc=amer,dc=mycorp,dc=com"
Set objNamespaceLDAP = GetObject("LDAP:")
Set objMyObject = objNamespaceLDAP.OpenDSObject(strPath, vbNullString, _
    vbNullString, 0)
```

From now on, most of the scripts will use GetObject for simplicity, but if you need to, you can just as easily use IADsOpenDSObject::OpenDSObject without modifying any of the other code.

Simple Manipulation of ADSI Objects

Let's now take a look at simple manipulation of Active Directory objects using ADSI. We are using Active Directory as the primary target for these scripts, but the underlying concepts are the same for any supported ADSI namespace and automation language. All the scripts use GetObject to instantiate objects and are assuming you are logged in already with an account that has administrative privileges over the objects manipulated.

If you aren't, you need to use `IADsOpenDSObject::OpenDSObject` as shown earlier in the chapter.

The easiest way to show how to manipulate objects with ADSI is through a series of real-world examples, the sort of simple tasks that form the building blocks of everyday scripting. To that end, imagine that you want to perform the following tasks on the *mycorp.com* Active Directory forest:

1. Create an Organizational Unit called Sales.
2. Create two users in the Sales OU.
3. Iterate through the Sales OU and delete each user.
4. Delete the Organizational Unit.

This list of tasks is a great introduction to how ADSI works because we will reference some of the major interfaces using these examples.

Creating the OU

The creation process for the Sales Organizational Unit is the same as for any object. First you need to get a pointer to the container in which you want to create the object. You do that using the following code:

```
Set objContainer = GetObject("LDAP://dc=mycorp,dc=com")
```

Because we are creating a container of other objects, rather than a leaf object, you can use the IADsContainer interface methods and properties. The `IADsContainer::Create` method is used to create a container object, as shown in the following code:

```
Set objSalesOU = objContainer.Create("organizationalUnit", "ou=Sales")
```

Here we pass two arguments to `IADsContainer::Create`: the objectclass of the class of object you wish to create and the Relative Distinguished Name (RDN) of the object itself. We use the `ou=` prefix because the type of object is an Organizational Unit. Most other objects use the `cn=` prefix for the RDN.

The `IADsContainer` interface enables you to create, delete, and manage other Active Directory objects directly from a container. Think of it as the interface that allows you to manage the directory hierarchy. A second interface called `IADs` goes hand in hand with `IADsContainer`, but while `IADsContainer` works only on containers, `IADs` will work on any object.

To commit the object creation to Active Directory, we now have to call `IADs::SetInfo`:

```
objSalesOU.SetInfo
```

ADSI implements a caching mechanism in which object creation and modification are first written to an area of memory called the property cache on the client executing the script. Each object has its own property cache, and each cache has to be explicitly written out to Active Directory using `IADs::SetInfo` for any creations or modifications to be physically written to Active Directory. This may sound counterintuitive, but in fact makes sense for a number of reasons, mostly involved with reducing network traffic. The property cache is discussed in more detail in Chapter 22.

Each object has a number of properties, some mandatory and some optional. Mandatory properties have to be defined during the creation of an object. They serve to uniquely identify the object from its other class members and are necessary to make the object usable in Active Directory. If you need to create an object with a large number of mandatory properties, it makes sense to write them all into a cache first and then commit them to Active Directory in one operation, rather than perform a sequence of SetInfo operations.

Although the Organizational Unit example has no other mandatory properties, other objects do. For example, in Windows 2000 Active Directory, user, group, and computer objects require sAMAccountName to be set before they can be written out successfully. In addition, you can also choose to set any of the optional properties before you use IADs::SetInfo.

Putting it all together, we have our first simple script that creates an OU:

```
Option Explicit
Dim objContainer, objSalesOU
Set objContainer = GetObject("LDAP://dc=mycorp,dc=com")
Set objSalesOU = objContainer.Create("organizationalUnit", "ou=Sales")
objSalesOU.SetInfo
```

Creating the Users

We will now move to the second task of creating two user objects. Creating user objects is not much different from creating an OU in the previous task. We use the same IADsContainer::Create method again, as in the following sample. This sample requires that you leverage objSalesOU from the previous example:

```
Dim objUser1, objUser2
Set objUser1 = objSalesOU.Create("user", "cn=Sue Peace")
objUser1.Put "sAMAccountName", "SueP"
objUser1.SetInfo
Set objUser2 = objSalesOU.Create("user", "cn=Keith Cooper")
objUser2.Put "sAMAccountName", "KeithC"
objUser2.SetInfo
```

The IADs::Put method is used here to set the SAM Account Name. The SAM Account Name is the name of the user as it would have appeared in previous versions of NT and is used to communicate with down-level NT domains and clients. It is still required because Active Directory supports accessing resources in down-level Windows NT domains, which use the SAM Account Name.

Windows Server 2003 Active Directory changed the mandatory requirement of the sAMAccountName attribute being populated during object creation. If you do not specify it, sAMAccountName will be set to a random value, such as $KJK000-H4GJL6AQOV1I.

It is also worth pointing out that the IADs::SetInfo calls can be put at the end of the script if you want to do that. As long as they go in the right order (i.e., the OU must exist before the user objects within that OU exist), the following works:

```
Option Explicit
Dim objContainer, objSalesOU
Dim objUser1, objUser2
Set objContainer = GetObject("LDAP://dc=mycorp,dc=com")
Set objSalesOU = objContainer.Create("organizationalUnit", "ou=Sales")
Set objUser1 = objSalesOU.Create("user", "cn=Sue Peace")
objUser1.Put "sAMAccountName", "SueP"
Set objUser2 = objSalesOU.Create("user", "cn=Keith Cooper")
objUser2.Put "sAMAccountName", "KeithC"
objSalesOU.SetInfo
objUser1.SetInfo
objUser2.SetInfo
```

This works because the property cache is the only thing being updated until the SetInfo call is issued. Because ADSI works against the property cache and not against Active Directory directly, you could put off the SetInfo calls until the end of your scripts. There is no special benefit to doing scripts this way, and it can lead to confusion if you believe incorrectly that properties exist in the underlying service during later portions of the script. In addition, if you bunch up cache writes and the server crashes, none of your writes will have gone through, which you could see as a good thing. However, we will not be using this method as we prefer to flush the cache as soon as feasible. Bunching caches to write at the end of a script encourages developers to neglect proper error checking and progress logging to a file from within scripts.

Tearing Down What Was Created

As you've seen, creating objects is a breeze with ADSI. Deleting objects is also very straightforward. Let's iterate through the Sales OU and delete the two users we just created:

```
Dim objUser
For Each objUser in objSalesOU
  objUser.DeleteObject(0)
Next
```

We used a For Each loop to enumerate over the objects in objSalesOU. The objUser variable will get set to a reference of each child object in the Sales OU. We then use IADsDeleteOps::DeleteObject method to delete the object. The value 0 must be passed in to DeleteObject, but it does not hold any special significance (it is reserved for later use).

The final step is to delete the Sales OU using the same method that we used to delete users (`IADsDeleteOps::DeleteObject`):

```
objSalesOU.DeleteObject(0)
Set objSalesOU = Nothing
```

The `IADsDeleteOps::DeleteObject` method can delete all the objects within a container, so it wasn't really necessary for us to delete each user object individually. We could have instead used `DeleteObject` on the Sales OU to delete the OU and all child objects within the OU. This method should be used with care since a lot of objects can be wiped out by using `DeleteObject` on the wrong container. If this is a serious concern and you would like more control over the deletions, consider using the `IADsContainer::Delete` method, which can only be used to delete leaf objects and childless sub containers.

 The `Nothing` keyword in VBScript is used to disassociate an object variable from any object. This prevents you from being able to use the variable later in your code. Setting the value of each object to `Nothing` may seem less than worthwhile when the script is due to end soon. However, you must get into this habit, and we can't stress its importance enough. After you have deleted an object from the underlying directory service, the property cache for that object still exists. If you do not remove the reference to it, and you use it again later, it refers to data that no longer exists. Trying to do a `SetInfo` (or a `GetInfo`, which is covered in the next chapter) on a deleted object's property cache generates a failure.

Summary

Hopefully, you now understand the basics of ADSI enough to be useful. It's a very robust API that allows you to interface to all aspects of Active Directory as well as Windows NT, Windows 2000, and Windows Server 2003 servers. Even though the majority of this chapter covers Microsoft operating systems, the code does use the LDAP namespace and is portable to many other directory services. One of ADSI's biggest strengths is its ability to communicate with a variety of directory services using either LDAP or a provider-specific namespace.

In the next chapter, we will cover the IADs interface in more depth along with a discussion of the Property Cache. A chapter covering ADO will follow and should give you all the necessary tools to query and manipulate Active Directory.

## CHAPTER 22

IADs and the Property Cache

Each object in a directory has a series of attributes, or properties, that uniquely define it. Although properties can vary from object to object, ADSI supports the manipulation of a core set of six properties common to all objects using the IADs interface. These properties are common to all objects because IADs is the most basic interface in ADSI.

The IADs Properties

The IADs properties are as follows:

Class
> The object's schema class

GUID
> The object's Globally Unique ID (GUID)

Name
> The object's name

ADsPath
> The ADsPath to the object in the current namespace

Parent
> The ADsPath to the object's parent

Schema
> The ADsPath to the object's schema class

Each of these properties has a corresponding property method in the IADs interface. You can use the property method, which has the same name as the property, to access that property's value. Example 22-1 contains code to display the six IADs properties for a user object.

Example 22-1. Using the explicit property methods to display the six IADs properties

```
Option Explicit

Dim objUser 'An ADSI User object
Dim str     'A text string

' User object using the LDAP namespace
Set objUser = GetObject("LDAP://cn=Administrator,cn=Users,dc=mycorp,dc=com")
str = str & "Name: " & objUser.Name & vbCrLf
str = str & "GUID: " & objUser.GUID & vbCrLf
str = str & "Class: " & objUser.Class & vbCrLf
str = str & "ADsPath: " & objUser.ADsPath & vbCrLf
str = str & "Parent: " & objUser.Parent & vbCrLf
str = str & "Schema: " & objUser.Schema & vbCrLf & vbCrLf

WScript.Echo str

Set objUser = Nothing
```

To begin, we declare two variables (`str` and `objUser`), invoke the `GetObject` method to create a reference to the user object, and assign it to `objUser`. We then set the `str` variable to the string `"Name:"` and apply the IADs::Name property method (i.e., `objUser.Name`) to retrieve the `Name` property's value (i.e., Administrator). The carriage-return line-feed constant (`vbCrLf`) specifies to move to the start of a new line. At this point, `str` represents the string `"Name: Administrator"`.

In the next line, we use the IADs::GUID property method (`objUser.GUID`) to retrieve the GUID property's value (i.e., {D83F1060-1E71-11CF-B1F3-02608C9E7553}). We are appending the GUID to previous value set in `str` so the new `str` represents the `Name` property value and the `GUID` property value.

Using IADs::Get and IADs::Put

While you can use property methods to access most of an object's properties, you can also use the IADs interface's IADs::Get and IADs::Put methods to retrieve any attribute on the object.

In other words, the following two sets of statements are equivalent:

```
strName = objUser.Description
objUser.Description = strName
strName = objUser.Get("description")
objUser.Put "description", strName
```

However, using the IADs::Get and IADs::Put methods is more of a performance hit as it involves internally doing a search for the property specified. Compared to this, the direct use of a property is what is known as a *direct vtable binding* per the COM documentation and is the faster of the two. IADs::Get and IADs::Put should be used only when a generic browser or program is written to work with any ADSI object. See Table 22-1 for the full set of methods and property methods for the IADs interface.

Table 22-1. *The main IADs methods and properties*

IADs methods and properties	Action
Get method	Retrieves a single item from the property cache
Put method	Sets a single item in the property cache
GetEx method	Retrieves single or multivalued items from the property cache
PutEx method	Sets single or multivalued items in the property cache
GetInfo method	Retrieves all of an object's properties into the property cache
GetInfoEx method	Retrieves one or more of an object's properties into the cache
SetInfo method	Writes out all the items in the property cache to the directory
get_Name method	Gets the name of the object
get_GUID method	Gets the GUID of the object
get_Class method	Gets the schema class name of the object
get_ADsPath method	Gets the ADsPath of the object
get_Parent method	Gets the parent ADsPath of the object
get_Schema method	Gets the ADsPath of the object's schema class
Class property	Represents the schema class of the object
GUID property	Represents the GUID of the object
Name property	Represents the name of the object
AdsPath property	Represents the ADsPath of the object
Parent property	Represents the ADsPath to the parent of this object
Schema property	Represents the ADsPath of the object's schema class

For example, the next script shows how you use `IADs::Get` and `IADs::Put` to retrieve, change, and return the mail property. After we set the `objGroup` variable to the pointer to the Managers group, we use the `IADs::Get` method (`objGroup.Get`) with the "mail" argument to retrieve the mail property's value. The `WScript.Echo` method displays the results in a window.

Changing the value and returning it to the property cache is just as simple. You use the `IADs::Put` method with the argument "mail." You don't put the argument in parentheses when you use the `IADs::Put` method; the method is a sub-procedure, not a function, and it doesn't return a value. The string that follows the `IADs::Put` function contains the Managers group's new mail contact address. To write the new mail property to Active Directory, you use `IADs::SetInfo`:

```
Option Explicit
Dim objGroup
Set objGroup = GetObject("LDAP://cn=Managers,ou=Sales,dc=mycorp,dc=com")
WScript.Echo objGroup.Get("mail")
objGroup.Put "mail", "agl1@mycorp.com"
objGroup.SetInfo
```

The preceding sample will fail if the Managers group does not have a value set initially for the `mail` attribute. The error you will receive is `Active Directory: The directory property cannot be found in the cache`.

The Property Cache

Having looked at properties and property methods, let's take a look at the property cache, a location in memory on the local machine running the script that stores properties for objects. Each object that you bind to has a personal property cache; the OS creates this cache the instant the bind succeeds. However, the OS doesn't immediately populate the cache with values.

When you use the `IADs::Get` method to retrieve an object's property, ADSI doesn't go to Active Directory to retrieve the value. Instead, ADSI reads the value from the property cache on the client executing the script. If ADSI doesn't find the property in the property cache when the call comes in, the system implicitly executes an `IADs::GetInfo` call to read all the properties for the current object into the cache. (You also can explicitly use the `IADs::GetInfo` method to populate the property cache with an object's properties.) The `IADs::Get` method then reads the appropriate value from the newly created cache.

 Strictly speaking, the previous paragraph isn't 100% accurate. Calling `IADs::GetInfo` will not return constructed attributes. For more information on loading constructed attributes, see *http://msdn.microsoft .com/en-us/library/aa705926(VS.85).aspx*.

Microsoft designed the property cache with efficiency in mind. The property cache lets you access an object's properties with a minimum number of calls, thereby minimizing network traffic. Retrieving all of an object's properties with one `IADs::GetInfo` call is more efficient than individually retrieving each property. Similarly, the process of writing all of an object's properties first to the cache and then to Active Directory with one `IADs::SetInfo` call is more efficient than writing each property individually to Active Directory.

Be Careful

The `IADs::GetInfo` and `IADs::SetInfo` methods are two of the most important methods you'll use. However, you need to be aware of two possible problems.

The first problem can arise if you try to access a property that doesn't have a value. For example, when you create a group object, the mail property doesn't automatically receive a value; you must provide a value, such as *agl1@mycorp.com*. When you use the `IADs::GetInfo` method, only those properties that have values appear in the property cache. Thus, if you don't give the mail property a value and you use `IADs::GetInfo`, the mail property value won't be in the property cache. If you try to access a property that doesn't exist in the cache, the script will throw an error that you need to catch.

 Later on we talk about navigating the property cache. If you want to see a good example of how this actually works, try this: create a new object of type group, which has around 21 properties set by the system by default. You then use IADs::GetInfo in a script and display the number of properties, and possibly their names, in a dialog box. Then set the description. Now, when you rerun the script, you will find that you have one more property in the cache than you did before the description. In other words, the description does not appear in the cache until you do an IADs::GetInfo after it has been set.

Another problem can arise if you forget to use IADs::SetInfo after modifying a property. For example, suppose you want to change the Managers group's mail property value and you create the script shown in Example 22-2.

Example 22-2. Making the mistake of forgetting the SetInfo call

```
Option Explicit

Dim objGroup   'An ADSI group object
Set objGroup = GetObject("LDAP://cn=Managers,ou=Sales,dc=mycorp,dc=com")

'**********************************************************************
'Get and write the mail property value, which forces an
'implicit GetInfo call
'**********************************************************************
WScript.Echo objGroup.Get("mail")

'**********************************************************************
'Set the new mail address in the cache
'**********************************************************************
objGroup.Put "mail", "new-address@mycorp.com"

'**********************************************************************
'Use an explicit GetInfo call to again retrieve all items into the cache
'**********************************************************************
objGroup.GetInfo

WScript.Echo objGroup.mail
```

In Example 22-2, we set the objGroup variable to the pointer to the Managers group. To display the current mail property value in a window, we use the WScript.Echo method with the IADs::Get method, which forces an implicit IADs::GetInfo call. We then set the new value for the objGroup's mail property, after which we use an explicit IADs::GetInfo call to again retrieve all the object's properties into the cache. Finally, we use the WScript.Echo method to display the results in a window.

When you run the script, two windows pop up. To your dismay, both windows state the original value of the mail property, which means that the system didn't write the new mail address to Active Directory. This cache write didn't occur because you need to explicitly call the IADs::SetInfo method to write out data from the cache to Active Directory. To fix the script, you need to insert the line:

```
objGroup.SetInfo
```

between the line setting the new mail address and the line making the explicit IADs::GetInfo call.

More Complexities of Property Access: IADs::GetEx and IADs::PutEx

Using the IADs interface's IADs::Get method works well for properties with a single value; however, some properties have multiple values, such as a user with several telephone numbers. If a property stores multiple values, you need to use the IADs interface's IADs::GetEx and IADs::PutEx methods to retrieve and return the values.

You also can use IADs::GetEx and IADs::PutEx for single-value properties.

Using IADs::GetEx

The following script shows how to use IADs::GetEx. In this script, we pass the multiple-value property as an argument to the IADs::GetEx method. We then use a For Each… Next loop on the resulting list:

```
Option Explicit
Dim objUser          'An ADSI user object
Dim arrPhoneList     'An array of phone numbers
Dim strPhoneNumber   'An individual phone number
Set objUser=GetObject("LDAP://cn=administrator,cn=Users,dc=mycorp,dc=com")
arrPhoneList = objUser.GetEx("otherTelephone")
For Each strPhoneNumber In arrPhoneList
  WScript.Echo strPhoneNumber
Next
```

When we make the IADs::GetEx call, the system makes an implicit IADs::GetInfoEx call rather than an implicit IADs::GetInfo call to Active Directory. You can use an explicit IADs::GetInfoEx call to get one or more properties if you don't want to use IADs::GetInfo to get all the property values. However, few scriptwriters use IADs::GetInfoEx for this purpose, because they typically use implicit calls or use IADs::GetInfo to read all values into the property cache. In addition, if you use IADs::GetEx for every property retrieval rather than using IADs::GetInfo, your underlying network traffic will increase. Instead of sending one request to the server for all the information, you'll be sending several requests for smaller amounts of information.

Although `IADs::GetInfoEx` isn't a good substitute for `IADs::GetInfo`, it works well for selectively reading properties into the property cache. Example 22-3 shows how to selectively retrieve only two properties.

Example 22-3. Selectively reading properties into the property cache using the GetInfoEx method

```
Option Explicit

Dim objUser  'An ADSI user object
Dim arrProps 'An array of properties to return

Set objUser=GetObject("LDAP://cn=administrator,cn=Users,dc=mycorp,dc=com")

'**********************************************************************
'Set the list of properties to return
'**********************************************************************
ArrProps = Array("cn", "distinguishedName")

'**********************************************************************
'Get the specified properties
'**********************************************************************
objUser.GetInfoEx arrProps, 0

WScript.Echo objUser.cn & vbTab & objUser.get("distinguishedName")
```

After we set the `objUser` variable, we create an array containing the properties we want (i.e., `cn` and `ADsPath`). Next, we pass that array to the `IADs::GetInfoEx` method as the first parameter. (The second parameter must be 0 for all actions; however, it is reserved and could be used in a later version of ADSI.) Then, the last line uses the `WScript.Echo` method to print the `cn` and `ADsPath` attributes, separating them with a tab.

Using IADs::PutEx

To set multivalue properties, you use the `IADs::PutEx` method. This is slightly more complicated than using `IADs::GetEx`. Suppose a property already has three values (e.g., pager numbers), and you want to put in two more. You must let `IADs::PutEx` know whether it needs to overwrite, update, or add to the existing values. You use the constants in Table 22-2 to tell `IADs::PutEx` what to do.

Table 22-2. The constants for updating the property cache with the PutEx method

Constant name	Value	Action
ADS_PROPERTY_CLEAR	1	Use when clearing all values
ADS_PROPERTY_UPDATE	2	Use when replacing all existing values
ADS_PROPERTY_APPEND	3	Use when adding to existing values
ADS_PROPERTY_DELETE	4	Use when deleting specific values

For complete documentation on these constants, refer to *http://msdn .microsoft.com/en-us/library/aa772282(VS.85).aspx*.

Use the constant name only if you're using VB. If you use VBScript with the WSH, you must either define the constants, as we've done in Example 22-4, or use the values directly. The four values are fairly straightforward to use, as the example script shows.

Example 22-4. Using constants with the PutEx method to update the property cache

```
Option Explicit

Const ADS_PROPERTY_CLEAR = 1
Const ADS_PROPERTY_UPDATE = 2
Const ADS_PROPERTY_APPEND = 3
Const ADS_PROPERTY_DELETE = 4

Dim objUser   'An ADSI User object
Dim strPager 'A text string holding a phone number
Dim arrPager 'An array of pager numbers
Set objUser=GetObject("LDAP://cn=Administrator,cn=Users,dc=mycorp,dc=com")

'**********************************************************************
'Set three pager numbers for the Administrator account
'**********************************************************************
objUser.PutEx ADS_PROPERTY_UPDATE, "otherPager", _
  Array("123-1234", "234-2345", "345-3456")
objUser.SetInfo
objUser.GetInfo
arrPager = objUser.GetEx("otherPager")
For Each strPager in arrPager
  WScript.Echo strPager
Next

'**********************************************************************
'Delete the first and last number
'**********************************************************************
objUser.PutEx ADS_PROPERTY_DELETE, "otherPager", Array("123-1234", "345-3456")
objUser.SetInfo
objUser.GetInfo
arrPager = objUser.GetEx("otherPager")
For Each strPager in arrPager
  WScript.Echo strPager
Next

'**********************************************************************
'Add a new pager number without deleting the remaining number
'**********************************************************************
objUser.PutEx ADS_PROPERTY_APPEND, "otherPager", Array("456-4567")
objUser.SetInfo
objUser.GetInfo
arrPager = objUser.GetEx("otherPager")
```

```
For Each strPager in arrPager
  WScript.Echo strPager
Next

'***********************************************************************
'Delete all values
'***********************************************************************
objUser.PutEx ADS_PROPERTY_CLEAR, "otherPager", vbNull
objUser.SetInfo
objUser.GetInfo
arrPager = objUser.GetEx("otherPager")
For Each strPager in arrPager
  WScript.Echo strPager
Next
```

After binding to the user object, three pager numbers are set for the Administrator account, wiping out any existing values. The property cache is then reloaded explicitly to make sure it contains the new values that were just set. Now, a `For Each` loop is used to go through the newly set property to show the individual pager numbers. The first and last pager numbers of the new property are deleted in the cache and written to Active Directory with `SetInfo`.

At this point, Active Directory should contain only one pager number, which is displayed by looping through the values again. Next we append a number to the value held for that property in the cache and subsequently write it out to Active Directory, leaving two numbers in Active Directory for that property. Looping through the values again shows there are two numbers. Finally, all values in the property cache for that property are deleted, and the changes are updated in Active Directory. Using the `For Each` loop one last time should show no values.

Knowing now that you can access all of an object's properties from the cache individually, it would make sense if there were a way to count the number of items, display their names as well as their values, and so on. For this purpose, Microsoft provided three interfaces: `IADsPropertyList`, `IADsPropertyEntry`, and `IADsPropertyValue`.

Manipulating the Property Cache

There will be times when you need to write a script that queries all the values that have been set in the underlying directory for a particular object. For example, you may need to write a script that queries all the property values that have been set for a particular user.

Discovering the set property values for an object can be a long, tedious job. Fortunately, ADSI provides a quick method. If someone has set a value for a property, it must be in that object's property cache. So all you need to do is walk through the property cache, displaying and optionally modifying each item as you go.

In this section, we'll describe the property cache mechanics and show you how to write scripts that use several ADSI methods and properties to add individual values, add a set of values, walk through the property cache, and write modifications to the cache and to the directory. Although these examples access the Lightweight Directory Access Protocol (LDAP) namespace, you can just as easily substitute the WinNT namespace in any of the scripts and run them against Windows NT servers.

Details of the property cache interfaces can be found in the MSDN Library at: *http://msdn.microsoft.com/en-us/library/aa772166(VS.85).aspx.*

Property Cache Mechanics

Every object has properties. When you perform an explicit `IADs::GetInfo` call (or an implicit `IADs::GetInfo` call using `IADs::Get`) on an object that you previously bound to, the OS loads all the properties for that specific object into that object's property cache (with the exception of constructed attributes). Consider the property cache a simple list of properties. The `PropertyList` object represents this list. You can use several `IADsPropertyList` methods to navigate through the list and access items. For example, you can navigate the list and access each item, every *n*th item, or one particular item based on its name.

Each item in the property list is a property entry represented by the `PropertyEntry` object. You use the `IADsPropertyEntry` interface to access property entries. A property entry can have one or more property values. To access values in a property entry, you use the `IADsPropertyValue` interface.

To summarize, use `IADsPropertyList` to navigate through and access property entries in the property list. Use `IADsPropertyEntry` when you want to manipulate a property. Use `IADsPropertyValue` to access the values of that property entry.

Adding Individual Values

To show you how to add an individual value, we'll expand on one of the examples from the previous section: the `otherPager` property of the `User` object. The `otherPager` property is an array of text strings representing multiple pager numbers.

Consider that any property represents data. Data can take several forms, including a string, an integer, or a Boolean value. In the cache, each property has two attributes: one attribute specifies the type of data the property represents, and the other attribute specifies the value of that data type. For example, each `otherPager` property has two attributes: a Unicode string (the type of data) and the pager number (the value of that Unicode string). The `User` object's `lastLogon` property, which specifies the time the user last logged on, has the two attributes: a `LargeInteger` (type of data) and a date/time stamp (the value of that `LargeInteger`).

The `pager` and `lastLogon` properties are instances of the `PropertyValue` object, so you manipulate them with the method and property methods of the `IADsPropertyValue` interface. For example, you use the `IADsPropertyValue::ADsType` property method to set the PropertyValue's type of data. Table 22-3 shows some of the corresponding constant names and values that you can set for the IADsPropertyValue::ADsType property.

Table 22-3. Constants for the IADsPropertyValue::ADsType property

Constant name	IADsPropertyValue property method (if appropriate)	Value
ADSTYPE_INVALID	None	0
ADSTYPE_DN_STRING	IADsPropertyValue::DNString	1
ADSTYPE_CASE_EXACT_STRING	IADsPropertyValue::CaseExactString	2
ADSTYPE_CASE_IGNORE_STRING	IADsPropertyValue::CaseIgnoreString	3
ADSTYPE_PRINTABLE_STRING	IADsPropertyValue::PrintableString	4
ADSTYPE_NUMERIC_STRING	IADsPropertyValue::NumericString	5
ADSTYPE_BOOLEAN	IADsPropertyValue::Boolean	6
ADSTYPE_INTEGER	IADsPropertyValue::Integer	7
ADSTYPE_OCTET_STRING	IADsPropertyValue::OctetString	8
ADSTYPE_UTC_TIME	IADsPropertyValue::UTCTime	9
ADSTYPE_LARGE_INTEGER	IADsPropertyValue::LargeInteger	10
ADSTYPE_PROV_SPECIFIC	None	11
ADSTYPE_OBJECT_CLASS	None	12
ADSTYPE_CASEIGNORE_LIST	None	13
ADSTYPE_OCTET_LIST	None	14
ADSTYPE_PATH	None	15
ADSTYPE_POSTALADDRESS	None	16
ADSTYPE_TIMESTAMP	None	17
ADSTYPE_BACKLINK	None	18
ADSTYPE_TYPEDNAME	None	19
ADSTYPE_HOLD	None	20
ADSTYPE_NETADDRESS	None	21
ADSTYPE_REPLICAPOINTER	None	22
ADSTYPE_FAXNUMBER	None	23
ADSTYPE_EMAIL	None	24
ADSTYPE_NT_SECURITY_DESCRIPTOR	IADsPropertyValue::SecurityDescriptor	25
ADSTYPE_UNKNOWN	None	26

For complete documentation on ADsTypes, visit *http://msdn.microsoft .com/en-us/library/aa772240(VS.85).aspx.*

Suppose you want to add a `PropertyValue` object with the value of "Hi There!" The two attributes of `PropertyValue` that need to be set include a case-sensitive string (i.e., the type of data, or `IADsPropertyValue::ADsType property`) and "Hi There!" (i.e., the value of that case-sensitive string, or the `IADsPropertyValue::CaseExactString` property). The `IADsPropertyValue::ADsType` constant for a case-sensitive string is ADSTYPE_CASE_EXACT_STRING, which has a numeric value of 2. As shown in Table 22-3, `IADsPropertyValue::CaseExactString` is one of a number of `IADsProperty Value` property methods, each relating to a specific data type. It is the value in `IADsPropertyValue::ADsType` that determines which of the property methods are actually used to get and set the data.

The following script shows how to create this new `PropertyValue` object. We begin by setting the ADSTYPE_CASE_EXACT_STRING constant to its numeric value (i.e., 2) and declaring the `objPropValue` variable. As we mentioned earlier, if you use VBScript with WSH, you must either define the constants, as the script does, or use the values directly:

```
Const ADSTYPE_CASE_EXACT_STRING = 2
Dim objPropValue    'An ADSI PropertyValue object
Set objPropValue = CreateObject("PropertyValue")
objPropValue.ADsType = ADSTYPE_CASE_EXACT_STRING
objPropValue.CaseExactString = "Hi There!"
```

We use VBScript's `CreateObject` method to create an instance of the `PropertyValue` object and set it to the `objPropValue` variable. Then two attributes are assigned to the `PropertyValue` object. The `objPropValue`'s `IADsPropertyValue::ADsType` property method is used to assign the property's data type to the ADSTYPE_CASE_EX-ACT_STRING constant. Finally, we use `objPropValue`'s `IADsProperty Value::CaseExactString` property method to assign the property's value to "Hi There!"

Adding Sets of Values

As we mentioned previously, some properties hold one value (e.g., the `lastLogon` property); others hold multiple values in an array (e.g., the `pager` property). The `PropertyEntry` object holds the entire set of values for a property, be it one value or many values.

However, the `PropertyEntry` object does more than store values. This object's properties dictate how you can manipulate those values. The `PropertyEntry` object supports the `IADsPropertyEntry` interface that has four property methods:

IADsPropertyEntry::Name
> The `IADsPropertyEntry::Name` property method sets the name of the property that you want to manipulate (e.g., `pager`).

IADsPropertyEntry::Values
> The `IADsPropertyEntry::Values` property method sets an array containing those values you want to manipulate (e.g., the pager numbers).

`IADsPropertyEntry::ADsType`

The `IADsPropertyEntry::ADsType` property method determines the data type of those values (e.g., Unicode string).

`IADsPropertyEntry::ControlCode`

The `IADsPropertyEntry::ControlCode` property method tells the cache whether to overwrite, update, or add to the property's existing values. You use the constants in Table 22-2 with the `IADsPropertyEntry::ControlCode` property. These constants are the same as the constants for the `IADs::PutEx` method described earlier. Because `IADsPropertyEntry::ControlCode` constants work the same way as the `IADs::PutEx` method constants, we won't go through them again here.

The next script shows how to create a `PropertyEntry` object from one property value:

```
Const ADSTYPE_CASE_IGNORE_STRING = 3
Const ADS_PROPERTY_UPDATE = 2
Dim objPropValue 'An ADSI PropertyValue object
Dim objPropEntry 'An ADSI PropertyEntry object
Set objPropValue = CreateObject("PropertyValue")
objPropValue.ADsType = ADSTYPE_CASE_IGNORE_STRING
objPropValue.CaseIgnoreString = "0123-456-7890"
Set objPropEntry = CreateObject("PropertyEntry")
objPropEntry.Name = "pager"
objPropEntry.Values = Array(objPropValue)
objPropEntry.ADsType = ADSTYPE_CASE_IGNORE_STRING
objPropEntry.ControlCode = ADS_PROPERTY_UPDATE
```

The first part of the script is similar to the previous one. We begin by setting the constants to their numeric values and declaring the variables. Next , we create an instance of the `PropertyValue` object and set it to the `objPropValue` variable. We then use the `IADsPropertyValue::ADsType` property method to assign the property's data type to the ADSTYPE_CASE_IGNORE_STRING constant and the `IADsPropertyValue::Case IgnoreString` property method to assign the property's value to 0123-456-7890.

The second part of the script begins by creating an instance of the `PropertyEntry` object and setting it to the `objPropEntry` variable. Then all four `PropertyEntry` properties are set. For the `IADsPropertyEntry::Values` property, you must use the VBScript `Array()` function to force the values into an array, even if you set only one value. For the `IADsPropertyEntry::ControlCode` property, you're replacing the existing values with the ones you're passing in.

Walking Through the Property Cache

For any object, the property cache consists of `PropertyEntry` objects that correspond to each property. When you use the `IADs::Get` method, it reads the cache's `PropertyEntry` for that particular property.

As we've previously mentioned, whenever you call `IADsOpenDSObject::OpenDSObject` or `GetObject`, as explained later, the object that is returned can use the IADs interface in addition to any interface designed for that object. The `IADsPropertyList` interface also is directly available for any object. It is of no real use without a call to `GetInfo` first, without which the property cache will be empty. Once the cache is populated, however, the methods and properties come into their own. Table 22-4 lists the `IADsProperty List` methods and properties.

Table 22-4. IADsPropertyList methods and properties

IADsPropertyList methods and properties	Action
Next method	Retrieves the value of the next item in the property list
Skip method	Skips a number of items in the property list
Reset method	Puts the pointer back to the beginning of the list
Add method	Adds a new property to the list
Remove method	Removes a property from the list
Item method	Gets an item from the property list
GetPropertyItem method	Gets an item in the property list
PutPropertyItem method	Puts an item in the property list
ResetPropertyItem method	Resets an item in the property list back to its original value
PurgePropertyList method	Deletes all items in the property list
PropertyCount property	The number of properties in the property list

 For complete documentation on the `IADsPropertyList` interface, visit *http://msdn.microsoft.com/en-us/library/aa706102(VS.85).aspx*.

The `PropertyList` object represents the entire set of properties for an object. The methods and property methods of the `IADsPropertyList` interface can be used to manipulate the `PropertyList` object. Example 22-5 uses several of those methods and property methods to demonstrate three ways of walking through the property cache.

Example 22-5. Walking through the property cache with the IADsPropertyList interface

```
Option Explicit

'*********************************************************************
'Force error checking within the code using the Err.Number property
'method in approaches 2 and 3
'*********************************************************************
On Error Resume Next

'*********************************************************************
'Declare the variables
'*********************************************************************
Dim objGroup      'The group whose property list you want to investigate
Dim strText       'A text string that displays results in one message box
```

```
Dim intPropCount  'The number of properties
Dim intIndex      'The index used while looping through the property list
Dim objPropEntry  'An individual property entry used in a loop

Set objGroup = GetObject("LDAP://cn=Managers,ou=Sales,dc=mycorp,dc=com")
objGroup.GetInfo

intPropCount = objGroup.PropertyCount
WScript.Echo "There are " & intPropCount & " values in the property cache."

'**********************************************************************
'Approach 1: PropertyCount property method
'**********************************************************************
strText = ""
For intIndex = 0 To (intPropCount-1)
  strText = strText & objGroup.Item(intIndex).Name & vbTab _
  & objGroup.Item(intIndex).ADsType & vbCrLf
Next
WScript.Echo strText

'**********************************************************************
'Approach 2: Next method
'**********************************************************************
strText = ""
Set objPropEntry = objGroup.Next
While (IsNull(objPropEntry) = False And Err.Number = 0)
  strText = strText & objPropEntry.Name & vbTab & objPropEntry.ADsType _
          & vbCrLf
  Set objPropEntry = objGroup.Next
Wend
WScript.Echo strText
Set objPropEntry = Nothing

'**********************************************************************
'Approach 3: Next and Skip methods
'**********************************************************************
strText = ""
objGroup.Reset
Set objPropEntry = objGroup.Next
While (IsNull(objPropEntry) = False And Err.Number = 0)
  strText = strText & objPropEntry.Name & vbTab & objPropEntry.ADsType _
          & vbCrLf
  objGroup.Skip(2)
  Set objPropEntry = objGroup.Next
Wend
WScript.Echo strText
Set objPropEntry = Nothing
```

The script begins by using VBScript's Option Explicit statement (which requires you to declare all variables before using them) and the On Error Resume Next statement (which allows you to do error handling). Then, after declaring the variables, the GetObject method is used to bind to the group whose property cache we want to look at. In this case, we want to view the properties for the Manager group object. Next, the IADs::GetInfo method is called to load the property cache for this group. Since we won't be using the `IADs::Get` method in the script, the system won't implicitly use the `IADs::GetInfo` method to load the cache, so we have to explicitly load it in.

Each object in `objGroup` has a `PropertyList` object, so we use the `IADsProperty List::PropertyCount` property method to count each `PropertyList` object. We store the count for later use by setting it to the `intPropCount` variable, and we print it out in a message box using WSH's `Echo` method.

We now know how many properties `objGroup` has, but we need to find out the values of those properties. We can use one of three approaches to walk through the property cache to get this information.

Approach 1: Using the IADsPropertyList::PropertyCount property method

We begin by walking through the property list by counting the items in the index 0 through `intPropCount-1`. We need to specify this index, because the property list index starts at 0 rather than 1. For example, a property list with 15 items has an index ranging from 0 to 14.

For each item in the index, you concatenate (&) two property methods to retrieve the property's `IADs::Name` and `IADsPropertyValue::ADsType`. The script processes concatenated statements from left to right, so it first uses the `IADsPropertyList::Item` method with the `intIndex` value as the item number to retrieve a property entry, to which it applies the `IADs::Name` property method to get the property's name. The script then uses the same process to retrieve the same property entry, to which it applies the `IADsPropertyValue::ADsType` property method to get the property's datatype.

Forcing the script to process `IADsPropertyList::Item` twice is inefficient. We processed it twice only to illustrate how to walk through the property list. The concatenated code includes more than just the two property methods. The code also concatenates a tab (`vbTab`) between the two property methods and a carriage-return line-feed (`vbCrLf`), or new line, after the second property method. But even more important, the code first concatenates the existing `strText` variable onto the front (i.e., `strText = strText & property method 1 & property method 2`), which means that, in the output, these property values are appended to the existing `strText` string. As a result, the WSH displays all the property values in one message box if you use WSH's *wscript.exe* scripting engine to run the script. If you're using WSH's *cscript.exe* scripting engine, using this append technique makes no difference. If you don't concatenate the `strText` variable (i.e., `strText = property method 1 & property method 2`), WSH displays a separate message box for each property.

When the script finishes looping through the property list index, it prints the appended `strText` string in the message box. Approaches 2 and 3 also use the append technique to display all their output in one message box.

Approach 2: Using the IADsPropertyList::Next method

We start this approach by resetting the `strText` variable to a zero-length string to ensure that no values from the previous approach are left in the string. Then the `IADsProper` `tyList::Next` method is called to retrieve a copy of the first property entry and set the result to the `objPropEntry` variable. Because we called the `IADsPropertyList::Next` method, we can use a while loop to iterate through the cache until we encounter a null value, which specifies that we're at the end of the list.

Providing that the first property entry isn't a null entry, we enter the while loop. The `And Err.Number = 0` code designates a test to see whether an error has occurred. A value of 0 indicates no error; any other value specifies an error. If a valid entry (i.e., not a null entry) is retrieved and an error hasn't occurred (i.e., the error number is equal to 0), we enter the loop. Within the loop, the property name and data type are appended to the `strText` string in a similar manner as before. To move to the next property entry in the property cache, we again call the `IADsPropertyList::Next` method. As long as this value isn't null and isn't generating an error code, the process continues until it hits a null entry, which means we're at the end of the list. The wend keyword signifies the end of the while loop. Finally, the results are printed.

Approach 3: Using the IADsPropertyList::Next and IADsPropertyList::Skip methods

The code in this approach is identical to the code used in approach 2, except for the addition of two lines. The `IADsPropertyList::Reset` property method sets the property list pointer to the first property entry in the cache. If we don't use the `IADsProperty` `List::Reset` property method, the pointer will be at the end of the cache, which would generate a null entry. The `IADsPropertyList::Skip` code tells the `IADsProperty` `List::Next` property method to skip the next two property entries. In other words, the `IADsPropertyList::Next` property method is retrieving every third property, so this approach returns only property entries 1, 4, 7, 10, and so on.

Writing the Modifications

Now that we've shown how to walk through the cache, next we will review how to write modifications to the cache and back to the directory. Example 22-6 illustrates these procedures. This script is an amalgam of the code in the earlier examples. As such, it shows how to assemble the pieces of code into a usable script.

Example 22-6. Writing modifications to the cache and back to the directory

```
Option Explicit
'***********************************************************************
'Force error checking within the code using the Err.Number property
'method in approaches 2 and 3
```

```
'************************************************************************
On Error Resume Next

'************************************************************************
'Declare the constants and variables
'************************************************************************
Const ADSTYPE_CASE_IGNORE_STRING = 3
Const ADS_PROPERTY_UPDATE = 2

Dim objPropValue    'An ADSI PropertyValue object
Dim objPropEntry    'An ADSI PropertyEntry object
Dim objUser         'The user whose property list you want to investigate
Dim strText         'A text string that displays results in one message box
Dim intPropCount    'The number of properties
Dim intIndex        'The index used while looping through the property list

Set objUser = GetObject("LDAP://cn=Brian Desmond,ou=Sales,dc=mycorp,dc=com")
objUser.GetInfo

'************************************************************************
'Section A: Calculate the property count, and enumerate each
'property's name and datatype
'************************************************************************
intPropCount = objUser.PropertyCount
WScript.Echo "There are " & intPropCount _
  & " values in the property cache before adding the new one."

strText = ""
For intIndex = 0 To (intPropCount-1)
  strText = strText & objUser.Item(intIndex).Name & vbTab _
    & objUser.Item(intIndex).ADsType & vbCrLf
Next
WScript.Echo strText

'************************************************************************
'Section B: Create a property entry, and write it to the cache
'************************************************************************
Set objPropValue = CreateObject("PropertyValue")
objPropValue.ADsType = ADSTYPE_CASE_IGNORE_STRING
objPropValue.CaseExactString = "0123-456-7890"

Set objPropEntry = CreateObject("PropertyEntry")
objPropEntry.Name = "pager"
objPropEntry.Values = Array(objPropValue)
objPropEntry.ADsType = ADSTYPE_CASE_IGNORE_STRING
objPropEntry.ControlCode = ADS_PROPERTY_UPDATE

objUser.PutPropertyItem(objPropEntry)

'************************************************************************
'Section C: Write out the cache to Active Directory and read the new
'cache explicitly back in from the object
'************************************************************************
```

```
objUser.SetInfo
objUser.GetInfo

'**********************************************************************
'Section D: Recalculate the property count, and re-enumerate each
'property's name and datatype to see the changes
'**********************************************************************
intPropCount = objUser.PropertyCount

WScript.Echo "There are " & intPropCount _
  & " values in the property cache after adding the new one."

strText = ""
For intIndex = 0 To (intPropCount-1)
  strText = strText & objUser.Item(intIndex).Name _
    & vbTab & objUser.Item(intIndex).ADsType & vbCrLf
Next
WScript.Echo strText
```

The script begins with `Option Explicit` and `On Error Resume Next`, after which it sets the constants, declares the variables, and sets the `objUser` variable to the AlistairGLN user object. The script then divides into four sections:

Section A

Determines the `User` object's property count and lists each property's name and data type.

Section B

Creates a property entry and writes it to the cache. The last line uses the `IADsPropertyList::PutPropertyItem` method to write the new property entry for `objUser` to the cache. However, the `IADs::SetInfo` method must be used to write this entry to the directory.

Section C

Contains new code. The first line uses the `IADs::SetInfo` method to write the cache to the directory. The second line uses the explicit `IADs::GetInfo` method to read it back into the cache. Although the second line might not seem necessary, it is. If we don't use an explicit `IADs::GetInfo` call, we'll be accessing the same cache that we accessed before we added the new property entry. The explicit `IADs::GetInfo` call retrieves any new properties that anyone else has updated since the last implicit or explicit `IADs::GetInfo` call.

Section D

Recalculates the property count and reenumerates each property's name and data type so that we can see the modifications. If we see the property count increase by one after we write the cache to the directory, the script has successfully executed.

Walking the Property Cache: The Solution

Example 22-7 is quite long. It walks through the property cache for an object and prints the name, data type, and values of each entry. Some of the properties are not printable strings, so printing them in a text format makes little sense. Thus, this script prints only the text strings. We used a VBScript dictionary object to map the data type integers (**ADsType**) to descriptive names. A dictionary is similar in nature to an associative array or hash, which are common in other programming languages. After instantiating a dictionary object, you can use the **Add** method to add new key value pairs to it.

Example 22-7. Walking through the property cache of an object

```
Option Explicit
On Error Resume Next

'**********************************************************************
'Declare the hash (dictionary), constants and variables
'**********************************************************************
Dim dicADsType
Set dicADsType = CreateObject("Scripting.Dictionary")
dicADsType.Add 0, "INVALID"
dicADsType.Add 1, "DN_STRING"
dicADsType.Add 2, "CASE_EXACT_STRING"
dicADsType.Add 3, "CASE_IGNORE_STRING"
dicADsType.Add 4, "PRINTABLE_STRING"
dicADsType.Add 5, "NUMERIC_STRING"
dicADsType.Add 6, "BOOLEAN"
dicADsType.Add 7, "INTEGER"
dicADsType.Add 8, "OCTET_STRING"
dicADsType.Add 9, "UTC_TIME"
dicADsType.Add 10, "LARGE_INTEGER"
dicADsType.Add 11, "PROV_SPECIFIC"
dicADsType.Add 12, "OBJECT_CLASS"
dicADsType.Add 13, "CASEIGNORE_LIST"
dicADsType.Add 14, "OCTET_LIST"
dicADsType.Add 15, "PATH"
dicADsType.Add 16, "POSTALADDRESS"
dicADsType.Add 17, "TIMESTAMP"
dicADsType.Add 18, "BACKLINK"
dicADsType.Add 19, "TYPEDNAME"
dicADsType.Add 20, "HOLD"
dicADsType.Add 21, "NETADDRESS"
dicADsType.Add 22, "REPLICAPOINTER"
dicADsType.Add 23, "FAXNUMBER"
dicADsType.Add 24, "EMAIL"
dicADsType.Add 25, "NT_SECURITY_DESCRIPTOR"
dicADsType.Add 26, "UNKNOWN"

Const ADS_PROPERTY_CLEAR = 1
Const ADS_PROPERTY_UPDATE = 2
Const ADS_PROPERTY_APPEND = 3
Const ADS_PROPERTY_DELETE = 4

Dim objPropValue    'An individual property value within a loop
Dim objPropEntry    'An ADSI PropertyEntry object
Dim objObject       'The object whose property list we wish to investigate
Dim strText         'A text string used to display results in one go
Dim intPropCount    'The number of properties in
```

```
Dim intIndex        'The index used while looping through the property list
Dim intCount        'Used to display property values in a numbered sequence

Set objObject = GetObject("LDAP://cn=administrator,cn=users,dc=mycorp,dc=com")
objObject.GetInfo
if (Err.Number > 0) Then
   Wscript.Echo "Object not found, returning..."
   Wscript.Quit
End if

'**********************************************************************
'Write out the current property cache total to the string that is
'storing output
'**********************************************************************
intPropCount = objObject.PropertyCount
strText = "There are " & intPropCount & _
          " values in the property cache." & vbCrLf

'**********************************************************************
'The extra vbTabs used in the first loop are to space the results so
'that they are nicely formatted with the list of values in the second loop
'**********************************************************************
For intIndex = 0 To (intPropCount-1)

   Set objPropEntry = objObject.Item(intIndex)
   strText = strText & objPropEntry.Name & vbCrLf

   strText = strText & vbTab & "Type:" & vbTab & vbTab & _
             dicADsType.Item(objPropEntry.ADsType) & vbCrLf

   '**********************************************************************
   'Go through each property value in the property entry and use the AdsType
   'to print out the appropriate value, prefixed by a count (intCount), i.e.:
   '
   '   Value #1: Vicky Launders
   '   Value #2: Alistair Lowe-Norris
   '   Value #3: Robbie Allen
   '**********************************************************************
   intCount = 1

   For Each objPropValue In objPropEntry.Values

      If (dicADsType(objPropValue.ADsType) = "STRING") Then
         strText = strText & vbTab & "Value #" & intCount & ":" _
           & vbTab & objPropValue.DNString & vbCrLf

      ElseIf (dicADsType(objPropValue.ADsType) = "CASE_EXACT_STRING") Then
         strText = strText & vbTab & "Value #" & intCount & ":" _
           & vbTab & objPropValue.CaseExactString & vbCrLf

      ElseIf (dicADsType(objPropValue.ADsType) = "CASE_IGNORE_STRING") Then
         strText = strText & vbTab & "Value #" & intCount & ":" _
           & vbTab & objPropValue.CaseIgnoreString & vbCrLf

      ElseIf (dicADsType(objPropValue.ADsType) = "PRINTABLE_STRING") Then
```

```
    strText = strText & vbTab & "Value #" & intCount & ":" _
        & vbTab & objPropValue.PrintableString & vbCrLf

    ElseIf (dicADsType(objPropValue.ADsType) = "NUMERIC_STRING") Then
        strText = strText & vbTab & "Value #" & intCount & ":" _
            & vbTab & objPropValue.NumericString & vbCrLf

    ElseIf (dicADsType(objPropValue.ADsType) = "BOOLEAN") Then
        strText = strText & vbTab & "Value #" & intCount & ":" _
            & vbTab & CStr(objPropValue.Boolean) & vbCrLf

    ElseIf (dicADsType(objPropValue.ADsType) = "INTEGER") Then
        strText = strText & vbTab & "Value #" & intCount & ":" _
            & vbTab & objPropValue.Integer & vbCrLf

    End If

    intCount=intCount+1

  Next
Next

WScript.Echo strText
```

This script also illustrates how you can just as easily use the WinNT namespace rather
than the LDAP namespace to display properties of objects, and how you can run the
script against Windows NT domains and Windows NT or later member servers rather
than Active Directory.

The script displays every value in the property cache for an object. However, there may
come a time when you wish to see the entire potential property cache for an object and
list which of all possible values have been set. To do that, you need to query the formal
schema class definition for the object. This leads us to the final section on the property
cache.

Walking the Property Cache Using the Formal Schema Class Definition

There is one other way to walk the property list for a particular object: using its schema
class details. Chapter 4 explained how the schema is the blueprint for objects in Active
Directory. As each schema class actually is stored in Active Directory, you can navigate
the object's properties by using the IADsClass interface to display each individual item
according to its formal name in the schema class. To do this, we first obtain a reference
to the object in the normal manner. We then obtain a reference to the schema class for
that object. We can do this using the IADs::Schema property method, which returns the
full ADsPath of the schema class. For example, the user objectclass in the *mycorp*
.com domain has the following schema ADsPath:

    LDAP://cn=User,cn=Schema,cn=Configuration,dc=mycorp,dc=com

Then we can use the `IADsClass::MandatoryProperties` and `IADsClass::OptionalProper`ties methods to retrieve the appropriate properties. The following example nicely brings together `IADs::GetEx` for retrieving multiple properties and writing to a file, which is required due to the large number of properties.

Example 22-8 uses `On Error Resume Next` because all properties may not display, and the program will fail if any do not. The script also differs from the previous script in that it lists all possible properties and whether they've been set. The previous example listed only those that had been set. The following script is also generic; it will print out the property cache for any object class. Just change the `ADsPath` passed to `GetObject`.

Example 22-8. Walking the property cache using the formal schema class definition

```
Option Explicit
'**********************************************************************
'Force error checking within the code using the Err.Number property
'method in approaches 2 and 3
'**********************************************************************
On Error Resume Next

'**********************************************************************
'Declare the constants and variables
'**********************************************************************
Dim objObject    'Active Directory object
Dim objClass     'ADSI Class object
Dim objProp      'An individual property
Dim intCount     'Incremental counter for display
Dim fileadsect   'A FileSystemObject
Dim outTextFile  'A TextStream Object

'**********************************************************************
'Create a VBScript file object and use it to open a text file. The
'second parameter specifies to overwrite any existing file that exists.
'**********************************************************************
Set fileadsect = CreateObject("Scripting.FileSystemObject")
Set outTextFile = fileadsect.CreateTextFile("c:\out.txt", TRUE)

'**********************************************************************
'Bind to the object and get a pointer to the appropriate schema class,
'i.e., User in this case
'**********************************************************************
Set objObject = GetObject("LDAP://cn=administrator,cn=Users,dc=mycorp,dc=com")
Set objClass = GetObject(objObject.Schema)

intCount = 1

'**********************************************************************
'Iterate through all the mandatory properties
'**********************************************************************
For Each objProp in objClass.MandatoryProperties
  EnumerateProperties objProp, outTextFile, objObject
  intCount = intCount + 1
Next
```

```
'***********************************************************************
'Iterate through all the optional properties
'***********************************************************************
For Each objProp in objClass.OptionalProperties
  EnumerateProperties objProp, outTextFile, objObject
  intCount = intCount + 1
Next

outTextFile.Close

'***********************************************************************
'Subroutine EnumerateProperties
'***********************************************************************
Sub EnumerateProperties(ByVal objProp, ByVal tsFile, ByVal objObj)

  Dim objProperty   'ADSI Property object
  Dim arrElement    'Array of elements

  '***********************************************************************
  'Get pointer to the schema property object
  '***********************************************************************
  Set objProperty = GetObject("LDAP://Schema/" & objProp)

  '***********************************************************************
  'Check whether property requires GetEx using IADsProperty::MultiValued
  '***********************************************************************
  If objProperty.MultiValued Then
    tsFile.WriteLine intCount & ") " & objProp & _
      " (" & objProperty.Syntax & ") (MULTI-VALUED)"

    '***********************************************************************
    'Check whether array returned from GetEx is empty using VBScript
    'function
    '***********************************************************************
    If (IsEmpty(objObj.GetEx(objProp))) Then
      tsFile.WriteLine vbTab & "= " & "NO VALUES SET!"
    Else
      For Each arrElement in objObj.GetEx(objProp)
        tsFile.WriteLine vbTab & "= " & arrElement
      Next
    End If

  Else
    tsFile.WriteLine intCount & ") " & objProp _
      & " (" & objProperty.Syntax & ")"

    Err.Clear
    If Err=0 Then
      tsFile.WriteLine vbTab & "= " & objObj.Get(objProp)
    Else
      tsFile.WriteLine vbTab & "= " & "Not Set!"
    End If

  End If
End Sub
```

Checking for Errors in VBScript

It is worthwhile to look at error handling in a little more detail now. Normally errors that occur in a script are termed fatal errors. This means that execution of the script terminates whenever an error occurs. When this happens, a dialog box opens and gives you the unique number and description of the error. While this is useful, sometimes you may like to set errors to be nonfatal, so that execution continues after the error. To do this, you include the following line in your code:

```
On Error Resume Next
```

Once you have done this, any line with an error is ignored. This can cause confusion, as can be seen from the following code. Note the missing P in LDAP:

```
Option Explicit
On Error Resume Next
Dim objGroup
Set objGroup = GetObject("LDAP://cn=Managers,ou=Sales,dc=mycorp,dc=com")
objGroup.GetInfo
WScript.Echo objGroup.Description
objGroup.Description = "My new group description goes here"
objGroup.GetInfo
WScript.Echo objGroup.Description
```

This script fails to execute any of the lines after the On Error Resume Next statement, as the first LDAP call into the objGroup variable failed. However, it will not terminate as usual with an error after the GetObject line, due to the On Error statement. To get around this, you should add a couple lines to do error checking. Example 22-9 is a good example of error checking in a different script.

Example 22-9. Error checking in VBScript

```
On Error Resume Next

'*********************************************************************
'Clear errors
'*********************************************************************
Err.Clear

'*********************************************************************
'Get a pointer to the Administrator account
'*********************************************************************
Set objUser = GetObject ("LDAP://cn=Administrator,cn=Users,dc=mycorp,dc=com")
If Err.Number = &H80005000 Then
  WScript.Echo "Bad ADSI path!" & vbCrLf & "Err. Number: " _
    & vbTab & CStr(Hex(Err.Number)) & vbCrLf & "Err. Descr.: " _
    & vbTab & Err.Description
  WScript.Quit
End If

'*********************************************************************
'Explicitly call GetInfo for completeness
'*********************************************************************
```

```
objUser.GetInfo

'************************************************************************
'Clear any previous errors
'************************************************************************
Err.Clear

'************************************************************************
'Try and get a pointer to the "moose" attribute of the user (which
'doesn't exist)
'************************************************************************
x = objUser.Get("moose")

'************************************************************************
'Check for property does not exist error
'************************************************************************
If Err.Number = &H8000500D Then
  WScript.Echo "No such property!" & vbCrLf & "Err. Number: " _
    & vbTab & CStr(Hex(Err.Number)) & vbCrLf & "Err. Descr.: " _
    & vbTab & Err.Description
End If
```

This is a simple example; the path does exist and the moose property does not exist for the user. ADSI errors start at 80005 in hexadecimal, and 8000500D is the error indicating that there is no such property. The &H prefix indicates that the following string is a hexadecimal number. You must use the Err::Clear method from the Err interface to clear any existing error information, prior to making a call that could generate an error. If an error has occurred, the value of Err.Number is nonzero; if Err.Number is 0, no error occurred. If an error has occurred, Err.Description contains any description that has been set for that error.

Because most calls to the Err interface will be to retrieve the Err::Number property, the Err::Number property is set as the default property method, meaning that you don't have to state it explicitly. For example, these two statements are equivalent:

```
If Err = &H8000500D Then
If Err.Number = &H8000500D Then
```

In addition, as Hex(0) is the same as 0, most sample code that you will see using VBScript looks like this:

```
On Error Resume Next
'Some_code_goes_here
Err.Clear

Set x = GetObject(something_goes_here)
If Err = 0 Then
  'No error occurred
  Some_success_code_goes_here
Else
  'Error occurred
  Some_failure_code_goes_here
End If
```

Finally, to reset error checking back to the default as if the `On Error Resume Next` statement had not been included, we use the following code:

```
'The last character is a zero, not a capital "o"
On Error Goto 0
```

You can find a full list of ADSI errors in the MSDN library at *http://msdn.microsoft.com/en-us/library/aa772195(VS.85).aspx*.

Summary

Over the last two chapters, we've covered the interfaces, methods, and property methods that allow you to use access and manipulate generic objects in Active Directory. These interfaces include:

- `IADs`
- `IADsContainer` (covered more fully later)
- `IADsPropertyList`
- `IADsPropertyEntry`
- `IADsPropertyValue`

We've also looked at how to supply credentials to authenticate with alternate credentials using the `ADsOpenDSObject` interface as well as how to work with the error handling capabilities of VBScript.

In the next chapter, we cover how to search Active Directory using a database query interface called ADO.

## CHAPTER 23

Using ADO for Searching

Microsoft's ADO technology lets you conduct database searches and retrieve the results through a flexible interface called record sets. ADO also lets you update information in a database directly or with stored procedures. Since Microsoft created an ADO database provider for ADSI (the ADSI OLE DB provider), you can also use ADO's database query technology to query Active Directory. However, the ADSI OLE DB provider is currently read-only, so many of the useful ADO methods for updating data aren't available. You can use ADO only for searching and retrieving objects, but despite the read-only limitation, using ADO is still a boon. It is significantly faster to search Active Directory using ADO than it is to use ADSI to enumerate each object recursively down a branch. Even using `IADsContainer::Filter` is slow in comparison. So if you need to search Active Directory rapidly for attributes that match certain criteria, ADO is exactly what you should use. The ADO object model consists of nine objects (`Command`, `Connection`, `Error`, `Field`, `Parameter`, `Property`, `Record`, `Recordset`, and `Streams`) and four collection objects (`Errors`, `Fields`, `Parameters`, and `Properties`). However, some of these objects aren't useful if you're using the ADSI OLE DB provider, as they are more often used for accessing full-fledged database services. For example, the `Parameter` object lets you pass parameters to stored procedures, but this object is of little use because the ADSI provider doesn't support stored procedures.

The objects that are appropriate to ADSI in a read-only environment are the `Command`, `Connection`, `Error`, `Field`, `Property`, and `Recordset` objects. We use them to show you how to perform complex searches. For a full description of the ADO object model and the available functions, check out the following in the MSDN Library at: *http://msdn .microsoft.com/en-us/library/ms675532(VS.85).aspx*.

One point to note: ADO is written to work with all types of databases , so there are a number of ways to do exactly the same thing. We will attempt to cover examples of each different way as they crop up so that you will be able to choose the method that suits you best or that you are familiar with.

The First Search

The easiest way to explain basic searching using ADO is with an example. Here we'll build an ADO query to search and display the distinguished names of all users in Active Directory. You can create a simple script to do this search in six steps.

Step 1: Define the Constants and Variables

For this script, you need to define one constant and three variables . The constant is adStateOpen, which we set to 1. If you're using VBScript, you use this constant later to determine whether you made a successful connection to the database. The two main variables are objConn (an ADO Connection object that lets you connect to the AD database) and objRS (an ADO Recordset object that holds the retrieved resultset). The third variable holds the output of the resultset, as shown in the following example:

```
Option Explicit
Const adStateOpen = 1
Dim objConn     'ADO Connection object
Dim objRS       'ADO Recordset object
```

The Option Explicit statement at the beginning of the script is optional, but we recommend that you include it. This statement forces the script to declare variables, so you can quickly spot errors.

Step 2: Establish an ADO Database Connection

To perform an ADO query, you need to establish an ADO connection, which is completely separate from any ADSI connections you opened with IADsOpenDSObject::Open DSObject. Before you can establish this connection, you must create an ADO Connection object to use. This object can be created the same way you create a filesystem object: use the CreateObject method, with "ADODB.Connection" as a parameter. You use the ADODB prefix to create all ADO objects, and Connection is the top-level object in the ADO object model:

```
Set objConn = CreateObject("ADODB.Connection")
```

Just as you use different programmatic identifiers (ProgIDs) (e.g., WinNT:, LDAP:) to tell ADSI which directory to access, you use different OLE DB providers to tell ADO which query syntax to use. An OLE DB provider implements OLE DB interfaces so that different applications can use the same uniform process to access data. The ADSI OLE DB connector supports two forms of syntax: the SQL dialect and the LDAP dialect. Although you can use the SQL dialect to query the ADSI namespace, most scriptwriters use the LDAP dialect because Active Directory is an LDAP Directory. However, the default for the Connection object's read/write property, objConn.Provider, is MSDASQL, which specifies the use of SQL syntax. Because you want to use the ADSI provider, you need to set objConn.Provider to "ADsDSOObject", which specifies the use of the LDAP syntax. By setting this specific provider, you force the script to use not only a specific syntax but also a specific set of arguments in the calls to the Connection object's methods.

```
objConn.Provider = "ADsDSOObject"
```

Step 3: Open the ADO Connection

You can open a connection to the directory by calling the Connection::Open method. When describing the methods and property methods of COM interfaces in text, the established notation is to use a double colon (::) separator. For example, Connection::Open specifies the Open method of the Connection object, as shown in the following example:

```
objConn.Open _
    "", "CN=Administrator,CN=Users,dc=mycorp,dc=com", "mypass"
```

As the code shows, the Open method takes three parameters. The first parameter is the Connection::ConnectionString parameter, which contains information that the script needs to establish a connection to the data source. In this case, it is blank. The second parameter contains the user DN, UPN, or legacy domain\user to bind with, and the third is the user's password.

In this code, you're authenticating with a username DN, UPN, or legacy Domain \UserID (the second parameter) and the user's password (the third parameter). You can leave the first parameter blank. Here's why: in ADO, you can perform the same task many ways because the Command, Connection, and Recordset objects heavily interrelate. If you set the properties of one object, you can use those same properties to open the connection of another object as long as you're not setting any new options. Such is the case in the preceding section of code; you're opening the connection without setting any new options. You then use an If…Then…Else statement to see whether the Open call worked. If the call succeeded (i.e., the connection state has a value of 1), the script prints the message "Authentication Successful" and proceeds to the query. If the call didn't work (i.e., the connection state has a value of 0), the script prints the message "Authentication Failed" and quits, setting the returned error code to 1:

```
If objConn.State = 1 Then
    WScript.Echo "Authentication Successful!"
Else
    WScript.Echo "Authentication Failed."
    WScript.Quit(1)
End If
```

Step 4: Execute the Query

The Connection::Execute method is used to perform a query. Connection::Execute accepts a string containing four arguments separated by semicolons:

```
Set objRS = objConn.Execute _
  ("<LDAP://dc=mycorp,dc=com>;(&(objectCategory=person)" _
  & "(objectClass=user));Name,distinguishedName;SubTree")
```

 If the string contains spaces before or after the semicolons, the code will fail. It's easy to forget this, and it's very annoying to try to debug, as the error just states that a parameter is invalid. You must also remember to enclose the parameter in parentheses because you're passing the Exe cute method's result to a variable.

The four arguments for any LDAP query you want to execute are:

Search base

The search base specifies the point in the directory from which the search will start. You must use a full ADsPath to specify the search base and enclose the ADsPath in angle brackets (< >). In this script, we are starting from the directory's root (i.e., LDAP://dc=mycorp,dc=com).

Filter

The filter defines criteria to match objects with. You must enclose this argument in parentheses. You also must use the format defined in RFC 2254. Filters are covered in greater detail later in the Section Understanding Search Filters. The previous script used the search filter (&(objectCategory=person)(object Class=user)), which means that only user objects will be returned.

Attributes

The attributes argument is a comma-delimited list of attributes to return. You must specify each attribute individually. Unlike the IADs::Get method, which executes an implicit GetInfo call to obtain all attributes, this ADO search returns only the specified attributes in the resultset. In this case, the ADO search will return the Name and distinguishedName attributes. The distinguishedName is a useful attribute to retrieve because it lets you easily use ADSI to bind to that object. You then can perform an explicit GetInfo to obtain all the non-constructed attributes for that object.

Scope

The scope specifies how far down from the query's starting point (i.e., search base) to search. You can specify one of three string constants: Base, OneLevel, or Subtree. If you set the scope to Base, the ADO search will only check the object specified by the search base for a match to the search filter. If you set the scope to OneLevel, the ADO search checks any object directly under the search base, one level down. If you set the scope to Subtree, as this script does, the ADO search checks the search base and every container and object under the search base.

Step 5: Navigate Through the Resultset

The objRS variable holds the resultset, also known as the recordset. Recordset objects have a table-like structure. The structure's columns are fields, and the rows are records. Fields correspond to the attributes you want to return and assume the titles of those attributes (e.g., Name or distinguishedName). ADO also numbers the fields from left to right, starting with 0. Thus, you can access fields using attribute names or index numbers. Records correspond to the values of those attributes.

To manage the members of objRS, the simplest approach is to use the Recordset::Move Next method (which navigates to the next record in the resultset) while checking the Recordset::EOF (end-of-file) method. The RecordSet::EOF method returns true if you're at the end of the resultset. The following code sample uses both of these methods:

```
While Not objRS.EOF
    Wscript.Echo objRS.Fields.Item("Name").Value _
        & vbCrLf & objRS.Fields.Item("distinguishedName").Value
    objRS.MoveNext
Wend
```

As this section of code shows, we're using these two methods in a simple while loop to move through each record. If Recordset::EOF returns a value of false (i.e., you're not at the end of the resultset), the script outputs the contents of the record for each field and moves on to the next record. If Recordset::EOF returns a value of true (i.e., end of the recordset), then the script exits the while loop.

To access the values of each matching object, we are using objRS.Fields, which is a Fields collection object. As with all collections, Fields has a method called Item. The Fields::Item method takes an argument that equates to either the name of the field or its index number. The Fields::Item method returns a Field object, which has a

Value property method that allows us to get the value for that specific property of the object. In other words, the code:

```
objRS.Fields.Item("Name").Value
```

returns the value of the individual field called Name from the collection of all possible fields in the recordset. We'll come back to this more in the later examples on navigating resultsets.

Step 6: Close the ADO Connection

The Connection::Close method is used to close the ADO connection to the directory. To be complete, you may also want to set the Recordset object to Nothing to make sure it doesn't mistakenly get reused. That isn't mandatory if your script is done at that point, because it will automatically get cleaned up, but it is good practice nonetheless. That way, if you later add code to the end of the script, you can't mistakenly reuse the now-defunct objRS variable without reinitializing it first. Here is example code illustrating how to properly close down an ADO session:

```
Set objRS = Nothing
objConn.Close
```

The Entire Script for a Simple Search

The following is the entire script:

```
Option Explicit
Const adStateOpen = 1
Dim objConn    'ADO Connection object
Dim objRS      'ADO Recordset object
Set objConn = CreateObject("ADODB.Connection")
objConn.Provider = "ADSDSOObject"
objConn.Open "","CN=Administrator,CN=Users,dc=mycorp,dc=com", "mypass"
If objConn.State = adStateOpen Then
  WScript.Echo "Authentication Successful!"
Else
  WScript.Echo "Authentication Failed."
  WScript.Quit(1)
End If
 Set objRS = objConn.Execute _
  ("<LDAP://dc=mycorp,dc=com>;(&(objectCategory=person)" _
  & "(objectClass=user));Name,distinguishedName;SubTree")
 While Not objRS.EOF
  Wscript.Echo objRS.Fields.Item("Name").Value _
    & vbCrLf & objRS.Fields.Item("distinguishedName").Value
  objRS.MoveNext
Wend
objRS.Close()
Set objRS = Nothing
objConn.Close
Set objConn = Nothing
```

While we open and close the connection within the short script, we could keep the connection open for every query if we had many queries to execute. This is how ADO is normally used.

Understanding Search Filters

When you use the LDAP dialect with the ADSI OLE DB provider to conduct a search, you must use an LDAP search filter to specify your search criteria. In a simple case, (objectclass=user) would be used to select every object with the user objectClass under the search base. You can in fact use a filter to match the presence of a value (or not) for any attribute of an object. This enables you to create powerful searches with complex criteria. For example, you can search for any group object that has a certain user as a member and that has a description matching a certain substring.

Filters must follow the format specified in RFC 2254, *The String Representation of LDAP Search Filters*. You can download RFC 2254 from *http://www.ietf.org/rfc/rfc2254.txt*.

Although filters let you conduct powerful searches, working with them can seem complex because of the format used, known as prefix notation. To make it easier to understand, we have divided the discussion of filters into two parts: items within a filter and items connecting filters.

Items Within a Filter

Within a filter, you can have three types of items:

Operators

A filter can include one of three operators . The equal-to (=) operator checks for exact equivalence. An example is (name=janet). The greater-than-or-equal-to (>=) and less-than-or-equal-to (<=) operators check for compliance with a range. Examples are (size>=5) and (size<=20).

The equal-to operator can be modified to specify a bitwise comparison. The format of the filter is attribute:matching_rule_oid:=value. The two matching rule OIDs are 1.2.840.113556.1.4.803 for a bitwise AND match and 1.2.840.113556.1.4.804 for a bitwise OR match. For example, the filter (userAccountControl: 1.2.840.113556.1.4.803:=2) searches for objects that have bit 1 (value 2) enabled, which means they are marked as disabled.

Attributes

> You can include attributes in filters when you want to determine whether an attribute exists. You simply specify the attribute, followed by the = operator and an asterisk (*). For example, the (description=*) filter searches for objects that have the description attribute populated.

Substrings

> You can include substrings in filters when you want to search for objects with specific strings. Test for substrings by placing the attribute type (e.g., cn for common name, sn for surname) to the left of the = operator and the substring you're searching for to the right. Use the * character to specify where that substring occurs in the string. The (cn=Keith*) filter searches for common name (CN) attributes that begin with the substring "Keith"; the (cn=*Cooper) filter searches for CN strings that end with the substring "Cooper." Depending on the search, the latter form of substring searches can take a long time to return. Under Windows Server 2003 and higher, the substring searches perform much better than previously.

You can place several substrings together by using an asterisk character several times. For example, the (cn=Kei*Coo*) filter searches for two substrings in the string: the first substring begins with "Kei," followed by the second substring that begins with "Coo." Similarly, the (cn=*ith*per) filter searches for strings that have two substrings: the first substring ends in "ith" followed by the second substring that ends in "per."

The resultset of a substring search might contain objects that you don't want. For example, if you use the filter (cn=Kei*Coo*) to search for the object representing "Keith Cooper," your resultset might contain two objects: one representing "Keith Cooper" and another representing "Keith Coolidge." To address that issue, you can connect multiple filter strings together to refine your search even more.

Connecting Filters

Compound filters can be created by using the ampersand (&), the vertical bar (|), and the exclamation mark (!). Let's start by creating a filter to find all computers whose common name begins with the letter a. The following is the filter for this search:

    (&(objectCategory=computer)(cn=a*))

This filter actually consists of two filters: (objectCategory=computer) and (cn=a*), but because you're enclosing the filters in parentheses, you're treating them as one filter. The & prefix specifies the use of the logical AND operator. In other words, you're searching for objects that are in the computer objectCategory and have a cn that begins with the letter a.

You can continue to add additional filters to narrow the search even more. Suppose that in computers whose cn begins with the letter a, you want to find only those computers whose dNSHostName ends with the substring *mycorp.net*. To perform this search, you use the following filter:

```
(&(objectCategory=computer)(cn=a*)(dNSHostName=*mycorp.net))
```

You also can widen a search. Instead of using the & operator, you use the | prefix, which specifies the logical OR operator. For example, if you want to find all group or user objects, you use the following filter:

```
(|(objectCategory=group)(&(objectCategory=person)(objectclass=user)))
```

You can nest sets of filters, as long as each filter conforms to the correct notation. For example, if you want to find all groups whose cn begins with the letter a or whose description begins with the substring "Special groups," you use the following filter:

```
(&(objectCategory=group)(|(cn=a*)(description=Special groups*)))
```

So far, we've been searching for objects that have a certain characteristic. You can also search for objects that don't have a certain characteristic. Use the ! prefix, which specifies the NOT, or negation, operator. For example, you can search for all objects that do not have an objectClass equal to user with the following filter:

```
(!(objectClass=user))
```

By combining the &, |, and ! operators, you can perform powerful searches. For example, consider the following query:

```
(&
    (|(objectCategory=container)(objectCategory=organizationalUnit))
    (!(description=*))
    (|(cn=*cor*)(cn=J*))
)
```

This query is searching for any container or organizational unit (OU) that doesn't contain the description property and whose cn contains the letters "cor" or starts with the letter J. Here's how to include this filter in a script:

```
filterStr = _
    "(&(|(objectCategory=container)(objectCategory=organizationalUnit))" & _
    "(!(description=*))" & _
    "(|(cn=*cor*)(cn=J*))" & _
    ")"
```

There are no spaces in the string, yet the quotation marks do not overly detract from the formatting.

As you can see, this is a very powerful specification.

 If a value you are trying to match contains an asterisk, forward slash, backslash, NUL, or parenthesis, which are special characters used in filters, those characters must be specially encoded with escape sequences. These escape sequences are the hexadecimal representation of the ASCII values of the characters; e.g., an asterisk should be encoded as \2a, and a backslash should be encoded as \5c. Please see Search Filter Syntax in the MSDN Library: *http://msdn.microsoft.com/en-us/library/ aa746475.aspx.*

Optimizing Searches

When you are searching Active Directory using LDAP filters, there are some important guidelines to follow that can help reduce load on the domain controllers, increase the performance of your scripts and applications, and reduce the amount of traffic generated on the network. It is also important to socialize these concepts with others as much as possible. It takes only a couple of badly written search filters in a heavily used application to severely impact the performance of your domain controllers!

Efficient Searching

Understanding how to write efficient search criteria is the first important step to optimizing searches. By understanding a few key points, you can greatly improve the performance of your searches. It is also important to reuse data retrieved from searches or connections to Active Directory as much as possible. Microsoft has provided a paper on creating more efficient Active Directory Enabled applications. This paper has a lot of detailed information concerning efficient queries. You can find the paper at the URL: *http://msdn.microsoft.com/en-us/library/ms808539.aspx*.

The following list describes several key points to remember about searching:

- Use at least one indexed attribute per search. Certain attributes are marked as "indexed" in Active Directory, which allows for fast pattern matching. They are typically single-valued and unique, which means searches using indexed attributes can determine which objects match them very quickly. If you don't use indexed attributes, the database equivalent of a full table scan must be done to determine the matches.

- Use `objectCategory` or a combination of `objectClass` and `objectCategory` in every search. The problem with using only `objectClass` is that it is not indexed in a default Active Directory installation prior to Windows Server 2008. `objectCategory`, on the other hand, is indexed by default and much more efficient to use. See the next section for more information.

- Try to limit the use of trailing (`name=*llen`) or middle match (`name=*lle*`) searches. Active Directory, by default, is not optimized to handle these types of searches, and they should be avoided if possible. The use of these queries disables the ability to use the attribute's index and forces the AD to check every entry in directory for that attribute. In some cases, these types of searches can take anywhere from 10–15 seconds to several hours to complete! If there is an attribute in your directory that is often queried in this way, you may consider enabling a Tuple or Medial Index for the attribute. See Chapter 4 and the discussion on the `searchFlags` schema attribute.

- Avoid using the NOT (!) operator in search filters unless absolutely required. The use of a NOT operator on an indexed attribute precludes the use of the index, which forces Active Directory to look at every object within the scope of the search.

Another "gotcha" when using NOT is that the result set can return "false positives" with objects that you do not have permission to view the attribute on, even if the attribute has the value you are trying to find.

- Limit use of bitwise matching filters as they severely impact the use of the attribute's index.

- In Windows 2000 Active Directory, try to enumerate back link attributes versus querying forward link attributes. Although the attributes are implicitly linked, searching against the forward link is considerably slower than enumerating the back link. For example, if you want to find which objects someone manages, you can query the managedBy forward link attribute of all objects or you can enumerate the managedObjects back link attribute of the user in question. Another example is the forward link member and back link memberOf attributes used for specifying group membership. This shortcoming is corrected in Windows Server 2003 and higher, and querying the forward link has comparable performance as enumerating the back link.

- Use the appropriate search scope. Avoid using subtree searches unless you truly want to search more than one level down. If you only want to search directly below the search base, use the OneLevel scope.

- Use paged searching for queries that can potentially return thousands of entries. Most subtree searches should have paging enabled unless you are positive the search will not return more than 1,000 entries or do not want it to return more than 1,000 entries.

 Microsoft allows this limit to be modified by changing the Max-ResultSize value in the directory's LDAP policy as indicated at *http: //support.microsoft.com/kb/315071*. There are multiple issues that can result from modifying this policy, and therefore we highly discourage using this method to solve page size issues; instead, use paged searching.

- Reuse ADO Connection and Command objects as much as possible. ADO Connection and Command objects can be used for multiple searches, so there is no need to create additional ones.

ObjectClass Versus ObjectCategory

It is important to understand the differences between objectClass and objectCategory and how they should be used during searches. The first point to be aware of from a searching standpoint is that objectClass is not indexed. Initial concerns of the indexing code in the Windows 2000 alpha and beta periods indicated that indexed attributes should be unique single-valued attributes. Even though the indexing process was corrected to allow for efficient indexing and retrieval of multivalued attributes, objectClass indexing was not implemented by default in Active Directory. It is possible to index this attribute, however, and numerous large companies have found it quite desirable from a performance standpoint. See the discussion on searchFlags in Chapter 4 for more information.

 Windows Server 2008 domain controllers implicitly index objectClass regardless of the searchFlags setting for the attribute.

Another major difference is that objectClass is a multivalued attribute that contains the objectClass hierarchy for an instantiated object. For example, a user object has the following values as part of its objectClass attribute:

- top
- person
- organizationalPerson
- user

That is because the user class inherits from the organizationalPerson class, which inherits from the person class, which inherits from the top class. When a class inherits from another, the attributes of the inherited class (also known as the parent class) are available for the inheriting class to use. A class can inherit attributes from abstract and structural classes, which would show up in the objectClass attribute for an instantiated object, but auxiliary classes that get statically associated with a particular class do not. Statically associated auxiliary classes allow for a grouping of attributes to be associated with one or more classes in a similar manner to just adding attributes directly to a class's definition, and this association can be determined by looking at the schema. If your Active Directory is in Window Server 2003 forest functional mode or higher, then dynamic associated auxiliary classes will show up in the objectClass attribute for an instantiated object. This is because you can dynamically associate any appropriate auxiliary class on an object whenever you wish.

ObjectCategory, on the other hand, is a single-value *indexed* attribute, which specifies a classification for a type of object. ObjectCategory is intended to be an easy way to query for a certain "category" of objects, such as "Person." As an example, both user and contact objects have an objectcategory of Person, so by simply searching for (objectcategory=Person), you could possibly retrieve both user and contact objects.

For the reasons listed previously, queries should use objectCategory or a combination of objectClass and objectCategory as part of the search filter. The primary reasons for not using just objectClass is that it is not indexed and is multivalued, which does not make for an efficient query. The other classic problem with using only objectClass is that you can end up with more object types than you were expecting. This is a common problem with using (objectClass=user). You would think you'd only get user objects back using that filter, but you can also potentially get computer objects as well, since the computer `objectClass` is inherited from the user class (therefore causing it to be one of the values for the `objectClass` attribute for every computer object). And even though it would be efficient to use only `objectCategory` because it is indexed, it falls into the same trap as `objectClass`, because additional objects other than the one you are targeting may get returned (e.g., user objects and contact objects). It is for these reasons that you should try to use a combination of `objectClass` and `objectCategory` in your searches.

Several examples are included next to illustrate what using various combinations of `objectClass` and `objectCategory` can return:

People (i.e., Users and Contacts)
> `(objectCategory=person)`

Contacts
> `(&(objectClass=contact)(objectCategory=person))`

Users
> `(&(objectClass=user)(objectCategory=person))`

Users and computers (not optimized)
> `(objectClass=user)`

Users and computers (optimized)
> `(&(|(objectCategory=person)(objectCategory=computer))(objectClass=user))`

Groups
> `(&(objectClass=group)(objectCategory=group))`

Containers
> `(&(objectClass=container)(objectCategory=container))`

Organizational Units
> `(&(objectClass=organizationalunit)(objectCategory=organizationalUnit))`

Advanced Search Function: SearchAD

We will now take many of the concepts from this chapter and apply them in a useful example called SearchAD. SearchAD can be included in any VBScript and used immediately as is.

SearchAD takes five parameters and returns a Boolean indicating whether it succeeded or failed in the search. You should recognize most of these parameters:

- The base distinguished name to start the search from
- A valid ADO criteria string
- The depth that you wish to search, represented by one of the exact strings `Base`, `OneLevel`, or `SubTree`
- The comma-separated list of attributes that is to be returned

- A variable that will hold the returned results of the search in an array

The last parameter does not have any values when passed in, but if SearchAD is successful, the array contains the resultset.

Here is an example use of SearchAD:

```
bolIsSuccess = SearchAD("LDAP://ou=Finance,dc=mycorp,dc=com", _
    "(cn=a*)", "Base", "cn,description", arrSearchResults)
```

You can also use it as part of an If…Then condition:

```
If SearchAD("LDAP://dc=mycorp,dc=com", "(description=moose)", "SubTree", _
    "ADsPath,cn,description", arrSearchResults) Then
    'success code using arrSearchResults
Else
    'failure code
End If
```

The array that is returned is a two-dimensional array of attributes that match the criteria. If there were 12 results returned for the preceding query, this is how you access the results:

```
arrSearchResults(0,0) 'ADsPath of first result
arrSearchResults(0,1) 'CN of first result
arrSearchResults(0,2) 'Description of first result
arrSearchResults(1,0) 'ADsPath of second result
arrSearchResults(1,1) 'CN of second result
arrSearchResults(1,2) 'Description of second result
arrSearchResults(2,0) 'ADsPath of third result
arrSearchResults(2,1) 'CN of third result
arrSearchResults(2,2) 'Description of third result
arrSearchResults(3,0) 'ADsPath of fourth result
arrSearchResults(3,1) 'CN of fourth result
arrSearchResults(3,2) 'Description of fourth result
.

.

.
arrSearchResults(11,0) 'ADsPath of 11th result
arrSearchResults(11,1) 'CN of 11th result
arrSearchResults(11,2) 'Description of 11th result
```

You can loop through these values in your own code using VBScript's built-in function UBound to find the maximum upper bound of an array:

```
UBound(arrSearchResults,1) 'This results in a value of 11
UBound(arrSearchResults,2) 'This results in a value of 2
```

The first UBound gives the upper bound of the array's first dimension, and the second gives the upper bound of the second dimension. Thus, you can loop through an index from 0 to these values to iterate through the array. For example:

```
'Iterate through the entire set of records
For i=0 To UBound(arrSearchResults,1)
  'Now for each record iterate through the list of that record's values
  For j=0 To UBound(arrSearchResults,2)
    'Do something with arrSearchResults(i,j), e.g., the next line
```

```
        MsgBox arrSearchResults(i,j)
    Next
  Next
```

So, without further ado, here is Example 23-1, which contains the SearchAD function.

Example 23-1. SearchAD, an advanced search function

```
'**************************************************************************
'SearchAD Function (returns Boolean success or failure)
'**************************************************************************
Function SearchAD(ByVal strLDAPBase, ByVal strCriteria, ByVal strDepth, _
  ByVal strAttributeList, ByRef arrResults())

    Dim objConn, objComm, objRS
    Dim objDisconRS, intArrayIndex, attrib
    Dim intAttributeArrayIndex, arrAttributes, arrAttributesUb


    '**********************************************************************
    'Split out attributes to build disconnected recordset
    '**********************************************************************

    arrAttributes = Split(strAttributeList,",")
    arrAttributesUb = UBound(arrAttributes)


    On Error Resume Next


    '**********************************************************************
    'Create a disconnected recordset that we will use
    ' for temporary data storage
    '**********************************************************************

    Const adUseClient = 3
    Const adVarChar = 200
    Const maxCharacters = 255

    Set objDisconRS = CreateObject("ADODB.Recordset")
    objDisconRS.CursorLocation = adUseClient
    For intAttributeArrayIndex = 0 To arrAttributesUb
      attrib=arrAttributes(intAttributeArrayIndex)
      objDisconRS.Fields.Append attrib, adVarChar, MaxCharacters
    Next
    objDisconRS.Open


    '**********************************************************************
    'Used to specify an unsuccessful ADO connection
    '**********************************************************************

    Const adStateClosed = 0


    '**********************************************************************
    'Defined in ADS_SCOPEENUM (in the ADSI documentation) for a full
    'subtree search starting at the defined root
    '**********************************************************************

    Const ADS_SCOPE_SUBTREE = 2

    Set objConn = CreateObject("ADODB.Connection")
    Set objComm = CreateObject("ADODB.Command")
    Set objRS = CreateObject("ADODB.Recordset")
```

```
objConn.Provider = "ADSDSOObject"
objConn.Open "", vbNullString, vbNullString

'**********************************************************************
'If connection failed, then return FALSE
'**********************************************************************
If objConn.State = adStateClosed Then
  SearchAD = False
  Exit Function
End If


'**********************************************************************
'Link the now-open connection with the empty command object
'**********************************************************************
Set objComm.ActiveConnection = objConn


'**********************************************************************
'Populate the command object in order to execute a query through the
'linked connection. Set the text of the query command (i.e., the search),
'the max number of results to return, the timeout in seconds to wait
'for the query, and whether the results are to be cached.
'**********************************************************************
objComm.CommandText = "<" & strLDAPBase & ">;" & strCriteria & ";" _
  & strAttributeList & ";" & strDepth
objComm.Properties("Page Size") = 1000
objComm.Properties("Timeout") = 60
objComm.Properties("searchscope") = ADS_SCOPE_SUBTREE
objComm.Properties("Cache Results") = False


'**********************************************************************
'Execute the command through the linked connection
'**********************************************************************
Err.Clear
Set objRS = objComm.Execute


'**********************************************************************
'If there was an error, then return FALSE
'**********************************************************************
If Err Then
  objConn.Close
  Set objRS = Nothing
  SearchAD = False
Else
  '**********************************************************************
  'If we're pointing at the end of the resultset already (EOF) then there
  'were no records returned (although the query did search the AD), so
  'return FALSE
  '**********************************************************************
  If objRS.EOF Then
    objConn.Close
    Set objRS = Nothing
    SearchAD = False
  Else
    'Loop through the resultset and populate the disconnected recordset,
```

```
'which we will then use to build the array
While Not objRS.EOF
  objDisconRS.AddNew
  For intAttributeArrayIndex = 0 To arrAttributesUb
    attrib=arrAttributes(intAttributeArrayIndex)
    objDisconRS.Fields.Item(attrib) = objRS.Fields.Item(attrib)
  Next
  objDisconRS.Update
  objRS.MoveNext
Wend

'*********************************************************************
'Close the connection
'*********************************************************************
objConn.Close
Set objRS = Nothing

'*********************************************************************
'Now in order to place all the resulting attributes into the array that
'we'll pass back out, we need to redimension the array so that it is
'large enough to hold the records. The array is multidimensional in
'order to hold all the attribute fields.
'*********************************************************************

ReDim arrResults((objDisconRS.RecordCount - 1),arrAttributesUb)

'*********************************************************************
'Loop through the newly redimensioned array, starting at zero, and add
'each field to the array
'*********************************************************************
intArrayIndex = 0
objDisconRS.MoveFirst
While Not objDisconRS.EOF
  For intAttributeArrayIndex=0 To arrAttributesUb
    attrib=arrAttributes(intAttributeArrayIndex)
    arrResults(intArrayIndex,intAttributeArrayIndex) = _
                          objDisconRS.Fields.Item(attrib)
  Next
  intArrayIndex = intArrayIndex + 1
  objDisconRS.MoveNext
Wend
Set objDisconRS = Nothing
SearchAD = True
    End If
  End If
End Function
```

Summary

In this chapter, we reviewed the basics of ADO, which provides a robust search interface for Active Directory. While originally intended for databases, ADO was adapted to Active Directory to allow queries based on LDAP search filters. Several techniques for optimizing searches in Active Directory were reviewed, including a discussion of using objectClass versus objectCategory. We ended the chapter by covering a fully functional SearchAD procedure that can be used as-is in any VBScript to easily search Active Directory based on specified criteria. SearchAD hides all the underlying ADO logic, including connection setup, query execution, and recordset manipulation.

After providing a good background for ADSI and ADO in the last three chapters, we are now ready to move to more practical applications. The next several chapters show some of the capabilities these interfaces provide and a lot of sample code to get you started.

## CHAPTER 24

Users and Groups

In this chapter, we will show you how to automate the creation and manipulation of user and group accounts. Although tools to create user and group accounts already exist (e.g., the Windows 2000 Resource Kit's *Addusers* utility), ADSI's versatility lets you quickly write a script that creates 1,000 fully featured user or group accounts based on whatever business logic you require. You can also create command-line utilities or web-based interfaces using the techniques shown in this chapter to perform such functions as unlocking locked-out user accounts or adding users to groups.

Creating a Simple User Account

You can quickly create a user account with minimal attributes with ADSI. The following code shows how to create a user on a local computer and in an Active Directory domain:

```
Option Explicit
Dim objDomain, objUser

'Creating a local user on a computer or member server
'Valid for Windows NT/2000/2003/2008
Set objComputer = GetObject("WinNT://MYCOMPUTER,Computer")
Set objUser = objComputer.Create("user","vlaunders")
objUser.SetInfo

'Creating a user in Active Directory
Set objDomain = GetObject("LDAP://cn=Users,dc=mycorp,dc=com")
Set objUser = objDomain.Create("user", "cn=vlaunders")
objUser.Put "sAMAccountName", "vlaunders"
objUser.Put "userPrincipalName", "vlaunders@mycorp.com"
objUser.SetInfo
```

The code is composed of two sections. The first section uses the WinNT provider to create a user account on a local computer that could be a member server or part of a workgroup. The second section uses the LDAP provider to create a user account in an Active Directory domain.

When you create users in an Active Directory domain, you need to be aware of two important User object attributes: **sAMAccountName** and **userPrincipalName**. The User object has several mandatory attributes. The system sets many of these mandatory attributes, except for one, sAMAccountName, which allows Active Directory-based clients to interact with older clients and NT domains. You must set the sAMAccountName attribute before you call IADs::SetInfo or the creation will fail. The userPrincipalName attribute isn't mandatory, but it is recommend so users can log on using an email-style address, as defined in RFC 2822, *Internet Message Format* at *http://www.ietf.org/rfc/rfc2822.txt*.

> Windows Server 2003 Active Directory changed the mandatory requirement of sAMAccountName being populated during object creation. If you do not specify it, you will get a randomly generated sAMAccountName such as $KJK000-H4GJL6AQOV1I.

Creating a Full-Featured User Account

Creating user accounts as we've done previously is fine for an introduction, but typically you'll need to set many more attributes to make them usable in your environment. The approaches you use to create fully featured users in the NT and Active Directory environments differ slightly; Active Directory offers considerably more properties than NT, such as the office and home addresses of users, as well as lists of email addresses and pager, fax, and phone numbers.

You can manipulate User objects with a special interface called IADsUser. IADsUser's methods and property methods let you directly set many of the User object's property values. Tables 24-1, 24-2, and 24-3 contain the methods, read-write property methods, and read-only property methods, respectively, for the IADsUser interface. The corresponding Active Directory attribute is included in parentheses for the property methods that can be set with the LDAP provider.

Table 24-1. IADsUser methods

Method	Description
IADsUser::ChangePassword	Changes the existing password.
IADsUser::SetPassword	Sets a new password without needing the old one.
IADsUser::Groups	Gets a list of groups of which the user is a member. You can use the IADsMembers interface to iterate through the list.

Table 24-2. IADsUser read-write property methods

Property method	Available with WinNT or LDAP?
IADsUser::AccountDisabled	WinNT, LDAP (userAccountControl mask).
IADsUser::AccountExpirationDate	WinNT, LDAP (accountExpires).
IADsUser::Department	LDAP (department).

Property method	Available with WinNT or LDAP?
IADsUser::Description	WinNT, LDAP (description).
IADsUser::Division	LDAP (division).
IADsUser::EmailAddress	LDAP (mail).
IADsUser::EmployeeID	LDAP (employeeID).
IADsUser::FaxNumber	LDAP (facsimileTelephoneNumber).
IADsUser::FirstName	LDAP (givenName).
IADsUser::FullName	WinNT, LDAP (displayName).
IADsUser::GraceLoginsAllowed	Neither.
IADsUser::GraceLoginsRemaining	Neither.
IADsUser::HomeDirectory	WinNT, LDAP (homeDirectory).
IADsUser::HomePage	LDAP (wWWHomePage).
IADsUser::IsAccountLocked	WinNT, LDAP (userFlags/lockoutTime). This method is unreliable for determining locked status with the LDAP provider; only use it with the WinNT provider.
IADsUser::Languages	LDAP (languages).
IADsUser::LastName	LDAP (sn).
IADsUser::LoginHours	WinNT, LDAP (logonHours).
IADsUser::LoginScript	WinNT, LDAP (scriptPath).
IADsUser::LoginWorkstations	WinNT, LDAP (userWorkstations).
IADsUser::Manager	LDAP (manager).
IADsUser::MaxLogins	WinNT.
IADsUser::MaxStorage	WinNT, LDAP (maxStorage).
IADsUser::NamePrefix	LDAP (personalTitle).
IADsUser::NameSuffix	LDAP (generationQualifier).
IADsUser::OfficeLocations	LDAP (physicalDeliveryOfficeName).
IADsUser::OtherName	LDAP (middleName).
IADsUser::PasswordExpirationDate	WinNT.
IADsUser::PasswordMinimumLength	WinNT.
IADsUser::PasswordRequired	WinNT, LDAP (userAccountControl mask).
IADsUser::Picture	LDAP (thumbNailPhoto).
IADsUser::PostalAddresses	LDAP (postalAddress).
IADsUser::PostalCodes	LDAP (postalCode).
IADsUser::Profile	WinNT, LDAP (profilePath).
IADsUser::RequireUniquePassword	WinNT.
IADsUser::SeeAlso	LDAP (seeAlso).

Property method	Available with WinNT or LDAP?
IADsUser::TelephoneHome	LDAP (homePhone).
IADsUser::TelephoneMobile	LDAP (mobile).
IADsUser::TelephoneNumber	LDAP (telephoneNumber).
IADsUser::TelephonePager	LDAP (pager).
IADsUser::Title	LDAP (title).

Table 24-3. IADsUser read-only property methods

Property method	Available with WinNT or LDAP?
IADsUser::BadLoginAddress	Neither
IADsUser::BadLoginCount	WinNT, LDAP (badPwdCount)
IADsUser::LastFailedLogin	LDAP (badPasswordTime)
IADsUser::LastLogin	WinNT, LDAP (lastLogin)
IADsUser::LastLogoff	WinNT, LDAP (lastLogoff)
IADsUser::PasswordLastChanged	LDAP (pwdLastSet)

For more information on IADsUser, check out the following location in the MSDN Library at: *http://msdn.microsoft.com/en-us/library/aa746340(VS.85).aspx*.

Now let's apply some of this knowledge to an example of how to create a fully featured user in Active Directory.

The `IADsUser::IsAccountLocked` method has never worked properly with the LDAP Provider. It can give a false reading of the current locked status of the account. There is a new attribute in Windows Server 2003 called `msDS-User-Account-Control-Computed`, which will show expired and locked status. Unfortunately the attribute is constructed so you cannot use it for a query, but you can return the value for any objects returned from another query. Like the normal `userAccountControl` attribute, this attribute is a bitmask. It will correctly identify if the user is locked or expired. When the account is locked, bit 4 (value 16) will be set. When the account password is expired, bit 23 (8388608) will be set.

LDAP Provider

Example 24-1 shows how to create a fully featured user in Active Directory. The property name `userFlags` changes to `userAccountControl` for the extended settings. Home directory attributes are set along with creation of the home directory folder if it doesn't exist. However, the account is not modified to disallow the password to be changed by the user. In Active Directory with the LDAP provider, this requires changing permissions on the user object and cannot be done with a simple flag change in the `userAccountControl` attribute. The password set operation is implemented prior to enabling the account; this is required when you have a password length policy. Other minor differences exist, such as the use of more constants and property methods. Active Directory lets you set many property values for users, including multivalue properties that you set via an array. For example, you can list several telephone numbers for the TelephoneNumber, TelephoneMobile, and TelephoneHome properties. Through the use of constants, you can even set up Active Directory to let users log on with smart cards.

Example 24-1. Creating a full-featured user account in Active Directory

```
Option Explicit

'**********************************************************************
'WshShell::Run constants
'**********************************************************************
Const vbMinimizedNoFocus = 6


'**********************************************************************
'Flag constants. See the sidebar on "Boolean Arithmetic with
'Hexadecimal Values."
'**********************************************************************
Const UF_SCRIPT = &H1
Const UF_ACCOUNTDISABLE = &H2
Const UF_HOMEDIR_REQUIRED = &H8
Const UF_PASSWD_NOTREQD = &H20
Const UF_PASSWORD_CANT_CHANGE = &H40
Const UF_ENCRYPTED_TEXT_PASSWORD_ALLOWED = &H80
Const UF_DONT_EXPIRE_PASSWD = &H10000
Const UF_MNS_LOGON_ACCOUNT = &H20000
Const UF_SMARTCARD_REQUIRED = &H40000
Const UF_TRUSTED_FOR_DELEGATION = &H80000
Const UF_NOT_DELEGATED = &H100000

Const ADS_PROPERTY_UPDATE = 2

Dim objDomain, objUser, fso, intUserFlags, intNewUserFlags
Dim fldUserHomedir, wshShell

Set objDomain = GetObject("LDAP://cn=Users,dc=mycorp,dc=com")
Set objUser = objDomain.Create("user","cn=vlaunders")
objUser.Put "sAMAccountName", "vlaunders"
objUser.Put "userPrincipalName", "vlaunders@mycorp.com"

'**********************************************************************
'Write the newly created object out from the property cache and read
'all the properties for the object, including the ones set by the
'system on creation
'**********************************************************************
objUser.SetInfo
objUser.GetInfo

'**********************************************************************
'Set the password
'**********************************************************************
objUser.SetPassword "thepassword$1"
```

```
'**********************************************************************
'Set the properties
'**********************************************************************
objUser.AccountDisabled = False
objUser.AccountExpirationDate = "02/05/01"
objUser.Description = "My description goes here!"
objUser.LoginScript = "login.vbs"
objUser.Profile = "\\MYDOMAIN\DFS\Users\vlaunders\profile"
objUser.PasswordRequired = True
objUser.TelephoneHome = Array("0123-555-7890")
objUser.PutEx ADS_PROPERTY_UPDATE, "otherHomePhone", _
  Array("0123 555 7891", "0123 555 7892")
objUser.TelephoneNumber = Array("0123 555 7890")
objUser.PutEx ADS_PROPERTY_UPDATE, "otherTelephone", _
  Array("0123 555 7891", "0123 555 7892")
objUser.TelephoneMobile = Array("0123 555 7890")
objUser.PutEx ADS_PROPERTY_UPDATE, "otherMobile", _
  Array("0123 555 7891", "0123 555 7892")
objUser.NamePrefix = "Ms."
objUser.FirstName = "Victoria"
objUser.LastName = "Launders"
objUser.DisplayName = "Victoria Launders"

'**********************************************************************
'Set the drive that you'll map to
'**********************************************************************
objUser.HomeDirectory = "\\MYDOMAIN\DFS\Users\vlaunders"
objUser.Put "homeDrive", "Z:"

'**********************************************************************
'Set all the properties for the user and read back the data, including
'any defaults, so that you can set the flags
'**********************************************************************
objUser.SetInfo
objUser.GetInfo

'**********************************************************************
'Create the home directory
'**********************************************************************
Set fso = CreateObject("Scripting.FileSystemObject")
If Not fso.FolderExists("\\MYDOMAIN\DFS\Users\vlaunders") Then
  Set fldUserHomedir = fso.CreateFolder("\\MYDOMAIN\DFS\Users\vlaunders")
End If

'**********************************************************************
'Set full rights for the user to the home directory
'**********************************************************************
Set wshShell = WScript.CreateObject("Wscript.Shell")
wshShell.Run "cacls.exe \\MYDOMAIN\DFS\Users\vlaunders /e /g vlaunders:F", _
vbMinimizedNoFocus, True
```

Boolean Arithmetic with Hexadecimal Values

Assume that you want an attribute of an object (e.g., userFlags of the User object) to set eight values. You use an 8-bit binary number to represent those eight values. If you want the attribute to hold 11 values, you use an 11-bit binary number.

The binary system is a base-2 system in which 0 typically represents a false condition and 1 typically represents a true condition. In this example, 0 means the value isn't set, and 1 means the value is set. If you want to set only the third and eighth values of an 8-value attribute, you set the third and eighth bits of an 8-bit binary number to 1, or &B10000100. (You read binary numbers from right to left.) The prefix &B specifies that the number is binary.

However, attributes store data as decimal values. Thus, you need to convert the binary number into a decimal value, which is base-10. For example, the binary number &B10000100 translates into:

$$2^7 + 2^2 = 128 + 4 = 132$$

You use the Boolean AND operator to check whether a bit is set and the OR operator to set a bit. For example, suppose you want to see whether the fourth bit is set in an 8-bit binary number that has a decimal value of 132. You can check for the existence of this bit using the AND operator to compare the number to a binary mask indicating that the fourth bit is set. The equation to do this is:

&B10000100 AND &B00001000 = &B00000000

You solve this equation by resolving the AND operation for each bit individually. For example, the first bit in &B10000100 is 0, and the first bit in &B00001000 is 0: 0 AND 0 is 0. The second bit in &B10000100 is 0, and the second bit in &B00001000 is 0: 0 AND is 0. The third bit in &B10000100 is 1, and the third bit in &B00001000 is 0; 1 AND 0 is 0. When you calculate all eight bits, the result is &B00000000. In other words, the fourth bit isn't set.

1	0	0	0	0	1	0	0
0	0	0	0	1	0	0	0
0	0	0	0	0	0	0	0

Suppose you want to test whether the third bit is set:

&B10000100 AND &B0000100 = &B00000100

Because the third bit in &B10000100 is 1, and the third bit in &B0000100 is 1, the resulting bit is 1 (1 AND 1 is 1), which specifies that the value for the third bit is set.

1	0	0	0	0	1	0	0
0	0	0	0	0	1	0	0
0	0	0	0	0	1	0	0

Let's translate this binary equation into decimal and hex equations:

&B10000100 AND &B0000100 = &B00000100
132 AND 4 = 4
&H84 AND &H4 = &H4

If the return value is 0 or &H0, the bit isn't set. If the return value is the bit's actual value (in this case, 4 or &H4), the bit is set.

```
132 OR 8 = 140
&H84 OR &H8 = &H8C
```

Just like the AND operator, the OR operator works with binary, decimal, and hex systems. Taking the example just given, let's try to set the third bit, which happens to be already set:

```
&B10000100 OR &B0000100 = &B10000100
132 OR 4 = 132
&H84 OR &H4 = &H84
```

1	0	0	0	0	1	0	0
0	0	0	0	0	1	0	0
1	**0**	**0**	**0**	**0**	**1**	**0**	**0**

In other words, the result is the new value with that bit set. Because that bit was already set, nothing changes. Let's try setting the fourth bit, which isn't already set:

```
&B10000100 OR &B00001000 = &B10001100
```

1	0	0	0	0	1	0	0
0	0	0	0	1	0	0	0
1	**0**	**0**	**0**	**1**	**1**	**0**	**0**

The result includes a newly set fourth bit. You can even set two bits at once. For example, here's how you set the fourth and fifth bits:

```
&B10000100 OR &B00011000 = &B10011100
132 OR 24 = 156
&H84 OR &H18 = &H9C
```

1	0	0	0	0	1	0	0
0	0	0	1	1	0	0	0
1	**0**	**0**	**1**	**1**	**1**	**0**	**0**

Although the Boolean mathematics is straightforward, luckily you don't have to include this code in a script. Instead, you typically use constants. For example, if you declare the constant:

```
Const UF_DONT_EXPIRE_PASSWD = &H10000
```

you just need to specify that constant in the script. To determine this bit's existence, use the code:

```
If intUserFlags And UF_DONT_EXPIRE_PASSWD = 0 Then
 'UF_DONT_EXPIRE_PASSWD is not set
Else
 'UF_DONT_EXPIRE_PASSWD is set
End If
```

You set bits in a similar fashion. For example, to set the &H10000 bit, use the code:

```
intUserFlags = intUserFlags Or UF_DONT_EXPIRE_PASSWD
```

We created the home directory by obtaining a reference to a FileSystemObject object and calling the `FileSystemObject::CreateFolder` method if the directory doesn't already exist. The permissions were set by running the *cacls.exe* command using the `WshShell::Run` method. When calling `WshShell::Run`, you need to include three parameters. The first parameter is the command you want to execute; the second parameter can be any of the following constant values that describe how you want to treat the new window produced by executing the command:

```
Const vbHide = 0             ' hides the window
Const vbNormalFocus = 1      ' displays the window
Const vbMinimizedFocus = 2   ' minimizes the window with focus
Const vbMaximizedFocus = 3   ' maximizes the window with focus
Const vbNormalNoFocus = 4    ' displays the window w/o focus
Const vbMinimizedNoFocus = 6 ' minimizes the window w/o focus
```

The last parameter to the `WshShell::Run` method should be to set to true if you want the script to wait until CACLS finishes before continuing to the next line.

 As an alternative to using CACLS to set permissions, you could write a script that makes use of the interfaces described in Chapter 25, or you could use the *ADsSecurity.dll* provided in the Platform SDK.

Creating Many User Accounts

User-specific scripts work well if you have to create only a few user accounts. If you need to create many user accounts at one time, or if you create new accounts often, using a script with an input file is more efficient. The input file includes the user data so that you can use the script to create any user account. For example, the output shown below represents the *users-to-create.txt* input file that provides the user data for the universal script in Example 24-2. Although this input file includes only four data sets, you can include as many data sets as you want. You include a data set for each user account that you want to create:

```
vlaunders:12/09/01:The description:Victoria Launders:onebanana
aglowenorris:08/07/00:Another user:Alistair Lowe-Norris:twobanana
kbemowski:03/03/03:A third user:Karen Bemowski:threebanana
jkellett:08/09/99:A fourth user:Jenneth Kellett:four
```

Example 24-2. Creating many user accounts using a script with an input file

```
Option Explicit

Const ForReading = 1

Dim objDomain, objUser, fso, tsInputFile, strLine, arrInput
Dim fldUserHomedir, wshShell

Set objDomain = GetObject("LDAP://cn=Users,dc=mycorp,dc=com")
Set fso = CreateObject("Scripting.FileSystemObject")
```

```
'**********************************************************************
'Open the text file as a text stream for reading.
'Don't create a file if users-to-create.txt doesn't exist
'**********************************************************************
Set tsInputFile = fso.OpenTextFile("c:\users-to-create.txt", ForReading, False)

'**********************************************************************
'Execute the lines inside the loop, as long as you're not at the end
'of the file
'**********************************************************************
While Not tsInputFile.AtEndOfStream

  '**********************************************************************
  'Read a line, and use the Split function to split the data set into
  'its separate parts
  '**********************************************************************
  strLine = tsInputFile.ReadLine
  arrInput = Split(strLine, ":")

  Set objUser = objDomain.Create("user","cn=" & arrInput(0))
  objUser.Put "sAMAccountName", arrInput(0)
  objUser.Put "userPrincipalName", arrInput(0) & "@mycorp.com"

  '**********************************************************************
  'Write the newly created object out from the property cache
  'Read all the properties for the object, including
  'the ones set by the system on creation
  '**********************************************************************
  objUser.SetInfo
  objUser.GetInfo

  '**********************************************************************
  'Set the password
  '**********************************************************************
  objUser.SetPassword arrInput(4)

  '**********************************************************************
  'Set the properties
  '**********************************************************************
  objUser.AccountDisabled = False
  objUser.AccountExpirationDate = arrInput(1)
  objUser.Description = arrInput(2)
  objUser.LoginScript = "\\MYDOMAIN\DFS\Loginscripts\" & arrInput(0) & ".vbs"
  objUser.Profile = "\\MYDOMAIN\DFS\Users\" & arrInput(0) & "\profile"
  objUser.PasswordRequired = True
  objUser.DisplayName = arrInput(3)

  '**********************************************************************
  'Set the drive that you'll map to
  '**********************************************************************
  objUser.HomeDirectory = "\\MYDOMAIN\DFS\Users\" & arrInput(0)
  objUser.Put "homeDrive", "Z:"
  objUser.SetInfo
```

```
'****************************************************************
'Create the home directory
'****************************************************************
If Not fso.FolderExists("\\MYDOMAIN\DFS\Users\" & arrInput(0)) Then
  Set fldUserHomedir = fso.CreateFolder("\\MYDOMAIN\DFS\Users\" & arrInput(0))
End If

'****************************************************************
'Set full rights for the user to the home directory
'****************************************************************
Set wshShell = WScript.CreateObject("Wscript.Shell")
wshShell.Run "cacls \\MYDOMAIN\DFS\Users\" & arrInput(0) _
  & " /e /g " & arrInput(0) & ":F", 1, True

'****************************************************************
'Stop referencing this user
'****************************************************************
Set objUser = Nothing
Wend

'Close the file
tsInputFile.Close
```

As the output shows, each data set goes on a separate line. A data set can contain as many values as you want. The data sets in the *users-to-create.txt* file have five values: username, expiration date, description, full name, and password. You use colons to separate the values.[*]

The script reads in the user data to create the user accounts. As the script shows, you use FileSystemObject (FSO) and TextStream (TS) objects to manipulate the user data. For information about FSO and TS objects, see *http://msdn.microsoft.com/en-us/library/6kxy1a51(VS.85).aspx*. After you create a reference to an FSO object and assign that reference to the `fso` variable, apply the `FileSystemObject::OpenTextFile` method to open the *users-to-create.txt* file, setting the user data to the `tsInputFile` TS variable. Then use a while loop with the `TextStream::AtEndOfStream` method to loop through each line in `tsInputFile` until the end of the file. Once you reach the end of the file, use the `TextStream::Close` method to end the script.

The interior of the while loop is the heart of the script. Begin the while loop by applying the `TextStream::ReadLine` method to read in one line of `tsInputFile` at a time. The `strLine` string variable holds the retrieved data from that line, which you pass to VBScript's `Split` function. Using the colon as the separator, this function splits the data set into its five parts, assigning the data to the `arrInput` array variable. This array has index values that correspond to the five parts: 0 represents the username, 1 represents the expiration date, 2 represents the description, 3 represents the full name, and 4 represents the password.

---

[*] While comma-separate-value (CSV) files are the norm for this sort of thing, the comma is more often used in properties that will be added for users, so the colon is used here instead.

The code in the middle of the while loop is similar to the code used earlier. After we create a reference to an ADSI User object and assign that reference to the `objUser` variable, we set that user's property values (including the home drive). We then use `IADs::SetInfo`, set the password, create the home directory, and set the directory permissions. However, instead of explicitly specifying each user's username, expiration date, description, full name, and password in the code, we specify the appropriate array index value. For example, for those property values in which you need to specify the username, you specify `arrInput(0)` instead of vlaunders, aglowenorris, kbemowski, or jkellett.

The while loop ends with setting `objUser` to `Nothing`. We need to clear `objUser` because we use this variable again when the `TextStream::ReadLine` method reads in the next line from `tsInputFile` to create the next user account.

Instead of reading in user data from a text file, you can read in data from other sources, such as a web-based form, a Microsoft Word document, an Excel spreadsheet, a database, or even a specially formatted Microsoft Outlook email message. You also can use command-line arguments to pass in user data, as we will show in a later example.

Modifying Many User Accounts

Once you have created the user accounts in a domain, you will more than likely need to modify them at some point. The modifications may consist only of changing individual properties of a user, such as the description or name fields. In these cases, you can perform the change manually or write a command-line script as shown in the next section. In some situations, you will need to make a large number of changes to your user accounts, as would be the case if you changed the name of a login script and wanted to point all users to the new script.

In most cases with Active Directory domains, you will want to use ADO to find objects, as explained in Chapter 23. So for our next example, let's say that we want to change the login script for all users in the domain that have a department attribute equal to "Sales." Example 24-3 shows how this can be done using ADO.

Example 24-3. Modifying the login script for all users in Sales

```
Option Explicit
On Error Resume Next
Dim objConn, objComm, objRS, objUser
Dim strBase, strFilter, strAttrs, strScope
'**********************************************************************
'Set the ADO search criteria
'**********************************************************************
strBase   = "<LDAP://dc=mycorp,dc=com>;"
strFilter = "(&(objectclass=user)(objectcategory=person)(department=Sales));"
strAttrs  = "ADsPath;"
strScope  = "Subtree"
```

```
set objConn = CreateObject("ADODB.Connection")
objConn.Provider = "ADsDSOObject"
objConn.Open
'*********************************************************************
'Need to enable Paging in case there are more than 1000 objects returned
'*********************************************************************
Set objComm = CreateObject("ADODB.Command")
Set objComm.ActiveConnection = objConn
objComm.CommandText = strBase & strFilter & strAttrs & strScope
objComm.Properties("Page Size") = 1000
Set objRS = objComm.Execute()
While not objRS.EOF
  Set objUser = GetObject( objRS.Fields.Item("ADsPath").Value )
  objUser.LoginScript = "login-sales.vbs"
  objUser.SetInfo
  if Err.Number <> 0 Then
     Wscript.Echo objUser.Name & " error occurred"
     Err.Clear
  Else
     Wscript.Echo objUser.Name & " modified"
  End if
  Set objUser = Nothing
  objRS.MoveNext
Wend
```

Note that we enabled Paging by setting up an ADO Command option and set the Page Size property to 1,000. This will ensure that we get all matching records. If we did not set Page Size, the maximum number of records returned would be whatever the administrative limit is for your Active Directory (the default is 1,000).

Account Unlocker Utility

Imagine that you need a utility that quickly enables and unlocks an NT or Active Directory user account. The account was locked because the password was entered incorrectly too many times in succession. Writing a user-specific script is inefficient if you have many users. Using an input file to pass in the needed user data to a script also is inefficient. You'd have to create the input file just before running the script, because you can't predict whose account you need to unlock. The best approach is to use command-line arguments to pass in the user data as you need it. Example 24-4 uses this approach to enable and unlock an Active Directory user account. If you have a mixed NT and Active Directory network, you can even combine these two utilities into one script.

Example 24-4. Account unlocker utility for Active Directory using the LDAP provider

```
'*********************************************************************
'How to unlock and enable a Active Directory user via arguments
' to this script
' Parameters should be <domain> <username>, where domain specifies
' a fully qualified AD domain like dc=mycorp,dc=com
'*********************************************************************
```

```
Option Explicit

Dim wshArgs, objUser, strOutput, arrSearchResults

On Error Resume Next

'************************************************************************
'Get the arguments
'************************************************************************
Set wshArgs = Wscript.Arguments

'************************************************************************
'If no arguments passed in, then quit
'************************************************************************
If wshArgs.Count = 0 Then
  WScript.Echo "ERROR: No arguments passed in." & vbCrLf & vbCrLf _
    & "Please use AD-UNLOCK <domain> <username>" & vbCrLf & vbCrLf
  WScript.Quit
End If

'************************************************************************
'Error checking of the arguments could go here if we wanted to
'************************************************************************

'************************************************************************
'Use SearchAD function from the end of Chapter 22 to scan the entire
'Active Directory for this user and return the ADsPath. If the search
'failed for whatever reason, then quit
'************************************************************************
If Not SearchAD("LDAP://" & wshArgs(0), _
  "(&(objectcategory=person)(objectClass=user)(sAMAccountName=" _
    & wshArgs(1) & "))", "SubTree", "ADsPath", arrSearchResults) Then

  WScript.Echo "ERROR: No users found." & vbCrLf & vbCrLf
  WScript.Quit
Else
  '************************************************************************
  'Attempt to bind to the first ADsPath specified in the array
  '(as there should be only one)
  '************************************************************************
  Set objUser = GetObject(arrSearchResults(0,0))
  If Err Then
    Wscript.Echo "Error: Could not bind to the following user: " & vbCrLf _
      & vbCrLf & arrSearchResults(0,0) & vbCrLf & vbCrLf
    WScript.Quit
  Else
    strOutput = "Connected to user " & arrSearchResults(0,0) & vbCrLf
  End If

  '************************************************************************
  'Attempt to enable the user (but don't quit if you fail)
  '************************************************************************
  Err.Clear
  objUser.AccountDisabled = False
  objUser.SetInfo
```

```
If Err Then
  strOutput = strOutput & vbTab & "Error: Could not enable the user." & vbCrLf
Else
  strOutput = strOutput & vbTab & "User enabled." & vbCrLf
End If

'**********************************************************************
'Attempt to unlock the user
'**********************************************************************
Err.Clear
objUser.IsAccountLocked = False
objUser.SetInfo
If Err Then
  strOutput = strOutput & vbTab & "Error: Could not unlock the user." & vbCrLf
Else
  strOutput = strOutput & vbTab & "User unlocked." & vbCrLf
End If

  WScript.Echo strOutput
End If
```

You pass in two arguments, domain and username, to the script. We use the `Wscript::Arguments` property method to retrieve the arguments; it stores the arguments as a collection, indexing them from 0 to the number of arguments minus 1. The `wshArgs` collection in the script includes the argument `wshArgs(0)`, which represents the domain, and `wshArgs(1)`, which represents the username.

We use the `WshArguments::Count` method to count the number of arguments. If the count is 0, the script sends an error message and then quits. Use the `Wscript.Echo` method to display the error message so that you can use *cscript.exe* or *wscript.exe* to run the script. If you use the VBScript `MsgBox` function (which displays messages as dialog boxes) in a script that you run from *cscript.exe*, the error messages will not be displayed in the command window.

If the connection attempt fails, the script writes an error message and then quits. If the attempt succeeds, the script puts the output from that attempt into the `strOutput` text string variable. That way, if you're running *wscript.exe* rather than *cscript.exe*, the results appear in one dialog box.

The next two sections attempt to enable and unlock the user account. However, the script doesn't quit if an attempt fails. The `Err::Clear` method, which works only if you enable `On Error Resume Next`, clears the error object so that you can detect the next error.

Whether an attempt succeeds or fails, the output goes to the `strOutput` string variable, where it's appended to any existing text. The `vbTab` constant and the `vbCrLf` constant ensure that any new text that we concatenate appears in separate indented lines underneath the user's ADsPath. Finally, we use the `WScript::Echo` method to print the results in `strOutput`.

Although more elegant and efficient, using the LDAP provider is a little tricky because users can exist in any container anywhere in a domain tree. Thus, you can't immediately attempt to bind to the user account because you don't know the ADsPath. You first must conduct an ADO search to obtain the ADsPath.

At the end of Chapter 23, we showed how to use ADO to construct the Active Directory search routine SearchAD. We use the routine here to search Active Directory for the user's ADsPath and store it in `arrSearchResults(0,0)`. The search is executed using a set of arguments, including `wshArgs(0)` and `wshArgs(1)`. If you put the individual filters on separate lines and substitute the domain and username for `wshArgs(0)` and `wshArgs(1)`, the set of arguments looks something like this:

```
LDAP://dc=mycorp,dc=com
(&(objectcategory=person)(objectClass=user)(sAMAccountName=vlaunders))
ADsPath
SubTree
arrSearchResults
```

If the search fails, the script displays an error message and then quits. If the search succeeds, the script attempts to bind to the ADsPath. The rest of the script proceeds similarly to the one for Windows NT.

 This script requires you to know which user is currently locked out. If you need to find all users who are locked out in an Active Directory domain, check out the command-line tool unlock.exe freely available on the web site *http://www.joeware.net*. Unlock will quickly find and unlock all locked out accounts.

This script is simple but powerful. You can easily add to the script to perform other tasks, such as changing passwords and account expiration dates.

Creating a Group

Now we will move on to creating groups. Creating a group is very similar to creating a user. You use the same `IADsContainer::Create` method:

```
Set objGroup = objSalesOU.Create("group", "cn=Managers")
objGroup.Put "sAMAccountName", "Managers"
objGroup.SetInfo
```

This code assumes we already have a pointer to an OU in the `objSalesOU` variable. The `IADs::Put` method is used to set the `sAMAccountName`, a mandatory attribute in Windows 2000 Active Directory with no default value, just like with users.

The `IADsGroup` interface that operates on group objects supports four methods and one property that are specific to the group object, as listed in Table 24-4.

Table 24-4. The IADsGroup interface

IADsGroup methods and properties	Action
Add	Adds users to the group as members
Remove	Removes user members from the group
IsMember	Tests to see if a user is a member of a group
Members	Returns a list of all the members of the group
Description	Returns the text describing the group

In Example 24-5, we show how to create a group with both the WinNT and LDAP providers.

Example 24-5. Creating a group with both the WinNT and LDAP providers

```
Option Explicit

Dim objDomain, objGroup, objComputer

'Creating a group in a Windows NT domain
Set objDomain = GetObject("WinNT://MYDOMAIN")
Set objGroup = objDomain.Create("group","MyGroup")
objGroup.SetInfo

'Creating a local group on a computer or member server
'Valid for Windows NT, Windows 200x
Set objComputer = GetObject("WinNT://MYCOMPUTER")
Set objGroup = objComputer.Create("group","My Group")
objGroup.SetInfo

'Creating a group in Active Directory
Set objDomain = GetObject("LDAP://cn=Users,dc=mycorp,dc=com")
Set objGroup = objDomain.Create("group","cn=My Group")
objGroup.Put "sAMAccountName", "MyGroup"
objGroup.SetInfo
```

Adding Members to a Group

Adding objects as members of a group can be done with `IADsGroup::Add`, a simple method that takes the DN of the object to be added:

```
objGroup.Add("LDAP://cn=Sue Peace,cn=Users,dc=mycorp,dc=com")
objGroup.Add("LDAP://cn=Keith Cooper,cn=Users,dc=mycorp,dc=com")
```

Groups can contain virtually any other type of object as a member, including users, computers, and other groups.

Adding Many USER Groups to Groups

In Chapter 13, we described the need to add many user groups as members of several permission groups. Example 24-6 contains the code necessary to implement this functionality. It scans for all groups prefixed with USER_ and DRUP_. It then adds all the USER groups to each DRUP group, except for the group where the suffix matches. In other words, all USER_ groups except USER_Finance are added to DRUP_Finance. This was why the names were set up this way.

Example 24-6. Adding many user groups as members of several permission groups

```
'**************************************************************************
'Search the entire AD for all groups starting USER_ and return the cn
'and AdsPath variables in the following structure
'
'  arrUSERGroup(index,0) = cn attributes
'  arrUSERGroup(index,1) = ADsPath attribute
'
'where index goes from 0 to (the maximum number of results returned -1)
'**************************************************************************
If (SearchAD("LDAP://dc=mycorp,dc=com", _
      "(&(objectCategory=group)(cn=USER_*))", _
         "SubTree", "cn,ADsPath", arrUSERGroup)) Then

  '**************************************************************************
  'As above but for DRUP_ groups
  '**************************************************************************
  If (SearchAD("LDAP://dc=mycorp,dc=com", _
      "(&(objectCategory=group)(cn=DRUP_*))", _
         "SubTree", "cn,ADsPath", arrDRUPGroup)) Then

    '**************************************************************************
    'Set up an index to allow us to iterate through the USER_ groups. The
    'Ubound function here counts the maximum number of rows returned
    '**************************************************************************
    arrUSERGroupsUb = Ubound(arrUSERGroups)
    For intUSERGroupIndex = 0 To arrUSERGroupsUb
      '**************************************************************************
      'As above but for DRUP_ groups
      '**************************************************************************
      arrDRUPGroupsUb = Ubound(arrDRUPGroups)
      For intDRUPGroupIndex = 0 To arrDRUPGroupsUb
        '**************************************************************************
        'Extract the portion of the name that corresponds to all letters after
        'the "USER_" or "DRUP_" parts (i.e., five letters)
        '**************************************************************************
        txtUSERGroupSuffixName = Right(arrUSERGroup(intUSERGroupIndex,0), _
          Len(arrUSERGroup(intUSERGroupIndex,0))-5)
        txtDRUPGroupSuffixName = Right(arrDRUPGroup(intDRUPGroupIndex,0), _
          Len(arrDRUPGroup(intDRUPGroupIndex,0))-5)
        '**************************************************************************
        'If the two extracted strings are not the same, then add the USER group
        'to the DRUP group
        '**************************************************************************
```

```
         If Not txtUSERGroupSuffixName = txtDRUPGroupSuffixName Then
           Set objDRUPGroup = GetObject(arrDRUPGroup(intDRUPGroupIndex,1))
           If NOT objDRUPGroup.IsMember(arrUSERGroup(intUSERGROUPIndex,1)) Then
             objDRUPGroup.Add(arrUSERGroup(intUSERGroupIndex,1))
             objDRUPGroup.SetInfo
           End If
         End If
     Next
   Next
 End If
End If
```

 These searches make use of the ADO search function called SearchAD discussed in Chapter 23.

Evaluating Group Membership

The `IADsGroup::IsMember` method takes one argument, the DN of the object to check, just as **Add** and **Remove** do. It returns a Boolean, i.e., true or false. That allows you to use it in an **If … Then** statement like this:

```
Set objGroup = GetObject("LDAP://cn=Managers,ou=Sales," _
    & "dc=mycorp,dc=com")
If objGroup.IsMember("LDAP://cn=Vicky Launders,ou=Sales," _
    & "dc=mycorp,dc=com") Then
    WScript.Echo "Is a Member!"
Else
    WScript.Echo "Is NOT a Member!"
End If
```

To get a list of members in a group, the `IADsGroup::Members` method can be used. The `IADsGroup::Members` function is different from the other `IADsGroup` methods we have shown so far, since it returns a pointer to an `IADsMembers` object. Table 24-5 shows the two methods `IADsMembers` support.

Table 24-5. The IADsMembers interface

IADsMembers methods	Action
Count	The number of items in the container. If there is a filter set, only the number of items that match the filter are returned.
Filter	A filter, consisting of an array of object class strings, that can restrict the number of objects returned during enumeration of the container.

There are a number of ways of enumerating the members of a group. The For Each …
In … Next loop is the most common. This is how it works:

```
Set objGroup = GetObject("LDAP://cn=Managers,ou=Sales," _
    & "dc=mycorp,dc=com")
WScript.Echo "Number of members of the group: " & objGroup.Members.Count
For Each objMember In objGroup.Members
    WScript.Echo objMember.Name
Next
```

This script displays the number of members and then prints each member's name. As
the For loop executes, objMember ends up holding an IADs object representing each
member of the group.

Another useful feature of IADsMembers is the Filter method. It can be used to filter
certain object classes during enumeration just like you can with containers. To view
only the members of a group that are users, you would modify the previous example
to do the following:

```
objMembers = objGroup.Members
objMembers.Filter = Array("User")
For Each objMember In objMembers
    WScript.Echo objMember.Name
Next
```

Summary

In this chapter, we looked at how to create and manipulate properties of user and group
objects in Active Directory and the Windows NT SAM. We used this knowledge to
show how to write a script to create thousands of users easily from a set of data in a file
or from a database. We then showed how to create simple tools, such as an account
unlocker, that you can use in your day-to-day management of Active Directory. Next
we showed how to create groups and modify group members. Finally, we reviewed
how to determine group membership and iterate through all the members of a group.

## CHAPTER 25

Permissions and Auditing

Security descriptors (SDs), access control lists (ACLs), and access control entries (ACEs) have been used for files and directories on NTFS filesystems for years. The same concepts apply to securing Active Directory objects as well. While the information in this chapter is focused on Active Directory, the principles of creating a SD that contains a discretionary access control list (DACL) and system access control list (SACL) can map over to NTFS files and directories.

ADSI provides four main interfaces we can use:

IADsAccessControlEntry
: Manipulates individual ACEs that represent access or audit permissions for specific users or groups to objects and properties in Active Directory

IADsAccessControlList
: Manages collections of ACEs for an object

IADsSecurityDescriptor
: Manages the different sets of ACLs to an object

IADsSecurityUtility
: Gets, sets, and retrieves security descriptors for an object

All of the ADSI security interfaces can be found in the MSDN Library at *http://msdn .microsoft.com/en-us/library/aa746481.aspx.*

 If you haven't read Chapter 13 in its entirety, you may find this chapter a little confusing.

How to Create an ACE Using ADSI

Microsoft has a habit of calling a shovel a ground insertion earth management device (GIEMD for short); that is, they like to give names that are not always intuitive to the average person. The contents of the five properties of the ACE object are not all immediately obvious from the names. In addition, as Microsoft uses the ACE for system audit and permissions entries, a number of values that can go into the properties make sense only in a particular context. To complicate matters further, one property (AceFlags) is a catchall area that currently serves as the location for two completely different sets of information.

Creating an ACE is a simple matter, getting it right is a lot more difficult. To set up an ACE, you need the following basic pieces of information:

AccessMask
> What permissions you want to set

AceType
> Whether you are setting allow/deny permissions or auditing for an object or property

Trustee
> Who to apply the permissions to

AceFlags
> What inheritance options you want and, if it is an audit entry, whether you are monitoring successes or failures

Flags
> Determines whether or not the object type is inherited or not

ObjectType
> Indicates what type of ADSI object the permission is for

InheritedObjectType
> What the ACE applies to if not just the entire object

We will now go through several examples to show you what the seven properties of an ACE will contain based on certain security settings. Let's start with the simple example: giving a user full control permissions to an Organizational Unit. That means the information in Table 25-1 gets stored as an ACE on the SD of the Organizational Unit itself.

Table 25-1. Contents of the ACE properties when giving a user full control permissions to an Organizational Unit

Name of the property	Value to be stored
Trustee	Names the user who is to have the permission.
AccessMask	Gives full control (i.e., give every permission).
AceType	This is an allow permission.
AceFlags	The permission applies to this object. Child objects inherit this ACE.
Flags	Neither ObjectType nor InheritedObjectType is set.
ObjectType	Null.
InheritedObjectType	Null.

The user (`Trustee`) is allowed (`AceType`) full control (`AccessMask`) to the current object and all objects down the tree (`AceFlags`). The last three properties in the table are not used here, as the permission is a simple one that is being applied to an entire object.

If we were auditing successful and failed modifications to the entire Organizational Unit by the user, the contents of the audit ACE on the Organizational Unit would look like Table 25-2.

Table 25-2. Contents of the ACE properties when auditing successful modifications to an Organizational Unit and all children by a user

Name of the property	Value to be stored
Trustee	Names the user who is to be audited.
AccessMask	Gives full control (i.e., audit every action).
AceType	This is an audit ACE.
AceFlags	The auditing applies to this object. Child objects inherit this ACE. This ACE audits successes and failures.
Flags	Neither ObjectType nor InheritedObjectType is set.
ObjectType	Null.
InheritedObjectType	Null.

In this case, we are auditing (`AceType`) successful and failed (`AceFlags`) modifications of all types (`AccessMask`) by a user (`Trustee`) for this object and all children (`AceFlags`).

 Note the changes to `AceFlags` as compared to the previous permissions entry. While a permissions entry uses `AceType` to indicate whether it is set to allow or deny, an auditing entry uses `AceFlags` to indicate whether it is auditing successes or failures.

Let's take a look at a more complex example: giving the same user the ability to set the description for user objects within the entire branch beneath an Organizational Unit, as shown in Table 25-3. Again, this ACE is set on the SD of the Organizational Unit, yet it doesn't actually apply to the Organizational Unit itself. This ACE applies to the description attribute of user objects, so the Organizational Unit acts only as a carrier. The ACE is inherited down the tree by all objects, but only ever directly affects users. As soon as an object is created in one of those containers, the ACE is instantly added as an ACE on the SD of the object via inheritance rules. When access is being checked, if the object is a user, the ACE is "in effect" and allows the trustee to make the specified change.

Be careful with adding audit entries to Active Directory prior to Windows Server 2008. Auditing imparts significant overhead to a domain controller's workload, and it is easily possible to enable too much auditing. Too much auditing can cause the domain to not function properly or perform its functions very slowly as well as fill the security log with many entries that may not be very useful.

Table 25-3. Contents of the ACE properties for a more complex example

Name of the property	Value to be stored
Trustee	Names the user who is to have the permission.
AccessMask	Gives write access to a specific property.
AceType	This is an allow permission.
AceFlags	The permission is inherited only and does not apply to this object. Child objects inherit this ACE.
Flags	Both ObjectType and InheritedObjectType are set.
ObjectType	This is the schemaIDGUID of the description attribute. [a]
InheritedObjectType	This is the schemaIDGUID of the User class.

[a] Globally Unique Identifiers (GUIDs) are used in the schema to distinguish objects and object attributes uniquely across your forest. Specifying that a GUID is used somewhere means that you are using a unique identifier for that item.

The user (Trustee) is allowed (AceType) write access (AccessMask) to a specific attribute of a specific object class (AccessMask and Flags), namely, the description (ObjectType) of user objects (InheritedObjectType). The ACE does not apply to the current object (AceFlags), so the current object is acting only as a propagator of the ACE down the tree (AceFlags).

To audit successful and failed modifications to the description of user objects within the entire branch beneath an Organizational Unit, the contents of the audit ACE on the Organizational Unit would look like Table 25-4.

Table 25-4. Contents of the ACE properties when auditing successful modifications to an Organizational Unit and all children by a user

Name of the property	Value to be stored
Trustee	Names the user who is to be audited.
AccessMask	Gives write access to a specific property.
AceType	This is an audit ACE.
AceFlags	The auditing is inherited only and does not apply to this object. Child objects inherit this ACE. This ACE audits successes and failures.
Flags	Both ObjectType and InheritedObjectType are set.
ObjectType	This is the schemaIDGUID of the description attribute.
InheritedObjectType	This is the schemaIDGUID of the User class.

We are auditing (`AceType`) successful and failed (`AceFlags`) write access (`AccessMask`) to a specific attribute of a specific object class (`AccessMask` and `Flags`) by a user (`Trustee`), namely, the `description` (`ObjectType`) of *user* objects (`InheritedObject Type`). The ACE does not apply to the current object (`AceFlags`), so the current object is acting only as a propagator of the ACE down the tree (`AceFlags`).

Each ACE property uses a set of values that correspond to the text populating the following tables. Let's consider each of the properties of an ACE in turn to examine the values that can be stored within.

Trustee

The `Trustee` is the group or user receiving the permissions defined in the `AccessMask` and `AceType` fields or the user or group that is being audited. The `Trustee` can take any of the following forms:

Domain accounts
> These are the logon names used in previous versions of Windows NT, in the form *domain\useraccount*, where *domain* is the name of the Windows NT domain that contains the user and *useraccount* is the `sAMAccountName` property of the specified user. An example is AMER\jsmith. This is still valid for Active Directory domains.

Well-known security principals
> These represent special identities defined by the Windows security system, such as Everyone, Authenticated Users, System, Creator Owner, etc. The objects representing the security principals are stored in the Well-Known Security Principals container beneath the Configuration container.

Built-in groups
> These represent the built-in user groups defined by the Windows NT security system. They have the form BUILTIN*groupname* where *groupname* is the name of the built-in group. The objects representing the built-in groups are stored in the Builtin container beneath the domain container. An example is BUILTIN\Administrators.

Security Identifiers (SIDs)
> These are specified in string format and represent the `objectSID` property of the specified user or group in Active Directory. An example is `S-1-5-99-427-9`.

User Principal Name (UPN)
> This is the `userPrincipalName` property of the specified user or group in Active Directory. An example is *Nicole.Hansknecht@mycorp.com*.

When using a Trustee in an ACE, you should always try to use a group, not a user. Groups are far more flexible in that you can easily change who has permissions or easily grant more trustees the same permission by adding more users to the group. You also need to be very careful of the scope of the group. For example, a domain local group is not a good group scope to use for granting write access to an object in the configuration container in a multidomain forest because the domain local groups are effective only on domain controllers from the domain the groups exist in. If you find you can write to a configuration container object on a domain controller from one domain but not on a domain controller in another domain, there is a good chance your access was granted through a domain local group.

AccessMask

The AccessMask specifies the single or multiple permissions you are setting or auditing for the ACE. Note that this property does not determine whether you are allowing or denying the permission or whether you are auditing successful or failed access, only what the permission is.

If you are applying the permissions to a specific object or property, you also need to specify the relevant GUID of the object or property that you are giving rights to in the ObjectType or InheritedObjectType properties.

The largest set of values applies to the AccessMask, which is probably what you would expect. See Table 25-5.

Table 25-5. AccessMask constants

ADSI name	Decimal value	Hex value	Description
ADS_RIGHT_GENERIC_READ	2,147,483,648	&H80000000	Right to read from the Security Descriptor, to examine the object and its children, and to read all properties
ADS_RIGHT_GENERIC_WRITE	1,073,741,824	&H40000000	Right to write all properties, write to the DACL, and add/remove the object from the tree
ADS_RIGHT_GENERIC_EXECUTE	536,870,912	&H20000000	Right to list children of the object
ADS_RIGHT_GENERIC_ALL	268,435,456	&H10000000	Right to create/delete children, delete the tree, read/write properties, examine the object and its children, add/remove the object from the tree,

ADSI name	Decimal value	Hex value	Description
			and read/write with an extended right
ADS_RIGHT_ACCESS_SYSTEM_SECURITY	16,777,216	&H1000000	Right to get or set the SACL in the SD of the object
ADS_RIGHT_SYNCHRONIZE	1,048,576	&H100000	Right to use the object for synchronization (see ADSI documentation for more information)
ADS_RIGHT_WRITE_OWNER	524,288	&H80000	Right to assume ownership of the object; no right to grant ownership to others (User must be a trustee of the object)
ADS_RIGHT_WRITE_DAC	262,144	&H40000	Right to write to the DACL of the object
ADS_RIGHT_READ_CONTROL	131,072	&H20000	Right to read from the security descriptor of the object
ADS_RIGHT_DELETE	65,536	&H10000	Right to delete the object
ADS_RIGHT_DS_CONTROL_ACCESS	256	&H100	Right to perform an application-specific extension on the object (GUID=extended right)
ADS_RIGHT_DS_LIST_OBJECT	128	&H80	Right to examine the object (if this is missing, the object is hidden from the user)
ADS_RIGHT_DS_DELETE_TREE	64	&H40	Right to delete all children of this object, regardless of the permission on the children
ADS_RIGHT_DS_WRITE_PROP	32	&H20	Right to write properties of the object (GUID=specific property; no GUID=all properties)
ADS_RIGHT_DS_READ_PROP	16	&H10	Right to read properties of the object (GUID=specific property; no GUID=all properties)
ADS_RIGHT_DS_SELF	8	&H8	Right to invoke a validated write update
ADS_RIGHT_ACTRL_DS_LIST	4	&H4	Right to examine children of the object
ADS_RIGHT_DS_DELETE_CHILD	2	&H2	Right to delete children of the object (GUID=specific child object class; no

ADSI name	Decimal value	Hex value	Description
			GUID=all child object classes)
ADS_RIGHT_DS_CREATE_CHILD	1	&H1	Right to create children of the object (GUID=specific child object class; no GUID=all child object classes)
No name defined	-1	&HFFFFFFFFFFFFFFFF	Full control
No name defined	983551	&HF01FF	Full control, alternate value

These values were taken from the ADSI documentation for the ADS_RIGHTS_ENUM enumerated type available from the MSDN Library under the section described at the beginning of the chapter.

The value in the first column is the constant name that Microsoft defined for ADSI. This works fine if you are programming in VB or VC++ or scripting in a language that can make use of the available ADSI libraries, but with VBScript these constants are not defined. In other words, you have to define them in each script you use. To save you time, just copy the Const definitions from any of the ACE scripts provided on the O'Reilly web site for this book. We've included the values in both decimal and in hex for two reasons. First, we will be using hex in the scripts; the decimal values are there in case you want to use them for your own preference. Second, Microsoft defines all their constants in hexadecimal, so that is what you will see in the ADSI documentation. &H is the prefix for a hex number in VBScript, so if you want to specify that a group can list, create, and delete all children, you would use the value &H7, consisting of the rights ADS_RIGHT_ACTRL_DS_LIST + ADS_RIGHT_DS_DELETE_CHILD + ADS_RIGHT_DS_CREATE_CHILD.

The last two values have no name and are what you use if you want to define full control permissions. Note that in this case, most programmers tend to use the decimal value −1 even if they have used hexadecimal values elsewhere.

The GUIDs relating to properties and children are discussed further under the ACE Flags property.

You probably noticed two different numeric values for full control in Table 26-5. While −1 is the "official" value for full control, you will often find 983551 set in some ACEs that were configured as full control. 983551 is the combination of the following:

- `ADS_RIGHT_WRITE_OWNER`
- `ADS_RIGHT_WRITE_DAC`
- `ADS_RIGHT_READ_CONTROL`
- `ADS_RIGHT_DELETE`
- `ADS_RIGHT_DS_CONTROL_ACCESS`
- `ADS_RIGHT_DS_LIST_OBJECT`
- `ADS_RIGHT_DS_DELETE_TREE`
- `ADS_RIGHT_DS_WRITE_PROP`
- `ADS_RIGHT_DS_READ_PROP`
- `ADS_RIGHT_DS_SELF`
- `ADS_RIGHT_ACTRL_DS_LIST`
- `ADS_RIGHT_DS_DELETE_CHILD`
- `ADS_RIGHT_DS_CREATE_CHILD`

AceType

This property dictates whether the ACE denies permissions, allows permissions, or audits use of permissions (whether success or failure is defined in `AceFlags`). The values set here depend on whether the ACE applies to a specific object/property or just applies generally. See Table 25-6.

Table 25-6. AceType constants

ADSI name	Decimal value	Hex value	Description
`ADS_ACETYPE_SYS TEM_ALARM_OBJECT`	8	&H8	Not used.
`ADS_ACETYPE_SYS TEM_AUDIT_OBJECT`	7	&H7	This is a system-audit entry ACE using a GUID.
`ADS_ACE TYPE_ACCESS_DENIED_OBJECT`	6	&H6	This is an access-denied ACE using a GUID.
`ADS_ACE TYPE_ACCESS_ALLOWED_OBJECT`	5	&H5	This is an access-allowed ACE using a GUID.
`ADS_ACETYPE_SYSTEM_AUDIT`	2	&H2	This is a system-audit entry ACE using a Windows NT Security Descriptor.
`ADS_ACETYPE_ACCESS_DENIED`	1	&H1	This is an access-denied ACE using a Windows NT Security Descriptor.

ADSI name	Decimal value	Hex value	Description
ADS_ACETYPE_ACCESS_ALLOWED	0	&H0	This is an access-allowed ACE using a Windows NT Security Descriptor.

 Only one value can be set at any one time. This is why the values are not 1, 2, 4, and so on.

These values were taken from the ADSI documentation for the ADS_ACETYPE_ENUM enumerated type available from the MSDN Library under the section described at the beginning of the chapter.

Those ACEs that have a GUID in ObjectType or InheritedObjectType use the top four _OBJECT values. Any ACEs that do not refer to a specific GUID use the bottom three.

AceFlags

This catchall location stores two sets of information: inheritance and auditing. First it stores whether its children can inherit this ACE, whether the ACE applies to this object or is only acting as a propagator to pass it on to other objects, and whether the ACE itself is inherited. Second, for system-audit ACEs, this property indicates whether audit events are generated for success, failure, or both of the AccessMask permissions. See Table 25-7.

Table 25-7. AceFlags constants

ADSI name	Decimal value	Hex value	Description
ADS_ACEFLAG_FAILED_ACCESS	128	&H80	Used in the SACL only; indicates to generate audit messages for failed access attempts
ADS_ACEFLAG_SUCCESS FUL_ACCESS	64	&H40	Used in the SACL only; indicates whether to generate audit messages for successful access attempts
ADS_ACE FLAG_VALID_INHERIT_FLAGS	31	&H1F	Indicates whether the inherit flags for this ACE are valid (set only by the system)
ADS_ACEFLAG_INHERITED_ACE	16	&H10	Indicates whether this ACE was inherited (set only by the system)
ADS_ACEFLAG_INHERIT_ONLY_ACE	8	&H8	Indicates an inherit-only ACE that does not exercise access controls on the object to which it is attached
ADS_ACEFLAG_NO_PROPA GATE_INHERIT_ACE	4	&H4	Child objects will not inherit this ACE
ADS_ACEFLAG_INHERIT_ACE	2	&H2	Child objects will inherit this ACE

These values were taken from the ADSI documentation for the `ADS_ACEFLAG_ENUM` enumerated type available from the MSDN Library under the section described at the beginning of the chapter.

There are three unusual aspects to this property:

- The two SACL flags should surely be in `AceType`, not `AceFlags`, since `AceType` already indicates the allow or deny aspects of a DACL ACE. Strangely, they are here instead.

- The `ADS_ACEFLAG_INHERIT_ONLY_ACE` indicates that the object that this ACE is attached to is acting only as a carrier for the object, rather than being affected by the ACE itself.

- Flags of this nature in ADSI are normally are intended to indicate the presence or absence of something. The flag is set or it is not, giving us two states for whatever the flag refers to. Take a look at the last two flags in the table. The `ADS_ACE FLAG_INHERIT_ACE` flag indicates that the ACE will be propagated down to child objects throughout the section of the tree below this object. If the `ADS_ACE FLAG_INHERIT_ACE` flag is set, `ADS_ACEFLAG_NO_PROPAGATE_INHERIT_ACE` will not be set. If `ADS_ACEFLAG_NO_PROPAGATE_INHERIT_ACE` is set, `ADS_ACEFLAG_INHERIT_ACE` is not, and this prevents the ACE from being inherited by subsequent generations of objects. Don't try to set both at the same time.

Flags, ObjectType, and InheritedObjectType

For the ACE to know whether it contains an `ObjectType` or `InheritedObjectType` field, it contains a `Flags` property. This can have only four values. If the value is 0, neither object is present in the ACE. The other three values (1, 2, and 3) are made up from the two constants displayed in Table 25-8.

Table 25-8. Flag type constants

ADSI name	Decimal value	Hex value	Description
ADS_FLAG_INHERI TED_OBJECT_TYPE_PRESENT	2	&H2	Indicates that an InheritedObject Type is present in the ACE
ADS_FLAG_OBJECT_TYPE_PRESENT	1	&H1	Indicates that an ObjectType is present in the ACE

These values were taken from the ADSI documentation for the `ADS_FLAGTYPE_ENUM` enumerated type available from the MSDN Library under the section described at the beginning of the chapter.

The `ObjectType` and `InheritedObjectType` fields store GUIDs or null values that indicate what the ACE actually applies to. Table 25-9 explains it much better.

Table 25-9. How to use ObjectType and InheritedObjectType

ACE requirement	AceFlags	Flags	ObjectType	InheritedObjectType
Permissions are to apply to entire current object.	Effective on current object; not inherited by child objects	Neither	Null (ignored but still set)	Null (ignored but still set)
Permissions are to apply to a specific attribute of the current object.	Effective on current object; not inherited by child objects	Object Type only	schemaIDGUID of the attributeSchema object that defines the attribute in the schema or rightsGuid of the controlAccessRight object that defines the extended right, property set, or validated right in the extended-rights container	Null (ignored but still set)
Permissions are to apply to all child objects.	Not effective on current object; inherited by children	Object Type only	Null[a]	Null (ignored but still set)
Permissions are to apply to child objects that are of a specific class.	Not effective on current object; inherited by children	Object Type only	schemaIDGUID of the classSchema object that defines the class in the schema or rightsGuid of the controlAccessRight object that defines the extended right, property set, or validated right in the extended-rights container	Null (ignored but still set)
Permissions are to apply to a specific attribute of specific child objects.	Not effective on current object; inherited by children	Both	schemaIDGUID of the attributeSchema object that defines the attribute in the schema or rightsGuid of the controlAccessRight object that defines the extended right, property set, or validated right in the extended-rights container	schemaIDGUID of the classSchema object that defines the class in the schema

[a] Setting null for the ObjectType field in the third entry signifies that this ACE applies to all child objects; this is the only time that you do not use a GUID in this property. The system understands that a null value for a required ObjectType field is the same as providing the GUIDs for every possible child object all at once.

You do not need to set null items that are ignored; they will be set to null by the system on creation of the ACE.

Note that Flags, ObjectType, and InheritedObjectType have defaults of 0, null, and null, respectively.

A Simple ADSI Example

All of the seven ACE properties are set using property methods of the same names as those in an ADSI interface called `IADsAccessControlEntry`. The ACEs that are created using this are then modified using `IADsAccessControlList` and `IADsSecurityDescriptor`.

Let's go through an example now so you can see how it all fits together. Example 25-1 shows a section of VBScript code that creates an ACE that allows ANewGroup full access to the myOU organizational unit and all its children.

Example 25-1. A simple ADSI example

```
Option Explicit

'Declare constants
Const FULL_CONTROL = -1
Const ADS_ACETYPE_ACCESS_ALLOWED = 0
Const ADS_FLAG_INHERITED_OBJECT_TYPE_PRESENT = 2

'Declare variables
Dim objObject    'Any object
Dim objSecDesc   'SecurityDescriptor
Dim objDACL      'AccessControlList
Dim objNewACE    'AccessControlEntry

'Create the new ACE and populate it
Set objNewACE = CreateObject("AccessControlEntry")
objNewACE.Trustee = "AMER\ANewGroup"
objNewACE.AccessMask = FULL_CONTROL
objNewACE.AceType = ADS_ACETYPE_ACCESS_ALLOWED
objNewACE.AceFlags = ADS_FLAG_INHERITED_OBJECT_TYPE_PRESENT

'Add the new ACE to the object and write it to the AD
Set objObject = GetObject("LDAP://ou=myOU,dc=amer,dc=mycorp,dc=com")

'Use IADs::Get to retrieve the SD for the object
Set objSecDesc = objObject.Get("ntSecurityDescriptor")

'Use IADsSecurityDescriptor:: DiscretionaryAcl to retrieve the existing DACL
Set objDACL = objSecDesc.DiscretionaryAcl

'Use IADsAccessControlList::AddACE to add an ACE to an existing DACL
objDACL.AddAce objNewACE

'Use IADsSecurityDescriptor:: DiscretionaryAcl to put back the modified DACL
objSecDesc.DiscretionaryAcl = objDACL

'Use IADs::Put to replace the SD for the object
objObject.Put "ntSecurityDescriptor", Array(objSecDesc)

'Write out the property cache using IADs::SetInfo
objObject.SetInfo
```

A common error seen by script writers writing their own ACL manipulation scripts is the dreaded "The security ID structure is invalid" error, or error –2147023559. The number one cause of this error is a trustee that cannot be resolved to a SID.

Discussion

First we create the new ACE. This requires use of a `CreateObject` function call to create a new empty instance of an ACE object. We then have to set the four fields that we need. The `Trustee` is the user or group that will have the permission to the myOU object. The `AccessMask` value set to –1 indicates that full permission is being set. To say whether the full permissions are allowed or denied, we use a 0 in the `AceType` field, which indicates that the ACE is a permissions-allowed ACE. Finally, the `AceFlags` field is set to 2 so that child objects will inherit this ACE. This means that the ACE now allows ANewGroup full access to the myOU organizational unit and all its children.

We then go through binding to the object to get the security descriptor and ultimately the DACL so that we can add the new ACE to the DACL. Once that is done, we reverse the steps and set the security descriptor for the object, writing out the property cache as the last step.

A Complex ADSI Example

Example 25-2 is an example of a real-life problem that gets asked nearly every week in the Microsoft newsgroups: how to delegate the ability to unlock an account, reset a password, and set the flag that the account must change password on the next logon.

Example 25-2. Delegating unlock, password reset, and must change password flag

```
Option Explicit

'Modify these to change your trustee and target for the ACL mod
Const TRUSTEE="AMER\PasswordAdmin"
Const OBJPATH="ou=myOU,dc=amer,dc=mycorp,dc=com"

'Attribute, Class, Control Access Right constants
Const ATTRIB_LOCKOUTTIME_GUID = "{28630EBF-41D5-11D1-A9C1-0000F80367C1}"
Const ATTRIB_PWDLASTSET_GUID = "{BF967A0A-0DE6-11D0-A285-00AA003049E2}"
Const CLASS_USER_GUID = "{BF967ABA-0DE6-11D0-A285-00AA003049E2}"
Const CAR_RESETPWD_GUID = "{00299570-246D-11D0-A768-00AA006E0529}"

'AccessMask constants
Const ADS_RIGHT_GENERIC_READ = &H80000000
Const ADS_RIGHT_GENERIC_WRITE = &H40000000
Const ADS_RIGHT_GENERIC_EXECUTE = &H20000000
Const ADS_RIGHT_GENERIC_ALL = &H10000000
Const ADS_RIGHT_ACCESS_SYSTEM_SECURITY = &H1000000
Const ADS_RIGHT_SYNCHRONIZE = &H100000
Const ADS_RIGHT_WRITE_OWNER = &H80000
```

```
Const ADS_RIGHT_WRITE_DAC = &H40000
Const ADS_RIGHT_READ_CONTROL = &H20000
Const ADS_RIGHT_DELETE = &H10000
Const ADS_RIGHT_DS_CONTROL_ACCESS = &H100
Const ADS_RIGHT_DS_LIST_OBJECT = &H80
Const ADS_RIGHT_DS_DELETE_TREE = &H40
Const ADS_RIGHT_DS_WRITE_PROP = &H20
Const ADS_RIGHT_DS_READ_PROP = &H10
Const ADS_RIGHT_DS_SELF = &H8
Const ADS_RIGHT_ACTRL_DS_LIST = &H4
Const ADS_RIGHT_DS_DELETE_CHILD = &H2
Const ADS_RIGHT_DS_CREATE_CHILD = &H1
Const FULL_CONTROL = -1

'AceType constants
Const ADS_ACETYPE_SYSTEM_AUDIT_OBJECT = &H7
Const ADS_ACETYPE_ACCESS_DENIED_OBJECT = &H6
Const ADS_ACETYPE_ACCESS_ALLOWED_OBJECT = &H5
Const ADS_ACETYPE_SYSTEM_AUDIT = &H2
Const ADS_ACETYPE_ACCESS_DENIED = &H1
Const ADS_ACETYPE_ACCESS_ALLOWED = &H0

'AceFlags constants
Const ADS_ACEFLAG_FAILED_ACCESS = &H80
Const ADS_ACEFLAG_SUCCESSFUL_ACCESS = &H40
Const ADS_ACEFLAG_VALID_INHERIT_FLAGS = &H1F
Const ADS_ACEFLAG_INHERITED_ACE = &H10
Const ADS_ACEFLAG_INHERIT_ONLY_ACE = &H8
Const ADS_ACEFLAG_NO_PROPAGATE_INHERIT_ACE = &H4
Const ADS_ACEFLAG_INHERIT_ACE = &H2

'Flags constants
Const ADS_FLAG_INHERITED_OBJECT_TYPE_PRESENT = &H2
Const ADS_FLAG_OBJECT_TYPE_PRESENT = &H1

'Declare variables
Dim objObject      'Any object
Dim objSecDesc     'SecurityDescriptor
Dim objDACL        'AccessControlList
Dim objNewACE_1    'AccessControlEntry
Dim objNewACE_2    'AccessControlEntry
Dim objNewACE_3    'AccessControlEntry

'Create new ACE, Unlock User Objects
Set objNewACE_1 = CreateObject("AccessControlEntry")
objNewACE_1.Trustee = TRUSTEE
objNewACE_1.AccessMask = ADS_RIGHT_DS_WRITE_PROP or ADS_RIGHT_DS_READ_PROP
objNewACE_1.AceType = ADS_ACETYPE_ACCESS_ALLOWED_OBJECT
objNewACE_1.AceFlags = ADS_ACEFLAG_INHERIT_ONLY_ACE _
                                      or ADS_ACEFLAG_INHERIT_ACE
objNewACE_1.Flags= ADS_FLAG_OBJECT_TYPE_PRESENT _
                       or ADS_FLAG_INHERITED_OBJECT_TYPE_PRESENT
objNewACE_1.ObjectType= ATTRIB_LOCKOUTTIME_GUID
objNewACE_1.InheritedObjectType = CLASS_USER_GUID
```

```
'Create new ACE, Set/Clear Must change password on next logon
Set objNewACE_2 = CreateObject("AccessControlEntry")
objNewACE_2.Trustee = TRUSTEE
objNewACE_2.AccessMask = ADS_RIGHT_DS_WRITE_PROP or ADS_RIGHT_DS_READ_PROP
objNewACE_2.AceType = ADS_ACETYPE_ACCESS_ALLOWED_OBJECT
objNewACE_2.AceFlags = ADS_ACEFLAG_INHERIT_ONLY_ACE _
                                           or ADS_ACEFLAG_INHERIT_ACE
objNewACE_2.Flags= ADS_FLAG_OBJECT_TYPE_PRESENT _
                                 or ADS_FLAG_INHERITED_OBJECT_TYPE_PRESENT
objNewACE_2.ObjectType= ATTRIB_PWDLASTSET_GUID
objNewACE_2.InheritedObjectType = CLASS_USER_GUID

'Create new ACE, Reset Password
Set objNewACE_3 = CreateObject("AccessControlEntry")
objNewACE_3.Trustee = TRUSTEE
objNewACE_3.AccessMask = ADS_RIGHT_DS_CONTROL_ACCESS
objNewACE_3.AceType = ADS_ACETYPE_ACCESS_ALLOWED_OBJECT
objNewACE_3.AceFlags = ADS_ACEFLAG_INHERIT_ONLY_ACE _
                                           or ADS_ACEFLAG_INHERIT_ACE
objNewACE_3.Flags= ADS_FLAG_OBJECT_TYPE_PRESENT _
                                 or ADS_FLAG_INHERITED_OBJECT_TYPE_PRESENT
objNewACE_3.ObjectType= CAR_RESETPWD_GUID
objNewACE_3.InheritedObjectType = CLASS_USER_GUID

'Add the new ACE to the object and write it to the AD
Set objObject = GetObject("LDAP://" & OBJPATH)

'Use IADs::Get to retrieve the SD for the object
Set objSecDesc = objObject.Get("ntSecurityDescriptor")

'Use IADsSecurityDescriptor:: DiscretionaryAcl to retrieve the existing DACL
Set objDACL = objSecDesc.DiscretionaryAcl

'Use IADsAccessControlList::AddACE to add ACEs to an existing DACL
objDACL.AddAce objNewACE_1     ' Add Unlock
objDACL.AddAce objNewACE_2     ' Add Set/Clear must change password
objDACL.AddAce objNewACE_3     ' Add Reset password

'Use IADsSecurityDescriptor:: DiscretionaryAcl to put back the modified DACL
objSecDesc.DiscretionaryAcl = objDACL

'Use IADs::Put to replace the SD for the object
objObject.Put "ntSecurityDescriptor", Array(objSecDesc)

'Write out the property cache using IADs::SetInfo
objObject.SetInfo
```

 If you run this script multiple times, you will see the same ACEs being added to the ACL over and over again. It is a very simple script and does not check to see whether the permissions have already been delegated, and the security interface itself is not smart enough to prevent the duplicates. You should thus be careful not to run this script more than once for a given target path.

Discussion

The first thing you will notice is that this script is longer than the last. Do not let that confuse or scare you; it is still quite simple. At the top of the script are two lines that you modify to specify which group (or user) the delegation is being applied for and the object to which the delegation is being applied to. This small change makes it much easier to modify the script for your use; you do not have to go looking for other places to make changes.

The next section of the script is dedicated to defining constants for the attributes, classes, and control access rights we are delegating. Once you get past the simple examples of allowing full control to everything or read access to everything, you need to start specifying actual object class types, attributes, control access rights, property sets, and validated writes. Unfortunately, the security interfaces aren't intelligent enough to take simple names like user or `lockoutTime` and set the proper values in the ACEs, so we need to know the proper values and specify them ourselves. For classes and attributes, we need to use the `schemaIDGUID` attribute from the `classSchema` and `attributeSchema` objects involved. For control access rights, property sets, and validated rights, we need to use the `rightsGUID` attribute of the `controlAccessRight` objects in the `cn=extended-rights` container of the configuration naming context.

Now there is a long section of various constants defined for the security interfaces specifying values for the various types of permissions that can be granted, whether they are inherited, etc. These values are from Tables 25-5 through 25-8.

Finally, we reach the core piece of the script, what really makes it different from the simple example—the creation of three new ACEs:

1. Unlock Account
2. Set/Clear "User Must Change Password On Next Logon" Flag
3. Reset Password

Unlock account

The first ACE delegates the ability to unlock a user account. In Active Directory, the attribute that controls whether or not an account is locked is the `lockoutTime` attribute; if the value is 0, the account is definitely unlocked. The delegate will need write access so the value can be set to 0 to clear the attribute when it is locked. It would be incorrect to assume that the delegate can already read the `lockoutTime` value, so it is best to grant Read Property (RP) as well as Write Property (WP). While this RP may not be needed initially, it may be needed later if Active Directory is locked down. In order to grant RP and WP, you specify an `AccessMask` of `ADS_RIGHT_DS_WRITE_PROP` combined with `ADS_RIGHT_DS_READ_PROP`. Because these are bit flags, we combine them with the or keyword.

Since we are granting permissions to a specific object and attribute, `ADS_ACE TYPE_AC-CESS_ALLOWED_OBJECT` has to be specified instead of `ADS_ACE TYPE_ACCESS_ALLOWED` for the value of `AceType`. This is exactly as specified in Table 25-6.

The next property to be set is the `AceFlags` property, which specifies inheritance. This ACE should only be inherited to user objects, so it requires two flags to be specified that must again be combined with the or keyword:

- `ADS_ACEFLAG_INHERIT_ONLY_ACE` to specify that the object we are applying the ACL to should not apply the ACE to itself (i.e., the OU shouldn't apply this).

- `ADS_ACEFLAG_INHERIT_ACE` to specify that the children of the object should apply the ACE (i.e., objects under the OU should apply this).

Finally, we come to the most confusing part of the ACE: the `inheritedObjectType` and the `objectType` combined with the `Flags` property. The ACE needs to apply to a specific attribute on a specific objectclass; this means that both the `inheritedObjectType` and `objectType` properties will be populated. That indicates that the two bit flags `ADS_FLAG_OBJECT_TYPE_PRESENT` and `ADS_FLAG_INHERITED_OBJECT_TYPE_PRESENT` both must be combined in the `Flags` property with the or keyword. If you think about it, that part is pretty straightforward; the flag values are well named. So now, what do you use for the `objectType` and `inheritedObjectType` properties? It is actually quite easy once you get the hang of it, even though the names aren't intuitive. The objectclass that you need to have inherit this ACE is placed into the `inheritedObjectType` property; in this case, it is the user class, so you set this property to the `schemaIDGUID` value of the user class. That leaves the `objectType` property, and you only have one piece of information left, the attribute you want to delegate, so you set the property equal to the `schemaIDGUID` of the `lockoutTime` attribute.

Set/clear "User Must Change Password On Next Logon" flag

This ACE is very similar to the previous Unlock Account ACE; in fact, the only difference is the `objectType` property. The new value is the `schemaIDGUID` of the attribute `pwdLastSet`. Under Windows NT, this capability was handled through a bit flag. Active Directory tracks this now by tracking the last time the password was changed. If the value is set to 0, it means the account must change the password on the next logon. If the value has any other value, it is the time the password was last set and is used to determine the password age for expiration. So once again, only a simple RP and WP needs to be granted, so take the values from the previous ACE and simply change the `objectType` from the `lockoutTime` attribute to the `pwdLastSet` attribute.

Reset Password

The final ACE is the Reset Password ACE. This one is a little more involved, but still only has two properties that are different from the Unlock Account ACE. You will recall the discussion from Chapter 13 about property sets, control access rights, and validated writes; well, resetting a password involves more than writing a single attribute from a permission standpoint. Resetting a password actually updates several attributes, so Microsoft has assigned a special right to signify that someone can do this. It is similar to specifying an attribute to be delegated in that you store a GUID for the control access right into the objectType attribute. It is different in that you must get a different GUID, the rightsGuid, from a controlAccessRight object, not an attributeSchema object. These controlAccessRight objects are stored in the cn=extended-rights container of the configuration NC.

The other difference is that you must specify a special AccessMask value. Reset Password isn't an attribute or even a set of attributes you are granting access to, so granting RP and WP doesn't make sense. Because this is a special operation, you instead grant Control Access (CA) permission. This is specified by setting the AccessMask property with ADS_RIGHT_DS_CONTROL_ACCESS.

Making Your Own ACEs

This script should show you how to handle a vast majority of your delegation work via scripts. You only need to fill in the properties of the ACE to describe what you want. For many delegations, you can use the Unlock Account ACE as a model and simply modify the objectType and inheritedObjectType properties. You can change a Grant to a Deny by changing the AceType from ADS_ACETYPE_ACCESS_ALLOWED_OBJECT to ADS_ACE TYPE_ACCESS_DENIED_OBJECT.

Delegate member attribute on groups

The inheritedObjectType should be the schemaIDGUID for the group class ({BF967A9C-0DE6-11D0-A285-00AA003049E2}). The objectType should be the schemaIDGUID for the member attribute ({BF9679C0-0DE6-11D0-A285-00AA003049E2}). As for the rest of the ACE, you can either grant or deny RP or WP or both.

Delegate ability to view Confidential Attribute

As mentioned in Chapter 13, Microsoft does not provide a mechanism to easily grant granular delegated access to attributes marked as Confidential. You are now armed with the information required to write a script to delegate this permission. Two permissions need to be present in order to read a Confidential attribute: the first is obviously RP, and the second is CA. So in order to grant the ability to read a confidential attribute that you added to your schema called socialSecurityNumber, you would retrieve the schemaIDGUID from the schema for the attribute and set the objectType property with that value. You would set the inheritedObjectType property to the schemaIDG UID for the user class. Finally, you would set the AccessMask to RP and CA by using the or keyword.

How to implement other delegations

All delegation is a combination of very simple values. Sometimes it isn't always easy to ascertain what values should be set for what properties of the Security interface. To help with this, use the GUI or some other delegation tool such as DSACLS to set up some delegation, and then simply list out the ACL and see what values are set. Once you have done this two or three times, you will be able to quickly put together new scripts to delegate anything you need. To assist you in this process, the last script of this chapter will output the entire security descriptor of any object you specify showing raw numeric values for each property, as well as the "decoded" constant names, attributes, classes, property sets, extended rights, and validated writes.

Creating Security Descriptors

If you are creating an object from scratch and you don't want it to receive the default DACL and SACL that would normally be applied to objects created, you can write your own DACL and SACL for an object. As you would expect, there are a number of properties associated with security descriptors and ACLs that you need to set. SDs and ACLs can be manipulated with the `IADsAccessControlList` interface (see Table 25-10) and the `IADsSecurityDescriptor` interface (see Table 25-11). We'll go through these briefly now and then move on to some more examples.

Table 25-10. IADsAccessControlList methods and properties

IADsAccessControlList methods and properties	Action
AddAce method	Adds an ACE to an ACL
RemoveAce method	Removes an ACE from an ACL
CopyAccessList method	Copies the current ACL
AclRevision property	Shows the revision of the ACL (always set to 4; see later text)
AceCount property	Indicates the number of ACEs in the ACL

Table 25-11. IADsSecurityDescriptor methods and properties

IADsSecurityDescriptor methods and properties	Action
CopySecurityDescriptor method	A copy of an existing SD.
Revision property	The revision of the SD (always set to 4, as noted earlier).
Control property	A set of flags indicating various aspects of the SD (see later text). Generally, you will not need to set this property; instead, you can set the properties listed in this table.
Owner property	The SID of the owner. If this field is null, no owner is set.
OwnerDefaulted property	A Boolean value indicating whether the owner is derived by the default mechanism when created (i.e., assembled out of all the inherited ACEs

IADsSecurityDescriptor methods and properties	Action
	passed down by its parents) rather than explicitly set by the person or application that created the SD in the first place.
Group property	The SID of the object's primary group, if appropriate. If this field is null, no primary group exists.
GroupDefaulted property	A Boolean value indicating that the group is derived by the default mechanism rather than explicitly set by the person or application that created the SD in the first place.
DiscretionaryAcl property	The discretionary ACL that holds permissions ACEs. The SE_DACL_PRESENT flag must be set in the Control property if a DACL exists. If the flag is set and yet this field is null, full access is allowed to everyone.
DaclDefaulted property	A Boolean value indicating that the DACL is derived by the default mechanism rather than explicitly set by the person or application that created the SD in the first place. This is ignored unless SE_DACL_PRESENT is set.
SystemAcl property	The system ACL that holds auditing ACEs. The SE_SACL_PRESENT flag must be set in the Control property if a SACL exists.
SaclDefaulted property	A Boolean value indicating that the SACL is derived by the default mechanism rather than explicitly set by the person or application that created the SD in the first place. This is ignored unless SE_SACL_PRESENT is set.

Every SD and ACL has a revision level to define the data structures in use. The SD revision level has never changed, so it is fixed at revision level 1. The ACL revision, on the other hand, has gone through several revisions and is now at revision level 4.

Having a revision allows Microsoft to update the security data structures to allow for new properties and concepts. This lets Active Directory know what version of the structures are used so it can properly interpret them.

The Control property can take a number of flags that help to define the properties of an SD. See Table 25-12 for a full description.

Table 25-12. Control constants

ADSI name	Decimal value	Hex value	Description
ADS_SD_CONTROL_SE_OWNER_DEFAULTED	1	&H1	This Boolean flag, when set, indicates that the SID pointed to by the Owner field was provided by the default mechanism rather than set by the person or application that created the SD in the first place. This may affect the treatment of the SID with respect to inheritance of an owner.
ADS_SD_CONTROL_SE_GROUP_DEFAULTED	2	&H2	This Boolean flag, when set, indicates that the SID in the Group field was provided by the default mechanism rather

ADSI name	Decimal value	Hex value	Description
			than explicitly set by the person or application that created the SD in the first place. This may affect the treatment of the SID with respect to inheritance of a primary group.
ADS_SD_CONTROL_SE_DACL_PRESENT	4	&H4	This Boolean flag, when set, indicates that the security descriptor contains a DACL. If this flag is set and the `Discre tionaryAcl` field of the SD is null, an empty (but present) ACL is explicitly being specified.
ADS_SD_CONTROL_SE_DACL_DEFAULTED	8	&H8	This Boolean flag, when set, indicates that the field was provided by the default mechanism rather than explicitly set by the person or application that created the SD in the first place. This may affect the treatment of the ACL with respect to inheritance of an ACL. This flag is ignored if the `SE_DACL_PRESENT` flag is not set.
ADS_SD_CONTROL_SE_SACL_PRESENT	16	&H10	This Boolean flag, when set, indicates that the security descriptor contains a SACL.
ADS_SD_CONTROL_SE_SACL_DEFAULTED	32	&H20	This Boolean flag, when set, Indicates that the ACL pointed to by the `System Acl` field was provided by the default mechanism rather than explicitly set by the person or application that created the SD in the first place. This may affect the treatment of the ACL with respect to inheritance of an ACL. This flag is ignored if the `SE_SACL_PRESENT` flag is not set.
ADS_SD_CON TROL_SE_DACL_AUTO_INHERIT_REQ	256	&H100	The DACL of the SD must be inherited.
ADS_SD_CON TROL_SE_SACL_AUTO_INHERIT_REQ	512	&H200	The SACL of the SD must be inherited.
ADS_SD_CON TROL_SE_DACL_AUTO_INHERITED	1,024	&H400	The DACL of the SD supports auto-propagation of inheritable ACEs to existing child objects.
ADS_SD_CON TROL_SE_SACL_AUTO_INHERITED	2,048	&H800	The SACL of the SD supports auto-propagation of inheritable ACEs to existing child objects.

ADSI name	Decimal value	Hex value	Description
ADS_SD_CONTROL_SE_DACL_PROTECTED	4,096	&H1000	The DACL of the SD is protected and will not be modified when new rights propagate through the tree.
ADS_SD_CONTROL_SE_SACL_PROTECTED	8,192	&H2000	The SACL of the SD is protected and will not be modified when new rights propagate through the tree.
ADS_SD_CONTROL_SE_SELF_RELATIVE	32,768	&H8000	The SD is held in a contiguous block of memory.

These values were taken from the ADSI documentation for the ADS_SD_CONTROL_ENUM enumerated type available from the MSDN Library under the section described at the beginning of the chapter.

In your ADSI code, it is possible to specify that the DACL or SACL is either null or empty. While in both cases each ACL contains no ACEs, there is a big difference between the effects of each setting. Specifically, any ACL that has been set to null (vbNull) grants full permissions to everyone, while an ACL that exists but contains no ACEs (i.e., is empty) grants no permissions to anyone at all.

Now we have enough information to be able to create our own SD. Example 25-3 does exactly that. While we have defined all of the SD constants, to save space we have defined only the ACE constants that we are using. Also note that this code is not 100% complete; the object creation code is not included.

Example 25-3. Creating your own security descriptor

```
Option Explicit

'AccessMask constants
Const ADS_RIGHT_DS_LIST_OBJECT = &H80

'AceType constants
Const ADS_ACETYPE_ACCESS_DENIED = &H1

'AceFlags constants
Const ADS_ACEFLAG_INHERIT_ACE = &H2

'Security Descriptor constants
Const ADS_SD_CONTROL_SE_OWNER_DEFAULTED = &H1
Const ADS_SD_CONTROL_SE_GROUP_DEFAULTED = &H2
Const ADS_SD_CONTROL_SE_DACL_PRESENT = &H4
Const ADS_SD_CONTROL_SE_DACL_DEFAULTED = &H8
Const ADS_SD_CONTROL_SE_SACL_PRESENT = &H10
Const ADS_SD_CONTROL_SE_SACL_DEFAULTED = &H20
Const ADS_SD_CONTROL_SE_DACL_AUTO_INHERIT_REQ = &H100
Const ADS_SD_CONTROL_SE_SACL_AUTO_INHERIT_REQ = &H200
```

```
Const ADS_SD_CONTROL_SE_DACL_AUTO_INHERITED = &H400
Const ADS_SD_CONTROL_SE_SACL_AUTO_INHERITED = &H800
Const ADS_SD_CONTROL_SE_DACL_PROTECTED = &H1000
Const ADS_SD_CONTROL_SE_SACL_PROTECTED = &H2000

'Security Descriptor and ACL Revision numbers
Const ACL_REVISION_DS = 4
Const SECURITY_DESCRIPTOR_REVISION = 1

'Declare general variables
Dim objNewObject            'The new object
Dim objSecDesc              'SecurityDescriptor
Dim objDACL                 'AccessControlList object containing permission ACEs
Dim objSACL                 'AccessControlList object containing audit ACEs
Dim objNewACE               'AccessControlEntry

'Set no permission to view the object for members of DenyGroup
Set objNewACE = CreateObject("AccessControlEntry")
objNewACE.Trustee = "AMER\DenyGroup"
objNewACE.AccessMask = ADS_RIGHT_DS_LIST_OBJECT
objNewACE.AceType = ADS_ACETYPE_ACCESS_DENIED
objNewACE.AceFlags = ADS_ACEFLAG_INHERIT_ACE

'Create a new DACL and add the ACE as the sole entry
Set objDACL = CreateObject("AccessControlList")
ObjDACL.AceCount = 1
ObjDACL.AclRevision = ACL_REVISION_DS
ObjDACL.AddAce objNewACE
Set objNewACE - Nothing

'Create the SD for the object. Set the SD to use the DACL supplied rather
'than the default one. Set the SD to use the default SACL that will be
'generated from inherited ACEs and defaultSD.
Set objSecDesc = CreateObject("SecurityDescriptor")
objSecDesc.Revision = SECURITY_DESCRIPTOR_REVISION
objSecDesc.OwnerDefaulted = True
objSecDesc.GroupDefaulted = True
objSecDesc.DiscretionaryAcl = objDACL
objSecDesc.DaclDefaulted = False
objSecDesc.SaclDefaulted = True

'**************************************************************************
'Create the objObject first [this code is not included here]
'The variable objNewObject should point at the new object
'**************************************************************************

'Assign the SD to the existing object
objNewObject.Put "ntSecurityDescriptor", objSecDesc
objNewObject.SetInfo
```

Listing the Security Descriptor of an Object

A good example of a useful real-world task is when you are curious to see what ACEs have been set on an object, such as a domain or Organizational Unit. Example 25-4 is a piece of code that can be used as the basis for checking through an Active Directory forest looking for irregularities or that can be used to help you build the proper values for your own delegation script. The code is fairly simple but very long, due to the fact that it has to check every constant for both the SACL and DACL of each object.

Example 25-4. Examining the security descriptor of an object

```
Option Explicit

'Declare the variables
Dim objObject, objRootDSE, objSchema, objExtRights, objEnum, objSD
Dim objDACL, objSACL, objACE
Dim SchemaGuids, CARGuids, SDCtlD, AccMaskD, ACEFlagsD, FlagsD
Dim strDC, strSchemaPath, strConfigPath, strGUID, strLDAPPath

'AccessMask constants
Const FULL_CONTROL                       = -1
Const FULL_CONTROL2                      = &HF01FF

Const ADS_RIGHT_GENERIC_READ             = &H80000000
Const ADS_RIGHT_GENERIC_WRITE            = &H40000000
Const ADS_RIGHT_GENERIC_EXECUTE          = &H20000000
Const ADS_RIGHT_GENERIC_ALL              = &H10000000
Const ADS_RIGHT_ACCESS_SYSTEM_SECURITY   = &H1000000
Const ADS_RIGHT_SYNCHRONIZE              = &H100000
Const ADS_RIGHT_WRITE_OWNER              = &H80000
Const ADS_RIGHT_WRITE_DAC                = &H40000
Const ADS_RIGHT_READ_CONTROL             = &H20000
Const ADS_RIGHT_DELETE                   = &H10000
Const ADS_RIGHT_DS_CONTROL_ACCESS        = &H100
Const ADS_RIGHT_DS_LIST_OBJECT           = &H80
Const ADS_RIGHT_DS_DELETE_TREE           = &H40
Const ADS_RIGHT_DS_WRITE_PROP            = &H20
Const ADS_RIGHT_DS_READ_PROP             = &H10
Const ADS_RIGHT_DS_SELF                  = &H8
Const ADS_RIGHT_ACTRL_DS_LIST            = &H4
Const ADS_RIGHT_DS_DELETE_CHILD          = &H2
Const ADS_RIGHT_DS_CREATE_CHILD          = &H1

'AccessMask Dictionary for Flag enumeration
Set AccMaskD = CreateObject("Scripting.Dictionary")
AccMaskD.Add FULL_CONTROL, "FULL_CONTROL"
AccMaskD.Add FULL_CONTROL2, "FULL_CONTROL2"
AccMaskD.Add ADS_RIGHT_GENERIC_READ, "ADS_RIGHT_GENERIC_READ"
AccMaskD.Add ADS_RIGHT_GENERIC_WRITE, "ADS_RIGHT_GENERIC_WRITE"
AccMaskD.Add ADS_RIGHT_GENERIC_EXECUTE, "ADS_RIGHT_GENERIC_EXECUTE"
AccMaskD.Add ADS_RIGHT_GENERIC_ALL, "ADS_RIGHT_GENERIC_ALL"
AccMaskD.Add ADS_RIGHT_ACCESS_SYSTEM_SECURITY, "ADS_RIGHT_ACCESS_SYSTEM_SECURITY"
AccMaskD.Add ADS_RIGHT_SYNCHRONIZE, "ADS_RIGHT_SYNCHRONIZE"
AccMaskD.Add ADS_RIGHT_WRITE_OWNER, "ADS_RIGHT_WRITE_OWNER"
AccMaskD.Add ADS_RIGHT_WRITE_DAC, "ADS_RIGHT_WRITE_DAC"
AccMaskD.Add ADS_RIGHT_READ_CONTROL, "ADS_RIGHT_READ_CONTROL"
AccMaskD.Add ADS_RIGHT_DELETE, "ADS_RIGHT_DELETE"
AccMaskD.Add ADS_RIGHT_DS_CONTROL_ACCESS, "ADS_RIGHT_DS_CONTROL_ACCESS"
AccMaskD.Add ADS_RIGHT_DS_LIST_OBJECT, "ADS_RIGHT_DS_LIST_OBJECT"
```

```
AccMaskD.Add ADS_RIGHT_DS_DELETE_TREE, "ADS_RIGHT_DS_DELETE_TREE"
AccMaskD.Add ADS_RIGHT_DS_WRITE_PROP, "ADS_RIGHT_DS_WRITE_PROP"
AccMaskD.Add ADS_RIGHT_DS_READ_PROP, "ADS_RIGHT_DS_READ_PROP"
AccMaskD.Add ADS_RIGHT_DS_SELF, "ADS_RIGHT_DS_SELF"
AccMaskD.Add ADS_RIGHT_ACTRL_DS_LIST, "ADS_RIGHT_ACTRL_DS_LIST"
AccMaskD.Add ADS_RIGHT_DS_DELETE_CHILD, "ADS_RIGHT_DS_DELETE_CHILD"
AccMaskD.Add ADS_RIGHT_DS_CREATE_CHILD, "ADS_RIGHT_DS_CREATE_CHILD"

'AceType constants
Const ADS_ACETYPE_SYSTEM_AUDIT_OBJECT    = &H7
Const ADS_ACETYPE_ACCESS_DENIED_OBJECT   = &H6
Const ADS_ACETYPE_ACCESS_ALLOWED_OBJECT  = &H5

Const ADS_ACETYPE_SYSTEM_AUDIT           = &H2
Const ADS_ACETYPE_ACCESS_DENIED          = &H1
Const ADS_ACETYPE_ACCESS_ALLOWED         = &H0

'AceFlags constants
Const ADS_ACEFLAG_FAILED_ACCESS              = &H80
Const ADS_ACEFLAG_SUCCESSFUL_ACCESS          = &H40
Const ADS_ACEFLAG_VALID_INHERIT_FLAGS        = &H1F
Const ADS_ACEFLAG_INHERITED_ACE              = &H10
Const ADS_ACEFLAG_INHERIT_ONLY_ACE           = &H8
Const ADS_ACEFLAG_NO_PROPAGATE_INHERIT_ACE   = &H4
Const ADS_ACEFLAG_INHERIT_ACE                = &H2

'AceFlags Dictionary for Flag enumeration
Set ACEFlagsD = CreateObject("Scripting.Dictionary")
ACEFlagsD.Add ADS_ACEFLAG_FAILED_ACCESS, "ADS_ACEFLAG_FAILED_ACCESS"
ACEFlagsD.Add ADS_ACEFLAG_SUCCESSFUL_ACCESS, "ADS_ACEFLAG_SUCCESSFUL_ACCESS"
ACEFlagsD.Add ADS_ACEFLAG_VALID_INHERIT_FLAGS, "ADS_ACEFLAG_VALID_INHERIT_FLAGS"
ACEFlagsD.Add ADS_ACEFLAG_INHERITED_ACE, "ADS_ACEFLAG_INHERITED_ACE"
ACEFlagsD.Add ADS_ACEFLAG_INHERIT_ONLY_ACE, "ADS_ACEFLAG_INHERIT_ONLY_ACE"
ACEFlagsD.Add ADS_ACEFLAG_NO_PROPAGATE_INHERIT_ACE, _
                                "ADS_ACEFLAG_NO_PROPAGATE_INHERIT_ACE"
ACEFlagsD.Add ADS_ACEFLAG_INHERIT_ACE, "ADS_ACEFLAG_INHERIT_ACE"


'Security Descriptor constants
Const ADS_SD_CONTROL_SE_SACL_PROTECTED        = &H2000
Const ADS_SD_CONTROL_SE_DACL_PROTECTED        = &H1000
Const ADS_SD_CONTROL_SE_DACL_AUTO_INHERITED   = &H400
Const ADS_SD_CONTROL_SE_SACL_AUTO_INHERITED   = &H800
Const ADS_SD_CONTROL_SE_SACL_AUTO_INHERIT_REQ = &H200
Const ADS_SD_CONTROL_SE_DACL_AUTO_INHERIT_REQ = &H100
Const ADS_SD_CONTROL_SE_SACL_DEFAULTED        = &H20
Const ADS_SD_CONTROL_SE_SACL_PRESENT          = &H10
Const ADS_SD_CONTROL_SE_DACL_DEFAULTED        = &H8
Const ADS_SD_CONTROL_SE_DACL_PRESENT          = &H4
Const ADS_SD_CONTROL_SE_GROUP_DEFAULTED       = &H2
Const ADS_SD_CONTROL_SE_OWNER_DEFAULTED       = &H1

'Security Descriptor Dictionary for Flag enumeration
Set SDCtlD = CreateObject("Scripting.Dictionary")
SDCtlD.Add ADS_SD_CONTROL_SE_SACL_PROTECTED, "ADS_SD_CONTROL_SE_SACL_PROTECTED"
```

```
SDCtlD.Add ADS_SD_CONTROL_SE_DACL_PROTECTED, "ADS_SD_CONTROL_SE_DACL_PROTECTED"
SDCtlD.Add ADS_SD_CONTROL_SE_SACL_AUTO_INHERITED, _
                              "ADS_SD_CONTROL_SE_SACL_AUTO_INHERITED"

SDCtlD.Add ADS_SD_CONTROL_SE_DACL_AUTO_INHERITED, _
                              "ADS_SD_CONTROL_SE_DACL_AUTO_INHERITED"
SDCtlD.Add ADS_SD_CONTROL_SE_SACL_AUTO_INHERIT_REQ, _
                          "ADS_SD_CONTROL_SE_SACL_AUTO_INHERIT_REQ"
SDCtlD.Add ADS_SD_CONTROL_SE_DACL_AUTO_INHERIT_REQ, _
                          "ADS_SD_CONTROL_SE_DACL_AUTO_INHERIT_REQ"
SDCtlD.Add ADS_SD_CONTROL_SE_SACL_DEFAULTED, "ADS_SD_CONTROL_SE_SACL_DEFAULTED"
SDCtlD.Add ADS_SD_CONTROL_SE_SACL_PRESENT, "ADS_SD_CONTROL_SE_SACL_PRESENT"
SDCtlD.Add ADS_SD_CONTROL_SE_DACL_DEFAULTED, "ADS_SD_CONTROL_SE_DACL_DEFAULTED"
SDCtlD.Add ADS_SD_CONTROL_SE_DACL_PRESENT, "ADS_SD_CONTROL_SE_DACL_PRESENT"
SDCtlD.Add ADS_SD_CONTROL_SE_GROUP_DEFAULTED, "ADS_SD_CONTROL_SE_GROUP_DEFAULTED"
SDCtlD.Add ADS_SD_CONTROL_SE_OWNER_DEFAULTED, "ADS_SD_CONTROL_SE_OWNER_DEFAULTED"

'Flags constants
Const ADS_FLAG_INHERITED_OBJECT_TYPE_PRESENT = &H2
Const ADS_FLAG_OBJECT_TYPE_PRESENT           = &H1

'Flags Dictionary for Flag enumeration
Set FlagsD = CreateObject("Scripting.Dictionary")
FlagsD.Add ADS_FLAG_INHERITED_OBJECT_TYPE_PRESENT, _
                          "ADS_FLAG_INHERITED_OBJECT_TYPE_PRESENT"
FlagsD.Add ADS_FLAG_OBJECT_TYPE_PRESENT, "ADS_FLAG_OBJECT_TYPE_PRESENT"

' Misc Constants
Const ADS_SECURITY_INFO_SACL   = &H8
Const ADS_SECURITY_INFO_DACL   = &H4
Const ADS_SECURITY_INFO_GROUP  = &H2
Const ADS_SECURITY_INFO_OWNER  = &H1
Const ADS_OPTION_SECURITY_MASK = &H3           ' Security mask for options
Const ADS_OPTION_SERVERNAME = 0
Const E_ADS_PROPERTY_NOT_FOUND = &H8000500D  ' Property not found in cache

'Main Script Logic Begin
'Retrieve parameter, display usage if necessary
If (WScript.Arguments.Count <> 1) Then
  Out "Usage: sdlist ADsPath"
  Out "   Ex: sdlist LDAP://dc=mycorp,dc=com"
  WScript.Quit
End If
strLDAPPath=WScript.Arguments.item(0)

'Bind to object
Out "Opening object - " & strLDAPPath
Set objObject = GetObject(strLDAPPath)
strDC = objObject.GetOption(ADS_OPTION_SERVERNAME)
Out "Using domain controller: " & strDC

'Connect to RootDSE, retrieve Schema/Config NCs
Out "Opening RootDSE"
Set objRootDSE = GetObject("LDAP://" & strDC & "/RootDSE")
strSchemaPath = objRootDSE.Get("schemaNamingContext")
```

```
strConfigPath = objRootDSE.Get("configurationNamingContext")

'Connect to schema and retrieve schemaIDGUIDs of attributes and classes
'  schemaIDGUID attribute is an octet string
'Build dictionary object to hold values
Out "Opening Schema"
Set objSchema = GetObject("LDAP://" & strSchemaPath)
Out "Retrieving classes and attributes"
objSchema.Filter=Array("attributeSchema","classSchema")
Set SchemaGuids = CreateObject("Scripting.Dictionary")
For Each objEnum In objSchema
  strGUID=GuidToStr(objEnum.schemaIDGUID)
  SchemaGuids.add UCase(strGUID),objEnum.lDAPDisplayName
Next

'Connect to extended-rights container and retrieve rightsGuids of CA objects
'  rightsGuid is a unicode string
'Build dictionary object to hold values
'  handle validated writes special, MS duplicated a rightsGuid
Out "Opening Extended-Rights container"
Set objExtRights = GetObject("LDAP://cn=extended-rights," & strConfigPath)
Out "Retrieving Property Sets, Extended Rights, and Validated Rights"
objExtRights.Filter=Array("controlAccessRight")
Set CARGuids = CreateObject("Scripting.Dictionary")
For Each objEnum In objExtRights
  strGUID="{" & objEnum.rightsGuid & "}"
  if objEnum.validAccesses = 8 then strGUID = "VWRITE - " & strGUID
  CARGuids.add UCase(strGUID),objEnum.displayName
Next

'Retrieve Security Descriptor
'  Need to check if the property not found in cache error was thrown as it
'  indicates person running script has insufficient rights

On Error Resume Next
Set objSD = objObject.Get("nTSecurityDescriptor")
If Err = E_ADS_PROPERTY_NOT_FOUND Then
  Out ""
  Out "You do not have access to the DACL..."
  WScript.Quit
End If
On Error Goto 0

'Write out the SDs general information
Out ""
Out "=================================================================="
Out "Security Descriptor"
Out "  SD revision is : " & objSD.Revision
Out "  SD Owner is    : " & objSD.Owner
Out "  SD Group is    : " & objSD.Group
Out "  Control Flags " & HexStr(objSD.Control)
DisplayFlags GetFlagStrs(objSD.Control,SDCtlD),"      "
Out "++++++++++++++++++++++++++++++++++++++++++++++++++++++++++++++++++++"

'Write out the DACL general information
```

```
Set objDACL = objSD.DiscretionaryAcl
Out "Discretionary ACL"
Out "  DACL revision : " & objDACL.AclRevision
Out "  DACL ACE Count: " & objDACL.AceCount
Out "-----------------------------------------------------------------"

'Loop through ACEs
EnumACEs(objDACL)
Out "-----------------------------------------------------------------"
Out "-----------------------------------------------------------------"

'Retrieve SACL
'    The SACL requires enhanced permissions to retrieve. Because of this
'    and how the Security Interface works, the script disconnects from the
'    the object and reconnects and attempts to set the options to retrieve
'    the SACL. If it fails, throw an error.
Set objObject = Nothing
Set objObject = GetObject(strLDAPPath)
objObject.SetOption ADS_OPTION_SECURITY_MASK, ADS_SECURITY_INFO_OWNER _
                                      Or ADS_SECURITY_INFO_GROUP _
                                      Or ADS_SECURITY_INFO_DACL _
                                      Or ADS_SECURITY_INFO_SACL

On Error Resume Next
Set objSD = objObject.Get("nTSecurityDescriptor")
If Err = E_ADS_PROPERTY_NOT_FOUND Then
  Out ""
  Out "You do not have access to the SACL..."
  WScript.Quit
End If
On Error Goto 0

'Write out the SACL general information
Set objSACL = objSD.SystemAcl
Out "System ACL"
Out "  SACL revision : " & objSACL.AclRevision
Out "  SACL ACE Count: " & objSACL.AceCount
Out "-----------------------------------------------------------------"

'Loop through ACEs
EnumACEs(objSACL)
Out "-----------------------------------------------------------------"

'Main Script Logic End
'Subroutines

'Output Routine, change this routine to redirect output
Sub Out(str)
  WScript.Echo str
End Sub

'Convert a binary GUID to a string GUID
'    Convert GUID octet string to Hex characters then arrange in proper order
'    and add brackets {}
Function GuidToStr(Guid)
```

```
    Dim i, str
    str = " "
    For i = 1 To Lenb(Guid)
       str = str & Right("0" & Hex(Ascb(Midb(Guid, i, 1)))), 2)
    Next

    GuidToStr = "{"
    For i = 1 to 4
       GuidToStr = GuidToStr & Mid(str,10-(i*2),2)
    Next
    GuidToStr = GuidToStr & "-"
    For i = 1 to 2
       GuidToStr = GuidToStr & Mid(str,14-(i*2),2)
    Next
    GuidToStr = GuidToStr & "-"
    For i = 1 to 2
       GuidToStr = GuidToStr & Mid(str,18-(i*2),2)
    Next
    GuidToStr = GuidToStr & "-"
    For i = 1 to 2
       GuidToStr = GuidToStr & Mid(str,16+(i*2),2)
    Next
    GuidToStr = GuidToStr & "-"
    For i = 1 to 6
       GuidToStr = GuidToStr & Mid(str,20+(i*2),2)
    Next
    GuidToStr = GuidToStr & "}"
End Function

'Convert integer to Hexidecimal string for output - format (0xnnnn)
Function HexStr(val)
   HexStr = "(0x" & Hex(val) & ")"
End Function

'Get list of Flag strings for given bit flag value and Dictionary
'  Loops through the keys of a dictionary object and executes a bitwise-AND
'  against value and each key. If there is a match, adds key's matching item
Function GetFlagStrs(val,ByRef dict)
   Dim keys, keycnt, i, ar(), flgcnt
   flgcnt=0
   keys = dict.Keys
   keycnt = UBound(keys)
   For i = 0 To keycnt
      If ((val and keys(i)) = keys(i)) Then
         Redim Preserve ar(flgcnt)
         ar(flgcnt) = dict(keys(i)) & "   " & HexStr(keys(i))
         flgcnt = flgcnt + 1
      End If
   Next
   GetFlagStrs=ar
End Function

'Loop through Array and display strings with fill padding
Sub DisplayFlags(ar,fill)
   Dim str
```

```
    For Each str In ar
        Out fill & str
    Next
End Sub

'Convert ACETYPE value to string
'    ACETYPE is NOT a bitflag attribute.
Function AceTypeToStr(acetype)
    Select Case acetype
        Case ADS_ACETYPE_SYSTEM_AUDIT_OBJECT
            AceTypeToStr = "ADS_ACETYPE_SYSTEM_AUDIT_OBJECT"
        Case ADS_ACETYPE_ACCESS_DENIED_OBJECT
            AceTypeToStr = "ADS_ACETYPE_ACCESS_DENIED_OBJECT"
        Case ADS_ACETYPE_ACCESS_ALLOWED_OBJECT
            AceTypeToStr = "ADS_ACETYPE_ACCESS_ALLOWED_OBJECT"
        Case ADS_ACETYPE_SYSTEM_AUDIT
            AceTypeToStr = "ADS_ACETYPE_SYSTEM_AUDIT"
        Case ADS_ACETYPE_ACCESS_DENIED
            AceTypeToStr = "ADS_ACETYPE_ACCESS_DENIED"
        Case ADS_ACETYPE_ACCESS_ALLOWED
            AceTypeToStr = "ADS_ACETYPE_ACCESS_ALLOWED"
        Case Else
            AceTypeToStr = "Unknown"
    End Select
    AceTypeToStr = AceTypeToStr & " " & HexStr(acetype)
End Function

'Resolves a GUID to a schema objects or a Control Access Right object
Function GuidToObj(guid, access)
    Dim str
    guid = UCase(guid)
    If (guid <> "") Then
        If (SchemaGuids.Exists(guid)) Then
            str = SchemaGuids(guid)
        End If
        If (str = "") Then
            If (access and ADS_RIGHT_DS_SELF) Then
                guid = "VWRITE - " & guid
            End If
            If (CARGuids.Exists(guid)) Then
                str = CARGuids(guid)
            End If
        End If
        If (str = "") Then str = "__UNKNOWN__"
        GuidToObj = str & " (" & guid & ")"

    Else
        GuidToObj = "__NONE__"
    End If
End Function

'Loop through ACES from ACL and display information about each ACE
Sub EnumACEs(ByRef objACL)
    dim intACECount
    intACECount = 1
```

```
  For Each objACE In objACL
    Out "  ACE #" & intACECount
    Out "    Trustee               : " & objACE.Trustee
    Out "    AceType               : " & AceTypeToStr(objACE.AceType)
    Out "    AceFlags " & HexStr(objACE.AceFlags)
    DisplayFlags GetFlagStrs(objACE.AceFlags,ACEFlagsD), "            "
    Out "    Access Mask Flags " & HexStr(objACE.AccessMask)
    DisplayFlags GetFlagStrs(objACE.AccessMask,AccMaskD), "            "
    Out "    Flags " & HexStr(objACE.Flags)
    DisplayFlags GetFlagStrs(objACE.Flags,FlagsD), "           "
    Out "    Object Type          : " _
                & GuidToObj(objACE.ObjectType,objACE.AccessMask)
    Out "    Inherited Object Type : " _
        & GuidToObj(objACE.InheritedObjectType,objACE.AccessMask)
    Out ""
    intAceCount = intACECount + 1
  Next
End Sub
```

Summary

This chapter took a detailed look at the four main interfaces that you can use to manipulate and iterate over permissions and auditing entries for objects and attributes in your organization:

- IADsAccessControlEntry
- IADsAccessControlList
- IADsSecurityDescriptor
- IADsSecurityUtility

You should now have the tools in your programming belt necessary to modify the permissions in Active Directory as needed.

## CHAPTER 26

Extending the Schema and the Active Directory Snap-ins

This chapter takes a look at two different areas: programmatically extending the schema and customizing the functionality of the Active Directory administrative MMC snap-ins. Although these topics may seem very different, they share the common thread of storing and presenting information beyond what Active Directory is configured to do by default. They are also related because you will often want to include new schema extensions in the Active Directory snap-ins.

In the first half of the chapter, we take a look at how you can manipulate the schema to include new attributes and classes. In the second half, we describe how to modify the various components of the Active Directory Users and Computers (ADUC) snap-in to include customized display names and menus. While we will focus on ADUC, the techniques presented in this chapter can be used to modify any of the Active Directory administrative snap-ins.

Modifying the Schema with ADSI

We've shown you how the schema works in Chapter 4 and how to design extensions in Chapter 14. Now let's take a look at how to query and manipulate the schema using ADSI.

IADsClass and IADsProperty

In addition to being able to query and update schema objects as you can any other type of object with the `IADs` interface, there are two main schema-specific interfaces available: `IADsClass` and `IADsProperty`. Each of these interfaces has a variety of useful methods and property methods to allow you to set mandatory properties for classes, optional properties for classes, maximum values for attributes, and so on.

First, let's compare accessing and modifying the schema by directly using the attributes we are interested in versus using the `IADsClass` and `IADsProperty` methods. This first code section uses attributes directly:

```
objAttribute.Put "isSingleValued", False
objAttribute.Put "attributeId", "1.3.6.1.4.1.999999.1.1.28"
arrMustContain = objSchemaClass.Get("mustContain")
arrMayContain = objSchemaClass.Get("mayContain")
```

Now we will use the ADSI schema interfaces to do the same thing:

```
objAttribute.MultiValued = True
objAttribute.OID = "1.3.6.1.4.1.999999.1.1.28"
arrMustContain = objSchemaClass.MandatoryProperties
arrMayContain = objSchemaClass.OptionalProperties
```

This makes use of `IADsClass::Manda-toryProperties`, `IADsProperty::MultiValued`, `IADsProperty::OID`, and `IADsClass::OptionalProperties`. As you can see, it's not hard to convert the code. However, we feel that including code that directly modifies the properties themselves gives you some idea of what you are actually changing and helps you to refer back to the definitions presented in Chapter 4.

More details on these three interfaces can be found in the MSDN Library at *http://msdn.microsoft.com/en-us/library/aa746465(VS.85).aspx*.

Creating the Mycorp-LanguagesSpoken Attribute

We will create an example attribute called `Mycorp-LanguagesSpoken`. It is to be a multivalued, indexed attribute that can hold an array of case-sensitive strings of between 1 and 50 characters. The name is prefixed with *Mycorp*, so it is obvious that *Mycorp* created the attribute.

Mycorp's Schema Manager has decided that the OID for this attribute is to be 1.3.6.1.4.1.999999.1.1.28. This is worked out as follows:

- Mycorp's root OID namespace is 1.3.6.1.4.1.999999.
- Mycorp's new attributes use 1.3.6.1.4.1.999999.1.1.*xxxx* (where *xxxx* increments from 1).
- Mycorp's new classes use 1.3.6.1.4.1.999999.1.2.*xxxx* (where *xxxx* increments from 1).
- The attribute is to be the 28th new attribute created by Mycorp.

The code to create such an attribute is included in Example 26-1.

Example 26-1. Creating the MyCorp-LanguagesSpoken attribute

```
Option Explicit
Dim objAttribute
Dim objSchemaContainer

Set objSchemaContainer = _
```

```
GetObject("LDAP://cn=Schema,cn=Configuration,dc=mycorp,dc=com")

Set objAttribute = objSchemaContainer.Create("attributeSchema", _
                                    "cn=Mycorp-LanguagesSpoken")

'Write out mandatory attributes
objAttribute.Put "attributeId", "1.3.6.1.4.1.999999.1.1.28"
objAttribute.Put "oMSyntax", 27
objAttribute.Put "attributeSyntax", "2.5.5.3"
objAttribute.Put "isSingleValued", False
objAttribute.Put "lDAPDisplayName", "myCorp-LanguagesSpoken"

'Create the attribute
objAttribute.SetInfo

'Write out optional attributes
objAttribute.GetInfo
objAttribute.Put "description", "Indicates the languages that " & _
                                    "a user speaks"
objAttribute.Put "rangeLower", 1
objAttribute.Put "rangeUpper", 50
objAttribute.Put "searchFlags", 1
objAttribute.SetInfo
```

Here is the corresponding LDIF file:

```
dn:
  CN=Mycorp-LanguagesSpoken,CN=Schema,CN=Configuration,DC=mycorp,DC=com
changetype: add
objectClass: attributeSchema
adminDescription: Indicates the languages that a user speaks
attributeID: 1.3.6.1.4.1.999999.1.1.28
attributeSyntax: 2.5.5.3
oMSyntax: 27
isSingleValued: FALSE
rangeLower: 1
rangeUpper: 50
adminDisplayName: Mycorp-LanguagesSpoken
searchFlags: 1
lDAPDisplayName: myCorp-LanguagesSpoken
```

That was fairly straightforward. Remember to change the attributeID attribute to correspond to your own OID namespace if you use the code. Figure 26-1 shows the newly created attribute using the Schema Manager snap-in.

Creating the FinanceUser class

We will now create a new class called Mycorp-FinanceUser. It is to be a structural class so that others can create instances of it within containers. It will have the new Mycorp-LanguagesSpoken as an attribute, as well as inheriting from the User class. The OID for the class will be 1.3.6.1.4.1.999999.1.2.4, representing the fourth class we've created under our base OID. Example 26-2 contains the code to create the class.

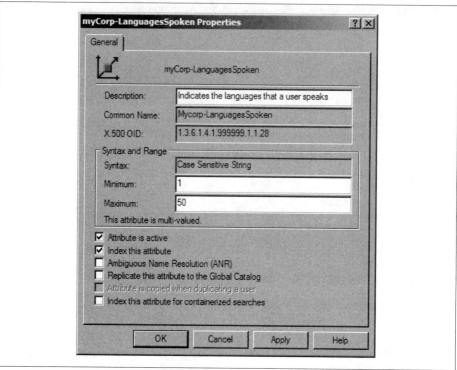

Figure 26-1. The Mycorp-LanguagesSpoken attribute viewed using the Schema Manager snap-in

Example 26-2. Creating the Mycorp-FinanceUser class

```
Option Explicit
Const ADS_PROPERTY_APPEND = 3

Dim objAttribute, objSchemaContainer, objClass

Set objSchemaContainer = _
  GetObject("LDAP://cn=Schema,cn=Configuration,dc=mycorp,dc=com")

Set objClass = objSchemaContainer.Create("classSchema", _
                                         "cn=Mycorp-FinanceUser")

'Write out mandatory attributes
objClass.Put "governsId", "1.3.6.1.4.1.999999.1.2.4"
objClass.Put "objectClassCategory", 1 'Structural Class
objClass.Put "subClassOf", "user"
objClass.Put "lDAPDisplayName", "mycorp-FinanceUser"
objClass.Put "adminDescription", "Indicates a Financial User"
objClass.Put "mustContain", "myCorp-LanguagesSpoken"

'Create the class
objClass.SetInfo
```

Here is the corresponding LDIF file:

```
dn:
 CN=Mycorp-FinanceUser,CN=Schema,CN=Configuration,DC=mycorp,DC=com
changetype: add
objectClass: classSchema
adminDescription: Indicates a Financial User
subClassOf: user
governsID: 1.3.6.1.4.1.999999.1.2.4
mustContain: myCorp-LanguagesSpoken
adminDisplayName: Mycorp-FinanceUser
objectClassCategory: 1
lDAPDisplayName: mycorp-FinanceUser
```

Figure 26-2 is the Schema Manager view of the newly created Mycorp-FinanceUser class.

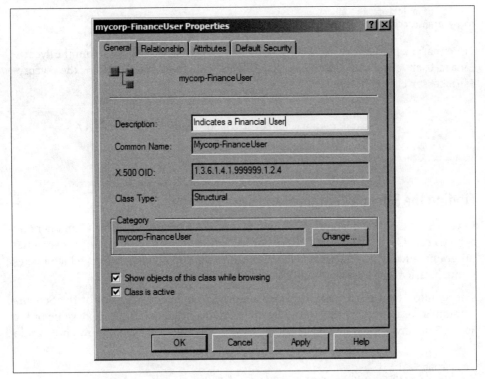

Figure 26-2. The Mycorp-FinanceUser class viewed using the Schema Manager snap-in

Creating instances of the new class

Finally, we want to create a new Mycorp-FinanceUser object. First, we have to get a reference to the Schema Container and create the object with all the mandatory attributes. Example 26-3 shows what this would look like.

Example 26-3. Creating an instance mycorp-FinanceUser

```
Option Explicit
Dim objContainer, objMycorpFinanceUser

Set objContainer = _
  GetObject("LDAP://ou=Finance Users,dc=Mycorp,dc=com")

'Create the new Mycorp-FinanceUser object
Set objMycorpFinanceUser = objContainer.Create("Mycorp-FinanceUser", _
  "cn=SimonWilliams")

'Set the mandatory properties
objMycorpFinanceUser.Put "sAMAccountName", "SimonWilliams"
objMycorpFinanceUser.Put "Mycorp-LanguagesSpoken", _
  Array("English", "French", "German")

'Write the object to the AD
objMycorpFinanceUser.SetInfo
```

Note that the mandatory properties include `Mycorp-LanguagesSpoken` from the `Mycorp-FinanceUser` class and `sAMAccountName` from the `User` class, which the `Mycorp-FinanceUser` class inherits from.

 `sAMAccountName` is not required for Windows Server 2003 and newer Active Directories as well as ADAM instances.

Finding the Schema Container and Schema FSMO

In your scripts or applications, it is good practice to locate the Schema Container and Schema FSMO dynamically instead of hardcoding those values. By finding those values programmatically, your scripts become much more forest-independent, which makes it much easier to transport to other forests in the future.

The solution to find the Schema Container is an easy one. The DN of the Schema Container for a forest can be found by querying the `schemaNamingContext` value of the `RootDSE` on any domain controller in the forest. The following code shows how to do that:

```
Option Explicit
Dim objRootDSE, objSchemaContainer, strSchemaPath

'Get the Root DSE from a random DC
Set objRootDSE = GetObject("LDAP://RootDSE")
'Get the Schema NC path for the domain
strSchemaPath = objRootDSE.Get("schemaNamingContext")
'Connect to the schema container on a random DC
Set objSchemaContainer = GetObject("LDAP://" & strSchemaPath)
```

The first `GetObject` call retrieves the RootDSE. Next we simply get the `schemaNamingContext` attribute and pass that to another `GetObject` call (or the `IADsOpenDSObject::OpenDSObject` method if you prefer to authenticate), which will return a reference to the Schema Container on a random domain controller. If you want to make changes without forcing the FSMO role to your currently connected server, you need to change the last line to connect to the server currently holding the Schema FSMO. This can be done in several additional steps:

```
Option Explicit
Dim objNTDS, objServer, strFSMORoleOwner, objSchemaContainer
Set objNTDS = GetObject("LDAP://" & objSchemaContainer.Get("fSMORoleOwner"))
Set objServer = GetObject( objNTDS.Parent )
strFSMORoleOwner = objServer.Get("dNSHostName")
'Connect to the schema container on the server holding the
'Schema Master FSMO role
Set objSchemaContainer = _
  GetObject("LDAP://" & strFSMORoleOwner & "/" & strSchemaPath)
```

The `fSMORoleOwner` attribute of the Schema Container actually contains the NTDS Settings DN of the domain controller holding the Schema FSMO. For example:

```
cn=NTDS Settings,cn=MOOSE,cn=Servers,cn=Main-Headquarters-
Site,cn=Sites,cn=Configuration,dc=mycorp,dc=com
```

From this, you can retrieve the distinguished name of the parent container that holds an attribute called `dNSHostName` that contains the DNS host name of the domain controller that object represents.

Transferring the Schema FSMO Role

If you want to transfer the Schema FSMO role to a specific server, just set the `becomeSchemaMaster` attribute to 1 on the RootDSE for that server. The script will need to either run under the credentials of someone in the Schema Admins group to perform this transfer or use `IADsOpenDSObject::OpenDSObject` and authenticate as someone in Schema Admins. The moment we write out the property cache, the proposed master contacts the current master and requests the role and any updates to the Schema NC that it has yet to see. Here is the code to do the transfer:

```
Option Explicit
Const DC_TO_TRANSFER_FSMO_TO = "niles.mycorp.com"
Dim objRootDSE, objSchemaContainer, strSchemaPath
Dim strSchemaPath, objSchemaContainer, strServerName
Dim strFSMORoleOwner, objNTDS, objServer
'Get the Root DSE
Set objRootDSE = GetObject("LDAP://" & DC_TO_TRANSFER_FSMO_TO & _
                           "/RootDSE")
'Request a Schema Master transfer
objRootDSE.Put "becomeSchemaMaster", 1
objRootDSE.SetInfo
```

At this point, the transfer has been requested. We now need to connect to the Schema NC and wait until the **fSMORoleOwner** attribute points to our new server:

```
'Get the Schema NC path for the domain
strSchemaPath = objRootDSE.Get("schemaNamingContext")
'Connect to the schema container on my DC
Set objSchemaContainer = GetObject("LDAP://" & DC_TO_TRANSFER_TO _
  & "/" & strSchemaPath)
'Initialize the while loop by indicating that the server is not the one
'we are looking for
strServerName = ""
'While the Server Name is not the one we are looking for, keep searching
While Not strServerName = DC_TO_TRANSFER_FSMO_TO
  'Get the FSMO Role Owner attribute
  strFSMORoleOwner = objSchemaContainer.Get("fSMORoleOwner")
  Set objNTDS = GetObject("LDAP://" &  strFSMORoleOwner )
  Set objServer = GetObject( objNTDS.Parent )
  strServerName = objServer.Get("dNSHostName")

  Set objNTDS = Nothing
  Set objServer = Nothing
  ' Sleep 2 seconds
  WScript.Sleep 2000
  objSchemaContainer.GetInfo()
Wend
'At this point in the code, the role has been
'transferred, so we can continue
```

You should not use the code exactly as written here because there is no error checking. Without error checking, there is no guarantee that the original writing of the **becomeSchemaMaster** attribute actually worked. There is also no guarantee that the attachment to the **DC_TO_TRANSFER_FSMO_TO** server actually worked, either. So if either of these or anything else went wrong, we may never exit the while loop. Even if both of these conditions worked, we may set the value, and the DC may attempt to contact the current Schema FSMO to find that it is unavailable. Again, we go into an infinite loop and the code never terminates. You certainly should include a timeout value as a second condition to the while loop to trap an occurrence of this problem.

Forcing a Reload of the Schema Cache

If you need to reload the schema cache, Microsoft recommends that you do so once you've finished all your writes. While the cache is being reloaded, any new queries are served from the old cache and will continue to be served by the old cache until the new one comes online. Microsoft specifically states that working threads that are referencing the old cache once a reload is finished will continue to reference the old cache. Only new threads will reference the new cache.

Reloading the cache using ADSI is very simple. Simply set the **schemaUpdateNow** attribute to 1 on the RootDSE of a DC. The following code shows how to do this:

```
Option Explicit
Dim objRootDSE, strDC
strDC = "dc01"
'Get the Root DSE
Set objRootDSE = GetObject("LDAP://" & strDC & "/RootDSE")
'Reload the cache on that DC
objRootDSE.Put "schemaUpdateNow", 1
```

It can also be done in LDIF with the following file:

```
dn:
changetype: modify
add: schemaUpdateNow
schemaUpdateNow: 1
-
```

Adding an Attribute to the Partial Attribute Set

If you identify an attribute that you would like to be part of the partial attribute set and thus accessible via the global catalog, it is straightforward to add it. To add an attribute, the isMemberOfPartialAttributeSet attribute for the attributeSchema object must be set to true. Example 26-4 shows how to add the myCorp-SpokenLanguages attribute to the partial attribute set.

Example 26-4. GC-Enabling the myCorp-SpokenLanguages attribute

```
Option Explicit
Const ATTR_TO_ADD = "myCorp-LanguagesSpoken"

Dim objRootDSE, objSchemaContainer
Dim strFSMORoleOwner, strSchemaPath

'Get the Root DSE from a random DC
Set objRootDSE = GetObject("LDAP://RootDSE")

'Get the Schema NC path for the domain
strSchemaPath = objRootDSE.Get("schemaNamingContext")

'Connect to the schema container on a random DC
Set objSchemaContainer = GetObject("LDAP://" & strSchemaPath)

'Get the Schema FSMO DNS name
Dim objNTDS, objServer
Set objNTDS = GetObject("LDAP://" & objSchemaContainer.Get("fSMORoleOwner") )
Set objServer = GetObject( objNTDS.Parent )
strFSMORoleOwner = objServer.Get("dNSHostName")

'Connect to Schema FSMO and Get the attribute
Dim objAttr
Set objAttr = GetObject("LDAP://" & strFSMORoleOwner & "/" & _
                "cn=" & ATTR_TO_ADD & "," & strSchemaPath)

'Set the property to true
```

```
objAttr.Put "isMemberOfPartialAttributeSet", True
objAttr.SetInfo
```

 Under Windows 2000, anytime an attribute is added to the partial attribute set, a full sync of the global catalog contents is initiated to all global catalogs in the forest. Because this can have a significant impact on replication and network performance, it should be done with caution. This limitation was removed in Windows Server 2003.

Customizing the Active Directory Administrative Snap-ins

In many cases, you may want to modify Active Directory Users and Computers (ADUC) to display additional attributes, perhaps even ones you've created. Continuing the schema extension example from the beginning of the chapter, let's say that you decide you want the myCorp-LanguagesSpoken attribute to be displayed in ADUC so others can view the languages a user speaks. Fortunately, the Active Directory snap-ins are largely customizable by modifying one or more attributes in Active Directory. You can also extend the functionality of a snap-in using WSH, VB, or any other COM-based language.

The rest of the chapter is devoted to reviewing the components behind the Active Directory administrative snap-ins and how you can modify them to meet your needs. These components include:

Display Specifiers
> Objects in Active Directory that contain localized user interface information

Property Pages
> Tabbed dialog box that displays information

Context Menus
> Menu displayed after right-clicking an object (e.g., user)

Icons
> Image displayed when viewing a particular class

Display Names
> User-friendly names displayed for attributes and classes (e.g., Last Name)

Creation Wizard
> Wizard interface used to create an object

Display Specifiers

Display specifiers are objects stored in Active Directory that contain information on how to display and manage objects for a specific object class through the Active Directory snap-ins. These display specifiers are held in the Configuration Naming Context

---

under the `DisplaySpecifiers` container. Within the `DisplaySpecifiers` container, there is a container for each supported locale, in a path similar to this:

```
LDAP://cn=409,cn=DisplaySpecifiers,cn=Configuration,dc=mycorp,dc=com
```

The preceding container contains the display specifiers for the U.S./English locale of 409. If you wanted to create or manage display specifiers for a different locale, you just create a new container with the relevant hexadecimal code for the locale and populate it with the relevant display specifier objects. For example, 409 in hex represents 1,033 in decimal, and 1,033 is the U.S./English locale. If we created 809 (2,057 in decimal), we would get the U.K./English locale, and if we created 40C (1,036 in decimal), we would get the French locale. The currently installed locale values can be found in the registry at `HKLM\SYSTEM\CurrentControlSet\Control\ContentIndex\Language`. Having display specifiers per locale enables you to support a wide variety of languages for a geographically disperse client base.

Each of the locale-specific containers has a series of objects of the `displaySpecifier` class. The object names are in the form of *ObjectClass-Display*. The user class has one called *User-Display*, the computer class has one called *Computer-Display*, and so on. To extend the interface for a specific object class for a particular language, you just need to modify the appropriate attributes on the `displaySpecifier` object that represents the class in that container.

Here's a simple example. The `classDisplayName` attribute exists on all `displaySpecifier` objects. Let's say we use the ADSI Edit tool from the Support Tools to open up the *Group-Display* object and change this attribute from Group to *Moose*. If we right-click on any container in the ADUC tool, a context menu normally appears, allowing us to create a new user, group, or Organizational Unit (among other things). After making the edit and reopening ADUC, it allows us to create a new User, *Moose*, or Organizational Unit. The way that the **group** class was displayed in the interface has been changed. If we wanted to change the display specifier for the French locale as well as or instead of the U.S./English locale, we would go to (or create) the 40C container and apply the change to the *Group-Display* object.

Let's now review some of the other customizations you can make.

Property Pages

You can see the array of property pages that exist by opening the properties of any object in ADUC. You can add property pages to these and display your own here. For this to work, though, the property page has to exist as a Component Object Model (COM) object that supports the `IShellExitInit` and `IShellPropSheetExt` interfaces. This means that the property page has to be created first in Visual Basic, Visual C++, or something similar.

Creating the object is the hardest part. Actually telling the system to use it is easy. Once the property page COM object exists, it will have a Globally Unique Identifier (GUID).

You then use ADSI Edit to go to the display specifier object representing the class that you wish to modify and alter the `adminPropertyPages` or `shellPropertyPages` attributes. These attributes are multivalued and store data in the following form:

```
2, {AB4909C2-6BEA-11D2-B1B6-00C04F9914BD}
1, {AB123CDE-ABCD-1124-ABAB-00CC4DD11223}
```

The first item represents the order number in which the sheets should appear. The second represents the UUID. A third optional parameter can be used to store extended information, such as data passed to the property page as it is displayed.

To add your own property page to a class, you edit either the `Shell` or `Admin` property page attribute, depending on whether you want the default (shell) or administrator UI to be modified, and add in a line like the preceding form. It really is that simple. You can even modify the existing pages, if any exist, and resequence them to your liking.

Context Menus

When you right-click an object in ADUC, a context menu pops up. You can add your own entries to this context menu. Context menu items are held in the `shellContext Menu` attribute for the default UI and `adminContextMenu` attribute for the admin UI in each `displaySpecifier` object. Items that should appear in both go into the `contextMenu` attribute.

The items that you add to the context menus can launch an application or create an instance of a COM object. The data takes the following form in the relevant attributes:

```
1,Extra &Data..., E:\MYPROG.EXE
2,&Extended Attributes...,C:\MYSCRIPT.VBS
3,{DB4909C2-GDEA-11D2-B1B6-00C04F9914BD}
```

Notice that the last item is a COM object. It is denoted by its GUID. The COM object must have been created to support the `IShellExtInit` and `IContextMenu` interfaces. Extra data can be passed to the COM object by including it as a third parameter on the line. The former two items are much more important to administrators. Here you can see that we added two extra items to the menu. These items are an executable program and a VBScript script. Any type of application is valid. The second parameter is the string you want to appear on the context menu. Use of an ampersand (&) character before a letter denotes that letter as the accelerator. Thus, when the menu is being displayed using the previous code example, typing "d" selects the first option, and "e" selects the second.

Being able to add scripts and programs to a context menu is a very powerful capability. Couple these scripts and programs with ADSI, and you have a way of extending the snap-ins Microsoft provides to deliver completely customized functionality based on your business or organizational needs. For example, let's say that you want to extend the schema and include a new, optional `myCorp-LanguagesSpoken` attribute for the User class. You can go to the *User-Display* object for the appropriate locale and modify the contextMenu attribute (so it is available to both users and administrators) to include an ADSI script that displays that attribute in a message box. The following code is all that is needed:

```
Option Explicit
Dim wshArgs, objUser
Set wshArgs = WScript.Arguments
Set objUser = GetObject(wshArgs(0))
MsgBox objUser.Get("myCorp-LanguagesSpoken"),,"Languages Spoken"
```

The script does nothing more than bind to the object's distinguished name that is passed in as an argument to the program, and print out the attribute in a MsgBox with an appropriate title, as shown in Figure 26-3.

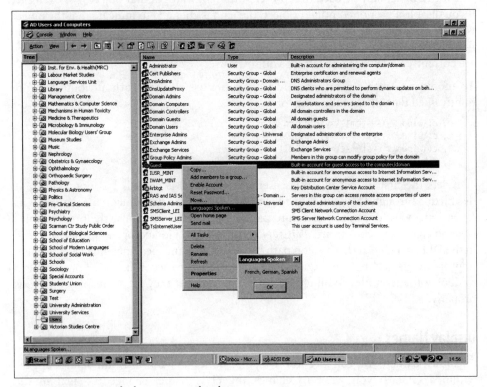

Figure 26-3. Viewing the languages spoken by a user

The Guest user object was right-clicked, which popped up a context menu that includes Languages Spoken. You can see that it is actually the string "&Languages Spoken…" being displayed if you look at the text in the bottom-left corner of the window. When we click the item or press the L key, a dialog box generated by the script is displayed on the screen. Normally the dialog box and the context menu would not be displayed together, but we have done so in this screen to show you the process.

You could also write a script or program that allowed you to modify the mycorp-LanguagesSpoken attribute and have it appear only on the administrator's context menus. Then you can use the ADUC tool to manage your users and this extra attribute, without ever needing to actually develop an entirely new interface if you don't want to.

Icons

When you look at a container of objects in ADUC, it shows you an icon for each object that is appropriate to the specific object class for that object. The icons for Organizational Units look different than those for containers, users, and printers, for example. The icon can actually be used to represent different states of that object. For example, if you disable a user or computer object, the icon is changed to indicate that the object is disabled. All in all, 16 different state icons can be defined for any object class. The first three represent the states closed (the default state), open, and disabled; the last 13 are currently undefined and left for your own use.

To modify the icon for an object class, simply use the `iconPath` attribute to store multivalued data of the following form:

```
0, c:\windows\system32\myicon.ico
1, c:\windows\system32\myicons.dll, 0
2, c:\windows\system32\myicons.dll, 2
3, c:\windows\system32\myicons.dll, 7
```

This sets the first four icon values. Remember that 0 is closed, 1 is open, and 2 is disabled; 3 through 15 are undefined. The first one uses a proper icon file with an ICO extension and so doesn't need a third parameter. The last three use the first (0), third (2), and eighth (7) icons from *MYICONS.DLL*, using an index for the set of icons held in the DLL, starting at 0. The icon path has to exist on the local machine for any client to properly display the icon. Remember to take that into account, since you may need to deploy the icon files to all clients in an enterprise if they are to display the icons properly.

Display Names

As shown earlier, you can alter the way that both class and attribute names appear within a GUI. If you want to change the class name, change the text in the `classDisplayName` property of the relevant `displaySpecifier` object. If you want to change what attributes names appear as, then you need to modify the multivalued attribute `attributeDisplayNames`. Attribute values take the form of a comma-delimited string as follows:

```
mobile,Mobile Number
physicalDeliveryOfficeName,Office Location
extensionAttribute1,My First Extended Attribute
```

The first value is the LDAP name corresponding to the attribute in the schema, and the second is the name that it is to be displayed as. Note that you shouldn't insert a space between the comma and the second value unless you want the name to be preceded by a space.

Leaf or Container

When you view objects in the ADUC, some display as containers and some display as leaf objects. Most objects that you are concerned with actually act as containers, even if you see them displayed as leaf objects. Take a printer on a computer, for example. If that printer is published as a `printQueue` object to Active Directory, the object is located as a leaf object within the computer object that it is published on. The computer object acts as a container for any print queues that it publishes. User, computer, and group objects by default are not displayed as containers. ADUC in fact has an option on the View menu to change this, called "View users, groups, and computers as containers." However, all objects get treated in this fashion, and you can modify any object's default setting by going to the `displaySpecifier` and changing the Boolean value of `treatAsLeaf` to true or false as required.

Object Creation Wizard

When you create a user, group, or Organizational Unit, ADUC presents a simple wizard to allow you to specify the relevant data for that object. It is possible for administrators to modify the default behavior in one of two ways. Administrators can replace the existing wizard entirely, if one exists, or they can just add extra pages to the wizard. Only one wizard can ever exist, so you either create a new one or modify the existing one. Let's say that you want to have the wizard ask for the value for the `myCorp-Langua gesSpoken` attribute for the `User` class. As the existing User creation wizard does not allow data to be input for this attribute, you can replace the entire wizard with a new one of your own, or you can place a new page into the wizard to receive data on this attribute. With property pages, we need to create new wizards or creation wizard extensions (extra pages to existing wizards) as COM objects that support the `IDsAdmin NewObjExt` interface. New wizards that replace the default wizards in use by the system are known as primary extensions, and they replace the core set of pages that would be used to create the object. Primary extensions support creation wizard extensions; you can define a primary extension for all users, for example, and later add a couple of extra pages using a creation wizard extension if you require.

If you are replacing the wizard entirely with a primary extension, modify the `creationWizard` attribute of the relevant `displaySpecifier` object to hold the GUID of the COM object. If you are just providing creation wizard extensions, you specify the order that the pages should appear, followed by the UUID in the `createWizardExt` multivalued attribute. The format is the same as for property pages.

Summary

In this chapter, we covered how to query and manipulate the Active Directory Schema, including how to locate and transfer the Schema FSMO. The schema cache and its importance was also briefly touched on, along with information on how to determine which attributes of an object are in the GC and how to add an attribute to the GC if necessary.

The second part of the chapter focused on how to customize the Active Directory administrative MMC snap-ins by modifying displaySpecifier objects. We described how to manipulate each of the major snap-in components, including property pages, context menus, icons, display names and the object creation wizard.

## CHAPTER 27

Scripting with WMI

The Windows Management Instrumentation (WMI) API was developed by Microsoft in 1998 in response to the ever-growing need for developers and system administrators to have a common, scriptable API to manage the components of the Windows operating systems. Before WMI, if you wanted to manage some component of the operating system, you had to resort to using one of the component-specific Win32 APIs, such as the Registry API or Event Log API. Each API typically had its own implementation quirks and required way too much work to do simple tasks. The other big problem with the Win32 APIs was that Microsoft's scripting languages such as VBScript could not use them. This really limited how much an inexperienced programmer or system administrator could do to programmatically manage systems. WMI changes all this by providing a single API that can be used to query and manage the Event Log, the Registry, processes, the filesystem, or any other operating system component.

You may be wondering at this point: this is a book on Active Directory, so why do I need to care about a system management API? Even if your sole job in life is to manage Active Directory, WMI can benefit you in at least two ways. First, Active Directory runs on top of Windows Server. These servers need to be managed (i.e., Event Log settings configured, Registry modified, applications installed, etc.) and monitored (i.e., filesystem space, services running, etc.). You can choose to do all of those tasks manually, or you can use WMI to automate them. For each task you automate, the total cost of ownership to support Active Directory is reduced, and you help ensure your servers stay consistent. In the Windows Server 2003 release, there are several new WMI hooks into Active Directory to monitor things such as trusts and replication.

In this chapter, we will give a brief introduction to the concepts and terminology behind WMI and then delve into several sample scripts showing how to make use of it. We will cover some system-specific tasks, such as managing services, the Event Log, and the Registry, which should give you a good grounding in some of the fundamentals of WMI. In the second half of the chapter, we will review how WMI can be used to access and monitor Active Directory.

In a single chapter, we can go into only so much detail about the internals of WMI; we won't be covering some of the more advanced topics. If you are interested in more information than what this chapter provides, we recommend checking out the MSDN Library or one of the WMI books available on the market. You can access the WMI SDK documentation by going to the MSDN Library web page: *http://msdn.microsoft .com/en-us/library/aa394582(VS.85).aspx*.

Origins of WMI

There have been several industry initiatives over the years to develop a model for managing systems and devices that would be robust enough to meet the needs of most vendors. Several protocols and frameworks have been developed to address the problem. The Simple Network Management Protocol (SNMP) is probably the most notable, but is pretty simple in its implementation and does not provide many features most vendors need for a single management framework.

The Distributed Management Task Force (DMTF) was created in the early 1990s to address the management framework problem. They developed the Web-Based Enterprise Management (WBEM) standard, which attempts to unify the management frameworks utilizing web technologies. As part of the WBEM standard, they also created the Common Information Model (CIM) , which is the language used for describing management data in an object-oriented way. The WBEM/CIM standards have garnered a lot of industry support in recent years and provide the basis for WMI.

For more information on WBEM/CIM, check out the DMTF website: *http://www.dmtf .org*.

WMI Architecture

The WMI architecture is composed of two primary layers: the CIM infrastructure, which includes the CIMOM and CIM Repository, and the WMI providers. Although the concepts Microsoft uses are very similar to the WBEM/CIM standards, they did not implement one very important component: the use of web technologies for the transport mechanism. Instead of using HTTP to transport messages between the WMI infrastructure and clients, Microsoft uses COM and DCOM, two Microsoft-specific technologies. This limits the use of WMI to only Microsoft platforms.

That being said, the capabilities to manage Microsoft-based platforms with WMI are nearly unlimited. More and more vendors are utilizing WMI not only to manage components of the Microsoft OS, but also to manage their own applications. Microsoft has also become heavily invested in WMI by providing WMI providers for nearly all of its major applications, including Active Directory, Exchange 2000 and Exchange 2003, and DNS.

CIMOM and CIM Repository

The CIM Repository is the primary warehouse for management data. It contains the static data that does not change very frequently, such as memory or disk size. The CIMOM or CIM Object Manager handles requests from clients, retrieves data from the CIM Repository, and returns it to the client. The CIMOM also provides an event service, so that clients can register for events and be notified dynamically when they occur. For dynamic data, such as performance monitor counters, the CIMOM will interact directly with a WMI provider instead of retrieving the data directly from the CIM Repository. The CIM Repository cannot store all possible data that is needed by the various WMI providers. The storage requirements would be significant, not to mention that a lot of the data would become out-of-date almost immediately after it was stored.

WMI Providers

The WMI providers contain much of the intelligence behind WMI. Typically a provider will be implemented for each individual managed component, such as the Event Log or Active Directory Trusts. Each provider is responsible for interacting with its managed component and can perform certain functions implemented by methods on classes representing that component. Also, as described earlier, some providers interact with the CIMOM to provide dynamic data that cannot be held in the CIM Repository.

Each WMI provider is also associated with a namespace. The namespace is used to segregate where WMI providers store their data and class definitions. Think of it as a filesystem. You could store all of your files in a single directory, but it would be hard to manage. By storing data and class definitions for providers under different namespaces, you don't have to worry about confusing the EventLog provider with the Active Directory Trust provider. Table 27-1 contains the more commonly used and AD-related WMI providers and the associated namespace.

Table 27-1. Some of the commonly used and AD-related WMI providers

Provider	Namespace
Win32 provider	root\cimv2
EventLog provider	root\cimv2
Registry provider	root\default
Active Directory provider	root\directory\LDAP

Provider	Namespace
Replication provider	*root\MicrosoftActiveDirectory*
Trustmon provider	*root\MicrosoftActiveDirectory*
DNS provider	*root\MicrosoftDNS*

Getting Started with WMI Scripting

Once you have a basic understanding of the WMI architecture, scripting with WMI is easy. In fact, once you understand how to reference, enumerate, and query objects of a particular class with WMI, it is straightforward to adapt the code to work with any managed component.

Referencing an Object

To reference objects in WMI, you use a UNC-style path name. An example of how to reference the C: drive on a computer called dc1 looks like the following:

```
\\dc1\root\CIMv2:Win32_LogicalDisk.DeviceID="C:"
```

The format should be easy to follow. The first part of the path (\\dc1\) is a reference to the computer on which the object resides. To reference the computer on which the script is running, you can use a "." for the computer name. The second part (root \CIMv2) is the namespace the object resides in. The third part (Win32_LogicalDisk) is the class of the object to reference. The fourth part is the key/value pairs representing the object. Generically, the path can be shown as follows:

```
\\ComputerName\NameSpace:ClassName.KeyName="KeyValue"[,KeyName2="KeyValue2"...]
```

Now that we know how to reference WMI objects, let's go ahead and instantiate an object using VBScript's GetObject function. For GetObject to understand that we are referencing WMI objects, we have to include one additional piece of information: the moniker. Just as we've been using the LDAP: and WinNT: progIDs to reference Active Directory and SAM-based objects in ADSI, we need to use the winmgmts: moniker when we are dealing with WMI objects:

```
Set objDisk = GetObject("winmgmts:\\dc1\root\CIMv2:Win32_LogicalDisk.DeviceID='C:'")
```

Note that if you want to reference the C: logical drive on the local computer, you can leave off the computer name and namespace path. The GetObject call would then look like this:

```
Set objDisk = GetObject("winmgmts:Win32_LogicalDisk.DeviceID='C:'")
```

We have left out the namespace path to show that a script can use a default namespace. *root\CIMv2* is the default namespace; however, this is configurable, and it is not advised to assume this will be the default on any systems you do not directly control. Also, when accessing a provider that uses any other namespace or when referencing a remote object, you need to include the namespace path.

Enumerating Objects of a Particular Class

Now let's look at an example. We want to view all logical disks on a machine, not just a particular disk. To do so, we need to use the InstancesOf method on a WMI object pointing to the namespace of the provider that contains the class. This example shows InstancesOf in use:

```
Option Explicit
Dim strComputer, objWMI, objDisks, objDisk
strComputer = "."
Set objWMI = GetObject("winmgmts:\\" & strComputer & "\root\cimv2")
Set objDisks = objWMI.InstancesOf("Win32_LogicalDisk")
For Each objDisk In objDisks
  WScript.Echo "DeviceID: " &  objDisk.DeviceID
  WScript.Echo "FileSystem: " &  objDisk.FileSystem
  WScript.Echo "FreeSpace: " & objDisk.FreeSpace
  WScript.Echo "Name: " & objDisk.Name
  WScript.Echo "Size: " & objDisk.Size
  WScript.Echo ""
Next
WScript.Echo "The script has completed successfully."
```

Here we get a WMI object pointing to the root\CIMv2 namespace, after which we call the InstancesOf method and pass the Win32_LogicalDisk class. The InstancesOf method returns a collection of Win32_LogicalDisk objects, which we then iterate over with a For Each loop.

As you can imagine, this is very powerful and allows you to easily retrieve a list of all the logical disks, services, or processes on a computer. The only issue is that we needed to know which property methods of the Win32_LogicalDisk class we wanted to see. We can instead retrieve all properties of the Win32_LogicalDisk class using the Properties_ method on each object:

```
Option Explicit
Dim strComputer, strWMIClass
Dim objWMI, objDisks, objDisk, objProp

strComputer = "."
strWMIClass = "Win32_LogicalDisk"

Set objWMI = GetObject("winmgmts:\\" & strComputer & "\root\cimv2")
Set objDisks = objWMI.InstancesOf(strWMIClass)
For Each objDisk In objDisks
    For Each objProp In objDisk.Properties_
```

```
     ' Print out NULL if the property is blank
     If IsNull(objProp.Value) Then
        WScript.Echo " " & objProp.Name & " : NULL"
     Else
     ' If the value is an array, we need to iterate through each element
     ' of the array
        If objProp.IsArray = TRUE Then
           For I = LBound(objProp.Value) To UBound(objProp.Value)
              WScript.echo " " & objProp.Name & " : " & objProp.Value(I)
           Next
        Else
        ' If the property was  not NULL or an array, we will print it
           WScript.echo " " & objProp.Name & " : " & objProp.Value
        End If
     End If
     Next
     WScript.Echo ""
Next
WScript.Echo "The script has completed successfully."
```

Searching with WQL

So far we've shown how to instantiate specific objects, such as a logical drive, and also how to enumerate all the objects of a particular class using the `InstancesOf` method. Knowing how to do both of these functions will take us a long way with WMI, but we are missing one other important capability: the ability to find objects that meet certain criteria.

The creators of WMI found an elegant way to handle this problem. They implemented a subset of the Structured Query Language (SQL) known as the WMI Query Language (WQL). WQL greatly increases the power of WMI by giving the programmer ultimate control over locating objects.

With WQL, we can even perform the same function as the `InstancesOf` method we used earlier. The following query will retrieve all the `Win32_LogicalDisk` objects on the system:

```
select * from Win32_LogicalDisk
```

We can use any property available on `Win32_LogicalDisk` objects as criteria in our search. As an example, let's say we wanted to find all NTFS logical disks that have less than 100 MB of available space. The query would look like the following:

```
select * from Win32_LogicalDisk
where FreeSpace < 104857600
and    filesystem = 'NTFS'
```

In order to put WQL to use, we first need to get a WMI object to the namespace we want to query. After we've done that, we can call the `ExecQuery` method on that object and pass the WQL query to use. The next example uses the "less than 100 MB" query we just described to print out all logical disks on the local computer that match that criterion:

```
Option Explicit
Dim strComputer, objWMI, objDisks, objDisk
strComputer = "."
Set objWMI = GetObject("winmgmts:\\" & strComputer & "\root\cimv2")
Set objDisks = objWMI.ExecQuery _
        ("select * from Win32_LogicalDisk " & _
         "where FreeSpace < 104857600 " & _
         "and filesystem = 'NTFS' ")
For Each objDisk In objDisks
  WScript.Echo "DeviceID: " & objDisk.DeviceID
  WScript.Echo "Description: " & objDisk.Description
  WScript.Echo "FileSystem: " & objDisk.FileSystem
  WScript.Echo "FreeSpace: " & objDisk.FreeSpace
Next
WScript.Echo "The script has completed successfully."
```

Authentication with WMI

So far, the examples we've shown assume that the caller of the script has the necessary rights to access the WMI information on the target machine. In many cases in which you are trying to automate a task, this may not be the case. Luckily, using alternate credentials in WMI is very straightforward.

Previously, to connect to a WMI namespace, we would have used the following:

```
strComputer = "dc1"
Set objWMI = GetObject("winmgmts:\\" & strComputer & "\root\cimv2")
```

But let's say that the person calling the script does not have any privileges on the *dc1* computer. We must now use the following:

```
strComputer = "dc1.mycorp.com"
strUserName = "administrator"
strPassword = "password"

Set objLocator = CreateObject("WbemScripting.SWbemLocator")
Set objWMI = objLocator.ConnectServer(strComputer, "root\cimv2", _
                              strUserName, strPassword)
```

We've replaced the single call to GetObject with a call to CreateObject to instantiate a WbemScripting.SWbemLocator object. The SWbemLocator object has a method called ConnectServer, which allows us to specify the target machine, username, and password to authenticate with. You can then use the object returned from ConnectServer to get the instances of a class, perform a WQL search, or any other function.

This was quick introduction to WMI scripting. We will be covering additional tasks, such as invoking an action or modifying properties of an object, as we walk through specific examples later in the chapter.

WMI Tools

There are several tools available to query and browse WMI information. These tools can be very useful in situations in which you want to access WMI information, but do not want to write a script to do it.

WMI from a Command Line

The WMI command-line tool (WMIC) is a powerful tool that can expose virtually any WMI information you want to access. It is available in Windows XP and Windows Server 2003 (and higher). Unfortunately, WMIC does not run on Windows 2000, but it can still be used to query WMI on a Windows 2000 machine.

WMIC maps certain WMI classes to "aliases." Aliases are used as shorthand so that you only need to type "logicaldisk" instead of "Win32_LogicalDisk." An easy way to get started with WMIC is to type the alias name of the class you are interested in. A list of all the objects that match that alias/class will be listed.

```
wmic:root\cli>logicaldisk list brief
DeviceID  DriveType  FreeSpace     ProviderName  Size         VolumeName
A:        2
C:        3          1540900864                  4296498688   W2K
D:        3          15499956224                 15568003072
Z:        5          0                           576038912    NR1EFRE_EN
```

Most aliases have a `list brief` subcommand that will display a subset of the properties for each object. You can run similar queries for services, CPUs, processes, and so on. For a complete list of the aliases, type `alias` at the WMIC prompt.

The creators of WMIC didn't stop with simple lists. You can also utilize WQL to do more complex queries. This next example displays all logical disks with a drivetype of 3 (local hard drive):

```
wmic:root\cli>logicaldisk where (drivetype = '3') list brief
DeviceID  DriveType  FreeSpace     ProviderName  Size         VolumeName
C:        3          1540806144                  4296498688   W2K
D:        3          15499956224                 15568003072
```

We have barely touched the surface of the capabilities of WMIC. You can invoke actions, such as creating or killing a process or service, and modify WMI data through WMIC as well. For more information, check out the Support WebCast "WMIC: A New Approach to Managing Windows Infrastructure from a Command Line," available at *http://support.microsoft.com/kb/325427*. Help information is also available by going to Start→Help, and search on WMIC.

WMI from the Web

Included as sample applications with the original WMI SDK, the WMI CIM Studio and WMI Object browser are web-based applications that provide much more benefit than just being example applications provided in the SDK. The following is a list of the tools and their purpose:

- The WMI CIM Studio is a generic WMI management tool that allows you to browse namespaces, instantiate objects, view the instances of a class, run methods, edit properties, and even perform WQL queries.
- The WMI Object Browser allows you to view the properties for a specific object, look at the class hierarchy, view any associations, run methods, and edit properties for an object.
- The WMI Event Registration allows you to create, view, and configure event consumers.
- The WMI Event Viewer displays events of configured event consumers.

The web-based WMI tools can be obtained separately from the WMI SDK at: *http://www.microsoft.com/downloads/details.aspx?FamilyID=6430f853-1120-48db-8cc5-f2abdc3ed314.*

WMI SDK

The WMI SDK provides the complete WMI reference documentation, along with numerous sample scripts and programs. It also includes the web-based WMI tools described in the previous section. The WMI SDK can be downloaded from the Platform SDK site located at: *http://www.microsoft.com/msdownload/platformsdk/sdkupdate/.*

Scriptomatic Version 2.0; WMI Scripting Tool

The Microsoft "Scripting Guys" have made an extremely useful tool freely available for creating basic WMI scripts. It allows you to browse a machine's namespaces and classes to select the items you are interested in and then generates a basic script to display the associated properties. You have the option to create scripts in several scripting languages, including VBScript, Perl, JScript, and Python. This tool can be downloaded from the Microsoft website and is located at: *http://www.microsoft.com/downloads/details.aspx?FamilyID=09dfc342-648b-4119-b7eb-783b0f7d1178.*

Manipulating Services

Querying services is simple to do with WMI. The `Win32_Service` class is the WMI representation of a service. The `Win32_Service` class contains a lot of property methods that provide information about the service; the most useful ones have been listed in Table 27-2.

Table 27-2. Useful Win32_Service properties

Property	Description
AcceptPause	Returns a Boolean indicating whether the service can be paused.
AcceptStop	Returns a Boolean indicating whether the service can be stopped.
Description	Description of the service.
DisplayName	Display name of the service.
Name	Unique string identifier for the service.
PathName	Fully qualified path to the service executable.
Started	Boolean indicating whether the service has been started.
StartMode	String specifying the start mode of the service. Will be one of Automatic, Manual, or Disabled.
StartName	Account under which the service runs.
State	Current state of the service. Will be one of Stopped, Start Pending, Stop Pending, Running, Continue Pending, Pause Pending, Paused, or Unknown.

The following script retrieves all the running services on a machine. All we need to do is use a WQL query that finds all **Win32_Service** objects that have a state of "Running":

```
Option Explicit
Dim strComputer, objWMI, objServices, objService
strComputer = "."

Set objWMI = GetObject("winmgmts:\\" & strComputer & "\root\cimv2")
Set objServices = objWMI.ExecQuery _
    ("SELECT * FROM Win32_Service WHERE State = 'Running'")
For Each objService In objServices
   WScript.Echo objService.DisplayName
   WScript.Echo " Name: " & objService.Name
   WScript.Echo " PathName: " & objService.PathName
   WScript.Echo " Started: " & objService.Started
   WScript.Echo " StartMode: " & objService.StartMode
   WScript.Echo " StartName: " & objService.StartName
   WScript.Echo " State: " & objService.State
   WScript.Echo ""
Next
WScript.Echo "The script has completed successfully."
```

Before you can start to manipulate the status of a service, you have to be able to find any dependent services. A dependent service requires the parent service to be running while it is running. If you try to stop the parent service without first stopping all dependent services, you will get an error. The following example shows how to find all dependent services for the IIS Admin service:

```
Option Explicit
Dim strService, strComputer, objWMI, objServiceList, objService
strService = "IISADMIN"
strComputer = "."

Set objWMI = GetObject("winmgmts:\\" & strComputer & "\root\cimv2")
```

```
Set objServiceList = objWMI.ExecQuery( _
        "Associators of {Win32_Service.Name='" & strService & "'} " & _
        "Where AssocClass=Win32_DependentService Role=Antecedent" )

WScript.Echo "List of dependent services for " & strService & ":"
For Each objService In objServiceList
  WScript.Echo " " & objService.DisplayName
Next
WScript.Echo "The script has completed successfully."
```

You may have noticed the WQL query in this example is a little different than the ones we've used so far. We used something called the *Associators* for a class. One of the fundamental concepts within WMI is class association, which allows you to perform queries to retrieve objects that have dependencies or associations to a given object. *Associators* come into play in lot of situations, but a great example of them is with service dependencies. Some services are dependent on others in order to run. Using the `Associators of` clause within a WQL query allows you to find each dependent service.

Now that we can get a list of a service's dependent services, we can write scripts to stop, start, and restart a service. Table 27-3 lists the useful methods available to the `Win32_Service` class.

Table 27-3. Useful Win32_Service methods

Property	Description
ChangeStartMode	Changes the start mode for the service. Pass in Automatic, Manual, or Disabled.
PauseService	Pause a service.
ResumeService	Resume a service.
StartService	Start a service.
StopService	Stop a service.

Example 27-1 shows how to restart a service. Because there is no `RestartService` method available in WMI, you have to simulate a restart by stopping all dependent services, stopping the target service, and then starting the target service and any dependent services.

Example 27-1. Using Win32_Service methods to simulate a RestartService method

```
Option Explicit
Dim strService, strComputer
Dim objWMI, objServiceList, objService

strService  = "IISADMIN"
strComputer = "."

WScript.Echo "Restarting " & strService & "..."

' Stop dependent services
Set objWMI = GetObject("winmgmts:\\" & strComputer & "\root\cimv2")
Set objServiceList = objWMI.ExecQuery("Associators of " _
```

```
                    & "{Win32_Service.Name='" & strService & "'} Where " _
                    & "AssocClass=Win32_DependentService " & "Role=Antecedent" )
For Each objService In objServiceList
    WScript.Echo " Stopping " & objService.Name
    objService.StopService()
Next
WScript.Sleep 10000    ' Pause to allow services to stop

' Stop target service
Set objService = objWMI.Get("Win32_Service.Name='" & strService & "'")
WScript.Echo " Stopping " & objService.Name
objService.StopService()
WScript.Sleep 10000    ' Pause to allow service to stop

' Start target service
Set objService = objWMI.Get("Win32_Service.Name='" & strService & "'")
WScript.Echo " Starting " & objService.Name
objService.StartService()
WScript.Sleep 10000    ' Pause to allow service to start

' Start dependent services
Set objServiceList = objWMI.ExecQuery("Associators of " _
                    & "{Win32_Service.Name='" & strService & "'} Where " _
                    & "AssocClass=Win32_DependentService " & "Role=Antecedent" )
For Each objService In objServiceList
    WScript.Echo " Starting " & objService.Name
    objService.StartService()
Next
WScript.Echo "The script has completed successfully."
```

Querying the Event Logs

The Event Logs are typically a system administrator's first line of inquiry when trying to troubleshoot problems. Because they are so important, it is also important to see how we can make use of them with WMI. The two major components that we need to be concerned with are the Event Logs themselves and the events contained within each Event Log. We will first focus on properties of Event Logs.

The Win32_NTEventLogFile class represents an Event Log. Table 27-4 contains several Win32_NTEventLogFile properties that can be used to query or modify properties of an Event Log.

Table 27-4. Useful Win32_NTEventLogFile properties

Property	Description
FileSize	Size of the Event Log file in bytes.
LogFileName	Standard name used for describing the Event Log (e.g., Application).
MaxFileSize	Max size in bytes that the Event Log file can reach. This is a writeable property.
Name	Fully qualified path to the Event Log file.
NumberOfRecords	Total number of records in the Event Log.

Property	Description
OverwriteOutDated	Number of days after which events can be overwritten. This is a writeable property with 0 indicating to overwrite events as needed, 1–365 being the number of days to wait before overwriting, and 4294967295 indicating that events should never be overwritten.
OverwritePolicy	Text description of the overwrite policy (as specified by the OverwriteOutDated property). Can be one of WhenNeeded, OutDated, or Never.
Sources	Array of registered sources that may write entries to the Event Log.

Let's look at an example that displays all of the properties listed in Table 27-4 for each Event Log and sets the MaxFileSize and OverwriteOutDated properties if they have not already been set to the correct values. Since we want to iterate over all Event Logs, we will pass Win32_NTEventLogFile to the InstancesOf method. Example 27-2 shows how to accomplish this.

Example 27-2. Displaying properties of the Event Log using Win32_NTEventLogFile

```
Option Explicit
Dim strComputer, intMaxFileSize, intOverwriteOutDated
Dim objWMI, objELF, objEL

strComputer = "."
intMaxFileSize = 10 * 1024 * 1024    ' << 10MB
intOverwriteOutDated = 180           ' << 6 months

Set objWMI = GetObject("winmgmts:\\" & strComputer & "\root\cimv2")
Set objELF = objWMI.InstancesOf("Win32_NTEventLogFile")
' Iterate over each Event Log
For Each objEL In objELF
   WScript.Echo objEL.LogFileName & " Log:"
   WScript.Echo " FileSize: " & objEL.FileSize

   ' If the size has not been set yet, set it
   If objEL.MaxFileSize <> intMaxFileSize Then
      WScript.Echo " ** Setting MaxFileSize: " & intMaxFileSize & " (new) " & _
                 objEL.MaxFileSize & " (current)"
      objEL.MaxFileSize = intMaxFileSize
      objEL.Put_
   Else
      WScript.Echo " MaxFileSize: " & objEL.MaxFileSize
   End If

   WScript.Echo " Name: " & objEL.Name
   WScript.Echo " NumberOfRecords: " & objEL.NumberOfRecords

   ' If the overwrite date has not been set, set it
   WScript.Echo " OverwritePolicy: " & objEL.OverwritePolicy
   If objEL.OverwriteOutDated <> intOverwriteOutDated Then
      WScript.Echo " ** Setting OverwriteOutDated: " & _
                 intOverwriteOutDated & " (new) " & _
                 objEL.OverwriteOutDated & " (current)"
      objEL.OverwriteOutDated = intOverwriteOutdated
```

```
      objEL.Put_
    Else
       WScript.Echo " OverwriteOutDated: " & objEL.OverwriteOutDated
    End If

    WScript.Echo ""
Next
WScript.Echo "The script has completed successfully."
```

Note that for the MaxFileSize and OverwriteOutDated properties, we set them only if they haven't been set already. To set properties, simply set the property method equal to the new value. To commit the change, you must use the Put_ method. Using Put_ is very similar to SetInfo in ADSI. WMI implements a caching mechanism very similar to the Property Cache described in Chapter 22. If we did not call Put_, the new values would never have been written back to the system.

The Event Logs contain a wealth of information about the health and status of the system and hosted applications. With WMI, system administrators can write simple to complex queries to find specific events in any of the Event Logs. The Win32_NTLogEvent class represents individual event entries in an Event Log. Table 27-5 contains several useful properties that are available for Win32_NTLogEvent objects.

Table 27-5. Useful Win32_NTLogEvent properties

Property	Description
CategoryString	Category name if present.
EventCode	The event number (or ID) for the event.
EventType	Numeric value representing severity of the event. See Type for the string version.
LogFile	Event Log name the event is contained in. LogFile and RecordNumber are used as keys to uniquely identify an event.
Message	Event message text.
RecordNumber	The number associated with the event. RecordNumber is unique within an Event Log.
SourceName	Name of source that generated the error.
Type	String representing the severity of the event. Will be one of Error, Warning, Informational, Security audit success, or Security audit failure.
User	User that was logged on when event was generated.

In the next example, we will retrieve all events that match certain criteria. Let's say that we want to find all Information events in the System Event Log that have an event code of 5778 and were generated after November 1, 2005. The WQL for this query works out to be:

```
Select * from Win32_NTLogEvent
    Where Type = 'Information'
    And Logfile = 'System'
    and EventCode = 5778
    and TimeGenerated > '2005/11/01'
```

Once we have the WQL query, the rest of the code is very similar to many of the previous examples:

```
Option Explicit
Dim strComputer, objWMI, objEvents, objEvent
strComputer = "."

Set objWMI = GetObject("winmgmts:\\" & strComputer & "\root\cimv2")
Set objEvents = objWMI.ExecQuery _
    ("Select * from Win32_NTLogEvent Where Logfile = 'System' " & _
    "and EventCode = 5778 and Type = 'Information' " & _
    "and TimeGenerated > '20080801000000.000000-000' ")

WScript.Echo "Total events that match criteria: " & objEvents.Count
For Each objEvent In objEvents
    WScript.Echo " CategoryString: " & objEvent.CategoryString
    WScript.Echo " EventType: " & objEvent.EventType
    WScript.Echo " LogFile: " & objEvent.LogFile
    WScript.Echo " Message: " & objEvent.Message
    WScript.Echo " RecordNumber: " & objEvent.RecordNumber
    WScript.Echo " SourceName: " & objEvent.SourceName
    WScript.Echo " TimeGenerated: " & objEvent.TimeGenerated
    WScript.Echo " Type: " & objEvent.Type
    WScript.Echo " User: " & objEvent.User
    WScript.Echo ""
Next
WScript.Echo "The script has completed successfully."
```

Monitoring Trusts

New to Windows Server 2003 is the Trustmon WMI provider. The Trustmon provider allows you to query the list of trusts supported on a domain controller and determine if they are working correctly. The Trustmon provider consists of three classes, but the primary one is the `Microsoft_DomainTrustStatus` class, which represents each trust the domain controller knows about. The Trustmon provider is contained under the root \MicrosoftActiveDirectory namespace. Note that this namespace is different than for the Active Directory provider, which is contained under root\directory\ldap.

Table 27-6 provides a list of the property methods available to this class.

Table 27-6. Microsoft_DomainTrustStatus properties

Property	Description
Flatname	NetBIOS name for the domain.
SID	SID for the domain.
TrustAttributes	Flag indicating special properties of the trust. Can be any combination of the following: • 0x1 (nontransitive) • 0x2 (uplevel clients only) • 0x40000 (tree parent)

Property	Description
	• 0x80000 (tree root)
TrustDCName	Name of the domain controller the trust is set up with.
TrustDirection	Integer representing direction of the trust. Valid values include:
	• 1 (inbound)
	• 2 (outbound)
	• 3 (bidirectional)
TrustedDomain	Naming of trusted domain.
TrustIsOK	Boolean indicating whether the trust is functioning properly.
TrustStatus	Integer representing the status for the trust. 0 indicates no failure.
TrustStatusString	Textual description of status for the trust.
TrustType	Integer representing the type of trust. Valid values include:
	• 1 (downlevel)
	• 2 (uplevel)
	• 3 (Kerberos realm)
	• 4 (DCE)

As you can see from Table 27-6, the `Microsoft_DomainTrustStatus` class provides just about all the information you'd want to know concerning a trust. The following example shows how easy it is to enumerate all the trusts using this class:

```
Option Explicit
Dim strComputer, objWMI, objTrusts, objTrust
strComputer - "."

Set objWMI = GetObject("winmgmts:\\" & strComputer & _
                "\root\MicrosoftActiveDirectory")
Set objTrusts = objWMI.ExecQuery("Select * from Microsoft_DomainTrustStatus")

For Each objTrust In objTrusts
  WScript.Echo objTrust.TrustedDomain
  WScript.Echo " TrustedAttributes: " & objTrust.TrustAttributes
  WScript.Echo " TrustedDCName: "     & objTrust.TrustedDCName
  WScript.Echo " TrustedDirection: "  & objTrust.TrustDirection
  WScript.Echo " TrustIsOk: "         & objTrust.TrustIsOK
  WScript.Echo " TrustStatus: "       & objTrust.TrustStatus
  WScript.Echo " TrustStatusString: " & objTrust.TrustStatusString
  WScript.Echo " TrustType: "         & objTrust.TrustType
  WScript.Echo ""
Next
WScript.Echo "The script has completed successfully."
```

Next, let's illustrate a script that finds any trust that has some kind of failure. All we need to do is modify the WQL query in the previous example to include a `whereTrustIsOk = False` clause. We then print out the `TrustStatusString` property, which will return a description of the failure:

```
Option Explicit
Dim strComputer, objWMI, objTrusts, objTrust
strComputer = "."

Set objWMI = GetObject("winmgmts:\\" & strComputer & _
                    "\root\MicrosoftActiveDirectory")
Set objTrusts = objWMI.ExecQuery("Select * from Microsoft_DomainTrustStatus " & _
                    "where TrustIsOk = False ")

If objTrusts.Count = 0 Then
   WScript.Echo "There are no trust failures"
Else
  For Each objTrust In objTrusts
     WScript.Echo objTrust.TrustedDomain & " - " & objTrust.TrustStatusString
     WScript.Echo ""
   Next
End If
WScript.Echo "The script has completed successfully."
```

One of the neat features of the Trustmon provider is that it is configurable. Through WMI, you can modify what type of checks it does to determine trust failures and also how long to cache information it retrieves. All of this is done with the `Microsoft_Trust Provider` class. Table 27-7 contains a list of all property methods for this class.

Table 27-7. Microsoft_TrustProvider properties

Property	Description
TrustListLifetime	Number of minutes to cache the last trust enumeration (20 is the default).
TrustStatusLifetime	Number of minutes to cache the last trust status request (3 is the default).
TrustCheckLevel	Number representing the type of check to perform against each trust during enumeration (2 is the default). Valid values include:
	• 0 (enumerate only)
	• 1 (enumerate with SC_QUERY)
	• 2 (enumerate with password check)
	• 3 (enumerate with SC_RESET)
ReturnAll	Boolean indicating whether both trusting and trusted domains are enumerated. True is the default, which indicates to check both trusting and trusted domains.

Now we will show a simple script that changes the default settings for the Trustmon provider. In the following example, we set the `TrustListLifetime` to 15 minutes, the `TrustStatusLifetime` to five minutes, and the `TrustCheckLevel` to 1:

```
Option Explicit
Dim strComputer, objTrustProv
strComputer = "."

Set objTrustProv = GetObject("winmgmts:\\" & strComputer & _
                    "\root\MicrosoftActiveDirectory:Microsoft_TrustProvider=@")

objTrustProv.TrustListLifetime    = 15    ' 15 minutes
```

```
objTrustProv.TrustStatusLifetime = 5      ' 5 minutes
objTrustProv.TrustCheckLevel     = 1      ' Enumerate with SC_QUERY
objTrustProv.Put_
WScript.Echo "The script has completed successfully."
```

The Trustmon provider is a great example of how to utilize WMI in the Active Directory space. What previously could only have been done with command-line utilities or MMC snap-ins can now be done programmatically very easily.

Monitoring Replication

The WMI Replication provider is another good example of how Microsoft is leveraging WMI to help with monitoring Active Directory. Like the Trustmon provider, the Replication provider is only available with Windows Server 2003 and later, and is contained under the root\MicrosoftActiveDirectory namespace. It provides classes to list the replication partners for a domain controller, view the supported Naming Contexts for a domain controller, and also see the pending replication operations.

Table 27-8 contains some of the more useful properties for the MSAD_ReplNeighbor class, which represents a replication partner (or neighbor) for a given domain controller.

Table 27-8. Useful MSAD_ReplNeighbor properties

Property	Description
IsDeletedSourceDsa	Boolean indicating whether the source DC has been deleted.
LastSyncResult	Number representing the result of the last sync operation with this neighbor. A value of 0 indicates success.
NamingContextDN	DN of the Naming Context for which the partners replicate.
NumConsecutiveSyncFailures	Number of consecutive sync failures between the two neighbors.
SourceDsaCN	CN of the replication neighbor.
SourceDsaSite	Site the replication neighbor is in.
TimeOfLastSyncAttempt	Time of the last sync attempt.
TimeOfLastSyncSuccess	Time of last successful sync attempt.

There are actually several property methods available other than what is shown in Table 27-8, so in the following example, we will enumerate all the replication neighbors and print out every property available to the MSAD_ReplNeighbor class:

```
Option Explicit
Dim strComputer, objWMI, objReplNeighbors, objReplNeighbor, objProp
strComputer = "."

Set objWMI = GetObject("winmgmts:\\" & strComputer & _
                    "\root\MicrosoftActiveDirectory")
Set objReplNeighbors = objWMI.ExecQuery("Select * from MSAD_ReplNeighbor")

For Each objReplNeighbor In objReplNeighbors
```

```
    WScript.Echo objReplNeighbor.SourceDsaCN & "/" & _
            objReplNeighbor.NamingContextDN & ":"
   For Each objProp In objReplNeighbor.Properties_
      If IsNull(objProp.Value) Then
         WScript.Echo " " & objProp.Name & " : NULL"
      Else
         WScript.Echo " " & objProp.Name & " : " & objProp.Value
      End If
   Next
   WScript.Echo ""
Next
WScript.Echo "The script has completed successfully."
```

Now that we can find all of the replication neighbors for a given domain controller, we will take a look at any outstanding replication operations. The MSAD_ReplPendingOp class represents a pending replication operation. The class has several property methods, and some of the more useful ones are listed in Table 27-9.

Table 27-9. Useful MSAD_ReplPendingOp properties

Property	Description
DsaDN	DN of replication neighbor
NamingContextDN	DN of Naming Context that holds the object being synced
PositionInQ	Number representing the position in the replication queue
TimeEnqueued	Date representing when operation was put in the queue

The next example is not much different from most of our others. We simply query all MSAD_ReplPendingOp objects for a particular host. If zero are returned, that signifies there are no pending replication operations on the host:

```
Option Explicit
Dim strComputer, objWMI, objRepOps, objRepOp
strComputer = "."

Set objWMI = GetObject("winmgmts:\\" & strComputer & _
                   "\root\MicrosoftActiveDirectory")
Set objRepOps = objWMI.ExecQuery("Select * from MSAD_ReplPendingOp")

If objRepOps.Count = 0 Then
  WScript.Echo "There are no pending replication operations"
Else
  For Each objRepOp in objRepOps
    WScript.Echo objRepOp.DsaDN
    WScript.Echo objRepOp.NamingContextDN
    WScript.Echo objRepOp.PositionInQ
    WScript.Echo objRepOp.TimeEnqueued
  Next
End If
WScript.Echo "The script has completed successfully."
```

Summary

In this chapter, we gave a quick introduction into the WMI architecture and the concepts behind it. We then covered some of the tools available for querying and modifying WMI data. Next, we went through several examples for querying and manipulating services and the Event Logs. The last part of the chapter covered the WMI hooks into Active Directory, including the WMI providers for Trustmon and Replication monitoring.

In the next chapter, we will put our WMI knowledge to use as we work with the WMI DNS Provider. We will use WMI to configure Microsoft DNS server settings programmatically and manipulate zones and resource records.

## CHAPTER 28

Scripting DNS

DNS is a core technology of Active Directory that cannot be overlooked. Although features such as Active Directory Integrated DNS can take a lot of the hassle of managing DNS servers and zones out of your hands, you still have to set up the initial zone configurations. Unfortunately, lack of a good DNS API has always been a big gap for managing a Microsoft DNS server environment. The only way to automate maintenance and management of Microsoft DNS has been by executing Dnscmd commands from within a batch, VBScript, or Perl script. Over time, Microsoft has continued to improve Dnscmd, and as of Windows 2000, it provides just about every option you need to manage DNS server configuration, zones, and resource records using a command line. In Windows Server 2003, it even allows you to manage Application Partitions! Microsoft also provides the DNS MMC snap-in for those who want to manage DNS via a GUI, although it is not very suitable for managing large environments or making bulk modifications.

Microsoft's answer to the DNS API issue is WMI. As explained in Chapter 27, WMI is one of Microsoft's APIs for managing and monitoring systems and services. With the WMI DNS provider, you have complete programmatic control over a Microsoft DNS environment, much as you do with Dnscmd from a command line.

In this chapter, we will cover the WMI DNS provider at length, including the properties and methods available for the primary WMI DNS classes. Several sample scripts will be shown, which will give you a head start on developing scripts to manage your own DNS environment.

DNS Provider Overview

The DNS WMI provider was first released as part of the Windows 2000 Resource Kit Supplement 1, but unfortunately it was not ready for prime time. That version was buggy, did not include all the documented features, and in several cases behaved differently than what the documentation described. Also, since the DNS provider was included as part of a Resource Kit, it was not fully supported by Microsoft, which means that if you encountered problems, you were largely on your own. That said, much of the functionality you probably need is present in the Windows 2000 version, so it may be suitable. You can download the Windows 2000 DNS provider separately from the Resource Kit via FTP from *ftp://ftp.microsoft.com/reskit/win2000/dnsprov.zip*.

Beginning with Windows Server 2003, the DNS provider is fully functional and supported. It is installed automatically whenever you install the DNS Server service. You can also install it separately as described in the next section. This may be necessary when doing development with the provider on a machine that does not have the DNS Server installed.

 For our purposes, all sample code has been tested using the Windows Server 2008 DNS provider.

Installing the DNS Provider

You do not need to manually install the provider if you are installing the DNS Server service on a Windows Server 2003 or better server because it gets installed with the service.

If you downloaded the DNS provider files for Windows 2000 (*dnsschema.mof* and *dnsprov.dll*), you will first need to copy them to the *%SystemRoot%\System32\wbem* directory. Next, you'll need to compile the DNS managed object format (MOF) file by executing mofcomp *filename* from a command line. With Windows 2000, the DNS MOF file is named *dnsschema.mof*, and beginning with Windows Server 2003, it is called *dnsprov.mof*. The output of the command should look like the following:

```
C:\WINDOWS\system32\wbem>mofcomp dnsprov.mof
Microsoft (R) 32-bit MOF Compiler Version 5.2.3628.0
Copyright (c) Microsoft Corp. 1997-2001. All rights reserved.
Parsing MOF file: dnsprov.mof
MOF file has been successfully parsed
Storing data in the repository...
Done!
```

The last step is to register the DNS provider DLL by executing *regsvr32 dnsprov.dll* from a command line. You should see a dialog box with the following:

```
DllRegisterServer in dnsprov.dll succeeded.
```

At this point, you will be able to use the DNS provider from your scripts.

Managing DNS with the DNS Provider

The three main areas of interest when it comes to managing DNS include server configuration, zone management, and creation and deletion of resource records. The DNS provider has several classes to manipulate each of these components. With the MicrosoftDNS_Server class, you can manipulate server configuration settings, start and stop the DNS service, and initiate scavenging. The `MicrosoftDNS_Zone` class allows you to create, delete, and modify zone configuration. The `MicrosoftDNS_ResourceRecord` class and its child classes provide methods for manipulating the various resource record types. Each of these will be explained in more detail in the next few sections.

Several additional classes are also supported by the DNS provider to manage other aspects of DNS, including the root hints (`MicrosoftDNS_RootHints`), DNS cache (`MicrosoftDNS_Cache`), and server statistics (`MicrosoftDNS_Statistics`). For more information on these classes, including sample scripts in VBScript and Perl, check out the following section in the MSDN Library: *http://msdn.microsoft.com/en-us/library/ms682125(VS.85).aspx*.

Manipulating DNS Server Configuration

There are close to 50 different settings that can be configured on a Microsoft DNS server. They range from default scavenging and logging settings to settings that customize the DNS server behavior, such as how zone transfers will be sent to secondaries and whether to round-robin multiple A-record responses.

The DNS provider is mapped to the root\MicrosoftDNS namespace. A DNS server is represented by an instance of a `MicrosoftDNS_Server` class, which is derived from the `CIM_Service` class. Table 28-1 contains all the property methods available in the `MicrosoftDNS_Server` class.

Table 28-1. MicrosoftDNS_Server class properties

Property name	Property description
AddressAnswerLimit	Max number of records to return for address requests (e.g., A records).
AllowUpdate	Determines whether DDNS updates are allowed.
AutoCacheUpdate	Indicates whether the DNS server will dynamically attempt to update its root hints (also known as cache) file.
AutoConfigFileZones	Indicates which standard primary zones that are authoritative for the name of the DNS server must be updated when the name server changes.
BindSecondaries	Determines the format zone transfers (AXFR) will be sent as to non-Microsoft DNS servers.
BootMethod	Determines where the server will read its zone information.
DefaultAgingState	For AD-integrated zones, the default scavenging interval in hours.
DefaultNoRefreshInterval	For AD-integrated zones, the default no-refresh interval in hours.
DefaultRefreshInterval	For AD-integrated zones, the default refresh interval in hours.
DisableAutoReverseZones	Determines whether the server automatically creates reverse zones.
DisjointsNets	Indicates whether the default port binding for a socket used to send queries to remote DNS servers can be overridden.
DsAvailable	Indicates whether Active Directory is available on the server.
DsPollingInterval	For AD-integrated zones, the interval in seconds to poll Active Directory for updates.

Property name	Property description
DsTombstoneInterval	For AD-integrated zones, the length of time in seconds that tombstoned records (i.e., deleted) records should remain in Active Directory.
EdnsCacheTimeout	Length of time, in seconds, the cached EDNS version information is cached.
EnableDirectoryPartitionSupport	Flag indicating whether application partition support has been enabled.
EnableDnsSec	Flag indicating whether DNSSEC resource records are returned if queried.
EnableEDnsProbes	When TRUE, the DNS server always responds with OPT resource records according to RFC 2671, unless the remote server has indicated it does not support EDNS in a prior exchange. When FALSE, the DNS server responds to queries with OPTs only if OPTs are sent in the original query.
EventLogLevel	Determines the type of events (e.g., errors or warnings) that will be logged to the DNS Event Log.
ForwardDelegations	Determines whether queries to delegated subzones are forwarded.
Forwarders	List of IPs the server forwards queries to.
ForwardingTimeout	Time in seconds to wait for a response from a forwarded query.
IsSlave	Indicates whether the DNS server is a slave.
ListenAddresses	List of addresses the DNS server can receive queries on.
LocalNetPriority	If TRUE, records for IPs on the same net are given a higher priority.
LogFileMaxSize	Max size in bytes of the DNS server log.
LogFilePath	Filename and path to DNS server log.
LogIPFilterList	List of IPs used to filter entries written to the DNS server log.
LogLevel	Determines what events should be written to the system log.
LooseWildcarding	Indicates whether the server supports wildcarding (e.g., * MX records).
MaxCacheTTL	Max time in seconds to leave a recursive query in the local cache.
MaxNegativeCacheTTL	Max time in seconds to leave a recursive query that resulted in an error in the local cache.
Name	FQDN or IP of server.
NameCheckFlag	Indicates the set of eligible characters to be used in DNS names.
NoRecursion	Flag indicating whether the server will perform recursive lookups.
RecursionRetry	Time in seconds before retrying a recursive lookup.
RecursionTimeout	Time in seconds before the DNS server gives up recursive query.
RoundRobin	Flag indicating whether the server will round-robin addresses returned from a query that returns multiple A records.
RpcProtocol	Protocol to run administrative RPC over.
ScavengingInterval	Interval in hours between initiating scavenges.
SecureResponses	Indicates whether the DNS server exclusively saves records of names in the same subtree as the server that provided them.
SendPort	Port on which the DNS server sends UDP queries to other servers.
ServerAddresses	List of IP addresses for the server.

Property name	Property description
StrictFileParsing	Indicates whether the DNS server parses zone file strictly, which means if bad data is encountered, the zone will fail to load.
UpdateOptions	Flag that restricts the type of records that can be updated via DDNS.
Version	DNS server version.
WriteAuthorityNS	Flag indicating whether the server includes NS and SOA records in the authority section on successful response.
XfrConnectTimeout	Number of seconds server waits for a successful TCP connection to a remote server when attempting a zone transfer.

The `MicrosoftDNS_Server` class also provides a few methods to initiate certain actions on the DNS server. Perhaps two of the most useful are `StartService` and `StopService`, which allow you to start and stop the DNS service. Table 28-2 contains the list of methods available to the `MicrosoftDNS_Server` class.

Table 28-2. MicrosoftDNS_Server class methods

Method name	Method description
GetDistinguishedName	For AD-integrated zones, gets the DN of the zone
StartScavenging	Starts the scavenging process for zones that have scavenging enabled
StartService	Starts the DNS service
StopService	Stops the DNS service

Listing a DNS Server's Properties

The first step in programmatically managing your DNS server configuration is to see what settings you currently have and determine whether any need to be modified. With WMI, it is really easy to list all properties for the server. The following example shows how to do it:

```
Option Explicit
Dim objDNS, objDNSServer, objProp, i
Set objDNS = GetObject("winMgmts:root\MicrosoftDNS")
' Replace the "." below with a server name to run
' this script against a remote server
Set objDNSServer = objDNS.Get("MicrosoftDNS_Server.Name="".""")

WScript.Echo objDNSServer.Properties_.Item("Name") & ":"
For Each objProp In objDNSServer.Properties_
  If IsNull(objProp.Value) Then
    WScript.Echo " " & objProp.Name & " : NULL"
  Else
    If objProp.IsArray = TRUE Then
      For I = LBound(objProp.Value) To UBound(objProp.Value)
        WScript.Echo " " & objProp.Name & " : " & objProp.Value(I)
      Next
    Else
```

```
        WScript.Echo " " & objProp.Name & " : " & objProp.Value
      End If
    End If
  Next
  WScript.Echo "The script has completed successfully."
```

After getting a WMI object for the DNS provider (**root\MicrosoftDNS**), we get a **MicrosoftDNS_Server** object by looking for the "." instance. Because there can only be one instance of **MicrosoftDNS_Server** running on any given computer, we do not need to worry about multiple objects. After getting a **MicrosoftDNS_Server** object, we iterate through all the properties of the object and print each one out. Note that we have added special checks for values that contain arrays to print each element of the array. In that case, we use **Lbound** and **Ubound** to iterate over all the values for the array.

Configuring a DNS server

Now that we can see what values have been set on our DNS server, we may want to change some of them. To do so is very straightforward. We simply need to set the property method (e.g., **EventLogLevel**) to the correct value. This example shows how it can be done:

```
Option Explicit

On Error Resume Next
Dim objDNS, objDNSServer

Set objDNS = GetObject("winMgmts:root\MicrosoftDNS")
Set objDNSServer = objDNS.Get("MicrosoftDNS_Server.Name="".""")

WScript.Echo objDNSServer.Name & ":"
objDNSServer.EventLogLevel = 4
objDNSServer.LooseWildcarding = True
objDNSServer.MaxCacheTTL = 900
objDNSServer.MaxNegativeCacheTTL = 60
objDNSServer.AllowUpdate = 3
objDNSServer.Put_

If Err Then
  WScript.Echo " Error occurred: " & Err.Description
Else
  WScript.Echo " Change successful"
End If
WScript.Echo "The script has completed successfully."
```

Note that we had to call **Put_** at the end. If we didn't, none of the changes would have been committed.

The preceding example only functions properly when run against Windows Server 2003 DNS servers.

Restarting the DNS Service

After making changes to DNS settings, you typically will need to restart the DNS service for them to take effect. We can utilize the StopService and StartService methods as shown in the following example to do this:

```
Option Explicit
On Error Resume Next
Dim objDNS, objDNSServer

Set objDNS = GetObject("winMgmts:root\MicrosoftDNS")
Set objDNSServer = objDNS.Get("MicrosoftDNS_Server.Name=""."""")

objDNSServer.StopService
If Err Then
  WScript.Echo "StopService failed: " & Err.Description
  WScript.Quit
End If

objDNSServer.StartService
If Err Then
  WScript.Echo "StartService failed: " & Err.Description
  WScript.Quit
End If

WScript.Echo "Restart successful"
```

DNS Server Configuration Check Script

Building on the examples we've used so far in this chapter, we can now move forward with writing a robust DNS server configuration check script. A configuration check script can be very important, especially in large environments where you may have many DNS servers. Unless you have a script that routinely checks the configuration on all of your DNS servers, it is very likely that those servers will not have an identical configuration. If this is true, when problems pop up over time, you may end up spending considerably more time troubleshooting because of the discrepancies between the servers.

To accomplish the configuration checking, we will store each setting in a VBScript Dictionary object. For those coming from other languages such as Perl, a Dictionary object is the VBScript analog of a hash or associative array. It is not extremely flexible but works well in situations such as what we need. Another option would be to store the settings in a text file and read them into a Dictionary object when the script starts up. Example 28-1 contains the configuration check code.

Example 28-1. DNS Server configuration check script

```
Option Explicit
On Error Resume Next

Dim arrServers
Dim strUsername, strPassword
Dim dicDNSConfig

' Array of DNS servers to check
arrServers = Array("dns1.mycorp.com","dns2.mycorp.com")

' User and password that can modify the config on the DNS servers
strUsername = "dnsadmin"
strPassword = "Securednspwd!"

' This dictionary object will contain the key value pairs for all the settings
' that you want to check and configure on the DNS servers
Set dicDNSConfig = CreateObject("Scripting.Dictionary")
dicDNSConfig.Add "AllowUpdate",            1
dicDNSConfig.Add "LooseWildCarding",       True
dicDNSConfig.Add "MaxCacheTTL",            900
dicDNSConfig.Add "MaxNegativeCacheTTL",    60
dicDNSConfig.Add "EventLogLevel",          0
dicDNSConfig.Add "StrictFileParsing",      True
dicDNSConfig.Add "DisableAutoReverseZones", True

Dim arrDNSConfigKeys
arrDNSConfigKeys = dicDNSConfig.keys

Dim objLocator
Set objLocator = CreateObject("WbemScripting.SWbemLocator")

Dim x, y, boolRestart
For x = LBound(arrServers) To UBound(arrServers)
  boolRestart = False

  WScript.Echo arrServers(x)

  Dim objDNS, objDNSServer
  Set objDNS = objLocator.ConnectServer(arrServers(x), "root\MicrosoftDNS", _
                                 strUserName, strPassword)
  Set objDNSServer = objDNS.Get("MicrosoftDNS_Server.Name="".""")

  For y = 0 To dicDNSConfig.Count - 1
    Dim strKey
    strKey = arrDNSConfigKeys(y)

    WScript.Echo "  Checking " & strKey
    If dicDNSConfig.Item(strKey) <> objDNSServer.Properties_.Item(strKey) Then
      objDNSServer.Properties_.Item(strKey).value = dicDNSConfig(strKey)
      objDNSServer.Put_
      boolRestart = True
      If Err Then
        WScript.Echo "    Error setting " & strKey & " : " & Err.Description
        WScript.Quit
```

```
         Else
            WScript.Echo "      " & strKey & " updated"
         End If
      End If
   Next

   If boolRestart Then
      objDNSServer.StopService
      If Err Then
         WScript.Echo "StopService failed: " & Err.Description
         WScript.Quit
      End If

      objDNSServer.StartService
      If Err Then
         WScript.Echo "StartService failed: " & Err.Description
         WScript.Quit
      End If
      WScript.Echo "Restarted"
   End If

   WScript.Echo ""
Next
WScript.Echo "The script has completed successfully."
```

Besides the use of the `Dictionary` object, most of the script is a combination of the other three examples shown so far in this chapter. We added a server array so that you can check multiple servers at once. Then for each server, the script simply checks each key in the `Dictionary` object to see whether the value for it matches that on the DNS server. If not, it modifies the server and commits the change via `Put_`. After it's done looping through all the settings, it restarts the DNS service if a change has been made to its configuration. If a change has not been made, it proceeds to the next server.

One enhancement that would make the process even more automated would be to dynamically query the list of DNS servers instead of hard coding them in an array. You would simply need to query the NS record for one or more zones that your DNS servers are authoritative for. As long as an NS record is added for each new name server, the script would automatically pick it up in subsequent runs. Later in the chapter, we will show how to query DNS with the DNS provider.

Creating and Manipulating Zones

The `MicrosoftDNS_Zone` class provides a plethora of properties and methods to aid in managing your zones. Even if you are using AD-integrated zones, which help reduce the amount of work it takes to maintain DNS, you will inevitably need to configure settings on a zone or create additional zones. Tables 28-3 and 28-4 present the list of available properties and methods for the `MicrosoftDNS_Zone` class.

Table 28-3. MicrosoftDNS_Zone class properties

Property name	Property description
Aging	Specifies aging and scavenging behavior. Zero indicates scavenging is disabled.
AllowUpdate	Flag indicating whether dynamic updates are allowed.
AutoCreated	Flag indicating whether the zone was auto-created.
AvailForScavengeTime	Specifies the time when the server may attempt scavenging the zone.
DataFile	Name of zone file.
DisableWINSRecordReplication	If TRUE, WINS record replication is disabled.
DsIntegrated	Specified if zone is AD integrated.
ForwarderSlave	Indicates whether the DNS server acts as a slave when resolving the names for the specified forward zone. Applicable to Forward zones only.
ForwarderTimeout	Indicates the time, in seconds, a DNS server forwarding a query for the name under the forward zone waits for resolution from the forwarder before attempting to resolve the query itself. This parameter is applicable to the Forward zones only.
LastSuccessfulSoaCheck	Number of seconds since the beginning of January 1, 1970 GMT, since the SOA serial number for the zone was last checked.
LastSuccessfulXfr	Number of seconds since the beginning of January 1, 1970 GMT, since the zone was last transferred from a master server.
LocalMasterServers	Local IP addresses of the master DNS servers for this zone. If set, these masters override the MasterServers found in Active Directory.
MasterServers	IP addresses of the master DNS servers for this zone.
NoRefreshInterval	Specifies the time interval between the last update of a record's timestamp and the earliest moment when the timestamp can be refreshed.
Notify	If set to 1, the master server will notify secondaries of zone updates.
NotifyServers	IP address of DNS servers to notify when changes occur to this zone
Paused	Flag indicating whether the zone is paused and therefore not responding to requests.
RefreshInterval	Interval indicated how often records with nonzero timestamps are expected to be refreshed. Records that are not refreshed in this time window may be scavenged.
Reverse	If TRUE, zone is a reverse (in-addr.arpa) zone. If FALSE, zone is a forward zone.
ScavengeServers	Array of strings that enumerates the list of IP addresses of DNS servers that are allowed to perform scavenging of stale records of this zone. If the list is not specified, any primary DNS server authoritative for the zone is allowed to scavenge the zone when other prerequisites are met.
SecondaryServers	Array of strings enumerating IP addresses of DNS servers allowed to receive this zone through zone replication.
SecureSecondaries	Flag indicating whether zone transfers are allowed only to servers specified in `Secondar iesIPAddressesArray`.
Shutdown	If TRUE, zone has expired (or shutdown).
UseWins	Flag indicating whether zone uses WINS lookups.

Property name	Property description
ZoneType	Type of zone. It will be either DS Integrated, Primary, or Secondary.

Table 28-4. MicrosoftDNS_Zone class methods

Method name	Method description
AgeAllRecords	Age part or all of a zone.
ChangeZoneType	Convert zone to one of the following types: DS integrated, Primary, Secondary, Stub, Stub-DS integrated, or Forward.
CreateZone	Create a new zone.
ForceRefresh	Forces secondary to update its zone from master.
GetDistinguishedName	Get distinguished name of the zone.
PauseZone	Causes the DNS server to not respond to queries for the zone.
ReloadZone	Reload the contents of the zone. This may be necessary after making changes to a zone that you want to take effect immediately.
ResetSecondaries	Specify list of secondaries.
ResumeZone	Causes the DNS server to start responding to queries for the zone again.
UpdateFromDS	Reloads the zone information from Active Directory. This is only valid for AD-integrated zones.
WriteBackZone	Save zone data to a file.

Creating a Zone

Creating a zone with the DNS provider is a straightforward operation. You simply need to get a WMI object for the DNS namespace, instantiate an object from the `MicrosoftDNS_Zone` class, and call `CreateZone` on that object. The next example shows how to do this:

```
Option Explicit
On Error Resume Next

Dim strNewZone, objDNS, objDNSZone, strNull
strNewZone = "mycorp.com."

Set objDNS = GetObject("winMgmts:root\MicrosoftDNS")
Set objDNSZone = objDNS.Get("MicrosoftDNS_Zone")
' Zone type 0 is a primary zone
strNull = objDNSZone.CreateZone(strNewZone, 0, True)

If Err Then
  WScript.Echo "Error occurred creating zone: " & Err.Description
Else
  WScript.Echo "Zone created..."
End If
```

The three parameters we passed into `CreateZone()` include the zone name, zone type flag, and DS-integrated flag. When the DS-integrated flag is set to true, the primary zone will be AD-integrated; if it is false, it will be a standard primary zone. At the time of this writing, Microsoft had conflicting documentation about these parameters and their valid values.

Configuring a Zone

Configuring a zone is not too different from configuring a server. The primary difference is how you instantiate a `MicrosoftDNS_Zone` object. To use the `Get()` method on a WMI (`SWbemServices`) object, you have to specify the keys for the class you want to instantiate. For the `MicrosoftDNS_Zone` class, the keys include `ContainerName`, `DnsServerName`, and `Name`. In this case, `ContainerName` and `Name` are the name of the zone. We retrieve the `DnsServerName` by getting a `MicrosoftDNS_Server` object as we've done earlier in the chapter.

Example 28-2 first lists all of the properties of the *mycorp.com.* zone before it modifies the `AllowUpdate` property and commits the change.

Example 28-2. Configuring a zone

```
Option Explicit
On Error Resume Next

Dim strZone, objDNS, objDNSServer, objDNSZone, objProp
strZone = "mycorp.com."

Set objDNS = GetObject("winMgmts:root\MicrosoftDNS")
Set objDNSServer = objDNS.Get("MicrosoftDNS_Server.Name="".""")
Set objDNSZone = objDNS.Get("MicrosoftDNS_Zone.ContainerName=""" & strZone & _
                            """,DnsServerName=""" & objDNSServer.Name & _
                            """,Name=""" & strZone & """")

' List all of the properties of the zone
WScript.Echo objDNSZone.Name
For Each objProp In objDNSZone.Properties_
  If IsNull(objProp.Value) Then
    WScript.Echo " " & objProp.Name & " : NULL"
  Else
    If objProp.IsArray = TRUE Then
      For I = LBound(objProp.Value) To UBound(objProp.Value)
        WScript.Echo " " & objProp.Name & " : " & objProp.Value(I)
      Next
    Else
      WScript.Echo " " & objProp.Name & " : " & objProp.Value
    End If
  End If
Next

' Modify the zone
objDNSZone.AllowUpdate = 1
objDNSZone.Put_

WScript.Echo ""
```

```
If Err Then
  WScript.Echo "Error occurred: " & Err.Description
Else
  WScript.Echo "Change successful"
End If
```

Listing the Zones on a Server

The last zone example we will show lists the configured zones on a specific DNS server. To make the following example a little more robust, we've added logic to make the script configurable so it can be run against any DNS server. That is accomplished by using the ConnectServer method on the SWbemLocator object:

```
Option Explicit
Dim strServer, strUsername, strPassword
strServer = "dns1.mycorp.com"
strUsername = "dnsadmin"
strPassword = "Securednspwd!"

Dim objLocator, objDNS, objDNSServer, objZones, objZone
Set objLocator = CreateObject("WbemScripting.SWbemLocator")
Set objDNS = objLocator.ConnectServer(strServer, "root\MicrosoftDNS", _
                                 strUsername, strPassword)
Set objDNSServer = objDNS.Get("MicrosoftDNS_Server.Name=""."""")
Set objZones = objDNS.ExecQuery("Select * from MicrosoftDNS_Zone " & _
                        "Where DnsServerName = '" & _
                        objDNSServer.Name & "'")
WScript.Echo objDNSServer.Name
For Each objZone In objZones
  WScript.Echo " " & objZOne.Name
Next
WScript.Echo "The script has completed successfully."
```

To retrieve the list of zones, we used a WQL query with ExecQuery to find all MicrosoftDNS_Zone objects that had a DnsServerName equal to the name of the server we are connecting to.

Creating and Manipulating Resource Records

Resource records are the basic unit of information in DNS. A DNS server's primary job is to respond to queries for resource records. Most people don't realize they are generating resource record queries with nearly every network-based operation they do, including accessing a website, pinging a host via its *Fully Qualified Domain Name* (FQDN), or logging into Active Directory.

Resource records come in many different flavors or types. Each type corresponds to a certain type of name or address lookup. Each record type also has additional information encoded with the record that represents things such as the *time to live* (TTL) of the record. The following is a textual example of what a CNAME record looks like:

```
www.mycorp.com.  1800  IN  CNAME  www1.mycorp.com.
```

Or, more generically:

```
Owner  TTL  Class  Type  RR-Data
```

Now let's break down the record into its individual parts:

Owner
> The owner of the resource record. This field is typically what is specified during a query for the particular type.

TTL
> The time to live, or length of time a nonauthoritative DNS server should cache the record. After the TTL expires, a nonauthoritative server should requery for an authoritative answer.

Class
> Resource record classification. In nearly all cases, this will be "IN" for Internet.

Type
> Name of the resource record type. Each type has a standard name that is used in zones (e.g., CNAME, A, PTR, SRV).

RR-Data
> Resource record specific data. When you perform a query, you are typically looking for the information returned as part of the RR-Data.

The WMI DNS provider fully supports querying and manipulating resource records. In Tables 28-5 and 28-6, the supported properties and methods are listed for the `Micro softDNS_ResourceRecord` class, which implements a generic interface for resource records.

Table 28-5. MicrosoftDNS_ResourceRecord class properties

Property name	Property description
ContainerName	Name of container (e.g., zone name) that holds the RR
DnsServerName	FQDN of the server that contains the RR
DomainName	FQDN of the domain that contains the RR
OwnerName	Owner of the RR
RecordClass	Class of the RR; 1 represents IN
RecordData	Resource record data
TextRepresentation	Textual representation of the RR—e.g., *www.mycorp.com.* 1800 IN CNAME *www1.mycorp.com*
Timestamp	Time RR was last refreshed
TTL	Time to live or maximum time a DNS server is supposed to cache the RR

Table 28-6. MicrosoftDNS_ResourceRecord class methods

Method name	Method description
CreateInstanceFromTextRepresentation	Creates a new instance of a MicrosoftDNS_ResourceRecord subclass based on the textual representation of the resource record, server name, and container or zone name. A reference to the new object is returned as an out parameter.
GetObjectByTextRepresentation	Gets an instance of the appropriate MicrosoftDNS_ResourceRecord subclass as specified by the textual representation of the resource record, server name, and container or zone name.

The MicrosoftDNS_ResourceRecord class by itself is not enough. There are over two dozen different types of resource records with many having additional fields that would not have corresponding methods in the generic interface. To solve this problem, subclasses of MicrosoftDNS_ResourceRecord were created for each supported record type. Each subclass provides specific methods to access any field supported by the resource record type. Each supported resource record has a subclass with a name in the format of MicrosoftDNS_<RR Type>Type.

To show just how different resource records can be, let's take a look at an A record:

```
www.mycorp.com.  1800  IN  A  192.10.4.5
```

Now let's compare that with an SRV record:

```
_ldap._tcp.dc._msdcs.mycorp.com 1800  IN  SRV  0 100 389 dc1.mycorp.com.
```

As you can see, the SRV record has several additional fields. By using the MicrosoftDNS_SRVType subclass, we can access each field with methods provided by the class.

The complete list of supported resource record types is provided in Table 28-7.

Table 28-7. DNS provider supported resource records

Resource record type	DNS provider class	RFC	Description
A	MicrosoftDNS_Atype	RFC1035	Name-to-IPv4 address mapping
AAAA	MicrosoftDNS_AAAAType	RFC1886	Name-to-IPv6 address mapping
AFSDB	MicrosoftDNS_AFSDBType	RFC1183	Andrew File System (AFS) Database Server record
ATMA	MicrosoftDNS_ATMAType	N/A	ATM-address-to-name mapping
CNAME	MicrosoftDNS_CNAMEType	RFC1035	Canonical (alias) name
HINFO	MicrosoftDNS_HINFOType	RFC1035	Host information
ISDN	MicrosoftDNS_ISDNType	RFC1183	Integrated services digital network (ISDN) record
KEY	MicrosoftDNS_KEYType	RFC2535	KEY record
MB	MicrosoftDNS_MBType	RFC1035	Mailbox record
MD	MicrosoftDNS_MDType	RFC1035	Mail agent
MF	MicrosoftDNS_MFType	RFC1035	Mail forwarding agent
MG	MicrosoftDNS_MGType	RFC1035	Mail group record

Resource record type	DNS provider class	RFC	Description
MINFO	MicrosoftDNS_MINFOType	RFC1035	Mail information record
MR	MicrosoftDNS_MRType	RFC1035	Mailbox rename record
MX	MicrosoftDNS_MXType	RFC1035	Mail exchanger
NS	MicrosoftDNS_NSType	RFC1035	Name server
NXT	MicrosoftDNS_NXTType	RFC2535	Next record
PTR	MicrosoftDNS_PTRType	RFC1035	Address-to-name mapping record
RP	MicrosoftDNS_RPTType	RFC1183	Responsible person
RT	MicrosoftDNS_RTType	RFC1183	Route through record
SIG	MicrosoftDNS_SIGType	RFC2535	Signature record
SOA	MicrosoftDNS_SOAType	RFC1035	Start of authority
SRV	MicrosoftDNS_SRVType	RFC2052	Service record
TXT	MicrosoftDNS_TXTType	RFC1035	Text record
WINS	MicrosoftDNS_WINSType	N/A	WINS server
WINSR	MicrosoftDNS_WINSRType	N/A	WINS reverse-lookup
WKS	MicrosoftDNS_WKSType	RFC1035	Well-known services
X25	MicrosoftDNS_X25Type	RFC1183	X.121 Address-to-name mapping

Finding Resource Records in a Zone

With the marriage of DNS and WMI, querying DNS has never been so easy. By using WQL, you can write complex query routines that would not have been possible previously. To list all of the resource records on a server, you simply need to execute the WQL query select * from MicrosoftDNS_ResourceRecord against the target server. The following example shows what this would look like if the script is run on a DNS server:

```
Set objDNS = GetObject("winMgmts:root\MicrosoftDNS")
Set objRR = objDNS.ExecQuery("Select * from MicrosoftDNS_ResourceRecord ")

For Each objInst In objRR
  WScript.Echo objInst.TextRepresentation
Next
WScript.Echo "The script has completed successfully."
```

The TextRepresentation method is available to all resource record types since it is defined in MicrosoftDNS_ResourceRecord. It will return a text string representing the resource record, such as the following:

```
www.mycorp.com. IN  A  192.10.4.5
```

If you want to limit the query to only a specific zone, change the WQL query to include criteria for ContainerName, such as the following:

```
Select * from MicrosoftDNS_ResourceRecord Where ContainerName = 'ZoneName'
```

Since Active Directory uses DNS to store all of the Global Catalog servers in a forest and domain controllers in a domain, you can write scripts to utilize DNS to access this information and integrate it into your applications. The following example does exactly this by selecting all SRV records with a particular OwnerName. To find all Global Catalog servers in a forest, simply query **_ldap._tcp.gc._msdcs.<ForestDNSName>**, and to find all domain controllers in a domain, query **_ldap._tcp.dc._msdcs.<DomainDNSName>**:

```
Option Explicit

Dim strDomain
strDomain = "mycorp.com"

Dim objDNS, objRRs, objRR
Set objDNS = GetObject("winMgmts:root\MicrosoftDNS")
Set objRRs = objDNS.ExecQuery("Select * from MicrosoftDNS_SRVType " & _
                    "Where OwnerName = '_ldap._tcp.gc._msdcs." & _
                    strDomain & "'")
WScript.Echo "Global Catalogs for " & strDomain
For Each objRR In objRRs
   WScript.Echo "  " & objRR.DomainName
Next

WScript.Echo

Set objRRs = objDNS.ExecQuery("Select * from MicrosoftDNS_SRVType " & _
                    "Where OwnerName = '_ldap._tcp.dc._msdcs." & _
                    strDomain & "'")
WScript.Echo "Domain Controllers for " & strDomain
For Each objRR In objRRs
   WScript.Echo "  " & objRR.DomainName
Next
WScript.Echo "The script has completed successfully."
```

Creating Resource Records

With the DNS provider, creating resource records is also very easy to do. The MicrosoftDNS_ResourceRecord::CreateInstanceFromTextRepresentation method takes the server name to create the record on, the domain name, and the text representation of the resource record as in parameters. It also provides an out parameter, which will be an object representing the newly created record.

Example 28-3 goes through the process of creating both A and PTR records. Both records are typically necessary when adding a new host to DNS.

Example 28-3. Creating A and PTR resource records

```
Option Explicit

Dim strRR, strReverseRR, strDomain, strReverseDomain

' A record to add
strRR = "testb.mycorp.com. IN A 192.32.64.13"
```

```
strDomain = "mycorp.com"

' PTR record to add
strReverseRR = "13.64.32.192.in-addr.arpa IN PTR testb.mycorp.com"
strReverseDomain = "192.in-addr.arpa."

Dim objDNS, objRR, objDNSServer, objRR2, objOutParam
Set objDNS = GetObject("winMgmts:root\MicrosoftDNS")
Set objRR = objDNS.Get("MicrosoftDNS_ResourceRecord")
Set objDNSServer = objDNS.Get("MicrosoftDNS_Server.Name=""".""")

' Create the A record
Dim strNull
strNull = objRR.CreateInstanceFromTextRepresentation( _
                objDNSServer.Name, _
                strDomain, _
                strRR, _
                objOutParam)

Set objRR2 = objDNS.Get(objOutParam)
WScript.Echo "Created Record: " & objRR2.TextRepresentation
Set objOutParam = Nothing

' Create the PTR record
strNull = objRR.CreateInstanceFromTextRepresentation( _
                objDNSServer.Name, _
                strReverseDomain, _
                strReverseRR, _
                objOutParam)

Set objRR2 = objDNS.Get(objOutParam)
WScript.Echo "Created Record: " & objRR2.TextRepresentation
```

Summary

The WMI DNS provider fills a much-needed gap for programmatic management of a Microsoft DNS environment. In this chapter, we reviewed how to install the DNS provider, including some of the caveats for using it on Windows 2000. We then covered the classes used for managing server configuration, along with each of the available server settings. Next, we showed how to create and manipulate zones with the DNS provider. Finally, we covered the various resource record types and their associated WMI classes.

## CHAPTER 29

Programming the Directory with the .NET Framework

In 2002, Microsoft announced a major new initiative called ".NET" that was intended to fundamentally change the way software is written for the Windows platform. Something called ".NET Framework" would provide a unified, cross-language programming model and a "managed" runtime environment for this code, which would take care of the messy details such as memory management, making software development easier.

The .NET Framework, now on version 3.5, has seen three major releases, expanding the capability of the programming library substantially. The landscape for directory services programming has also expanded dramatically. In fact, over the last five years or so, the .NET directory services programming interfaces have seen the only really substantial investment by Microsoft in interfaces for programming the directory.

While a skeptic might suggest this is because .NET was just playing catch up, the reality is that now, more than ever before, the .NET Framework is *the* place for Windows developers of all stripes to access the directory. It is also the case that we have a lot more to talk about than we did last time. Let's dig in.

Why .NET?

Why bother learning about .NET? After all, many AD administrators have been scripting happily for years with VBScript, ADSI, WMI, and a pile of command-line tools. We have been getting along just fine. This .NET stuff is really for the enterprise developers writing line of business applications, is it not?

First, let's be clear that .NET may not be for everyone. There are many techniques available for programming the directory, and you may not need to move away from the tools and techniques you already use. However, there are some compelling reasons to consider it:

- Powerful features that were once only available to C++ developers are now being exposed in the .NET Framework. This makes it easier for the vast majority of us who do not program in C++ to get to these features.

- Microsoft has a powerful new web development platform called ASP.NET that vastly improves how we can build applications for the web. Many AD development tasks lend themselves to web-based deployment. We'll see more about ASP.NET in Chapter 30.

- Microsoft has a new command shell called PowerShell that is based on the .NET Framework. PowerShell completely changes the equation for how shell programmers and scripters can program and administrate Windows. We'll see more about PowerShell in Chapter 31.

Choosing a .NET Programming Language

As we previously mentioned, .NET is a programming environment that can be accessed from many different languages. In fact, the runtime environment for .NET (or "managed") code is called the Common Language Runtime or CLR. The runtime is fundamentally object-oriented, but is otherwise neutral to the language syntax used to program it. At the time of this writing, there are dozens of different languages that can be used to write .NET code, from the time-honored COBOL to experimental languages like F#.

Microsoft itself ships tools for several of these languages, including C#, Visual Basic.NET (or VB.NET), C++, and JScript.NET. It is fair to say that most .NET developers use either C# or VB.NET, with Microsoft itself using C# for the vast majority of their own work. C# as a language looks a bit like C++, but a lot more like Java. However, for most of us, our background is in writing VBScript code, so for this book we will present all of the examples in VB.NET.

This decision will likely make a few people grumpy, but it is the best compromise. For those who are put off by this decision, please take consolation in the fact that the thing that really matters is learning the framework itself. The language details are not usually that important. In fact, the languages are often so similar that there are many free tools that can translate code from one language to another with no loss at all.

Unfortunately, there is no way we can explain the basics of programming .NET or any specific languages features. Those sorts of primers already exist on the Internet and in bookstores. Instead, we will take the approach of keeping things simple enough to not require a lot of background and additional depth.

Choosing a Development Tool

Since the last version of this book, the landscape for .NET development tools has expanded as much as the framework itself. Today, you have a lot of choices for how you can write .NET code. The primary decision to make is whether you want to use an integrated development environment (IDE) for your development tasks. IDE's simplify development by making it easier to organize your code files and build them into executables.

.NET IDE Options

Back in the days of Visual Studio.NET 2002, Microsoft was basically the only game in town for .NET IDEs. However, that story has changed significantly. Not only does Visual Studio 2008 come in a variety of different packages, some of them completely free, but there are other non-Microsoft products available to choose from such as SharpDevelop from IC# Code (*http://www.sharpdevelop.net*) and Primal Code.NET by HALLoGRAM Publishing (*http://www.hallogram.com*).

The point here is that there are many options and quite a few of them are free. It is not necessary to buy an expensive tool to write .NET code. Although we do not endorse a particular tool, we will say that most .NET developers use Microsoft's Visual Studio, and the free Express versions (*http://www.microsoft.com/express/*) are suitable for our needs, so that is a reasonable place to start.

.NET Development Without an IDE

Although an IDE can be nice, we do not actually need one to write code for the .NET Framework. In fact, Microsoft provides a free downloadable SDK with all versions of the framework that includes all the tools we need to build .NET code. Though it is rarely done, it is certainly possible to dive right in with Notepad and a command prompt! There are also a variety of tools available such as Snippet Compiler by Jeff Key (*http://www.sliver.com/dotnet/SnippetCompiler/*) that provide an experience similar to scripting, but with compiled code.

.NET Framework Versions

At the time of this writing, Microsoft has released versions 1.0, 1.1, 2.0, 3.0, and 3.5 of the .NET Framework. It can be confusing to understand which .NET features are available in which releases, which release came bundled with which operating system release and how code written for one version will work on another version. Let's unravel all that. Both .NET 3.0 and 3.5 require .NET 2.0 to be installed because they are not actually standalone releases. NET 3.5 also requires Service Pack 1 for .NET 2.0 to be installed.

First, a few general notes on .NET Framework versions:

- It is not a problem to install multiple versions of the framework on the same machine. They happily coexist when installed side by side.

- By default, code compiled against a specific version of the framework will run against that same version of the framework if it is installed on the machine from which it is executed. However, if that version of the framework is not installed where the code is running but a newer version *is* installed, it will load against the newer version.

- Generally speaking, code written against an earlier version of the framework will run with no problems against a later version of the framework. There are a few backwards compatibility problems, but they are rare overall.

- Make sure you have installed the latest service packs as they are released.

Which .NET Framework Comes with Which OS?

Depending on the operating system (OS) of the machine where you want to execute .NET code, a version of the framework may already be included. Table 29-1 summarizes which OS has what.

Table 29-1. .NET Framework/Windows OS cross-reference

Operating system	Included framework versions
Windows 2000	None
Windows XP	None
Windows Server 2003	1.1
Windows Server 2003 R2	1.1, 2.0
Windows Vista	2.0, 3.0
Windows Server 2008	2.0, 3.0

This basically means that unless you control the infrastructure and have made provisions to install some version of .NET through other means, you cannot assume any version of the .NET Framework is available unless the operating system is Windows Server 2003 or higher. You may install whatever version(s) of the framework you wish on any machine, with the exception that .NET 2.0 is the last version of the framework supported on Windows 2000.

> At this time, the Server Core install of Windows Server 2008 does not support the .NET Framework. No version of the .NET Framework can be installed on it. This means that .NET code cannot execute on a Server Core machine.
>
> However, this does not mean you cannot administrate a Server Core domain controller with .NET code. It simply means that the code must execute elsewhere and access the domain controller remotely over the network.

Unfortunately, once we include service packs and other factors, the matrix of possible options for .NET Framework installation across all of the different OS versions can get a little hairy. We will not attempt to document this completely and instead defer to Microsoft's own deployment guides for the details:

- .NET 1.0: *http://msdn.microsoft.com/en-us/library/ms994336.aspx*
- .NET 1.1: *http://msdn.microsoft.com/en-us/library/ms994339.aspx*
- .NET 2.0: *http://msdn.microsoft.com/en-us/library/aa480237.aspx*
- .NET 3.0: *http://msdn.microsoft.com/en-us/library/aa480173.aspx*
- .NET 3.5: *http://msdn.microsoft.com/en-us/library/cc160717.aspx*

Directory Programming Features by .NET Framework Release

The .NET Framework includes a huge number of classes and other programming types. In order to keep things organized, these types are arranged in hierarchical groupings called namespaces. The core components of the framework are arranged under the System namespace.

There are now four main namespaces specifically used for directory services programming:

- System.DirectoryServices (SDS)
- System.DirectoryServices.ActiveDirectory (SDS.AD)
- System.DirectoryServices.Protocols (SDS.P)
- System.DirectoryServices.AccountManagement (SDS.AM)

This does not include all of the other types we might need to access to perform additional programming tasks and also ignores access to WMI, which is also something that .NET can do, but is not something we will cover at all in this book.

 For brevity, we will refer to the namespaces by the above abbreviations throughout the text.

Assemblies Versus Namespaces

In order to keep the framework modular, major pieces of functionality are compiled into separate components called assemblies. An assembly is essentially just a DLL. An assembly can contain types in multiple different namespaces, and namespaces can span across different assemblies. Do not let this confuse you though.

There are three important things to know here:

- In order to use a type in a specific assembly, our code must reference that assembly.
- The directory services programming features are bundled into separate assemblies from the rest of the .NET Framework so that code that does not need these features does not need to load the types contained in these assemblies.
- By default, none of the various projects types in Visual Studio reference *any* of the directory services programming assemblies, so we must remember to add that reference first. This will likely apply to whatever tool you end up using for development.

Summary of Namespaces, Assemblies, and Framework Versions

Table 29-2 summarizes which namespace is available in which .NET Framework release.

Table 29-2. Directory services namespaces by framework release

Namespace	Assembly	Version
System.DirectoryServices	*System.DirectoryServices.dll*	1.0+
System.DirectoryServices.ActiveDirectory	*System.DirectoryServices.dll*	2.0+
System.DirectoryServices.Protocols	*System.DirectoryServices.Protocols.dll*	2.0+
System.DirectoryServices.AccountManagement	*System.DirectoryServices.AccountManagement.dll*	3.5

The bottom line is that .NET 2.0 contains the majority of the available features, but you need .NET 3.5 to get all of them. Looking at Table 29-1, this also implies that you may need to get one of the newer versions of .NET installed where you want to run your code.

 Our recommendation is that you at least use .NET 2.0, and we will assume .NET 2.0 unless otherwise noted. Use the latest service packs as well.

Directory Services Programming Landscape

First, let's take a high-level view of how all of the various pieces fit together.

As you might imagine, the .NET Framework does not attempt to implement the entire operating system from the ground up, but instead uses existing operating system services to some extent or another and repackages them in the more consistent .NET programming model. All of the .NET directory services features leverage existing operating system functionality, some of which we have already covered in this book.

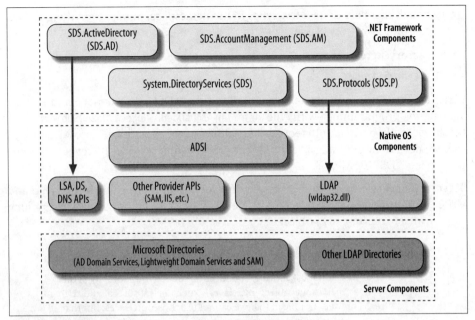

Figure 29-1. Windows Directory Services API mode

Figure 29-1 depicts how the various pieces fit together.

As with most software architectures, the model is built up in layers from low-level components to high-level ones. At the top, we see how the various .NET components fit together and depend on each other.

Right at the center of the diagram, we see ADSI and how it depends on various lower level operating system components. You will find it reassuring that much of the investment you have already made in learning ADSI from this book and other sources will directly carry over to your .NET programming activities.

Now, let's dig into the high-level details of each namespace in turn.

System.DirectoryServices Overview

The `System.DirectoryServices` namespace (`SDS`) is the primary namespace we use for programming directory services in .NET. It is the oldest namespace, having been included with .NET since the very first 1.0 release.

`SDS` is basically just a simple interop layer over the existing ADSI programming model. Most of what you already know about ADSI will apply directly to `SDS`. `SDS` is in many ways more like a stripped-down version of ADSI, but in other ways is more powerful. In all cases, it is ADSI that does the bulk of the work, with the underlying components it depends on doing the actual heavy lifting.

Even though there are quite a few types in the namespace, almost everything in SDS revolves around two core classes:

- `DirectoryEntry`
- `DirectorySearcher`

`DirectoryEntry` is essentially a wrapper around the ADSI `IADs` interface and is most similar to programming with the familiar `IADsOpenDSObject.OpenDSObject` and `GetObject` methods. In fact, `DirectoryEntry` allows us to "drop down" into ADSI whenever we need to by exposing a `NativeObject` property that provides direct access to the underlying ADSI COM object.

`DirectoryEntry` is used to connect to the directory, refer to specific objects, read and write their attributes, create new objects, delete objects, and move objects. Everything starts with a `DirectoryEntry` object.

 By stripped down, we mean that SDS supports the core interfaces in ADSI such as `IADs` and `IADsContainer`, but does not directly support any of the so-called "persistent object interfaces" such as `IADsGroup` and `IADsUser`. This does not mean that we cannot use those interfaces, but that we may need to jump through some additional hoops to get to them.

`DirectorySearcher` is the more interesting part of SDS. As its name would imply, it allows us to search the directory via LDAP queries. In the ADSI scripting world, we use ADO for querying the directory via the ADSI OLE DB provider while we use `GetObject` to access specific objects and perform modifications. This approach made it easier for developers accustomed to querying SQL databases to learn LDAP, but the two models were never well-integrated and ADO gets a little clunky when special features need to be accessed. Additionally, many of the powerful advanced LDAP query features supported by Active Directory never got exposed to ADO, so developers using this technology were basically out of luck.

`DirectorySearcher` is a different approach. Instead of using a similar pattern and having .NET developers use the classes in `System.Data` for executing LDAP searches, the designers of the framework gave us a component purpose-built for doing LDAP queries. The main advantages are:

- Tight integration with `DirectoryEntry` and the other supporting classes in SDS.
- Works in terms of LDAP-specific search concepts such as search base, query scope and filter instead of using SQL terminology that may not apply.
- Special features such as paged searches and timeout settings are cleanly supported via strongly-typed properties.
- All of the advanced Active Directory search features exposed by ADSI are supported (as of .NET 2.0 anyway; .NET 1.0 and 1.1 were more basic).

We will see how some of this looks when we show some examples in the upcoming sections.

 The .NET Framework data access components in System.Data still support OLE DB data sources. This means that the OLE DB provider we used with ADO in VB and VBScript can still be used with .NET as well. It may seem like the natural thing to do for those programmers coming from that background. Don't do it!

Besides having all of the same clumsiness issues that ADO always suffered from, it is not as fast and is completely unnecessary now that we have DirectorySearcher.

While we are issuing warnings, VB.NET also supports a GetObject method for backwards compatibility reasons. Don't use this for accessing Active Directory objects either. Use DirectoryEntry instead.

Under the hood, DirectorySearcher accomplishes its magic by interoperating with a low level ADSI interface called IDirectorySearch. IDirectorySearch has been in ADSI for a long time, but VB and VBScript developers could not call it directly as it was designed only for C++ developers. The ADSI OLE DB provider we use in VBScript is actually another wrapper around IDirectorySearch that adapts IDirectorySearch to the ADO programming model. With DirectorySearcher, we get a component designed for LDAP programming and with all the special features exposed.

Other nice things in System.DirectoryServices

As of .NET 2.0, the .NET Framework has first-class support for Windows security objects such as security descriptors, DACLs, ACEs, and SIDs. SDS follows suit and provides support for the full complement of Active Directory security-descriptor manipulation functions. The classes that support this are much faster and more powerful than the ADSI-based interfaces we used to program them before such as IADsSecurityDescriptor.

We usually do not spend much time writing code that manipulates security descriptors, but full support for these features is welcome in the cases when we do.

System.DirectoryServices Summary

- SDS is the primary namespace we use for .NET directory services programming.
- DirectoryEntry and DirectorySearcher are the two main classes.
- SDS is based on ADSI, so much of our ADSI knowledge applies directly.
- SDS is a little stripped down compared to full ADSI, but works well in general.
- DirectorySearcher is a better query interface than what we had before.

System.DirectoryServices.ActiveDirectory Overview

SDS.AD was added to .NET in version 2.0 and instantly added a ton of new functionality, nearly tripling the number of classes available previously. As the name might imply, SDS.AD provides support for performing operations on Active Directory specifically. When we say Active Directory, we include both AD Domain Services and Lightweight Domain Services (AD LDS, formerly ADAM).

SDS.AD provides access to functions that previously were difficult or impossible for developers using languages other than C++ to access. The functions can be grouped into the following categories:

- Active Directory infrastructure (forests, domains, global catalogs, domain controllers, sites, etc.)
- Replication
- Trusts
- Directory Schema

SDS.AD accomplishes this goal by using a clever design to marry the ADSI programming model to a set of non-LDAP RPC interfaces with function names like DsGetDCName. As we will see, SDS.AD is integrated tightly with SDS, making it easy to move between the two namespaces as needed.

Why use System.DirectoryServices.ActiveDirectory?

You may be looking at the list from the previous section and thinking that the number of times you needed or wanted to be able to write code to create a trust could be counted on one hand (or less), and you might be right. In fact, much of the functionality exposed by SDS.AD is stuff that most of us never need to automate. The tasks involving SDS.AD classes are infrequent and other tools are often more appropriate to accomplish those tasks.

The sweet spot for SDS.AD is in the first point, which is the access to Active Directory infrastructure components. The ability to do things like enumerate domains and domain controllers is helpful and very easy to use here. Additionally, SDS.AD provides access to the full power of the DC Locator component of Windows and allows us to access all of the advanced features of DC Locator such as finding domain controllers in specific sites and forcing rediscovery. For more information on DC Locator, refer to Chapter 6. This was never available to us at all via ADSI or SDS before.

With this in mind, we will proceed to ignore all of the other more obscure features of SDS.AD and instead concentrate on the infrastructure features in our upcoming examples.

System.DirectoryServices.ActiveDirectory summary

- Added in .NET 2.0.
- Provides many powerful features that we not previously available to most programmers.
- Tightly integrated with SDS.
- Some of the functions supported are a bit obscure, but the infrastructure features are always useful.

System.DirectoryServices.Protocols Overview

SDS.P was also added to .NET in the version 2.0 release. Unlike SDS.AD, which layers new capabilities on top of the existing ADSI-based SDS, SDS.P is a completely different animal. Referring back to Figure 29-1, we see that SDS.P does not layer on top of ADSI at all, but instead sits directly on top of the core Windows LDAP library, *wldap32.dll*. We also see that SDS.P does not overlap with SDS at all.

In a nutshell, SDS.P gives us a completely different model for programming LDAP. Instead of using the "object-centric" metaphor of ADSI where you create programmatic objects that point to specific objects in the directory in order to manipulate them, SDS.P applies the "connection-centric" metaphor inherent in the standards-based LDAP API design. For example, in SDS.P we create a DirectoryConnection object to connect to the underlying directory, and then we perform operations on that connection by sending it messages such as search requests and receiving messages such as search responses in response.

SDS.P implements just about every feature of the underlying LDAP API, bringing the full power of LDAP to the programmer, including many features not even supported by ADSI and thus not possible in SDS. It also provides the opportunity to get the best possible performance from LDAP in scenarios where performance trumps productivity (i.e. not usually scripting).

The downside of this is that SDS.P is more complicated and demands that you learn all of the intimate details of LDAP and AD programming. Basically, it is provided to support the needs of systems programmers much more so than administrators or even normal enterprise developers.

Why use System.DirectoryServices.Protocols?

For most of us, the answer is that we will probably never need to. This namespace is not for us, so we can safely ignore it.

However, there are definitely specific scenarios where SDS.P really is needed or desirable, and we can at least list a few of them:

- You need access to obscure AD LDAP features not supported by ADSI such as the phantom root or stats controls.

- You are programming against a non-Microsoft LDAP directory and ADSI does not mesh well with it.

- You are writing a highly scalable multithreaded server application and need the full support for asynchronous queries and maximum performance not available with ADSI.

- You use SSL with your LDAP programming and need to override the SSL certificate verification policy so that certain error conditions that would cause an ADSI connection to fail can be ignored.

You need to query a directory using the DSML protocol instead of the LDAP protocol. At the same time, the difference in complexity between writing AD code in VBScript and LDAP API code in C++ is much larger than the difference between programming SDS and SDS.P in VB.NET. If you are inclined to get your hands dirty and are pretty comfortable with LDAP, feel free to check it out. We will provide one simple sample and leave it at that.

System.DirectoryServices.Protocols summary

- Powerful, low-level library for programming LDAP directly (no ADSI).

- Not intended for use by typical administrators and enterprise developers; intended for systems programmers.

- In specific situations, it may be the only way to accomplish a particular goal, but most of these scenarios are uncommon.

- Probably safe to ignore by most of us.

System.DirectoryServices.AccountManagement Overview

Since its introduction in NET 1.0, SDS has often been criticized for being too difficult to use for performing common tasks for managing users and groups. It was a step down from the approach provided by ADSI before it. Microsoft did not really do anything to address this shortcoming in .NET 2.0, but the 3.5 release changed this significantly.

In .NET 3.5, Microsoft introduced a new namespace and assembly called SDS.AM. Also called "The Principal API," SDS.AM significantly simplifies the tasks associated with managing directory security principals such as users, computers, and groups.

These are the design goals of SDS.AM:

- Provide a unified design for managing security principals that works the same across all three of Microsoft's primary directory platforms: AD Domain Services, AD Lightweight Domain Services and the local machine SAM database.

- Reduce the need to understand LDAP programming or the underlying details of the store being accessed.

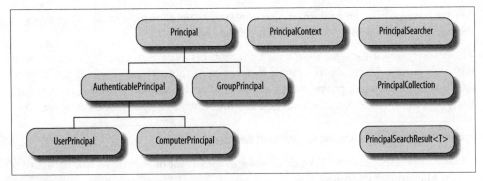

Figure 29-2. Primary classes in System.DirectoryServices.AccountManagement

- Make the design flexible so that it can be extended to provide custom functionality and "drop down" into SDS whenever more power is needed.

Referring back to Figure 29-1, we see that SDS.AM layers on top of SDS with a bit of overlap with SDS.P as well. For the most part, SDS.AM is based on SDS and thus ADSI. In a way, we could say that SDS.AM reintroduces features ADSI always had with the IADsUser, IADsComputer, and IADsGroup interfaces, but in actuality it does ADSI one better. Because SDS.AM is much newer, it allowed the designers to purposefully include support for AD Lightweight Directory Services and also take advantage of many .NET programming features that simplify development tasks. We will see this when we dive into the examples.

Referring to Figure 29-2, we see that there are just a few primary classes within SDS.AM. On the left, we see a class called Principal with several other classes underneath of it. The lines here are significant because they indicate an inheritance relationship. UserPrincipal derives from AuthenticablePrincipal, which derives from Principal, etc. Principal is essentially the center of the universe in SDS.AM. We can also derive our own classes from any of these classes as a way to extend SDS.AM to our own directory customizations.

PrincipalContext is a helper class used to create different types of Principal objects. Its primary job is to specify which type of directory we are accessing.

PrincipalSearcher and the classes underneath of it are used for finding Principal objects in the directory and work in conjunction with PrincipalContext and Principal.

Why use System.DirectoryServices.AccountManagement?

Unlike SDS.P, SDS.AM really is intended to be used by most of us. It significantly simplifies many common tasks and is much easier to use than any of the other directory services programming namespaces. It provides such a high degree of abstraction that it makes it possible for a programmer to know almost nothing about LDAP, ADSI, or the underlying directory model to accomplish common tasks. It is by far the most productive

API we have been given to date. It also contains a comparatively small set of types in the namespace, so it takes little effort to get started with.

The primary downside with SDS.AM is that it requires .NET 3.5, and that does not ship with any current Microsoft operating systems as of this writing. Thus, if we want to use it, we have to make provisions to get it installed somehow. However, the productivity benefits are significant. We suggest you find a way to get this done where possible.

System.DirectoryServices.AccountManagement summary

- New namespace in .NET 3.5 designed specifically for managing security principals in Microsoft directories
- Requires the least knowledge about LDAP and the underlying directories of any of the other namespaces
- Provides a highly productive developer experience

.NET Directory Services Programming by Example

Now, let's switch focus and dive into some code. Unfortunately, there is no possible way we can do much more than scratch the surface of all of the types of things we can do with .NET directory services programming. This topic could easily fill an entire book (and has a few times already). If you need a deeper reference, *The .NET Developer's Guide to Directory Services Programming* by Kaplan and Dunn (Addison-Wesley) is an excellent option.

Conventions for the code samples:

- Unless otherwise stated, assume we are using .NET 2.0.
- For brevity, we will skip error handling and object cleanup code that we really should be using in most "real" work.
- Assume that we are using a simple console application type for our samples, but do not let that imply that you can only build console applications. All of these samples may be used in any .NET application type.
- Assume we have an assembly reference to *System.DirectoryServices.dll* and have imported namespaces for SDS and SDS.AD via the following block of code.

```
Imports System.DirectoryServices
Imports System.DirectoryServices.ActiveDirectory
```

Like VBScript and VB6, VB.NET supports a programming technique called "late binding." Late binding allows us to refer to properties or methods on an object that may not be explicitly available on the current class. This is mostly helpful when working with COM interfaces in .NET.

However, C# does not have such a feature and requires complex "reflection" code to accomplish the same goal. For that reason, we will avoid using any late binding in our samples. SDS provides other ways to accomplish the same tasks anyway, so late binding is not really necessary. You can add the Option Strict and Option Explicit directives in your code to disable late binding if you wish.

Additionally, VB.NET is not case-sensitive but C# is, so we'll use proper case in all of our examples.

Connecting to the Directory

There are two basic options available for connecting to the directory:

- Use DirectorySearcher
- Use one of the infrastructure classes in SDS.AD

Let's look at some examples of each in turn. As we previously learned, LDAP directories support a special object called *RootDSE* that allows the programmer to query the directory for information such as the partitions it contains, so we will start there.

```
'connect to rootDSE using "serverless binding"
Dim rootDSE As New DirectoryEntry("LDAP://RootDSE")
'this uses the full constructor to do the same thing
Dim rootDSE2 As New DirectoryEntry( _
    "LDAP://RootDSE", _
    Nothing, _
    Nothing, _
    AuthenticationTypes.Secure _
    )
'same as first but specifying a specific domain
Dim rootDSE3 As New DirectoryEntry( _
    "LDAP://mycorp.com/RootDSE")
'now we are using explicit credentials and
'Secure (negotiate) authentication
Dim rootDSE4 As New DirectoryEntry( _
    "LDAP://rootDSE", _
    "someuser@mycorp.com", _
    "Password1", _
    AuthenticationTypes.Secure _
    )
'bind to LDS rootDSE as an AD LDS user using
'simple bind and SSL to protect the credentials
'on the network
Dim ldsRootDSE As New DirectoryEntry( _
    "LDAP://adldsserver.com/RootDSE", _
```

```
          "otheruser@adlds", _
          "Password1", _
          AuthenticationTypes.SecureSocketsLayer _
          )
```

The first thing we notice is that this looks quite a bit like `GetObject` or `OpenDSObject` in ADSI. This is no accident. The same technology is being used and the same rules apply. In .NET, we use a feature called "method overloading" to specify multiple constructors for the same object. This makes it easy to either use the defaults or to specify explicit credentials and other options whenever we need to. We also show an example of connecting to AD LDS at the end. Again, the same rules apply except that we cannot use "serverless binding" with AD LDS and must specify a server name.

In the AD LDS example, we connect using SSL and use LDAP simple bind instead of Windows secure bind.

 There is no flag to specify a simple bind. Instead, we supply non-null credentials and specify an `AuthenticationType` other than `Secure`. It is a little confusing at first, but it actually works the same way in ADSI as well. If we still want to do a secure bind with a Windows user and also use SSL, we simply combine the flags like:

```
          AuthenticationTypes.Secure Or
              AuthenticationTypes.SecureSocketsLayer
```

There are many other flags available, but we simply do not have room to explain them all. They are the same flags available in ADSI in the `ADS_AUTHENTICATION_ENUM`, just with slightly different names that use .NET standards. Reference *http://msdn.microsoft.com/en-us/library/ system.directoryservices.authenticationtypes.aspx* for a listing of possible `AuthenticationTypes`.

Now, let's read some attributes and connect to the domain root object:

```
'now, let's get the defaultNamingContext for this domain
Dim ncName As string = DirectCast( _
    rootDSE.Properties("defaultNamingContext").Value, _
    String)
Dim ncRoot As New DirectoryEntry("LDAP://" + ncName)
'now, let's use SDS.AD to do the same thing
'in one line of code!
Dim ncRoot2 As DirectoryEntry = _
    Domain.GetCurrentDomain().GetDirectoryEntry()
```

In this example, we show how to read LDAP attributes from our `DirectoryEntry` we created previously. Instead of using `Get` and `GetEx` like we do in ADSI, .NET implements a `PropertyCollection` that contains `PropertyValueCollection` objects. The `Value` property on `PropertyValueCollection` is a helper that returns:

- A null reference (`Nothing`) if the attribute is not set or not available
- A single value as `Object` if the attribute has a single value

- An array of `Object` values if the attribute is multivalued

This is handy, so we will use it frequently. Since attributes in AD can be of many different data types and .NET converts them to specific data types the same way that ADSI does, they are returned as `Object`. This means we must convert them back into the type they really are.

After that, we use the `defaultNamingContext` attribute value from `RootDSE` to build another `DirectoryEntry`, this time pointing to the domain partition root object.

Next, we use an alternate approach to accomplish the same goal in a single line of code using the `Domain` class. Obviously, this is less work and quite handy. Let's show some other examples with the `Domain` class.

```
'create a Domain-type DirectoryContext pointing to
'a specific domain with default credentials
Dim context1 As New DirectoryContext( _
    DirectoryContextType.Domain, _
    "othercorpdomain.com" _
    )
'build a Domain object with the context
Dim domain1 As Domain = Domain.GetDomain(context1)
'create a Domain-type DirectoryContext pointing to
'a specific domain with alternate plaintext credentials
Dim context2 As New DirectoryContext( _
    DirectoryContextType.Domain, _
    "othercorpdomain.com", _
    "someuser@mycorp.com", _
    "Password1" _
    )
Dim domain2 As Domain = Domain.GetDomain(context2)
```

With `SDS.AD`, we use an object called `DirectoryContext` as a way to build all sorts of different types of objects such as domains, forests, specific servers, and even AD LDS configuration sets or AD application partitions. We see this pattern repeated in `SDS.AM` with the `PrincipalContext` class.

 We do not set `AuthenticationTypes` with `DirectoryContext` in the same way we can when building a `DirectoryEntry`. The underlying code sets all the right defaults for us, including `Signing` and `Sealing`, although there is no option to use either SSL or simple bind. `SDS.AD` only supports Windows authentication for both AD DS and LDS.

As we said before, `SDS.AD` provides a vast array of AD management features, and we do not have room to even scratch the surface. Some of our favorite features include the ability to expand the complete domain tree and locate global catalog servers from which you can directly construct a `DirectorySearcher` for searching the GC. We'll part with one final example showing how to enumerate domain controllers in a specific domain, since nearly everyone has to do this from time to time:

```
Dim currentDomain As Domain = Domain.GetCurrentDomain()
For Each dc As DomainController _
    In currentDomain.FindAllDomainControllers()
    'We can do whatever we want now that we have all the DCs...
    Console.WriteLine(dc.Name)
Next
```

The example is trivially easy, and that is really the whole point. SDS.AD takes tasks that can range from annoying to nearly impossible and makes them easy to accomplish.

The IDisposable Interface and Directory Services Programming

The .NET Framework provides an interface called IDisposable that is applied to many objects throughout the framework. IDisposable has a single method called Dispose with the intended use being that developers are encouraged to call the Dispose method on objects when they are done with them rather than allowing the .NET runtime to clean these objects through the normal garbage collection mechanism. The reason this is sometimes necessary is that .NET objects that interoperate with native resources via COM and direct API calls often hold references to memory and other operating system resources that are not managed directly by the runtime. Even though well-designed objects that also implement a Finalize method will eventually cause these resources to be released when the runtime's garbage collector gets around to calling it, that may take longer than would be desirable otherwise, especially in cases where small .NET objects reference expensive native resources.

Developers may either call the Dispose method directly or use the Using statement to do this automatically (variants of which are available in both VB.NET and C#). The Using statement is the preferred method and looks like this:

```
Dim entry As New DirectoryEntry("LDAP://RootDSE")
Using (entry)
    'do something with the DirectoryEntry here…
End Using
```

The reason we mention this is that many objects in the .NET directory services programming namespaces implement the IDisposable interface, including DirectoryEntry, DirectorySearcher, and SearchResultCollection, and significant chunks of the types in SDS.AD, SDS.AM, and SDS.P. This should come as no surprise, as we have seen how much all these namespaces depend on underlying native APIs.

Even though our code samples do not demonstrate this, it is always a good idea to wrap your IDisposable objects in a Using block. In short-lived programs, the difference is likely to be minimal, but it can make a huge difference in resource usage for applications that instantiate many of these objects or with long-lived processes such as those that are typical in .NET web applications.

We said that these objects will eventually get cleaned up by the garbage collector one way or the other, and for the most part that is true. However, in the case of the SearchResultCollection, it is not. It currently has a limitation that does not allow the Finalize method that is called by the garbage collector to release the underlying native resource. As such, you should always wrap SearchResultCollection in a Using block.

Searching the Directory

One of the primary reasons we have a directory in the first place is to look up information in it, so it stands to reason that searching the directory is one of the things we'll do most often. Let's look at some basic examples of searching with `DirectorySearcher`:

```
Dim root As DirectoryEntry = _
    Domain.GetCurrentDomain().GetDirectoryEntry()
Dim searcher As New DirectorySearcher(root)
searcher.Filter = "(&(objectCategory=person)(objectClass=user))"
searcher.SearchScope = SearchScope.SubTree
'We only want this attribute returned, so specify it
searcher.PropertiesToLoad.Add("sAMAccountName")
'enable paging by setting a non-zero page size
searcher.PageSize = 1000
Dim src As SearchResultCollection
Using (src)
    src = searcher.FindAll()
    For Each result As SearchResult In src
        Console.WriteLine(result.Properties("sAMAccountName")(0))
    Next
End Using
```

A `DirectorySearcher` object always needs a `DirectoryEntry` to use as a way of establishing the connection to the directory and determine which object will be the base of the search. In our example, we use our previous shortcut with `SDS.AD` to build a `DirectoryEntry` pointing to the domain partition root object for this purpose. Note that you can build a `DirectorySearcher` without specifying this and SDS will try to do this for you, but it is nearly always better to be explicit about your intent in your code.

We use a standard filter for finding user objects and set the scope to `SubTree`, even though that is not technically necessary since it is the default. We also add the `sAMAccountName` attribute to the list of `PropertiesToLoad` to specify that we want only that attribute returned instead of the default of "all" as per normal LDAP rules.

 From a performance perspective, it is important to supply values to `PropertiesToLoad` as a normal procedure. If we do not, the directory will return Active Directory default attribute values for each matched object. This results in a significant waste of network bandwidth, especially for searches that return many results. It is also worth noting that if we wish to return operational or constructed attributes such as `canonicalName` or `allowedAttributesEffective`, we must specify them in `PropertiesToLoad` as they are never returned in a default search.

We also set the `PageSize` to 1000 to enable paged searches. As with other ADSI-based searches, we do not explicitly loop through the pages of results returned by the server under the hood. ADSI does this for us. Generally speaking, it is always a good idea to enable paged searches as we usually want to get all of the results, even if there are more than 1000. If there are less than 1000, the paging request does not hurt anything.

To enumerate the results, we use a `For Each` loop against the `SearchResultCollection` object returned by the call to `FindAll`. Note that this approach provides better performance than using a `For` loop based on the `Count` property of the `SearchResultCollection`. This has to do with the fact that in order to get the `Count`, the entire search must be executed under the hood anyway. Using `For Each` instead fetches the results as they are returned.

Notice that like `DirectoryEntry`, the `SearchResult` class also has a `Properties` property that provides access to the attribute values returned by the search. They behave similarly except that `SearchResult` objects are strictly read-only and the `ResultPropertyValueCollection` does not have a handy `Value` property like the `PropertyValueCollection`, so we must access the first value returned by indexing into the array. Make sure that if you access an attribute that might be null, you first check to see if the `SearchResult` contains that attribute using the `Contains` method or else indexing into the array will result in an error:

```
If result.Properties.Contains("displayName") Then
    Console.WriteLine(result.Properties("displayName")(0))
End If
```

 The `SearchResult` class contains a method called `GetDirectoryEntry` that will return the `DirectoryEntry` object for any given result using the same security context and connection information supplied to the original `DirectoryEntry` used to build the `SearchRoot` for the Directory Searcher. While it may seem tempting to use this method to access the property cache to read attributes from the search, this is a bad idea from a performance perspective. The reason is that creating a `DirectoryEntry` object results in at least one and usually two additional searches to the directory to fill the property cache for each object. Since the `SearchResult` object already contains the results we asked for in our search, it makes no sense to access this data again in a less efficient way. Always use the `SearchResult` when you need to read attribute values from a search.

The appropriate case to call the `GetDirectoryEntry` method is when you need to perform modifications on the returned object. `SearchResult` objects are read-only, so we must have a `DirectoryEntry` if we need to perform a modification.

`DirectorySearcher` is also the place where many of the special features in AD LDAP are lurking. As of .NET 2.0, `DirectorySearcher` provides access to things like *Attribute Scope Queries, Directory Synchronization, Virtual List Views, Deleted Object Searches,* and *Extended DN Queries.* Once again, we are pressed for space in this book, but check out some of the other resources available to find out how to use these advanced features if you find yourself in need of them.

Basics of Modifying the Directory

Now that we have some of the basics covered, let's turn our attention to modifying the directory. After all, searching is only useful if someone puts some objects in the directory first.

We have a few options when it comes to modifying the directory. SDS allows us to create, modify, or delete just about any type of object in the directory we can think of, as long as we know how. It is our workhorse for modifications, so we will start with it.

On the other hand, much of an administrator's life tends to revolve around modifying security principals in the directory such as users, computers, and groups. As we've already learned, a new namespace in .NET 3.5, SDS.AM, gives us a simple, powerful way to manipulate those types of objects specifically. In the next section, we will show some samples for performing those tasks, using both namespaces for contrast.

Finally, SDS.AD again provides us with a rich set of features for modifying AD infrastructure objects such as sites, trusts, and the schema (which is almost always a bad idea to modify in code, but is sometimes necessary). This essentially allows you to build your own versions of the AD Domains and Trusts, Sites and Services, and Schema Management MMC snap-ins, if you so desire. Unfortunately, we won't be showing you how. We just wanted you to know where to look if the need arises.

You cannot perform modification operations on a read-only domain controller. If you attempt to do so, the DC will issue a write referral to a writable DC. This may or may not work.

The other problem with writes to RODCs is that if the write referral did work, the change would go to a different DC than the DC you were trying to access, so a subsequent read to the original RODC will not have the new data until replication completes. This can cause chaos in an application that does not anticipate this.

By default, ADSI asks for writable DCs, so this may or may not actually be a problem. However, the best solution to this problem is to be explicit in your intentions and ask for a writable DC. Fortunately, .NET provides a clean way to do this as of SP1 of .NET 2.0. The LocatorOptions enumeration now provides a WriteableRequired value that can be specified, so make sure you use the overloaded versions of methods for locating DCs (such as Domain.FindDomainController) that allow you to specify LocatorOptions.WriteableRequired when needed.

In order for ADSI on machines running Windows XP or Windows Server 2003 to contact an RODC, you will need to install the compatibility package available from *http://support.microsoft.com/kb/944043*.

For more details on application compatibility guidance for RODCs, see Microsoft's reference *http://technet2.microsoft.com/windows server2008/en/library/53673855-3678-47e9-bb9f-acac8c1fb1781033 .mspx?mfr=true*.

Basic add example

Let's get started with a simple example: adding a new OU under the root of the domain:

```
Dim root As DirectoryEntry = _
    Domain.GetCurrentDomain().GetDirectoryEntry()
Dim newOU As DirectoryEntry = _
    root.Children.Add("OU=New OU", "organizationalUnit")
newOU.Properties("description").Value = "A new OU"
newOU.CommitChanges()
```

Adding a new object to the directory using DirectoryEntry revolves around using the Add method on the Children property of the DirectoryEntry object that will be parent of the newly added object. The first parameter of the Add method takes the relative distinguished name (RDN) of the new object. For a default Windows Server 2008 Active Directory, this will always be CN=xxx, UID=xxx, OU=xxx, or DC=xxx, as those are the four default RDN attribute IDs. With AD LDS, there is more flexibility. The second parameter indicates the objectClass of the new object.

The second thing to notice is that the Add method returns a new DirectoryEntry object. This object is not yet persisted in the directory, but instead exists in memory until we actually call the CommitChanges method. This allows us to set additional attributes on the object before it is first saved, and it is important because some objects define mandatory attributes that must be set on the object at create time, or they define attributes that can only be set at create time (schema objects are an example here). Here, we show adding a description attribute to demonstrate how this works, although description is not mandatory and could be added after the fact.

Basic remove examples

Removing objects is simple. Let's save some time and just remove the OU we just created. We will reuse the same variables we already initialized:

```
root.Children.Remove(newOU)
```

Once again, we use the Children property on DirectoryEntry, this time calling its Remove method. The Remove method takes another DirectoryEntry object as its parameter, which indicates the object to be removed. As long as the object passed in is a child of the parent and we have the necessary permissions, the deletion happens immediately.

If we instead want to delete an object and all of its descendants, we must use a slightly different approach. For simplicity, let's pretend "New OU" from our creation example now has a bunch of child objects, including other containers with children:

```
newOU.DeleteTree()
```

Here, we call the DeleteTree method on the object that we wish to delete along with all of its descendants. This is a little different than the previous example where we removed a single object via the Remove method on the parent object's Children property.

The overall point here is that we must know which type of deletion we want to perform and use the appropriate technique, and that in both cases, the deletion is immediate. Hopefully it goes without saying that we must be extremely careful when deleting objects in general!

Moving and renaming objects

In ADSI, we have a multipurpose method called MoveHere that we use for doing object moves, object renames, or both operations at the same time. SDS attempts to simplify this model by providing separate MoveTo and Rename methods instead.

MoveTo provides two overloads. One allows us to simply move the object while the second overload allows us to move and rename at the same time. Let's take a look. In our example, we have two DirectoryEntry objects pointing to OUs in our domain, and we wish to move one OU under the other:

```
Dim firstOU As New DirectoryEntry( _
    "LDAP://OU=First OU,DC=mycorp,DC=com")
Dim newParent as New DirectoryEntry( _
    "LDAP://OU=Second OU,DC=mycorp,DC=com")
'choose one or the other!!!
'this one moves without renaming
firstOU.MoveTo(newParent)
'this one moves and renames
firstOU.MoveTo(newParent, "OU=Child OU")
```

In the last line where we rename the object while moving it, we supply the new name in RDN format as we did in the creation sample. We also use this same approach when using the Rename method to change an objects name without moving it. Let's rename our second OU from the previous sample:

```
Dim toBeRenamed As New DirectoryEntry( _
    "LDAP://OU=Second OU,DC=mycorp,DC=com")
toBeRenamed.Rename("OU=A different name")
```

Modifying existing objects

The final aspect of modification basics is changing attribute values on existing objects. For the most part, this works exactly the same way we saw in our create example where we added an attribute value between the time we initially created and saved it to the directory. We set the desired attribute to the value we need and call CommitChanges when we are done:

```
Dim entry as New DirectoryEntry( _
    "LDAP://CN=test,OU=People,DC=mycorp,DC=com")
entry.Properties("displayName").Value = "new name"
entry.Properties("description").Value = "new description"
entry.CommitChanges()
```

Using the Value property replaces the existing value with the new value or sets the attribute if it was not set previously.

If the attribute is multivalued and we wish to modify incrementally instead of replacing the whole thing, we should instead use the Add and Remove methods to add and remove specific values. We can also replace an entire multivalued attribute using the Value property again. To remove all attribute values, call the Clear method.

The other main thing to keep in mind is that we must supply data in the appropriate data type for the attribute value being set. Most directory attributes are strings, but some take numeric, date, or binary data, so check the schema reference documentation to know for sure.

Managing Users

Now that we have the basics of directory modifications mastered, let's look at a few user management examples. As we have learned by now, effective user management comes down to knowing many of the picky little details about how data is stored in the directory and how to change it to get the results we need. Let's start with a simple user creation sample:

```
Dim parent As DirectoryEntry = New DirectoryEntry( _
    "LDAP://OU=people,DC=mycorp,DC=com")
Dim user As DirectoryEntry = _
    parent.Children.Add("CN=test.user", "user")
user.Properties("sAMAccountName").Value = "test.user"
user.Properties("userPrincipalName").Value = "test.user@mycorp.com"
user.CommitChanges()
```

This looks fairly similar to our previous example of creating an OU, except that we set some different attributes for the user object. The problem with this is that this user will not have a password and will be disabled by default, so it is not very useful yet. Additionally, if we have a password policy in place requiring passwords, we cannot enable the user until after we have set a password. Let's revise our sample:

```
Dim parent As DirectoryEntry = New DirectoryEntry( _
    "LDAP://OU=people,DC=mycorp,DC=com")
Dim user As DirectoryEntry = _
    parent.Children.Add("CN=test.user", "user")
user.Properties("sAMAccountName").Value = "test.user"
user.Properties("userPrincipalName").Value = "test.user@mydomain.com"
user.CommitChanges()

'This is how we call an IADsUser method
user.Invoke("SetPassword", New Object() {"Password1"})
'This is how we call an IADsUser property method
user.InvokeSet("AccountDisabled", New Object() {False})
'or we could do this which is faster:
user.Properties("userAccountControl").Value = 512 'normal

'force change password at next logon
user.Properties("pwdLastSet").Value = 0
user.CommitChanges()
```

Suddenly, our sample is getting a little complex. First, notice that we use a method on DirectoryEntry called Invoke to call methods on underlying ADSI interfaces. In this case, we call IADsUser.SetPassword. Invoke takes an array of objects as its other argument because the method we could be calling under the hood might take any number of different arguments of any type and we need a generic mechanism to make this work, although in this case it really just wanted a single string.

Next, we see a call to InvokeSet. While Invoke is used for calling ADSI methods, InvokeGet and InvokeSet are used specifically for calling the set and get versions of ADSI properties—in this case, IADsUser.AccountDisabled. We also show how you could set userAccountControl directly instead of using the ADSI property, although we cheat a little by setting a direct numeric value instead of changing the single bit we need to flip in order to remove the disabled flag. In general, setting this attribute to an arbitrary value is bad practice. Instead, we should manipulate the individual bit flags to avoid overwriting other settings and make our intentions in our code more clear.

Finally, we set the pwdLastSet attribute to 0 to force the user to change their password at next login and call the CommitChanges method to update the object in the directory.

We also see that we have to do this whole thing in three steps. We cannot call SetPassword on an object that has not been created yet and we cannot enable an object that has no password, so all three steps are needed.

Now, let's pretend we need to add a user to AD LDS. In this case, we use a totally different method to enable the user. Instead of using userAccountControl, AD LDS uses the msds-userAccountDisabled Boolean attribute (set to False as you might guess). While this is certainly easier to deal with than flipping individual bits on userAccount Control, the problem is that we need different code for different stores and have to keep track of all these details.

Once we throw in all of the rest of the user management functions such as setting home directory, account expiration, and so on, it gets messy quickly.

Managing users with System.DirectoryServices.AccountManagement

Now, let's take a look at how SDS.AM attempts to simplify this by creating the same user again:

```
Dim principalContext As new PrincipalContext( _
    ContextType.Domain, _
    "MyCorp", _
    "OU=People,DC=mycorp,DC=com")
Dim newUser As New UserPrincipal( _
    principalContext, "test.user", "Password1", True)
```

Obviously, this is much simpler. The fourth parameter tells SDS.AM that we would like the user enabled during the creation. In fact, the only real LDAP thing we need to know here is the distinguished name of the container we want to put the user in.

Where it gets even nicer is the fact that we can create a user in either the local SAM database or AD LDS simply by varying how we build the initial `PrincipalContext` object. The second line of code stays the same.

```
Dim samContext As New PrincipalContext(ContextType.Machine)
Dim ldsContext As New PrincipalContext( _
    ContextType.ApplicationDirectory, _
    "localhost:50000", "OU=Users,O=Demo")
```

Unlike with `SDS` where we use the `Invoke` and `InvokeSet` methods to call into the underlying ADSI interface members, `SDS.AM` provides strongly typed .NET properties and methods that allow us to manipulate users, groups, and computers in a friendlier way. For example, we now have methods such as `SetPassword`, `ExpirePasswordNow`, `IsAccountLockedOut`, and `UnlockAccount`, and properties such as `LastPasswordSet` and `UserCannotChangePassword` to make all of these operations that were once difficult, or at least annoying, both simple and easy to understand.

The productivity gains with `SDS.AM` do not stop there. `SDS.AM` also provides:

- The full set of user and computer provisioning functions including read, update, move, and delete functions.

- A comprehensive set of group management functions, including provisioning of groups and expansion of group membership for both groups and users.

- A set of functions for finding principals in the directory that require little, if any, LDAP knowledge.

- An extensibility model that allows us to create our own `Principal` classes that support our own schema modifications or other relevant AD schema that are not directly supported in the "out of box" `Principal` classes.

- A high-performance bind authentication component for performing LDAP authentication in a scalable, dependable way.

Again, we can only scratch the surface here. To dig a little deeper, check out the MSDN magazine article "Look It Up" by Wilansky and Kaplan from the January 2008 issue (*http://msdn.microsoft.com/en-us/magazine/cc135979.aspx*).

Overriding SSL Server Certificate Verification with SDS.P

As promised, we have up to this point totally avoided any examples having to do with `SDS.P`, suggesting that it really is not intended for most programmers and not worth attempting to cover in a high-level introduction such as this one. We also promised one simple sample to show you what it looks like. This sample is also relevant because it is something you cannot do in ADSI at all.

The scenario is that your code needs to connect to an LDAP directory, possibly AD DS or LDS, but also maybe a non-Microsoft LDAP directory, and we need to use SSL. Unfortunately, there is a problem with the server's SSL certificate. Perhaps the subject name on the certificate does not match the DNS name we must use to access the server or perhaps we do not trust the certificate's issuer on our client or perhaps the certificate has expired. ADSI *does* support SSL/LDAP operations, but it will fail with a "Server Not Operational" error if there is anything wrong with the server's certificate. This behavior cannot be changed, so with ADSI we are out of luck.

However, the Windows LDAP API *does* provide more options here (ADSI simply does not expose access to this advanced feature). Since SDS.P provides nearly the entire scope of Windows LDAP functionality, we also have access to this feature in SDS.P and can override the SSL verification logic:

```vb
Public Module MyModule
    Sub Main()
        Dim con As New LdapConnection( _
            new LdapDirectoryIdentifier( _
                "badserver.com:636", True, False))
        con.SessionOptions.SecureSocketLayer = True
        con.SessionOptions.VerifyServerCertificate = _
            AddressOf ServerCallback
        con.Credential = New NetworkCredential("", "")
        con.SessionOptions.SecureSocketLayer = True
        con.AuthType = AuthType.Anonymous
        con.Bind()
        'do a RootDSE search and get the currentTime attribute
        Dim search As New SearchRequest( _
            "", _
            "(objectClass=*)", _
            SearchScope.Base, _
            New String(){"currentTime"} _
            )
        Dim response As SearchResponse = _
            DirectCast(con.SendRequest(search), SearchResponse)
        For Each entry As SearchResultEntry In response.Entries
            Console.WriteLine(entry.Attributes("currentTime")(0))
        Next
    End Sub

    Function ServerCallback( _
        ByVal connection As LdapConnection, _
        ByVal certificate As X509Certificate _
        ) As Boolean
    'ignore errors; do not even check the certificate
    'just return true
        Return True
    End Function
End Module
```

Even though we have tried to scare you with the complexity of SDS.P, the code turns out to be fairly simple.

The main trick here is that we define a method called ServerCallback that implements a method signature of a specific delegate (basically a .NET callback function) defined in SDS.P called VerifyServerCertificateCallback. We tell our LdapConnection to call our callback function during SSL certificate verification by using the AddressOf keyword on the `SessionOptions.VerifyServerCertificate` member to point to our method. `ServerCallback` simply returns `True`, instructing the underlying code to accept the certificate presented by the server and ignore any errors. We could write something more intelligent by looking at the data in the certificate that is passed to us if we wished.

 We are not recommending you should ignore SSL errors as a general practice. This is usually a bad idea, especially in cases where the infrastructure is not something you directly control. SSL is there is help protect us. It is better to try to fix the problem with the server's certificate instead, but using the correct host name or adding required trusted root certificates.

The rest of the code just sets up the connection to use SSL and anonymous authentication and connects to the directory using the `Bind` method. After that, we show a simple `RootDSE` search, a *Base* scope query with a null search base specified, and return the `currentTime` attribute to demonstrate a simple search operation. However, the point here is not to demonstrate the search, but to show the SSL verification. We would not even get past the `Bind` method without our SSL verification override if there was a problem with the server's certificate.

Summary

.NET, now in version 3.5, is here to stay, and Microsoft continues to invest in these resources for developers while the options in native code APIs have been largely unchanged for years now. Not only does .NET allow us to do the same things we are used to doing in our other tools, but it also provides access to features that were previously only available to C++ developers and new approaches that make development easier.

.NET is also an essential tool to learn for tackling other new technologies such as ASP.NET web development and Windows PowerShell.

In this chapter, we took a quick tour of the now-expansive landscape of directory services development namespace in .NET, including the following:

- `System.DirectoryServices`
- `System.DirectoryServices.ActiveDirectory`
- `System.DirectoryServices.AccountManagement`
- `System.DirectoryServices.Protocols`

A single chapter can only scratch the surface of what we can do, but hopefully we have given you enough to get your feet wet and generate some excitement about the possibilities.

## CHAPTER 30

PowerShell Basics

The goal of this chapter is to give you a basic understanding of what Windows PowerShell is, how it can help you, and a quick reference source for PowerShell constructs. We'll take a look at the PowerShell language, the built-in cmdlets, and how to integrate PowerShell with technologies like WMI.

PowerShell is more than just a shell. It's a scripting platform, a programming language, a development environment, and a replacement for the legacy Windows command shell, *cmd.exe*. Automation is a key facet of running a successful IT operation, and Windows PowerShell extends the ability to automate across numerous Microsoft and third-party technologies in an easy and cohesive manner.

Exploring the PowerShell

As with any shell, PowerShell has a number of basic features that you should be familiar with as you move through this chapter.

Variables and Objects

Variables are named data storage that you can use in PowerShell to store whatever you want. Variables are always prefixed with a $ sign followed by a name of your choosing. For example, if you wanted to store *Brian* in a variable called $FirstName, you would run $FirstName = "Brian".

Variables also have scope. Scope determines which level of access is provided to variables (and also functions) within the PowerShell environment. Table 30-1 details the three possible scopes for your variables. You need to remember scope when you start working with scripts and functions as you may find that variables you were looking to use are not always accessible.

Table 30-1. Scopes

Scope	Description
Local	Limited to the current function
Script	Limited to the context of the current executing script, with the exception of dot-sourced scripts
Global	Available across all scopes

 When you launch a script with a period in front of the name, the script is said to be "dot sourced". Dot sourcing takes all the variables in the script and makes them available to the calling scope. An example of where this might be useful is if you had a script that had a series of library functions you wanted to make available. If you wanted to dot source `c:\scripts\Myfunctions.ps1`, you would run:

```
c:\scripts\Myfunctions.ps1
```

Nearly everything we work with in PowerShell is an *object* of some kind. If you're a programmer, objects in PowerShell are just like objects in any other language. You can think of an object as a structured way to store data. There are two important facets of objects throughout this chapter—properties and methods.

Properties describe a given aspect of an object. For example, a user could have a property of `Name`. Properties are accessed by using a period. If you wanted to access the `Name` property of the `$user` variable, you would run `$user.name`.

A method is code that can be executed by the object. For example, a user could have a method called `Rename`. Methods are called by using a period and passing any parameters between parentheses. If you wanted to execute the `Rename` method of the object stored in `$user`, you would run `$user.Rename("George")`.

Working with Quotes

In most languages, quotes are used to wrap *strings*. PowerShell is no different as we saw earlier when we stored the string *Brian* in `$FirstName`. One thing you need to be cognizant of is how PowerShell behaves when you quote variables.

More specifically, PowerShell behaves differently whether you use the single quote, ', or double quotes, ". If you want to store a literal string without expanding variables, use the single quote. Conversely, if you want to expand variables in a string, use double quotes. `Write-Output 'Your current path is $pwd'` would print *Your current path is $pwd*. If you executed `Write-Output "Your current path is $pwd"`, PowerShell would output *Your current path is C:*.

Profiles

PowerShell profiles are scripts that run each time you load PowerShell. There are two types of profiles: user-specific and host-specific. Table 30-2 details the locations where you can store a profile. If you wanted to run a series of commands each time PowerShel loads, such as loading snap-ins you use often, you would place those commands in your profile. You can access the path to your profile by accessing the **$profile** variable.

 We'll discuss the key information about snap-ins later in this chapter.

Table 30-2. PowerShell profile locations

Path	Description
%windir%\system32\WindowsPowerShell\v1.0\profile.ps1	Applies to all users and instances of PowerShell.
%windir%\system32\WindowsPowerShell\v1.0\Microsoft.PowerShell_profile.ps1	Applies to all users but only the Microsoft.PowerShell instance of PowerShell. Other applications which host PowerShell will not apply this profile.
%UserProfile%\My Documents\WindowsPowerShell\profile.ps1	Applies to all instances of PowerShell run by the current user.
%UserProfile%\My Documents\WindowsPowerShell\Microsoft.PowerShell_profile.ps1	Applies only to the Microsoft.PowerShell instance of PowerShell run by the current user. Other applications which host PowerShell will not apply this profile.

Working with the Pipeline

The concept of a pipeline has been around for decades, but PowerShell has taken the pipeline to a new level. A pipeline is traditionally defined as the redirecting of the textual output of one process into the input of another process. However, this is text output, which has to be parsed, reparsed, modified, and passed along. Oftentimes, there is a lot of data loss along the way with this model.

PowerShell changes this paradigm by passing .NET objects in the pipeline. As a result the data which is passed is high fidelity compared to the typical text output which often loses detail every step of the way.

The $_ Expression

You'll see throughout this chapter that we frequently use **$_** in our scripts and commands. When you are working with the pipeline, you often need to refer to the current object being passed. **$_** is a shortcut for doing this. We'll cover a number of scenarios where the **$_** expression is critical as we go through this chapter.

Pipeline by Example

In order to demonstrate the difference between the traditional command-shell pipeline and the PowerShell pipeline, let's explore a common task—find all files in a folder structure that are greater than 1 MB in size.

First, let's look at how you'd do this in the traditional Windows command shell:

```
for /f "tokens=*" %F in ('dir /s /b') do @(if %~zF GTR 1048576 echo %F)
```

The same task can be accomplished in PowerShell using the following command:

```
dir C:\ -Recurse | Where-Object { $_.Length -gt 1mb } | `
    ForEach-Object{ $_.FullName }
```

 Dir is an alias for the Get-ChildItem cmdlet.

While the PowerShell command is certainly easier to read, there's definitely not an obvious benefit as it's even a bit longer than the DOS command. Consider if you needed to expand upon this example to determine additional information such as timestamps on the file, or even to filter on those timestamps:

```
# To output the last time the file was accessed and when it was created
dir c:\ -Recurse | ?{$_.Length -gt 1mb} | Format-Table `
    FullName,LastAccessTime,CreationTime

# Now... all files greater than 1 MB and not accessed in the last month
dir c:\ -Recurse | ?{($_.Length -gt 1mb) -And ($_.LastAccessTime `
    -lt (Get-Date).AddMonths( 1))}
```

 Notice that we use the $_ expression in these examples to refer to the current object being passed by the dir cmdlet. We'll cover the semantics of the filtering shortcut, ?, used here a bit later in the chapter.

These samples are possible in PowerShell because PowerShell returns an object for each result returned by the dir command. If you're familiar with .NET, the object returned is actually an instance of the System.IO.FileInfo class.

Cmdlets

PowerShell cmdlets are a key piece of the overall PowerShell environment. Out of the box, Windows PowerShell brings to the table numerous cmdlets that you can leverage in your scripts. As PowerShell has continued to evolve, third party software developers have begun releasing cmdlets for their own products, further enhancing the PowerShell environment. Microsoft makes the information required for anyone to build cmdlets available in the Windows SDK.

The Cmdlet Naming Scheme

Windows PowerShell brings predictability and discoverability by providing a standard naming scheme for cmdlets. Every cmdlet is named in a *Verb-Noun* fashion, and the list of approved verbs is defined by Microsoft. Table 30-3 details a list of approved verbs by category.

A few examples of this naming schema revolve around Windows services. If you wanted to get the list of all the services on a system, you could run the `Get-Service` cmdlet. To start a service, you could use the `Start-Service` cmdlet. Predictably, a list of processes is accessible with the `Get-Process` cmdlet.

While it's not required, we recommend that as a best practice you name the functions in your PowerShell scripts using the *Verb-Noun* model we've discussed.

 The list of verbs in Table 30-3 is simply a list of approved verbs. You can use other verbs and you will come across cmdlets that do, but as a best practice you should limit yourself to the verbs in Table 30-3.

Table 30-3. Approved verbs

Common verbs	Communication verbs	Data verbs	Diagnostic verbs	Lifecycle verbs	Security verbs
Add	Connect	Backup	Debug	Disable	Block
Clear	Disconnect	Checkpoint	Measure	Enable	Grant
Copy	Read	Compare	Ping	Install	Revoke
Get	Receive	Convert	Resolve	Restart	Unblock
Join	Send	ConvertFrom	Test	Resume	Security
Lock	Write	ConvertTo	Trace	Start	
Move		Dismount		Stop	
New		Export		Suspend	
Remove		Import		Uninstall	
Rename		Initialize			
Select		Limit			
Set		Merge			
Split		Mount			
Unlock		Restore			
		Update			
		Out			

Cmdlet Parameters

Nearly all of the cmdlets (and scripts) you work with in PowerShell will accept parameters, or arguments. Any information you need to provide to a cmdlet in order for it to run will be specified as a parameter. There are two types of parameters—named and positional.

Named parameters are passed by name. If, for example, you were to run `Get-ChildItem -Recurse -Path c:\windows`, you would have supplied two named parameters: `-Recurse` and `-Path`.

Positional parameters are assumed based on where they exist in the command sequence. Many of the default parameters for cmdlets, such as `-Path` for `Get-ChildItem`, are capable of acting as positional parameters. If you ran `Get-ChildItem C:\Windows`, PowerShell would assign *C:\Windows* to `-Path`, as `-Path` is also a positional parameter.

Parameters can also act as switches. Switches are parameters that, when specified, set a condition to true; when they are omitted, the condition is assumed to be false. The `-Recurse` parameter supplied to `Get-ChildItem` earlier is an example of a switch. If and only if `-Recurse` is specified, `Get-ChildItem` behaves recursively.

Working with Built-in Cmdlets

Table 30-4 covers many of the cmdlets that PowerShell includes out of the box. The list is far too long for us to discuss each cmdlet, but, as a rule, you can run the `Get-Help` cmdlet to access that cmdlet's help. For example, if you wanted to access help on the `Where-Object` cmdlet, you could run `Get-Help Where-Object`. You can supply the `-detailed` argument to the `Get-Help` cmdlet for even more information.

Table 30-4. PowerShell built-in cmdlets

Add-Content	Get-Location	Push-Location	Update-Type Data
Add-History	Get-Member	Read-Host	Where-Object
Add-Member	Get-PfxCertifi cate	Remove-Item	Write-Debug
Add-PSSnapin	Get-Process	Remove-ItemProperty	Write-Error
Clear-Content	Get-PSDrive	Remove-PSDrive	Write-Host
Clear-Item	Get-PSProvider	Remove-PSSnapin	Write-Out put
Clear-ItemProperty	Get-PSSnapin	Remove-Variable	Write-Pro gress
Clear-Variable	Get-Service	Rename-Item	
Compare-Object	Get-TraceSource	Rename-ItemProperty	

ConvertFrom-SecureString	Get-UICulture	Resolve-Path
Convert-Path	Get-Unique	Restart-Service
ConvertTo-Html	Get-Variable	Resume-Service
ConvertTo-SecureString	Get-WmiObject	Select-Object
Copy-Item	Group-Object	Select-String
Copy-ItemProperty	Import-Alias	Set-Acl
Export-Alias	Import-Clixml	Set-Alias
Export-Clixml	Import-Csv	Set-AuthenticodeSignature
Export-Console	Invoke-Expression	Set-Content
Export-Csv	Invoke-History	Set-Date
ForEach-Object	Invoke-Item	Set-ExecutionPolicy
Format-Custom	Join-Path	Set-Item
Format-List	Measure-Command	Set-ItemProperty
Format-Table	Measure-Object	Set-Location
Format-Wide	Move-Item	Set-PSDebug
Get-Acl	Move-ItemProperty	Set-Service
Get-Alias	New-Alias	Set-TraceSource
Get-AuthenticodeSignature	New-Item	Set-Variable
Get-ChildItem	New-ItemProperty	Sort-Object
Get-Command	New-Object	Split-Path
Get-Content	New-PSDrive	Start-Service
Get-Credential	New-Service	Start-Sleep
Get-Culture	New-TimeSpan	Start-Transcript
Get-Date	New-Variable	Stop-Process
Get-EventLog	Out-Default	Stop-Service
Get-ExecutionPolicy	Out-File	Stop-Transcript
Get-Help	Out-Host	Suspend-Service
Get-History	Out-Null	Tee-Object
Get-Host	Out-Printer	Test-Path
Get-Item	Out-String	Trace-Command
Get-ItemProperty	Pop-Location	Update-FormatData

When you're looking to learn a new technology, or even how to work with a new facet of an existing one, having the tools to understand how the technology works can make the learning process much easier. PowerShell provides three cmdlets that are indispensable in this situation: Get-Help, Get-Command, and Get-Member.

Get-Help

Get-Help is one of the first places you should turn when you're trying to understand how a cmdlet works, or even to look for a cmdlet that does what you need to do. There are a number of parameters you can specify for the Get-Help cmdlet:

Name
> Specifies the name of the cmdlet or *about topic* you want to get help for. You can specify wildcards as well, so to see all the about help files, you could run:
>
> ```
> Get-Help about_*
> ```

Component
> Displays help for a given component.

Functionality
> Displays help for a given functionality.

Role
> Displays help for a given role.

Category
> Displays help for a given category.

Full
> Specifies you want *all* the help available for the cmdlet. Since this switch leads to a large amount of information being printed, you'll probably want to leverage the built-in **help** function, which displays information in a paged fashion, instead. For example, if you wanted to get a full listing for the Get-Command cmdlet, you could run:
>
> ```
> help Get-Command -full
> ```

Detailed
> Specifies you want more than just basic help, but not all the help as is the case with the -Full switch.

Examples
> Specifies you want just the examples for the cmdlet, e.g., Get-Help Get-Help -Examples.

Get-Command

The Get-Command cmdlet, also accessible via the gcm alias, allows you to discover what cmdlets, functions, and scripts are available. The following is a partial list of the parameters for Get-Command:

Name

Specifies the name of the command you want to display, e.g., `Get-Command Get-ChildItem`. You can specify wildcards as well, similar to `Get-Help`.

Verb

You can use the `-Verb` parameter to query PowerShell for all of the cmdlets using a given verb. If, for example, you wanted to display all of the `Get` and `Set` verbs, you could run:

```
Get-Command -Verb Get,Set
```

Noun

Similar to the `-Verb` parameter, the `-Noun` parameter allows you to query PowerShell for all of the cmdlets using a specific noun. If, for example, you wanted to display all of the cmdlets using the `Service` verb, you could run:

```
Get-Command -Noun Service
```

PSSnapin

If you want to see the cmdlets defined in a given snap-in, you can use the `-PSSnapin` switch. If, for example, you wanted to view all of the cmdlets in the Quest AD Management snap-in (discussed in Chapter 31), you could run:

```
Get-Command -PSSnapin Quest.ActiveRoles.ADManagement
```

Get-Member

The `Get-Member` cmdlet, also accessible with the `gm` alias, can tell you about the properties and methods of an object in PowerShell. A common example of using this cmdlet is if you needed to know what properties were available for filtering or formatting your output. A partial list of the parameters available is:

InputObject

If you wanted to supply a specific object to `Get-Member` in lieu of leveraging the pipeline, you will need the `-InputObject` argument. If, for example, you wanted to examine the first element in the `$dirs` array, you could run:

```
Get-Member -InputObject $dir[0]
```

MemberType

If you want to filter on what types of members are outputted, you can use this switch. The most common member types you'll likely want to filter on are `Property` and `Method`. If you wanted to see all the properties of the output from the dir cmdlet, you could run:

```
dir | Get-Member -MemberType Property
```

Managing the Environment

Like any command shell, you'll need to work with and manipulate your environment in PowerShell. The environment comprises such thing as what directory you're working in, and the properties of the current shell.

Set-Location

The Set-Location cmdlet is aliased to cd and works similar to the cd command under a typical DOS shell.

Set-ExecutionPolicy

Execution policies govern the use of scripts. By default, you are not permitted to run any PowerShell scripts. Table 30-5 details the possible execution policies that you can set using Set-ExecutionPolicy.

Table 30-5. Execution policies

Execution Policy	Description
Restricted	No scripts are permitted to execute.
AllSigned	Only scripts that are digitally signed are permitted to execute.
RemoteSigned	Scripts that are downloaded or marked as being from the Internet are required to be digitally signed in order to execute.
Unrestricted	All scripts are permitted to execute.

 PowerShell also takes in to consideration your Internet Explorer security zone configuration settings when determining what execution policy to apply to a script. For more information on this, refer to the blog entry at *http://blogs.msdn.com/powershell/archive/2007/03/07/how-does-the -remotesigned-execution-policy-work.aspx*.

Get-PSSnapin

Snap-ins are .NET assemblies that contain a collection of cmdlets and/or providers for use within PowerShell. If you want to see which snapins are currently loaded in the shell, you can execute the Get-PSSnapin cmdlet. You can optionally specify the following parameters to customize the output of the Get-PSSnapin cmdlet:

Name
    Specify the name of one or more snap-ins to limit the cmdlet to.

Registered
    This switch will display all of the snap-ins PowerShell is aware of, regardless of whether or not they are currently loaded.

If you simply wanted to list all of the loaded snap-ins, you could run `Get-PSSnapin`. To extend the view to registered snap-ins, run:

```
Get-PSSnapin -Registered
```

Add-PSSnapin

In order to use a snap-in, you need to load it. The Add-PSSnapin cmdlet will load a given list of snap-ins either by name or via the pipeline. If you use a particular snap-in a lot, add the `Add-PsSnapin` command in your profile to load snap-ins for you.

If you wanted to automatically load all the snap-ins you have registered, you could run:

```
Get-PSSnapin -Registered | Add-PsSnapin
```

Formatting Output

Often times, you'll find that the manner in which cmdlet output is displayed is less than optimal. PowerShell provides, with the `Format` verb, a number of cmdlets that allow you to control the output style via the pipeline.

Format-List

The `Format-List` cmdlet, aliased to `fl`, allows you to display the output of a cmdlet in a list style. You can use the `-Property` parameter to specify which properties are output to the shell. In this example, we get the status of the *lanmanserver* service and display a filtered list of properties in list format:

```
PS C:\> Get-Service lanmanserver | fl Name,DisplayName,Status
Name        : lanmanserver
DisplayName : Server
Status      : Running
```

Format-Table

The `Format-Table` cmdlet, aliased to `ft`, allows you to display the output of a cmdlet in a tabular format. Much like the `Format-List` cmdlet, you can use the `-Property` parameter to specify which properties are output to the shell. In this example, we output the status of the last four services output by the `Get-Service` cmdlet in tabular format:

```
PS C:\> Get-Service | Select -Last 4 | ft Name,DisplayName,Status

Name            DisplayName                     Status
----            -----------                     ------
wuauserv        Automatic Updates               Running
WZCSVC          Wireless Configuration          Running
Xmlprov         Network Provisioning Service    Stopped
XobniService    XobniService                    Running
```

The `Format-Table` cmdlet has a number of parameters that are worth discussing:

AutoSize
>   The -AutoSize parameter formats the table so that the columns are the minimum width necessary to display their contents. This is a popular parameter because it is very useful when you have several properties and you want them to fit nicely on the screen.

HideTableHeaders
>   If you don't want to see the table headers, specify the -HideTableHeaders switch.

GroupBy
>   -GroupBy is a useful parameter that allows you to group the output in a cmdlet by a given property. If you wanted to display the contents of the C:\Windows folder grouped by file extension, you could run:

```
dir C:\WINDOWS | ft -GroupBy Extension
```

>   You can also use -GroupBy with the Format-List cmdlet.

InputObject
>   If you want to display an existing object in lieu of depending on the pipeline, you can specify that object to the -InputObject parameter. You can also use -InputObject with the Format-List cmdlet.

Out-Null

The Out-Null cmdlet simply disposes of information piped to it in lieu of printing it to the console.

Processing and Filtering Output

When you're working with the output of a cmdlet, you may need to process or filter that output before passing it to another cmdlet in the pipeline. Two important cmdlets for this activity are Foreach-Object and Where-Object.

Foreach-Object

The foreach-object cmdlet, aliased to %, processes each item in the pipeline and executes a given set of commands for each object. There are a few parameters of foreach-object that you'll want to be familiar with:

Process
>   A script block that executes the foreach element in the pipe.

InputObject
>   If you want to display an existing object in lieu of depending on the pipeline, you can specify that object to the -InputObject parameter.

Begin

If you'd like to execute some code prior to running the code specified in `-Process`, you can specify `-Begin`. In this example, we print *Started* followed by the name of each item in the current directory:

```
dir | % -Begin {Write-Host "Started"} -Process {$_.Name}
```

End

Similar to the `-Begin` parameter, `-End` allows you to execute some code at the conclusion of processing each item in the pipeline. In this example, we print *Complete* to the shell following the display of each item in the current directory:

```
dir | % -Process {$_.Name} -End {Write-Host "Complete"}
```

 `-End` is the last code block executed, but, as with `-Begin`, it is only processed once and does not have access to `$_`.

Where-Object

The `Where-Object` cmdlet, aliased to `?`, allows you to execute a block of code that determines, for each item in the pipeline, whether or not that object will be passed further down the pipeline. The `Where-Object` cmdlet is what you should use if you need to filter output:

FilterScript

The `-FilterScript` parameter provides the code that will execute for each item in the pipeline. If the result of the code is `$true`, the object will be passed on. Otherwise, it will be dropped.

InputObject

If you want to display an existing object in lieu of depending on the pipeline, you can specify that object to the `-InputObject` parameter.

If, for example, you wanted to gather a list of all the files in a folder that were greater than 10 megabytes in size, you could run:

```
dir C:\windows | ?{$_.Length -gt 10mb}
```

If, for example, you wanted to get a list of services that are currently stopped, you could run:

```
Get-Service | ?{$_.Status -eq "Stopped"}
```

Importing Information

Very often you'll find that your scripts need to work with information stored in files. For importing information from the filesystem, PowerShell provides a number of cmdlets that we'll explore here.

Get-Content

The Get-Content cmdlet, aliased to gc, imports the contents of a file and creates an array with each line representing a separate entry in the array. There are a number of parameters you'll want to be familiar with when working with the Get-Content cmdlet:

Path
> This is the file or path to a series of files you want to work with.

Include
> If you want to process a certain set of files specified in -Path, you can provide a filter here. If, for example, you wanted to process all of the text files, you could specify -Include *.txt.

Exclude
> If you want to process a certain set of files specified in -Path, except for those matching a filter, you can provide that filter here. If, for example, you wanted to exclude all of the executable files, you could specify -Exclude *.exe.

TotalCount
> -TotalCount limits the number of lines read from the file.

If you had a text file called *MyServerList.txt* with a list of server names, one per line, you could read those server names into an array variable $servers by running:

```
$servers = Get-Content c:\temp\MyServerList.txt
```

If you wanted to only read the first 10 servers in *MyServerList.txt*, you could run:

```
$servers = gc c:\temp\MyServerList.txt -TotalCount 10
```

 We used the alias of Get-Content, gc, in the preceding example.

Import-Csv

Comma-separated value (CSV) files are easily one of the most common formats for exchanging data between systems. PowerShell makes working with CSVs easy by providing the Import-Csv cmdlet, which will process a given CSV file. One limitation is that PowerShell expects the first line to contain a header row that contains the names of the columns. PowerShell uses these to create the objects stored in the array Import-CSV builds.

If you wanted to import a file called *MyUsers.csv*, you could run $users = Import-Csv MyUsers.csv. If you subsequently ran $users[0], you would be able to see the names of the columns that PowerShell has converted to properties of the objects and, of course, the data in the first line of the CSV.

Import-CliXml

If you need to import objects serialized to the filesystem using `Export-CliXml`, you can use the `Import-CliXml` cmdlet. We'll discuss `Export-CliXml` in more detail in the next section. If you wanted to import MyObjects.xml and store it in `$myObjects`, you could run:

```
$myObjects = Import-CliXml MyObjects.xml
```

Exporting Information

As you might expect, PowerShell includes cmdlets that export information, much like the cmdlets that import data.

Export-Csv

If you want to export an object or a series of objects to a CSV file, you can pass them to the `Export-Csv` cmdlet. There are a few parameters that you should be aware of when working with the `Export-Csv` cmdlet:

Path
> This is the file you want to export to.

InputObject
> If you want to display an existing object in lieu of depending on the pipeline, you can specify that object to the `-InputObject` parameter.

NoTypeInformation
> When specified, this switch tells PowerShell to exclude type information from the export.

If you wanted to export a listing of the services currently loaded on a machine in CSV format, you could run this command:

```
Get-Service | Select Name,DisplayName,Status | Export-Csv MyServices.csv -NoTypeInformation
```

Export-CliXml

Serialization is a term that, in the context of our discussion, means taking an object (or a series of objects) and converting them to a format that can be persisted to the filesystem. XML is the format PowerShell allows us to serialize objects to in conjunction with the `Export-CliXml` cmdlet. As discussed earlier, if you want to deserialize an object, you would use the `Import-CliXml` cmdlet. There are a few parameters that you should be aware of when working with the `Export-CliXml` cmdlet:

Path
> This is the file you want to export to.

InputObject
> If you want to display an existing object in lieu of depending on the pipeline, you can specify that object to the -InputObject parameter.

If you wanted to export the objects returned by the Get-Process cmdlet, you could run:

```
Get-Process | Export-CliXml CurrentProcesses.xml
```

If you had an array of objects, $myArray, that you wanted to save, you could run:

```
Export-CliXml myArray.xml -InputObject $myArray
```

Out-File

The Out-File cmdlet will export cmdlet output to a text file exactly as it is displayed on the screen. There are a few parameters that you should be aware of when working with the Out-File cmdlet:

FilePath
> This is the file you want to export to.

Append
> When specified, this switch instructs the cmdlet to append data to the end of an existing file.

InputObject
> If you want to display an existing object in lieu of depending on the pipeline, you can specify that object to the -InputObject parameter.

If you wanted to export the list of processes running on the machine to a text file called *MyProcesses.txt*, you could run:

```
Get-Process | Out-File MyProcesses.txt
```

Building PowerShell Scripts

PowerShell *scripts* are text files that contain a series of PowerShell commands that are run sequentially. Typically, scripts also contain functions that you can reference throughout the script, and sometimes from the PowerShell console at large. Scripts are always stored in a file named with a *.ps1* extension. To execute a script, you would pass the fully qualified or relative path followed by any arguments. To run MyScript.ps1, which is in the current directory, you would run .\MyScript.ps1.

If you want to structure your scripts to use the pipeline, you will want to use a process block as well as optional begin and end blocks. The syntax is similar to the following:

```
begin
{
    # This code is executed once at the beginning of the script
}
process
{
```

```
    # This code is executed for each object in the pipeline
}
end
{
    # This code is executed once at the end of the script

}
```

Any time you prefix a line with the # symbol, you are making a comment.
Comments are ignored by PowerShell and are purely for making your
scripts easier to understand.

To access the current pipeline object in the pipeline during the process block, you would
use the $_ variable. In this example we simply print each object in the pipeline:

```
begin
{
    Write-Host "Starting"
}
process
{
    Write-Host $_
}
end
{
    Write-Host "Complete"
}
```

Arguments

PowerShell exposes any arguments to your scripts through the $args array variable. If
you want to check how many arguments have been passed, you can access
$args.Count. Since $args is an array, you can loop through the contents as described
later in this chapter in the section on loops.

Any arguments which are declared as named or positional arguments
in the script declaration will not be included in the $args array variable.
Refer to the discussion on the param keyword in the section on Functions
for more information about declaring arguments.

If you want to have a formal definition of the arguments your script expects, you should
start your script with a param block, which we discuss shortly in the section on functions.

Functions

You can simply place PowerShell commands in the script, or you can organize your script into *functions*. Functions allow you to create blocks of code that can be called repeatedly throughout the script without having the code in your script more than once.

You define a function with the function keyword followed by a unique name for the function. The syntax is similar to the following:

```
function FunctionName()
{
    #code
}
```

If, for example, you wanted to define a function that simply printed the current date and time to the console, you could write something like this:

```
Function PrintDateTime()
{
    Get-Date
}
```

Quite often, however, functions will accept parameters that customize the behavior of the function. If you want to specify parameters, you need to use the param keyword in conjunction with function:

```
function FunctionName()
{
    param($parameter1, $parameter2)
    #code
}
```

If, for example, you wanted to define a function that added two numbers together, you could write code like this:

```
function Add()
{
    param([int32]$numberA, [int32]$numberB)
    $numberA + $numberB
}
```

In the preceding example, we also told PowerShell the *type* of the variables we expected. By telling PowerShell that we were expecting 32-bit integers, we allow PowerShell to make sure that if, for example, a string was passed, an error would result. This saves us from having to write our own parameter-verification code here. You can simply omit the bracketed type information if you don't need this functionality.

When calling functions, you should use syntax similar to the following:

```
$result = Add 1 2
```

This will store 3 in $result. If you delimit the parameters with commas or include parentheses as is expected in many scripting languages, PowerShell will display an error.

Error Handling

Handling errors is an important tenet of scripting such that you can ensure that your scripts continue executing even when the unexpected occurs. There are two ways to handle errors in PowerShell: the first is with the -ErrorAction parameter, and the second is through the use of trap blocks.

The -ErrorAction parameter can be passed to cmdlets and scripts and will define what action PowerShell should take when an error occurs. Table 30-6 details the possible error actions.

Table 30-6. Error-action preferences

Error Action	Description
Continue	The default setting. PowerShell will print an error message but continue executing.
SilentlyContinue	PowerShell will continue processing, but will not print the error message.
Stop	PowerShell will halt processing and display the error message.
Inquire	PowerShell will display the error message and prompt the user for action.

You can access the current error-action setting from your scripts by examining the $ErrorActionPreference variable.

When you want to handle an exception in the body of your script, you can use a trap block. The syntax for a trap block is:

```
trap
{
    # error handling code
    # break or continue
}
```

After you execute the error-handling code, you can specify the break or continue keyword. If you specify break, PowerShell will halt execution of your function or script. If you specify continue, PowerShell will proceed with the processing of your function or script. If you do not specify break or continue, PowerShell will proceed without handling the error.

If you want to cause an error, you can use the *throw* keyword. For example, *throw "A serious error has occurred."*

Flow Control

Flow control statements allow scripts to branch depending on different conditions. Different types of flow-control statements, such as conditional statements and loops, exist in PowerShell.

Conditional Statements

The most common type of conditional statement is undoubtedly the If block. If blocks allow your code to make decisions based on logical operators and comparison operators. Table 30-7 details a list of logical operators, and Table 30-8 details a list of comparison operators.

Table 30-7. Logical operators

Operator	Description
-and	Performs a logical AND
-or	Performs a logical OR
-xor	Performs a logical XOR
-not	Performs a logical NOT

Table 30-8. Comparison operators

Operator	Description	Example
-eq	Equal	If($val -eq $anotherVal){"They are the Same"}
-ne	Not equal	If($val -ne $anotherVal){"Not the Same"}
-gt	Greater than	If($number -gt 10){"Number is 11 or Higher"}
-ge	Greater than or equal to	If($number -ge 10){"Number is 10 or higher"}
-lt	Less than	If($number -lt 10){"Number is Less than 10"}
-le	Less than or equal to	If($number -le 10){"Number is 10 or Lower"}
-like	Wildcard compare	If($val -like "*found*"){"Value has found in it"}
-notlike	Negative wild card compare	If($val -notlike "*missing*"){"Value doesn't have missing in it"}
-match	Regular expression (regex) compare	If($val -match "^Begin"){"Starts with Begin"}
-notmatch	Negative regular expression (regex) compare	If($val -notmatch "Done$"){"Doesn't end with Done"}
-contains	Containment operator for arrays	If($array -contains $value){"$value is in the array"}
-notcontains	Negative containment operator for arrays	If($array -notcontains $value){"$value is missing from array"}

 Most of the comparison operators in Table 30-8 have case-sensitive equivalents. To access the case-sensitive equivalent, prefix the operator name with a c. For example, if you wanted to test for case-sensitive equality, you would use -ceq.

The syntax of the `if, elseif,` and `else` statements is:

```
if (condition)
{
    #Code to execute
}
elseif (condition)
{
    #Code to execute
}
else
{
    #Code to execute
}
```

For example, if you wanted to test whether a variable was less than, greater than, or equal to 10, you could run code similar to this:

```
$value = 17
if ($value -lt 10)
{
    Write-Output "$value is less than 10"
}
elseif ($value -gt 10)
{
    Write-Output "$value is greater than 10"
}
else
{
    Write-Output "$value is equal to 10"
}
```

Switch statements allow you to check if a variable matches a series of conditions and then take action. If, for example, we wanted to execute some code depending on what letter was stored in `$value`, we could do something like this:

```
$value = "b"
switch ($value)
{
    "a"   { '$value is equal to a' }
    "b"   { '$value is equal to b' }
    "c"   { '$value is equal to c' }
    default { '$value is not equal to a, b, or c" }
}
```

One neat trick with the `switch` statement is that you can pass the -file argument, and the switch statement will execute for each line in the file:

```
switch -file myfile.txt
{
    #...
}
```

Loops

Loops allow you to execute code either until a condition is true or a predetermined number of times. For example, if you had an array of objects that you needed to process, you would typically use a foreach loop. If you wanted to run some code until a condition occurred, you would use a while loop. For more information on arrays, see the upcoming sidebar "Working with Arrays."

The syntax of a foreach loop is:

```
foreach($item in $array)
{
    #code
}
```

If you wanted to process an array, you could run some code similar to the following:

```
$myArray = @("entry 1", "entry 2", "entry 3")
foreach($item in $myArray)
{
    Write-Output "The current item is $item."
}
```

 There is an important difference between the foreach statement and the alias foreach. The alias foreach is an alias for the Foreach-Object cmdlet. This difference is critical as the foreach statement does *not* accept piped input and the foreach-object cmdlet does not accept the syntax of foreach.

For the most part, you should never notice this difference since PowerShell has logic that determines which foreach to use, but knowing this difference could be important in case you get snagged.

The for loop is very closely related to the foreach loop. The difference is that the for loop runs a defined number of times tracked by a *counter variable*. The syntax of a for loop is:

```
for(initialization; condition; increment)
{
    #code
}
```

If you wanted to execute some code 100 times, you could use a for loop similar to the following:

```
for($i = 0; $i -lt 100; $i++)
{
    Write-Output "`$i is currently $i"
}
```

The preceding example is an example of using an escape statement. Since we are using double quotes, PowerShell would replace both occurrences of $i with the current value. By prefixing $i with the backtick, PowerShell ignores that instance of $i.

Working with Arrays

Arrays, also known as collections, are used to store lists of objects of the same type. You can create arrays using the @() construct, e.g., $array = @($object1,$object2,$object3). When you want to reference a specific element of an array, you reference that element by *index*. Indexes refer to the position in the array, with the first element being in position zero. For example, to reference the second element of $array, you would use $array[1].

Hash tables are special types of arrays that store key/value pairs. Each key must be unique and refer to a single value. You can also create hash tables by using the @{} construct, e.g., $hash = @{"localhost"="127.0.0.1"; "server2"="192.168.1.100"}. When you want to refer to an element in a hash table, you refer to that element by its key. To access the IP of server2 in $hash, you would run $hash["server2"].

We use while loops to run a block of code until a condition becomes false. The syntax of a while loop is:

```
while($condition)
{
    #code
}
```

A common example where you might use a while loop is when you need to wait for specific user input, perhaps to receive confirmation. Here's an example of waiting for a user to type in "yes":

```
Write-Host "We need confirmation to proceed!"
while ($input -notmatch "yes")
{
        $input = Read-Host "Type `"yes`" to continue:"
}
```

All of the loop structures we've explored so far allow you to use the break and continue statements to manage the execution of the loop. If you need to immediately exit a loop, you would use the break statement. This example is an infinite while loop that we exit when $i exceeds 100:

```
while($true)
{
    $i++
    if($i -gt 100)
    {
        break
```

```
        }
    }
```

Continue statements return you to the beginning of a loop, bypassing the remainder of the loop body. The following is an example of the continue statement in a script that searches *myFile.txt* and prints lines that don't contain the string "Michigan":

```
foreach($entry in (Get-Content myFile.txt))
{
    if($entry -match "Michigan")
    {
        Write-Host "Line contains Michigan"
        continue
    }
    Write-Host "$entry"
}
```

The Get-Content cmdlet allows us to read the contents of an item such as a text file and process them one line at a time.

Using WMI

PowerShell fully exposes WMI through the Get-WMIObject cmdlet (alias gwmi). There are a number of parameters you'll want to take a look at when using the Get-WMIObject cmdlet:

Class

The -Class parameter specifies the WMI class you want to retrieve. In this example, we retrieve the contents of the Win32_ComputerSystem class for the current machine:

```
Get-WMIObject Win32_ComputerSystem

Domain              : WORKGROUP
Manufacturer        : Dell Inc.
Model               : Dimension 4700
Name                : BRIAN-WKS01
PrimaryOwnerName    : Brian Desmond
TotalPhysicalMemory : 3219177472
```

Property

If you want to filter the properties returned from a WMI class, you can use the -Property parameter. In this example, we retrieve two properties from the Win32_OperatingSystem class:

```
Get-WmiObject Win32_OperatingSystem -Property `
    SystemDirectory,Version
SystemDirectory : C:\WINDOWS\system32
Version         : 5.2.3790
```

Namespace

The -Namespace parameter works in conjunction with -Class to tell WMI where the class is located. For example, if you wanted to see the ICMP settings for the Windows Firewall, you could use the HNet_FwICMPSettings class from the Root \Microsoft\HomeNet namespace:

```
gwmi -Name Root\Microsoft\HomeNet -Class HNet_FwIcmpSettings

AllowInboundEchoRequest                : False
AllowInboundMaskRequest                : False
AllowInboundRouterRequest              : False
AllowInboundTimestampRequest           : False
AllowOutboundDestinationUnreachable    : False
AllowOutboundParameterProblem          : False
AllowOutboundSourceQuench              : False
AllowOutboundTimeExceeded              : False
AllowRedirect                          : False
Name                                   : Default
```

 Notice that in this example, we used the gwmi alias to Get-WMIObject.

ComputerName

You can provide the -ComputerName parameter with a list of remote machine names to connect to, and Get-WMIObject will execute the WMI query against each of those machines. In this example, we connect to two remote machines specified in $servers to collect Win32_ComputerSystem info:

```
$servers = "Win2k8x64dc1","Win2k8x64dc2"
gwmi Win32_ComputerSystem -ComputerName $servers

Domain              : corp.lab
Manufacturer        : VMware, Inc.
Model               : VMware Virtual Platform
Name                : WIN2K8X64DC1
PrimaryOwnerName    : Windows User
TotalPhysicalMemory : 1072447488

Domain              : corp.lab
Manufacturer        : VMware, Inc.
Model               : VMware Virtual Platform
Name                : WIN2K8X64DC2
PrimaryOwnerName    : Windows User
TotalPhysicalMemory : 535576576
```

Filter

The -Filter parameter allows you to specify a filter for the WMI engine to apply to each result returned. If, for example, you ran Get-WMIObject Win32_Service without a filter, you would get a listing of every service on the machine. In this example, we use the -Filter parameter to limit the results to information about the *Browser* service:

```
gwmi Win32_Service -Filter "name='Browser'"

ExitCode  : 1077
Name      : Browser
ProcessId : 0
StartMode : Disabled
State     : Stopped
Status    : OK
```

Query

If you're used to working with WMI from VBScript, for example, you probably are used to running WQL queries to retrieve information from WMI. In this example, we use the -Query parameter to specify a query that returns information about the *NetLogon* service:

```
$query = "SELECT * FROM Win32_Service WHERE Name='Netlogon'"
gwmi -Query $query

ExitCode  : 0
Name      : Netlogon
ProcessId : 584
StartMode : Auto
State     : Running
Status    : OK
```

There are a couple of free tools we recommend that will make working with WMI much easier:

- Scriptomatic available from *http://www.microsoft.com/DownLoads/details.aspx ?familyid=09DFC342-648B-4119-B7EB-783B0F7D1178*.
- WMIExplorer available from *http://thepowershellguy.com/blogs/posh/archive/tags/ WMI+Explorer/default.aspx*
- PowerTab available from *http://thepowershellguy.com/blogs/posh/pages/powertab .aspx*

Summary

In this chapter, we've taken a look at the Windows PowerShell language and environment. We took a look at the cmdlets that PowerShell is centered around and how to work with them. The pipeline is an extremely powerful component of PowerShell that allows you to pass objects between cmdlets for manipulation without any loss of fidelity. PowerShell exposes WMI and the .NET framework to you for use in addition to the cmdlets available, and we took a look at how to work with WMI as well. In Chapter 31, we explore how to use PowerShell specifically for managing Active Directory.

Scripting Active Directory with PowerShell

This chapter will show you how take advantage of Windows PowerShell to execute common Active Directory administration tasks. Over the course of this chapter, we'll examine tasks centered on management of users, groups, computers, and organizational units. After mastering these elements, we will go on to assemble a PowerShell script that can be used to populate an Active Directory test domain. As a capstone to this activity, we will look at a number of third-party PowerShell snap-ins that can extend the script built in this chapter.

If you haven't already, take a few minutes to review Chapter 29 for an introduction to managing Active Directory with .NET.

Becoming Familiar with .NET

Working with Windows PowerShell doesn't require that you understand all the intricacies of .NET or even be a developer. However, having a basic grasp of the .NET classes used for working with Active Directory will make you much more productive. In this section, we'll take a look at the key .NET classes used throughout this chapter and how to leverage them in PowerShell. The majority of these classes are located in the `System.DirectoryServices` *namespace*, which we'll abbreviate as `SDS` throughout this chapter.

DirectoryEntry

Almost anytime you need to represent an object in Active Directory, chances are you'll be using the `DirectoryEntry` class. This is so common that PowerShell actually includes a shortcut for referencing objects in Active Directory. If you prefix a distinguished name with [ADSI], PowerShell will create a `DirectoryEntry` object for you. For example, you could build a `DirectoryEntry` for a user *bdesmond* like this:

```
[ADSI]"LDAP://cn=bdesmond,cn=users,dc=corp,dc=lab"
```

```
distinguishedName
-----------------
{cn=bdesmond,cn=users,dc=corp,dc=lab}
```

> You will often see the use of [ADSI] in scripts or samples on the Internet since it makes code shorter and easier to read. If you're wondering what is happening behind the scenes, the equivalent PowerShell command to the previous code sample would be:
>
> ```
> New-Object System.DirectoryServices.DirectoryEntry `
> "LDAP://cn=bdesmond,cn=users,dc=corp,dc=lab"
> ```
>
> [ADSI] is an example of a *type accelerator*.

DirectorySearcher

The `DirectorySearcher` class is, as its name implies, for searching for objects in Active Directory. It's important to remember that the search results returned from a `DirectorySearcher` are `SearchResult` objects, not `DirectoryEntry` objects.

> If you need to get the `DirectoryEntry` object (such as for making an update to the search result), call `SearchResult.GetDirectoryEntry()`.

In this example, we will search the domain for user *bdesmond*:

```
$filter = "(sAMAccountName=bdesmond)"
$ds = New-Object DirectoryServices.DirectorySearcher([ADSI]"", $filter)
$ds.FindOne()
```

Notice how we were able to embed an [ADSI] shortcut within our script. In this case, by providing an empty string to [ADSI], the `DirectoryEntry` class will represent the root of the current domain.

Domain

.NET provides a `Domain` class in the `SDS.ActiveDirectory` namespace that allows you to query and manipulate domains in the forest. If you wanted to get the `Domain` object representing the current domain, you could run this code:

```
[DirectoryServices.ActiveDirectory.Domain]::GetCurrentDomain()
```

When you need to access a *static* member of a class, you must use `::` to do so. `GetCurrentDomain()` is a static method in the `Domain` class.

Forest

.NET provides a `Forest` class in the `SDS.ActiveDirectory` namespace that allows you to query and manipulate the forest. If you wanted to get the `Forest` object representing the current forest, you could run this code:

```
[DirectoryServices.ActiveDirectory.Forest]::GetCurrentForest()
```

DirectoryContext

Many of the classes in the `SDS.ActiveDirectory` namespace require that you specify additional hints for them to succeed. The `DirectoryContext` class encapsulations all of this information including the ability for you to specify explicit credentials to operate under. Table 31-1 provides a list of valid context types.

In this example, we create a `DirectoryContext` for binding to the forest *corp.lab* using explicit credentials:

```
$context = New-Object
System.DirectoryServices.ActiveDirectory.DirectoryContext('Forest', `
    "corp.lab",'jUser',"P@ssWOrd!22")
[DirectoryServices.ActiveDirectory.Forest]::GetForest($context)
```

Table 31-1. Directory contexts

Context	Description
Domain	The DNS name of a domain
Forest	The DNS name of a forest
DirectoryServer	The DNS name of a domain controller or AD LDS instance
ConfigurationSet	Represents a service connection point (SCP) for an AD LDS instance
ApplicationPartition	The DNS name of an application partition

DomainController

The `DomainController` class in the `SDS.ActiveDirectory` namespace not surprisingly represents a domain controller. You can use the `DomainController` class as a wrapper for performing DC Locator calls as well as for tasks such as moving a FSMO role. In this example, we find a domain controller in the *corp.lab* domain:

```
$context = New-Object DirectoryServices.ActiveDirectory.DirectoryContext('Domain',`
    "corp.lab")
[DirectoryServices.ActiveDirectory.DomainController]::FindOne($context)
```

GlobalCatalog

The `GlobalCatalog` class in the `SDS.ActiveDirectory` namespace is an extension of the `DomainController` class that specifically represents global catalogs. You can use the `GlobalCatalog` class as a wrapper for performing DC Locator calls as well as for tasks such as promoting a domain controller to a global catalog. In this example, we find a global catalog in the *corp.lab* forest:

```
$context = New-Object DirectoryServices.ActiveDirectory.DirectoryContext('Forest',`
    "corp.lab")
[DirectoryServices.ActiveDirectory.GlobalCatalog]::FindOne($context)
```

 Notice that we specify a forest-level `DirectoryContext` in this example. Global catalogs are a forest-level configuration item, so it would not make sense to specify a specific domain.

ApplicationPartition

You can access a list of application partitions in the forest via the Forest class. This list is a collection of `ApplicationPartition` objects. In this example, we return a list of application partitions in the current forest:

```
$forest = [DirectoryServices.ActiveDirectory.Forest]::GetCurrentForest()
$forest.ApplicationPartitions
```

 The `ApplicationPartition` class is located in the `SDS.ActiveDirectory` namespace.

Understanding Client-Side Processing

Before we dive into building our script, it is important to take a minute to understand what is actually happening under the covers when you run ADSI code under Power-Shell. Figure 31-1 illustrates how PowerShell interacts with Active Directory to execute the following code sample:

```
# Script To Change User CN and Display Name
$user = [ADSI]"LDAP://CN=Jsmith,OU=MyUsers,DC=Corp,DC=lab"
$user.DisplayName = "Jon Smith"
$user.GivenName = "Jon"
$user.SetInfo()
```

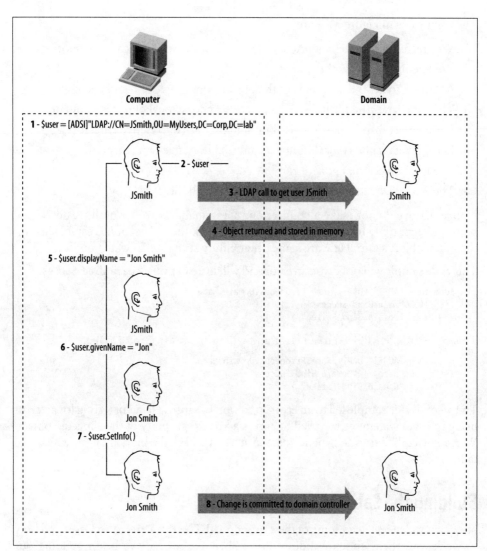

Figure 31-1. Client-side object processing

The eight steps in Figure 31-1 are:

1. We create a reference to an Active Directory object in our local in-memory cache.
2. We attempt to access the user.
3. A request to get the attributes of the object from Active Directory is made.
4. The data is returned from Active Directory and the local object is populated.
5. Local object display name is set (but not committed to Active Directory).
6. Local object name is set (but not committed to Active Directory).
7. The local object changes are committed.
8. The Active Directory object is modified to match the local copy.

Notice that we do not make a connection to a domain controller until we access the object the first time. It is a common mistake to think the connection is established on the initial object setup. Here are some other failure scenarios to watch out for.

This code sample will not cause an error and will instead print `Domain Bind Successful`:

```
$domain = [ADSI]"LDAP://Some.Erroneous.Domain.Name"
If($?){ "Domain Bind Successful" } `
    else{ "Domain Bind Failed" }
```

This code sample will lead to an error and will print `Domain Bind Failed`:

```
$domain = [ADSI]"LDAP://Some.Erroneous.Domain.Name"
If($domain.name) { "Domain Bind Successful" } `
    else{ "Domain Bind Failed" }
```

The second code sample led to an error condition because instead of testing for an error using the (`$?`) statement, we tried to access a known property of the expected object. When PowerShell tries to expand `$domain.name`, it makes the bind attempt, which will fail.

Building the Lab Build Script

Now that we've reviewed some of the common .NET Active Directory classes and how to work with them under Windows PowerShell, we're ready to begin building our script. We'll first take a look at some boilerplate setup code for the script, and then we'll begin building the functions necessary to support the logic of our script.

Setup

To kick off our script, we're going to need to lay the foundation for our code. The code sample below is the code we will start off with:

```
Param($dc, $domain, $count=10)
# Script Setup
if($dc -ne $null)
{
```

```
    $ldapConnectionString = "LDAP://$dc/"
    $domainDN = ([ADSI]"LDAP://$dc").distinguishedName[0]
}
else
{
    $ldapConnectionString = "LDAP://"
    $domainDN = ([ADSI]"").distinguishedName[0]
}
if(!$domain){$domain = $domainDN -Replace "dc=", "" -Replace ",", "."}
```

In this section we define what we want to accept from the command line as parameters (also called arguments). The `Param` statement defines which parameters we want to accept:

```
Param($dc, $domain, $count=10)
```

Our script will accept three parameters:

$dc

This value, if supplied, is used as the domain controller to connect to when we make our Active Directory connections. This is an optional parameter, and the code is smart enough to locate a domain controller for us if we don't specify **$dc**.

$domain

We will use $domain to create the `userPrincipalName` for user objects. If **$domain** is not specified, the code will generate it by using the distinguished name of the discovered Domain:

```
if(!$domain){$domain = $DomainDN -Replace "dc=", "" -Replace ",", "."}
```

$count

This parameter specifies how many `OrganizationalUnit` objects to create. By default we will create 10 child `OrganizationalUnit` objects, 50 `User` objects (5 per child `OrganizationalUnit`), and 50 `Computer` objects (5 per child `OrganizationalUnit`) for each test `OrganizationalUnit`.

After the `Param` statement, our code parses the parameters passed and builds two local variables which will be used later on. First, we check to see if a **$dc** was passed and use this information to determine the **$LdapConnectionString** and **$DomainDN**:

$ldapConnectionString

This string (which contains the object's `distinguishedName`) is used to get the Active Directory objects. If no domain controller is passed, we use "LDAP://" as the string.

$domlitainDN

The distinguished name of the domain.

If $dc was passed we create an LDAP connection string to that DC and then return the `distinguishedName` by making a connection to the server and requesting the property. For example, if **-dc Win2k8x64DC1.corp.lab** is passed we would end up with $LdapCon nectionString as *LDAP://Win2k8x64DC1.corp.lab/* and $domainDN as *DC=corp,DC=lab*.

If $dc is null, then we assume the user wants to just discover this information using the current user domain. In this case we set the $LdapConnectionString to *LDAP://*, and we make a connection to Active Directory using an empty string and return the distinguishedName of the domain that was discovered. After this section of code is run, we should have all the information we need to get started.

Creating Organizational Units

Since we're going to need a place to store the objects our script creates, we'll start off by building the organizational unit code. Like any other Active Directory object, we can create organizational units in PowerShell by using the ADSI interface provided by the DirectoryEntry class. The code below is a complete function for creating an organizational unit object:

```
Function New-ADOU {
  Param($Name, $OU)

  $root = "${LdapConnectionString}${OU}"
  $BaseOU = [ADSI]$root
  $NewOU = $BaseOU.Create("organizationalUnit", "ou=$Name")
  $NewOU.SetInfo()
  $NewOU.DistinguishedName
}
```

First we start with the function statement, which names the function and sets up the parameters for the function. Our parameters are:

$Name
  The name of the new organizational unit

$OU
  Distinguished name of the path in AD under which we want to create to the new organizational unit

The next three lines are where we establish the location to create the new Organizational Unit. $root is the combination of the $LdapConnectionString and the distinguished Name of the parent that was passed. $BaseOU is the object returned when we request the $root from the Domain.

```
$root = "${LdapConnectionString}${OU}"
$BaseOU = [ADSI]$root
```

The final three lines are where the real work is done.

```
$NewOU = $BaseOU.Create("organizationalUnit", "ou=$Name")
$NewOU.SetInfo()
$NewOU.DistinguishedName
```

Here we create a local instance of the new organizational unit using the Create() method. Then, we call SetInfo() to commit the new object to Active Directory. Finally, we return the disinguishedName. You might think it is odd that we only return the distinguishedName, but we do that because this information will be used later to create child objects.

Creating User Accounts

Users are a key part of any Active Directory deployment, and a lab would not be complete without some test users. The code sample in this section creates a basic user account in the directory:

```
Function New-ADUser {
  Param($Name, $Password="P@ssw0rd", $OU)

  $root = "${LdapConnectionString}${OU}"
  $UserOU = [ADSI]$Root
  $userObj = $UserOU.Create("User", "CN=$Name")

  # Set samAccountName and userPrincipalName
  $userObj.Put("samAccountName", "$Name")
  $userObj.Put("userPrincipalName", ("{0}@{1}" -f $Name, $Domain))
  $userObj.SetInfo()

  # Set Password
  $userObj.PsBase.Invoke("SetPassword", $Password)

  # Enable Account
  $userObj.PsBase.InvokeSet('AccountDisabled', $false)
  $userObj.SetInfo()
  $userObj.DistinguishedName
}
```

First we start with the function statement, which names the function and sets up the parameters for the function. Our parameters are:

$name

> This is our user's name. We will use this parameter to populate the cn, sAMAccount Name, and userPrincipalName attributes.

$password

> $password specifies the password to use for the user account. If you don't specify a value for $password, the default of *P@ssw0rd* will be used instead.

 The value you specify for $password must meet the domain's password policy, or the password set call will fail.

$OU

> This is the distinguishedName of the destination organizational unit where the account should be created.

The following code is where we setup the Active Directory connection. Just as we did with the New-ADOU function, we establish a connection to Active Directory using the `$LdapConnectionString` and the `distinguishedName` of the destination organizational unit. We send the string to ADSI and assign the object to `$UserOU`.

Once we've setup the parent OU in `$UserOU`, we can call `Create()` method on the Object, passing the class of the object (user) and `$name`. This code returns a user object locally that we store in `$UserObj`:

```
# Creating Connection String
$root = "${LdapConnectionString}${OU}"

# Creating Account in OU
$UserOU = [ADSI]$Root
$userObj = $UserOU.Create("User", "CN=$Name")
```

Before we can commit these changes, we have to setup several attributes of the account. We use the `Put()` method to set these values. The code below sets the `sAMAccountName` to be the same as the `$name`:

```
$userObj.Put("samAccountName", "$Name")
```

Set the `userPrincipalName` to *$name@$domain*:

```
$userObj.Put("userPrincipalName", ("{0}@{1}" -f $Name, $Domain))
```

 The -f parameter called in the code above is a wrapper for the .NET `String.Format()` method.

Finally we use `SetInfo()` to commit the changes to Active Directory, as without this line the object is not written to Active Directory.

```
$userObj.Setinfo()
```

In this section we set the users password and commit the changes to the Active Directory Server:

```
$userObj.PsBase.Invoke("SetPassword", $Password)
```

Now that we have valid user with a valid password, we can enable the account:

```
$userObj.PsBase.InvokeSet('AccountDisabled', $false)
$userObj.SetInfo()
```

Finally we return the `distinguishedName` of the user:

```
$userObj.DistinguishedName
```

This concludes the `New-ADUser` function, and you can easily expand this function as necessary.

Creating Computer Accounts

This function creates a computer object in a given OU. If you compare the code to the previous sample for creating user objects, you'll find that it's really quite similar.

```
Function New-ADComputer {
  Param($Name, $OU)

  # Creating Connection String
  $root = "${LdapConnectionString}${OU}"

  # Creating Account in OU
  $CompOU = [ADSI]$Root
  $CompObj = $CompOU.Create("computer", "cn=$Name")

  # Set samAccountName
  $CompObj.Put("samAccountName", "$Name`$")
  $CompObj.SetInfo()

  # Enable Account
  $CompObj.PsBase.InvokeSet('AccountDisabled', $false)
  $CompObj.SetInfo()

  $CompObj.DistinguishedName
}
```

Since the code very closely resembles the previous sample, we'll only take a look at the important differences. The first difference is when we call the **Create()** method as we if we want a computer object and not a user.

```
$CompObj = $CompOU.Create("computer", "cn=$Name")
```

Computer accounts always append a $ sign to the end of the account name. In order to do this in PowerShell, we need to escape the $ by using a backtick `. For more information on the use of the backtick, see Chapter 30.

```
$CompObj.Put("samAccountName", "$Name`$")
```

If, for example, $Name was *Server 1*, the preceding code would set sAMAccountName to *Server1$*.

Creating Groups

Users are usually members of groups, so our script will have the capability to create groups and also to add users to those groups. The group creation code is similar to creating users and computers:

```
Function New-ADGroup {
  Param($Name, $OU)

  $Root = "${LdapConnectionString}${OU}"
  $GroupOU = [ADSI]$Root

  $GroupObj = $GroupOU.Create("group", "cn=$Name")
```

```
$GroupObj.Put("samAccountName", "$Name")
$GroupObj.Put("groupType", "2147483656")
$GroupObj.SetInfo()

$GroupObj.DistinguishedName
}
```

In the case of groups we have to change Create() call to make the object of class group:

```
$GroupObj = $GroupOU.Create("group", "cn=$Name")
```

We also specify that this group is a universal security group:

```
$GroupObj.Put("groupType", "2147483656")
```

Adding group members

Now that we have the code to create a group, we need to be able to add members to the group:

```
Function Add-GroupMember {
    Param($Member, $Group)
    $Root = "${LdapConnectionString}${Group}"
    $GroupObj = [ADSI]$Root
    $GroupObj.Add("LDAP://$Member")
}
```

Here we define two parameters:

$Member

    The distinguished name of the object you want to add to the group

$group

    The distinguished name of the group to add the object to

Since the group already exists, we don't need to create anything here, and instead we call the Add() method, which accepts the distinguished name of a group member to add to the group:

```
$GroupObj.Add("LDAP://$Member")
```

 ADSI requires that you prefix the distinguished name of the object to add to a group with *LDAP://*.

Putting It All Together

At this point, we've built the functions to create all of the major object types our lab will contain. Let's quickly take a look at the core functions we've created so far:

- New-ADOU
- New-ADUser

- New-ADComputer
- New-ADGroup
- Add-GroupMember

Using these functions, we are going to build a script that executes the following tasks. Following execution, we will have a domain populated with enough objects to make a lab environment suitable for basic testing. The logical flow of our script will be:

1. Create an OU called *TestOU*.
2. Create an OU for computers called *TestComputers*.
3. Create an OU for users called *TestUser*.
4. Create an OU for groups called *TestGroups*.
5. Create $count base OUs in the *TestOU*.
6. Simulate a tree structure by creating four child OUs in each base OU.
7. In each of the child OUs, create five users and five computers.
8. Create two hundred groups and add the users to the groups.

Example 31-1 shows our completed script.

Example 31-1. Complete lab build script

```
#A TestOU OU
Write-Host " + Creating TestOU"
$TestOU = New-ADOU -name TestOU -OU $DomainDN

#A TestGroups OU
Write-Host " + Creating TestGroups OU"
$TestGroups = New-ADOU -Name TestGroups -OU $DomainDN

#Create x number of OUs Under TestOU
foreach($i in 1..$Count)
{
  $lvl1Child = New-ADOU -Name "LvL1ChildOU$i" -OU $TestOU
  Write-Progress "Creating OUs LvL1ChildOU$i" -Status "Updating" `
    -PercentComplete ($i / $Count * 100)
  # Each of the Level 1 OUs will have 4 Child OUs
  foreach($x in 1..4)
  {
    $lvl2Child = New-ADOU -Name "LvL2Child${i}${x}" -OU $lvl1Child
    Write-Progress "Creating Child OUs LvL2Child${i}${x}" `
        -Status "Updating" -PercentComplete ($x/4*100) -Id 1
    #Each Level 2 OU should have 5 users Accounts and 5 Machines Accounts
    foreach($y in 1..5)
    {
      Write-Progress "Creating Child Users/Computers [x${i}${x}${y}]" `
        -status "Updating" -PercentComplete ($y/5*100) -Id 2
      New-ADUser -Name "usr${i}${x}${y}" -OU $lvl2Child | Out-Null
      New-ADComputer -Name "srv${i}${x}${y}" -OU $lvl2Child | Out-Null
    }
  }
}
```

```
}

# Find all the Users
$props = @(1.1)
$Root = "${LdapConnectionString}${TestOU}"
Write-Host " + Finding all users in [$root]"
$base = [ADSI]"$Root"
$filter = "(&(objectCategory=person)(objectClass=user))"
$ds = New-Object DirectoryServices.DirectorySearcher($base, `
    $filter, $props)
$ds.PageSize = 1000
$users = $ds.FindAll()

$eUsers = $users | ?{$_.path.Split("=")[1] -Match "(2|4|6|8|0),OU$"} | `
    %{$_.Path.Split("/")[2]}
$oUsers = $users | ?{$_.Path.Split("=")[1] -Match "(1|3|5|7|9),OU$"} | `
    %{$_.Path.Split("/")[2]}

foreach($i in 1..5)
{
  $NewGrp = New-ADGroup -Name "TestGrp$i" -OU $TestGroups
  if($i % 2 -eq 0)
  {
    Write-Host "    - Adding even numbered users to Group [$NewGrp]"
    $eUsers | %{Add-GroupMember -Member $_ -Group $NewGrp}
  }
  else
  {
    Write-Host "    - Adding odd numbered users to Group [$NewGrp]"
    $oUsers | %{ Add-GroupMember -Member $_ -Group $NewGrp}
  }
}
```

Example 31-1 can certainly be intimidating at first, but when broken down it's not too bad. Let's take a look at the first three lines:

```
#A TestOU OU
Write-Host " + Creating TestOU"
$TestOU = New-ADOU -Name TestOU -OU $DomainDN
```

The Write-Host line simply outputs that we are creating an organizational unit called *TestOU*. *TestOU* will be the parent of all of our subsequently created OUs, users, and computers. It's important to note that we are storing the result of the New-ADOU call in a variable called $TestOU.

The next important block of code is where we begin creating the child OU hierarchy for our environment:

```
#Create x number of OUs Under TestOU
foreach($i in 1..$Count)
{
  $lvl1Child = New-ADOU -Name "LvL1ChildOU$i" -OU $TestOU
  Write-Progress "Creating OUs LvL1ChildOU$i" -Status "Updating" `
    -PercentComplete ($i / $Count * 100)
```

This section of the code is where it may seem to start getting really complicated. We use a series of three nested **foreach** loops, and this is the first one. This first loop creates the first level of the OU hierarchy. The code creates an OU called *LvL1ChildOU$i*, where $i is the counter in our loop:

```
$lvl1Child = New-ADOU -Name "LvL1ChildOU$i" -OU $TestOU
```

The resulting OU's distinguished name is stored in a variable called **$lvl1Child**, which we'll use in the subsequent loop.

> The **Write-Progress** command allows PowerShell to provide real-time status of long-running commands. If you specify a large value for **$count** at the beginning of this script, you may find that it takes some time to run. For more information on **Write-Progress**, see *http://technet .microsoft.com/en-us/library/bb978680.aspx*.

In the following loop, we create our second-level child OUs. We will once again leverage our **New-ADOU** function to create child OUs called *LvL2Child$i$x* (where $i and $x are our counter variables) in the *LvL1Child OU*. While it's not strictly required to give each OU a unique name using $i, doing so gives us OU names that are globally unique within the test environment. Similar to before, we capture the output of **New-ADOU** in **$lvl2Child** which we'll use in the subsequent loop.

In this final loop, we create the users and computers in the given child OU. In order to complete this task, we will leverage the **New-ADUser** function to create users called **usr$i$x$y** in the LvL2child OU, and the **New-ADComputer** to create computers called **srv$i$x$y**. We are using counter variables $i, $x, and $y to ensure that each object is uniquely named.

```
#Each Level 2 OU should have 5 users Accounts and 5 Machines Accounts
foreach($y in 1..5)
{
    Write-Progress "Creating Child Users/Computers [x${i}${x}${y}]" `
        -status "Updating" -PercentComplete ($y/5*100) -Id 2
    New-ADUser -Name "usr${i}${x}${y}" -OU $lvl2Child | Out-Null
    New-ADComputer -Name "srv${i}${x}${y}" -OU $lvl2Child | Out-Null
}
```

> We are piping the output of **New-ADUser** and **New-ADComputer** to **Out-Null** since we don't need the return values. Piping the output to **Out-Null** prevents PowerShell from printing the return value to the console each time.

Now that we've created all of the user objects that are going to exist in our lab, we can embark upon creating groups and adding users to them. In this script, every user will be a member of a number of groups, so we'll begin by retrieving all of the users we created in the script:

```
# Find all the Users
$props = @(1.1)
$Root = "${LdapConnectionString}${TestOU}"
Write-Host " + Finding all users in [$root]"
$base = [ADSI]"$Root"
$filter = "(&(objectCategory=person)(objectClass=user))"
$ds = New-Object DirectoryServices.DirectorySearcher($base, `
    $filter, $props)
$ds.PageSize = 1000
$users = $ds.FindAll()
```

Since we're using a `DirectorySearcher` to retrieve the users, there are three properties we have to set:

`$base`

> This is where to base our search; in this case it's `$TestOU`.

`$filter`

> This is the LDAP filter to search with. Since we're looking for all the users, we'll use `(&(objectCategory=person)(objectClass=user))`.

`$prop`

> This is an array of properties to return. In our case, we are using the special property `1.1`, which indicates that only distinguished names should be returned.

After building the `DirectorySearcher`, we can call `FindAll()` to return the search results. ADSI will automatically handle paging of the search results in increments of 1,000, which is what we set `$ds.PageSize` to.

The logic for deciding which users go in which groups is based on whether the username generated earlier has an even or odd number in it. We split the users into two groups: even users, `$eUsers`, and odd users, `$oUsers`. The code here uses a regular expression that matches on even or odd numbers in the distinguished name:

```
$eUsers = $users | ?{$_.path.Split("=")[1] -Match "(2|4|6|8|0),OU$"} | `
    %{$_.Path.Split("/")[2]}
$oUsers = $users | ?{$_.Path.Split("=")[1] -Match "(1|3|5|7|9),OU$"} | `
    %{$_.Path.Split("/")[2]}
```

 Modular arithmetic operators return the remainder of a division operation, thus any odd number modulus 2 will return 1. So, for example, 4 % 2 will return 0 whereas 5 % 2 will return 1.

The final step is to create the groups and add the users to them. We are going to add even numbered users (stored in $eUsers) to groups with an even number, and odd numbered users (stored in $oUsers) to groups with an odd number. We determine whether or not a group is even-numbered by using the modular arithmetic operator, %.

```
foreach($i in 1..5)
{
    $NewGrp = New-ADGroup -Name "TestGrp$i" -OU $TestGroups
```

```
if($i%2 -eq 0)
{
  Write-Host "   - Adding Even Users to Group [$NewGrp]"
  $eUsers | %{Add-UsertoGroup -user $_ -Group $NewGrp}
}
else
{
  Write-Host "   - Adding Odd Users to Group [$NewGrp]"
  $oUsers | %{Add-UsertoGroup -user $_ -Group $NewGrp}
}
}
```

This concludes the assembly of a PowerShell script that you can use to populate an Active Directory domain with a sizeable amount of test data. Our script creates an organizational unit hierarchy, fills the hierarchy with users and computers, and then adds users to groups. We created a number of PowerShell functions that you can add to your library including New-ADOU, New-ADUser, New-ADComputer, Add-GroupMember, and some generic script setup code. You can easily leverage these functions in other PowerShell scripts.

Working with Forests and Domains

Manipulating forest and domain properties are both very common Active Directory tasks when writing scripts. As we discussed early in the chapter, PowerShell exposes these task through the .NET Framework.

Gathering Forest Information

This code snippet will get a **Forest** object and put it in the variable called **$forest**:

```
$forest = [System.DirectoryServices.ActiveDirectory.Forest]::GetCurrentForest()
```

GetCurrentForest() is a method that returns a **Forest** object for the current user context. As you can see in output below, forest objects have quite a few properties that can be utilized in scripts:

```
PS> $forest

Name                   : corp.lab
Sites                  : {Default-First-Site-Name}
Domains                : {corp.lab}
GlobalCatalogs         : {Win2k8x64dc1.corp.lab, Win2k8x64DC2.corp.lab}
ApplicationPartitions  : {DC=ForestDnsZones,DC=corp,DC=lab,
                           DC=DomainDnsZones,DC=corp,DC=lab}
ForestMode             : Windows2003Forest
RootDomain             : corp.lab
Schema                 : CN=Schema,CN=Configuration,DC=corp,DC=lab
SchemaRoleOwner        : Win2k8x64dc1.corp.lab
NamingRoleOwner        : Win2k8x64dc1.corp.lab
```

You can get the name of the forest root (Name), a listing of sites, child domains, and global catalogs (Sites, Domains, and GlobalCatalogs, respectively), the functional level (ForestMode), and the owners of the schema master and domain naming master FSMOs (SchemaRoleOwner and NamingRoleOwner, respectively).

In addition to properties, the Forest class also has a number of methods you can use to manipulate the forest. You can pipe $forest to Get-Member to get a listing of these methods. Since we only want to see the members and the associated type of each member, we are going to use Format-Table to control the output:

```
PS>$forest | Get-Member -MemberType Method | `
    Format-Table Name,MemberType -Auto
```

Name	MemberType
CreateLocalSideOfTrustRelationship	Method
CreateTrustRelationship	Method
DeleteLocalSideOfTrustRelationship	Method
DeleteTrustRelationship	Method
FindAllDiscoverableGlobalCatalogs	Method
FindAllGlobalCatalogs	Method
FindGlobalCatalog	Method
GetAllTrustRelationships	Method
GetSelectiveAuthenticationStatus	Method
GetSidFilteringStatus	Method
GetTrustRelationship	Method
RaiseForestFunctionality	Method
RepairTrustRelationship	Method
SetSelectiveAuthenticationStatus	Method
SetSidFilteringStatus	Method
UpdateLocalSideOfTrustRelationship	Method
UpdateTrustRelationship	Method
VerifyOutboundTrustRelationship	Method
VerifyTrustRelationship	Method

The output above has been trimmed to only show Active Directory-specific methods.

While we haven't got the space to cover all of these methods, the names alone should demonstrate the scope of control the Forest class offers. For a reference to the Forest class, visit *http://msdn.microsoft.com/en-us/library/system.directoryservices.activedirectory.forest.aspx*. One example is getting a global catalog from the list of global catalogs across the forest:

```
PS> $forest.GlobalCatalogs | Select -First 1
Forest                : corp.lab
CurrentTime           : 7/19/2008 2:40:07 PM
HighestCommittedUsn   : 1859774
OSVersion             : Windows Serverr 2008 Enterprise
Roles                 : {SchemaRole, NamingRole, PdcRole, RidRole}
```

```
Domain                      : corp.lab
IPAddress                   : fe80::6d92:4ce9:be59:2af4%10
SiteName                    : Default-First-Site-Name
SyncFromAllServersCallback  :
InboundConnections          : {3b12048f-91e7-45c5-9234-34e30438b977}
OutboundConnections         : {b12b66dc-54d5-4428-b38b-45eeae3080f4}
Name                        : Win2k8x64dc1.corp.lab
Partitions                  : {DC=corp,DC=lab,CN=Configuration,DC=corp,DC=lab,
```

If you want to return a table of all the sites in the forest and the servers in them, you could run code similar to this:

```
PS> $forest.Sites | Format-Table Name,Servers
Name                             : Default-First-Site-Name
Domains                          : {corp.lab}
Subnets                          : {}
Servers                          : {Win2k8x64dc1.corp.lab,
                                    Win2k8x64DC2.corp.lab}
AdjacentSites                    : {}
SiteLinks                        : {DEFAULTIPSITELINK}
InterSiteTopologyGenerator       : Win2k8x64dc1.corp.lab
Options                          : None
Location                         :
BridgeheadServers                : {}
PreferredSmtpBridgeheadServers   : {}
PreferredRpcBridgeheadServers    : {}
IntraSiteReplicationSchedule     :
DirectoryServices.ActiveDirectory.ActiveDirectorySchedule
```

Gathering Domain Information

When it comes to collecting information about a domain, there are a couple ways to start. The first option is to begin with the Forest object we created earlier ($forest):

```
$domain = $forest.Domains | ?{$_.Name -eq "corp.lab"}
```

This searches the list of domains in the forest for *corp.lab* and returns the Domain object for it. The second route is to start from scratch and use the Domain class to generate a Domain object for the current domain:

```
$domain = [System.DirectoryServices.ActiveDirectory.Domain]::GetCurrentDomain()
```

Now that we have a Domain object, let's see what it has to offer:

```
PS> $domain
Forest                  : corp.lab
DomainControllers       : {Win2k8x64dc1.corp.lab, Win2k8x64DC2.corp.lab}
Children                : {}
DomainMode              : Windows2003Domain
Parent                  :
PdcRoleOwner            : Win2k8x64dc1.corp.lab
RidRoleOwner            : Win2k8x64dc1.corp.lab
InfrastructureRoleOwner : Win2k8x64DC2.corp.lab
Name                    : corp.lab
```

Similar to the Forest object, we can see the name of the domain (Name), the forest (Forest) and parent domain (Parent) it lives under, a listing of domain controllers (DomainControllers) and FSMO role owners (PdcRoleOwner, RidRoleOwner, and InfrastructureRoleOwner), and the functional level (DomainMode).

As with the Forest object, you can use Get-Member to see what methods are available:

```
PS> $domain | Get-Member -MemberType Method | `
    Format-Table Name,MemberType -Auto


Name                                 MemberType
----                                 ----------
CreateLocalSideOfTrustRelationship   Method
CreateTrustRelationship              Method
DeleteLocalSideOfTrustRelationship   Method
DeleteTrustRelationship              Method
FindAllDiscoverableDomainControllers Method
FindAllDomainControllers             Method
FindDomainController                 Method
GetAllTrustRelationships             Method
GetDirectoryEntry                    Method
GetSelectiveAuthenticationStatus     Method
GetSidFilteringStatus                Method
GetTrustRelationship                 Method
RaiseDomainFunctionality             Method
RepairTrustRelationship              Method
SetSelectiveAuthenticationStatus     Method
SetSidFilteringStatus                Method
UpdateLocalSideOfTrustRelationship   Method
UpdateTrustRelationship              Method
VerifyOutboundTrustRelationship      Method
VerifyTrustRelationship              Method
```

While a complete discussion of the Domain object is out of scope for this book, you can reference *http://msdn.microsoft.com/en-us/library/system.directoryservices.activedirectory.domain.aspx* for the documentation.

If you want to retrieve the Name, OS, Site, and Highest Committed USN for each domain controller in the domain, you could run this command:

```
$domain.DomainControllers | `
    Format-Table Name,OSVersion,SiteName,HighestCommittedUsn -Auto
```

The following command triggers the KCC on each domain controller in the domain:

```
$domain.DomainControllers | %{$_.CheckReplicationConsistency()}
```

This command returns any domain controllers that returned an error last time they tried to replicate:

```
$domain.DomainControllers | %{$_.GetAllReplicationNeighbors()} | `
    ?{$_.LastSyncResult -ne 0}
```

If you want to mark each domain controller in the domain as a global catalog, you could run this command:

```
$domain.DomainControllers | %{$_.EnableGlobalCatalog()}
```

Transferring domain and forest FSMO roles is a two-step process. The first step is to get the FSMO role type for the role you want to transfer. This code stores each of the role types in a variable:

```
$IFM = [DirectoryServices.ActiveDirectory.ActiveDirectoryRole]::`
    InfrastructureRole
$PDC = [DirectoryServices.ActiveDirectory.ActiveDirectoryRole]::PdcRole
$RID = [DirectoryServices.ActiveDirectory.ActiveDirectoryRole]::RidRole
$DomainMaster = `
    [DirectoryServices.ActiveDirectory.ActiveDirectoryRole]::NamingRole
$SchemaMaster = `
    [DirectoryServices.ActiveDirectory.ActiveDirectoryRole]::SchemaRole
```

The next step is to find the domain controller you want to transfer the FSMO role to:

```
$dc = $domain.DomainControllers | ?{$_.Name -eq "<DC Name>"}
```

Once we've identified the domain controller, we call `TransferRoleOwnership()`, specifying the type of role we want to transfer. In this example, we will transfer the infrastructure master:

```
$dc.TransferRoleOwnership($IFM)
```

Understanding Group Policy

Scripting Group Policy has historically been a task that was not easily accomplished. SDM Software, a third party software vendor, offers a number of free Group Policy cmdlets on their website. You can download these cmdlets from *http://www.sdmsoft ware.com/freeware.php*.

Group Policy Refresh Cmdlet

The `Update-SDMgp` cmdlet allows you to remotely refresh Group Policy data on a machine from PowerShell. There are a number of parameters:

Target
:   This mandatory parameter is the name of the remote computer on which to trigger a Group Policy refresh.

Username
:   Use this parameter when you need to enter alternate credentials to connect to the remote system.

Password <SecureString>
:   This is the password for the user specified in the `Username` parameter.

Computer
:   Indicates that Group Policy refresh should only target the computer-specific settings.

User

Indicates that Group Policy refresh should only target the user-specific settings.

Force

This parameter tells the remote refresh to issue a forced refresh.

Logoff

This parameter tells the remote refresh to issue a refresh and then logoff the current user.

Boot

This parameter tells the remote refresh to issue a refresh and then reboot the remote system.

Sync

This tells the remote machine to issue a *sync* command, which will cause the next foreground refresh event to occur synchronously.

Ignore

When used with the `Force`, `Boot`, and `Logoff` switches, the reboot or logoff will not occur.

In this example, we refresh Group Policy on machine *win2k8x64dc2*:

```
Update-SDMgp "win2k8x64DC2"
```

To force the refresh on *win2k8x64dc2*, add the `-force` switch:

```
Update-SDMgp "win2k8x64DC2" -force
```

To refresh just the computer policy on *win2k8x64dc2*, add the `-computer` switch:

```
Update-SDMgp "win2k8x64DC2" -computer
```

If you had a list of machines stored in a variable called `$list`, you could run this command to refresh the Group Policy on each machine:

```
$list | %{Update-SDMgp $_}
```

GPMC Cmdlets

SDM Software ships a second package of cmdlets that allow you to manipulate Group Policy objects in Active Directory. Table 31-2 provides a listing of those cmdlets as of version 1.2 of the package.

Table 31-2. SDM Software GPMC cmdlets

Cmdlet	Description
Add-SDMgplink	Links a Group Policy to a location in Active Directory
Add-SDMgpoSecurity	Adds a user or group permission to a GPO
Add-SDMSOMSecurity	This cmdlet modifies the ACL on SOM objects (e.g., sites, domains, and OUs) to allow group policy specific permissions to be applied to trustees (i.e., users and groups)
Export-SDMgpo	Exports the specified GPO to a location specified

Cmdlet	Description
Get-SDMgplink	Get all the GPOs linked at a given location in Active Directory
Get-SDMgpo	Gets a GPO Object by Name. Use * for all
Get-SDMgpoBackups	Gets a GPO from a local backup
Get-SDMgpoSecurity	Gets the security settings for a specific GPO
Get-SDMSOMSecurity	Gets the security from a specific location in Active Directory
Import-SDMgpo	Imports a specific GPO from a backup location
New-SDMgpo	Creates a new Group Policy
Remove-SDMgplink	Removes a specific gpLink from given location
Remove-SDMgpo	Deletes a Group Policy object by name
Remove-SDMgpoSecurity	Removes a specific Group Policy Permission
Remove-SDMSOMSecurity	Removes a GPO specific permission from the location
Restore-SDMgpo	Restores a Group Policy from a backup path

There are some additional cmdlets that are exclusively for Windows Vista Service Pack 1 and later and Windows Server 2008:

- `Get-SDMStarterGPO`
- `Get-SDMWMIFilter`
- `New-SDMStarterGPO`
- `Copy-SDMStarterGPO`
- `Out-SDMgpsettingsreport`
- `Out-SDMRSOPLoggingReport`
- `Remove-SDMWMIFilterLink`
- `Remove-SDMStarterGPO`

You could use the GPMC cmdlets discussed here to extend the domain build script we created earlier in this chapter. This code will create group policy objects in Active Directory and link them to the base OUs:

```
Add-PSSnapin SDMSoftware.PowerShell.GPMC -ea 0

# Insert this code before the first foreach block
# Create Group Policies
1..$count | %{New-SDMgpo "TestGPO$_"}

# Insert this code immediately before the second foreach block
#Link policies on the base OUs
1..$count | %{Add-SDMgplink -Name "TestGPO$_" `
    -Scope "OU=LvL1ChildOU${_},${TestOU}" -Location -1}
```

If you wanted to back all of your Group Policy objects up to the filesystem, you could run this command:

```
Get-SDMgpo * | Export-SDMgpo -Location c:\temp\backups
```

To generate HTML reports for each Group Policy object, you could run this code:

```
Get-SDMgpo *  | %{$_ | Out-SDMgpsettingsreport `
    -FileName "c:\temp\$($_.Name).html" -ReportHTML}
```

Quest Cmdlets

Quest Software has released a number of free Active Directory-oriented cmdlets for
PowerShell. These cmdlets make many of the tasks we've written code for earlier in
this chapter quite easy. Visit *www.quest.com/PowerShell* to download the Quest Active
Directory cmdlets. Table 31-3 provides a description of the cmdlets available from
Quest Software.

Table 31-3. Quest Software Active Directory cmdlets

Cmdlet	Description
Add-QADGroupMember	Adds a user to a group.
Add-QADPasswordSetting sObjectAppliesTo	Use this cmdlet to apply a password settings object to users or global security groups.
Connect-QADService	This cmdlet establishes a connection to any LDAP server using the current credentials unless otherwise specified.
Convert-QADAttribute Value	Convert attribute values of a directory object to the specified .NET type. For example, convert ObjectSid to friendly string from Byte[ ] array.
Disable-QADUser	Disables a user.
Disconnect-QADService	Disconnects connection established from a Connect-QADService call.
Enable-QADUser	Enables a user.
Get-QADComputer	Gets a computer object from Active Directory by using the DN, SID, GUID, Domain\Name, or LDAP Filter.
Get-QADGroup	Gets a group object from Active Directory by using the DN, SID, GUID, Domain\Name, or LDAP Filter.
Get-QADGroupMember	Gets group members for a group.
Get-QADObject	Gets an object from Active Directory by using the DN, SID, GUID, Domain\Name or LDAP Filter.
Get-QADPasswordSetting sObject	Retrieves a password-settings object.
Get-QADPSSnapinSettings	View the default settings for Quest cmdlets.
Get-QADUser	Gets a user object from Active Directory by using the DN, SID, GUID, Domain\Name, or LDAP filter.
Move-QADObject	Moves an Active Directory object to a new location.
New-QADGroup	Creates a new group.
New-QADObject	Creates a new object. This is for objects that do not have a specific cmdlet to create them, such as an OU.

Cmdlet	Description
New-QADPasswordSettingsObject	Creates a new password settings object.
New-QADUser	Creates a new user.
Remove-QADGroupMember	Removes a member from the specified group.
Remove-QADObject	Deletes an object from Active Directory.
Remove-QADPasswordSettingsObjectAppliesTo	Unlinks a password-settings object from specified users or groups.
Rename-QADObject	Renames an Active Directory object.
Set-QADGroup	Sets an Active Directory property on a group.
Set-QADObject	Sets an Active Directory property on an object.
Set-QADPSSnapinSettings	Sets a default setting for the Quest snap-ins.
Set-QADUser	Sets an Active Directory property on a user.
Unlock-QADUser	Unlocks a user account.

While there are too many cmdlets provided in this package to provide examples for all of them, we have created samples showing all of the tasks we implemented earlier in this chapter.

You can use the New-QADObject cmdlet to create an organizational unit:

```
$BaseOU = New-QADObject -Type OrganizationalUnit `
                        -ParentContainer "DC=Corp,DC=Lab" `
                        -Name QuestTestOU
```

The following code sample creates a computer using the New-QADObject cmdlet:

```
New-QADObject -ParentContainer $BaseOU.dn `
              -Name "QuestServer1" `
              -ObjectAttributes @{"sAMAccountName"="QuestServer1`$"} `
              -Type "Computer"
```

The following code sample creates a user using the New-QADUser cmdlet:

```
New-QADUser -ParentContainer $BaseOU.dn `
            -Name "QuestUser1" `
            -SamAccountName "QuestUser1" `
            -UserPrincipalName "QuestUser1@DC=Corp,DC=Lab" `
            -UserPass "!P@ssw0rd22!"
```

The following code sample creates a group using the New-QADGroup cmdlet:

```
New-QADGroup -ParentContainer $BaseOU.dn `
             -Name "QuestTestGrp$_" `
             -sAMAccountName "QuestTestGrp$_"
```

If you wanted to add the user *QuestUser1* to a group, you could use the following code sample:

```
Get-QADUser QuestUser1 | Add-QADGroupMember -Identity "QuestTestGrp"
```

PowerShell makes working with comma-separated value (CSV) files quite easy with the `Import-CSV` cmdlet. Example 31-2 shows you how to import a CSV file containing a series of users into Active Directory.

Example 31-2. Importing a CSV of users into Active Directory

```
$users = Import-Csv c:\temp\myusersV2.csv
$OU = "OU=MyUsers,DC=corp,DC=lab"

foreach($user in $users)
{
    $props = @{}
    $propNames = $user | Get-Member -MemberType Properties | %{$_.name}
    foreach($prop in $propNames)
    {
        $value = $user.$prop -replace "'|`"", ""
        $props += @{$prop = $value}
    }
    New-QADUser -Name $user.DisplayName -ObjectAttributes $props `
        -Parent $OU
}
```

The first part of this script uses `Import-CSV` to parse the CSV file. We then store the OU we will create the users under in `$OU`:

```
$users = Import-Csv c:\temp\myusers.csv
$OU = "OU=MyUsers,DC=corp,DC=lab"
```

 This script expects that the CSV file has a header row and that header row contains valid Active Directory attribute names and values.

The next section is where we parse the CSV header and make a table with valid property name and value pairs. For example, `@{sAMAccountName=Jdoe7}`. This is very important because to make this script work we are taking advantage of a special parameter that the Quest cmdlets support called `ObjectAttributes`:

```
foreach($user in $users)
{
    $props = @{}
    $propNames = $user | Get-Member -MemberType Properties | %{$_.name}
    foreach($prop in $propNames)
    {
        $value = $user.$prop -replace "'|`"", ""
        $props += @{$prop = $value}
    }
```

Once we have parsed the CSV, we can pass the results to the `New-QADUser` cmdlet:

```
New-QADUser -Name $user.DisplayName -ObjectAttributes $props `
    -Parent $OU
```

Summary

This chapter covered many common Active Directory automation tasks using Windows PowerShell. After building functions that manipulated users, computers, groups, and organizational units, we assembled them all to build a script that can populate an Active Directory domain with a configurable amount of test data. We also took a look at some of the .NET classes that you can use to work with forest and domain settings from PowerShell.

As Windows PowerShell has continued to gain acceptance in the community, third party software vendors have begun shipping PowerShell cmdlets. SDM Software and Quest Software both ship free cmdlet packages for working with Active Directory. We took a look at a few samples of both and also built a script to import a CSV of users into Active Directory.

## CHAPTER 32

Scripting Basic Exchange 2003 Tasks

In this chapter, we will show you how to automate manipulating some of the basic Exchange settings, specifically concerning users (and by extension inetOrgPersons), groups, and contacts. Although tools to manage Exchange settings already exist (e.g., Active Directory Users and Computers), scripting allows you quickly handle mailbox-enabling or moving thousands of users based on whatever business logic you require. Simple scripts can take the place of Exchange migration or management utilities that you would possibly otherwise need to purchase.

This chapter covers Exchange 2003. The concepts presented in this chapter will generally not work with Exchange 2007. Since there are still a very large number of Exchange 2003 deployments, we've elected to leave this chapter in the 4th Edition. Chapter 33 covers the concepts discussed in this chapter with respect to Exchange 2007.

Notes on Managing Exchange

Managing Exchange is a little different from managing most other Microsoft applications. The computer where you run the tools or scripts must be a member of a domain in the forest where the Exchange organization resides; this is true whether you are using a script or the GUI. Also, Exchange doesn't allow you to select other organizations to manage. This can be troublesome for someone managing multiple Exchange organizations, or a mobile worker who moves between sites or companies and likes to run her workstation in workgroup mode instead of being a member of any specific domain.

Permissions are very important and are often misunderstood in Exchange. Permissions can be set up very simply or in a very complicated way; it is tough to find a middle ground. The simplest method is to give Domain Admin access to your Exchange administrators. This is pretty standard in small companies where the Exchange administrators are doing all aspects of administration. But this practice is usually unacceptable in larger companies where separation of duties and more security is required. Please see the section on Exchange Delegation for more discussion and details on permissions.

Exchange Management Tools

Most of the scripts in this chapter require that the Exchange Management Tools from the Exchange media are loaded. Specifically, many will need the Collaboration Data Objects for Exchange Management (CDOEXM) installed and registered, and that is only installed with the Exchange Management Tools. Although it is possible to load and register the specific DLLs involved, Microsoft does not support that configuration. Additionally, Microsoft does not support loading Outlook and the Exchange Management Tools on the same machine, though they generally interact just fine.

 The primary issue that has been publicly reported when running Outlook and the Exchange Management Tools on the same machine is profile switching in Outlook when Exchange System Manager (ESM) is running. The solution is to simply close out Outlook and ESM, and then you can restart Outlook and choose the alternate profile. If you wish to relaunch ESM then, that will work fine as well.

For more details on the Microsoft guideline, see Microsoft Knowledge Base Article 266418 at *http://support.microsoft.com/kb/266418/.*

Installation of the tools for most Windows operating systems requires Internet Information Services (IIS), World Wide Web (WWW) service, Simple Mail Transport Protocol (SMTP) service, and the appropriate Admin Pack to be installed on the machine. Windows XP SP2 has eased this requirement to only needing IIS and the Windows Server 2003 Admin Pack. Once the tools are loaded, these requirements can be removed because they aren't actually used. You install the tools by running *<driveletter>:\setup \i386\setup.exe* on the Exchange media; replace *<driveletter>:* with the drive letter of the CD-ROM drive. Once the installation starts, follow the prompts to the component selection screen. Select Custom, then select Install next to Microsoft Exchange System Management Tools. Finally, click Next and complete the remainder of the prompts. The Exchange Server 2003 Management Tools cannot be installed on Windows Vista or Windows Server 2008, but only on Windows XP and Windows Server 2000/2003.

Mail-Enabling Versus Mailbox-Enabling

Exchange has two primary mechanisms for hooking users into the mail system. The first mechanism is called mailbox-enabling and associates a mailbox in the Exchange organization to a user. This is the normal setting for users in most organizations that allows them to log into the Exchange system with Outlook, Outlook Web Access (OWA), or other mail clients that can communicate through standard mail interfaces such as POP3 or IMAP.

The second mechanism is called mail-enabling; this connects one or more email addresses to the user that are external to the Exchange organization. This is used for someone who needs to log into the forest, but does not want a mailbox in the Exchange organization. For example, Dr. Amy Gramzow of the Acme Consulting Company could be on a long-term assignment at MyCorp, Inc. and have any email sent that is sent to her at *DrAmy@MyCorp.com* forwarded to her *AGramzow@AcmeConsulting.com* mailbox so that she doesn't have to manage multiple mailboxes.

Mail-enabling is also used to make Exchange aware of contacts and groups. These objects can't be authenticated, so creating a mailbox for them doesn't make sense; they must be mail-enabled instead of mailbox-enabled. Contacts will almost always have an external email address associated with them; a group, on the other hand, will be used as a distribution list to forward messages on to multiple recipients, which could be internal to the organization or outside of it.

Exchange Delegation

Exchange delegation is a delicate and complicated topic. It is discussed in this chapter with the scripts so that it is fresh in your mind and so that you understand the level of permissions required to do the tasks that are illustrated.

Most of the Exchange permissions are granted through access control lists (ACLs) on objects in Active Directory. These permissions in Active Directory can be delegated in a very granular way. Exchange consolidates the permissions into three main layers of delegation called *roles*:

- Exchange View Only Administrator allows you to look at the Exchange System.
- Exchange Administrator allows you to fully administer Exchange Server computer information.
- Exchange Full Administrator allows you to fully administer Exchange.

Be aware that none of these Exchange Roles give you access rights on user objects themselves. You can be an Exchange Full Administrator and not be able to mailbox-enable a single user. For that, you need to determine what rights you want the Exchange Administrators to have on user objects and grant them separately.

Unfortunately, it is beyond the scope of this book to dig into all of the various ways to delegate rights to Active Directory objects. We will assume for the remainder of this chapter that any administrator who needs to make changes to a user or group, such as mail-enabling or mailbox-enabling a user, mail-enabling a distribution group, creating a contact, and so on, is a member of the Account Operators group with the additional permissions outlined in the next paragraph delegated in Active Directory.

By default, Account Operators have permissions to manage user objects, inetOrgPerson objects, and group objects. They do not have permissions to manage contacts or query-based distribution lists. In order for an Account Operator to be able to fully manage mail-specific contents of Active Directory, you must grant permissions separately to create, delete, and manage contacts (i.e., objects with an objectClass of contact), and query-based distribution groups (i.e., objects with an objectClass of `msExchDynamicDistributionList`) have to be added separately. For details on Active Directory security and delegation, see Chapter 13.

In this security-aware world we now live in, it would be lax to not discuss delegation best practices. Security best practices dictate a separation of duties for different types of administrators. This is also known as the principle of least privilege. Exchange is definitely large enough to follow this type of model and has a couple of levels where these separations can most logically be made.

The first level involves the Help Desk or Call Center Exchange troubleshooters. These are people who you don't want making changes. You only want them to look at what is in place so they can properly escalate to the next level of support if the issue is truly an Exchange issue. These administrators will just need view-only access to Exchange and Active Directory; this would map to the Exchange View-Only Admin Role.

The second level are the Exchange Data Administrators, administrators who are responsible for manipulating which users do and don't get mailboxes, as well as managing contacts and distribution lists. They will need to be able to manipulate users and other mail-enabled objects, but not manipulate the overall Exchange system configuration. This level is often automated, and the functionality is often wrapped into some sort of provisioning system as the requests and responses should be standardized. This level of permission will need Exchange view access and various create/delete/change permissions on the user, contact, and group objects in the forest. This would map to the Exchange View-Only Admin Role, coupled with the specially delegated Account Operator permissions as specified earlier. The primary tool these administrators use will be the Active Directory Users and Computers (ADUC) snap-in.

 This functionality, placed in a custom web-based application with a proper authentication and authorization system, could be pushed to the Help Desk or even out to the business users so that business management can directly manage who can and can't have email access based on rules specified by Exchange Administrators.

Finally, you have Exchange Service Administrators; these are the main Exchange administrators who are actually managing the overall service. They need to be able to manipulate the servers and the system configuration, but don't generally need to manipulate the mail objects, such as users, groups, and contacts. This level would map to Exchange Admin or Exchange Full Admin Roles. This level also requires local Administrator rights on the Exchange Servers. There could be times that these administrators will need additional permissions in Active Directory on User objects, most notably if they are moving mailboxes or reconnecting mailboxes. The primary tool these administrators will use will be the Exchange System Manager (ESM) snap-in.

Depending on the size of your company and the security concerns you have, you may have none of these divisions, a subset of these divisions, or possibly even more divisions.

Mail-Enabling a User

You can easily mail-enable a user with very little code using ADSI and CDOEXM. The following code shows you how to mail-enable a single user specified by a known DN:

```
' This code mail enables a user.
Option Explicit
Dim strUserDN, strEmailAddr, objUser
' ------ SCRIPT CONFIGURATION ------
strUserDN = "<UserDN>"    ' e.g. cn=DrAmy,cn=Users,dc=mycorp,dc=com
strEmailAddr = "<EmailAddress>"  'e.g. Agramzow@AcmeConsulting.com
' ------ END CONFIGURATION ---------
Set objUser = GetObject("LDAP://" & strUserDN)
objUser.MailEnable strEmailAddr
objUser.Put "internetEncoding",1310720
objUser.SetInfo()
WScript.Echo "Successfully mail-enabled user."
```

 Mail-enabling a user requires Exchange Data Administrator permissions.

This should all be familiar, with the exception of `MailEnable`. `MailEnable` is a method of the `IMailRecipient` CDOEXM interface. For a user, it takes a single argument: the email address to associate with the user. In the background, the specific changes made by the `MailEnable` method are on the **user** object in Active Directory and include changes to the following attributes:

- `targetAddress`
- `mailNickname`
- `mAPIRecipient`
- `legacyExchangeDN`

 You are probably looking at that list of attributes and thinking, "Hey, I can just populate those attributes with LDAP calls; I don't even need to use CDOEXM!" To be honest, that is almost true. It is only "almost" true for two reasons: first, depending on which knowledge base articles you read, you will find confusion on whether or not setting the LDAP attributes is supported by Microsoft or not. Second, you actually don't need to set all of those attributes; the minimum attributes needed are `mailNickname` and `targetAddress`.

In addition to those attributes, the `internetEncoding` attribute should also be set for proper message handling. This is the attribute that is updated if you go into the Advanced tab of the Internet Address Properties screen in ADUC. The default value for this attribute is 1310720, which tells Exchange to use the default settings of the Internet

Mail Service. You can specify other values to force email to be converted to various formats. Table 32-1 contains the list of alternate values for the `internetEncoding` attribute.

Table 32-1. internetEncoding attribute values.

Value	Meaning
1310720	Use Internet Mail Service settings
917504	Allow plain text
1441792	Allow plain text or HTML
2228224	Allow plain text/uuencoding
131072	Allow plain text/uuencoding with BinHex

Once all of those attributes are in place, the Recipient Update Service (RUS) sets additional attributes on the user object to make it useable for Exchange.

 Everywhere the `objectClass user` is specified, `inetOrgPerson` can be inserted in its place; for all intents and purposes, these objects are interchangeable in Exchange.

Table 32-2 lists all methods and properties of the `IMailRecipient` interface.

Table 32-2. IMailRecipient properties and methods

Type	Name	Description
Property	Alias	Specifies alias for email address generation. Also known as `mailNickname`; does not apply to groups.
	ForwardingStyle	Specifies whether email is also delivered to alternative email address.
	ForwardTo	Specifies the URL path to the recipient to which mail is forwarded.
	HideFromAddressBook	Specifies whether the recipient is displayed in the address book.
	IncomingLimit	Specifies the maximum size, in KB, of a message sent to this recipient.
	OutgoingLimit	Specifies the maximum size, in KB, of a message that this user can send.
	ProxyAddresses	List of proxy addresses for the recipient. See note about `proxyAddresses` below.
	RestrictedAddresses	Specifies whether messages from the addresses listed in RestrictedAddressList are to be accepted or rejected.
	RestrictedAddressList	Specifies a list of Microsoft Active Directory paths of senders to be accepted or rejected.
	SMTPEmail	Specifies primary SMTP address used for the recipient. Does not apply to groups.
	TargetAddress	Specifies the delivery address to which email for this recipient should be sent. This property is read-only.
Method	MailEnable	Enables a recipient to receive mail. Recipient can be a user, folder, contact, or group.
	MailDisable	Disables mail to a recipient.

Mail-Disabling a User

Now that you have seen how to mail-enable a user, it is a good time to show a code sample illustrating mail-disabling a user:

```
' This code mail disables a user.
Option Explicit
Dim strUserDN, objUser
' ------ SCRIPT CONFIGURATION ------
strUserDN = "<UserDN>"    ' e.g. cn=DrAmy,cn=Users,dc=mycorp,dc=com
' ------ END CONFIGURATION ---------
Set objUser = GetObject("LDAP://" & strUserDN)
objUser.MailDisable
objUser.SetInfo()
WScript.Echo "Successfully mail-disabled user."
```

 Mail-disabling a user requires Exchange Data Administrator permissions.

Once again, this is a very simple script with one new method, the `MailDisable` method. This method is aptly named in that it mail-disables a user, and that is all it does. Unfortunately, you cannot use this method to mailbox-disable a user. So when you call this method, you should be sure that the user is mail-enabled versus mailbox-enabled. If you use this method on a mailbox-enabled user, you will get an error such as "E-mail addresses cannot be removed from this user because it has a mailbox." The quick way to ascertain whether a user has a mailbox versus being simply mail-enabled is to check for the existence of the homeMDB attribute. If a user object has homeMDB populated, there is an associated mailbox for that account.

Creating and Mail-Enabling a Contact

A contact in Exchange 2000 or above is similar to a custom recipient in Exchange 5.5. Contacts can be created in Active Directory like a user is created, and mail-enabling a contact is identical to mail-enabling a user. Because the users and groups chapter didn't discuss creating a contact, it will be wrapped into the script here. You can shorten the following script down to just mail-enabling of an existing contact or by using the script shown in the previous section and substituting in the contact DN for the user DN:

```
' This code creates and then mail-enables a contact.
Option Explicit
Dim strOU, strContactCN, strEmailAddr, strDisplayName,
Dim objOU, objContact
' ------ SCRIPT CONFIGURATION ------
strOU = "<OU>" ' e.g. ou=Contacts,dc=mycorp,dc=com
strContactCN = "<ContactCN>" ' e.g. cn=DrAmy
strEmailAddr = "<EmailAddress>" 'e.g. Agramzow@AcmeConsulting.com
```

```
strDisplayName = "<Display Name>" 'e.g. Dr. Amy Gramzow
' ------ END CONFIGURATION ---------
' Create Contact
Set objOU = GetObject("LDAP://" & strOU)
Set objContact = objOU.Create("contact",strContactCN)
objContact.Put "displayName", strDisplayName
objContact.SetInfo
WScript.Echo "Successfully created contact."
' Mail-Enable Contact
objContact.MailEnable strEmailAddr
objContact.Put "internetEncoding", 1310720
objContact.SetInfo()
WScript.Echo "Successfully mail-enabled contact."
```

Mail-enabling a contact requires Exchange Data Administrator permissions.

Creating a contact is very simple; there are no mandatory attributes, though a Display Name (displayName) is usually set so that the cn isn't used for display in the Global Address List (GAL) when the contact is mail-enabled. You will note that the mail-enable process is exactly the same as it is done for user objects; simply specify the external email address as the parameter to the MailEnable method.

Mail-Disabling a Contact

Mail-disabling a contact is exactly like mail-disabling a user:

```
' This code mail disables a contact.
Option Explicit
Dim strContactDN, objContact
' ------ SCRIPT CONFIGURATION ------
strContactDN = "<ContactDN>"    ' e.g. cn=DrAmy,ou=Contacts,dc=mycorp,dc=com
' ------ END CONFIGURATION ---------
set objContact = GetObject("LDAP://" & strContactDN)
objContact.MailDisable
objContact.SetInfo()
WScript.Echo "Successfully mail-disabled contact."
```

Mail-disabling a contact requires Exchange Data Administrator permissions.

It was mentioned previously that you needed to know if the user was mail-enabled or mailbox-enabled. This is not the case with contacts because they cannot be mailbox-enabled; you can always use the MailDisable method for Exchange contacts.

Mail-Enabling a Group (Distribution List)

A mail-enabled **group** is a group that is used as an Exchange Distribution List. You send email to the group's email address, and all users and contacts in the group that are known to Exchange (either mail- or mailbox-enabled) will receive a copy of the message:

```
' This code mail enables a group.
Option Explicit
Dim strGroupDN, objGroup
' ------ SCRIPT CONFIGURATION ------
strGroupDN = "<GroupDN>"    ' e.g. cn=MyDL,ou=Groups,dc=mycorp,dc=com
' ------ END CONFIGURATION ---------
Set objGroup = GetObject("LDAP://" & strGroupDN)
objGroup.MailEnable
objGroup.SetInfo()
WScript.Echo "Successfully mail-enabled group."
```

 Mail-enabling a group requires Exchange Data Administrator permissions.

You probably noticed that the email address wasn't specified when the `MailEnable` method was called. The email address is automatically created based on the `sAMAccountName` of the group. Unfortunately, CDOEXM does not allow you to specify the address for the group. It is possible to modify the email address programmatically, but you will need to modify the multivalued attribute called **proxyAddresses** directly. This attribute controls the addresses available for a given mail object within the Exchange system.

The **proxyAddresses** attribute is a collection of addresses for a given mail object. Each value is of the form prefix:address—e.g., *SMTP:DrAmy@MyCorp.com*. The two prefixes you will always find are smtp and x400, which specify addresses for those mandatory protocols.

The prefix can be in all capital letters or all lowercase; if capitalized, it means that the address is the primary address for that protocol. For example, a prefix with an uppercase SMTP: means the address is the primary SMTP address. A prefix with a lowercase smtp: means the address is a secondary address. You must always have one and only one primary address per protocol. You can, however, add multiple secondary addresses.

One final note on **proxyAddresses**: the attribute values *MUST* be unique across the entire forest. Exchange queries for proxy addresses on a regular basis throughout the day, and duplicates can cause considerable confusion and several additional queries to resolve the confusion. The GUI tools will look for duplicates, but if you change these values programmatically, it is up to you to verify that the values are unique.

Group scope for distribution lists is important. If you have a single domain forest, you are free to use any group scope you wish: Domain Local, Global, or Universal. In a single domain forest, there is no benefit to not using Universal groups. If you have a multidomain forest, you should stick to Universal groups. All group expansion is handled by querying global catalogs, and Universal groups are the only groups that are guaranteed to have their membership present on all global catalogs in a forest. Universal Group Caching does not help with this, as group expansion requires actual queries to a global catalog.

Mail-Disabling a Group

Mail-disabling a group is exactly like mail-disabling a contact:

```
' This code mail disables a group.
Option Explicit
Dim strGroupDN, objGroup
' ------ SCRIPT CONFIGURATION ------
strGroupDN = "<GroupDN>"   ' e.g. cn=MyDL,ou=Groups,dc=mycorp,dc=com
' ------ END CONFIGURATION ---------
Set objGroup = GetObject("LDAP://" & strGroupDN)
objGroup.MailDisable
objGroup.SetInfo()
WScript.Echo "Successfully mail-disabled group."
```

Mail-disabling a group requires Exchange Data Administrator permissions.

Mailbox-Enabling a User

You can easily mailbox-enable a user with very little code using ADSI and CDOEXM. The following code shows you how to mailbox-enable a single user specified by a known DN:

```
' This code creates a mailbox for a user.
Option Explicit
Dim strUserDN, strEmailAddr, objUser
' ------ SCRIPT CONFIGURATION ------
strUserDN = "<UserDN>"   ' e.g. cn=DrAmy,cn=Users,dc=mycorp,dc=com
strHomeMDB = "<Home MDB DN>"
' e.g. CN=Mailbox Store (SERVER),CN=First Storage Group,CN=InformationStore,
' CN=SERVER,CN=Servers,CN=First Administrative Group,CN=Administrative Groups,
'      CN=MYCORP,CN=Microsoft Exchange,CN=Services,
'      CN=Configuration,DC=mycorp,DC=com"
' ------ END CONFIGURATION ---------
Set objUser = GetObject("LDAP://" & strUserDN)
objUser.CreateMailBox strHomeMDB
objUser.SetInfo()
WScript.Echo "Successfully mailbox-enabled user."
```

Mailbox-enabling a user requires Exchange Data Administrator permissions.

That should all be familiar with the exception of `CreateMailBox`. `CreateMailBox` is a method of the `IMailBoxStore` CDOEXM interface. This method takes a single argument, the LDAP URL of the mail store object, to create the mailbox in. In the background, the specific changes made by the `CreateMailBox` method are on the **user** object in Active Directory and include changes to the following attributes:

- `mDBUseDefaults`
- `msExchUserAccountControl`
- `homeMTA`
- `msExchHomeServerName`
- `homeMDB`
- `mailNickname`
- `msExchMailboxGuid`
- `msExchMailboxSecurityDescriptor`
- `legacyExchangeDN`

Once all of those attributes are in place, the Recipient Update Service (RUS) sets additional attributes on the user object. The mailbox cannot be used nor receive email until the RUS has gone through this stamping process.

 As with mail-enabling a user, mailbox-enabling a user can be accomplished with just setting a few LDAP attributes. Also as before, depending on what knowledge base articles you read, you will find confusion on whether or not setting the LDAP attributes is supported or not by Microsoft. You actually don't need to set all of those attributes; the minimum attributes needed are `mailNickname` and any of `homeMDB`, `home MTA`, or `msExchHomeServerName`.

Table 32-3 lists all methods and properties of the `IMailBoxStore` interface.

Table 32-3. IMailBoxStore properties and methods

Type	Name	Description
Property	DaysBeforeGarbageCollection	Specifies the number of days deleted mail is retained before it is permanently deleted.
	Delegates	Specifies the list of distinguishedNames of all users that can send email on behalf of the user.
	EnableStoreDefaults	Specifies whether to use default limits for mailbox store limits (quotas).

Type	Name	Description
	GarbageCollectionOnlyAfterBackup	Specifies whether deleted messages can only be permanently deleted after the mailbox has been backed up.
	HardLimit	Specifies the maximum mailbox size, in KB, over which sending and receiving mail is disabled.
	HomeMDB	Specifies the distinguishedName of the mailbox store of the recipient. This property is read only.
	OverQuotaLimit	Specifies a size limit, in KB, of a mailbox. If this limit is exceeded, sending mail is disabled.
	OverrideStoreGarbageCollection	Indicates whether this mailbox should use the garbage collection properties set on the mailbox or the properties set on the database.
	RecipientLimit	Specifies the maximum number of people to whom the recipient can send mail.
	StoreQuota	Specifies the maximum size, in KB, allowed for the mailbox.
Method	CreateMailBox	Creates a mailbox.
	DeleteMailBox	Deletes a mailbox.
	MoveMailBox	Moves a mailbox.

Mailbox-Disabling a User (Mailbox Deletion)

Now that you have seen how to mailbox-enable a user, it seems a good time to show a code sample illustrating this concept:

```
' This code removes a user's mailbox.
Option Explicit
Dim strUserDN, objUser
' ------ SCRIPT CONFIGURATION ------
strUserDN = "<UserDN>"    ' e.g. cn=DrAmy,cn=Users,dc=mycorp,dc=com
' ------ END CONFIGURATION ---------
Set objUser = GetObject("LDAP://" & strUserDN)
objUser.DeleteMailBox
objUser.SetInfo()
WScript.Echo "Successfully deleted user's mailbox."
```

 Mailbox-disabling a user requires Exchange Data Administrator permissions.

Once again, this is a very simple script with one new method, the `DeleteMailBox` method. Unfortunately, you cannot use this method to mail-disable a user. So when you call this method, you should be sure that the user is mailbox-enabled versus mail-enabled. If you use this method on a mail-enabled user, you will get an error such as "This user does not have a mailbox." The quick way to ascertain whether a user has a mailbox or is simply mail-enabled is to check for the existence of the homeMDB attribute. If a user object has homeMDB populated, there is an associated mailbox for that account.

The DeleteMailBox method is actually not well named because it doesn't really delete the mailbox. In actuality, it disconnects the mailbox from the user. The mailbox, by default, will still exist in the exchange store for 30 days and can be reconnected to the same or any other user object that doesn't have a mailbox associated with it. To actually delete the mailbox, you need to purge the mailbox.

Purging a Disconnected Mailbox

In order to truly delete a mailbox out of the store, you must purge the mailbox. The following code shows how to purge a mailbox:

```
' This code purges a deleted mailbox.
Option Explicit
Dim strComputer, strMailbox, objWMI, objDiscMbx, objMbx
' ------ SCRIPT CONFIGURATION ------
strComputer = "<Exchange Server>" 'e.g. ExchServer2
strMailbox = "<Mailbox Alias>"    'e.g. DrAmy
' ------ END CONFIGURATION ---------
Set objWMI = GetObject("winmgmts:\\" & strComputer & _
                       "\root\MicrosoftExchangeV2")
Set objDiscMbx = objWMI.ExecQuery("Select * from Exchange_Mailbox WHERE " _
                        & "MailboxDisplayName='" & strMailbox & "'",,48)
For Each objMbx In objDiscMbx
   objMbx.Purge
Next
Wscript.Echo "Successfully purged mailbox."
```

Purging a mailbox requires Exchange Service Administrator permissions.

This script doesn't need CDOEXM; it actually does what it needs to do through Windows Management Instrumentation (WMI). Chapter 27 is entirely devoted to WMI, so the documentation here will be sparse. Suffice to say, this script executes a query against the Exchange server using the WMI Exchange_Mailbox class, which is available in Exchange 2003 only, and asks for all mailboxes with the specified name. It then loops through the returned mailboxes and executes the Purge method against each, which effectively removes it from the store. After a purge, the mailbox can only be recovered by restoring from a backup. If there have been multiple mailboxes disconnected from the given user in the last 30 days, there will be multiple mailboxes to purge.

If you want to narrow down which specific mailboxes are being returned by the query, there are other attributes you can query against, such as `DateDiscoveredAbsentInDS` or `LastLogonTime` properties. See the `Exchange_Mailbox` class documentation in MSDN at *http://msdn.micro soft.com/en-us/library/aa143732.aspx.*

Reconnecting a Disconnected Mailbox

After a mailbox has been disconnected, and prior to it being purged or exceeding its retention period, it can be reconnected to a user object that doesn't currently have a mailbox associated with it. The following code shows how to reconnect a mailbox:

```
' This code reconnects a mailbox to a user.
Option Explicit
Dim strComputer, strUser, strMailbox, objWMI, objDiscMbx, objMbx
strComputer = "<Exchange Server>" ' e.g. ExchServer2
' ------ SCRIPT CONFIGURATION ------
strUser = "<Userid>"                ' e.g. DrAmy
strMailbox = "<Mailbox Alias>"      ' e.g. DrAmy
' ------ END CONFIGURATION ---------
 Set objWMI = GetObject("winmgmts:\\" & strComputer & _
                    "\root\MicrosoftExchangeV2")
Set objDiscMbx = objWMI.ExecQuery("Select * from Exchange_Mailbox WHERE " _
                    & "MailboxDisplayName='" & strMailbox & "'",,48)
For Each objMbx In objDiscMbx
   objMbx.Reconnect strUser
Next
WScript.Echo "Successfully reconnected mailbox."
```

Reconnecting a mailbox requires Exchange Service Administrator permissions, plus additional permissions on user objects. See the earlier section "Exchange Delegation."

This script is like the purge mailbox script and doesn't need CDOEXM; it also does what it needs to do through Windows Management Instrumentation (WMI). This script executes a query against the Exchange server using the WMI `Exchange_Mailbox` class (which is available in Exchange 2003) and asks for all mailboxes with the specified name. It then loops through the returned mailboxes and executes the **Reconnect** method against the mailbox returned. Unfortunately, there are some rather serious flaws with the implementation of the **Reconnect** method, which severely limits its usability in some environments.

The first flaw is that the WMI **Reconnect** method must be run directly on the Exchange Server with the disconnected mailbox so that the script must run on the Exchange server. You can't, for instance, have a script that runs from a workstation that will reconnect mailboxes on any of your Exchange servers.

The second flaw is that you cannot specify the domain of the user you want to reconnect to the mailbox. In a single domain Exchange environment, this will be fine. Trying to reconnect a mailbox in a forest with the same user name in multiple domains could give unexpected results.

Moving a Mailbox

There are times when you want to move mailboxes from one Exchange server to another. The reason for the move may be for a migration from an older Exchange server to a new one (e.g., Exchange 5.5 to Exchange 2003) to better load balance mailboxes between Exchange Servers, or any number of other reasons. This is a very simple task to handle through a CDOEXM script. The following code shows how to move a mailbox:

```
' This code moves a mailbox.
Option Explicit
Dim strUserDN, strServer, strSGName, strMailStoreName, strSearch
Dim objSrv, strSg, strSGUrl, strMBUrl, objUser
' ------ SCRIPT CONFIGURATION ------
strUserDN = "<UserDN>" ' e.g. cn=DrAmy,cn=Users,dc=mycorp,dc=com
strServer = "<Exchange Server>"        ' e.g. ExchServer2
strSGName = "<Storage Group Name>"        ' e.g. SG1
strMailStoreName = "<MailBox Store Name>" ' e.g. DB1
' ------ END CONFIGURATION ---------
' Find Storage Group URL and Generate Mailbox Store URL
strSearch = "cn=" & strSGName  & ","
Set objSrv = CreateObject("CDOEXM.ExchangeServer")
objSrv.DataSource.Open strServer
For Each strSg In objSrv.StorageGroups
    If InStr(1, strSg, strSearch, 1) > 0 Then
        strSGUrl = strSg
        Exit For
    End If
Next
strMBUrl = "LDAP://cn=" & strMailStoreName & "," & strSGUrl
' Attach to user and move mailbox
Set objUser = GetObject("LDAP://" & strUserDN)
objUser.MoveMailbox(strMBUrl)
WScript.Echo "Successfully moved mailbox."
```

 Moving a mailbox requires Exchange Service Administrator permissions, plus additional permissions on user objects. See the earlier section "Exchange Delegation."

The main work of moving a mailbox is handled by the `MoveMailBox` method of the `IMailBoxStore` interface. The trickiest aspect is getting the argument you need to specify for the move, which is the Home MDB URL for the database you want to move the user to. Previously in the MailBox-Enable script, the absolute path of the Home MDB object was specified. The method used here allows you to specify three well-known components (server, storage group, store name), which can be used to determine the proper value.

A mailbox move is an odd operation in terms of permissions. Logically, moving a mailbox is basically a combination of create and delete operations, which is something an Exchange Data Administrator can do just fine. However, to actually move a mailbox, you must have Exchange Administrator Role permissions, with a subset of the permissions that Exchange Data Administrator permissions have on user objects. See Microsoft Knowledge Base Article 842033 at *http://support.microsoft.com/kb/842033* for details of the permissions needed.

If you don't handle user mailbox administration through an automated web site, it is recommended that you delegate permissions to the attributes listed in the knowledge base articles to some Active Directory group. Once delegated, add the Exchange Administrator Role users to that group and have them handle all mailbox moves.

Enumerating Disconnected Mailboxes

If you want to know which disconnected mailboxes exist on an Exchange server, you can simply enumerate them. The following code shows how to enumerate disconnected mailboxes:

```
' This code enumerates disconnected mailboxes.
Option Explicit
Dim strComputer, objWMI, objDiscMbx, objMbx
' ------ SCRIPT CONFIGURATION ------
strComputer = "<Exchange Server>" 'e.g. ExchServer2
' ------ END CONFIGURATION ---------
Set objWMI - GetObject("winmgmts:\\" & strComputer & _
                    "\root\MicrosoftExchangeV2")
Set objDiscMbx = objWMI.ExecQuery("Select * from Exchange_Mailbox",,48)
For Each objMbx In objDiscMbx
  If (objMbx.DateDiscoveredAbsentInDS <> "") then
     WScript.Echo objMbx.MailBoxDisplayName & " " & _
                objMbx.DateDiscoveredAbsentInDS
  End If
Next
WScript.Echo "Successfully enumerated disconnected mailboxes."
```

 Although viewing mailbox details in the Exchange System Manager (ESM) requires only Exchange View-Only Administrator role access, in order to do this with a script, the WMI provider also requires local administrator permissions on the Exchange server.

Just like the Purge Mailbox and Reconnect Mailbox scripts, this script uses the WMI **Exchange_Mailbox** class to gather the requested information.

Viewing Mailbox Sizes and Message Counts

A common task is to look at an Exchange server and determine the sizes and counts of messages on the server for all mailboxes. The following code shows how simple this is to do:

```
' This code enumerates mailbox sizes and message counts.
Option Explicit
Dim strComputer, objWMI, objMbxs, objMbx
' ------ SCRIPT CONFIGURATION ------
strComputer = "<Exchange Server>" 'e.g. ExchServer2
' ------ END CONFIGURATION ---------
 Set objWMI = GetObject("winmgmts:\\" & strComputer & _
                        "\root\MicrosoftExchangeV2")
Set objMbxs = objWMI.ExecQuery("Select * from Exchange_Mailbox",,48)
For Each objMbx In objMbxs
   WScript.Echo objMbx.MailBoxDisplayName & " " & objMbx.size & "KB  " _
                & objMbx.TotalItems & " items"
Next
WScript.Echo "Script completed successfully."
```

This script is very similar to the script to enumerate disconnected mailboxes. The same basic process is used; we have simply changed the initial query to select the record set to enumerate through. There are actually several properties that can be displayed this way. Table 32-4 lists the properties and their descriptions.

Table 32-4. Exchange_Mailbox properties

Property	Description
LegacyDN	legacyDN of the mailbox. This matches the legacyExchangeDN attribute of the user object in Active Directory.
MailboxGUID	Indicates the globally unique identifier (GUID) that links the mailbox to a user in Active Directory. This value is also populated in the user's Active Directory object as msExchMailboxGuid.
ServerName	Name of the server the mailbox resides on.
StorageGroupName	Indicates the name of the storage group that contains the mailbox.
StoreName	Indicates the name of the message database (MDB) that contains the mailbox.
AssocContentCount	Indicates the total number of messages associated with the mailbox folders.
DateDiscoveredAbsentInDS	Indicates when the store detected that the mailbox no longer had a corresponding user entry in Active Directory, i.e., when the mailbox was disconnected.
DeletedMessageSizeExtended	Indicates the cumulative size of all deleted messages that are still being retained according to retention policy settings.
LastLoggedOnUserAccount	Indicates the account name last used to log on to the mailbox. Note that this doesn't necessarily mean an interactive logon to the mailbox messages; this could be from someone viewing a calendar entry or other innocuous access.
LastLogoffTime	Indicates the time that the last user logged off. See note for LastLoggedOnUserAccount.
LastLogonTime	Indicates the time that the last user logged on. See note for LastLoggedOnUserAccount.

Property	Description
Size	Indicates cumulative size of all of the messages in the mailbox in kilobytes.
StorageLimitInfo	Contains the storage-limit settings on the mailbox.
TotalItems	Indicates the total number of messages in a mailbox.

Viewing All Store Details of All Mailboxes on a Server

The following code takes all of the properties from Table 32-2 and displays them for all mailboxes on a specified server:

```
' This code enumerates all store details about all mailboxes
' on a single specified server
Option Explicit
Dim strComputer, objWMI, objMbxs, objMbx
' ------ SCRIPT CONFIGURATION ------
strComputer = "<Exchange Server>" 'e.g. ExchServer2
' ------ END CONFIGURATION ---------
Set objWMI = GetObject("winmgmts:\\" & strComputer & _
                        "\root\MicrosoftExchangeV2")
Set objMbxs = objWMI.ExecQuery("Select * from Exchange_Mailbox",,48)
For Each objMbx In objMbxs
  WScript.Echo "LegacyDN: " _
                      & objMbx.LegacyDN
  WScript.Echo "MailBoxGUID: " _
                      & objMbx.MailboxGUID
  WScript.Echo "ServerName: " _
                      & objMbx.ServerName
  WScript.Echo "StorageGroupName: " _
                      & objMbx.StorageGroupName
  WScript.Echo "StoreName: " _
                      & objMbx.StoreName
  WScript.Echo "AssocContentCount: " _
                      & objMbx.AssocContentCount
  WScript.Echo "DateDiscoveredAbsentInDS: " _
                      & objMbx.DateDiscoveredAbsentInDS
  WScript.Echo "DeletedMessageSizeExtended: " _
                      & objMbx.DeletedMessageSizeExtended
  WScript.Echo "LastLoggedOnUserAccount: " _
                      & objMbx.LastLoggedOnUserAccount
  WScript.Echo "LastLogoffTime: " _
                      & objMbx.LastLogoffTime
  WScript.Echo "LastLogonTime: " _
                      & objMbx.LastLogonTime
  WScript.Echo "Size: " _
                      & objMbx.Size
  WScript.Echo "StorageLimitInfo: " _
                      & objMbx.StorageLimitInfo
  WScript.Echo "TotalItems: " _
                      & objMbx.TotalItems
  WScript.Echo ""
  WScript.Echo ""
```

```
Next
WScript.Echo "Script completed successfully."
```

Dumping All Store Details of All Mailboxes on All Servers in Exchange Org

The following code takes the preceding script and extends it by extracting all information from all Exchange servers and dumping it to a text file in semicolon delimited format:

```
'This script dumps all store details of all mailboxes in an
'Exchange ORG to a text file in semi-colon delimited format
Option Explicit
Dim objConn, objComm, objRS
Dim strBase, strFilter, strAttrs, strScope
Dim fso, outfile
Dim strComputer, objWMI, objMbx, objMbxs
' ------ SCRIPT CONFIGURATION ------
strConfigDN = "<Config NC DN>" 'e.g. cn=configuration,dc=mycorp,dc=com
' ------ END CONFIGURATION ---------

'Set the ADO search criteria
strBase   = "<LDAP:// " & strConfigDN & ">;"
strFilter = "(objectcategory=msExchExchangeServer);"
strAttrs  = "name;"
strScope  = "Subtree"
set objConn = CreateObject("ADODB.Connection")
objConn.Provider = "ADsDSOObject"
objConn.Open

'Need to enable Paging in case there are more than 1000 objects returned
Set objComm = CreateObject("ADODB.Command")
Set objComm.ActiveConnection = objConn
objComm.CommandText = strBase & strFilter & strAttrs & strScope
objComm.Properties("Page Size") = 1000
Set objRS = objComm.Execute()

'Create a VBScript file object and use it to open a text file. The
'second parameter specifies to overwrite any existing file that exists.
Set fso = CreateObject("Scripting.FileSystemObject")
Set outfile = fso.CreateTextFile("c:\out.txt", TRUE)

'Write header line to file
outfile.WriteLine "LegacyDN;" _
                & "MailBoxGUID;" _
                & "ServerName;" _
                & "StorageGroupName;" _
                & "StoreName;" _
                & "AssocContentCount;" _
                & "DateDiscoveredAbsentInDS;" _
                & "DeletedMessageSizeExtended;" _
                & "LastLoggedOnUserAccount;" _
                & "LastLogoffTime;" _
```

```
                    & "LastLogonTime;" _
                    & "Size;" _
                    & "StorageLimitInfo;" _
                    & "TotalItems"

 'Loop through all servers and dump all store info for all mailboxes
 While Not objRS.EOF
    strComputer = objRS.Fields.Item("name").Value
    Set objWMI = GetObject("winmgmts:\\" & strComputer & _
                          "\root\MicrosoftExchangeV2")
    Set objMbxs = objWMI.ExecQuery("Select * from Exchange_Mailbox",,48)
    For Each objMbx In objMbxs
      outfile.Write objMbx.LegacyDN
      outfile.Write ";" & objMbx.MailboxGUID
      outfile.Write ";" & objMbx.ServerName
      outfile.Write ";" & objMbx.StorageGroupName
      outfile.Write ";" & objMbx.StoreName
      outfile.Write ";" & objMbx.AssocContentCount
      outfile.Write ";" & objMbx.DateDiscoveredAbsentInDS
      outfile.Write ";" & objMbx.DeletedMessageSizeExtended
      outfile.Write ";" & objMbx.LastLoggedOnUserAccount
      outfile.Write ";" & objMbx.LastLogoffTime
      outfile.Write ";" & objMbx.LastLogonTime
      outfile.Write ";" & objMbx.Size
      outfile.Write ";" & objMbx.StorageLimitInfo
      outfile.WriteLine ";" & objMbx.TotalItems
    Next
    objRS.MoveNext
 Wend
 outfile.Close
```

 While viewing mailbox details in the Exchange System Manager (ESM) only requires Exchange View-Only Administrator role access, in order to do this with a script, the WMI provider also requires local administrator permissions on the Exchange server.

Summary

In this chapter, we had a basic discussion of some basic concepts of Exchange, such as mail- and mailbox-enabling Active Directory objects and delegation of Exchange permissions. Next, we looked at the mechanisms available to manipulate various Exchange properties of user, contact, and group objects in Active Directory via script interfaces. Then we used these mechanisms to mail- and mailbox-enable various objects, as well as several other admin tasks commonly handled through the Active Directory Users and Computers and Exchange System Manager Tools. Finally, we presented a script to gather all information available from the mailbox store through the IMailBoxStore interface for all mailboxes on all Exchange servers and dumped that information to a file in a semicolon delimited format. This script illustrated how you can take simple concepts and build them up to generate a great deal of useful information about your

---

environment. That simple dump could be used to analyze mailbox use in your organization or be used to track mailbox growth and trending information.

## CHAPTER 33

Scripting Basic Exchange 2007 Tasks

This chapter is about providing a brief jumpstart to managing Exchange 2007 recipients with PowerShell. While you can accomplish nearly all of the tasks in this chapter with the *Exchange Management Console* (EMC), managing large numbers of objects with the GUI never scales. In order to efficiently work with large scale environments, it's typically necessary to use scripts instead.

In this chapter we'll cover managing users, groups, and contacts, and end with a couple of larger scripts that bring together the skills taught in this chapter. If you're not familiar with PowerShell, take a few minutes to read Chapter 30 for an introduction to Power-Shell, and Chapter 31 provides an introduction to managing Active Directory objects with PowerShell.

Exchange Scripting Notes

In order to manage Exchange 2007 servers from your workstation, you'll need to have a couple of additional components installed. The first prerequisite is PowerShell. For more information about installing PowerShell, reference Chapter 30. The second prerequisite is the Exchange management tools. While Exchange 2007 will only run on 64-bit hardware, the management tools can run on 32-bit or 64-bit hardware. You can download the 32-bit management tools from *http://www.microsoft.com/downloads/de tails.aspx?FamilyID=6be38633-7248-4532-929b-76e9c677e802*.

 Unlike Exchange 2003 and earlier, Exchange 2007 is entirely supported to run the Exchange management tools on a machine that is also running Microsoft Outlook. The conflicts that precluded doing this safely in earlier versions are no longer an issue with Exchange 2007.

Once you've loaded the Exchange management tools, it is important to make sure you use the Exchange Management Shell shortcut on your Start menu in order to launch PowerShell. If you use the generic PowerShell shortcut, you will receive an error when

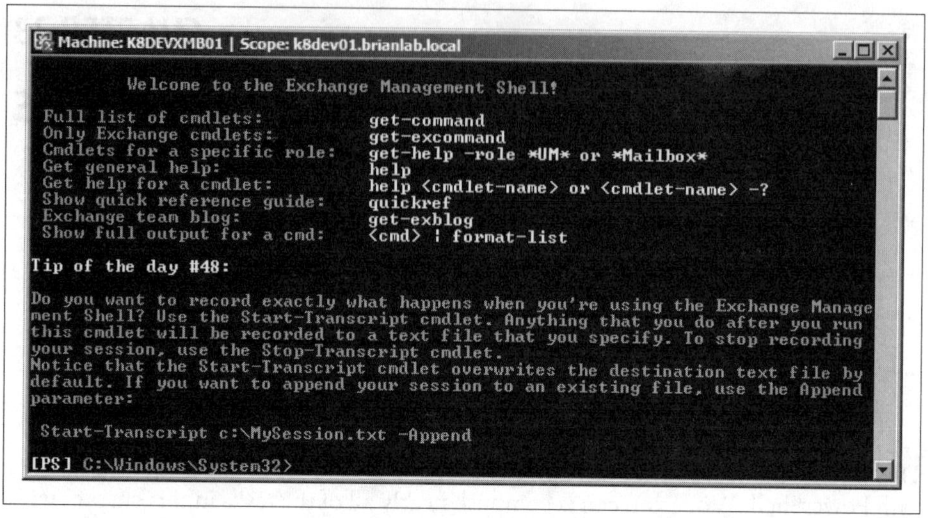

Figure 33-1. Exchange Management Shell

you try to run Exchange cmdlets. If you have launched the correct shortcut, your PowerShell window should look similar to Figure 33-1.

The Departure of the Recipient Update Service

Under Exchange 2000 and Exchange 2003, enabling an Active Directory object for Exchange was effectively a two step process. The first step was to set a few key attributes on the object (or use CDOEXM which did that for you), and the second step was to wait for the Exchange Recipient Update Service (RUS) to notice the changes to this object and finish enabling it. This asynchronous process caused many headaches for administrators over the years, and in Exchange 2007 the RUS has been eliminated.

Under Exchange 2007, the process for enabling an object is completely synchronous. When Exchange cmdlets are called to enable the object, all of the changes are made on the spot and the object is immediately ready to receive email (assuming the necessary changes have replicated throughout your Active Directory).

The downside to this change of procedure is that you can't simply set a few attributes and then expect Exchange to complete the process on your behalf. Unfortunately, this is how many provisioning systems operate. With Exchange 2007, if you want to continue to provision objects in an asynchronous fashion, you will need to call a couple of PowerShell cmdlets to finish the job. We'll discuss these steps later in this chapter.

The alternative is to modify your provisioning process to call the Exchange cmdlets directly for each affected object. One strategy we have seen used is to have the provisioning tool generate a text file of PowerShell commands that need to be run, and then a process that picks up this text file and executes it on a server with the Exchange Management Shell installed. If your provisioning system runs on Unix, you'll need to incorporate a mechanism such as FTP (or another file transfer protocol) to copy the file to a Windows machine that can execute the PowerShell commands.

Mail-Enabling Versus Mailbox-Enabling

Exchange has two primary mechanisms for hooking users into its mail system. The first mechanism is called mailbox-enabling, and this associates a mailbox in the Exchange organization to a user. This is the normal setting for users in most organizations that allows them to log into the Exchange system with Outlook, Outlook Web Access (OWA), or other mail clients that can communicate through standard mail interfaces such as POP3 or IMAP.

The second mechanism is called mail-enabling; this connects one or more email addresses to the user that are external to the Exchange organization. This is used for someone who needs to log into the forest, but does not want a mailbox in the Exchange organization. For example, Dr. Amy Gramzow of the Acme Consulting Company could be on a long-term assignment at MyCorp, Inc. and have any email that is sent to her at *DrAmy@MyCorp.com* forwarded to her *AGramzow@AcmeConsulting.com* mailbox so that she doesn't have to manage multiple mailboxes.

Mail-enabling is also used to make Exchange aware of contacts and groups. These objects can't be authenticated, so creating a mailbox for them doesn't make sense; they must be mail-enabled instead of mailbox-enabled. Contacts will almost always have an external email address associated with them; a group, on the other hand, will be used as a distribution list to forward messages on to multiple recipients, who could be internal to the organization or outside of it.

Exchange Cmdlet Primer

Rather than repeating some of the same notes each time we use a cmdlet in this chapter, there are a couple of common elements to all of the cmdlets we'll use that are worth covering up front. The first is the verbs that are common across all of them, and the second are the common parameters.

The common verbs and their behaviors we will see are:

Enable
> When you call an Enable cmdlet, an existing Active Directory object must be specified that will be updated to include Exchange specific attribute values.

Disable
> When you call a Disable cmdlet, an existing Active Directory object must be specified that will be updated to remove Exchange specific attribute values.

New
> When you call a New cmdlet, the cmdlet will create the relevant object (such as a user) in Active Directory and then populate the Exchange specific attribute values.

Remove

> When you call a Remove cmdlet, the cmdlet will *delete* the object from Active Directory.

Get

> Get cmdlets return data from Active Directory and/or Exchange.

Set

> Set cmdlets update properties or attributes of the specified object in Active Directory and/or Exchange.

The common parameters we will see across all of the cmdlets in this chapter include:

-Identity

> The identity parameter specifies the target object in Active Directory. This is usually a distinguished name (DN), username, or user principal name. We will make note of which format is appropriate throughout the chapter.

-Confirm

> Many of the cmdlets will prompt you to confirm that you wish to take an action. If you specify -confirm:$false in a command, you will not be prompted.

Managing Users

There are four tasks that we'll explore in this section:

- Mailbox- and mail-enabling users
- Mailbox- and mail-disabling users
- Displaying Exchange specific properties
- Moving user mailboxes

Throughout the examples in this section, we will assume that you are working with an existing user object in Active Directory. Where appropriate, we will make a note of the cmdlet you should substitute to create the user in the same transaction.

Mailbox-Enabling a User

In order to mailbox enable a user, you will need to call Enable-Mailbox and specify, at a minimum, the user object to enable (-Identity) and a target mailbox database (-TargetDatabase). In this example, we mailbox-enable user bdesmond (we've specified the identity as domain\username) and create the mailbox on server K8DEVXMB01 in mailbox database MB01SG01MS01:

```
[PS]    C:\>Enable-Mailbox    -Identity    "k8dev01\bdesmond" `
-Database "K8DEVXMB01\MB01SG01MS01"
    Name            Alias         ServerName    ProhibitSendQuota
    ----            -----         ----------    -----------------
    Brian Desmond   bdesmond      k8devxmb01    unlimited
```

As soon as `Enable-Mailbox` completes, the user's mailbox will be ready for use. For a complete description of how to use this cmdlet, visit *http://technet.microsoft.com/en-us/library/aa998251(EXCHG.80).aspx.*

If you need to create the Active Directory user in the same transaction, use the `New-Mailbox` cmdlet instead.

Mailbox-Disabling a User

In order to mailbox-enable a user, you will need to call `Disable-Mailbox` and specify at a minimum the user object to enable (`-Identity`). In this example, we will disable the mailbox for user bdesmond in domain k8dev01:

```
[PS] C:\>Disable-Mailbox -Identity "k8dev01\bdesmond"
```

If you don't want to be prompted, you can attach the `-confirm` parameter.

As soon as the `Disable-Mailbox` cmdlet completes, the mailbox will be marked as disconnected in the Exchange Mailbox Database. For a complete description of the usage for this cmdlet, visit *http://technet.microsoft.com/en-us/library/aa997210(EXCHG.80).aspx.*

If you use the `Remove-Mailbox` cmdlet, the user's account in Active Directory will be deleted!

Mail-Enabling a User

In order to mail-enable a user, you will need to call the `Enable-MailUser` cmdlet and specify, at a minimum, the user object to enable (`-Identity`) and the external email address the user should receive mail at (`-ExternalEmailAddress`). In this example, we will mail-enable user cdesmond at *carrie@mycorp.com*:

```
[PS]  C:\>Enable-MailUser  -Identity "k8dev01\cdesmond" -`
ExternalEmailAddress "carrie@mycorp.com"
    Name                        RecipientType
    ----                        -------------
    Carrie Desmond              MailUser
```

For more information about the `Enable-MailUser` cmdlet, visit *http://technet.microsoft.com/en-us/library/aa996549(EXCHG.80).aspx.*

If you need to create the Active Directory user in the same transaction, use the `New-MailUser` cmdlet instead.

Mail-Disabling a User

In order to disable an existing mail-enabled user, you will need to call the `Disable-MailUser` cmdlet and specify at a minimum the user object to disable (`-Identity`). In this example, we will disable mail-enabled user cdesmond:

```
[PS] C:\>Disable-MailUser -Identity "k8dev01\cdesmond"
```

If you don't want to be prompted, you can attach the `-confirm` parameter.

For more information about the `Disable-MailUser` cmdlet, visit *http://technet.microsoft.com/en-us/library/aa997465(EXCHG.80).aspx*.

If you use the `Remove-MailUser` cmdlet, the user's account in Active Directory will be deleted!

Viewing Mailbox Properties

You can use the `Get-Mailbox` cmdlet to display the properties of one or more mailboxes. If you specify the `-Identity` property, the properties of a given mailbox will be returned:

```
[PS] C:\>Get-Mailbox -Identity "k8dev01\bdesmond"
Name            Alias        ServerName   ProhibitSendQuota
----            -----        ----------   -----------------
Brian Desmond   bdesmond     k8devxmb01   unlimited
```

If you wanted to return all of the mailboxes on a server, you could specify the `-Server` parameter instead. In this example, we also specify which properties of the mailboxes we would like to view. By piping to `ft` (short for `Format-Table`), we tell PowerShell that we want a table style listing containing only a few specific attributes:

```
[PS]    C:\>Get-Mailbox    -Server    k8devxmb01    |    ft `
Name,PrimarySMTPAddress,ServerName
Name             PrimarySmtpAddress               ServerName
----             ------------------               ----------
Administrator    Administrator@k8dev01.b...       k8devxmb01
Brian Desmond    brian@briandesmond.com           k8devxmb01
```

There are over 104 properties to choose from in the output of `Get-Mail box`. If you're wondering how to come up with the correct property names to specify when filtering the output, try running `[PS] C:\>Get-Mailbox | Get-Member -MemberType Property`.

If you wanted to get information about a user's mailbox in Exchange, you could use the `Get-MailboxStatistics` cmdlet. In this example, we pipe the output to `fl` (short for `Format-List`), which tells PowerShell that we want a list-style display of the information, including all of the available properties for the mailbox:

```
[PS] C:\>Get-MailboxStatistics -Identity "k8dev01\bdesmond" | fl
    AssociatedItemCount    : 3
    DeletedItemCount       : 0
    DisconnectDate         :
    DisplayName            : Brian Desmond
    ItemCount              : 2
    LastLoggedOnUserAccount : K8DEV01\bdesmond
    LastLogoffTime         : 7/20/2008 11:18:42 PM
    LastLogonTime          : 7/20/2008 11:18:32 PM
    LegacyDN               : /O=K8DEVX01/OU=EXCHANGE ADMINISTRATIVE GROUP (FYDIBOH
                             F23SPDLT)/CN=RECIPIENTS/CN=BDESMOND
    MailboxGuid            : 49061a0e-c3a8-47b7-a1e2-ddaeb289614c
    ObjectClass            : Mailbox
    StorageLimitStatus     : BelowLimit
    TotalDeletedItemSize   : 0B
    TotalItemSize          : 4194B
    Database               : K8DEVXMB01\SG01\MB01SG01MS01
    ServerName             : K8DEVXMB01
    StorageGroupName       : SG01
    DatabaseName           : MB01SG01MS01
    Identity               : 49061a0e-c3a8-47b7-a1e2-ddaeb289614c
    IsValid                : True
    OriginatingServer      : k8devxmb01.k8dev01.brianlab.local
```

If you're looking for information about a mail-enabled user, use `Get-MailUser`.

For more information on the cmdlets discussed in this section, reference the documentation available at these links:

- `Get-Mailbox`

  http://technet.microsoft.com/en-us/library/bb123685(EXCHG.80).aspx

- `Get-MailboxStatistics`

  http://technet.microsoft.com/en-us/library/bb124612(EXCHG.80).aspx

- `Get-MailUser`

  http://technet.microsoft.com/en-us/library/aa997254(EXCHG.80).aspx

- Get-Member

  http://technet.microsoft.com/en-us/library/bb978623.aspx

- Format-List

  http://technet.microsoft.com/en-us/library/bb978736.aspx

- Format-Table

  http://technet.microsoft.com/en-us/library/bb978645.aspx

Moving a User Mailbox

In order to move a user's mailbox, you'll want to use the `Move-Mailbox` cmdlet and specify, at a minimum, the user object to move (`-Identity`) and a target mailbox database (`-TargetDatabase`). In this example, we will move user k8dev01\bdesmond to a new mailbox database, k8devxmb01\mb01sg01ms02:

```
[PS]  C:\>Move-Mailbox  -Identity  "k8dev01\bdesmond" `
-TargetDatabase "k8dev01xmb01\mb01sg01ms02"
```

 If you don't want to be prompted, you can attach the `-confirm` parameter.

When you call `Move-Mailbox`, PowerShell will provide a progress display in the console similar to Figure 33-2.

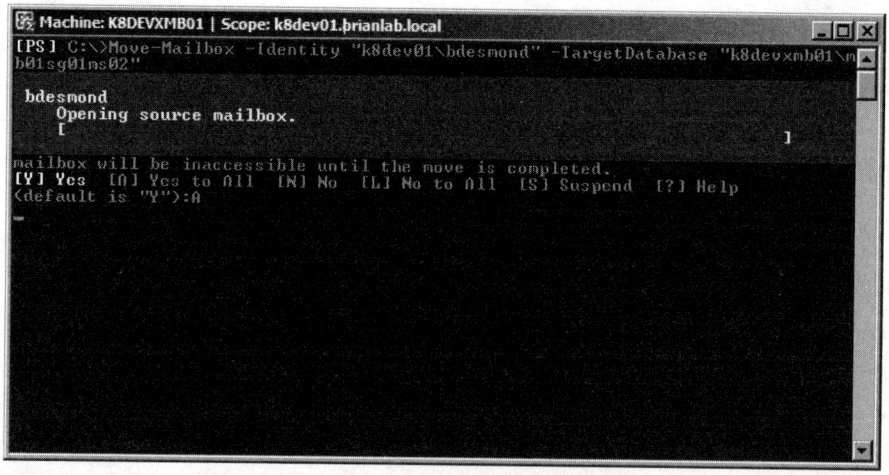

```
Machine: K8DEVXMB01 | Scope: k8dev01.brianlab.local
[PS] C:\>Move-Mailbox -Identity "k8dev01\bdesmond" -TargetDatabase "k8devxmb01\m
b01sg01ms02"

bdesmond
    Opening source mailbox.
    [                                                                          ]

mailbox will be inaccessible until the move is completed.
[Y] Yes  [A] Yes to All  [N] No  [L] No to All  [S] Suspend  [?] Help
<default is "Y">:A
```

Figure 33-2. Move mailbox progress

Typically, administrators need to move large numbers of mailboxes at a time. Rather than calling `Move-Mailbox` once per user, you can pipe the output of `Get-Mailbox` to `Move-Mailbox`. In this example, we'll move all of the mailboxes on server k8devxmb01 to the message store named mb01sg01ms01 on k8devxmb02:

```
[PS] C:\>Get-Mailbox -Server k8devxmb01 | `
Move-Mailbox -TargetDatabase "k8dev01xmb02\mb01sg01ms01"
```

If you run this command as-is, each mailbox will be moved individually. If you'd like to run multiple mailbox moves concurrently, specify the `-MaxThreads` parameter in the `Move-Mailbox` cmdlet call. You can specify a maximum of 30 threads; however, you should test how many concurrent moves your environment can handle. Take into account factors such as network and disk performance.

For a complete description of how to use this cmdlet, visit *http://technet.microsoft.com/en-us/library/aa997599(EXCHG.80).aspx*.

Provisioning Mailboxes Out-of-Band

If you need to enable mailboxes with an identity management system or other tool that doesn't have PowerShell capabilities, you'll need to either work out all attributes that need to be populated and their proper values, or you'll need to call a few cmdlets to complete the process for you. In order for this process to work, you'll need to have working Exchange email address policies (EAPs) in place. Email address policies define the rules Exchange uses to attach an email address to a user. Typically, EAPs define filtering criteria, such as the value of the company attribute or an *extension attribute*, which in turn define what objects (such as users, groups, or contacts) the EAP applies to.

If your identity management tool populates the correct attributes, you can trigger an EAP to be applied and then you can update the address lists in your organization. These steps will cause affected objects (users, groups, contacts, etc.) to be fully enabled for Exchange.

The steps to do this are:

1. Get-EmailAddressPolicy | Update-EmailAddressPolicy
2. Get-AddressList | Update-AddressList
3. Get-GlobalAddressList | Update-GlobalAddressList

 It's important that you run these steps serially in the order shown in order for them to work correctly.

In a large organization, this can take some time to run, so make sure you have an idea of how long this takes if you are scheduling these commands to run automatically.

Managing Groups

There are three tasks that we'll explore in this section:

- Mail-enabling and mail-disabling groups
- Displaying Exchange specific properties

Throughout the examples in this section, we will assume that you are working with an existing group object in Active Directory. Where appropriate, we will make a note of the cmdlet you should substitute to create the group in the same transaction.

Mail-Enabling a Group

In order to mail-enable a group, you'll need to call the `Enable-DistributionGroup` cmdlet and specify the group to mail-enable (`-Identity`). In this case we specify the complete distinguished name of the group:

```
[PS]    C:\>Enable-DistributionGroup    -Identity       `
"CN=Cool People,OU=Groups,DC=k8dev01,dc=brianlab,dc=local"
    Name            DisplayName         GroupType           PrimarySmtpAddress
    ----            -----------         ---------           ------------------
    Cool People     Cool People         Universal           CoolPeople@k8dev...
```

As soon as `Enable-DistributionGroup` completes, the distribution group will be ready for use. For a complete description of the usage for this cmdlet, visit *http://technet.microsoft.com/en-us/library/aa998916(EXCHG.80).aspx*.

> If you need to create the Active Directory group in the same transaction, use the `New-DistributionGroup` cmdlet instead.
>
> To create a dynamic distribution group, use `New-DynamicDistributionGroup`.

Mail-Disabling a Group

In order to disable an existing mail-enabled group, you will need to call the `Disable-DistributionGroup` cmdlet and specify at a minimum the group object to disable (`-Identity`):

```
[PS]    C:\>Disable-DistributionGroup    -Identity       `
"CN=CoolPeople,OU=Groups,DC=k8dev01,dc=brianlab,dc=local"
```

> If you don't want to be prompted, you can attach the `-confirm` parameter.

For more information about the `Disable-DistributionGroup` cmdlet, visit *http://technet .microsoft.com/en-us/library/aa997942(EXCHG.80).aspx.*

 If you use the `Remove-DistributionGroup` cmdlet, the group object in Active Directory will be deleted!

If you need to remove a dynamic distribution group, use the `Remove-DynamicDistributionGroup` cmdlet.

Managing Group Membership

The `Add-DistributionGroupMember` and `Remove-DistributionGroupMember` cmdlets are helpful when you need to add and remove group members. You can either specify a specific user to add to a group, or you can pipe a list of users to the cmdlets. In this example, we add one user, k8dev01\bdesmond to a group:

```
[PS]   C:\>Add-DistributionGroupMember  -Identity          `
"CN=Cool People,OU=Groups,DC=k8dev01,dc=brianlab,dc=local" `
-member "k8dev01\bdesmond"
```

In this example, we remove k8dev01\bdesmond:

```
[PS]   C:\>Remove-DistributionGroupMember  -Identity       `
"CN=CoolPeople,OU=Groups,DC=k8dev01,dc=brianlab,dc=local"  `
-member "k8dev01\bdesmond"
```

If you wanted to create a distribution group containing all of the users on a specific Exchange server, you could run a command similar to the following:

```
[PS]    C:\>Get-Mailbox   -Server   "k8devxmb01"     |
Add- DistributionGroupMember       -Identity         `
"CN=K8DEVXMB01Users,OU=Groups,DC=k8dev01,dc=brianlab,dc=local"
```

 If you are trying to update a group's membership, the preceding example will fail if a group already contains one of the users piped to it. In order to handle this situation gracefully, you need to specify the `-ErrorAction:Continue` parameter in your `Add-DistributionGroupMem` ber command. This will cause the cmdlet to proceed after an error. If you want to proceed after an error and also not print the errors to the console, specify `-ErrorAction:SilentlyContinue`.

For more information on the cmdlets discussed in this section, reference the documentation available at these links:

- `Add-DistributionGroupMember`

    http://technet.microsoft.com/en-us/library/bb124340(EXCHG.80).aspx

- `Remove-DistributionGroupMember`

    http://technet.microsoft.com/en-us/library/aa998016(EXCHG.80).aspx

Displaying Group Properties

You can use the `Get-DistributionGroup` cmdlet to display the properties of one or more groups. If you specify the `-Identity` property, the properties of a given group will be returned:

```
[PS]   C:\>Get-DistributionGroup    -Identity      `
"CN=CoolPeople,OU=Groups,DC=k8dev01,dc=brianlab,dc=local"
    Name              DisplayName      GroupType            PrimarySmtpAddress
    ----              -----------      ---------            ------------------
    Cool People       Cool People      Universal            CoolPeople@k8dev...
```

If you wanted to return all of your distribution groups, simply omit the `-Identity` parameter. As with the examples in the previous section on displaying mailbox information, you can use `Format-Table` and `Format-List` to manage how the information is displayed.

> To display information about a dynamic distribution group, use the `Get-DynamicDistributionGroup` cmdlet.

If you want to view all of the members of a given group, you can use the Get-DistributionGroupMember cmdlet. In this example, we display all of the members of the Cool People group:

```
[PS]   C:\>Get-DistributionGroupMember   -Identity       `
"CN=CoolPeople,OU=Groups,DC=k8dev01,dc=brianlab,dc=local"
    Name              RecipientType
    ----              -------------
    Administrator     UserMailbox
    bdesmond          Usermailbox
```

For more information on the cmdlets discussed in this section, reference the documentation available at these links:

- Get-DistributionGroup: *http://technet.microsoft.com/en-us/library/*
  bb124755(EXCHG.80).aspx
- Get-DistributionGroupMember: *http://technet.microsoft.com/en-us/library/*
  aa996367(EXCHG.80).aspx

Summary

In this chapter we took a look at a number of PowerShell commands that can be used for managing users and groups under Exchange 2007. We also looked at some handy tricks for leveraging the PowerShell pipeline capabilities to work with batches of objects. Exchange 2007 brings a different process for provisioning objects—there is no more Recipient Update Service (RUS). Thus, we took a brief look at a couple of strategies for working around this new behavior when you are using an identity management system to provision users and other objects to your Active Directory.

Index

We'd like to hear your suggestions for improving our indexes. Send email to *index@oreilly.com*.

About the Authors

Brian Desmond spends his days focused on Active Directory for some of the world's largest companies. A Microsoft MVP since 2004, Brian brings extensive knowledge of how Active Directory works and how to succesfully run Active Directory deployments large and small.

Joe Richards is a consultant/admin/tool writer and Microsoft MVP for Windows Server Directory Services. Joe updated the second edition of *Active Directory Cookbook*.

Robbie Allen Robbie Allen is an author, entrepreneur, and web industry veteran. He's worked in IT for the last 12 years and runs the popular sports website:*http://statsheet .com*. He is also the author of *Active Directory Cookbook*.

Alistair G. Lowe-Norris is an enterprise program manager for Microsoft U.K., although during the writing of this book he worked for Leicester University as the project manager and technical lead of the Rapid Deployment Program for Windows 2000.

Colophon

The animals on the cover of *Active Directory*, Fourth Edition, are a domestic cat (*felis silvetris*) and her kitten. The domestic cat is a descendant of the African wild cat, which first inhabited the planet one million years ago. Other early forerunners of the cat existed as many as 12 million years ago.

The domestic cat is one of the most popular house pets in the world. There are hundreds of breeds of domestic cats, which weigh anywhere from 5 to 30 pounds, with an average of 12 pounds. The cat is slightly longer than it is tall, with its body typically being longer than its tail. Domestic cats can be any of 80 different colors and patterns. They often live to be 15–20 years old; 10 years for a human life is about equal to 60 years for a cat.

The cat's gestation period is approximately two months, and each litter may contain three to seven cats. Mother cats teach their kittens to eat and to use litter boxes. Kittens ideally should not leave their mother's sides until the age of 12 weeks and are considered full grown at the age of about three years.

The cover image is a 19th-century engraving from Dover Pictorial Archive. The cover font is Adobe ITC Garamond. The text font is Linotype Birka; the heading font is Adobe Myriad Condensed; and the code font is LucasFont's TheSans Mono Condensed.

Related Titles from O'Reilly

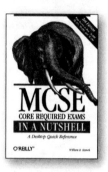

Windows Administration

Active Directory Cookbook, *2nd Edition*

Active Directory, *3rd Edition*

Big Book of Windows Hacks

DNS on Windows Server 2003, *3rd Edition*

Essential Microsoft Operations Manager

Essential SharePoint 2007, *2nd Edition*

Exchange Server Cookbook

Learning Windows Server 2003, *2nd Edition*

MCSE Core Elective Exams in a Nutshell

MCSE Core Required Exams in a Nutshell, *3rd Edition*

Monad (AKA PowerShell)

Securing Windows Server 2003

SharePoint Office Pocket Guide

SharePoint User's Guide

SharePoint 2007: The Definitive Guide

Windows Server 2003 in a Nutshell

Windows Server 2003 Network Administration

Windows Server 2003 Security Cookbook

Windows Server Cookbook

Windows Server Hacks

Windows Vista Annoyances

Windows XP Cookbook

Our books are available at most retail and online bookstores.

To order direct: 1-800-998-9938 • *order@oreilly.com* • *www.oreilly.com*

Online editions of most O'Reilly titles are available by subscription at *safari.oreilly.com*

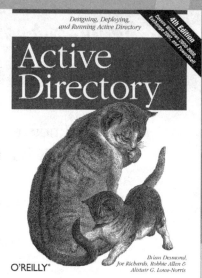